Best Wishes

[signature]

The Celtic,

Glasgow Irish

and the

Great War

The Storms Break

Scottish Football Season 1914–1915

ISBN 978-0-9541263-3-9

Illustrations and Photographic credits:

The author would like to thank the families of the individuals whose images appear in this publication. Acknowledgement is also due to a number of institutions, archives and museums that provided graphics. Thank you to Mike Strang for his work on the cartoon used on the dustcover. Thanks also to former Scots Guardsman Jack Murray for access to his postcard collection and to John McGlynn for his work on the original dustcover graphics.

Front and back cover:

The Glasgow Evening Times, O'Kane family and Mike Strang.

FOREWORD

Relatively few, except perhaps some in Whitehall, could have anticipated the looming cataclysm. There is a touch of sang - froid about the reaction of the correspondent who had covered Celtic's recent tour of Central Europe (including matches in Berlin and Leipzig) to the assassination of the Archduke Francis Ferdinand and his wife - ' I am afraid we shall not see the Prato or the Corso next summer' - but the deed was to trigger an unimaginable conflict which set in train changes whose ramifications still linger to this very day. The age of innocence was well and truly over by its end. The 'Great War' touched every level and facet of British society, as Ian McCallum makes clear in his graphic and impressive depiction of its impact on the Glasgow Irish and its most famous symbol, Celtic Football Club.

During its course, the *Glasgow Observer*, the chronicler of that community and a champion of its aspirations for Home Rule for the 'Ould Country', regularly printed details (with photos where available) of its dead and wounded not only with a subliminal ,political motive of pointing out to the wider world the sacrifices being made by the Glasgow (and West of Scotland) Irish, but also as a means of underlining the human, family dimension of the tragedy. In truth, no - one could escape the war in all its manifestations. Celtic players, when not called to the front, would be required to 'do their bit' for the war effort each weekday by working in shipyards, engineering works, iron foundries, pits and munitions factories. Jimmy McMenemy, the acme of coolness on a football pitch, would be consumed with anger and belligerent sentiments in London at the piteous sight of Belgian refugees, several thousands of whom would be billeted in an Irish community in Glasgow that had experience of exile and was unstinting in its generosity, with Celtic manager Willie Maley making a noteworthy contribution. And who could read the story of his nephew Josie's leave - taking of his family (headed by Tom of early Celtic fame) to join his regiment without a lump forming in the throat? Who, in reading of future Celt Hugh Hilley's joining up while under age, could imagine that it was but an initial instalment in an astonishing family saga? The Celtic story in World War 1, as Ian McCallum underlines, goes way beyond triumphs on the field of play, sending footballs to the front and displays of simulated trench warfare as part of the Army's recruiting drive.

In essence, this account is a depiction of a community emerging from the shadows. While not yet fully accepted in wider Scottish society, which still regarded it for reasons of race and religion as some form of underclass, it was beginning to make its mark, as illustrated most vividly by Glasgow ILP councillor John Wheatley demonstrating his leadership qualities during the 'Rent Strike' caused by greedy landlords trying to exploit the shortage of accommodation for war - workers flocking into the city. A few years after the cessation of hostilities, he would become the Minister of Health in the first Labour government, introducing the Housing Act which established the principle of - and groundwork for - the expansion of affordable municipal (or 'council') housing for the working class.

PAT WOODS

JULY 2014

Dedication

This book is dedicated to the forgotten and ignored generation of Celtic Football Club supporters who voluntarily responded to the bugle call at a time of dire national emergency. They shared with their fellow Glaswegians their own blood sacrifice and by doing so advanced the causes of understanding and toleration between communities.

Divided Loyalty

In 1898 the recruiting officer at the Connaught Rangers' depot in Galway received a letter from one Michael McDonough, who had enlisted the year before a year too young by recruiting rules. He had consequently been "claimed out by his mother for not being old enough to serve." He was gravely disappointed at being denied "the honour to ware [sic] the scarlet coat which Queen Victoria bestrode on my back." Now, however, he had come of age, and was determined "to take the honour to be a true brave soldier for Queen Victoria, for I am conscious [sic] enough that she is in want of brave soldiers now." McDonough had read in the papers of the troop movements to South Africa and India, and he was

> *full willing to leave my manson [sic] and go into the interiors of Africa to fight*
> *voluntarily [sic] for Queen Victoria and as far as there is life in my bones and*
> *breath in my body, I will not let any foreign invasion tramp on Queen's land.*

There was however, an important caveat that he felt he should mention. He pointed out that "if her [Victoria] or her leaders ever turns with cruelty on the Irish race, I will be the first that will raise my sword against her, " and in this regard he was sure that he would have "plenty of Irishmen at my side, for they are known to be the bravest race in the world."

They were sentiments shared by hundreds of thousands of his countrymen.

Contents

Illustrations

Acknowledgements

I wish to express my gratitude to the descendants of the individuals mentioned in the book, in particular, the Hilley family, the Angus family, the Gallacher family and the family of Thomas Maley. I would also like to thank the staff at the various libraries, archives, regimental museums and records offices for their assistance during my research, in particular, the Mitchell Library, the Scottish Football Association, the Scottish Football League, the National Archives, the National Archives of Ireland, the National Library of Scotland, the Queen's Own Highlanders (Seaforths and Camerons) Museum and the Irish Guards Museum.

I am grateful to the Glasgow Catholic Observer, the Glasgow Daily Record, the Glasgow Herald and the Glasgow Evening Times for permission to reproduce various graphics published in their period newspapers.

My thanks is also due to Pat Woods and Terry Dick, two great Celtic men, whose helpful advice and encouragement were crucial at various stages of the book.

A very particular thank you goes to Jamie Fox, both for his enthusiastic support for the Celtic, Glasgow Irish and the Great War project, and for his proof reading of the draft manuscripts. Without his in depth knowledge and incisive suggestions, the book would be much less than what it is.

I have made every reasonable effort to contact the copyright holders of material reproduced in this book. If any involuntary infringement of copyright has occurred, sincere apologies are offered and the owners of such copyright are requested to contact me.

All errors and omissions are, of course, entirely my own.

The author can be contacted by email at: ianmccallum@sky.com.

Ian McCallum

Glasgow

May 2014

"GATHER, GATHER, GATHER !"

Let Glasgow Flourish on Greater Fields

Prologue

The series of books, *The Celtic, Glasgow Irish and the Great War*, examines the social history, political atmosphere and wartime experiences of the Irish Roman Catholic community that had settled in Glasgow and central Scotland over the course of the nineteenth century. The books survey the community's support for and attitude to the British war effort over the course of the Great War seen through the prism of their greatest sporting achievement, the Celtic Football Club.

Book One	The Gathering Storms	
Book Two	**The Storms Break**	**Season 1914/15**
Book Three	The End of Innocence	Season 1915/16
Book Four	The Blood Sacrifice	Season 1916/17
Book Five	An Ocean of Blood	Season 1917/18
Book Six	The Never Ending Trials	Season 1918/19

The Storms Break is set within the context of the Glasgow Irish community's long-held aspiration for Home Rule for Ireland, and the conflicts and paradoxes of their dual Scots–Irish identity at a time of grave national emergency in Ireland and in Europe. The book examines the reaction of the Glasgow Irish to the social and moral pressures brought about by events at home and abroad as they unfolded over the first year of the Great War.

Central to the narrative is the Celtic football team's performances on the field of play and the club's reactions to political, military and footballing events as they unfolded over the course of the 1914/15 football season. Accused of not doing their bit, *The Storms Break* highlights the pressures applied to professional footballers to enlist into the military and examines the *middle-class* crusade to have *working-class* professional football suspended for the duration of the conflict.

The Storms Break also studies the race between the Celtic and Heart of Midlothian FC for the 1914/15 Scottish League title and examines the circumstances that led to a number of Hearts footballers famously enlisting into the army. It goes on to challenge the perception that their subsequent military service cost Heart of Midlothian the 1914/15 League Championship

Image Credit: www.naval-history.net

A BRITISH GENTLEMAN ABROAD

BERLIN, I JUNE 1914

As the British national anthem was played by the restaurant's string quartet, a Prussian officer seated at a table of military men rose from his chair. Snapping his heels together, he came rigidly to attention and saluted. The recipients of his salute were the members of the Celtic Football Club, then on the last night of their 1914 summer tour of Germany and central Europe. The Celtic manager, William Maley rose from his table, smiled and raised his glass to return the salute. Little did either man know that their respective nations would be at war with each other just weeks later.

William or Willie Maley as he was better known, was the very epitome of an Edwardian, middle class gentleman. He was well educated, well connected, well travelled and fiercely proud to be British. In fact, he was exactly the type of patriotic Briton who, when about to go abroad, would be routinely recruited by the British secret service as an information gatherer.

Born and raised among the British military and numbering very many British soldiers among his oldest and closest friends, Willie Maley was vastly knowledgeable on all matters military. He was capable of deducing information of intelligence value by simply noting the ranks and uniforms of officers, types of units, standard of equipment and the deportment of the soldiers that he came across while on tour. The Celtic club had toured the same counties in 1911, but by the summer of 1914 British diplomats were in no doubt as to Germany's imperialistic ambitions. In the Balkans, the Austro-Hungarian annexation of Bosnia and Herzegovina saw diplomatic relations between Russia and the German-Austro-Hungarian alliance deteriorate to the point where the British, potential allies of Russia, were becoming increasingly concerned. The attitude and demeanour of the native populations would therefore be of great interest to British intelligence, particularly the mood of any of the subject peoples from across the Austro-Hungarian Empire. The 1914 Celtic tour couldn't have been better timed had it been organised for them by British intelligence, it being conducted during the German and Austro-Hungarian annual military exercises. The massive conscript army of Imperial Germany alone could field five million men.

Later, the information gleaned from Maley's dining room encounter could have been added to his mental notes from previous encounters with the military in Leipzig, Dresden, Vienna, Budapest, and Potsdam where he organised a visit to a 'Zeppelin' base. The following day the Celtic party began their long journey home to Glasgow. As was usual for Celtic touring parties returning from abroad, they stopped off in London where they met up with Irish Parliamentary Party friends at Whitehall and at Westminster.

Some of Maley's very detailed and militarily astute comments and observations from the tour can be seen in 'The Man in the Know' sports column of the Glasgow Catholic Observer in June and July 1914. It was reported that when in Vienna the Celtic tourists encountered *several regiments of artillery and a regiment of Bersaglieri, light infantry recruited in the Tyrol. In Budapest, they'd seen regiments of Moravians, Honveds and Bohemians. The famous Prussian guard and the giant, menacing, German airships 'Zeppelins' soon to be dropping bombs on British homes were also mentioned. Overall, it was considered that the Germans and Austro-Hungarians were much better set up (equipped and trained) than the French. Ironically, considering it would be the Balkans that provided the spark that set the world ablaze, the surly, resentful attitude of the Bosnian Serb politicians and diplomats encountered while in Budapest was also noted and commented upon. After the assassination of the Austro-Hungarian heir in Sarajevo at the end of June, considered by many Irish Nationalists to be the price of Empire, it was thought unlikely that the Celtic would see the Prater or Corso next summer.*

Whether, Willie Maley was indeed an information gatherer we will probably never know. However, there is no doubt whatsoever that he would have been the right man, in the right place with the right experience, attitude and expertise for the task. As a confirmed and committed British imperialist, if he wasn't volunteering his observations to the secret service while stopped off in Whitehall, its intelligence analysts should have been reading the Glasgow Catholic Observer as the storms began to break over Europe.

THE STORMS BREAK

SCOTTISH FOOTBALL SEASON 1914 – 1915

IAN McCALLUM

Sergeant William Bailey

Sergeant William Bailey was a man of high renown,
Tooral looral looral looral loo,
In search of gallant young recruits he used to scour the town,
Tooral looral looral looral loo,
His face was full and swarthy, of medals he had forty,
And ribbons on his chest red white and blue,
It was he that looked the hero as he made the people stare O,
As he stood on Dunphy's corner tooral loo.

But alas for human greatness every dog he has his day,
Tooral looral looral looral loo,
And Sergeant William Bailey he is getting old and grey,
Tooral looral looral looral loo,
No longer youths are willing to take his dirty shilling,
And things for him are looking mighty blue,
In spite of fife and drumming no more recruits are coming,
For Sergeant William Bailey tooral loo.

Sergeant William Bailey what a wretched sight to see,
Tooral looral looral looral loo,
His back that once was firm and straight is almost bent in three,
Tooral looral looral looral loo,
Some rebel youths with placards have called his army blackguards,
And told the Irish youth just what to do,
He has lost his occupation let's sing in jubilation,
For Sergeant William Bailey tooral loo.

(Traditional)

Introduction

By 1914, Great Britain had for 100 years, been the sole and undisputed global superpower and was the possessor of the greatest empire the world had ever seen. Her possessions straddled the globe and at their zenith included nearly a quarter of the land surface and one quarter (400 million) of the world's population. The British diaspora largely populated colonial America and what were then known as the great white dominions of Canada, Australia and New Zealand. The peoples of the dominions regarded themselves still as distinctly British and remained emotionally and financially tied to Great Britain, which they regarded as the motherland. With colonies and naval bases on every continent, through the might of the Royal Navy, the long arm of British political influence was felt worldwide. The small, entirely volunteer British Army was scattered across the Empire, where the battalions stationed in the various colonies were employed mainly on policing duties. Great Britain's imperial power was at its zenith, but after two vicious little wars in South Africa with the Boer farmers, spanning the turn of the century, its thirst for colonies had abated and the empire was increasingly being viewed more as an economic bloc and a captive market for British industry. However, Britain's industrial might was on the wane and it was no longer the world's leading industrial power. From the 1870s, Britain's industrial and commercial strength had declined relative to that of the United States of America and Imperial Germany and both nations had overtaken Britain industrially. Despite that fact, Britain, bolstered by being the world's banker and by having a booming shipbuilding industry, remained the leading power in the world thanks to its financial resources, productive capacity, imperial possessions and the might of the Royal Navy.

On the eve of the war, Great Britain was a constitutional monarchy, edging its way towards democracy, but the right to vote was still largely dependent on wealth and 40 per cent of males and all women were still disenfranchised. The country was governed by a parliament with an elected House of Commons and a hereditary House of Lords. At that time, there were two great political parties, which vied to form the government, the Conservative/Liberal Unionists and the Liberals. The electorate saw the former as representing the Establishment, the middle and business classes, and the party attracted the support of Irish Unionist MPs due to its opposition to Irish Home Rule. The Liberal Party represented a wider cross section of society and presented a progressive, social liberal agenda, which included taxing the rich to pay for welfare reforms. The party also supported a limited form of devolved government for Ireland.

The third strongest party was the Irish Parliamentary Party (IPP), which represented Irish Nationalist aspirations for Ireland, mainly land reform and home rule. The IPP enjoyed the support of most Irish Nationalists, including most Glasgow Irish Nationalists. The fledgling socialists of the British Labour Party, who represented the lower or working classes, were only in fourth place. Finally, the All-For-Ireland League (AFIL) was another Irish Nationalist political party with MPs at Westminster. The party's main political aim was to unite all Irishmen behind home rule. The AFIL was more stridently Nationalist than the IPP and its aim was to distance Ireland from Great Britain through a greater degree of autonomy than the IPP envisaged, but to avoid at any cost the partitioning of Ireland. Perhaps counter-intuitively the AFIL took a serious view of Unionist objections to Home Rule. The league sought to allay what it held to be deep-seated and reasonable anxieties about Home Rule.

In the decade leading up to the Great War, Britain was a divided nation, riven by a number of major internal tensions: over Ireland, women's suffrage and long-running increasingly militant labour disputes. The country was one of the wealthiest on earth, but the disparity of wealth was staggering. In 1900 it was estimated that around 30 per cent of the British population lived on the verge of starvation. In what was a massively deferential class-driven age, the lower or working classes were expected to know their place in society and to respect those in the classes above them, particularly those members of what was known as the Establishment, a political, religious and financial elite who controlled and governed the country.

In 1906, a Liberal government was elected with a massive majority. It introduced a whole raft of social reforms, which included: worker compensation schemes for injuries at work, free medical tests and treatment for school children. In 1908 the foundations of the modern Welfare State were laid with the introduction of the first state pension of five shillings per week for those over seventy years of age and in 1911 the National Insurance Act, which provided insurance for workers unable to work through sickness. A very basic unemployment scheme for workers in certain industries prone to short-term lay-offs was also introduced. To pay for the social reforms, the Liberal government taxed the wealthy. The reforms were resisted in the middle- and upper-class Conservative party, which dominated the unelected House of Lords that had the power to veto indefinitely bills passed in the House of Commons. The political crisis caused by the Lords' rejection of the 1909 People's Budget led to the general election of 1910, which resulted in a hung parliament. The Liberal party under Herbert Asquith formed a new government only with the conditional support of the Irish Parliamentary Party (IPP) led by John Redmond MP, which held the balance of power.

Born in Co Wexford, the son of an Irish Nationalist MP, John Redmond was educated by the Jesuits at Clongowes Wood and later at Trinity College, Dublin. The Redmond family were among the few members of the Catholic landed class who had managed to hold onto their land through the period of the Penal Laws. His connections with the smaller landed gentry made him less of a fierce and relentless enemy of the landlord class than, for instance, Michael Davitt, who was the son of a small farmer evicted from his home while a child. However, Redmond did take part in the Land War (1879–82) and the Plan of Campaign (1886–91) and was briefly imprisoned in 1888 for incitement. By the turn of the twentieth century, he had united and taken over the leadership of the IPP and was seen as the Irish political successor to the immortal Daniel O'Connell and Charles Stewart Parnell. He lacked the charm of the former and the political guile and ruthlessness of the latter, but he was an immensely popular figure in his own right.

The IPP existed purely to deliver by constitutional means Irish Home Rule and land reform and was in most other aspects fairly conservative. It is important to understand exactly where John Redmond stood in the context of his subsequent, unequivocal support for the British during the Great War and to recognise the overwhelming popular support both he and his political position enjoyed in the first two years of the war. Redmond was deeply opposed to the use of physical force as a means to political ends. As a great admirer of the British House of Commons, he was committed to political change by constitutional means. He was convinced of the power of a still evolving constitutional British democracy and was sure he could gain land reform and Home Rule for the whole of Ireland on his terms.

By 1914, most constitutional Nationalists considered their aims for land reform, local government and education were well on the way to being achieved. The ability of tenants to buy their holdings through the Land Acts of 1881, 1903 and 1909 saw millions of acres back in the hands of the native Irish. On the subject of Home Rule, Redmond considered it politically, financially and practically undesirable that Ireland should be wholly independent of and outside the most economically powerful organisation on earth, the British Empire. Much the same economic reasons apply to modern day Britain and Ireland and their continued membership of the European Union. His vision was that Irish Home Rule was an interim step to All-Ireland autonomy. In his own words:

> I mean the restoration to Ireland of representative government in accordance with the constitutionally expressed will of a majority. ... I mean that the internal affairs of Ireland shall be regulated by an Irish Parliament ... that all Imperial affairs ... and common interests of the Empire shall continue to be regulated by the Imperial Parliament as at present. ... The Irish say to England, 'Retain every guarantee of the entire strength of the Empire and give up that which you have shown yourself incompetent to fulfil satisfactorily.'

Therefore, his vision was one in which an Irish parliament based in Dublin would be responsible for all internal Irish matters, but the Irish would retain representation and an Irish voice at Westminster, largely as exists with the devolved parliaments of the Scots and Welsh today. He further expected that in time Irish Home Rule would evolve into full autonomy on a dominion model similar to those of Australia and Canada.

Driven on by John Redmond, the Liberal party introduced the Parliament Act of 1911, which ended the power of hereditary peers to veto government bills indefinitely. Now the unelected peers of the realm could only hold up a bill for three years, before the said bill would automatically pass through the Lords. The Act was only pushed through the two houses of parliament with the support of the IPP and the threat to swamp the House of Lords with new Liberal peers. The curtailing of the veto powers of the Lords enabled the Liberals finally to push through the 1912 Home Rule for Ireland Bill in the spring of 1914. The implementation of the bill would see the creation of an Irish parliament in Dublin with very limited autonomy from London, and controlled by Roman Catholic, Irish Nationalist politicians. The enactment of the Irish Home Rule Bill had been bitterly opposed by the Ulster Unionists. Realising that their struggle to prevent the enactment of the Bill had been lost, and aided and abetted by the British Conservative Party, they tabled an amendment to the Bill proposing that Ulster be excluded from the constitutional change.

The resurgence and advances of Irish nationalism in the two decades prior to the Great War had resulted in an upsurge in Unionism, particularly Ulster Unionism, as a decidedly worried Protestant community in Ireland sought to strengthen ties with mainland Britain. By the spring of 1914, a political impasse over Home Rule had taken Ireland to the verge of civil war. Unionists and Nationalists armed their followers and formed paramilitary units: the predominantly

Unionist and Orange Ulster Volunteer Force (UVF) and the Nationalist, predominately Roman Catholic, Irish Volunteers. In mid-1914, John Redmond, took political control of the Irish Volunteers, while the UVF was led by Sir Edward Carson. Both forces illegally imported arms; however, the UVF, with much wealthier backers, was significantly better armed than the Nationalists. While the UVF could train with modern weapons including machine guns, the Nationalists listed pikes on their weapons list. In the summer of 1914 they confronted each other over the barrels of guns, determined to impose their vision of Ireland on the other community by force if necessary.

Carson's Call

In addition to the two main political protagonists in Ireland, there were at the time three other Nationalist organisations with their own visions of a New Ireland. First, there was a militant labour movement under Edinburgh Irish socialist and former British soldier James Connolly. He was motivated by the Marxist belief that socialism could only be achieved when a country was sufficiently industrialised for the proletariat to be strong enough to overthrow the bosses and their capitalist oppression. Born of Irish parents, Connolly believed the British establishment deliberately kept the south of Ireland agricultural and poor to serve the needs of the wider British economy. To Connolly, complete independence from Britain was essential if Ireland was ever to become a socialist state. By linking trade unionism with his aim of establishing a socialist workers' republic, he brought many of the urban working class, who previously had little interest in politics, into the Republican and therefore, by definition, the separatist fold. This was a re-emergence of the idea for a Republican revolution after a hundred years and was a growing force pushing for independence from Britain. James Connolly had many adherents in central Scotland with connections to the Independent Labour Party and to the Catholic Socialist Society. As far as the Unionists and Redmond's Nationalists were concerned, Connolly wrote in the socialist newspaper Forward in March 1911:

> We can detest them both. In fact, they represent the same principle in
> different stages of social development. The Tories are the conservatives
> of Irish feudalism; the United Irish Leaguers are the conservatives of a
> belated Irish capitalism. It is our business to help the latter against the
> former only when we can do so without prejudice to our own integrity as
> a movement.

During the Dublin Lockout of 1913, a workers militia known as the Irish Citizen Army was formed to protect the striking ITGWU workers from the Dublin Corporation sponsored violence of the Dublin police. Jim Larkin and James Connolly were the titular leaders of the organisation, but it was former British Army officer Captain Jack White who formed and trained the 300-strong Irish Citizen Army.

The second was Sinn Féin (*We Ourselves*), a movement founded by Arthur Griffith in 1905. Interestingly, it was Mary Lambert Butler, a cousin of Sir Edward Carson, who suggested the name to Griffith. His constitutional idea was for a dual monarchy, mimicking a similar concept that had worked well for Austria and Hungary, from which the plan took its title, the *Austrian Solution*. The idea was akin to a federal system in which the separate, but equal, kingdoms of Ireland and Britain were governed separately under the same monarch. The movement rejected Connolly's ideas of socialism and the violent overthrow of capitalism, although at times they did cooperate. They also rejected the IPP's constitutional approach. Arthur Griffith advocated a system of peaceful resistance in which an independent Irish parliament would be set up in Dublin to govern Ireland in defiance of the British government. In effect, the Irish Government would carry on the management of Irish internal affairs as if it were already independent, ignoring the usual British institutions, such as the courts and civil administration, as though they never existed. Although a former member of the IRB, Griffith was not really a Republican and Sinn Féin did not want an Irish republic. He was happy enough to see Ireland remain within the British Empire as long as it was to the material benefit of the Irish people. While he had initially denounced the 1912 Home Rule Bill as a 'grotesque abortion' of the national demand, he quickly rallied and called on separatists to make preparations for becoming the principal party of opposition in the Irish parliament. His organisation would later get the blame for the Easter Rising despite never actually supporting or taking part in it. The organisation had almost disappeared by 1914 although Griffith still published his newspaper Sinn Féin on an occasional basis, but he was on the verge of bankruptcy.

Third, there was a small, but dedicated number of men, not all Irish and not all Catholic, who believed that only a fully independent and republican Ireland would be acceptable. (*Republicanism has never been an exclusively Catholic enterprise.*) The Irish Republican Brotherhood (IRB) was a secret, non-sectarian, oath-bound organisation founded in Ireland in 1858 by James Stephens. The organisation believed the only way to overthrow British rule in Ireland was by force of arms and in 1914 the organisation was actively working to that end. The IRB in 1914 was no longer a mass organisation, as it had been in the 1860s. It had about 1300 members, mostly elderly Fenians organised into small centres throughout Ireland and in British cities with large Irish immigrant populations, like London, Liverpool and Glasgow. Although much reduced in numbers, its influence was felt across a broad cross section of Nationalist organisations that it had infiltrated, from cultural organisations, the Gaelic League and GAA, to the political party Sinn Féin, the Irish Industrial Committee and most significantly, from November 1913, the Irish Volunteers. Its influence, in short, was felt far beyond its own ranks.

Despite the objections and barriers put in its place, by the spring of 1914 the Irish Home Rule Bill had passed through all the administrative stages in both the House of Commons and the House of Lords, the cherished dream of millions of Irish Nationalists was about to be realised. John O'Brien and his party the AFIL had opposed the IPP's coercive 'Ulster must follow' policy, and had published in January 1914 specific concessions that would enable Ulster to join a Dublin parliament believing in 'any price for a United Ireland, but never partition'. The AFIL MPs abstained from the final vote passing the Act, describing it as a 'partition' deal. Notwithstanding, the vexed and still unresolved question of Ulster, the Irish Home Rule Bill was about to be passed into law and required only the King's signature. John Redmond, the Nationalist leader of the Irish Parliamentary Party (IPP), having led the Nationalist Irish to this point, was at the height of his popularity having apparently succeeded where more illustrious Irish patriots had failed. With Home Rule seemingly only a matter of time, the Catholic Irish were as politically strong as they had been for centuries.

Education reforms ensured that the Irish people were better educated than ever before, with illiteracy rates having fallen from around 50 per cent in 1861 to below 20 per cent in 1911. This resulted in a growing consciousness of Irish identity that in turn encouraged the revival of the Irish language and Celtic culture. An expanding Catholic business and professional middle class was prospering in Ireland, particularly in and around Dublin, and although there was still a long way to go, with very many serious social injustices still to be righted, to most politically minded Irish nationalist, overall, the future of Erin seemed set fair.

In the summer of 1914, the British government did not have their troubles to seek; it was said of Prime Minister Asquith: 'Very few prime ministers in history have been afflicted by so many plagues and in so short a space of time.' In addition to Ireland, and militant suffragettes starving themselves in the name of women's suffrage, the autumn and winter promised industrial disturbances on a previously unseen scale with the trade unions planning a general strike. The domestic strife at the heart of the British Empire was being carefully noted by her potential enemies abroad, where it seemed to many that a great power appeared to be sinking into decadence and decay. In Europe, the deteriorating diplomatic situation in the Balkans, where the Austro-Hungarian Empire was flexing its military muscle, encouraged by its Germanic cousins, was adding to the British government's concerns.

The German Empire, formed by the unification of the German states after the Prussian defeat of France in the 1870 Franco-Prussian War, appeared economically and militarily threatening. As a result, the major European nations entered into a whole series of treaties and mutual protection alliances designed by the politicians to maintain a balance of power and thus prevent a major war in Europe. The alliances fluctuated over the years prior to the Great War, but by 1914 the alignment was clear enough: Germany, Austro-Hungary and a very reluctant Italy, known as the Triple Alliance, were in one camp and in the other camp was the Triple Entente of France, Russia and a very reluctant Great Britain. In compliance with the numerous treaty obligations, the nations agreed either to come to each other's aid should they be attacked, or at least not to interfere in any conflict between the nations. Although the British too had been a signatory of a number of the treaties and alliance, her political aims in Europe had long been about maintaining a balance of power among the most powerful nations. As long as no single nation completely dominated, the British were happy enough to see the nations squabble among themselves, remaining in what was called at the time 'splendid isolation'. Britain's period of isolation was about to come to an abrupt end, as bound together by the treaties and agreements, like a line of manacled convicts, the major nations of Europe shuffled towards the lip of a cliff.

In the years preceding the Great War, a whole series of minor incidents and diplomatic slights combined to edge the nations ever closer to that precipice. On 28 June 1914, a consumptive Serbian youth named Gavrilo Princip stepped off a Sarajevo pavement and shot dead the heir presumptive of the Austro-Hungarian Empire. Sarajevo was the capital of Bosnia, a minor province of the Austro-Hungarian Empire only recently annexed from the failing Ottoman Empire. Bosnia was situated in the Balkans, a most unstable region of southern Europe populated by a volatile mix of Slavs, Serbs and Croats. The independently minded Bosnians were striving for autonomy, but if they had to be part of something, they would have chosen to be annexed by their ethnic cousins in the neighbouring independent state of Serbia. The shot that Princip fired into the Archduke's limousine is often called 'the fuse that set Europe ablaze'; that is a slight exaggeration, but the assassination certainly did not help the situation. What it did was to provide the excuse for Austria-Hungary to slap down the upstart Serbians whose influence in the region was growing. Austria-Hungary's reaction to the assassination of its heir (who was not greatly liked by the Emperor, Franz Josef, or his government) was three weeks in the cooking.

The Austro-Hungarians had convinced themselves that Belgrade was implicated in the assassination and decided to stamp their authority upon the Serbians, crushing the Nationalist movement in the region and cementing Austria-Hungary's influence in the Balkans. It did so by issuing an ultimatum to Serbia, which effectively nullified Serbia's sovereignty. Sir Edward Grey, the British Foreign Secretary, commented that he had 'never before seen one state address to another independent state a document of so formidable a character'. Austria-Hungary's expectation was that Serbia would reject the ultimatum, thereby giving her a pretext for launching a limited war against Serbia. However, the Serbians had Slavic ties with mighty Russia, an altogether different proposition for Austria-Hungary. Having recently watched Russia back down over Bosnia-Herzegovina, Austria-Hungary did not expect Russia to be drawn into the dispute, other than through diplomatic protest. However, it sought reassurances from Germany, that it would come to its aid should the unthinkable happen and Russia declare war. Imperial Germany readily agreed, even encouraging Austria-Hungary's warlike stance by issuing the infamous Blank Cheque. The Germans and particularly their military leadership were well aware that their actions risked turning a local dispute into a major European war, but they believed that war in Western Europe was inevitable and if it happened, better sooner than later. If sooner, they believed they could win the war and gain complete domination of Western Europe.

Despite Serbia endeavouring to placate them, the Austro-Hungarians, as planned, rejected the Serbian counter-offers and encouraged by Germany declared war on Serbia. Russia mobilised her vast army in support of the Serbs, Germany mobilised her armies in support of Austria and declared war on Russia on 1 August and on France two days later. Russia looked for support from her ally France and France looked to a very reluctant Great Britain. Although the British were allied to both France and Russia, it was a much looser worded agreement, one which placed a 'moral obligation' to come to the aid of the French. Or so they thought, until the French ambassador in London pulled a naval agreement out from his back pocket in which the British had agreed to protect northern French ports from German attack, in return for which the French looked after British interests in the Mediterranean.

With the Balkan crisis threatening to plunge the whole of Europe into war, British politicians were forced to turn their full attention away from domestic problems and to take close note of the deteriorating political situation in Europe. As late as 31 July, the British Prime Minister, Herbert Asquith, had told the Archbishop of Canterbury that Britain would not intervene in any European conflict. There had been little sympathy in Britain for Serbia up to this point and only a few people could have told you anything about it, including exactly where it was. Just about everyone who was anyone pleaded with the government not to become involved, including the governor of the Bank of England, who warned the Chancellor of the Exchequer, Lloyd George, of a possible financial collapse. With the exception of the armaments industry, big business desperately wanted to stay out of it and at the beginning of August the socialists of the Independent Labour Party organised a number of anti-war demonstrations around the country, including one on Glasgow Green.

Gavrilo Princip's pistol shots had pushed the Austro-Hungarians over the lip of the cliff and over the course of the first week of August 1914, the remaining nations were dragged into the abyss.

DEAR AULD GLESGA TOON

By 1911, 45 per cent of the population of Scotland lived in the industrial central belt of the country and Glasgow on the eve of the Great War was a metropolis of 1,000,000 people. It was one of the great cities of the British Empire, an industrial colossus and the sixth largest by population in Europe. The proudly Imperialistic Victorian city fathers had unashamedly adopted the title of Second City of the Empire. The city dominated the world in heavy engineering and shipbuilding and the term 'Clyde built' was a byword for engineering excellence. By the mid-1870s, the Clyde had replaced the Thames as the centre of British shipbuilding and by 1885, ten Scots firms produced 20 per cent of Britain's steel output. Railway locomotives built by the North British Locomotive Company based in Springburn were sold all over the world and accounted for half of Britain's total production. Overall, the Scottish engineering industry employed 78,000 workers. The shipbuilding, railway and heavy engineering industries in Glasgow and the west of Scotland had created a new social force, the *industrial working class*. Over two-thirds of all trade unionists in Scotland worked in Glasgow. The city itself was at the centre of an industrial Clydeside conurbation that stretched almost continuously for over fifty miles. The Glasgow and Scottish economy depended heavily on international trade, particularly with the countries of the British Empire. Yet despite the seeming invincibility of British industry, many sectors were in fact in decline. The reliance on heavy industry, whose markets were largely overseas, caused fluctuations in demand, which produced regular downturns and unemployment. The build-up of armaments in the decade preceding the Great War papered over the cracks in this increasingly outdated economic structure and the underlying social problems were forgotten.

Politically, the city was traditionally a Liberal stronghold, but at the turn of the twentieth century the Conservatives assumed control of the city council. The Scottish Labour movement was at last beginning to gain some traction; the first working-class representatives were elected to the town council in the 1890s and the city got its first Labour MP in 1906. The tens of thousands of Glasgow's seething population of over a million souls, 700,000 of whom were crammed into the city's three central square miles, lived in poverty. Hundreds of thousands of people of all religious and political persuasions were condemned to live restricted and unfulfilled lives, caught up in a never-ending cycle of toil and want. The lower or working class, which made up around 75 per cent of the population, was an irreverent ethnic melting pot of Scots Highlanders and Lowlanders, native Irish and Glasgow Irish, Jews, Italians, Poles and even a few English, a vibrant mix of the godly and ungodly, the former usually only on a Sunday. They lived cheek by jowl, irrespective of race or religious persuasion, in the ubiquitous soot-blackened grey sandstone tenement blocks laid out in a horseshoe to the north, south and east of the city, very many still in appalling slum conditions. The last cholera outbreak in the city was in the 1860s but diseases such as bronchitis, tuberculosis and pneumonia resulted in very high death rates. It was a dirty, unhealthy, hard-grafting and equally hard-drinking city (there were 1700 drinking establishments in the city in 1912) of predominantly low-paid, but increasingly militant, skilled, semi-skilled and unskilled manual workers.

As a result of the industrial revolution and the disastrous Irish potato famine of the mid-1840s, successive waves of Irish immigrants, mostly Roman Catholics, arrived in Glasgow and its satellite villages over the course of the nineteenth century. The Catholic Irish immigrants and their descendants settled in the most Protestant, anti-Catholic country in the whole of Europe, and as a result of their race and religion suffered decades of institutionalised racism, sectarianism and discrimination. They encountered an all-pervasive attitude that because of their race, and political and religious beliefs, they were lacking in loyalty and the qualities of responsible citizenship. This widely held perception resulted in the stigmatisation and social marginalisation of the Catholic Irish community.

Although the vast majority of the economic immigrants who fled Ireland to settle in Scotland were Roman Catholics, a significant number of Irish Protestants, mainly from Ulster, also settled in west central Scotland over the same period, driven out of Ireland by the same economic necessity as their Catholic neighbours. They too maintained very close links with family and friends left behind in the north of Ireland. For much of the nineteenth century they too suffered discrimination from the native Scots being regarded very much as Irish as opposed to Scots. By the turn of the twentieth century, the early Protestant Irish immigrants, having lost their distinctive Ulster brogue, had largely been absorbed into the wider Scots community. However, Irish Protestant immigrants who maintained links with what was regarded by most native Scots as a distinctly Irish Orange Order, were still labelled as Protestant Glasgow Irish. The descendants of the early Irish Catholic immigrants, born and raised in Glasgow and west central Scotland, began to be labelled the 'Glasgow Irish'. It was a title that became a euphemism for a Roman Catholic of Irish descent and was a term of derision and contempt. Although the title was aimed specifically at the Catholic Irish in Glasgow and its environs, the term was in general usage throughout central Scotland.

As a consequence of their social exclusion from the wider Glasgow society, the Glasgow Irish over the course of several decades established their own vibrant, socially supportive community. Largely as a result of racism and bigotry, the Glasgow Irish remained firmly lodged at the very bottom of the social and economic ladder. For the most part, they could only find work in the unskilled sectors of the job market. The racial discrimination and bigotry suffered by the vast majority of the Glasgow Irish ensured they were firmly entrenched on the lowest tier of the all-pervasive British class system, although the independent but seriously underfunded Catholic education system was another contributing factor. It took very little to tip them from being what was considered to be respectable poor to being unrespectable poor, which helped cement the negative stereotyping from which they already suffered.

On the eve of war, Archbishop John Aloysius McGuire was the religious leader of the Glasgow's Roman Catholic community. Born of Irish parents in Burrells Lane, off the High Street, Glasgow on 8 September 1851, he was educated at St Mungo's Academy, St Aloysius College and at Stoneyhurst College before studying law at Glasgow University. In 1871, he relinquished his studies and went to Rome. He was ordained a priest in 1875 and back in Glasgow, he worked under Archbishop Charles Eyre before being ordained a Bishop in 1894. In 1902, he was appointed Archbishop of Glasgow on the death of Archbishop Eyre. A man of the people, he was a supporter of the early socialist movement.

Cocooned in their own, socially self-sufficient community, the Glasgow Irish prospered within the financial and social constraints imposed upon them. Thanks mainly to a concerted drive for respectability over a period of twenty-five years, led in the main by the Roman Catholic Church, the Glasgow Irish had begun, finally, to emerge from the shadows and were increasingly interacting on equal terms with the wider Scottish community. The general perception among the Glasgow Irish at the turn of the twentieth century was that socially and economically progress was being made and that the Irish were no longer confined *exclusively* to the *low jobs* as was once the case. Glasgow employers were increasingly finding that the Irish were capable and reliable and, of course, business sense and self-interest overrode racism and bigotry. Even the Glasgow Catholic Observer, the Glasgow Irish newspaper, was moved to comment, 'in fairness most Glasgow employers were very impartial as to whom they employ'. With an expanding, increasingly well respected and largely accepted business and professional class, the community's ambition of acceptance, leading to full integration into the wider Glasgow community, seemed within touching distance.

The Glasgow Irish were a community in transition, toiling with overlapping identities – ethnic, religious and political. By the eve of the Great War, the social and cultural ties of the Glasgow Irish to the *auld country* remained immensely strong; as demonstrated in their membership of various Irish social and cultural organisations, however, as Scottish and Glaswegian influences increasingly affected the Glasgow Irish, there was an inevitable degree of ethnic fade. Therefore the children of the Irish immigrants born in Glasgow and Scotland were increasingly establishing emotional and cultural bonds in their own city and country of birth. They began to consider themselves as something different, not entirely Irish and not entirely Scots. The resulting Scots-Irish identity was one in which most of the younger generation of Glasgow Irish were completely comfortable and the latest generation of Glasgow Irish were becoming increasingly involved in the wider Glasgow community. They considered themselves to be stakeholders in their own city and felt a civic responsibility to contribute to the wider community. This latest generation of Glasgow Irish were better educated than ever before, and were now forcing their way into mainstream society. They were at the forefront of the drive challenging ancient injustices and were increasingly becoming involved in local politics, taking part in school boards, standing in parish board elections and participating in various cross-community projects. Over the first decade of the twentieth century, increasing numbers of the

Glasgow Irish were standing as candidates at local municipal elections. Reflecting the working and housing conditions that the community was forced to endure, they were increasingly finding cause with the socialists of the emerging Independent Labour Party (ILP). Glasgow Irish political leaders, such as John Wheatley and Patrick Dollan,

Rory Oge O'More Irish Warpipe Band at Celtic Park, 21 March 1914

hugely influenced local politics in Glasgow came to their socialist ideals through Irish nationalism.

When it came to national politics, the Glasgow Irish voter was joined at the hip to the causes of Irish Nationalism. For centuries the native Catholic Irish people had struggled, very often led by Irish Presbyterians, to win various degrees of autonomy or Home Rule, first from England, then from a united Great Britain and Ireland. The struggles, very often violent, had left the native Catholic Irish in particular with a reputation for endemic disloyalty to the British state. In the last decades of the nineteenth century a series of violent incidents on the British mainland, perpetrated by advanced Irish Republicans (the Fenians), had thrown the loyalty of the Irish living in Britain, including the Glasgow-born Irish, into question. The rebellious, disloyal reputation lingered on through their support for Irish Home Rule, despite it now being by peaceful, constitutional means.

By 1914, the Glasgow Irish's political support had for the best part of twenty-five years gone unconditionally to the constitutional Irish Nationalists of the Irish Parliamentary Party, led for the past fifteen years by the massively popular John Redmond MP. Encouraged by the IPP election machine, at general or by-elections for the British parliament, the Glasgow Irish vote conditionally went to the Liberal Party, largely, although not exclusively, because of its commitment to the introduction of Home Rule for Ireland. Over the early months of 1914, the Glasgow Irish community watched with increasing concern as the Home Rule debate took Ireland to the brink of civil war. In response to the Unionist/Orange faction in the north of Ireland forming the paramilitary Ulster Defence Force (UDF), in November 1913 the Irish Volunteers had been formed in Dublin. The Glasgow Irish formed their own Irish Volunteer battalions based in Glasgow and Clydebank in January 1914. Not to be outdone Glasgow's Orangemen also formed an UVF battalion, and on 23 May 1914 the Glasgow Herald was reporting that it was 2000 strong.

While remaining passionate about the fate of Ireland and their Roman Catholic faith, the Glasgow Irish community and its political and religious leaders were at the same time dedicated to self-improvement and the advancement of their community in Glasgow and Scotland. Their long-term and wholehearted support of constitutional nationalism in the guise of the IPP and its Home Rule movement had allowed them to advance both causes. By overwhelmingly foregoing the physical force republican tactics of the Fenians, the Glasgow Irish were demonstrating to their host society that they deserved its respect and that their contribution and support of constitutional Nationalism merited recognition.

For the Glasgow Irish and constitutional Irish Nationalists, the outbreak of the Great War threatened decades of political, social and economic progress as the British people watched the Nationalist Irish grapple with the paradox of Irish Nationalist political interests and support for the British war effort. For the first eighteen months of the Great War, enlistment into the British armed forces would be entirely voluntary and a matter for an individual's personal choice. As the British nation rose to the challenge of what would quickly become *Total War*, the Glasgow Irish were forced to decide whose side they were on.

From the start of the Great War, the Irish and by association the Glasgow Irish would come under close scrutiny regarding their loyalty and commitment to Great Britain and to the British war effort. Just how Scottish or British did third- or sometimes even fourth-generation Glasgow Irish feel and how much loyalty did the Scots-born Irish feel they owed to their homeland? How were they supposed to respond to the British nation's call to arms having suffered decades of bigotry, derision, racism and marginalisation? On a very personal level, the dilemma for the Glasgow Irish was understanding just how much loyalty they felt they owed to their local communities, to their neighbours and workmates? Exactly how marginalised and under siege did they as a community feel? Was it enough to stand on the sidelines of the war? Just how much moral pressure did the Glasgow Irish feel as they watched their neighbours march off to defend the community, including their own wives and children?

Conditioned for the best part of forty years by the Roman Catholic Church and their political leaders to strive for respectability, advancement and inclusion into the wider Scottish society, the Great War would provide an opportunity for the Glasgow Irish to demonstrate their commitment to their host society by contributing their share of the blood sacrifice. The question was, would the Glasgow Irish take the opportunity or adopt the old dictum that 'England's difficulty was Ireland's opportunity'?

CELTIC FOOTBALL CLUB

To understand something of the political and business atmosphere in which the directors and supporters of Celtic Football Club operated during the Great War, it is necessary to understand the political traditions and reputation of the club and its Glasgow Irish supporters over the first twenty-five years of its existence. The Celtic Football and Athletic Club was formed in the St Mary's League of the Cross hall at 67 East Rose Street on 6 November 1887. The club's Glasgow Irish founding fathers and later its directors were politically very active and outspoken on very many topics including social welfare, education, land reform in both Ireland and the Scottish Highlands, and British Imperialism. From the turn of the twentieth century, the Glasgow Irish had been flirting with the socialist policies of the Scottish Labour Party to which they were naturally drawn; however, the glittering prize for most people with Irish Nationalist sympathies was still Home Rule for Ireland. For the Glasgow Irish, all these political subjects were heavily influenced by their Roman Catholic religion and their Irish heritage. As the founding fathers led the Celtic to its pre-eminent position in Scottish football, the club itself became a highly visible vehicle and propaganda tool, advertising and promoting the political beliefs and aspirations of the Glasgow Irish community, the vast majority of whom supported Home Rule for Ireland. The cornerstone of their political beliefs, *constitutional* Irish Nationalism, is manifestly clear in their membership and adherence to the agenda and philosophies of the Home Government Branch of the Irish National League (INL) and its successor the United Irish League (UIL). Like the INL and UIL, the main political focus of the Glasgow-based Home Government Branch was Irish ¬– rather than Scottish or British – land reform and self-government for Ireland, while the protection of the interests of the Irish in Britain was secondary.

Formed by Irish protestant John Ferguson in 1871, the Home Government Branch came to dominate Irish politics completely in Scotland and its weekly meetings were known as the parliament of the Glasgow Irish. It raised considerable sums of money for the IPP and brought all the major Nationalist politicians of the time to Glasgow; Parnell, Davitt and John Redmond came and they were very happy to do so, recognising the importance of Glasgow Irish support. Rallied by the Irish Nationalists' mouthpiece, the Glasgow Observer, the Glasgow Irish vote conditionally went to the Liberal Party, which promised to deliver both Home Rule and land reform. John Ferguson and the Home Government Branch had a profound influence on the men involved in the founding and early development of Celtic FC. John Glass, Joe Shaughnessy, John O'Hara, Willie and Tom Maley, James McKay, James Kelly, Hugh and Arthur Murphy, the McKillop brothers, Joseph McGroary, James Quillan, Thomas White, and Thomas and Partick Colgan were all disciples and the list could go on. All shared Ferguson's, at times, paradoxical beliefs in a mix of socialism and capitalism, imperialism and Nationalism, both Irish and Scots versions. From around 1903, the UIL was effectively under the control of John Redmond, the leader of the Irish Parliamentary Party (IPP) since 1900. By 1914, the latest generations of Glasgow Irish had been supporting the aims of the IPP for the best part of twenty-five years, first under Charles Stewart Parnell and for the last fourteen years under the leadership of John Redmond. Very many had grown up with the dream of Irish Home Rule, which now seemed at last to be within touching distance.

Despite the passing of that generation of Glasgow Irish Nationalists who had felt closest to Ireland and who had founded, managed and eventually took ownership of the club, the Celtic directors and shareholders were still closely and publicly associated with Irish Nationalist causes. They still regularly supported and financially contributed to the cause of constitutional Nationalism in the form of the Irish Parliamentary Party led by John Redmond. In May 1909, the Celtic's secretary and manager, Willie Maley, organised the travel arrangements for the Home Government Branch delegates to the United Irish League conference in Manchester, while his brother Tom was at the same time lecturing at UIL meetings. At the end of October, Irish Nationalist MP Joe Devlin attended a Celtic versus Clyde game played at Shawfield. Accompanied by Celtic director John McKillop, the Belfast MP visited the Celtic dressing room after the game to congratulate the Bhoys on their 2–0 victory. *Wee Joe* was a lifelong supporter of the Celtic's Irish cousins, the Belfast Celtic FC.

In March 1911, John Redmond MP was the keynote speaker at a St Patrick's Day lecture in Glasgow. As a massively popular figure among the Glasgow Irish, over a thousand Nationalists packed into the hall to hear him speak, including Celtic's Tom Maley and his wife Elizabeth. Also in the crowd was Glasgow Irish socialist Willie Gallacher, by then a member of the Marxist inclined Social Democratic Federation, which was soon to morph into the British Socialist Party. A child of a mixed marriage, Gallacher once described how his Irish blood leapt as he listened to John Redmond tear into the subject of Home Rule like a man inspired. At the same time, former Celtic committeeman Arthur Murphy reopened the Home Government Branch, closed after internal disputes over its support of the ILP at the request of John Redmond, who became its honorary president. Later that year, a delegation of players and officials from Celtic FC returning from their European tour diverted into London where they met Irish Party MPs at Westminster.

John Redmond MP

In June 1913, Redmond and the IPP leadership came to Glasgow to muster support for the Home Rule Bill. At a meeting held in St Andrew's Halls in the city, 5000 Glasgow Nationalists crammed into the room to hear the leaders speak. The meeting was organised by the Glasgow Liberals including Celtic director Colonel John Shaughnessy. The attendance roll reads like a who's who of Celtic FC. In addition to Colonel Shaughnessy, fellow directors James Kelly and Michael Dunbar were present as were Celtic stalwarts Arthur Murphy, John S Henry, Pat Gaffney, Dr Scanlan and ex-bailie O'Hare. John Redmond was so popular in Glasgow, they even named an east end football team after him.

On the eve of the Great War, Celtic FC was the current Scottish League champions and holders of the Scottish FA Cup. A Scottish team, based in Glasgow, playing their football in Scotland and comprising mostly Scottish players, the Celtic was still regarded by most people, certainly in west central Scotland, as an Irish team. The reason for this was that over the course of the previous twenty-five years Celtic FC itself had emerged as a definition of Irishness and was the single greatest ethno-cultural focus for its Irish and Glasgow Irish supporters. For the consciously Irish Catholic community the club provided a sense of its own identity. As a hybrid, Scots-Irish institution, Celtic FC also provided a focus for the thousands of its supporters who, as a result of increasing numbers of mixed marriages and a widening ethnic drift, were aware of their own hybrid Scots-Irish identity and the often paradoxical political and social attitudes it engendered.

Celtic FC had been converted from a sporting social club whose remit was to raise funds for needy causes, to a very successful limited liability company in 1897. That the Celtic supporters themselves had much to do with the success of the club, there was no doubt. As early as 1900, the supporters were being widely acclaimed as being like none other. The Glasgow Herald newspaper put much of the success of the club down to its supporters: 'Enterprise, of course has a lot to do with the Celt's success but there must be other causes at work. These are not to be found on the surface. One, and perhaps the most important is the loyalty of the Celtic supporters.'

Although obviously rejoicing in the success of the team, whether the team was successful or not was of little consequence, for the team's sporting battles were merely representative of the community's struggles in life and they, like the club, could not be given up. That was why the Celtic's style of play mattered almost as much as the final result, for the team was a reflection of the best characteristics of the community and its principles. It was not simply that the team must win at all costs: it was the manner in which they won. The option of whether the Glasgow Irish would or would not support the Celtic was removed from them at birth. Irrespective of whether you were a man or a woman, young or old, football follower or not, being born Glasgow Irish meant you were born to and always would, irrespective of where you happened to be in the world, support the Celtic.

The general public's perception of and grudging attitude to the success of Celtic FC, whose directors were all Irish or Scots Irish Roman Catholics, was a reflection of the enmity endured by the Glasgow Irish community as a whole. The football club's cultural and religious heritage and the political beliefs of its founding fathers and vast majority of its supporters ensured it was regarded by the Scottish establishment with barely disguised animosity and suspicion, particularly when it came to the politics of Ireland and particularly of Home Rule. As the very high profile standard-bearer of the Glasgow Irish, the attitudes experienced by Celtic FC in many ways reflected the ambiguous position of the Glasgow Irish in Scotland and the Irish nation as part of the Union of Great Britain and Ireland.

In 1913, the Celtic Football and Athletic Club Ltd celebrated its twenty-fifth birthday. Over much of that period the club was seen by many as a Glasgow Irish standard-bearer, spearheading the Glasgow Irish community's drive towards respectability and inclusion and was already, after just a quarter of a century, both a Glasgow institution and the pride of the Glasgow Irish community from which it had sprung. Celtic FC and its founding fathers and later its directors, largely the same individuals or their descendants, had indeed played a very significant role in the advancement of their own Glasgow Irish community, both social and politically. Since its formation in November 1887, Celtic FC had become undeniably the most successful football club in Britain, which at that time meant the world.

Chapter One

The Internationalists

In late July 1914, in response to the situation in the Balkans, the various international treaties, alliances and promises of support that were supposed to keep Europe at peace, kicked in. The main protagonists formed up in their armed camps, which divided Europe into two rival alliances. In 1881, Germany and Austro-Hungary, allies since 1879, formed the Triple Alliance with Italy. Germany and Austro-Hungary had strong ethnic ties and shared borders, regions and a common language. The Germans and Austro-Hungarians agreed to come to each other's aid in the event of either being attacked. Both agreed to come to Italy's aid in the event of its being attacked by France, while Italy agreed to assist against an attack on either one by France and to remain neutral in the event of a war between Austro-Hungary and Russia. The treaty was ratified every five years, but Italy was very much both a reluctant and a junior partner in the alliance. It had joined mainly out of fear of France, but also for the additional diplomatic muscle it provided when in negotiations with Austro-Hungary over disputed Italian-speaking territories (Trento and Trieste), which had been annexed by the Austro-Hungarians. Still untrusting of the Austro-Hungarians, due to the disputed territories and their rivalry in the Balkans, Italy later entered into a secret treaty with France. Despite the Triple Alliance, the Italians felt their most deadly foe was still the Austro-Hungarians. On the outbreak of the war the Italians would refuse to side with the Germans and Austro-Hungarians and remained neutral.

The Triple Entente of France, Russia and Great Britain was formed over a period of several years. In 1890, Russia had allowed the Reinsurance Treaty signed between itself and Germany in 1887 to lapse. The treaty stated that both powers would remain neutral if either was involved in a war with a third. For Germany, the treaty was aimed at negating the possibility of a war against both France and Russia on two fronts. The lapsing of the treaty was a key landmark on the road to world war for it presented Germany with the possibility of being attacked simultaneously on two fronts. A year later Russia signed an agreement with France agreeing that they would consult each other should they find themselves at war. In a counter to the Triple Alliance, the Franco-Russian agreement was strengthened in 1892 by the signing of the Franco-Russian Military Convention. Britain, meanwhile, was being torn from self-imposed 'splendid isolation', which allowed the Europeans to squabble among themselves as long as British interests were not at risk. The emergence of a unified German state threatened to put an end to that policy.

At the beginning of the twentieth century, a massive German warship-building programme saw the British enter into a number of cordial agreements with France and Russia culminating in the Anglo-Russian Entente of 1907 and heralding the formation of the Triple Entente of Britain, France and Russia. The ententes were not binding military treaties, but instead they morally obligated the nations to come to each other's aid in time of war. In 1912, the British and French did sign a military agreement, the Anglo-French Naval Convention, in which Britain promised to defend the French coastline from naval attack, while the French promised to defend the Mediterranean and the Suez Canal.

In addition to the alliances between the major nations, there were other minor alliances and agreements, which would prove to be equally significant in the march to conflagration. Russia's pledge to support Serbia, and Britain's largely forgotten agreement to defend Belgian neutrality, were just two. A number of minor incidents and wars over the decade preceding the Great War, such as Japan's victory over Russia in 1903 and the Balkan War between Italy and Turkey in 1912 and 1913, all served to heighten tensions and aggravate nationalist sensitivities. In this atmosphere of international strain, the fiercely nationalistic states of Europe strengthened their armed forces and prepared for the war that most people felt was long overdue.

Over the first years of the war, the main protagonists as far as the British were concerned were Germany and later Turkey. The Austro-Hungarians and the Russians fought it out on the Eastern Front, while the British and French fought on the Western Front and later in 1915 in the Dardanelles and the Middle East.

GERMANY

The German state and army were headed by Queen Victoria's eldest grandson, Kaiser Wilhelm II. He was seldom seen out of uniform and was surrounded by a Prussian-dominated military entourage. Despite being the most industrially and socially advanced nation in Europe, the German political system was a throwback to the seventeenth century and the age of absolute monarchs. While an elected German parliament (the Reichstag) controlled domestic policies, the autocratic Kaiser personally made all-important political appointments and controlled both the all-powerful military and German foreign policy. On the run-up to war, Germany was very unsettled socially with the 1912 elections to the Reichstag resulting in the election of no fewer than 110 socialist deputies. This made it very difficult, if not impossible, for the Chancellor to liaise between the socialist-dominated Reichstag and the autocratic Kaiser, who was unconditionally supported by the ultra-right-wing German Army. Such was the scale of the unrest that the Chancellor believed that only a war, preferably a short sharp one, would prevent massive social upheaval and perhaps even a revolution. In addition, the German military believed that with Russia engaged in a massive rearmament programme, if war had to come, it would be better if it came before the programme could be completed. It was largely this despondent outlook that led to his decision to offer Germany's unconditional support to Austro-Hungary in its dispute with Serbia, commonly referred to as the Blank Cheque.

The unification of the German states under Bismarck had created a nation of 67 million from which it could draw manpower. After forty years of Prussian influence, militarism was institutionalised through the socially dominant role of the army in German culture. Every German male between the ages of seventeen and forty-five was liable for military service. A military ethos was spread throughout all social classes by the three years' universal military service. In peacetime, military service was very much like a social club with men serving together in the same regiment and affiliated reserve organisations throughout their service. The upper classes provided the officer corps for the regular army and reserves, forming a caste of military elite, mimicking the Prussian nobility's *Junker* class. The very highest military commanders were usually Prussian Army officers.

The German Army relied on compulsory service, which was designed to muster, with reserves, more than five million men. The German conscript system was so efficient that of the one million men called up each year only one-third was needed. The German army was one of the most efficient, well-trained and well-equipped forces in the world. At the core of the army was a very well trained officer corps, supported by a hundred thousand highly professional non-commissioned officers, who, true to Prussian military tradition, demanded and received unquestioned obedience from their soldiers. A particular strength of the very well-equipped German Army was its heavy artillery arm. Despite its much-vaunted efficiency, the German Army did have weaknesses, including a complicated chain of command with a rigid hierarchy, which discouraged delegation and initiative in commanders, an underdeveloped communications system between arms and a training regimen that produced *unthinking* soldiers who required constant supervision.

In response to the Franco-Russian military pact of 1894, the Germans were forced to consider and plan for an attack by these nations simultaneously. Count Alfred von Schlieffen, Chief of the German General Staff from 1891 to 1906, devised Germany's solution to the spectre of a war on two fronts. His recommended counter was simply to attack first. Germany recognised that it was not strong enough to combat both countries at the same time, therefore the plan relied on Germany's ability to defeat either individually, but that one country had to be defeated quickly before the other could come to the aid of its ally. He recommended that the French should be tackled first, believing that monolithic Russia would need six weeks to mobilise fully and launch an offensive. The Germans believed that if they could repeat their success in the Franco-Prussian war of 1870–71 when they crushed France in just thirty-three days, the bulk of the German Army could then be rushed to the Eastern Front to confront the Russians. Curiously, the German war planners barely considered the implications of the involvement of Great Britain, despite her being regarded as Germany's biggest obstacle to attaining the status of a world power.

Among the spoils of their victory in 1871, the Germans had annexed the French frontier provinces of Alsace and Lorraine. Count Schlieffen, well aware of the intensity of French feeling over their lost territory, surmised (correctly) that the French would first move to retake the lost provinces. He built this supposition into his plan and proposed a German fighting withdrawal on the frontier, while a massive right hook, composed of the bulk of the German Army, swept through neutral Belgium and into France, bypassing on either side of Paris to take the French forces being drawn into Alsace and Lorraine from the rear. The plan could be likened to a revolving door: if pressed heavily on one side, the other would swing round to hit you on the back. A vital component of Schlieffen's plan was that the western (right) wing of the armies must bypass Paris to the west with the 'right sleeve of the right hand man brushing the Channel'. He estimated the campaign would take thirty-nine days and much would depend on the vaunted German railway system's ability to move men and materiel quickly and efficiently.

On von Schlieffen's retirement in 1906, Count Helmuth von Moltke became Chief of the German General Staff. Although Moltke retained the Schlieffen Plan, over the next few years the plan was tinkered with and revised until the right wing no longer followed the coast but was pulled inland closer to the centre; however, it was still required to envelop Paris to the west. When the onslaught came, the weight of the German invasion forces in the west was colossal. There were almost 1.5 million men drawn up in seven massive armies: General Alexander von Kluck's First Army on the extreme right (northern) flank alone numbered over 320,000, while next to it in line, General Karl von Bulow's Second Army and General Max von Hausen's Third Army, numbered 260,000 and 180,000, respectively. They would carry out the assault with the German Fourth (180,000) and Fifth (200,000) Armies. The German Sixth Army (220,000) prepared to counter the expected French attack in Alsace and Lorraine, by retreating they would lure the French into the trap. The Seventh Army (125,000) was on the extreme left wing near the Swiss border. The Germans still had enough forces remaining to man the Eastern Front, with ten divisions to await the Russian onslaught. Under Prussian leadership and direction, the German military machine was awesome.

TURKEY

At the beginning of the twentieth century, to most people the name *Turkey* meant the exotic decadence of the infidel Turk, of Christian slavery, kasbahs and harems. Those more learned thought of the vast but declining Ottoman Empire, then known as the *Sick man of Europe*. The Ottoman Empire once comprised mainland Turkey, its possessions in the Balkans, which in the north almost reached Vienna, the Dodecanese Islands and the coastal regions of the Arabian subcontinent, which in the west included Israel, Syria, Libya, part of Arabia and Yemen. In the east, the Turks held sway over the Persian Gulf, Iraq and the Emirates. Six hundred years of expansion had resulted in a vast empire populated by a great mixture of nationalities and races. There were Arabs, Armenians, Kurds, Persians and Serbians all with different cultures, languages and religions, most of whom were extremely difficult to control, each having their own national and religious aspirations. In 1908, a revolution instigated by the Committee of Union and Progress, better known as the *Young Turks*, based in Salonika and with the support of the Turkish military, forced the despotic Sultan into constitutional change and to establish an elected Chamber of Deputies. Between 1908 and 1914, the Young Turks progressively gained more power and influence, usually as a result of some national emergency. However, Turkey continued to slide into decline, with major revolts in Arabia in 1908 and by the Albanians and Kurds in 1909. Despite their best efforts the Young Turks could not prevent significant swathes of their empire being lost through nationalist ambition and foreign expansionism.

In August 1914, strategically important Turkey apparently stood on the sidelines, a massive threat particularly to the Russians, but also to the British in Egypt. Although recently driven out of Europe in the First Balkan War fought against Serbia, Bulgaria and Greece, the old Ottoman Empire still held vast territories in Asia. It controlled almost all of the Arab Middle East and had ambitions in ethnically Turkish lands in the Russian Caucuses and in Central Asia. In the years immediately prior to the outbreak of the Great War, the Turkish Army was a poorly equipped and thoroughly demoralised lot. The army was manned mainly by peasants from Anatolia and by Arabs. All able-bodied males over eighteen years of age were liable to be called up. The

Turkish land forces consisted of three armies, which increased to four in September 1914. Their headquarters were at Constantinople, Baghdad, Damascus and Erzincan.

Ultimately, the Turks would field a total of nine armies, which would fight on five major fronts during the Great War. The number of corps allocated to each army varied, but two was usual. Two or three divisions formed a corps and in 1914, thirty-six divisions existed. Ultimately thirty-four additional divisions were mobilised. An infantry division comprised three regiments of three battalions; each battalion had four companies, a machine-gun company plus cavalry and artillery support units. On average, a Turkish infantry battalion at full strength contained twenty-four officers and 900 men. In practice, these numbers were seldom achieved and units comprising less than 450 all ranks were not unusual. In July 1914, there were 305 infantry battalions, both regular and reserve, and sixty-four machine-gun companies.

Throughout the period of the Great War, the Turkish Army would remain essentially manned by Turkish and Islamic peasants, but whether it was Digger from Melbourne, Paddy from Kildare or Jimmy fae the Calton, who faced Johnny Turk, they would all learn to respect the fighting qualities of the Turkish soldiers.

FRANCE

France had been England's traditional enemy for centuries and had been decisively crushed at the end of the Napoleonic wars. The defeat of Napoleon effectively ended France's pretensions of rivalling Britain's global superpower status. The French and British had cooperated in the mid-nineteenth century to see off a Russian thrust into the Mediterranean during the Crimean War. The Franco-Prussian War of 1870 saw France comprehensively defeated by the Prussians, thus ending any pretensions of being the dominant power in Western Europe. In addition, the country had been humiliated by the loss of two of her eastern provinces, Alsace and Lorraine. The loss of the two provinces would prevent any reconciliation between France and Germany. The defeat saw the creation of the French Third Republic, comprising a senate and an elected chamber of deputies. The growing power of Imperial Germany, which had a population almost double that of France, forced the French into an alliance with Russia, both agreeing to come to each other's aid if either were attacked by Germany. The alliance was seen in France as vital to national survival and liberal, freedom-loving French politicians actively cultivated relations with despotic, reactionary Russia. By the start of the twentieth century, France had recovered its confidence after the humiliation of the Franco-Prussian war debacle; however, over the period the country had remained an overwhelmingly agricultural nation and although it was self-sufficient in food, industrial development had stagnated and it lagged far behind Germany and Britain. Despite this, France, as one of the world's leading trading nations, was still very wealthy and regarded as a great power due to its overseas empire. By 1914, France had a global empire second only to that of Britain, with colonies in north and west Africa, Indochina, the Caribbean and in the Indian, Pacific and Atlantic Oceans. In 1914, France was governed by a coalition government of the centre right and centre left, under the leadership of conservative President Raymond Poincaré. As a native of the annexed province of Lorraine, he was a nationalist and in 1913 introduced policies to strengthen both the army and navy.

On the outbreak of war, France's military was just emerging from twenty years of disarray and despite a belated increase in funding in the year immediately prior to the outbreak of the war, it remained poorly equipped, trained and led. Its commanders had tactically and strategically learned very little from the Franco-Prussian war and, starved of funds, the army's training methods generally were outdated, with the infantry taught to advance in solid blocks and the cavalry still charging with lances and swords. From a population of around thirty-seven million, the French conscript army comprised some forty-seven divisions (823,000 men including over 46,000 colonial troops). The army was increased by almost 2.9 million men when reservists and territorials were mobilised over the first weeks of the war.

A new generation of young officers asserted that *attack* should be the new doctrine, which they felt best suited the French spirit of *élan* and conjured up the glory days of Napoleon Bonaparte with massive battalions of men smashing through enemy weak points. In fact there was still much about the French army that Napoleon would have been entirely familiar with. The French infantry went into battle dressed as they did in the Franco-Prussian War, in red kepis, blue coats and red trousers, their officers wearing white gloves and carrying swords. The regimental colours and military bands actually accompanied infantry battalions onto the battlefield. The cavalry, still a vital component of any army, were even more Napoleonic: the famous French cuirassiers were still sporting horsehair-plumed helmets, breastplates and knee-length boots. The French cavalry always had a reputation for excellence and it was said that they were never better than in 1914. A French infantryman was equipped with an obsolete Lebel eight-shot rifle. It was painfully slow to load and much inferior to the rifles carried by the German infantry. It came equipped with a needle bayonet, which had a nasty habit of breaking off in action. On the eve of war, the French Army suffered serious materiel shortcomings in comparison to the German Army. The French had 2,500 machine guns, the Germans 4,500. The artillery was the French Army's only redeeming feature: its 75 mm gun was the outstanding artillery piece of the war. A French field gun could fire almost twice as many rounds per minute as a British 18-pounder gun. However, the Germans had 6,000 of their roughly comparable 77 mm gun. The French had practically no heavy artillery.

The French military forces were commanded by sixty-three-year-old General Joseph Jacques (Papa) Joffre. Appointed Chief of the French General Staff in 1911, Joffre was largely responsible for the fatally flawed Plan XVII, which was a blueprint for the invasion of Germany. On the outbreak of war, the French fielded five armies. From north to south, these were the Fifth Army (254,000), the Fourth Army (193,000), the Third Army (168,000), the Second Army (200,000) and the First Army (265,000). Careful note of the dispositions and strengths of the French forces shows the greatest French strength lay on their right or southern flank, facing the relatively weak German Sixth Army in the annexed provinces of Alsace and Lorraine. Unfortunately, the French plan did not take into account the possibility that Germany would invade France through neutral Belgium.

BELGIUM

Belgium was a constitutional monarchy, whose king, Albert I (1875–1934), had succeeded his uncle, Leopold II, in 1908. The predominately Roman Catholic country was formed from political expediency and was specifically created to be a buffer between the warring French, Dutch and Germanic states in the aftermath of the Napoleonic wars. Despite its small size, with a population of just over seven million, Belgium was very prosperous, ranked commercially as the sixth in the world. The country was governed by a parliament of two houses, a senate and national assembly, with members elected by proportional representation. The king was nominally the head of the government, but delegated executive powers to a cabinet while retaining the right to initiate laws. The ruling Catholic Party had been in power since 1884. In an age of empires, Belgium had recently managed to get a slice of the imperial pie and was a colonial power. The Belgian government assumed control of the Congo Free State, renamed the Belgian Congo, from its late sovereign, King Leopold II, in 1908. The Belgian king had treated the resource-rich central African country, seventy-six times the size of Belgium itself, as his own private fiefdom, reducing the natives to absolute slaves. For twenty years the country was raped of its natural resources, particularly rubber and ivory, while its people were literally worked to death. Under Leopold's rule between 1885 and 1908, it is estimated that between ten and thirteen million Congolese died from mass murder, exhaustion, exposure, starvation or disease.

The country's military and political position was dictated by its geographical position. The country had for decades depended on its *guarantee* of neutrality, which provided very little incentive to spend money on its military forces. By 1914, little Catholic Belgium, as it would come to be portrayed, based its defence strategy on its well-publicised neutrality and on its formidable but as yet incomplete ring of fortresses. With a population of just over seven million, it could muster a field army of 190,000 men. The Belgian forces comprised a regular army, the gendarmerie and the civic guard. The gendarmerie formed an elite cavalry more than 3000 strong but the civic guard was of little military value. The army was organised into six divisions of all arms and the garrisons of the great fortresses at Antwerp, Liege and Namur. The largely conscript army was composed of around 14,000 regular soldiers with some 107,000 poorly trained conscripts or reservists in the field army. Another 5000 professional soldiers plus 60,000 older conscripts were allocated to garrison the forts. All parts of the military machine were ill equipped and badly trained, with Belgian army uniforms among the most outdated anywhere in Europe. The artillery and transport arms were particularly lacking. Most of the officers spoke French while most of the soldiers spoke Flemish. Belgium had no naval forces whatsoever.

GREAT BRITAIN

In 1914, Great Britain, which at that time included the whole of Ireland, boasted a population of forty six million, including 4.3 million in Ireland. A constitutional monarchy, it was governed by a parliament comprising a (not quite) democratically elected House of Commons and a hereditary House of Lords. The power of the latter to veto the decisions of the House of Commons had been severely curtailed in 1911. The king did not get unduly involved in politics and was informed rather than consulted by the elected representatives of the people. Of German descent, during the war the British royal family would be forced to change their family names: the King adopted the name Windsor, while Battenberg became Mountbatten, and Teck became Cambridge. The ruling political party had been the Liberals since 1906 and Herbert H Asquith had been the Prime Minister from 1908; however, from 1911 the Liberals remained in power only with the support of the Irish Nationalist Party led by John Redmond. Other important figures in the British Cabinet were Lloyd George, then Chancellor of the Exchequer, and Winston Churchill, the First Lord of the Admiralty. Canadian born, Andrew Bonar Law, leader of the Conservative-Unionist party led his majesty's official opposition in parliament. On the run-up to war Britain was riven by a number of major internal tensions over Ireland, women's suffrage and labour disputes. Ireland appeared to be on the verge of civil war, while the autumn and winter promised industrial disturbances on a previously unseen scale.

Unlike the great Continental armies that relied on conscription, the regular British Army was manned solely by volunteers. The small, but very professional British Army was widely regarded as a formidable fighting force, having been honed into shape by combat experience gained in various military emergencies throughout the Empire, including a vicious and enlightening fight in South Africa against the Boer famers. Prior to the outbreak of the Great War, the 240,000 strong regular British Army comprised entirely professional soldiers. The men enlisted voluntarily and after training, served in cavalry, artillery, infantry or service corps units. The army was stationed all over the world, but a Home Army, totalling around 120,000, was based in Britain and Ireland. The Home Army was, in the event of a war on the continent, earmarked to become the British Expeditionary Force (BEF) and to fight in Europe. On the eve of war, the regular army was 11,000 men under strength. With its worldwide commitments, successive British governments saw the army as primarily a police force for the empire, and historically it was very much the poor relation of the Royal Navy. The politicians regarded the massively powerful navy as the stalwart of British homeland defence and the long arm of British foreign policy, which often required gunboat diplomacy.

At the head of the armed forces sat the Secretary of State for War. A politician, he headed the Army Council, which comprised the heads of the staff departments. The regular army was split into two parts, home-based forces and those stationed abroad, mostly in India. The UK-based forces were divided into seven commands (Aldershot, Eastern, Irish, Northern, Scottish, Southern and Western). The army in India was borne upon the Indian establishment. The British Army consisted of a number of different branches: the infantry, cavalry, Royal Regiment of Artillery and the supporting corps comprising the Corps of Royal Engineers, the Army Medical Corps, the Army Service Corps, the Army Veterinary Corps, etc. Each of the branches was subdivided into different units, then, in the case of the infantry, into regiments, battalions (Bn), companies and platoons. The cavalry was organised into regiments, squadrons and troops, the artillery into brigades and batteries and the service corps into companies and detachments. Elements of all these units would, in turn, be allocated to larger tactical formations such as brigades, divisions and army corps. For example, an infantry battalion would be one of four grouped together to form an infantry brigade, while three such brigades made up an infantry division. Various sized units of artillery, cavalry and the supporting corps would also be allocated to an infantry division to achieve a balanced self-supporting formation. A number of divisions could then form an army corps. The composition, strengths, equipment allocation and roles of all the formations were adapted and modified throughout the war to take account of changes in manpower availability, tactical situation and technical developments.

An infantry division was the largest fighting formation on the battlefield. In addition to its twelve infantry battalions, it had attached artillery, engineer, transport, medical, signals and veterinary units (there were 5000 horses in a division). A full-strength infantry division would comprise in the region of 18,000 officers and men.

The vast majority of pre-war professional soldiers served in the infantry and prior to the outbreak of war, the regular infantry line regiments consisted of two active battalions, numbered the 1st and 2nd, and usually there was a reserve third battalion located at the regimental depot and responsible for training recruits. The two regular battalions were split between home service and foreign service, usually India, though other major overseas stations in 1914 were South Africa, Gibraltar, Burma, Malta and Egypt. The regular battalions were manned by volunteer soldiers, with the normal period of service being seven years with the colours, e.g. with one of the active battalions, and five years with the reserve forces subject to recall in an emergency. The cavalry, artillery and foot guards all had slightly different periods of service.

In addition to the regular army, there were a number of other sources from which the government could reinforce the professional army. The Regular Army Reserve was a pool of 145,000 experienced former professional soldiers, which was used to bring regular units up to full strength in times of national emergency. On being recalled, reservists were required to report immediately to the nearest military establishment before being issued with travel documents and dispatched to their own regimental depot. A Special Reserve of 63,000 men was also available to make good any deficiencies that existed after the regular reserve had been called up. The Special Reserve was formed during the Cardwell Reforms from many of the old militia units. It was a form of part-time soldiering in which men enlisted for six years and accepted the possibility of mobilisation in the event of a national emergency. After six months' full-time training on full pay, they reported for refresher training three or four weeks a year thereafter. Often special reservists went straight from training to a regular battalion on a period of attachment, which turned into a full-time commitment. In Ireland, the only form of part-time soldiering was the Special Reserve. Irish regiments, therefore, usually comprised at least two extra reserve battalions, while the North Irish Horse and the South Irish Horse were cavalry regiments composed entirely of special reservists.

Based at one of the various regimental training depots, a reserve battalion's role was to train and provide drafts for the two regular battalions and would not normally serve overseas. During an emergency, it would also administer the regular reservists recalled to active service before forwarding them to their battalions. Additionally, injured or wounded soldiers returning to duty after a period in hospital would be attached to reserve battalions prior to rejoining their units. On the outbreak of war, the men of the Reserves were mobilised and sent to join the regular army battalions to bring them up to their war establishment. The special reservists could be seen as a halfway house between full-time soldiers and the part-time soldiers of the Territorial Force.

The last in a series of major army reforms prior to the outbreak of the Great War came into force in 1908, with the creation of the Territorial Force. The Territorial Force (TF) was based on the old Rifle Volunteer battalions, raised and administered locally, but under central training control. It was envisaged that the TF would become a military school for the nation. The nominally 250,000 strong TF was originally planned to be a reserve for the Home Army with an overseas commitment. However, political pressure and vehement objections by the old volunteers to compulsory overseas service, forced the planners to drop the overseas commitment in favour of a voluntary commitment called 'Imperial Service'. The TF, if embodied, was liable to be called out for service in any part of the United Kingdom, but could not be sent overseas. The Territorial Force was therefore created as a home defence force, with a secondary role being to provide a trained pool of manpower in the event of a major conflict; however, the Imperial Service commitment allowed officers and men in time of national emergency to volunteer for service overseas. Under their terms of service, a volunteer would undertake to serve abroad, but only with his own unit, or with part of his own unit: he could not be drafted as an individual to any other unit unless he agreed. Haldane had hoped that the Imperial Service commitment would be taken up by around 20 per cent of the volunteers; in the event only around 1100 officers and 19,000 NCOs and men had taken up the obligation in 1913. Another variation on the TF terms of service was the Special Service Section: these individuals had volunteered to be called out in times of national emergency, whether their unit had been embodied or not. The men were required to be passed as fit for their duties and should be prepared to serve under the special circumstances for a period not to exceed one month. The organisation also had its own reservist list of former members, which theoretically should have been one-third the size of the whole TF, but by 1914 it stood at just 2000.

By 1912, the men joining the TF battalions came from all backgrounds and most by necessity held down full-time civilian jobs. A man wishing to join the Territorial Force could present himself at his local Territorial Force headquarters most nights, where he would be interviewed by one of the staff. A potential recruit was required to fulfil a number of conditions: he had to be between seventeen and thirty-five (often a blind eye was turned and fourteen and fifteen year olds were accepted) and the minimum height was 5ft 2in. Recruits were required to commit to four years' service, although they could resign at any time. This resulted in an enormous through flow as the initial enthusiasm waned and men simply failed to show. Men with previous service in the Volunteers or Territorial Force had to produce their discharge papers. Men with previous service in the regular army were required to produce their discharge and character certificates. All volunteers with no previous service were required to perform forty recruit drills (training periods), fire a recruit's course of musketry and attend an annual camp for eight or fifteen days to achieve their efficiency award. Men with previous service in the same branch of the service and recruits after their first year, were required to attend a minimum of ten drills, fire their annual course of musketry and attend the annual camp for eight or fifteen days to achieve their efficiency award. Men were allowed to re-engage for one, two, three or four years at any time during the last year of their engagement. In addition to the normal commitment to serve at home for four years, men were encouraged to volunteer for the Special Service Section or Imperial Service.

The TF was held in disdain both by the military authorities and by the general public and had received a bad press almost since its formation in 1908. A TF soldier only trained for a couple of hours on a weeknight and on an odd weekend during the month. They were also required to attend a fortnight's training camp once a year, but none of the training was compulsory. Just prior to the outbreak of war, the TF was over 47,000 men short of its establishment and there was a widespread feeling in military circles that they were a bit of a waste of time and effort. The general public saw the part-timers as something of a joke and bestowed upon the citizen soldiers of the TF numerous derogatory titles, such as 'Saturday night soldiers', 'Haldane's horse' and 'Featherbed heroes'. In some of the new TF battalions, the private club atmosphere of the Volunteers still prevailed and entire companies were manned by special interest groups: total abstainers, bankers, brewers, dockers, students, artisans or merchants. The 9th (Glasgow Highlanders) Bn Highland Light Infantry was largely composed of men with Highland roots including many Gaelic speakers. The 5th Bn Scottish Rifles thought themselves a cut above the rest, with very many of the men in their ranks university-educated members of the middle class. The social life available within the TF was undoubtedly a major attraction for men joining: every battalion had its shooting, rowing, football, cycling and billiards clubs and held annual events such as sports meetings or highland games. Many of the men looked on the two weeks' annual camp as a holiday. It was always held at the height of summer and two weeks in the countryside under canvas, away from the overcrowded slums, was indeed a holiday. Importantly for many working-class men, attendance at the annual camp meant they would be paid at army rates of pay for the two weeks, when they might otherwise be on holiday from work without pay.

The new TF battalions remained attached to the regiments to which their volunteer battalions had been affiliated. They were organised along the same modern lines as the professional army, together with higher formations, brigades and divisions, and all of the necessary support units (transport, medical, signals, engineers, artillery, etc.). Prior to the outbreak of the Great War, the existing TF battalions made up fourteen TF infantry divisions. The TF battalions were numbered consecutively after their regiment's reserve battalions and, depending on the size of the regimental area and population, they could be numbered 4th, 5th, 6th, 7th 8th, etc., and in some cases, such as the London regiments, much higher. Many TF battalions, especially the Highland regiments, had county names in their designations, such as the 4th (Ross-shire) Bn Seaforth Highlanders TF and the 6th (Renfrewshire) Bn Argyll and Sutherland Highlanders TF.

Finally, there also existed the National Reserve, a register maintained by the TF associations of older men with military experience. This Dad's Army type organisation consisted of retired officers and other ranks between the ages of forty-two and fifty-five and in 1913 it numbered at around 215,000.

NAVIES

In an age of empires, the major European belligerent nations, Britain, France and Germany, retained large naval forces to maintain links with their colonies. The Austro-Hungarians, Italians, Turks and Russians also maintained significant naval forces, but they were not comparable to the leading nations. By the outbreak of the Great War, the two most powerful navies were the British Royal Navy and the German Imperial Navy. The Royal Navy was controlled by the Admiralty, and presided over by two heads, the First Lord of the Admiralty (a political appointee) and the First Sea Lord (the senior naval officer). On the eve of the Great War these posts were occupied by Winston Churchill and Prince Louis of Battenberg. Prince Louis would soon be required to resign: his name and family considered too Germanic. For Britain, the Royal Navy was essential for communications over the vastness of her Empire and was a potent symbol of British power and reach. Trade blockades were a recognised form of coercive action and a British battleship sitting off a major port capable of blockading or shelling the city conveyed a diplomatic message much more forcefully than any ambassador ever could. With Britain importing vast quantities of its food, the Royal Navy also played an important role in protecting vital British trade routes. Great Britain was much more dependent on imported food supplies than Germany: pre-war free-trade policies had allowed a 'grain invasion' from America and Canada to shrink the domestic agricultural sector, after which British farmers largely concentrated on dairy and meat production. By 1914, Britain was importing 78 per cent of its wheat and flour and 52 per cent of its cereals and pulses. Despite British farmers specialising in meat and dairy produce, even these were imported in large quantities: 35 per cent of the meat, 43 per cent of the butter and 74 per cent of the cheese were imported. The Royal Navy was the largest and most powerful navy in the world and the British were immensely proud of their fleet. Since the days of Nelson, it had dominated and controlled the oceans of the world.

Germany, under Kaiser Wilhelm II, with pretensions of imperial greatness had acquired a few overseas colonies particularly in Africa and East Asia. Under the new head of the German Imperial Navy, Admiral Alfred von Tirpitz, Germany began a massive expansion of its fleet in 1897. The building programme sparked a naval arms race with Great Britain, and both nations spent awesome sums of money building massively powerful Dreadnought-type battleships in an attempt to narrow or maintain naval superiority. By 1914, the German Imperial Navy was much more powerful than the French and Russian navies and second only to the Royal Navy in overall size. The Germans thought that since the Royal Navy had worldwide commitments, they need only maintain their fleet at two-thirds the size of the Royal Navy to be able to match it in the North Sea. Although by the outbreak of the Great War Germany had not quite reached two-thirds parity, it did possess a massively powerful, ultra-modern battle fleet fully capable of taking on the Royal Navy's Home Fleet in open battle on the North Sea. With German naval forces largely concentrated in the North Sea and the Baltic, she could do little to protect her overseas possessions from the Entente forces.

The British had since the turn of the twentieth century recognised the dangers of the Imperial German Fleet dominating the North Sea, which would allow its battleships to blockade British ports and gain access to the North Atlantic where they could cut off British food supplies. The British Home Fleet was therefore reinforced and based at Scapa Flow in the Orkney Islands and at Rosyth on the Firth of Forth, tasked with preventing the German Imperial Fleet from breaking out of the North Sea and into the Atlantic where it could attack and disrupt British supply routes.

In addition to surface ships, by 1914 most major navies of the world possessed a number of new-fangled submarines in their fleets. Although regarded as having questionable military value, this arm of naval warfare had been slowly gaining credence and recognition over the first decade of the twentieth century, but, as usual, the British preoccupation with fair play had seen the arm sniffed at by many of the upper-middle-class senior naval officers, who regarded it as 'under-hand, sneaky and not quite British'.

One of the pioneers of submarines was Irishman John Phillip Holland, who was born in 1841 at Liscannor in Co Clare. Educated at the National School and by the Christian Brothers at Limerick, he developed an interest in scientific experiments and as early as 1859 was designing underwater craft. By 1873, he had joined his family in Boston where he worked for a time in an engineering firm before moving into teaching at St John's Catholic School in New Jersey. Around 1880 he submitted a design for a submarine to the American Navy, but it was rejected as being the work of science fiction. His brother, Michael, had joined the Fenian Brotherhood and introduced his brother to the physical force Irish Republicans. Amazingly, the Fenians, led by John Devoy, agreed to allocate money from its *Skirmishing Fund* to bankroll Holland's fantastic project. The Fenians saw the submarine as a way of striking at the British by attacking Royal Navy ships. Holland's underwater craft was duly built in New York in 1881 and officially titled *Holland II*, but was nicknamed the *Fenian Ram*. The craft marked an important stage in submarine development, but the project took too long to come to fruition so the Fenians withdrew their financial support. (The *Fenian Ram* was exhibited in Madison Square Gardens in 1916 to raise funds for the victims of the Easter Rising.) Holland then severed all links with the Fenians; indeed twenty years later he sold his designs to the British, who launched their own submarine designed by Holland in 1901.

By the outbreak of the Great War, the French possessed the most submarines (123), followed by the British (57), with the Germans (38) in third place. Despite some advances in design, including diesel engines, most were still highly unreliable and dangerous to operate and were largely restricted to coastal operations. All that would quickly change as the Germans grasped the value of the *Unterseeboot*, from which the famous 'U-boat' derived its ominous title. The Germans would be the first nation to employ the U-boat as a substitute for surface raiders, attacking allied merchant shipping and warships, and they would come to dominate undersea warfare during the Great War.

AIR FORCES

In August 1914 when the great European powers went to war, barely a decade had passed since the Wright brothers' first 20-second powered flight near Kitty Hawk, North Carolina. Since then, Louis Blériot in 1909 had made the first flight across the English Channel, Roland Garros had flown across the Mediterranean and in 1911 Italy became the first nation to use attack aircraft when it dropped grenades on Turkish troops in Libya. The potential of aircraft for military use, particularly for observation and reconnaissance, was not lost on the generals, but the technology was still too new and unreliable to play a major part in strategic thinking or planning. All the belligerent nations would enter the war with miniscule air assets compared to those deployed later in the conflict. None of the aircraft were designed specifically to drop bombs or had any type of gun, let alone a machine gun capable of firing through a rotating propeller. That, however, would soon change.

Germany, with around 246 aircraft, entered the war with more aircraft than either Britain or France, but much of Germany's efforts in the field of aeronautics were given over to the development of the airship. Although not justified by the results, the 'Zeppelin' throughout the Great War would for the British people become a byword for aerial terror.

Formed in 1913 as a flying company of six machines, at the outbreak of the war the Austro-Hungarian Air Service was composed of ten observation balloons and thirty-five aircraft. Despite being involved in conflict as recently as 1911, when it used aircraft to attack Turkish positions in Libya, Italy entered the war with around 115 aircraft in total, all only suitable for observation. Turkey's air arm was only founded in 1914 under the guidance of a French officer. Needless to say when Turkey entered the war he was quickly replaced by a German officer. When it entered the war the Ottoman air assets comprised just six landplanes, only four of which were operational, two seaplanes and an observation balloon.

France, as one of the pioneering nations of aviation, was at the forefront of aircraft development. French military aircraft participated in military manoeuvres for the first time in 1910. In 1914, the *Aviation Militaire* comprised about 160 aircraft in front-line service. On the outbreak of war, the Russian aviation service was the largest by far of all the nations, but very many of its 360 machines were unserviceable.

In Great Britain, the Royal Flying Corps had been created in May 1912 from the Air Battalion, Royal Engineers, which had been formed as a balloon unit. From January 1914, the service was reorganised into squadrons of three flights of four aircraft each, plus three reserve machines. Until July 1914, when the Royal Naval Air Service was created, Royal Navy aviators formed part of the Flying Corps. In August 1914, all available squadrons (four) comprising sixty aircraft were deployed to France with the BEF.

AND SO TO WAR

A British declaration of war would also commit her Empire, including India and her great white dominions, Australia, New Zealand and Canada, to the conflict. In the event of war, in Britain and Ireland the Home Army would be mobilised and as previously agreed by Anglo-French military planners, Britain would send the bulk of the Home Forces to the continent to join the French Army in the field. The force would be known as the British Expeditionary Force (BEF) and would consist initially of one cavalry and four infantry divisions comprising around 90,000 men. It was supposed to be six divisions, but two were held back after someone pointed out there would be literally no professional soldiers left to defend Britain. The BEF would still include the vast majority of regular soldiers who had been stationed in Britain and Ireland. At the beginning of August, the British Home Fleet moved north to its war station at Scapa Flow in the Orkney Islands, while the men of the Royal Naval Reserve mobilised and reported to their bases, including to Govan on the Clyde. Telegrams were flashed across the globe ordering the overseas battalions home from their policing duties throughout the Empire.

The war would be fought on an industrial scale never before experienced by mankind and every industrial and financial asset of the British Empire would in time be allocated to the war effort. Ironically and for once, the war was not one of British Imperial adventure, but was one that would quickly change from preventing German expansionism and conquest of mainland

Europe, to one of British national survival. Eventually, every man, woman and child would be required to put their shoulder to the wheel if the British nation was to survive. In addition to the military campaigns themselves, the first year of the war would be dominated by one subject above all others, *recruitment*, as Britain's small volunteer regular army was by necessity, rapidly and massively expanded. The recruitment campaign would lead to a phenomenon never before seen in the history of Great Britain, a Citizen's Army.

At the beginning of August 1914 the British politicians turned their attention, most with a great degree of relief, from the damnable question of Ireland to Europe. As Winston Churchill had commented a few days prior to the declaration of war, 'The parishes of Fermanagh and Tyrone faded into the mists and squalls of Ireland and a strange light began immediately, but by perceptible graduations, to fall and grow upon the map of Europe.'

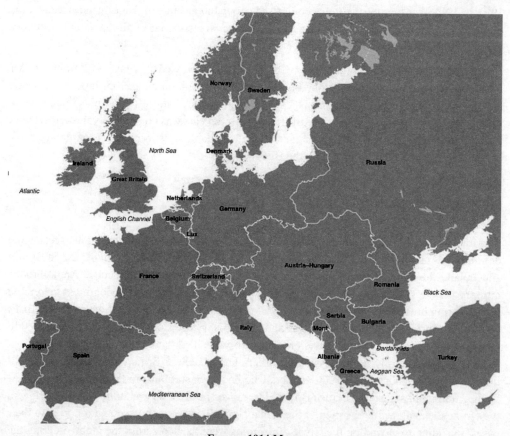

Europe 1914 Map

Chapter Two

A Just and Honourable War?

THE HOME FRONT

When the British parliament sat at the beginning of August, the deteriorating diplomatic situation in Europe had replaced the Irish crisis at the top of the political agenda. In response to the German note demanding passage for its armies through Belgium, Britain's ambassador in Berlin warned Germany that Belgian neutrality must be respected or Great Britain would declare war. On 4 August, with German troops already across the Belgian border, the Prime Minister answered questions on the status of the British treaty with the Belgians. He informed the House of Commons that the King had received an appeal from the King of the Belgians for the diplomatic intervention of Great Britain and that an official telegram insisting that the neutrality of Belgian territory be respected had been sent to the German government. A positive reply had been requested by midnight.

The history of the Kingdom of Belgium begins in 1839 with the creation of the independent, Catholic and democratic state. The area was a major junction between France, Germany and Holland, and over the previous 400 years been dominated in turn by Austria, Spain, France and Holland. With a view to creating a buffer zone between the constantly warring European powers and the English Channel, Britain, among others, guaranteed the Catholic kingdom's independence. The tiny state could not possibly hope to confront any of the major European powers on the battlefield, but by 1914 Belgium had constructed an extensive and fairly modern system of fortifications, which it hoped, alongside the country's declared neutrality, would deter potential aggressors. The Irish had a long-standing and sentimental relationship with the area and with the Flanders town of Louvain in particular. The religious persecutions of the Roman Catholic faith in Ireland under Elizabeth I and James I and VI of Scotland led to the suppression of monastic schools. Irish colleges were set up in a number of Catholic countries on mainland Europe, including Spain, Portugal, France and in what was now Belgium at Antwerp, Tournai and at Louvain. The Irish college of St Anthony's was founded in Louvain in 1602 specifically for the education of Irish priests. The Franciscans of St Anthony's also helped preserve the Irish language having printed religious books in the Irish tongue. As a result, by 1914, the Catholic library at Louvain was recognised as one of the most important repositories of the Irish language and early medieval books in Europe.

Had the British government publicly declared its determination to support its allies and been prepared to go to war earlier, the catastrophic situation may have been avoided. As it now stood, the Germans were astounded and dismayed that Britain was prepared to stand by the Belgians over what they called a 'scrap of paper' but at this late hour even if the Germans had wanted to stop, their war plan was too far advanced to halt.

In the days immediately before the war, the mood in Glasgow was, according to the Evening Times newspaper, 'Excitable'. So much so on Sunday 2 August it ran a couple of special editions devoted entirely to the war. The newsboys did a roaring trade, some charging double, and despite the newspaper vendors being closed, it being the Sabbath, 200,000 copies were sold. At dusk on 3 August, the British Foreign Secretary, Sir Edward Grey, watched the lamplighters light the gas lamps in the street outside his London home. Aware that a terrible European war was now inevitable, and affected by his own failure to stop it, he commented to a friend: 'The lamps are going out all over Europe, we shall not see them lit again in our lifetime.' He was not wrong; the consequences of the diplomatic failure would be far reaching, even beyond the catastrophic consequences of the immediate military conflict, and extend well beyond his death in 1933.

The British government, in response to the deteriorating situation on the continent, mobilised the Home Army, recalled all reservists to the colours and embodied the part-time soldiers of the Territorial Force. Thousands of the Glasgow Irish were among those reservists recalled to their regular army battalions. In the Gallacher home in Clydebank, twenty-six-year-old Willie Gallacher, the older brother of Celtic's Patsy Gallacher, was enjoying his terminal leave from the regular army. Willie had just completed seven years' service with the Highland Light Infantry (HLI) and was just a few weeks back from India and in the process of being discharged to the Reserve when war was declared. He probably did not even get a chance to hand in his uniform at Hamilton Barracks before being recalled to active service.

Despite her best efforts, a reluctant Great Britain was being dragged into the European morass. No nation goes to war unless it is in its own interest and that was certainly the case for the British in August 1914. While the German invasion of neutral Belgium was an important moral factor in the British decision to go to war, as important was what the act symbolised: the deliberate disregard for international law that the British could not afford to ignore. As an international trading nation, for the British the adherence of other nations to international law was vital to British economic interests across its vast Empire. If the British were seen to allow the Germans to flaunt international law, why would not a score of other nations scattered across the globe behave in a similar manner to the detriment of British trading interests.

In addition, it had long been a British article of faith that no nation should become a dominant power on the Continent. Britain could therefore not allow the Germans to defeat France and win a war that would see them control the Channel ports, threatening both British trade and the invasion of the British Isles. Better to fight alongside the French on the Continent now, than face a victorious Germany in the near future on her own. The German threat to Belgian neutrality allowed the British politicians to unite behind strategic self-interest and to sell the decision to go to war to the nation and Empire as a righteous cause, the freedom of small nations, which it undoubtedly was. The German invasion of neutral Belgium undoubtedly provided Great Britain with the strategic, moral and legal right for participation in the war. As far as the overwhelming majority of British, including the Irish, people were concerned it would be a *Just and Honourable War*.

At 2300 hrs (midnight 4–5 August by Central European time) with no German withdrawal forthcoming, Great Britain declared war on Germany. On 5 August, the Glasgow Herald reported that in London crowds of a hundred thousand gathered around Downing Street and

Buckingham Palace to hear the news. In response to their wild cheering and patriotic singing, the King and Queen appeared on the balcony several times after midnight. In Glasgow, it was late and raining heavily, so for the most part the streets were deserted. The few who were out and about awaiting developments, received the news with barely a murmur and there was no demonstration of any kind. In the same edition of the Glasgow Herald, a single column inch announced that the Admiralty had taken over two battleships ordered by the Turkish government and nearing completion. The decision would have far-reaching consequences for many of the Glasgow Irish and sons of Erin.

THE CELTIC CLUB 1914

Scottish Cup and League Winners 1913-14

By the start of the new 1914/15 season, Willie Maley's second great Celtic team were beginning to settle into the task, with most of the players now well established in their team positions. The success of this latest Celtic squad was further proof and justification of Maley's philosophy of evolutionary change and his policy of bringing local talent into the club as opposed to paying large transfer fees for established stars. The current pool of players emerged from the 1913/14 season as Scottish League champions and Scottish FA Cup winners from a three-year transition period of poor results, as judged by the club's own very high standards. In winning the 1913/14 League Championship, Celtic had lost just three times, conceding just fourteen goals in thirty-eight matches, the lowest ever in Scottish football.

The first team regulars included Charlie Shaw, the ever-reliable goalkeeper. He transferred to the club from Queens Park Rangers for the start of the previous season in a rare cash transfer for £500. Small for a goalkeeper at just 5ft 6in tall, he possessed safe hands and commanded his penalty box with the authority of a much bigger man. Born in Twechar, twenty-nine-year-old Charlie was married and in addition to playing professional football he owned a tobacconist and newsagents at Bridgeton Cross railway station, just a half mile from the stadium at Parkhead.

In the right back position was Alex McNair from Bo'ness. Known by fans as 'the Icicle', the nickname was a compliment to his intelligent, cool-headed play under pressure. Brought into the team in 1904, Alex was a model of consistency and one of the veterans of the current side. He was a survivor of Maley's first great team, which won six League Championships in a row and every competition it entered in 1908. A married man with one child, Alex lived in Larbert near Stirling and travelled daily through to Glasgow. He was employed as a grate fitter prior to becoming a professional footballer.

At left back was Joe Dodds, a brickwork labourer from Carluke, who was brought into the team in 1909 as a centre half. Joe was moved rearwards to left back on the departure of Jimmy Hay in 1911. The move was a stroke of genius as he and Alex McNair formed one of the greatest defensive pairings in the history of the club. Prior to joining Celtic full time, Joe, like his three brothers, was a member of the Territorial Force of part-time soldiers based in Carluke.

The right half was Ayrshireman 'Sunny' Jim Young from Kilmarnock. Jim joined the Celts on a free transfer from Bristol Rovers in 1903. The current team captain, he was another veteran of Maley's first great team, the six-in-a-row 1905 to 1910 championship-winning side. The epitome of the greatest team Scotland and Britain had ever seen, by 1914 Sunny Jim was already a Celtic legend with the Parkhead faithful having put in eleven years of outstanding service to the club. Jim was a married man and an iron turner to trade.

Centre half Peter Johnstone was a former Fife miner and diehard Celtic supporter. The ultimate utility player, Peter was signed to replace the great Peter Somers at inside left in 1908. He was a great favourite with the Celtic fans, who admired his courage and obvious commitment to the cause. He was dropped back into the midfield in August 1913. Married with two children, Peter was another Celt who took to retailing, but unlike the vast majority of his contemporaries who opened public houses, Peter had recently opened a newsagents shop in the Gallowgate. This was probably the influence of his in-laws, who were strictly pro temperance.

At left half, Johnny McMaster was a time-served electrician from Port Glasgow, who joined the Celts from Clydebank Juniors in May 1913. Despite a slight deafness, he was rock steady, seldom getting the praise his quiet effective performances deserved. A married man with two children, he lived in Glasgow while playing for the Celts.

At outside right, Andy McAtee was a coal miner from Cumbernauld. Brought into the side in September 1910, the former Croy and Mossend Hibernian winger was as fast as a gazelle and possessed a blistering shot. Both characteristics stemmed from massively powerful thighs, which at the time were likened to oak trunks. Married at the end of October 1913, Andy was living with his new wife in the village of Condorrat just a mile from his family home in the village of Smithstone.

At inside right, Patrick (Patsy) Gallacher was born in the poorhouse in Ramelton, Co Donegal, but was brought up in Clydebank. The diminutive footballing wizard was the darling of the Celtic faithful and the brightest star in a team of all stars. A carpenter to trade, he was brought to Celtic FC in October 1911. Nicknamed the 'Mighty Atom', Gallacher may have been small but he was as hard as nails and possessed legendary ball control. Hard working and possessing boundless energy, Patsy was an enormous asset to his team in defence as well as attack. By 1914, he was already well on the way to becoming, in the truest sense of the term, a Celtic legend.

At centre forward, Jimmy McColl was brought into the side for the 1913/14 season's Scottish Cup final replay at Ibrox. His two goals against Hibernian helped secure the cup for the Celts and his place in the first team. The fearless style of play of the twenty-one-year-old boy from St Anthony's reminded the fans of the Mighty Quinn in his heyday. He was soon to be christened 'Sniper' in recognition of his prestigious shooting ability. Small for a centre forward, McColl made up for his lack of height with enormous courage. Prior to making it in professional football, Jimmy followed his father into the shipyards where he worked as a riveter.

Rutherglen-born inside left Jimmy 'Napoleon' McMenemy was rescued from a tedious, labouring job in a chair factory to become one of the Celtic all-time greats. He signed for Willie Maley up a Union Street tenement close in 1902 and fought his way into the team the following year. 'Nap', as he was known to the fans, had all the attributes of a great footballer: fast, excellent ball control, passing and heading ability, good vision and a fierce shot. Napoleon led the line for the six-in-a-row championship-winning side and in 1914 his name would still have been first on the Celtic team sheet. The veteran of the side, at 34 years of age Jimmy showed no signs of slowing down.

The regular outside left was Johnny Browning. Largely underrated, he was quietly effective on the left wing at a time when wing play was a very large part of the Celtic game. Born in Dumbarton, this *Son of the Rock* was a baker to trade and had fought his way into the team midway through the 1912/13 season. Nicknamed the 'Smiler' on account of his dour personality, Johnny was brought into the team from that remarkable school of footballers, the Vale of Leven. Despite his apparent dourness, he reputedly did a good Harry Lauder impersonation and was something of a character in the dressing room. 'Smiler' Browning would be a fixture at outside left for the next seven years.

For a professional footballer, to have secured a regular place in the Celtic team was a life-changing event. Every player in the current squad came from a working-class background and football was their escape from the grinding poverty and squalor associated with their class. The majority of the players were unskilled labourers; many were miners and after their footballing careers came to an end with few exceptions they returned to the pits or to backbreaking manual labouring. While at Celtic FC the players were the best-paid footballers in Scotland with most receiving between £5 and £6 per week plus win bonuses. The Celtic's wage bill for season 1913/14 was £5800 for a squad of twenty-two players. In comparison the next wealthiest team in Scotland, Rangers, paid out £5300 for a playing squad of twenty-five players. The Celtic directors believed in quality rather than quantity and would rather have had a first squad of sixteen first-class players at £6 per week than twenty-five moderate players averaging half that sum. Despite Celtic FC's political affiliations and Irish Roman Catholic heritage, with the exception of the very first Celtic team, the club adopted a policy of employing players and staff irrespective of their creed or political leanings. The double-winning Celtic squad reflected the religious diversity with a mix of Roman Catholics and Protestants.

In what would become his final season, the great Jimmy Quinn's swansong cast a shadow over the club and the supporters doubted if they would ever see his likes again. Signed in 1902 from junior side Smithston Albion, Jimmy Quinn won six League Championship medals between 1905 and 1910 and five Scottish Cup winner's medals (1904, 1907, 1908, 1911 and 1912). First capped for Scotland in 1905, he won eleven full international honours and made eight appearances representing the Scottish League. The mighty James had, with one exception, been out of action for the double-winning season and Celtic struggled to find a quality centre forward let alone a replacement for the living legend. Bernie Connelly, George 'Dod' Whitehead and the magnificently named Londoner, Ebenezer Owers, brought in from Clyde FC, were all given a go, but in some way or other were found lacking. Finally, young Jimmy McColl, signed from St Anthony's in September 1913, was brought back to Parkhead and quickly made the position his own.

James Quinn

The 1913/14 Scottish Cup was won at Ibrox Park when the Bhoys defeated Hibernian FC after a replay in an all-Irish final. Hibernian FC was, like the Celtic, founded and supported by the immigrant Irish community, in this case from those who had settled in and around Leith and Edinburgh. Ibrox Park was situated in the south of the city and was the home of Celtic's old friends, but now greatest rivals, Glasgow Rangers. The stadium, a bastion of Irish Protestantism, had never before or since seen or heard the likes of it. Both sets of supporters, 40,000 strong and bedecked in emerald green, sang songs like 'God Save Ireland' and 'Wearing O' The Green'. The Celtic were lucky not to lose the first game, but thanks to two goals, one each from McColl and Browning, they overwhelmed Hibernian in the replay a few days later by four goals to one. The victory gave the Bhoys their ninth Scottish Cup and their third League and Cup double.

The only disappointment in what was a great season was the exit from the Glasgow Cup at the hands of 3rd Lanark FC (originally, the 3rd (Lanarkshire) Rifle Volunteers) after a goalless draw at Parkhead and a fluky late goal at Cathkin Park. Sweet revenge came in the form of a 6–0 drubbing of the 'Warriors' in the Charity Cup final when McMenemy scored two goals, and Dodds, McColl, McMaster and Johnstone all got a piece of the action. In what was a truly wonderful season, the Bhoys played a total of fifty-three games, won thirty-eight, lost six and drew nine. They scored 112 goals for and conceded twenty-four goals against. In the League only, the statistics were eighty-one goals for and an amazing fourteen against. For thirteen successive League and Scottish Cup games between 20 December 1913 and 21 February 1914, the Celtic had a single goal scored against them. Patsy Gallacher was the top scorer with twenty-one goals from thirty-seven starts and Charlie Shaw played in every one of the thirty-eight league games. The players who contributed to the success in large or small measure with appearances were: Shaw (38), McNair (32), Dodds (36), Young (34), Johnstone (36), McMaster (33), T McGregor (13), Davidson (5), Loney (2), McAtee (36), Gallacher (37), McMenemy (20), Browning (37), McColl (17), Quinn (1), Owers (14), Whitehead (7), Connelly (8), Crone (7), A McGregor (1), Cassidy (1) and Hill (2).

In addition to the first team regulars, there was a string of reserve players ready to step into the breach. At this time Celtic had no reserve team as such, but the highly transitory second string got run-outs at friendly, charity, benefit and minor cup games or were loaned out for spells to other teams. At the time, Celtic had a particularly close relationship with Ayr United

FC and dozens of players came and went between the clubs over the war years. Curiously, Willie Maley's eldest brother, Charles O'Malley, was a parish priest in Ayr, but apparently he showed very little interest in football. Also in the 1914/15 Celtic squad was Thomas McGregor, a quality fullback and standby for McNair or Dodds. Born in Laurieston, Stirlingshire, Tom was a first-class footballer, who even as a reserve managed to get selected for the Scotland squad. Standing in for McNair, he played in all the games during the European tour including the bruiser at Budapest against Burnley. Glaswegian Henry Jarvis was a wing half who came to Celtic in 1912 from Cambuslang Rangers. An electrician to trade, he worked full time at Fairfield Shipyard. As the understudy for the ever-reliable Jim Young, Henry spent much of his time on short-term loans. Edinburgh-born boy wonder, Michael Gilhooly, signed for Celtic as a sixteen year old in 1912 from Glencraig Celtic and was showing immense promise as a centre half. Against a regular halfback line of Young, Johnstone and McMasters, he was facing an uphill struggle to establish himself in the team. Maley recognised him as a very definite talent, but he was yet to get a run-out in a League game. The eighteen-year-old pulled on the hoops for friendlies or benefit games. Alex Gray was born in Bainsford near Falkirk and was a close neighbour of Alex McNair. Brought into the team from Stenhousemuir in 1912, he had been recommended to Celtic by Willie McOustra. When the Celtic signed Alex, Willie McOustra commented: 'Well, Willie, you have got some good players from the village, but you've got one of the best tonight.' Alex was a fast, tricky left-winger, whose only problems were the reliability of Johnny Browning and the reputation of Billy Crone. Fed out to Ayr United for the previous two seasons, he was now back training at Parkhead while working in the Parkhead Forge as an iron moulder. Billy Crone was a Belfast boy brought to the club from the Celtic's great friends and namesake Belfast Celtic. 'Handsome' Billy arrived at Parkhead in mid-1913 as cover for Patsy Gallacher and Jimmy McMenemy. Billy brought something of a reputation with him, but was struggling to live up to the hype. Joseph O'Kane, a young centre forward from Maryhill, was in the process of coming to the club. Willie Maley was not quite sure about him just yet, but he would get a run-out and would soon be off to Clydebank on loan.

Last, but by no means least, was the legendary Jimmy Quinn. Now in semi retirement, the Celts just simply refused to let him go. After years of physical abuse, his body was almost constantly breaking down injured. His best days were well gone but such was his persona and status, the club kept him, hoping against hope that he could make a comeback. Such was his reputation with fans of all clubs, the sports writers often speculated and hoped for the return of the 'Mighty' Quinn as he was famously and affectionately known. For the Celts, he was guaranteed a place in the first team whenever he was fit enough or whenever he could be persuaded, often against his better judgement, to step into the breach when the need was greatest.

Outwith the squad at Parkhead, there were a number of players who remained on Celtic's books, but who were loaned out to various clubs; Alex McGregor was at Dumbarton, James Wilson went to East Stirling, while Willie McStay, Bernie Connelly and Joe Cassidy were all at Ayr United. It was to be expected that a couple of the youngsters, Michael Gilhooly and Joe O'Kane, would also be farmed out to other clubs for the season. This *farming out* was the usual procedure at Celtic; not only did it get the players in question senior games and experience, but it saved Celtic from having to pay them. Several players who had been on the Celtic books during the 1913/14 season were let go. Outside left Archie McMillan, brought in from Kirkintilloch

Harp, was freed to go to Ayr United. Young Archie never really got a fair crack of the whip at Parkhead. The Glasgow Observer's sports correspondent, *the Man in the Know*, thought he should be nurtured, but was usually starved of the ball by the selfishness of Joe Cassidy; his chance to shine at Parkhead was missed. Andrew Davidson was a Glasgow University medical student, who despite making a major contribution to the success of the previous season was allowed to go to St Mirren.

For the successful 1913/14 Celtic squad, the highlight of the year was the annual end of season Continental tour of Europe. The team were due to set off from Glasgow on 14 May 1914 for a five-match jaunt around Germany, Austria and Hungary. A fortnight before, Willie Maley and the Celtic directors took in the English FA Cup final between Burnley and Liverpool at Crystal Palace in London. Maley was planning an exhibition match between the Scottish and English cup holders to be played probably in September. After watching an uninspiring final in which Burnley took the honours, the consensus was that the Scottish champions could give the English cup holders two goals of a start and still come up trumps. Little did they know at the time, but the two national cup holders would be meeting much sooner than September. The Bhoys set off for the Continent the day after beating Third Lanark 6–0 at Hampden Park to win the Glasgow Charity Cup. The following fourteen players were included in the party: Shaw, Dodds, McGregor, Young, Johnstone, McMaster, Jarvis, McAtee, Gallacher, McColl, McMenemy, Browning, Crone and the final place was taken by Frank Kelly, the son of Celtic chairman, James Kelly. The twenty-two-year-old was training to be an accountant, but as a talented outside right with blistering pace, he supplemented his pay by playing football, mostly with Motherwell FC. In addition to Willie Maley, directors James Kelly, Mick Dunbar and John McKillop, and trainer Willie Quinn assisted by Celtic legend Jimmy Quinn, accompanied the tourists. Finally, arguably the greatest Celtic supporter of all time, Charlie Quin, better known to the readership of the Glasgow Catholic Observer and the Glasgow Star as *the Man in the Know*, joined the touring party.

The Celtic tour was conducted during the annual military manoeuvres on the Continent and throughout their trip the Celtic party saw and were highly impressed by the military might of the German and Austro-Hungarian Armies. From the first morning when their train crossed the Rhine at Wessel, until they re-crossed the river a fortnight later, the Celtic party saw regiment after regiment conducting training exercises. Soldiers appeared to be everywhere. In Vienna, the team went to the open-air baths where they dined in bath sheets and met several batteries of artillerymen, cooling down after a hard day's training, as was a regiment recruited in the Tyrol called the Bersaglieri, whose members were sharpshooters. En route to Budapest, they experienced the much vaunted German railway system as it practised the rapid transportation of large numbers of troops. As the railway management prioritised troop trains, the Celtic tourists found their own train held up on occasion. In Budapest, they came across regiments of Moravians and Honveds and Celtic FC's Catholics followed a Bohemian regiment as it marched, accompanied by its band, to Sunday Mass. In Berlin they missed the review of the elite Prussian Guard due to the weather, but were suitably impressed as it goose-stepped down the Unter den Linden. In Berlin and Potsdam, they saw and marvelled at the new-fangled airships, the Zeppelins, and little did they imagine that the same airships would, within a few short months, become an object of aerial terror as they bombed British towns. Both German cities they likened to military camps. Military officers were even crowded into their hotels. One stood to salute the Celtic as the hotel played the British national anthem in their honour. The Celtic tourists thought the German and Austro-Hungarian soldiers were 'well set up', all very fine fellows with good manners; they were obviously from good families, especially the ones they met at Mass. They were much more impressive than the French soldiers that they had seen previously.

En route to Budapest from Vienna, the Celtic party was stopped at a customs post when Peter Johnstone's cases were searched. The magnificently attired customs officials discovered that he had ten extra packs of cigarettes. The officials were all for confiscating Peter's favourite smoke until someone noticed that he was part of the famous Celtic team. After posing for photographs and signing autographs, his supply of Woodbines was safe and the Celts continued on their journey.

Celtic v Burnley

On arrival in the Hungarian capital on 17 May, the Celtic played a friendly against local side Ferencvaros, which resulted in a 2–2 draw. Maley then discovered, much to his annoyance, that Celtic were scheduled to play a charity game against the English FA Cup winners Burnley. The game would be played for a trophy put up by a local businessman and grandly titled the Budapest Cup. The match turned into a very physical encounter, beyond what might be considered as typical of a Scottish or English cup game. A sports commentator suggested that a war correspondent should have sent in the match report and the encounter was nicknamed by those who saw it the Battle of Budapest. The match finished in an ill-tempered 1–1 draw after Burnley was awarded a controversial late penalty. As the players were leaving the pitch, Peter Johnstone got involved in a scuffle with Burnley's Jimmy Lindsay. The Ulsterman was mouthing off and Peter took exception to his comments. The pair had to be prised apart by club officials. The subsequent newspaper headlines highlighting the brawl, made unpleasant reading for the Celtic directors.

The next two games saw victories for the Celtic tourists; the Bhoys scored six goals against both Weiner Athletic in Vienna and Hertha FC in Berlin. On 30 May, the Celts were defeated 1–0 in a bruising encounter with the Leipzig Sports team in Leipzig. McAtee, McMaster and Patsy Gallacher were rested with Crone, Jarvis and Francis Kelly, son of the Celtic director, coming in as replacements. From the kick-off, the Bhoys had all the play but the goals they scored were chalked off. According to one eyewitness, the referee seemed more interested in the success of the Leipzig team than anyone else. In fact, the goal that won the game for the Germans was plainly fisted in, but allowed to stand. It was a battered and bruised Celtic side that staggered into the pavilion after the final whistle. Jimmy McMenemy in particular took some brutal punishment from a very physical German side. Two days later the Celts were back in Berlin where they beat Preussen FC 4–0 in the final game of the tour.

Soon after getting back from the Continental tour, the team and club officials went off on their summer break. For the players it was a casual month with some going on holiday. Wing wizard Patsy Gallacher went back to his home village of Ramelton, in Co Donegal, while goalkeeper Charlie Shaw went to Saltcoats for a fortnight. However, the players retained by Celtic for the new season continued to be paid over the close season and that meant putting in guest appearances at the numerous sports events throughout west central Scotland. Several players also appeared as five-a-side teams to play in the football competitions that were part and parcel of most sports events. The bigger the event, the better the prizes and the more powerful the Celtic combination. For example, the winning Celtic five who turned out at the Pollok Sports day included two youngsters, Joe Cassidy and Joe O'Kane. Cassidy was already on the Celtic books, but was farmed out to Ayr United, while young O'Kane was a Maryhill boy who Willie Maley had his eye on but had yet to sign. Meanwhile, the five who turned out for the Celtic at the two-day Rangers Sports meeting, Dodds, McColl, McAtee, Browning and Gray, were all members of the first team. For a successful five-a-side team, the prize was usually along the lines of a canteen of cutlery, pocket watches, clocks or travel cases. Willie Maley, ever the workaholic, was talent hunting along with Jimmy McMenemy at the replayed Junior Cup final at Cathkin Park on 7 June. On Wednesday 10 June, Maley along with a number of club directors, attended the City Chambers where they were presented with the Celtic's twelfth Glasgow Charity Cup. The following weekend he was at the East Kilbride Sports meeting judging the athletics.

At the end of June, Willie Maley took a break and spent a week or so on holiday at Tomintoul in the Scottish Highlands. His last few days there were spent contemplating the deteriorating political situation in Ireland and the assassination of the Austrian Archduke and his wife in Sarajevo on 28 June. He recalled that at one stage it was feared that the Celtic's 1914 Continental tour would be cancelled because of the deteriorating health of the Austrian Emperor Franz Joseph. He never thought the eighty-four-year-old monarch would survive his latest bout of illness and no one dreamed that it would be his heir and nephew that the Austro-Hungarians would be burying. Although the Celtic tourists never visited Sarajevo, they did meet at dinner several Bosnian and Herzegovinian diplomats in Budapest on state business. The Celts thought them oriental looking with their olive skins and red turbans, but they seemed gentlemanly enough. The Celtic party also picked up their mood of dissatisfaction with the Austro-Hungarian interference in Bosnian affairs. As Glasgow Irish, it was difficult not to feel some sympathy for small nations struggling with the aggression of a large imperialist power. Some of Maley's friends and acquaintances thought the murder of the Archduke and his wife was the price of empire and the Austro-Hungarians had to pay for their annexation of two small warlike states. Although he never imagined that any conflict in the Balkans would affect Great Britain or Ireland, it was feared that the Celtic would not tour central Europe next summer. On Willie Maley's return to Glasgow, July was spent finalising the programme for the Celtic Sports

Meeting. The world-renowned athletics meeting had been an annual event at Parkhead for the last twenty odd years and more or less ran itself. Only the current crop of touring international athletic stars of the track and field needed to be signed up, which involved a number of trips around the county including one to London.

At the beginning of August the players reported to Parkhead to start their pre-season training. As they sweated off the excess pounds under trainer Willie Quinn, the Bhoys swapped news of their holidays, compared close season training regimes and wondered at the latest outrages perpetrated by the mad women suffragettes, such as trying to blow up Rabbie Burns' Cottage. The possibility of war, both in Europe and much closer to home in Ireland, was undoubtedly the hottest topic of conversation. In Dublin, the Bachelor's Walk incident, where unarmed civilians had been shot dead by the military just days earlier, had taken Ireland to the very brink of civil war. The entire nation was outraged with even British newspapers demanding answers. Irish Nationalist leader John Redmond insisted and got an immediate public enquiry. The Glasgow Catholic Observer's headlines screamed 'Military Murder', while the Dubliners took to calling the battalion involved, the King's Own Scottish Borderers, the 'King's Own Murderers'.

In addition to the breaking news at home and in Ireland, the Bhoys sweating it out at Parkhead would also be recalling some of the military sights they had seen on their recent European tour. They had witnessed first hand the massive German and Austro-Hungarian conscript armies during their exercise season. It would have come as no surprise had they known that the Germans alone could field almost five million trained men in uniform almost at the drop of a hat. There was enough military expertise among the players and staff at Parkhead to be able to discuss the chances of the small 240,000 strong professional and entirely volunteer British Army, around half of which was used to police the Empire, should it be forced to confront the massive Continental conscript armies.

James Kelly JP

For the Bhoys, the season was due to start on 15 August with a very difficult away game against a young Heart of Midlothian team at Tynecastle. There were also a couple of charity games and a testimonial to be played before then by way of pre-season warm-ups.

When the Celtic squad turned up at Celtic Park to start pre season training, they discovered that much had changed at Parkhead over the close season. The old red, cement cycling track had been dug up to make room for additional terracing, which would allow an additional 20,000 spectators to be crammed into the stadium. The decision to remove the track had been taken eighteen months previously, with the last cycle race taking place on 18 May 1913. The club also had a new chairman since legendary ex-player James Kelly had resigned the post just a couple of days previously. He had taken over the position of chairman in 1909 on the death of John H McLaughlin. James Kelly JP was one of the Celtic originals. He had been the team captain in the club's very first game against Rangers and had been on the Celtic board since 1897. There was some talk in the newspapers of a rift in the boardroom, but the club categorically denied it. Charles Quin aka *the Man in the Know*, always ready to spring to the defence of the club, reported the reason for the resignation was simply to allow him to concentrate on his responsibilities as a local councillor, Justice of the Peace and other public work. He also pointed out that the former chairman still retained his place on the board. James Kelly was yet another publican, owning several public houses in his home village of Blantyre. With teenage sons, at or approaching serviceable age, the European crisis would have been a cause of some concern for forty-nine-year-old Kelly.

The new man in the chair was thirty-three-year-old Glasgow Irish solicitor Thomas White. Educated at Glasgow University, White was a fervent Irish Nationalist and a frequent speaker on Nationalist platforms. He was also the chairman of the Glasgow Star and Examiner, a newspaper that had been taken over by the Home Government Branch of the United Irish League in 1903. Tom White was the chairman of the branch at the time and already being a director of the newspaper, became chairman, taking over from Joe Devlin, the Irish Nationalist MP, when he became the general secretary of the United Irish League. The Glasgow Star was added to the newspaper stable of Charles Diamond, owner of the Glasgow Catholic Observer in 1908. A prodigy of Celtic founding father John Glass, Tom White had joined the Celtic board in 1906 aged just twenty-five and represented the club on the Glasgow Football Association, later becoming its president. When James Kelly resigned, Tom White was also the vice-president of the Scottish Football Association. Like so many of the early leaders at Celtic, Tom White was an early convert to socialism and was an election agent for the Scottish Labour Party. He would preside over the Celtic for a record thirty-three years and like James Kelly, would found a dynasty at Celtic.

In 1914, in addition to James Kelly and Tom White, the Celtic board included former player Mick Dunbar, who in 1914 was unmarried and living in Armadale Street, Dennistoun, with his schoolteacher sister. He and his brother Tom were successful publicans with three establishments in Glasgow's East End. Although not politically outspoken, Mick Dunbar never failed to put his hand into his pocket for the causes of Irish Nationalism. Voted onto the Celtic board in June 1897, he, along with Willie Maley and James Kelly, took most to do with the team itself. Mick and Willie Maley were great, lifelong friends.

Belfast-born Thomas Colgan joined the Celtic board in 1905 on the death of founding father John O'Hara. Yet another publican, Tom had long-standing Irish Nationalist credentials having been a member of the Home Government delegation to the Irish Race Convention in 1896. His brother Patrick Colgan was for many years the secretary of both the Archbishop Walsh Branch in Parkhead and the Home Government Branch of the Irish National League. Both brothers were long-term supporters of John Redmond and the IPP and regularly appeared on his political platforms and donated sizeable sums to its political war chest. Tom Colgan was himself something of a sportsman, taking active interest in athletic and football. As a young man, he was a sprinter and he played football for St Malachy's College, Belfast. He had been on the periphery of Celtic FC for some years and was among the original shareholders of the new limited company formed in 1897. By 1898, he and another brother John, who was a successful Antrim cattle dealer, held a considerable 400 club shares between them. In 1903, Tom Colgan married the daughter of fellow director James Grant, but tragically his young wife Mary Ellen died just nine months later aged just twenty-seven. By 1914 Tom was still a widower and spent much of his time commuting between Glasgow and Toomebridge, Antrim, where his ten-year-old daughter, Mary Ellen was in the care of his in-laws, the Grants. Among his business interests in Glasgow was the licence of the Old Vic public house on Govan Road.

Described as a genial Irishman, James Grant JP was first voted onto the Celtic committee in June 1896 and as the biggest single shareholder (with 400 and later 800 shares), was elected onto the board of directors in 1897. A wine and spirit merchant, he held several licences throughout the city including the Grant Arms in Argyll Street. He knew little of football and took little to do with the team. On conversion to limited liability he appears to have taken over the responsibility for the stadium from James McKay and was responsible for the improvements and extensions at the ground. His main claim to fame was building the famous or infamous Grant Stand at Parkhead. Although he had spent much of his working life in Glasgow, he maintained a home in Toomebridge, Co Antrim, where he was a local Justice of the Peace. By 1914 James Grant was terminally ill and spent most of his remaining time at his home in Toomebridge. His shares in the club would remain in the Colgan and Grant family until the 1990s.

Glasgow solicitor John Shaughnessy was the son of founding father Joseph Shaughnessy, who had died in 1906, and his Scottish wife Mary McDonald born at Fort Augustus in Lochaber. John was born in Rutherglen in 1868, and he and his siblings spent their summers with their mother's family in the Scottish Highlands. He followed in his father's footsteps by attending St Mungo's and St Aloysius' College in Glasgow and he later studied law at Glasgow University. In his youth, John Shaughnessy was himself something of a sportsman, playing junior football for his local team Rutherglen Glencairn. He played at outside left in the team that won the now defunct South Side Junior Cup and the Cambuslang and District League in their first season 1896/97. Two of his Glencairn contemporaries, Jimmy McMenemy and Alex Bennett, would go on to play for the Celtic. He and his siblings were also immersed in Celtic FC from a young age and were active members of the

**Col. Shaughnessy and William Maley
at Darnley Ranges circa 1913**

Celtic Harriers and the Celtic Cycling Club. In 1897, John Shaughnessy joined the Volunteer Movement, the Victorian version of the Territorial Army, and was accepted for a commission with the 1st Volunteer Bn Highland Light Infantry (later 5th Bn HLI). Just eighteen months later he transferred to 3rd (Lanarkshire) Rifle Volunteers. John Shaughnessy served with the volunteer battalion from 1899 and between then and 1907, was promoted through the ranks until he became a major and was appointed company commander. Over the eight years, John

Shaughnessy attended and passed a number of military courses including musketry instructor at Hythe, Kent, tactics, military engineering and supply and equipment. Although he could not be considered a crack shot, he took an active interest in shooting and was a member of the Darnley Range Committee. The Haldane Army reforms of 1908 heralded the end of the Volunteer movement including the old 3rd (Lanarkshire) Rifle Volunteers. The volunteer battalion was disbanded, only to reform immediately with the new title of the 7th Bn Cameronians (Scottish Rifles) Territorial Force (TF). As a recently promoted lieutenant colonel, John Shaughnessy assumed command of the new formation. He took the battalion to their annual camp at Troon in mid-July 1909 and every year thereafter until his retirement in 1913, after sixteen years' military service. After resigning his command of the battalion, he remained on the reserve officers list and commanded the Roman Catholic contingent of the National Reserve, which paraded in Glasgow at the beginning of July 1914.

Like his father, he was very active in local politics, particularly school boards, and he was the first Roman Catholic to gain a position on the Cathcart school board. Also like his father, he was a member of the Liberal Party and he was a natural bridge between Liberal and Irish Nationalists at a local level. As a member of the Glasgow Liberal Party he helped organise the visit of John Redmond to Glasgow in June 1913 and was among the 5000 people who packed into St Andrew's Hall in Glasgow to hear John Redmond speak on Irish Home Rule. As a Celtic director, he represented Celtic FC on a number of organisations, including the Glasgow Football Association. He joined the Celtic board in September 1911.

John McKillop was another of the original members of the club and was voted onto the board in 1897. He was the brother of Celtic committeeman and honorary club president, William McKillop, who died in 1909. The McKillop family arrived in Scotland at the height of the Great Famine and settled first in Catrine, Ayrshire where the older brothers went to work in the coalmines. A keen Ulster intellect, honed by a Scottish education saw the brothers move to Glasgow where John and James and later younger brother James, went into the grocery trade. From small beginnings the brother's business prospered and the McKillop brothers ultimately came to own the Grosvenor Restaurant once the chief, most popular eatery in Glasgow. John had taken the lead in running the family business while his brother William became involved in the Celtic project and later still in politics as an Irish Parliamentary Party (IPP) MP. Now aged sixty, John McKillop was unmarried and spent most of his time on the golf course at Lethamhill, near Riddrie, while younger brother, James, also a major Celtic shareholder, looked after the business. A fervent Celtic supporter, John left the running of the Celtic team to Maley, Kelly and Dunbar, but was involved in the business side of the company. Like his brother William, John McKillop was a long-term supporter of constitutional Irish Nationalism and the IPP. Although no great orator, he freely gave significant sums to various Irish causes and regularly appeared on their political platforms. By 1914, he had been unwell for some time. He had accompanied the Celtic tourists during their recent European tour, but halfway through he went to take a cure at Marienbad, at the time a famous Continental spa. Back in Glasgow, by the autumn his medical condition was deteriorating.

Last but by no means least was Mr Celtic himself, William Partick Maley. Born in a British Army barracks in Newry, Willie Maley was a very British Irishman. He was the son of Irishman Thomas Maley, a regular army sergeant who on his retirement from the military, attained the position of permanent staff instructor with the Rifle Volunteers based at Cathcart, near Glasgow. Maley and his four brothers grew up in a military environment and were steeped in army and regimental traditions. He developed a respect and admiration for the military that he would retain for the rest of his life. He regularly attended military functions socially and as a representative of the Celtic, and he ranked many soldiers among his personal friends. He was an honorary member of a number of warrant officers' and sergeants' messes and had a particular affection for his father's old regiment, the Royal Scots Fusiliers (RSF), whose depot was at Ayr. Having been associated with the club from its earliest days as a very talented player, by 1914, Willie Maley had held the post of secretary/manager for over twenty years. Having absorbed many of the ethics of a military lifestyle, such as personal discipline, hard work, self-improvement, respectability and loyalty, into his own character, he transferred the same ethics to his management of Celtic FC. A man of many facets and contradictions, he was at the same time a devout Roman Catholic and a Liberal socialist, a long-term advocate of constitutional Irish nationalism while being a fervent royalist and supporter of the establishment. Most of all he was a football genius, who by 1914 was already a legendary figure at Parkhead. He had over the previous twenty years built a number of teams that had completely dominated Scottish football, in particular, the Celtic squad of 1904, which won six league championships in a row between 1904 and 1910.

Willie Maley had dedicated his life to Celtic FC and had over the period built the Celtic into the most successful football club in Britain. His devotion to the club had, however, come at some personal cost. His marriage had broken down and on the eve of war forty-four-year-old Maley lived with his mother and two teenage sons in Glasgow's West End. The most high profile member of the Celtic management team, he was the public face of Celtic and represented the club on a number of associations; most notably he was a member of the Scottish Football League board.

Led first by John Glass, followed by John H McLaughlin and then by James Kelly, the Celtic management enjoyed a formidable reputation for business acumen among the hard-headed businessmen of Glasgow. It was a status that fully complimented the success and standing of the football team. With Celtic FC it was always business first and by 1914 the football club had acquired a reputation for a single-minded, at times ruthless, approach to the business side of the game. Always at the forefront of innovation and change, the Celtic management strove to maximise all revenue streams. By 1914, the Celtic did not even have a reserve team because it was felt a reserve team was not financially viable. By the eve of the Great War, Celtic was by some distance the most financially successful club in Scotland and ranked among the richest in the whole of Britain.

At the beginning of August 1914, Willie Maley was celebrating coming third in the Glasgow St Mungo's monthly golf competition with a score of seventy-one off a handicap of eight. At Parkhead, he and the Celtic directors were looking forward to the forthcoming annual Celtic sports meeting. It had been a glorious summer, but lately the weather had broken, mostly showers, but also occasional heavy driving rain replacing weeks of unbroken sunshine. With an eye on their sports meeting attendances Willie Maley and the directors hoped the squalls were not the end of the summer and that the stormy weather would soon pass.

IRELAND

On Sunday 1 August, with Ulster already intoxicated with Loyalism, Sir Edward Carson in reply to a journalist's question eagerly pledged the support of the UVF militiamen to the British government, not just in Ireland he trumpeted, but many would fight wherever they were asked to. That same day memorial masses were being said throughout Ireland for the victims of the Bachelor's Walk shooting and at Kilcoole on the Wicklow coast, Conor O'Brien landed 600 rifles, his portion from the Howth consignment. On 3 August, IPP leader John Redmond made his own dramatic pledge in the House of Commons in which he offered Irish Nationalist support to the British in the coming war. It was clear that he was supporting Britain because it was in Ireland's interest to do so. He opened his speech by highlighting Ireland's past grievances against Britain, adding that even ten years ago Irish Nationalist support would have been impossible, but insisted that the recent change in Britain's attitude towards Ireland, particularly the government's support for Home Rule, had created an entirely new situation. The Home Rulers, he declared:

> Stood with Britain against German militarism in the hour of crisis, 'to-day two large bodies of Volunteers exist in Ireland. I say to the Government, that they may to-morrow withdraw every one of their troops from Ireland. Ireland will be defended by her armed sons from invasion and for that purpose the armed Catholics in the South will be only too glad to join arms with the armed Protestant Ulstermen. Is it too much to hope that out of this situation a result may spring which will be good, not merely for the Empire, but for the future welfare and integrity of the Irish nation? Let the Irish Volunteers and the Ulster Volunteers defend Ireland while the British army concentrated on the Germans in Flanders.

Entirely unknown to John Redmond at the time, two letters from different sides of the great divide but mooting much the same idea had been published in the Dublin newspapers. One of them was from arch-Unionist Sir Arthur Conan Doyle:

> The chief point which has divided Protestant Ulster from the rest of Ireland is that Nationalists were not loyal to the Empire.

Then, recalling briefly the extent to which Irishmen, most with Nationalist leanings, had helped create that Empire, he went on:

> There is no possible reason why a man should not be a loyal Irishman and a loyal Imperialist also. ... A whole-hearted declaration of loyalty to the common ideal would at the present moment do much to allay the natural fears of Ulster and to strengthen the position of Ireland. Such a chance is unlikely to recur. I pray that the Irish leaders may understand its significance and put themselves in a position to take advantage of it.

The other letter, written from a different standpoint, was signed by MJ Judge, a most active Irish Volunteer who had been wounded in the scuffle on the way back from Howth with the rifles:

England might inspire confidence by restoring it. She could bestow confidence by immediately arming and equipping the Irish Volunteers. The Volunteers, properly armed and equipped, could preserve Ireland from invasion and England would be free to utilize her Army of Occupation for the defence of her own shores.

John Redmond could not have seen either of these letters, but those two trains of thought were included in his speech. The declarations of Irish support were very well received by the British and Irish public alike and both leaders were loudly hailed in the national newspapers. The Home Rule Act had already passed through the different stages that had stood between it and its final passage into law on

John Redmond presents colours to the Irish Volunteers 1913

receiving the royal signature. The next six weeks would see both sides locked in a final round of negotiation and struggle over Carson's amendment to the bill. The imminent passing into law of the Home Rule Act provided the British government with an opportunity to transform attitudes in Nationalist Ireland towards Britain. Although anti-English sentiment had by no means disappeared, throughout the island of Ireland attitudes had softened and any show of confidence in the Irish people and respect toward Irish nationhood would have been eagerly accepted and reciprocated.

John Redmond's pledge not to take advantage of England's difficulty is worth analysing, for this was the first step on a road that would ultimately lead to his own and his political party's destruction. By the time Redmond rose in parliament to make his historic pledge, Carson had already spoken privately to the government pledging the UVF's support. When John Redmond made his public declaration to stand by Britain, he effectively countered the Unionist's move to occupy the loyal and trusted high ground, which in future negotiations over Ulster would have given them a very powerful card to play had the Nationalists not followed suit. The Unionist thinking was how could the British not reward our unconditional loyalty when the disloyal and untrustworthy Nationalists, as usual, took advantage when England was at its most vulnerable? In addition, Redmond was also flinging a curved ball back into the British government's court. By accepting the Nationalist pledge, they were effectively recognising that the Irish had a right to bear arms in their own defence and that an armed Nationalist or Irish volunteer army would be legally defending Ireland, albeit alongside the UVF. This led naturally to calls for the British to arm and train the defenders including the Irish Volunteers, who badly needed arms and training instructors, much more so than the UVF. The Unionists now faced the options of either agreeing to defend Ireland alongside the Nationalists, which would show that common cause was possible. If common cause was possible then so was unity, therefore Home Rule for the whole of Ireland was also possible. Or if they refused to do so, they could be accused of undermining the British war effort and thereby undermining their own claim to unconditional loyalty. The Unionists were in a bit of a cleft stick when it came to future negotiations regarding an opt-out for Ulster: the British would only remember loyalty if it was in deeds and not just rhetoric. The Unionists left parliament that day without making any reply.

Redmond's pledge to defend Ireland was only possible of course because he felt the Home Rule Bill had been safely delivered and at this stage the Volunteers were only being asked to defend Ireland. Bearing in mind the Unionists' offer of unconditional loyalty, John Redmond had deliberately not demanded the full implementation of the Home Rule Bill as a condition of Nationalist support. Meanwhile, his senior military advisor, former British officer Colonel Maurice Moore, was urging Redmond to order the 10,000 British Army Reservists among the Irish Volunteers not to report for duty unless the Home Rule Bill was introduced immediately. Moore realised that once the reservists reported back to their regiments, the Irish Volunteers would lose most of its vital military instructors and much of its military effectiveness.

Colonel Moore's advice regarding the ex-servicemen among the Irish Volunteers was militarily sound, although how many of the reservists would have disregarded the recall to their old regiments is debatable. Regimental loyalty and their own sense of honour would most likely have seen a significant number ignore Colonel Moore's order. In Belfast on 6 August, the Irish News reported the departure on the previous day of 600 British Army reservists from the Irish Volunteers. In the event, Redmond refused to surrender the loyal and trusted high ground and give Carson and the Unionists the opportunity to cry Irish treachery. Unwilling to take the political flak, both in parliament and in the press, Redmond decided to let the reservists go. He was confident that his offer of the Irish Volunteers would be accepted and surmised that once the British War Office recognised the Volunteers as a legitimate defence force, it would issue the desperately needed weapons and then train the volunteers into what he hoped would be the nucleus of a future Irish army. With most military commentators predicting a short war, a British armed and trained Irish Nationalist force would be better able to match militarily the UVF when normal Irish politics resumed after the European conflict. The noises from the government were indeed encouraging and it appeared that the War Office would give the Irish Volunteers the official nod of approval.

Just to turn the heated debate up another few degrees, in Dublin Coroner Byrne presiding on the Bachelor's Walk enquiry delivered his verdict. He found that the three people killed during the shooting incident on Bachelor's Walk on 26 July (one was the mother of a serving soldier) had died from bullets fired from rifles of the King's Own Scottish Borderers (KOSB). He added, 'We strongly condemn the actions of the military in firing on unarmed citizens, as we are of the opinion that the circumstances existing at the time did not justify such action.' The jury considered that the government should compensate relatives of the dead.

THE BRITISH WARLORD

Lord Kitchener

Despite widespread political misgivings, on 5 August 1914, the sixty-four-year-old Anglo-Irish officer Field Marshal Earl Horatio Herbert Kitchener of Khartoum was appointed, almost by public demand, the Secretary of State for War. He was the first serving soldier to hold the post since the mid seventeenth century and was as such an immensely powerful figure within the British Cabinet. Once called an *accidental Irishman*, Kitchener's family were first-generation Anglo-Irish and as such he was not really in with the old Ascendancy Irish clique embedded within the British military establishment. Having said that, he was in Ireland long enough to be infected with the 'Protestant Master Race in an alien and hostile land syndrome'. His father was a retired Indian Army colonel, whose family came from the south of England. He bought property in Limerick and Kerry in the aftermath of the potato famine but the family only remained in Kerry for about fifteen years before Henry Kitchener moved them to Switzerland in an effort to improve the health of his wife, and the property was sold. At the outbreak of the Great War, Lord Kitchener was one of the most famous men in Britain and the Empire and was seen as its foremost soldier. He won fame initially during the failed attempt to rescue the Christian evangelist General Gordon at Khartoum. Later, rather dubious victories in the Sudan against a medieval army and against tough Boer farmers in South Africa brought him largely undeserved credit. Kitchener was behind the full implementation of the infamous concentration camp system during the Anglo-Boer War and despite fierce British public criticism over the civilian deaths in the camps, his eventual victory cemented his celebrity status with the public, who idolised him as the very epitome of British Imperialism.

On appointment as Secretary of State for War, Kitchener took on the political role as head of the military, but he also retained his position as a field marshal, and was therefore effectively Commander-in-Chief of the Army and in operational control. Kitchener was an immensely dominating figure, who intimidated most people with whom he came into contact. These included all politicians, whom he held in general contempt, but he reserved a particular contempt for the Liberals. Over the first months of the war he would completely dominate the British Cabinet in which he was second only to Prime Minister Asquith. His massive reputation and domineering character saw his Cabinet colleagues surrender to him almost total responsibility for the conduct of the war. According to Lloyd George, who was Chancellor of the Exchequer at the time:

> *In 1914 he [Kitchener] was practically a military dictator and his decisions upon any question affecting the war were final. The members of the Cabinet were frankly intimidated by his presence because of his repute*

and his enormous influence amongst all classes of the people. A word from
him was decisive and no one dared to challenge it in a Cabinet meeting.

The leader of the Conservatives Bonar Law would also comment: 'I doubt whether he [Asquith] possesses any influence with either K [Kitchener] or Churchill in military matters.'

Kitchener's dictatorial approach would eventually alienate both the Army Council and his own general staff, who also were in awe of him and whose views he largely ignored. Lord Kitchener was, however, one of the few people who realised that the war would not be over by Christmas, and that Britain's small volunteer army would need to be massively expanded if it was to oppose the vast European conscript armies taking the field.

At the first meeting of the wartime Cabinet, Kitchener stunned the politicians and the British High Command alike by announcing that in his opinion one million additional soldiers would be required sooner rather than later and that the war would probably last three years. Having quickly studied the French Battle Plan XVII to which the BEF was to conform, the French general staff and their war planners were added to the long list of people Kitchener thought incompetent. He warned the still shell-shocked Prime Minister and the War Cabinet that the Germans were likely to invade through Belgium and that the BEF should not deploy onto the French left flank as planned. Having just taken office, and probably because plans for the deployment of the BEF were already well advanced, Kitchener, for once, allowed himself to be persuaded by the British general staff to go along with the French plan. Once the politicians agreed to his demand to increase the size of the army, Kitchener refocused his considerable organisational abilities on raising his first half million men.

Kitchener immediately set himself three monumental tasks: (i) to raise, train and equip an army the size of which had never before been seen in Britain; (ii) to oversee British military strategy worldwide and (iii) to mobilise and reorganise British industry onto a war footing. There can be little doubt that Kitchener was the right man at the right time and place and that his contribution during the early phase of the war was vital, but few can doubt that as a soldier he was given far too much political power. Whereas his talent as a military organiser is without question, his talent as a military commander is debatable; he was most certainly not a statesman by any stretch of the imagination. By retaining supreme authority in all matters relating to the military, Kitchener, through the situation in Ireland regarding both Volunteer militias, by default also assumed enormous political power over Ireland.

As far as Ireland and the Irish was concerned, as an upper-class British officer, Kitchener held the traditional officer corps view, i.e. Ireland was and should remain part of the Empire and any sign of disloyalty from any quarter should not be tolerated. He distrusted and had a very low opinion of all volunteers, including Unionist ones, and he was determined that volunteers with Irish Nationalist sentiments, who may develop into an Irish Nationalist army, would not be encouraged or supported. Kitchener simply lacked the imagination or inclination to grasp the complexities of Irish politics and Anglo-Irish relations and Ireland would suffer accordingly. Acting on Kitchener's warning, the British Parliament sanctioned an immediate increase of five hundred thousand men for the regular army. Within days Kitchener called for an initial hundred thousand volunteers to create the first New Army, or Kitchener's first or K1 as it was popularly known, and a proclamation headed: 'Your Country needs you. A Call to Arms', was published on 7 August.

The idea of national conscription was anathema to the British people, but both the civil authorities and the general population expected all available men, particularly young single men, to respond voluntarily to the nation's call to arms simply as their patriotic duty. Very quickly enormous moral pressure would be brought to bear on all men of service age to volunteer for military service. Like just about everything else, Lord Kitchener had a very low opinion of peacetime army volunteers and had opposed the concept of the Territorial Force (TF) from its creation in 1908. Although he had very little personal experience of the volunteers, he decided they were a 'town-clerk's army' and dismissed them out of hand. He therefore decided against using them as a basis for raising the New Armies of citizen soldiers. No nationwide system existed to mount such an unprecedented recruitment campaign, therefore the massive expansion would largely depend, for the first hundred thousand recruits, on a national recruiting campaign and the rush of enthusiasm for the war. The TF administration and the regular army recruiting systems would have to muddle through as tens of thousands of recruits presented themselves for service. Then it would be down to an ad hoc collection of civic authorities, business interests and local committees made up of local dignitaries to raise the additional battalions or service battalions, as they would officially be known. This set-up produced very British, amateurish, parochial recruiting campaigns that encouraged a competitive spirit between everyone involved in the localised recruiting drives. Glasgow would soon begin to compare recruiting figures with Edinburgh, and Edinburgh with Liverpool, and Liverpool with Manchester, and so on. Leading citizens and the great and the good felt compelled to lead by example, taking a high-profile personal interest in raising battalions. This in turn encouraged everyone in the local community to do their bit for their recruiting figures and to fill up *their* Service units. This led to all sorts of organisations – churches, businesses, factories, offices, schools, universities, sporting clubs, etc. – all producing and publishing rolls of honour publicising how many of their members they had contributed to Kitchener's Army and how they were doing *their bit.*

THE FOURTH ESTATE

In an age before television and radio, it is difficult to overstate the power and influence of the fourth estate, not only because of its total circulation figures but also for the manner and tone in which it framed and interpreted events. Newspapers were the primary means of disseminating and receiving information and the period 1890 to 1920 would be known as the Golden Age of the print media. In 1914, over 200 Scottish titles were being published, of which 70 per cent were either Liberal or independent leaning. The Scottish Daily Record and Glasgow Evening Times, the two most popular newspapers in Glasgow, were selling over 150,000 copies per day. These figures increased considerably during the war with the Evening Times on occasion selling in excess of 350,000 copies. Similarly, the very popular Scottish weeklies, like the Dundee-based Weekly News, saw sales rise from 430,000 to almost 650,000 over the course of the war. Although the government quickly moved to censor the press, the Scottish newspapers were seen as being more independent than the British nationals, which were controlled by the likes of Dublin-born Lord Northcliffe, whose titles accounted for 29 per cent of the circulation of the London-based dailies. His brother, Lord Rothermere, was also a newspaper baron; he owned the Daily Mirror, the Glasgow Daily Record and Glasgow Evening News. Between them, the two brothers controlled nearly 50 per cent of the total circulation of daily newspapers and with a range of titles that went from the Times to the Daily Record they reached all classes of society.

Such was the power of the newspaper barons, the government trod very carefully when confronting the press and more often than not the newspapers printed what they liked. On 6 August 1914, the government established the Press Bureau and regulations contained within the Defence of the Realm Act (DORA) gave it the power to censor the British press for the first time. The new Press Bureau was completely independent of both the War Office and the Admiralty, the idea being to censor military news and telegraphs dispatched from the Front and then issue them to the press for publication. Lord Kitchener decided to appoint an official British Army war correspondent, whose dispatches were first censored at General Headquarters (GHQ) and then by Kitchener himself before being released to the press. In January 1915, after some pressure from the United States of America, the British government changed its policy and allowed selected journalists to report the war. Despite the censorship, two good examples of the power of the press were the 'Amiens Dispatch', which broke the story of the retreat from Mons at the end of August 1914 and which materially affected recruiting, and the story of the 'Shells Scandal' of 1915, which effectively brought down the Liberal government. Towards the end of the war, the politicians felt it would be safer if Lord Northcliffe were a part of the British government itself.

As politicians looked to justify the war to the people, they used the press and propaganda posters to get their message to the nation, often using rhetoric that reflected the scale of the crisis. The Great War became known as the war of 'big words': king, country, freedom, duty, democracy, liberty and civilisation were all regularly used in bold print headlines. 'Empathy' might be added when considering the Irish attitude to the invasion of little Catholic Belgium. 'The War,' argued the Cork Free Press, 'is against military despotism and in defence of the integrity of small nations. *Louvain* and *Rheims* alone are cries, which would stir the blood of Catholic Irishmen.' 'Ireland,' said the Westmeath Examiner, 'is at war with the forces of despotism.' Support for the war was almost universal, with the fate of little Belgium seeming to represent the aspirations of other little nations. In comparison to the threat posed by German militarism, British rule seemed positively benign to most people. However, not everyone could be easily influenced by political rhetoric, newspapers or propaganda. Tom Barry, future Chief of Staff of the IRA, wrote of his service in the British Army:

> In June 1915, in my seventeenth year, I had decided to see what this Great War was like. I cannot plead I went on the advice of John Redmond or any other politician, that if we fought for the British we would secure Home Rule for Ireland, nor can I say I understood what Home Rule meant. I was not influenced by the lurid appeal to fight to save Belgium or small nations. I knew nothing about nations, large or small. I went to the war for no other reason than that I wanted to see what war was like, to get a gun, to see new countries and to feel a grown man.

In addition to the national newspapers, the Roman Catholic community in Scotland had access to a number of publications aimed specifically at them, most notably the Glasgow Observer and the Glasgow Star, both of which covered mainly Glasgow and its environs but were also sold nationwide. The Observer's offshoot publication, the Catholic Herald, covered the Catholic communities in Aberdeen, Dundee, Edinburgh, Clydesdale and Lanarkshire. The Glasgow Observer was founded in 1885 by and for the Irish Catholic community in Scotland. Among the men who drove the original project through was Celtic founding father Dr John Conway. Charles Diamond, a Derry-born Catholic newspaper baron, Irish Nationalist and later Labour Party MP, acquired the publication in 1887. As the name suggests, the newspaper was very heavily influenced by the Roman Catholic Church in Scotland. In addition to the usual newspaper outlets, the ethnic community newspaper was sold every Sunday at the back of Catholic churches nationwide. Its sister paper, the Glasgow Star, was launched in 1903 as a direct competitor to the Observer by the Home Government Branch of the UIL. For two decades, the Observer, reflecting the staunchly pro-temperance beliefs of its owner Charles Diamond, had criticised the close association between the drinks trade and the Home Government Branch. The result was the Glasgow Star and Examiner, which trumpeted its Irish Nationalist and democratic beliefs on its banner. The Glasgow Star was added to the Diamond newspaper stable when it was acquired in 1908.

Although the Observer was sold throughout Scotland, the Glasgow Irish regarded it as their very own. Immensely influential and popular, the weekly broadsheet published on a Saturday was seen as representing the Catholic community's interests and contributed greatly to community cohesiveness. The newspaper championed constitutional Irish Nationalism and the campaigns for Irish Home Rule and land reform. Reflecting the anti-drink policy of the Catholic Church, the newspaper was staunchly pro-temperance. Although its designation as an Irish National and Catholic newspaper ensured it was parochial and partisan, it quickly developed into a vehicle that helped build bridges across community divides. Reflecting the goals and aspirations of the Glasgow Irish to be accepted by the wider community, it often highlighted and emphasised the Glasgow Irish's civic loyalty and their involvement and acceptance of wider responsibility, particularly on social and welfare matters. Initially, the newspaper was anti-socialist, reflecting the Roman Catholic Church's belief that socialism in the fullest sense and Catholicism could not be compatible. However, as early as 1891, the newspaper was making a distinction between the anti-clerical socialism of continental Europe and the labour movement in Scotland.

By 1914 with Home Rule seemingly achieved and the Nationalist-Liberal pact open to reappraisal, the attitude of Charles Diamond and his newly appointed managing editor, David Mitchel Quin, to the labour movement took a very definite tilt to the left and the newspaper began to publish Catholic Labour Notes. George Milligan, secretary of the Atlantic Branch of the Dockers Union, wrote the first column in January 1914. The newspaper led the first notes with an editorial, which resoundingly supported the concept that a Roman Catholic could support the labour movement. It argued that Roman Catholics could join the labour movement without alienating themselves from their Church. Although Roman Catholics could not be socialists in the full sense of the word, they were free to hold themselves aloof from secularism and atheism and to follow their conscience. Many in the Scottish labour movement saw the editorial as a momentous announcement and one that would carry beneficial results for the bulk of the Observer's readers.

The Celtic Football and Athletic Club was for the first ten years of its existence a community-based organisation, and as football became more popular, the Glasgow Catholic Observer took an increasing interest in all matters relating to the club. Its interest also reflected the community's sense of ownership and pride in the Celtic, a connection, pride and interest that never diminished, even after the club was converted into a public limited company in 1897 and became the property of its shareholders. The newspaper published a weekly column dedicated to everything Celtic. Several journalists wrote the column over the years, including Celtic legend Tom Maley, whose 'Tom Maley's Football Notes' provided an in-depth analysis of all Celtic affairs. The

Mr Charles Quin

longest running contributor to the column was Charles Quin, who had twenty years previously adopted the nom de plume *the Man in the Know*. Former schoolteacher and brother of the Observer's editor, David Mitchel Quin, Charlie was a passionate Celtic supporter, who had followed the club from its formation. At times outrageously biased towards Celtic, he had maintained a very close personal relationship with the Celtic hierarchy, particularly the Maley family, for over twenty-five years. The Glasgow Observer and *the Man in the Know* column was often used by the Celtic board to get the club's messages or versions of events out to the public. Unfortunately, since for the most part only the Glasgow or Scots Irish read the newspaper, their messages often failed to reach the wider Scottish public.

In addition to the aforementioned newspapers, the Glasgow Irish also had access to a number of Irish Nationalist or socialist publications, which, for as long as they were available, gave a counter view to the war as it affected Ireland and the Nationalist Irish. Very popular with the Glasgow Irish was the Freeman's Journal. The Dublin based publication was effectively the mouthpiece of John Redmond and the IPP and presented constitutional Nationalist views. Irish Freedom, Sinn Féin, Ireland, Irish Worker, Irish Volunteer and The Leader were all printed at some point in Glasgow and represented the advanced Nationalist and socialist-leaning views. These publications were all so anti-British establishment that they were political propaganda sheets. However, for those Glasgow Irish so inclined, the availability of publications expressing such diverse views, which covered the entire political spectrum, probably allowed them to make a reasonably balanced judgement of events. During the war, the advanced Nationalist and socialist publications, including the Independent Labour Party's mouthpiece Forward, would be closed down or threatened with closure and the editors and printers threatened with imprisonment and worse for publishing anti-recruitment propaganda.

PATRIOTS, DUPES AND FOOLS

To the modern mind, the image of tens of thousands of young men voluntarily marching off to Armageddon seems naive, irrational and mad, but it would be a mistake to see them as fools or dupes. Those current generations were the best educated, most patriotic the British nation had ever produced. Each 24 May was a public holiday and celebrated throughout Britain as Empire Day. Every village and town was decked with bunting and flags, special church services were held and for children it was a day of parties, picnics and treats. The object of the celebrations was to reinforce people's sense of pride in being British and to remind them of their links and responsibility for their Empire. The glories and triumphs of the British Empire were drummed into people, particularly children, from all angles and as far as they were concerned, irrespective of social rank, being born British was like owning a winning lottery ticket. No Empire Day would have been complete without at least one rendition by school or church choir of arch imperialist and anti-Catholic bigot Rudyard Kipling's 'Children's Song':

> Land of our birth, we pledge to thee
> Our love and toil in the years to be,
> When we are grown and take our place
> As men and woman with our race.
> Teach us to rule ourselves away,
> Controlled and cleanly night and day,
> That we may bring, if need arise,
> No maimed or worthless sacrifice.

Victorian and Edwardian schoolboys, particularly middle-class schoolboys, were indoctrinated with the ethics of honour, loyalty, chivalry and patriotism. The same ideas and principles were spread beyond the schools themselves through newspapers, novels, plays, comics and magazines. Schoolboys of all social classes devoured magazines and penny comic books with one of the most popular being The Boy's Own Paper. It was so well read among the Glasgow Irish boys of St Aloysius' College, that in December 1901 the headmaster felt compelled to urge the boys to read more than just the Boy's Own. The comic's basic themes were sport, adventure, military and hobbies. British military history often featured, including past victories, how the Empire was won, army and navy medals, and histories of famous British regiments. There were very few *working-class* heroes other than footballers and since the most interesting adventures, sports and hobbies were being carried out by the middle classes, who had the time and the money, the boys' papers concentrated largely on middle-class sports and interests, such as rugby, tennis, sailing and cricket as opposed to football or quoiting, and army officers as opposed to the other ranks. The paper thrilled its young readers with adventure stories set in exotic parts of the Empire, carried out by middle-class British, usually English, heroes, often army or naval officers, in tales of do and dare. Very often the English hero was supported in his exploits by his faithful lower class servant or lower rank soldier. The widely perceived racial superiority of the Anglo Saxon was displayed in the portrayal of the hero's lower class subordinates, who were depicted as being of an inferior race, often Scots or Irish. The Polar explorers Anglo-Irishman Sir Ernest Shackleton and the doomed Captain Scott and their adventures exemplified the type. The typical British middle-class male was portrayed as brave and dignified, stoic in the face of adversary, displaying the famous British stiff upper lip. He could be depended upon to do the right and honourable thing, leading what the British perceived to be lesser races and social classes by his example.

This concept of doing the right and honourable thing would be at the root of the tidal wave of support for the Belgians in August 1914. As far as the vast majority of the British people, including those of the island of Ireland, were concerned, the Germans and their allies were the aggressors and the war was a just and honourable one. The British people expected their government to do the right thing by honouring their obligations to the Belgian people set out in the Treaty of London.

In a modern age when words like patriotism, duty and national service do not have as much resonance as perhaps they once had, we cannot comprehend just how much they did mean to the Great War generations. In this atmosphere of 'doing ones bit' and 'doing the right thing', most people felt a personal moral obligation to contribute in some way to the war effort. The concept was not confined to the British Isles; in the great self-governing dominions, Canada, Australia and New Zealand, the same patriotic ethos was clearly evident. The emotional and cultural ties to what was regarded as the 'Motherland' ran deep and the commitment to the British Empire was total. On 10 August, the Glasgow Herald announced that Canada had offered two battle cruisers and an expeditionary force of 20,000 men, Australia offered her navy and 20,000 men and New Zealand 8000 men. In addition, Canada gifted to the British people one million 96-pound bags of flour. The British government gratefully accepted all the offers. Within days of the declaration of war, thousands of men of all social classes besieged Glasgow recruiting offices and the drill halls of the Territorial Force (TF), literally fighting with each other to enlist. These were largely the adventurers, romantics and the bloodthirsty itching to get into a fight.

All that said, the forces driving men to enlist were far more varied and complex than simply patriotism and idealism. Over the first few weeks of the war, for example, there was a major disruption in trade, therefore there was also a considerable number of unemployed banging on drill hall doors and barracks gates.

On 7 August an advertisement appealing for the first hundred thousand men appeared in the national newspapers. Lord Kitchener's stern moustachioed face stared from the page while his pointing finger seemed to challenge each man that 'Your Country Needs YOU'. He wanted a hundred thousand young, preferably single, men aged between nineteen and thirty. The volunteers enlisting were earmarked for specially created service battalions and the service involved enlisting for three years or until the war ended. Even before Kitchener's appeal, thousands of men were enlisting and between 4 and 8 August the total number of men attested over the entire country was 8191, a very large percentage of which were in London, where police were required to control the crowd outside the recruiting office in Great Scotland Yard. It represented an average daily intake of 1640 men, while the peacetime national intake for the regular army was less than 100 men per day.

With Lord Kitchener's announcement, a British male of fighting age now had three voluntary options for getting into the fray. He could join the regular army or Navy under normal conditions of service. He could join the TF, but would now be expected to sign the Imperial Service declaration and be prepared to serve overseas. Finally, he could volunteer to join Kitchener's new service battalions where he would serve for the duration of the war. Later in the war these distinctions, including the terms and conditions of enlistment, would blur and eventually men served wherever and with whatever type of unit they were sent to. See (Annex C)

Kitchener Recruiting Poster

Chapter Three

AUGUST

THE HOME FRONT

When hostilities broke out, a wave of unrestrained nationalism and enthusiasm for war swept through all the belligerent nations. All believed they were fighting for a righteous cause: the French were fighting for *la Patrie*, the Germans for the Fatherland, the Russians for Holy Mother Russia and the British for the freedom of small nations. In Germany (Adolf Hitler was in a cheering crowd in Munich), Austria, Russia, France and Britain, large crowds, mostly young and middle class, gathered to cheer the news that their country was at war. Within days, the British propaganda machine went into full swing. With the nation now at war, people of all social classes were caught up in a great outpouring of patriotic fervour. 'All over by Christmas' was the war cry.

On mobilisation, regular soldiers and reservists were ordered to report immediately to their units. The military was delighted with the response of the reservists, even some long-term deserters turned up. The Glasgow train stations were full of soldiers in uniform and reservists in civilian clothes making their way to the regimental depots and barracks all around the country. At the offices of Glasgow Corporation Tramways in Bath Street, 500 employees, every one a reservist, handed in their green tramway uniforms prior to joining their units. At the Glasgow and Greenock piers hundreds of Irish and Glasgow Irish soldiers and reservists were boarding the Irish ferries making their way to the Irish regimental depots. In Coatbridge, around 250 reservists, including eight of the town's postmen, left to join their units. The Post Office in Glasgow issued a warning that due to the numbers of postmen recalled to their battalions, they could not guarantee the usual postal service. This was initially a cause for concern at Parkhead with regards to the Celtic Sport Meeting, but the fears proved to be unfounded. In London, over 100 Members of Parliament, officers with the Reserves or Territorial Force (TF), immediately left Westminster to join their units.

With few exceptions, every political organisation, including the socialist Labour Party and the Trades Union Council (TUC), supported the war, though the Parliamentary Labour Party chairman Ramsey MacDonald resigned in protest. (*It cost him his membership of Moray Golf Club, which expelled him.*) In the belief that it would be a short war, the TUC went as far as to promise complete industrial peace for the duration of the war.

With British socialists split over the war, the Independent Labour Party (ILP) in Scotland quickly parted company with the Labour Party, adopting an anti-war stance. It had support from much of the Clydeside trade union leadership as the Trades Union Congress and the Co-op followed its lead. The ILP's propaganda organ, Forward, proclaimed in August that the war was being fought to satisfy the lust for industrial profit on the one hand, and the desire to promote the rise of the British military state on the other. That said, despite some fine rhetoric, the leadership of the ILP actually took a weak stance against the war. Of the seventeen ILP town councillors in Glasgow, only two came out against the war, John Wheatley and John S Taylor. Many Scottish socialists were also pacifists and the likes of John Mclean, Willie Gallacher, Harry McShane and Jimmy Maxton would also oppose the war. On the other side of the coin, Roman Catholic James O'Connor Kessack of the ILP, the leader of the Glasgow dockers and in 1910 the Labour parliamentary candidate for Camlachie, enlisted into the Scottish Horse in September 1914, received a commission in August 1915 and was killed in action in November 1916 serving with the Middlesex Regiment. His widow Margaret lived in Deerpark Garden, Tollcross. On 9 August, around 5000 anti-war demonstrators turned out for the Glasgow Peace rally organised by among others the Glasgow ILP, the Glasgow Trades Council and John McLean's British Socialist Party (BSP). Glasgow Irish spokesmen Patrick Dollan and John Wheatley, among others, addressed the crowd gathered on Glasgow Green, but these were a tiny minority of Scots and the event was not widely reported within the national press. Much of the meeting was interrupted by the comings and goings of the Glasgow Highlanders billeted in the People's Palace and their military band playing nearby. It took a very brave man indeed to publicly condemn the war amid the patriotic fervour. In Ireland, Sinn Féin opposed the war and immediately rekindled the anti-army recruiting campaign last used during the Anglo-Boer War.

At the junction of Glasgow's Argyll Street and Buchanan Street an anti-war speaker was addressing a sizeable crowd of around 1000 when he began to make anti-recruitment statements. He was first heckled, then dragged off his soapbox and assaulted by a man from the crowd. After being interviewed by police who actually witnessed the assault, the assailant was released; he then proceeded to ask for volunteers for the army and received the names of seventeen potential recruits from the crowd. On the Mound in Edinburgh, an antagonistic crowd broke up an anti-war rally.

Shortly after the mobilisation of the regular army, the government embodied the part-time soldiers of the Territorial Force (TF). In the city of Glasgow, the TF establishment amounted to 300 officers and 10,000 men. When notified of their embodiment, the men of the TF literally downed tools, left their places of employment and reported to their drill halls located in just about every city, town and village throughout the country. On arrival they received their £5 bounty as long as they were suitably attired, particularly if wearing serviceable footwear. The next four days were chaos as the men were administered, medically examined, inoculated and equipped. The sick, lame and lazy were weeded out and their places immediately filled by those clambering at the door of the drill hall to enlist. The new recruits were warned that they were required to sign the Imperial Service Declaration confirming that they were prepared to serve abroad and the first score or so actually got issued with something that resembled a uniform; the rest would need to train in their civilian clothes. With around 10,000 Glasgow territorials reporting for duty and needing billets, the army authorities requisitioned various public buildings, such as schools, church halls and the likes, all over the city. Over 400 Glasgow Territorials were billeted in St Aloysius' College. Many of them later attended several Masses at the nearby Jesuit Church.

The 9th (Glasgow Highlanders) Bn Highland Light Infantry (HLI) based at Greendyke Street opposite Glasgow Green, were accommodated for the most part in the nearby Paddy's Market or the *Briggait* as it was commonly known. The historic building had long been an emporium for selling fish wholesale and selling second-hand clothes. As the name suggests, it was the particular haunt and domain of the Glasgow Irish. The overflow went into the red sandstone and glass edifice that was the People's Palace, just a hundred yards from the battalion headquarters on Glasgow Green. If they lived nearby, the men were allowed to go home for the night. By Saturday 8 August, the 9th Bn HLI or Glesga Highlanders as they were more popularly known, had received orders to deploy to their war station. As the battalion marched from Greendyke Street to Queen Street Railway Station in the wee small hours, no one had the slightest idea of where they were going. Rumours were rife. Someone put it about that the Germans had invaded Scotland and the battalion was off to repel the Hun.

Among those Glesga Highlanders marching off to the railway station were Joseph Maley and his pal John Francis McKillop, both sons of famous Celtic Club families. Joseph or Josie as he was known to family and friends was the second son of Celtic legend and club founding father, Tom Maley. Josie was born in the Catholic Boy's Slatefield Industrial School, just a stone's throw from Celtic Park, where at the time of his birth his father was the school superintendent. His mother, Elizabeth, was also a qualified schoolteacher and was school matron. With his father deeply involved with the fledgling Celtic club, he and his three brothers, Tom, Willie and Charlie, would have spent many hours playing around Celtic Park. Now aged twenty-one, Josie was employed by Lloyds of London in their Glasgow office. He had been a member of the TF for some time and had attained the rank of corporal.

John Francis McKillop was the son of James McKillop, the youngest of the three McKillop brothers. The two elder brothers, John and William, had been involved in the Celtic project from its earliest days. Like his brothers, James McKillop was a major shareholder in Celtic. By 1914, John McKillop had been ill for some time and James now managed the McKillop business concerns. Like the Maley boys, John Francis would have spent time at Celtic Park as a boy, but was sent away in his youth to the exclusive Benedictine Ampleforth College. Prior to the outbreak of the war, nineteen-year-old John McKillop was employed in the insurance industry. Like his friend Josie Maley, John Francis was likely a member of the TF prior to the outbreak of the war.

The remaining TF units throughout the country were also deploying to join their brigades and divisions. Scotland provided two TF infantry divisions. The Lowland Division was headquartered in Glasgow and most of its units were drawn from west central Scotland such as the Glesga Highlanders and six other infantry battalions based in Glasgow. Among the Glasgow TF battalions deploying were the 8th Bn Cameronians (Scottish Rifles). The unit had a particular connection with the Garngad district, also known as *Little Ireland*. The battalion headquarters were based just a half-mile away in Cathedral Street and it recruited men mainly from the Garngad, Townhead, Springburn, Calton and Maryhill areas of the city. Such was the make-up of the battalion, it took on a decidedly Glasgow Irish flavour. Soon after its embodiment, the Lowland Division was assigned to coastal defence duties. The divisional headquarters moved to Bridge of Allan with brigades based at Stirling, Falkirk and Dunfermline. The Highland Division was headquartered at Perth with most of its units being drawn from the Highlands of Scotland. Renfrewshire and Argyllshire provided four infantry battalions. On 12 August, the Highland Division was ordered to move to Bedford, where it formed a part of the Central Defence Force. In addition to their guard duties, the divisions began what was expected to be a six-month training period. In November, the divisions would be retitled the 51st (Highland) Division and the 52nd (Lowland) Division.

A number of former Celtic FC players were also caught up in the general recall of reservists or in the public's enthusiasm for war. Among the first to be recalled having reserve commitments was Willie Nichol. Willie was a serving soldier with the Seaforth Highlanders when Willie Maley signed him in July 1911. The Seaforth Highlanders were based at Fort George near Inverness and Willie was turning out for Aberdeen FC as an amateur when Celtic persuaded him to buy himself out of the army and turn professional. One of a number of players brought in to replace the Mighty Quinn, Nichol was a burly centre forward who lacked the quality and speed of Quinn, but his robust style meant he could still do a job as a replacement. Willie Nichol played sixteen times for Celtic and scored nine goals before eventually joining Bristol City in May 1912. On the outbreak of war, he was immediately recalled to the Seaforth Highlanders.

Another old Bhoy who enlisted early was Patrick Slavin, who had been signed by Celtic from Fauldhouse Hibernian in February 1897. A talented outside right, he arrived at Celtic Park at an unfortunate time with the club in the throes of transforming from a charity into a limited company. Pat was seen only as a stopgap player before the club brought in some big names from England. A former member of the 10th Bn (Cyclists) Royal Scots TF, on enlisting he would serve with the 2nd Bn Royal Scots.

John Hastie was a Lanarkshire coal miner who learned his footballing trade with the quaintly named Glenbuck Cherrypickers, before being picked up by Celtic in 1910. After a spell out on loan to St Mirren, he came back to Celtic between 1911/12. He played nineteen times for the Bhoys at outside left, scoring four goals. While playing in the hoops, John was an enthusiastic member of the 5th Bn Royal Scots Fusiliers TF, based in his home village of Glenbuck, Lanarkshire.

Yet another Celtic old Bhoy who decided to *Take the Shilling* early in the war was Willie McOustra. Willie was signed from Ashfield in September 1899 and his competitive senior debut came in a 2–0 league victory at Queen's Park on 8 September 1900. He made thirty appearances for Celtic and scored nine goals before sustaining a bad knee injury and was sold to Tom Maley's Manchester City for what was at the time a sizeable fee. Now aged almost 34, he joined the regular army and at almost 5ft 9in was earmarked for the Scots Guards.

Thomas McAteer from Croy was a neighbour and friend of the mighty Jimmy Quinn. Tom, a former captain of Clyde FC, came to the Celtic towards the end of his playing career, but Willie Maley managed to get another two good seasons from him. He turned out twenty-eight times at centre half for the Bhoys before he retired in 1912. A coal miner with Baird and Co at Kilsyth, he hated and feared being down the pit and took the first opportunity to escape, joining the Cameron Highlanders at the beginning of September 1914. He served with the Cameron's 3rd (Reserve) Bn based at Invergordon during 1915 where he was the lynchpin of a very successful battalion football team.

Another old Celt who joined the Cameron Highlanders was John Young. John was on the Celtic's books between 1908 and 1913, but spent much of the time farmed out to other clubs, appearing just three times in the hoops. John finished he career as a professional player with Dundee Hibs before being released by Celtic in May 1913. A Calton Bhoy, John had recently married and was living in Ross Street when he responded to the call of Lochiel, Chief of the Cameron clan and joined the 5th (Service) Bn. Before he knew it, he was in Cameron Barracks, Inverness.

Willie Donnelly, the old Celtic goalie, joined the Royal Dublin Fusiliers. Born in Magherafelt, Willie's family settled in the Garngad in 1883 and by the turn of the century Willie was working as a steelworker in Blochairn. Playing in goal for Clyde FC, he could claim the astonishing feat of saving nineteen out of twenty-one penalty kicks. His goalkeeping reputation saw him brought in to Celtic as Dan McArthur's deputy in August 1900. He put in just five appearances for the Bhoys before going to Belfast Celtic in 1901.

Some of the Celtic old and bold would even return from abroad. John Colman, James McLaren and the two identical Strang twins, Willie and Sandy, came back to serve with the Canadian armed forces.

Among the young men who besieged the recruiting offices that first week of the war was Bridgeton boy Joseph McAree. Celtic daft, Joe was a promising young footballer. He was something of a prodigy of Tom Maley, who was then managing English first division side Bradford Park Avenue FC. The Celtic legend first came across Joe when he was the superintendent at the Slatefield Industrial School and had great hopes for the youngster. On the outbreak of war, Joe immediately gave up his job in the Beardmore Foundry at Dalmuir to join the regular army. After he enlisted at Stirling Castle he was sent to train with the 3rd (Reserve) Bn Argyll and Sutherland Highlanders first at Stirling, but soon afterwards the battalion moved to Woolwich, London.

On 7 August, the same day the first of Kitchener's advertisements appeared in the newspapers, the British Army's advance parties secretly left for France. The first major British loss of life was also reported in the press that day with the sinking of the cruiser *Amphion* the day previously. Over 130 men were lost including a number of Irish sailors, after she struck a mine in the North Sea. The first Glasgow Irish loss of life due to enemy action was James Gunn, a native of Camelon near Falkirk who was a stoker on board the *Amphion*.

The following day the government introduced the massively powerful Defence of the Realm Act (DORA). This gave the government sweeping new powers, including censorship of the press and communications, the authority to requisition buildings, land and horses and control of the railways. It also banned the public from buying binoculars (to prevent spying), flying kites and lighting bonfires (which could attract Zeppelins), feeding bread to wild animals (wasting food), or discussing military or naval matters. People were warned about discussing the war on trams and trains in case spies were listening. Spies and rooting them out became a short-lived national obsession after a number of notices appeared encouraging everyone to be on the lookout for suspicious characters, who may be enemy agents. In Kildare the police were busy arresting all with a Teutonic or oriental appearance. In most cases, it was later ascertained that the apprehended were not part of an espionage ring and they were discharged. Amongst the Kildare captives were two Russian Jews and three Belgian priests. A squad of English Territorials arrested a Glaswegian holidaying in the south of England. He was sketching some quaint houses beside a railway station that the soldiers were guarding. After questioning him, the man was taken into custody because the soldiers, unable to understand his *Glesga* accent, decided he was speaking German. Bird watchers and pigeon fanciers went in fear of arrest as the spy hunt gathered momentum. A real German spy, Lieutenant Karl Hans Lody, travelling as an American citizen, would land in Britain at the end of August and make his way to Edinburgh. The aim of his mission was the ship movements in and out of the naval dockyard at Rosyth on the Firth of Forth. As the war progressed, DORA would be amended and added to include British summer time hours, restricted pub opening times and weaker alcohol.

On 10 August, Glasgow magistrates appealed for men between the ages of thirty-five and fifty-five to enrol as special constables. Scores of Glasgow policemen were former soldiers and with reserve commitments had been recalled to their regiments, mostly the Scots or Irish Guards. On 12 August, Great Britain and France officially declared war on Germany's ally, Austria-Hungary and her Empire. The following day Austria-Hungary finally invaded Serbia, intending to teach the upstart Serbs a severe lesson. That same day the main elements of the British Expeditionary Force (BEF) began their move to France.

The command of the 90,000 strong BEF had been given to sixty-two-year-old Field Marshal Sir John French. Born in Kent, England, like most high-ranking officers of the time, Sir John French had Irish connections with his father having been born at Frenchpark, Co Roscommon where the family still retained a property. He and his five elder sisters lost their parents while young; their naval commander father John French died in 1854 and shortly afterwards their mother was confined in a mental institution. Sir John French's early life was dominated by his formidable sister Charlotte later Charlotte Despard. She was an independent spirit, a freethinker and later would be something of an affectionate embarrassment to Sir John in his army career. Charlotte converted to Catholicism and was a committed suffragette, being imprisoned in Holloway Prison twice for the cause

Charlotte Despard

of women's rights. She spent a lot of time in Ireland at the family property where she joined with Hanna Sheehy-Skeffington in forming the Irish Women's Franchise League. A vocal and practical supporter of the labour movement, both in Britain and Ireland, she financially supported the strikers during the Dublin lockout of 1913. A pacifist, she would campaign tirelessly against the war and later join Sinn Féin as a committed Irish Republican. Although she was immensely fond of her brother, she would be highly critical of him throughout his career and was an active member of *Cumann na mBan* at the same time as the IRA was attempting to assassinate Sir John. On her death in 1939, she was buried in the Republican plot at Glasnevin Cemetery.

In common with most of his peers and social class, Sir John French naturally had Unionist sympathies; however, he was by reputation apolitical and would not have allowed his views to interfere with his duty. He got his fingers burned after naively becoming embroiled in the Curragh incident and was forced to resign his position. Very much wiser, he was later credited with advising officers under his command: 'You will hear no politics from me, and I expect to hear none from you.' Subsequent to the Curragh incident, he gave several speeches strongly deprecating politics in the army. In August 1914, Sir John French was the natural choice for commanding the BEF, but he would prove to be indecisive and temperamentally unstable, prone to bouts of depression followed by over-optimism. Hot tempered, he had a volatile relationship with his subordinate commanders and believed, correctly, that the socially much better connected Sir Douglas Haig, commander of I Corps, was after his job.

Sir John French

Prior to deploying to France, Sir John was sent for by Lord Kitchener. Although the British Warlord had very untypically given way to politicians and staff officers regarding the deployment of the BEF, Kitchener was still very uneasy about its disposition when it arrived in France. He was concerned enough to have a final word with Sir John French before he departed. It is very difficult to issue a list of do's and don't's to an army commander about to take a force into active service. By definition the commander needs to be free to make and change plans as the combat situation develops. Irrespective of that fact, Lord Kitchener had a damn good go at it. With Sir John French standing at attention in front of his desk, Kitchener left him in absolutely no doubt that he was to safeguard the BEF at all cost. He hammered home the point that that his command was completely independent and he was not under any circumstances to come under the orders of the allied commander, General Joffre. If asked to participate in any forward movements in which the BEF might be unduly attacked, he was to consult with the government beforehand. He was warned specifically about being drawn into a position in which the BEF could possibly be overwhelmed and should the need arise he must withdraw towards to the Channel. Under no circumstances was he to allow the BEF to be bottled up and surrounded as the French had been at Sedan. After wishing Sir John French good luck, Kitchener dismissed him with a final glare and immediately went back to his paperwork. Sir John saluted, completed a smart about-turn and marched out of the office completely and utterly bemused.

Published weekly, the first wartime edition of the Glasgow Catholic Observer hit the news-stands on 8 August. Not yet quite in tune with the magnitude of the event, the newspaper was fairly low key regarding the war. There were updates on Ulster, the UFV and the Home Rule Bill, the enactment of which was eagerly awaited. The shooting incident at Bachelor's Walk was being covered with the public enquiry being reported on word for word. There were the usual parish announcements and advertisements, including one for orange marmalade. *The Man in the Know* was looking forward to the start of the new football season and more immediately to the annual Celtic Sports Meeting, the first without cycling included in the programme. There was also an open letter, 'A Catholic View of the Situation and Prospect', in which the war, as a 'Just and Honourable conflict', was vindicated from the Roman Catholic point of view. From the very beginning of the conflict, leading Catholic churchmen both in Scotland and to a lesser extent Ireland published articles in the newspapers justifying the war and encouraging Roman

Catholic participation in the conflict. The Glasgow Catholic Observer and Glasgow Star would pledge their Glasgow Irish readers to national unity, self-sacrifice, heroism and chivalry:

> Now as at all times in the history of the country, Catholics will be foremost in true patriotism and loyal support of authority. Happily, the government has, with few exceptions, the whole nation at its back. If war must come we shall all suffer in various degrees and ways and while our prayer is continuously 'Da pacem, Domine, in diebus nostris' [Give peace our Lord in our time], our aim will be to face the dark hours without boasting and without cowardice.

After Kitchener made his appeal there was an immediate increase of men arriving at the Army Recruiting Offices. There they found the recruiting staff completely overwhelmed by the numbers of potential recruits waiting to enlist. The system simply was not up to the task and very many men, put off by the long queues, gave up and went home. The War Office quickly identified the problem and after consulting with local authorities throughout the country, additional facilities for recruiters were made available, and within days new recruiting offices based on the various political parties local offices and staffed by their volunteer party workers were opened up in all the major British cities. In Glasgow the new *political* recruiting offices were opened on West Street, Bridgeton, David Street, off the Gallowgate, Monkland Street in Townhead, New City Road, Cumberland Street and Adelphi Street in the South Side, Dumbarton Road, Whiteinch, in the Gladstone Institute in Govan, Cathcart Road, Govanhill and at Pollok Street in Pollokshaws. The new offices were specifically for recruits aged nineteen to thirty wishing to enlist for general service under the New Army's terms and conditions. Recruits wishing to join the regular army under normal terms and conditions continued to do so at the main recruiting office in the Gallowgate or at West Nile Street in the city centre.

As the war entered its second week, the situation at the recruiting offices was improving with a significant rise in the numbers of recruits processed through the enlistment process. Between 9 and 15 August, nationwide over 43,000 men enlisted with the highest single day's figures being just over 8000 on 13 August. With the bottleneck at the recruiting offices apparently freed, the figures continued to show dramatic improvements and by 20 August Glasgow was producing between 200 and 300 recruits daily. Such was the improvement in the recruiting process that the next link in the recruiting process, the military depots, could not cope with the numbers of men arriving at their gates. This forced the political recruiting offices in Glasgow to be closed for a few days while the depots drew breath. By 25 August the Glasgow Herald was reporting that no fewer than 4000 men had been recruited through the political recruiting offices in the city and that the recruiting offices had now reopened.

Not everyone in the crowds milling around outside the recruiting offices were there to enlist. On 22 August, three men were caught pickpocketing in the crowd outside the army recruiting office in the Gallowgate. The following week they were sentenced to sixty days' imprisonment at Glasgow Central Police Court. It was also reported that the Territorial Force Associations, charged with administering the TF soldiers' separation allowance payments to the dependants of married men, were finally getting to grips with the backlog of late payments. In addition to the military allowances, supplementary assistance (relief) for families in need was available for a soldier's dependants from the Soldiers and Sailors Families Association. The Glasgow Herald itself had opened a 'Relief Fund', requesting silver coin donations, the smallest denomination of which was six pence. On 26 August, the newspaper announced that it had received a donation of 160 shillings (£8) from the St Andrew's RC Cathedral, which had been collected at evening service the previous Sunday. The fund on the date stood at 11,170 shillings (£558).

Shortly after Kitchener's demand for five hundred thousand men was granted, the Army Council agreed on the details of his proposed New Army, the outlines of which were announced to the national press. Six new infantry divisions with supporting troops would be added to the order of battle. These new divisions would form the First New Army and would soon be referred to as Kitchener's Army or K1. The new divisions would be numbered from the 9th to the 14th and each, except for the 14th, which would be a light division, would also carry a title showing its main area of recruitment. Two Celtic divisions were part of the K1 army and were titled the 9th (Scottish) and 10th (Irish). The titles given to the new divisions were not nationalistic; they were simply the military command areas from which most recruits were expected to be drawn and already recruits were being directed towards their new battalions and divisions. All the new divisions would quickly recruit well up to strength except the 12th (Eastern) Division, recruiting in the agricultural east of England then busy with the harvest, and the 10th (Irish) Division based at the Curragh.

In Ireland, the immediate effect of John Redmond's speech of support for the British war effort and his offer to guard the shores of Ireland against invasion with the Irish Volunteers, had been that even more Irishmen, both Protestant and Catholic, joined the Volunteers as opposed to the British Army. With the Irish harvest, a large proportion of the available Irish manpower already serving in the army or having reported to their units on mobilisation, thousands working away from home in England and Scotland, and many potential recruits already under orders with the Irish Volunteers, enlistment for the 10th (Irish) Division was always going to be slow. In Ulster, recruitment initially went well and in a cynical political move, many Unionists both in Ireland and in England compared the Ulster figures with those of the south, highlighting the poor recruitment figures of the 10th (Irish) Division and loudly suggesting that the Catholic Nationalist Irish were showing a distinct reticence to enlist. *The Nationalist Irish were not doing their bit, compared to the loyal Ulstermen. Was this the Nationalist Irish taking advantage of England's difficulty?* It was massively unfair, but as political point scoring it was very successful and it was a slur the Irish Nationalists would never entirely be able to shake off. In addition to their obvious commitment to Britain or Ulster, the enlistment of Protestant Ulstermen over the first four to six weeks of the war would have been heavily influenced by the numbers of lay-offs from factories and linen mills as they closed or went onto short time working due to the war. In Belfast, in particular, the industrial poor included Protestants and Catholics and both lived perilously close to the breadline.

Throughout the country, a significant proportion of the first hundred thousand were men who had lost their jobs due to the downturn in trade with Europe because of the war. The giant Singer factory in Clydebank, which employed over 16,000 workers, went onto short-time working, first two days then to just one day, and so many Celtic supporters worked at the factory that the development was noted with great concern at Celtic Park.

Over the first week or so of the war, life for most Glaswegians pretty much went on as usual. Unless that is you had a relative or friend who was a reservist or a member of the TF who had reported for duty. Or you were one of the people who were affected by the trade disruption that would see thousands of men laid off work. The Glasgow dockers, men and women at the numerous textile factories in Paisley, coal miners throughout central Scotland, all workforces that included very many Glasgow Irish, lost their jobs or went onto short-time work. The price of most commodities like food went up in a spate of panic buying, then fell back again over the course of the next fortnight. However, things were happening behind the scenes, the effects of which would soon be felt. The People's Palace on Glasgow Green and a number of church and school halls had been commandeered to accommodate the TF, and the military began to requisition horses straight off the streets and farms. The railways were brought under government control and travel overnight became more difficult.

CELTIC FC

By the end of the first week of August, the Celtic stadium at Parkhead was prepared for the annual Celtic Sports Meeting. The yearly event organised by Willie Maley was recognised as one of the best sports meetings in Britain, attracting the very best athletes from all over Europe. There were initially some concerns that the war might interfere with the meeting, but they were quickly dismissed by Maley, who insisted the event would carry on as normal. The two days of sports (Saturday 8th and Tuesday 11th) would feature a full range of track and field events, a five-a-side football competition in which eight of the senior Scottish

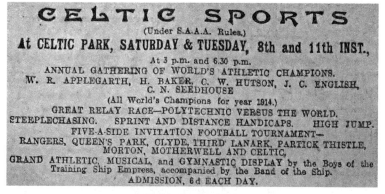

Celtic Sports 1914

clubs including Celtic and Rangers fielded sides, an eight-lap steeplechase and, as a novelty, the boys from the CTS *Empress*, a corrective training ship, would put on musical Indian club swinging and vaulting horse displays. Under the current circumstances, they would add a patriotic flavour to their performance. The Glasgow delinquents of the time were sentenced to the old *Empress* sailing ship moored in the Clyde for training under naval discipline and many of the boys took to the life and went on to join the Royal Navy. With the old cement cycling track gone, for the first time in many years cycling would not feature on the programme. The Celtic Sports Meeting was one of the most eagerly awaited athletics events of the year and as the Glasgow Evening Times put it, 'Three full hours of entertainment for a humble six pence'. Willie Maley arranged for all the war news arriving during the afternoon to be communicated to the crowd by megaphone or by board carried around the stadium. The Celtic would also unfurl their new League championship flag before the start of the sports. As it transpired, the event was one of the poorest anyone could remember. After weeks of blazing sunshine, it was completely spoiled by very heavy, continuous rain. The bad weather resulted in a very poor attendance of just 2000, massively down on previous years. The disastrous attendance was not helped by the thousands of Celtic supporters reporting for duty to their various military units. Even the five-a-side competition was a disaster, with both Celtic and Rangers being beaten in the semi-final by Queen's Park and Clyde respectively. Despite the disappointing drop in gate money, Celtic FC still donated the sizeable sum of one hundred guineas (£110) to the newly opened Glasgow Lord Provost's War Fund.

Saturday 15 August saw the opening game of the new season with the Scottish champions travelling through to Edinburgh. The Celtic would face a young and confident Heart of Midlothian team at Tynecastle. Hearts' manager, John McCartney, had been the manager/secretary for five years. When he arrived in the capital, an ageing Hearts team was languishing towards the lower half of the League table, having finished in eleventh position the two previous seasons. In his youth, Ayrshireman McCartney was a footballer of some repute and a junior football correspondent with some very definite views on how the game should be played. He played for and captained Rangers before moving to Springburn's Cowlairs in 1888. In September that year, he captained the Cowlairs team that was beaten 8–0 by Celtic in the second round of the Scottish Cup. John McCartney was a 'football' man to the bone. He was hugely complimentary towards Celtic's part in creating the Scottish League and launching professionalism – pointing out that the League saved the game north of the border. Without it, he wrote, football would have degenerated to something approaching the junior level. He was a great admirer of Celtic's first chairman John H. McLaughlin, whom he called 'The Parkhead Napoleon'. McLaughlin he thought was '*the most powerful, progressive and eloquent legislator Scotland has ever possessed',* and was way ahead of his time. John McCartney, Mick Dunbar and Willie Maley became firm lifelong friends.

McCartney had spent his first years at Tynecastle rebuilding the team in partnership with Elias Furst, Hearts' chairman. At the time, the ambitious Furst was also busy rebuilding the club's finances. After a couple of bad seasons during which Hearts, still containing much of the old team, continued to slide down the league, McCartney's new team started to take shape. Hearts finished fourth in season 1911/12, third in 1912/13 and third again in 1913/14. The League champions of 1913/14, Celtic, paid them the compliment of naming Hearts as the only team to beat them on merit that season. McCartney had managed to rebuild the team at a time when Hearts' chairman was also rebuilding much of Tynecastle Park, including a new £8000 stand capable of seating 4000 spectators. Money was therefore in short supply and to help pay for the new stand, McCartney was forced to sell his star striker. In February 1914, Percy Dawson went to Blackburn Rovers for a world-record fee of £2500. However, the astute John McCartney managed to screw £400 back to buy Liverpool centre forward Tom Gracie.

As it turned out Glaswegian, Gracie, was the final piece in the Hearts jigsaw, which included some outstanding talents, in particular, team captain, Bob Mercer, who was described at the time as the finest young defender in Scotland. He was skilful and intelligent and like Peter

Johnstone at Celtic, he preferred to play the ball out of defence rather than lumping it up the park. Brought into the side in 1909, Bob Mercer was the rock on which John McCartney would build his young side. He was twice capped for Scotland. At halfback, Peter Nellies was a miner to trade and a lifelong Hearts supporter. A junior and full Scotland internationalist, John McCartney stole him from under the nose of Rangers.

Bob Mercer Cigarette Card

At right back, Pat Crossan was the son of Irish Catholic parents. Born in the Midlothian shale-mining village of Addiewell, his parents had moved from Johnstone, Renfrewshire, just a few months before his birth. Pat was reputedly the fastest man in Scotland over 100 yards. Winger, Jimmy Speedie, was a principled young man, educated to higher grade at Boroughmuir School. He disliked the idea of being paid to play sport, so he signed on with Hearts as an amateur.

As McCartney watched his young side play during their close season tour of Denmark, he was confident they would mount a serious challenge over the coming season. He thought they might even win the League. The outbreak of the war saw two Hearts players with military commitments report for duty. Scottish internationalist George Sinclair was a reservist with the Royal Field Artillery and was a particular loss to the team. Neil Moreland was embodied with his TF battalion. Despite the loss of personnel, the Edinburgh side with one of the largest player pools in the Scottish league, remained upbeat as it welcomed the Scottish champions. The Heart of Midlothian would prove to be the Celtic's main challengers for the 1914/15 League flag.

The Bhoys had found it tough at Tynecastle over the previous few seasons, where they were guaranteed a particularly hostile reception from the Hearts supporters. The hostility came from the very obvious common heritage between Celtic and Hibernian, the latter being the Hearts' great Edinburgh rivals. Celtic had failed to score in the previous four meetings between the clubs and had failed to take full points at Tynecastle since the early part of season 1909/10. Celtic fielded a full-strength team, determined to get the season off to a good start and not repeat the mistakes of the previous season when they dropped five points out of the first twelve available.

The game turned into something of a cup tie, with every ball fought hard for. Hearts had the wind the first half, but Celtic were the better side and did everything right apart from creating scoring opportunities. Only Andy McAtee managed a worthwhile shot on the Hearts goal, but goalkeeper Boyd easily stopped it. Then against the run of play Hearts broke out and in what proved to be their only scoring opportunity in the first half, Wattie went through the Celtic defence to slip the ball past a helpless Charlie Shaw. The second half followed the same pattern with Celtic even more dominant, Hearts having two men playing on through injuries. Celtic failed to capitalise on scoring chances and must have guessed it was not going to be their day when McColl missed a penalty. It was his first penalty miss in five attempts. In a carbon copy of the events leading to their first goal, Hearts again broke away with only a few moments to go and scored their second goal through Tom Gracie. It was the first time in the game that the new Hearts centre managed to slip Peter Johnstone's iron grip. Hearts had but two clear chances throughout the match and took them both. It was the old tale of one team failing to create or squandering opportunities and the other taking them. Hearts goalie, Boyd, the fullbacks and Frew were stalwarts for the home team defence, while the Hearts performance was described as 'plucky, determined and full of grit'. Hearts captain, Bob Mercer, picked up a bad knee injury that would keep him out of the side for most of the season. The Edinburgh newspapers saw the game slightly differently from their sister rags based in Glasgow. They gave Hearts Harry Wattie the man of the match, describing his performance as 'outstanding'. For the Celts, Peter Johnstone played well, keeping Tom Gracie in his pocket for most of the game. It was a bitter defeat for Celtic made worse by the knowledge that it should never have happened. A crowd of 20,000 watched the game and everyone was duly impressed with the new stand, which unfortunately was not quite completed in time for the game.

The Bhoys should have known Saturday was going to be a bad day. Prior to travelling through to Edinburgh, Willie Maley met with representatives of Burnley to organise the replay for the drawn cup game in Budapest. He lost the toss of the coin for venue, and Celtic was required to travel south for the game, which was to be played on 1 September at Turf Moor. The trophy put up by a local newspaper proprietor was still in Hungary and most people thought it would not be seen until after the war, if ever. According to *the Man in the Know*, the illusive trophy was apparently a peculiar looking item, two-foot tall, slender, ungilded but encrusted all over in gems of dubious value and looking like a miner's safety lamp. As it transpired, both opinions were proved correct: the original was never seen (apparently it was the prize in a charity wrestling match) and it was very, very much later (May 1988) before a replacement vase was eventually seen at Parkhead. Under normal circumstances, Celtic would have expected to take a travelling support of some two or three hundred south for such a game. Now much fewer if any at all would be able to make the journey with the railways now under government control and the trains requisitioned for the war effort.

On Monday morning, the players reported to Parkhead smarting from the disappointing defeat at Tynecastle. To add to the gloom there had already been some suggestions in the press about how professional football and its players could contribute to the war effort. In response to the public mood of everyone doing their bit, Willie Maley informed the players that the directors would require them to learn how to drill and to shoot and that they were trying to tie up with other Glasgow clubs who were thinking along the same lines. The nearest shooting range was in the giant Beardmore Forge at Parkhead where the Glasgow battalions of the Irish Volunteers were regularly using the facility. The miniature rifle range was situated at the corner of Old Edinburgh Road and Duke Street and was one of the largest and best equipped in the country, having thirty target lanes and recreation and magazine rooms. In Edinburgh, Hearts and Hibernian were already taking part in military training together. Willie Maley's older brother, Tom Maley, was the manager at Bradford Park Avenue FC. In his youth, Tom was a non-commissioned officer with the old Rifle Volunteers and was now utilising his military experience to train the club's footballers to shoot. On Tuesday (18 August), Willie Maley's statement that the Celtic were considering having their players learn to drill and shoot was reported in the Scottish newspapers. That night the Bhoys crossed to the south side of the city to Ibrox Park for a benefit match in support of the Rangers goalkeeper Herbert Lock.

Englishman Lock was the Rangers' first choice goalie until he sustained a serious injury in a Glasgow Cup match against Partick Thistle in October 1912. The injury was serious enough that it put him out for the remainder of the season. He was replaced by John Hempsey and was unable to reclaim his No 1 jersey at Ibrox until January 1914. In the Celtic team, Crone replaced Gallacher, and a replacement came in for Browning, which were the only changes to the team that lost to Hearts. Rangers were missing four of their regulars. After only ten minutes play, Rangers defender Purcell came off worse after a collision with Crone. Having severely injured his ankle, he was unable to continue and forced to go off. In the days before substitutes, the Celtic directors sportingly agreed to him being replaced and Kelso came on in his place. In an open free-flowing and free-scoring game, McColl got three goals, while Crone, McMenemy and Peter Johnstone got one each. Rangers were allowed to run in their fourth goal on the final whistle to make the result look a bit closer than it actually was. Scorers for the Rangers were Cairns with two, and Gilchrist and Bowie with one each. A Clydebank Harrier made an attempt at the one-mile walking record at the half-time interval, but he failed. A crowd of 3000 turned out for the Rangers goalie and over £110 was taken at the gate.

SCOTTISH FOOTBALL

On Tuesday 11 August, the committee members of the SFA, including Celtic's new chairman, Thomas White, who was also the SFA vice-chairman, convened in Glasgow to make the draw for the first rounds of the Scottish Qualifying Cup. At the start of the meeting a number of letters were read out suggesting that the new football season, due to start in less than a week, be postponed until the end of hostilities. Only the member from Inverness agreed, stating that he thought it sacrilege to play football while solders might be dying. There was little support for his position so it was decided that the season would begin as planned but the issue could be reviewed again at the next meeting. A motion to call a special meeting to discuss the matter in more depth was also rejected. Within a few days of the outbreak of war, letters had begun to appear in the national press expressing disgust that fit men should be playing football while the country was at war. Pressure began to mount as some influential figures within the game took the same view. Thomas Forsyth, a solicitor, kirk elder and chairman of Airdrie FC, expressed his disgust at the stance taken by the SFA and threatened to resign. He later did so, but was initially persuaded to withdraw his resignation to fight the cause from within.

The Celtic board had already given some careful consideration to the matter and had decided that football should continue. In addition to the fact that they considered football to be a business enterprise in which they had invested a large amount of money and time, their attitude was that the ordinary working man would need something to take his mind off the horrors of war, including perhaps the sting of occasional military defeat. They further justified their decision with the fear that if football were stopped, the supporters would spend the now free Saturday afternoons in less salubrious pastimes. The board were also fearful that revenue streams, the money taken at the turnstiles in particular, could drop dramatically. Three thousand Glasgow dockers, almost 50 per cent of whom were Glasgow Irish, had already been laid off, as had thousands of Lanarkshire miners. A number of mills and factories including the giant Singer complex at Clydebank and the Paisley thread mills were on short-time working. There were suggestions that entry prices into grounds may have to be dropped. With thousands of spectators who were army reservists now recalled to the colours, many football clubs could soon be in financial difficulty.

The English football season was not due to begin until September; so the hierarchy of the game in England would address the matter of football and the war a week or so after the Scots. As in most things, where England went, the Scots tended to follow, but meanwhile in Scotland the season would continue as planned.

On 20 August the three ruling bodies of English football, the English Football Association (FA), the English Football League and the Southern League, met to discuss 'the national crisis'. Much to the relief of their Scottish counterparts they also agreed that football should continue. In line with the general opinion that the war would not last long, the FA felt there was a very important 'morale' factor that should be considered and thought 'a good game of football was just the thing to take one's mind off the war'. The English clubs agreed to show their commitment to the cause by supporting the various local and national war funds already springing up and to collect and donate footballs to the various military units in training. Had the English voted to cancel the football season, the Scots would have been compelled to follow suit. However, if the FA and SFA hierarchies thought that was the end of the matter, they would be sadly mistaken.

Willie Maley's comment to the newspapers about Celtic having their players learn to drill and shoot brought an indignant response from Disgusted, whose letter to the editor of the Daily Record was published on 21 August:

> Sir – Mr W. Maley's complacency raised my gorge. The emergency is here and now. Lord Kitchener says, 'Your country needs you.' What will our Colonial cousins think after travelling thousands of miles to uphold the flag when they behold crowds of our lusty sons chasing a bit of leather instead of pursuing Germans? It is incumbent on every man who is capable to learn to shoot straight and qualify for a place of honour in the fighting line to offer his services. This applies no less to spectators than the players. Must we have universal conscription before the gravity of the crisis is realised? If that comes all the gladiators of the football pitch will be commandeered.

The day after Disgusted's letter, the following from the Critic was published in the Glasgow Catholic Observer:

> Football! Stop! The critic says it;
> Football meantime I abhor;
> He's a coward knave who plays it;
> while his country is at war.

The Observer's staff poet, John Conway penned a reply:

> Why don't you go out to battle?
> Do you ever stop to think?
> It's nobler 'midst the cannons' rattle,
> Than fighting here with pen and ink.

Forgive me if for once I taunt you
(Loud in the army's praise you've sung),
Go and fight, if you want to,
Either that or 'haud yer tongue.

A cartoon appeared in the Evening Times on 22 August suggesting how professional football and its players could contribute to the National Relief Fund. The player's pretty sisters could sell kisses to the spectators, while the players themselves could go through the crowd before the game collecting donations.

Pretty Sisters Sell Kisses.
(Glasgow Evening Times)

They had chosen a bad time for collections at Parkhead: just the day before the entire Roman Catholic world was plunged into mourning on the death of Pope Pius X.

Other sports also came under the moral spotlight. The influential upper-class-controlled Jockey Club took the view that with so many people's jobs dependant on the sport, it would be a mistake to cancel the horse-racing season immediately.

THE HILLEY BHOYS

When war broke out in August 1914, the Hilley family were living at 174 Millburn Street, just off Garngad Hill. The Hilleys were a typical Glasgow Irish, Roman Catholic, Irish Nationalist, lower working class. The family were desperately poor and lodged firmly on the bottom rung of the social ladder. Edward and Susan with their young family in tow had arrived in Glasgow in 1891 from the Donegal village of Pettigo. On their arrival, they moved straight into the Glasgow

Irish enclave of the Garngad. The Garngad was a fairly small district, sandwiched between the Monkland Canal and a number of colossal chemical and steel complexes. It comprised only a dozen or so streets mostly running off the Garngad Hill and the Garngad road. Nicknamed the 'Good and the Bad', the Garngad was a Glasgow slum of the worst kind that lay just a mile to the north of the city, a part of the heavily industrialised St Rollox Parish. The Garngad was also known as Little Ireland, but that was simply because the Irish were the largest and the most vocal tribe among several others. Irish and Scottish Protestants, Highlanders, Jews, Italians and even some people from the Balkans, all equally poor, were crowded cheek by jowl into the dilapidated slum tenements.

By 1901 Edward and Susan's family comprised nine children: Margaret aged fifteen working in a nearby mill as a thread spinner, Patrick aged thirteen, William James aged twelve, John aged ten, Rose Ann aged eight, Thomas aged seven, Edward aged five, Bridget aged three and Hugh aged two. The Hilley family were next-door neighbours and great friends of the McGrory family, who also hailed from Donegal. In 1904, Edward and Susan were godparents to one of their children, a certain James (Jimmy) Edward McGrory. Jimmy's mother Catherine died when he was just twelve, and Jimmy, whose siblings were mostly girls, became lifelong friends with the Hilley boys. Jimmy McGrory was destined to become one of the all-time greats of Celtic FC and a living legend in the Garngad and beyond. Over the next ten years, the Hilley family remained on the 'Hill' at Millburn Street where the family grew with the addition of three more children, Charles, Cornelius and Susannah. The older Hilley children grew into young men and women, leaving school and taking up employment. For the most part they remained within their own ethnic and religious social circle and with their friends attended the local cinemas or dances and fetes organised by the Roman Catholic Church or Irish organisations, like the League of the Cross, the Catholic Young Men's Society and the Ancient Order of Hibernians. In time, the children began to leave the nest, Margaret first and then in 1908 the Hilley's eldest son Patrick married a local girl, Mary Josephine Reeves, from the Garngad Road. The young couple married in St Roch's Church then moved out of the district to their own tenement flat in the Gorbals. Ironically, in 1914 the family were as affluent as they were ever likely to be, with everyone in the household capable of work in full-time employment and contributing to the household coffers. At the time, Edward Hilley senior was working as a labourer in a local steelworks beside his twenty-five-year-old son, William James. Like most females of the period, Susan Hilley did not work, other than the eighteen hours a day of hard physical graft she put in looking after her large family.

Within a few days of war being declared, Garngad, like the rest of the country, was already being transformed. Scores of young local men were members of the Territorial Force and reported in to their drill halls, while others with army reserve commitments reported back to their regimental depots. Scores more of the Garngad's sons were already serving with the regular army and about to be deployed to France. Suddenly mothers were wearing worried expressions. Although everyone said it would be a short war, some were not so sure.

Over the next three months, three of the Hilley brothers would join the army. Each brother would feel compelled to enlist, responding to a different phase in the developing military situation. The first of the Hilley boys to respond to the emergency was Edward James Hilley, then aged nineteen, who after settling his affairs, answered Kitchener's first call in mid-August. Edward joined the regular army under normal terms of engagement and asked to serve with the Royal Artillery. He was posted to No 6 Royal Artillery Depot based at Maryhill in Glasgow where he was assigned to the Royal Field Artillery (RFA) and posted, after his six weeks basic training, as No 283 Gunner Edward Hilley to 50th Brigade (RFA). The brigade was attached to the newly formed Ninth (Scottish) Division, part of Kitchener's New Army (K1) then training in the south of England.

THE WAR FRONT

In France, General Sir John French issued orders in compliance with French operational plans instructing the BEF to move north towards the River Meuse where they would join up with their allies, by marching onto the French Fifth Army's left (western) flank. Once in position, the plan was for the joint force to advance north together, defeat the Germans and sweep them from Belgium. The French commanders expected to meet only light opposition. The Allies were in fact facing over 700,000 men in three huge German armies. The British were unaware that the French First and Second Armies on the extreme right (eastern) flank had been defeated over 14–20 August and the following day the French Third and Fourth Armies in the centre were also forced into retreat. As a result of these reverses, the commander of the Fifth Army, General Lanrezac, began to have doubts about the wisdom of the move and on 21 August halted his advance. Unfortunately, he forgot to tell the BEF, which continued its march north towards Mons. Tactically, matters deteriorated over the course of the day and General Lanrezac decided that the new situation was forcing him to retreat to save his army from defeat or capture. On 22 August, the French Fifth and Fourth armies on the BEF's right began to retreat south under constant pressure from the Germans. Meanwhile, the BEF had reached Mons, now nine miles ahead of the French Fifth Army and with a gap on their right of ten miles between them. The BEF was composed of a cavalry division of five brigades and I and II Corps, each of two infantry divisions. Each division consisted of three brigades each of four battalions of infantry with supporting units.

Over the course of 21 and 22 August, the infantry battalions trudged into positions in and around the town. It had been a long hot sore march and many of the reservists, having rejoined their battalions after several years in civilian life were suffering; their feet had grown soft and they were still breaking in stiff leather army boots. The men were exhausted and footsore; many were very badly blistered from marching on the French pave (cobbles) in their new boots. On arrival around Mons the BEF was deployed with I Corps, commanded by Scotsman General Sir Douglas Haig on the right, holding a salient to the east of the town with the troops deployed facing eastwards. On the left, General Smith-Dorian's II Corps (36,000 men) was holding a twenty-one-mile line along the Mons-Conde Canal's southern bank. To their left rear, the cavalry division was in contact with a French territorial division. The poorly trained French part-timers held the extreme left of the allied line.

The British and German forces first exchanged shots at around 0700 hrs on 22 August when Corporal Drummer Edward Thomas from Tipperary and his patrol from C Squadron 4th Royal

Irish Dragoon Guards encountered an enemy cavalry patrol north of Mons near the chateau of Ghislain. Corporal Thomas spotted a German cavalryman, mounted and about 400 yards away. Thomas took careful aim, fired off his shot and watched the man tumble from his horse; it was probably the first British shot of the war.

Over the course of the day, the British General Headquarters (GHQ), based a few miles to the rear at Le Cateau, began receiving reports from the Royal Flying Corps (RFC) of huge columns of enemy troops to the north. Sir John French, like most senior officers, particularly cavalry officers, was not greatly impressed with the new-fangled flying contraptions. That afternoon, he was even less convinced by the report of a huge column of enemy troops heading straight for them. This time the report was delivered to him personally by a slightly ridiculous looking, out of breath young flying corps pilot. The boy was standing before him, face covered in black oil except for the large two white circles around his eyes, which had been covered by his goggles. The general, while too courteous to tell the young pilot he thought him mistaken, politely dismissed the report as a very understandable exaggeration. Many years after the war, the pilot recounted his interview with Sir John. The general with his arm around the young pilot's shoulder proceeded to humour him, asking him all kinds of questions about his aeroplane: 'Was it very cold? What do you do if the engine stops? Wasn't it very dangerous?' As he spoke, General French led him out of the operations room and off for a cup of tea in the officers' mess. Unknown to Sir John, even more disturbing news was on its way to his headquarters, as its desperate messenger Lieutenant Spiers was being held up by thousands of Belgian refugees choking the roads leading southward. That same day the 2nd Bn Argylls was ordered up to the front from Boulogne and arrived by train at Valenciennes the following morning. On their arrival, they were informed that an additional infantry formation, the 19th Brigade, was to be formed from four battalions that had been on defence duties on the line of communications. The independent brigade included the 2nd Bn Royal Welsh Fusiliers, 1st Bn Cameronians (Scottish Rifles), 1st Bn Middlesex Regiment and the 2nd Bn Argylls. As part of the new brigade, the 2nd Argylls marched two hours to Onnaing from where they could hear the sound of the artillery guns.

On the outbreak of war, the Royal Navy, traditionally the mainstay of British Imperial power was forced to confront a changing strategic and tactical situation. With the largest and most powerful surface fleet in the world, British naval tactics typically involved a close blockade of enemy ports, taking the fight to the enemy. However, the Admiralty realised that the development of the submarine armed with torpedoes, and sea mines lain in likely approach and patrol routes meant the close blockade of enemy ports was fraught with risk. The British appreciating the change of circumstances adopted a strategy of blockading the North Sea, with in the north, the battleships of the British Home Fleet strung across the 200-mile wide channel between Norway and the Orkneys. To the south, the English Channel with sealed off by sea mines, the Dover patrol and British submarines. The strategy effectively turned the North Sea into a no man's land. The German fleet was unwilling to take on the British Grand Fleet in a head-to-head sea battle, and with the odd exception remained in home waters. T encourage the Germans to remain in port, on 28 August a British naval force ambushed a German naval patrol at Heligoland Bight. The Royal Navy sunk four German ships and severely damaged several others. The Germans lost over 1200 sailors, while the British lost no ships though thirty-five men were killed. It was a very minor engagement, but one that had a profound effect on the Kaiser. After the engagement he ordered that no further engagement that could result in the loss of capital ships should be undertaken without his express approval.

The German surface fleet was now effectively bottled up in port or confined to the North Sea. The German Navy did mount regular forays into the North Sea including shelling English coastal towns and sinking significant numbers of fishing trawlers, but they could not attack the British merchant fleet delivering vital food and raw materials from across the Atlantic to British west coast ports. As a result the German Navy was forced to expand and develop submarine warfare as the only way it could effectively contribute to the German war effort.

CELTIC FC

Dodds and McMenemy attack the Motherwell goal

Just as Sir John French was leading the young RFC pilot off for a cup of tea, Parkhead was filling up with around 17,000 of the Celtic faithful. On 22 August, Celtic were at home for the second league game of the season and were determined to make up for their surprise defeat at Tynecastle. Their opponents were an under strength Motherwell team, nicknamed the 'Steelmen' (from the major industry in the town), who arrived in Glasgow's east end missing four of their stalwarts. Despite the fact, Motherwell, as one of the few teams undefeated by Celtic the previous season, was expected to put up a decent show. Just like at Tynecastle the week previous, Celtic dominated right from the kick-off, with Peter Johnstone and McMenemy controlling the midfield for the home team. The Celtic attack, despite their midfield dominance, was subdued with Patsy Gallacher and McAtee putting in quiet, ineffectual performances. Strangely, the finest right wing in Scotland was up against a Motherwell left defence, which contained a very inexperienced, left back in the boy McGlade. The Motherwell forwards seldom troubled the Celtic's back line while at the other end a number of first half goals might have been scored were it not for a mix of bad luck and the skill of Motherwell keeper, Tom Allan, formerly of Hearts, who saved the visitors on a number of occasions. He was finally beaten by McColl who latched onto a through pass from McMenemy to score just before half-time. The second half followed the pattern of the first; Celtic had all the ball, but failed to make the most of it. Keeper Allan continued to excel but the Celtic forwards spurned a number of good scoring opportunities that on another day would have been taken. McColl's first half strike proved to be the only goal of the game, thereby securing the Bhoys their first points of the season. However, it could easily have been very different. Former Celt George 'Dod' Whitehead missed an absolute sitter late on. With only minutes to the final whistle, Motherwell launched a rare foray into the Celtic half. Charlie Shaw could only palm away a powerful shot from Hillhouse, which landed at the feet of Whitehead. It would have been easier for Dod to score but he somehow managed to slice his tap-in past the post, much to the relief of both Charlie Shaw and the Parkhead faithful. Had he scored it would have given the Steelmen an undeserved share of the points. Dod Whitehead would have better luck during the Great War when he was serving with the Royal Naval Division. His ship was torpedoed twice but he survived each time and played football again after the war. After just two games played, Celtic were in tenth position while their closest neighbours Clyde FC sat proudly on top of the league.

On 24 August, Celtic took a strong team to Maryhill in the north of the city for a charity game against Partick Thistle. The cause was one very close to the Celtic's heart, Roman Catholic schools. A crowd of 2500 turned up at Firhill to watch the game, which ended in a 2–2 draw. Celtic often used these types of game to try out new talent and on this occasion local boy Joe O'Kane pulled on the green and white hoops in his first senior team game for the Bhoys. Joe was a well-built local lad who prior to signing for Celtic was employed in the Maryhill gasworks. He was brought onto the Parkhead books the previous year from Maryhill Juniors aged just seventeen. The big centre forward had a very good game and scored on his debut after having already hit the post. Overall, O'Kane impressed and Willie Maley had high hopes for the lad. Despite impressing the manager, Joe would have to wait a while yet for his first competitive game for the Celtic. Johnny 'Smiler' Browning, Celtic's quietly effective left-winger, got the other goal. The Celtic team was; Shaw; McGregor and Dodds; Young, Johnstone and Jarvis; McAtee and Crone; O'Kane, Browning and Gray.

Amazingly, the following night Celtic was in action again. This time the evening kick-off saw the Bhoys over the river at Shawfield playing in a benefit match for Clyde's John Gilligan. In a period when a footballer's career was short and often cut much shorter by a game that was much more physical than the modern game, benefit or testimonial games were very important to the professional player. A footballer would usually be awarded a benefit game in recognition of good service to the club at the end of a long career or very often for a career brought to a sudden end by a bad injury. The takings at the gate would form the bulk of his severance pay and was a cash bonus before the player rejoined the normal man in the street, usually back working in the job he had done before he made it as a professional footballer. The more attractive the benefit game, the more spectators would come to watch and the larger the payout for the retiring player. Most of the big name players were happy enough to turn out on these occasions, as it was often a case of *there but for the grace of God*. The management of all the major clubs gave tacit support to the practice, but a balance had to be struck between the chance of a key player picking up an injury or a strain and attracting spectators who would pay to see the game.

Over 2000 spectators watched the game at Clyde, which ended in another draw, this time 1–1. The Londoner, Ebenezer Owers, only recently sent packing from Parkhead, came back to haunt Celtic by scoring for the home team. A punchy centre forward, at 5ft 10in tall and weighing eleven and a half stone, 'Ginger' Owers had come to Celtic from Clyde on loan at the beginning of December 1913. He was seen as a possible replacement for Jimmy Quinn and Ginger was delighted at the opportunity to show what he could do. He made his debut in the hoops against Third Lanark on 6 December, scoring twice in the 3–0 victory. He made a very significant contribution to Celtic completing the double in 1913/14, by scoring nine goals in total, including four in the 6–0 League home win over Ayr in December 1913. He played sixteen times for Celtic scoring an impressive eleven goals. After having a disastrous game in the drawn 1914 Scottish Cup Final against Hibernian, for which Ginger rather unfairly took most of the blame, he was dropped for the replay. Perhaps prematurely, Ginger Owers was sent back to Clyde where, much to his credit, he regained some of his excellent form towards the end of the 1913/14 season.

Although many of the Celtic stars were on show, the benefit game was really only a kick-about and a run-out for some of the Celtic second string. Alex Gray, a fast skilful left-winger just back at Parkhead from a spell at Ayr United, got Celtic's goal just before half-time. Gray was a very talented footballer, who just could not quite break into the first team, mainly due to the ever-reliable Johnny Browning. Also getting a run-out for the hoops was Edinburgh-born Michael Gilhooly. Willie Maley had great hopes for the young starlet, but with a team of established stars, Michael was another exceptional talent who simply could not break into the first team. Of course, the inevitable happened on the night when Alec McNair, the cornerstone of the Celtic defence, picked up an injury that would keep him out of the next two league games. The Celtic team at Shawfield was Shaw, McNair, T McGregor, Jarvis, Gilhooly, McMaster, A McGregor, Gallacher, McColl, Crone and Gray. If Willie Maley had concerns about McNair, his troubles paled into insignificance compared to those of Sir John French and the BEF.

THE WAR FRONT

As the referee was blowing the whistle to end the first half of the Celtic versus Motherwell game at Parkhead, Lieutenant Spiers, the British liaison officer at General Lanrezac's headquarters, was en route to the BEF GHQ located at Le Cateau. He was in a desperate rush and was exasperated by the constant hold-ups and delays caused by the roads being jammed with thousands of fleeing refugees. He arrived at the BEF around 2000 hrs and found the headquarters staff planning for the advance the next day. Spiers brought the astounding news that the French Fifth Army was in full retreat and confirmed the young pilot's reports that a large enemy force was closing in on the BEF. Planning for the advance was abruptly halted and new orders issued to prepare for a defensive battle with the British very much out on a limb and very much on their own. The desperate dash to GHQ by Lieutenant Spiers most certainly saved the entire British force from complete destruction.

The BEF immediately set about digging in, using picks and shovels, many borrowed from the locals. Both corps commanders were concerned about their ability to defend their positions, which had been adopted with a view of continuing the advance. Smith-Dorian in particular had the almost impossible task of defending a twenty-one-mile line. The battalions were tactically redeployed to defend the bridges with outposts positioned on the northern side of the canal to cover the approaches. The men dug their shell scrapes and awaited the expected onslaught. Later that night Sir John French received an unbelievable request from General Lanrezac, asking the BEF to launch a counter-attack against what he believed to be the right flank of the German army advancing onto the Fifth Army's retreating rear. His belief was badly mistaken: the German First Army, 320,000 strong, under General Alexander von Kluck, was in fact heading straight for the BEF and there was no flank for the British to attack. Sir John French dismissed the curious request out of hand but rather strangely, considering his own perilous situation, agreed to hold his positions at Mons for twenty-four hours.

Unaware of the exact location or strength of the British force, the German High Command believed the majority of the BEF was probably still around Ostend and Dunkirk. In fact, the German commander von Kluck wanted to take his First Army straight to the Channel ports, where he would take on the BEF before it got a chance to join the French, but von Bulow, commander of the Second Army, overruled him. Bulow was his nominal commander in the field and he ordered von Kluck to bring his force closer to the Second Army to guard its flank. Von Kluck protested, but was overruled by Supreme Headquarters. The Germans were therefore very surprised indeed when they stumbled into the British at Mons. Despite their overwhelming numerical superiority, over the course of the morning the German High Command fed their troops into the developing battle piecemeal, allowing a series of small-scale actions to develop. Had they launched a coordinated and concentrated full-scale assault using the entire weight of the four corps that they had at their disposal, history would most certainly have been very different.

Shortly after 0900 hrs on 23 August, the German guns were in position north of the canal and opened fire on the BEF's positions east of Mons. This was followed by an eight-battalion assault by infantry from the IX Corps. Approaching the British lines at Obourg and Nimy, they attacked the salient and were met by heavy rifle fire from the British infantry. The rifle fire cut the advancing German infantry to pieces as they attacked in solid company-strength blocks (150 men). The 4th Bn Royal Fusiliers with the 4th Middlesex Regiment were fighting around Nimy, an old industrial suburb north of Mons beside the canal. The position formed a salient or bulge, which jutted out of the line and was open to attack from three sides.

Lt. Maurice Dease VC

The 4th Bn Royal Fusiliers' machine gun officer was a twenty-four-year-old Irishman Lieutenant Maurice James Dease, a member of an ancient family of Catholic gentry from Mullingar in Co Westmeath. At around 1300 hrs, the Germans managed to cross the canal to the east of Nimy and began working between the 4th Royal Fusiliers and the 4th Middlesex Regiment, whom they threatened to surround. The position in the salient had become untenable and at around 1400 hrs the Middlesex began to withdraw followed by the Royal Fusiliers. Maurice Dease and his two teams of machine gunners remained on the railway bridge at Nimy covering the withdrawal. Over the next few hours the bridge was attacked by two battalions of German infantry (2000 men), but Maurice Dease, although wounded several times, refused to leave his guns and his men until he was eventually killed. He was posthumously awarded the first Victoria Cross of the Great War. One of his soldiers, Private Sidney Godley, continued to man the machine gun on his own, holding the enemy off until the entire battalion got away. He then coolly dismantled the gun and threw it into the canal before making his own escape. He too was awarded a Victoria Cross. Forty years later Sidney Godley recounted the incident in great detail to the BBC.

Along the canal to the west of Mons, the battle took longer to develop, but by 1100 hrs the defending battalions were coming under attack. At Mariette, three miles west of Mons, the Germans took advantage of Belgian civilians to advance while the British held their fire to allow the refugees to pass. Further west at Jemappes, the 1st Bn Royal Scots Fusiliers (Thomas Maley's old regiment) were defending the area around the bridge. For the Scots Fusiliers, Sunday morning broke with mist and a drizzly rain, but it would quickly clear to a hot humid morning. The church bells were calling the faithful to Mass and the locals were scurrying past their positions dressed in their Sunday best; war seemed very far away. By 1030 hrs the battalion was fighting off numerous assaults on its position and taking a heavy toll on the attackers as the rapid rifle fire tore through the German ranks. The British infantry could not believe the way the German infantry advanced to contact and a sergeant later commented:

> They were in solid square blocks, standing out sharply against the skyline. You couldn't help hitting them. ... We lay in our trenches with not a sound or sign to tell them of what was before them. They came closer and closer, and then our officers gave the word. They seemed to stagger like a drunk man hit suddenly between the eyes, after which they made a run for us shouting some outlandish cry that we couldn't make out.

A Gordon Highlander also described his battalion's first encounter with the Germans at Mons:

> Poor devils of infantry! They advanced in companies of 150 men in files five deep and our rifles have a flat trajectory up to 600 yards. Guess the result! We could steady our rifles on the trench and take deliberate aim. The first company were simply blasted away to heaven by a volley at 700 yards and in their insane formation every bullet was bound to find two billets.

As the day wore on, it was inevitable that the Germans would get across the canal in sufficient numbers and threaten to roll up the British line. By late afternoon, therefore, British battalions were planning their fighting withdrawals. By dusk all the battalions that had held the line were moving south. The British were falling back, but it was an ordered withdrawal and was in response to the tactical situation forced upon them by the French retreat.

In fact, the BEF as a whole had not been under any great pressure that first day; I Corps had barely fired a shot and II Corps' two divisions had held off four German divisions until well into the afternoon. Indeed, only half of its battalions had actually been involved in the fight. Over the course of the day, nine British battalions had effectively held off the four German divisions. The British losses for the day were in the region of 1600 killed, wounded or missing. German figures will never be known for certain, but they were very severe; figures range from a low 6000 to as high as 10,000. German commanders on the ground were astounded and appalled by the British firepower.

Sir John French had every intention of resuming the fight on 24 August, having been convinced by Sir Henry Wilson (a Curragh conspirator) that the German forces opposing the BEF were not in unbeatable numbers. Wilson further persuaded him that they should attack the next day. The British general staff then spent hours preparing plans for an attack northwards on 24 August. Late on 23 August with the attack plans complete, a wire arrived at British GHQ from the Allied Commander-in-Chief, General Joffre. The wire warned that the BEF was facing overwhelming numbers and that the French Fifth Army, led by Lanrezac, was now a full day's march to their rear. Sir John French finally accepted the inescapable fact that if the BEF did not retreat, it would be exposed on both flanks, surrounded and destroyed. Had the wire from Joffre not arrived at GHQ and had they followed Henry Wilson's attack plan, the BEF would have advanced into hell and been totally annihilated.

As the French forces continued to retreat south, the British were forced to deal with the Germans in close pursuit. After a very sharp engagement at La Cateau, where the British II Corps was forced to fight a stopping battle to break free of the pursuing German forces, the British Army began its epic, tactical withdrawal, known to posterity as the Retreat from Mons. The long trek would take the British back almost to the gates of Paris before they could halt, reorganise and turn to face the oncoming Germans. The retreat would last thirteen days and covered almost 200 miles. Along the way, on numerous occasions the retreating battalions were forced to turn around and fight their tormenting pursuers.

On 27 August, retreating with I Corps was the 2nd Bn Royal Munster Fusiliers, part of the 1st Guards Brigade. The battalion had halted in the early hours of the morning at the village of Fesmy. At about 0900 hrs, and prior to continuing the retreat, the battalion was ordered to take over the role of brigade rearguard. A short time later, a German cavalry patrol appeared just outside Fesmy. The Germans fired a few shots into the village and when the Munsters returned fire, they dismounted, took cover and waited for reinforcements. New orders arrived for the Munsters from brigade headquarters: they were to hold onto their positions until ordered or forced to retreat.

At around 1230 hrs, an order to retire immediately was sent to all the battalions of the 1st Brigade, but despite sending three dispatch riders, the Munsters did not receive the message until it was too late. The battalion was heavily attacked and after fierce fighting at Fesmy fell back, still fighting, to the area around Oisy, arriving there about 1730 hrs. It was then discovered that B Company was missing and the withdrawal was delayed for an hour until the company fought its way back to rejoin the battalion. The delay proved disastrous. The Germans managed to get ahead of the Munsters and cut them off as they fought their way back towards the village of Étreux. The Munsters attempted to break through, but despite several attacks, during which the commanding officer was killed, the remnants of the battalion, four wounded officers and 240 men, many also wounded, were driven back to an orchard on the outskirts of the village. There the Munsters fought on, completely surrounded, until their ammunition ran out and the survivors were forced to surrender. The 2nd Bn Royal Munster Fusiliers had fought off nine German battalions for the best part of six hours.

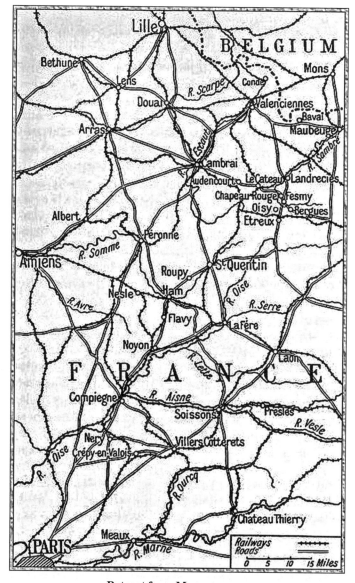

Retreat from Mons map

Their heroic fighting withdrawal and sacrifice delayed the German advance by those six hours and allowed I Corps to retire without having to fight a battle similar to that of II Corps at Le Cateau. The Germans later admitted to over 1500 wounded alone and acknowledged the heroic last stand of the Munsters by allowing the survivors to collect and bury their dead in the orchard. At Étreux, the Munsters lost 110 killed, hundreds more wounded and captured. The killed included sixteen Corkmen, Limerick lost twelve sons, Tralee lost nine while the fishing village of Balbriggan, a few miles north of Dublin, lost three men killed. Some of the Munsters had managed in the confusion to escape south, and five officers and 196 other ranks were mustered at Jonqueusea on 29 August. After the war, the orchard became a beautifully maintained British War Graves Commission cemetery, containing the graves of the Munsters killed during their heroic last stand.

The epic march saw men already tired from the march to Mons, stagger mile after mile in the heat and dust of a blazing French summer. By the end of August, the exhausted BEF had been marching, sometimes thirty miles a day, for almost a week. Often they were held up by thousands of refugees that marched alongside them carrying their few possessions. Men slept as they marched and snatched naps during the ten-minute halts, on average just four hours in twenty-four. I Corps had escaped lightly so far, thanks largely to the action of the Munsters at Étreux. On 29 August, the French Fifth Army launched a counter-attack at Guise-St Quentin, allowing the BEF finally to break cleanly with the pursuing Germans. By then the BEF was about on its knees; the men had to rest no matter the consequences. On 30 August the newly formed British III Corps (4th Division and 19th Brigade) moved onto II Corps' left flank. That same day Sir John French refused a French request to delay the BEF's retreat to fill a gap between them as they retired. Sir John French refused the request because he felt the BEF would need ten days recuperation before it could retake its place in the line. On 31 August the BEF crossed the Aisne and such was the exhausted condition of men and animals the day's march had to be shortened.

On 1 September, the 1st Bn Irish Guards with the 4th (Guards) Brigade were caught by the Germans in the forest at Villers-Cotterêts, south of Soissons and just 40 miles from Paris. The Irishmen, who had so recently cheered John Redmond at the gates of Wellington Barracks and sang 'A Nation Once Again' as they marched past the Houses of Parliament en route for France, were now exhausted. They were punch drunk with fatigue and had managed that night to grab a few minutes snatched sleep on the edge of a cold dank forest through which they were passing. Shook awake, they were on the march again by 0200 hrs and were then informed that they, along with the 2nd Bn Coldstream Guards, were now the 2nd Division's rearguard. After the heat and dust of the previous days, the morning broke wet, with a miserable drizzle that soaked the men, leaving them cold and wet, most having lost their greatcoats during the march. On reports of German cavalry in the area, the Irish Guards fell back into the forest, but it turned out not to be cavalry, but German infantry and they were already in the forest. The plantation was thickly planted with beech trees with the only fields of fire along the long forest rides that split the dense blocks of trees. The fighting was confused with the enemy appearing on both flanks and to the front. The Irishmen, covering the withdrawal of the Coldstream Guards, fought and fell back through the forest yielding ground slowly. Where men fell shot, they lay unnoticed in the dense vegetation while the battalions, unable to stop for their wounded, fought their way back to a line near Pisseleux. During the afternoon, the Irish Guards also fell back, covered by the Coldstream and Grenadier Guards, until they reformed in a wood north of the village. When the Irish Guards called their roll, the commanding officer, Lieutenant Colonel Morris, six officers and ninety men were missing or wounded. The fight at Villers-Cotterêts cost the 4th (Guards) Brigade over 300 officers and men, including two platoons of Grenadier Guards (seventy men), who had been cut off, surrounded and, fighting to the last man, killed at Rond de la Reine.

IRELAND

At Westminster, although the British government wished it otherwise, Irish politics went on. With the Home Rule Bill effectively in the bag, John Redmond's focus was on trying to prevent the permanent exclusion of six or eight northern Irish counties and the creation of an Ulster Unionist Protestant statelet. The thing that he cared for most in his world of politics was that 'not a single sod of Irish soil and not a single citizen of the Irish nation should be excluded from the operation of Irish self-government'. At this point, he also wanted and needed the official recognition, arming and training of the Irish Volunteers. The day war was declared, Redmond wrote a letter to the Prime Minister in which he made it clear to Asquith that he had taken a massive political gamble in making the offer of the Irish Volunteers and that he expected something in return. What he expected was absolutely no delay to the introduction of the Home Rule Bill, which only awaited the royal signature. He understood that the Amending Bill was still there, so he told Asquith that he would accept the immediate royal assent for the Home Rule Bill, with the proviso that the Act would not come into force until the Amending Bill was disposed of during the next session of parliament.

The Unionists saw the outbreak of war as an excuse to halt the progress of the Home Rule Bill in its tracks. Carson, needless to say, demanded that the bill should be suspended and the status quo should be preserved until parliament could turn its full attention back to the debate. Prior to the outbreak of the war, the Ulster Unionists had accepted that they were powerless to prevent the Home Rule Bill coming into force, but they were still determined not to be a milk cow for the agricultural south or be part what they regarded as a Popish state. Their political focus and aim had shifted to the permanent exclusion of as many of the northern counties as they could tease from the British government. After some bickering over parliamentary procedures, Asquith asked Redmond to trust him that the Home Rule Bill would go on the statute book without delay.

There was also the question of the political militias with both Redmond and Carson meeting with Lord Kitchener separately just days after the outbreak of war. Although civil enough, neither meeting went well for the Irish politicians. Kitchener began to lecture Carson on Irish politics to which the Unionist leader retorted: 'You're a damn clever fellow telling me what I ought to be doing.' Having offered the services of the UVF, Carson wanted his militia kept together as a separate formation within the British Army and asked for the word 'Ulster' to be incorporated into any title of any unit formed from the UVF men. Kitchener refused all Carson's points and the meeting broke up without any agreement.

Next it was John Redmond's turn to meet the formidable Secretary of State for War. He requested that the drill instructors who were army reservists and due to be recalled to their battalions, should be left with the Irish Volunteers and that his Volunteers be armed and trained as a national defence force, allowing the British garrisons to be withdrawn. Lord Kitchener simply blanked him, ignoring the point of arms and training, but made his own position clear: all he wanted from Ireland was recruits. When it came to the defence of Ireland, Kitchener was not impressed with the offer of either group of volunteers and told Redmond he planned to draft in English Territorials anyway, an organisation which he held in total contempt and thought fit only for garrison duties.

Kitchener had two very simplistic views on the matter of the Irish militias. He first thought that volunteers of any kind were a superfluous encumbrance at a moment when the supreme requirement was for men in the actual fighting line and that any encouragement of volunteers of any description, including the Territorials, simply gave men an excuse for shirking the war (the TF were not obliged to serve overseas). Secondly, volunteers outside the state's control were a danger to the British state. The threat was increased when there were two rival volunteer forces, which might fly at each other's throats, potentially diverting much needed military resources to deal with an internal security situation. It was little satisfaction that one of these militias was very inferior to the other in terms of arms and equipment. Hopefully, that fact would lessen the chance of any conflict between the two. It was an additional matter of personal satisfaction that the more powerfully armed force was, theoretically at least, loyal to the Empire and could be trusted to assist troops if any attack upon the Empire was begun by the other. This was a contingency that Kitchener would most certainly have taken into account when dealing with the UVF in particular and he was not prepared to change the status quo.

Lord Kitchener held Irish soldiers in very high regard and had no distrust of Irish soldiers serving in the regular regiments, no professional soldier ever had, but he had a deep distrust of any purely Irish military formation under Irish political control. At the back of Kitchener's mind was the determination: 'I will not arm England's potential enemies.' John Redmond was absolutely correct to push hard for the training and arming of the Irish Volunteers. A recent Royal Irish Constabulary (RIC) intelligence report had shown that the UVF possessed 53,300 rifles; the Irish Volunteers possessed only 10,400. After the disappointing meeting with Kitchener, Redmond wrote a furious letter to Asquith in which he warned that Ireland would take as a supreme affront the offer of the Volunteers being ignored. On 8 August, an official telegram was sent to Ireland. It read;

> His majesty's government recognises with deep gratitude the loyal help, which Ireland has offered in this grave hour. They hope to announce as soon as possible arrangements by which this offer can be made use of to the fullest possible extent.

The telegram was like manna from heaven for Redmond. From the tone of the telegram, it was plain that Asquith and his government favoured arming and training the Irish Volunteers.

In parliament on 10 August, John Redmond questioned the Prime Minister on the subject. From Hansard dated 10 August 1914:

Mr JOHN REDMOND: May I ask the Prime Minister whether there is any truth in the statement which has appeared in the newspapers that English Territorial regiments are to be sent to Ireland to replace the regiments to be withdrawn?

PRIME MINISTER: There is no truth in the statement. In the view of Lord Kitchener, the first necessity of the moment is to recruit the hundred thousand men whom he has asked for. He does not doubt, nor do I, that Ireland will contribute her full contingent. Subject to this, Lord Kitchener is anxious to lend any help that his own exigencies permit to the organisation and equipment of the Irish Volunteers. And we have shown our confidence in the willingness and capacity of the Irish to defend their own shores by countermanding the dispatch to Ireland of the English Territorials who, under the normal operation of our mobilisation scheme, would have gone there.

Mr JOHN REDMOND: May I ask the right hon gentleman whether he can say what steps the Government are going to take in this matter – that is to say, whether he would consider the advisability of the War Office, or some proper person, entering into consultation with the authorities, or the governing body, of the Volunteers in Dublin so as to concert some system whereby advantage might be taken at once of the situation which has arisen?

PRIME MINISTER: I know that Lord Kitchener is very anxious to do that. Of course, for the moment, the great difficulty, and the almost insuperable one, is the collecting of officers and non-commissioned officers for the organisation of the hundred thousand men for the Second Army which Lord Kitchener proposes to raise, but subject to that and concurrent with it, I think he will do everything in his power by consultation with gentlemen in Ireland to arrange for the full equipment and organisation of the Irish Volunteers.

In light of the exchanges in parliament and personal assurances given by Asquith to John Redmond in private, on 11 August the standing committee of the Irish Volunteers met in Dublin and unanimously passed the following resolution:

> *The Standing Committee desire, on behalf of the Irish Volunteers, to express their complete readiness to take joint action with the Ulster Volunteer Force for the defence of Ireland.*

The resolution was passed unanimously, but the adherents to physical force (IRB) on the committee, like IRB man Padraic Pearse, voted with deep reservations.

Unfortunately, neither Prime Minister Asquith and his government nor the Irish Nationalists built the intransigence, deceit and sheer bigotry of Field Marshal Lord Horatio Herbert Kitchener into their equations. At a Cabinet meeting on 12 August, Augustine Birrell, the Irish Chief Secretary, asked that the Irish Volunteers be accepted as an official military force. Asquith supported the 'immediate and complete recognition of the Volunteers'. Kitchener remained steadfastly opposed to the move, which he regarded as political *shenanigans*. Irrespective of what Asquith wanted, Kitchener was not prepared to act on any of the Prime Minister's suggestions or vague instructions. As usual Kitchener had convinced himself that he knew better and the Prime Minister, personally lacking the resolution, was incapable of facing down his intimidating Secretary of State for War and ordering him to comply. He was therefore simply ignored. Neither Asquith, nor anyone else in his government interested enough to care, had the strength of character to stand up to the dominating and dictatorial personality of Lord Kitchener. The drill instructors and reservists were duly withdrawn from both the Irish and Ulster Volunteers and no official recognition, arms or training would ever be forthcoming.

On the Unionist's side, they too were pressurising and threatening the government by using their UVF militia to extract political gain. After Asquith had promised Redmond that the Home Rule Bill would be introduced without delay, on 10 August, Carson told Asquith that the Ulster Unionists felt betrayed. He warned that he felt he must either resign his leadership of Ulster or go to Belfast to throw his lot in with his people and to join them in any action they may feel bound to undertake. The threat was clear and unambiguous. He added that all the difficulties could be avoided simply by postponing the Home Rule Bill. If it were postponed, Captain James Craig could offer Kitchener two divisions, 36,000 trained men with all their equipment, for immediate service abroad. Ulsterman James Craig was the son of a self-made whisky millionaire, a staunch Orangeman and MP for East Down. His strength lay in his organisational ability and feel for grass-roots opinion among the Protestants of East Ulster. He was once described as the very epitome of Ulster intransigence and is now recognised, much more so than Edward Carson, as the founding father of Northern Ireland. In addition to the two divisions, a similar number of men would be available for home service in Ulster. If Home Rule went ahead, of course, none of these men would be available. Asquith responded to the pressure by compromising, suggesting that further debate on Home Rule be adjourned to 26 August, by which time something could be worked out.

John Redmond's statesmanlike speech of 3 August now came back to bite and set him on a path from which he was unable to turn. His speech was so well received in Ireland that most moderate Nationalists, with Home Rule seemingly achieved, replaced the old Satan, England, with a new devil, Germany. The Irish Party's mouthpiece, the Freeman's Journal, of course, trumpeted 'Chorus of Approval from All Parts of Ireland' given to the Irish leader after his speech endorsing the British war effort. The newspaper printed numerous messages and telegrams of support from party groups and individual citizens. At the meeting of Kildare County Council on 22 August, the following resolution was adopted:

> *That in view of the present grave crisis, whereby our country is threatened with calamity, we, the Kildare County Council, endorse the action of Mr John E. Redmond, pledging the support of the National Volunteers to defend our shores against invasion, and hereby undertake in the event of our office staff taking up arms, to keep their respective offices open until their return. Our secretary is hereby directed to make the necessary arrangements for the purpose of carrying out this resolution into effect.*

Within the Irish Volunteer organisation, Redmond's speech had split the Provisional Committee into two unequal camps. The Ancient Order of Hibernians supported Redmond and headed up the larger group, while Eoin MacNeill headed the smaller but heavily IRB-infiltrated hard-line group. The hardliners were strongly supported by the Dublin County Board of Volunteers, who refused to have anything to do with helping the English government. Padraig Pearse and the IRB were effectively frozen out of decision-making within the Provisional Committee of the Volunteers over the next month, but soon events would take an unexpected and dramatic turn that would change all that.

John Redmond's Westminster speech had also horrified his Irish-American supporters, but like most things Irish, it was not quite as simple as it looked. Irish-Americans were more interested in the destruction of the British Empire than in Irish Home Rule, but Redmond desperately needed their financial support. In an attempt to justify his actions, he wrote to the President of the United Irish League in America. Unfortunately, he was married to a German and was running for the governorship of Pennsylvania, a state with a very large German vote. In his reply to Redmond, Michael Ryan would state quite openly that all his sympathies lay with Germany. He suggested the termination of the United Irish League and not another penny was received from them. To make matters even worse, the Irish-American press also turned against Redmond.

THE HOME FRONT

While II Corps were fighting at Le Cateau, German troops destroyed much of the medieval town and Irish college at Louvain, a war crime that echoed around the world, helping to vilify the term German Kultur. On 29 August, the Glasgow Herald reported:

> German soldiers furnished with bombs set fire to all parts of the town. The splendid Church of St Pierre, the University buildings, the library and the scientific establishments were delivered to the flames. Several notable citizens were shot. A town of 45,000 inhabitants, the intellectual metropolis of the Low Countries since the fifteenth century is now no more than a heap of ruins.

Ironically, considering the prolonged vilification and marginalisation of Roman Catholics by the British, a German anti-Catholic element would be introduced into British propaganda after the destruction of the university at Louvain and later the burning of Reims Cathedral by German troops. Although the anti-Catholic behaviour of the German Army as it rampaged through Belgium and France was, of course, exaggerated in the British press, the German Catholic hierarchy were concerned enough about anti-Catholic emotions in Germany that had been unleashed by the war to report their concerns to the Vatican. In response to the news of Louvain, a number of German shops were looted and set on fire in Dublin and on the British mainland.

As the tiny Belgian army fought against odds of 10–1, the newspaper headlines screamed: 'Poor, Gallant Little Belgium'. Nowhere else, outside of Belgium itself, did the destruction of Louvain rouse such intense indignation as in Ireland. Here the shock given to the whole civilised world by the German crime was the greater owing to the many Irish associations with Louvain and the peculiarly intimate relations that had existed for centuries with its university. Profound mourning for the irreparable loss of Irish memorials and Irish literary treasures was accompanied by fierce resentment against the authors of the wanton desecration and destruction, and demands for vengeance were made in the Nationalist press:

> A week or two ago there was a feeble attempt by a few Gaelic League cranks to obtain sympathy for German Kultur. It was claimed that Ireland owed a debt of gratitude to German linguists, such as Kuno Meyer, for their interest in the language and in Irish MSS. Now German Kultur is only alluded to with bitter sarcasm or with loathing and Irish soldiers are being called upon by their countrymen to avenge the brutality and savagery, which, it is declared, have placed the Kaiser and his soldiers outside the pale of civilisation. The feeling in Ireland is not surprising when the debt, which the Roman Catholic Church of the country owes to Louvain, is remembered.

More detailed newspapers reports of the event quickly appeared. The headlines now screamed, 'Poor Little Catholic Belgium'. Nuns and little girls had been raped, priests crucified on the doors of their churches, babies stuck on the bayonets of the Huns. In fact, the killings were part of a war policy known as *Schrecklichkeit* ('frightfulness'). Its purpose was to terrify civilians in occupied areas so that they would not rebel. Soon the British and Irish newspapers would be full of stories of atrocities committed by German troops on Belgian civilians. Although many of the incidents were exaggerated, many were true, with an estimated 6500 Belgian and French civilians murdered by the German Army in the first few weeks of the war. The US Ambassador to Belgium, Brand Whitlock, listed many in an official report to the US Secretary of State. Former IPP MP Tom Kettle was in Belgium buying arms for the Irish Volunteers when war broke out. He remained in Belgium as a war correspondent and would later confirm many of the accounts to a war crimes committee. The stories of raped girls, murdered babies, and priest and nuns executed struck a chord in the British and Irish psyche. Led by the British press, an international media crusade against German *Kultur* and Hunnish barbarism was begun.

Catholic City Destroyed
(Courtesy of Glasgow Observer)

The Glasgow Catholic Observer, published weekly, had to wait until 5 September when it headlined: 'GERMANY'S CAMPAIGN OF SAVAGERY. Historic Catholic City Wantonly Destroyed.' The outrage felt for small, independent Catholic Belgium, which had been invaded, pillaged and now largely occupied, ensured the sympathy of the Glasgow Irish, who could identify with a small country fighting for survival against a large imperial neighbour. Both the native Irish and the Glasgow Irish responded enthusiastically to calls from their Roman Catholic Church leaders and parish priests to support the British government and the war effort.

Highly ironic, was the fact that Belgium itself was a brutal colonial power, having assumed control of the Congo Free State in 1908. The conditions in the Congo were so bad that the British sent a diplomatic team to investigate the circumstances. In 1904, none other than Irish Republican martyr Sir Roger Casement submitted a report of the genocide in the Congo. His report and others were so damning that the diplomatic community insisted that the Congo be taken from the King and brought directly under the control of the Belgian government. The Belgian authorities, however, refused to hold a public enquiry into the atrocities and the inhuman practices. Although on a somewhat reduced scale, the human rights violations would continue under successive Belgian governments until the Congo finally gained its independence in 1960.

THE WAR FRONT

Back in France, the exhausted, though undefeated, BEF continued to trudge southward as August turned to September. For the French General Command, the first two weeks or so of the war had been disastrous. The French First and Second Armies on the right flank had been defeated over 14–20 August and the following day the Third and Fourth Armies in the centre were also forced into retreat. The knock-on effect of these reverses precipitated the withdrawal of the French Fifth Army immediately prior to the BEF's fight at Mons. Although the French battle plan was in disarray, General Joffre kept cool, ordering a slow withdrawal of the French armies. At the same time, he began transferring troops from the eastern flank to the west and Paris. There, a new French Sixth Army was being formed based on the Paris garrison. The Germans meanwhile, although still victorious and advancing, were well behind their schedule. After the battle at Le Cateau, von Kluck believed that he had destroyed the BEF and allowed his First Army to be drawn well ahead of General Karl von Bulow's Second Army advancing on his left. Von Kluck came to believe that if he could find the flank of the retreating French Fifth Army, he could deliver a fatal blow to the French ability to continue the war. On 29 August, the French Fifth Army launched a counter-attack on von Bulow's army at Guise-St Quentin. Stopping the Second Army in its tracks, it finally allowed the BEF to break cleanly from the pursuing Germans, gaining for themselves a day of desperately needed respite.

On 30 and 31 August the gap between von Kluck and von Bulow continued to grow as the latter halted and von Kluck continued with his advance. At the beginning of September, the Germans still believed that the Third, Fourth and Fifth Armies could and would deliver a decisive victory. By 1 September, von Kluck was across the River Oise, the last river barrier before Paris. His forward units were now only thirty miles from the French capital. At the same time Count Helmuth von Moltke, Chief of the German General Staff, headquartered in Luxembourg and remote in both time and space from the battlefield, abandoned the last vestiges of the Schlieffen Plan. Believing von Kluck still to be in line with von Bulow, he instructed von Kluck to shift toward the centre, driving any French forces away from Paris. He was also to move closer to von Bulow to protect the Second Army's right flank with a view of enveloping the French armies from both flanks. This decision meant von Kluck's army would bypass Paris to the east, exposing its own right flank to the rapidly forming French Sixth Army north of Paris. By the time the message reached von Kluck, he was already two days ahead of the German Second Army, whose right flank he was supposed to be protecting. He was completely unaware of the new French army forming on his own right flank. On 2 September, the French government abandoned Paris leaving its defence in the hands of its garrison.

For the BEF, the exhausting retreat continued for another four days. No further major engagements took place, but the cavalry screen saw action most days. On 3 September, the BEF crossed the Marne and on 6 September it halted and turned to face the Germans. The epic retreat had finally come to an end. The BEF was now in the area of Tournan, facing north, its left flank was just fifteen miles south-east of Paris and the spires of the city could be seen in the distance. The retreat had lasted thirteen days with just one major halt and covered a distance of 136 miles as the crow flies or nearer 200 miles as the men marched. The nearest French troops, the Fifth Army, were about fifteen miles away to the east and rear. The battles at Mons, Le Cateau and the various rearguard actions during the retreat cost the BEF around 14,000 casualties, dead, wounded or missing. Remarkably light given the circumstances, but a serious blow to such a small force. II Corps bore the brunt of the losses, but its first reinforcements of 10 per cent caught up with their units on 5 September and all base stores had been moved from Boulogne and Le Havre to St Nazaire, which assisted in the rapid replenishment of lost materiel.

For the 2nd Bn Munster Fusiliers the losses were so catastrophic that battle casualty replacements were insufficient to make up numbers, therefore the remnants of the battalion swopped roles with the 1st Bn Queen's Own Cameron Highlanders, who were transferred from army troops to the 1st (Guards) Brigade. Other British infantry battalions had also been very badly mauled. At Clary on 27 August, the 1st Bn Gordon Highlanders were surrounded and had approximately 500 men taken prisoner.

A similar fate befell the 2nd Bn Royal Dublin Fusiliers, who had only arrived at Le Cateau on 24 August with the 4th Division. The following day the battalion, nicknamed the 'Old Toughs' or the 'Dubs', marched from Le Cateau, north-west towards Cambrai near Haucourt. The battalion prepared and manned a defensive position until in the confusion of the withdrawal they were left behind and largely surrounded. Some of the *Dubs* managed to escape in small detachments, but many were cut off and taken prisoner. They would spend the next four years in the German prisoner of war camp at Limburg. Among those who escaped was Robert Downie from Springburn, a former pupil of St Aloysius' College and a mad keen Celtic supporter. At the time, twenty-one-year-old Robert had three brothers serving in the military. Overall, the Royal Dublin Fusiliers lost forty killed, scores more wounded and over 350 captured.

The Argyll and Sutherland Highlanders lost over 100 casualties, as did the Irish Guards. Also at Le Cateau, the 2nd Bn KOSB, the battalion involved at Bachelor's Walk, lost eight men killed, with scores wounded. Three platoons, 120 men, were surrounded and captured. Also captured was the officer commanding at Bachelor's Walk, Major Alfred Haig. Wounded in the shoulder, Haig reported to a field dressing station where he awoke from an opiate to find himself a prisoner of war. It should be noted that English and Welsh regiments suffered similar casualties under similar conditions, including the Royal Warwickshire Regiment, who were forced to temporarily amalgamate with the remnants of the 2nd Bn Royal Dublin Fusiliers.

On 4 September, General Joffre was apprised of von Kluck's change of direction. Miraculously, the German army was bypassing Paris to the east. Within hours, new orders were issued. The newly formed French Sixth Army, reinforced by the Paris garrison was ordered to attack into von Kluck's exposed right flank. The French Fifth Army and the BEF would also attack with the BEF moving into the gap between the two German armies. The Battle of the Marne was about to begin.

CELTIC FC

On 29 August, Celtic travelled to Love Street, Paisley, to play a St Mirren (Buddies) team that had finished the previous season with the wooden spoon. The Paisley club's directors took the failure to heart and invested in nine new players for the forthcoming season. The new boys included Andrew Davidson signed from Celtic during the close season. Davidson was a medical student at Glasgow University and although a highly talented left half, he lost out at Parkhead to McMaster having played just a half dozen games over the 1913/14 season. Andrew Davidson would qualify as a doctor and serve with the Royal Army Medical Corps (RAMC) during the Great War. He would later be knighted for his service to medicine. And signed from Blackburn FC was Hughie McGrory. Although a Garngad man, Hughie was no relation of future Celtic legend Jimmy McGrory. In the line-up against Celtic, Hughie would turn out forty-nine times for St Mirren before enlisting with the army. Despite the new signings, the home support must have feared the worst for their side against the Scottish champions.

On the day, Celtic were not at full strength, with Alec McNair and Jimmy McMenemy both missing. McNair had picked up an injury during the midweek benefit game against Clyde. The ever-ready and highly professional Tommy McGregor took his place. Powerful and fast, Tommy was a highly competent replacement, who had recently made the Scotland squad despite being a permanent replacement for Dodds or McNair. McMenemy was replaced by Browning with Alex Gray on the wing. Gray was back at Parkhead from Ayr and playing in his first league game for the Celts in well over a year.

The Celts were back at Love Street for the first time since the previous season's corresponding league fixture. Then the Bhoys had won by 3–0 after an ill-tempered game, which saw Johnny McMaster and Sowerby of St Mirren sent off near the end. As the players made their way to the pavilion, an incensed Celtic supporter named MacDougall assaulted

Liddell, the St. Mirren goalkeeper, clears, with M'Coll, the Celtic centre, running in. Liddell had an anxious afternoon.

Liddell, the St Mirren goalkeeper, clears from Jimmy McColl

Sowerby. A section of the crowd then invaded the park and in the ensuing melee a Paisley man named Thompson tried to pick the pocket of Willie Maley. Both MacDougall and Thompson were subsequently arrested and later at Paisley Police Court MacDougall was fined £3 and Thompson was sent to prison for three months hard labour. It came as no surprise therefore that this latest meeting of the two teams should be something of a hard, physical slugging match with both sides asking for and receiving no quarter.

St Mirren set their stall out from the kick-off and went toe to toe with Celtic in every department. Within a few minutes of the kick-off, Celtic got an indication that it might just be one of those days, when Charlie Shaw dropped a couple of balls in quick succession one almost crossing the line. So it proved to be as the home side took the lead after just five minutes. Clark latched onto some clever wing play by Englishman Sowerby to fire a terrific close-in shot past the helpless Charlie Shaw. Soon after the restart, the scorer took a kick to the face that left him in a state of total collapse and he was carried off the field for treatment. Patsy Gallacher equalised for the Celts five minutes later after a bad clearance by the St Mirren goalie, Liddell. The irrepressible Clark, bandaged and plastered, was back on the field and restored the Buddies lead in fifteen minutes. Page nodded another excellent crossed ball by Sowerby onto Clark, as he stood unmarked in the Celtic box leaving him an easy scoring opportunity that he gleefully accepted. Joe Dodds was not having the best of days having twice been posted absent while the St Mirren winger was setting up both goals for Clark, although, some would argue that on both occasions he was covering for McGregor. McColl again brought the Bhoys back level just before half-time. The teams went in at half-time for some much needed respite drawing 2–2. Just five minutes after the restart St Mirren went back into the lead with a fine goal from their excellent inside forward, Tom Page, who had gathered in a difficult ball, controlled it and took a shot in three skilful steps. The rough and tumble continued with Patsy Gallacher taking a kick in the face while trying to head what was for him a high ball. Clark lost his bandages and plasters but continued with his face covered in blood. Andy McAtee was next in the wars when he was kicked in the thigh and only the frantic efforts of trainer Quinn enabled the Croy man to remain in the game. Johnny Browning struggled to fill McMenemy's role but ensured a share of the points when he scored Celtic's third with fifteen minutes to go. Gallacher, McColl and Browning were the scorers for Celtic, but St Mirren's Tom Page was the undoubted man of the match. With Alex McNair missing, the Celts defence proved unstable and leaked goals. The Buddies had started without their regular keeper, Irishman Willie O'Hagen, who was out with an ankle injury, and it was Liddell their deputy keeper, slightly overawed by the occasion, who was to prove their weakest link. Were it not for the nervousness of the St Mirren goalie, Celtic could easily have left Love Street with no points. A crowd of 15,000 watched the massively entertaining but bruising encounter. The Celtic side on the day was Shaw, McGregor and Dodd, Young, Johnstone and McMaster, and McAtee, Gallacher, McColl, Browning and Gray. The home fans left greatly encouraged by their team's performance, which if replicated and maintained throughout the season, would see them finish much better placed than the previous season. The Celtic supporters were less happy: three games played, one loss, one shaky win and a draw. Celtic had slipped to eleventh place in the league; the faithful were disgruntled, but consoled themselves with the fact that it was still early in the season.

THE HOME FRONT

On the same day Celtic travelled to Paisley, an open letter from Prime Minister Asquith to the four Lord Mayors, or Lord Provost in Edinburgh's case, of the home nation capitals was published in the national newspapers. It was headed 'Rousing The Nation'. The Prime Minister asked in the letter that the civic leaders lead a combined effort to stimulate and mobilise public opinion into a national recruiting effort for the greatest conflict in which the nation had ever been involved. In response to the Asquith letter and in light of the dire situation in France, the nation sprung to arms. The result would be infantry battalions locally raised, known to posterity as the *pals battalions*. In Glasgow, the Corporation planned a committee meeting for the beginning of September when the city's response to the Prime Minister's appeal would be decided. Meanwhile, in view of the invasion threat, it was decided to form the Glasgow Citizens Training Force. The object of the force was to provide military training to men in the Glasgow district who were ineligible or, for business or other valid reasons, unable to enlist in the armed forces. A secondary responsibility was to encourage recruiting for and to give every possible assistance to the military. In addition to the city and town councils, many schools, colleges, universities, professions, factories, companies and sporting organisations responded to the Prime Minister's letter and got involved in the recruiting drive. The executive of the Glasgow Boy's Brigade battalion sent an urgent telegram to the Secretary of State for War in which companies of ex-members of the brigade were offered for service in the New Armies. The War Office wrote back explaining that only battalions of 1,000 men could be accepted. The Boy's Brigade companies would soon form the nucleus of the 16th (Service) Bn Highland Light Infantry (2nd Glasgow).

Many of the leading citizens, the great and the good of the various communities, also felt it their duty, in a community version of paterfamilias, to contribute and to lend their considerable social weight to the recruiting cause. Throughout the country, these powerful individuals sought to raise infantry battalions, usually on the back of their own considerable wealth and public reputations. The recruiting drive became something of a social event among the aristocracy and upper-class social elite. Recruits gained and contribution made to the effort became the 'in thing' for the season. The names of many of these individuals often found their way into the new battalions as subtitles. One such individual was Lieutenant Colonel Donald Cameron of Lochiel, Chief of the Cameron Clan. Using his considerable influence among his clansmen and the Highlanders living in Glasgow, plus the lure of the kilt, of course, he personally raised two new service battalions of Cameron Highlanders. The first battalion took his name as the 5th 'Lochiel's' (Service) Bn The Queen's Own Cameron Highlanders. His battalion included 150 men recruited from the Glasgow Stock Exchange. The 17th (Service) Bn Royal Scots were known as 'Rosebery's' after Lord Rosebery. The King's Liverpool Regiment contained four service battalions all raised by Lord Derby. The 15th Bn Royal Scots was named after Sir Robert Cranston. Another such individual who would have a profound effect on Celtic and the rest of Scottish football was Sir George McCrae, former secretary and shareholder of Heart of Midlothian FC. He would raise the 16th (Service) Bn Royal Scots, better known as McCrae's battalion.

The support offered to the British war effort by the constitutional Irish Nationalists and by the Roman Catholic Church in Scotland soothed any misgivings held by the politically aware Glasgow Irish Nationalists regarding their support of the British government. If there ever was any doubt about the Glasgow Irish and their commitment and loyalty to their new homeland, it was now completely dispelled. Encouraged by their priests, politicians, newspapers and their own enthusiasm for the war, the Glasgow Irish joined up in droves. The men voluntarily enlisting into the army were allowed to choose which regiment or arm of the services they wished to serve with and the vast majority of the Glasgow Irish found it easier and quicker to join their local Scottish regiments. It should also be noted that as individuals they were comfortable and confident enough, despite the alienation and marginalisation of their community, to join Scottish regiments. In England, the Irish and English Irish were also responding to the call and flocking to the colours. In addition to the new service battalions, in London and Liverpool the Irish joined their own battalions of the Territorial Force. In Liverpool, the 8th (Irish) Bn King's Liverpool Regiment (Irish republican James Connolly's old regiment) would raise three battalions while in London the 18th (County of London) Bn London Regiment (London Irish Rifles) would also raise three battalions.

On Tyneside, the response to the call for volunteers from the Irish community in Newcastle was so enthusiastic that the Irish-born Lord Mayor provided the Irish leadership to raise four new distinctively Irish service battalions for Kitchener's Army. By January 1915, 5500 Irishmen or sons of Irishmen had enlisted into the four specially designated Irish battalions of the Northumberland Fusiliers. The Irish battalions formed a Tyneside Irish Brigade comprising the 24th (Service) Bn (1st Tyneside Irish), 25th (Service) Bn (2nd Tyneside Irish), 26th (Service) Bn (3rd Tyneside Irish) and 27th (Service) Bn (4th Tyneside Irish). Two further reserve Irish battalions of the Northumberland Fusiliers were also raised from the Tyneside Irish community. The Tyneside Irish were among the first distinctly Irish units to be raised and many Irishmen from all over the country, including the Glasgow Irish, travelled to Newcastle to sign on with the Irish battalions. John Redmond would try very hard to have the four battalions of the Tyneside Irish Brigade sent to Ireland, where they would form part of the soon to be formed 16th (Irish) Division, but the snobbery of the divisional commander, who did not want 'slumbirds' in his division, effectively ruled it out.

The Tyneside Scottish community also raised a brigade of the Northumberland Fusiliers, but in the race to raise their brigades the Scots were beaten to the winning line by the Tyneside Irish. Indeed the entire British Empire was responding to the call of the motherland. In India, Australia, Canada, New Zealand and South Africa, units were being raised or expanded and prepared for service overseas. Many of these units were distinctly Irish, including the Canadian Irish Rangers and Canadian Irish Fusiliers. The Imperial Irish Horse, later the South African Irish Regiment, saw action in German South-West Africa.

Unlike on Tyneside, no such decisive Irish leadership emerged in Glasgow around which the Glasgow Irish could coalesce to form an identifiably Irish battalion; however, many of the Glasgow Irish who signed up in Glasgow chose to serve with Irish regiments and crossed the North Channel to regimental depots in Ireland.

In the same spirit of doing one's bit, and assuming that it would be a short war, the British business community also stepped up to the plate. Most, but not all the large concerns, like the mines and railway companies, promised to make up the wages of employees who, as reservists, TF soldiers or recruits, joined the colours and to allow their families to remain in company housing. They also guaranteed the men the same or equivalent jobs, paid at the same rate, when they returned from active service. The Clyde Navigation Trust, responsible for the management of the River Clyde, did likewise. Local authorities, which employed tens of thousands of men, also chipped in. On 26 August, the management of Glasgow Corporation Tramways announced that its employees now serving with the armed forces who had been recalled as reservists, embodied with their TF unit or joined up since the declaration of war, would be paid a portion of their wages. The sum, along with separation allowances paid to their dependants, would be equal to two-thirds of the employee's salary before joining the forces. Single men would be given an allowance equal to one-third of their salary. Normally the allowances paid by the employers would be in addition to and dependant on the pay and allowances being paid to the soldier by the military. With the best of intentions, the employers were opening something of a Pandora's box. Military pay was notoriously complex and depended on an infinite number of variables that affected a soldier's basic daily rate including arm of service, rank, time served, trade qualifications and proficiency to name but a few. To complicate matters even further, several emoluments were subject to variation from time to time. In response to the employers wishing to make up a part or all of the salaries, the army issued a pamphlet showing the basic Regular Army daily rates of pay and separation allowances for a number of arms and for the other ranks.

Many firms asked their employees to agree to a stoppage from their weekly wage to be donated to either their own or national relief funds. The 2000 workers with Niddrie and Benhar Coal Company agreed a voluntary levy in support of the national relief fund. The miners would give two pence per week while the war lasted, while surface workers and boys would give one penny. At the giant Parkhead Forge, Beardmore workers also contributed weekly to the relief funds. In addition to the allowance given to the serving employees by the management of Glasgow Corporation Tramways, the remaining employees pledged to give £3000 over six months, payable by weekly instalments to the National War Fund.

The public were bombarded at every turn for charitable donations, at work, in the streets, in church or chapel, and the level of voluntary donations was astounding. Scotland's contribution to the National Relief Fund at the end of August was: Glasgow £115,000, Edinburgh £79,000, Renfrewshire £36,000, Dundee £29,000, Aberdeen £10,000 and the Glasgow Irish bastion Coatbridge had raised £2600. These were colossal sums of money, and every penny was voluntarily and willingly given. The Celtic players on occasion gave sizeable sums from their wages, collected and donated on their behalf by the management. The various relief funds needed every penny. Up to the end of August the Glasgow Branch of the Soldiers and Sailors Families Association had received over 5500 applications for help from wives and dependants of volunteers. The problem was threefold. First, it was an administrative one with over the first two weeks of the war the number of wives and dependants eligible for the allowances jumping from 1500 to 250,000. Such a large increase completely overwhelmed the system, causing long delays in payment. Second, the army pay and separation allowances were paid monthly, causing hardship to families that were used to working on a weekly budget. Third, the allowance rate had not changed since the Boer War. It had not kept up with inflation and was therefore simply insufficient. Families in dire financial difficulties could appeal for help to the Soldiers and Sailors Families Association or the various national relief funds. In the Glasgow Star and Observer published at the beginning of September, Roman Catholics were being encouraged to bestir themselves and offer their services as visitors for the disbursement of relief distributed by the Soldiers and Sailors Families Association. John Warnock, an old Celtic committeeman, and his wife Sarah led the visitors' scheme in Springburn, Townhead and Garngad.

After the rush following Kitchener's first appeal, recruitment nationally had tailed off slightly towards the last week of August although there was still a steady flow. In an effort to stimulate recruitment, the editor of the English Daily Dispatch felt obliged to send telegrams to various civic leaders, including one to Sir Daniel MacAuley Stevenson, the Liberal Lord Provost of Glasgow. The editor wished the Lord Provost to publish an appeal to the 'Youth of England' to do their duty and enlist. Sir Daniel took great exception to the use of 'England' when the editor obviously meant Britain. In a very frosty reply, he reminded the editor that under no circumstances was Scotland to be assumed to be part of England. If the reference was to the entire country, the term 'Britain or British' was to be used. This would be a recurring theme throughout the war, where England was used to describe the other home nations, much to their irritation.

On 28 August, Lord Kitchener announced that the first hundred thousand recruits had enlisted. The first hundred thousand came to be regarded as the 'Cream of the Nation', the very best the country had to offer. They were the men who came when first called; they needed no coaxing or persuading, or no inducements. Kitchener then called for the second hundred thousand volunteers to come forward. The War Office raised the upper age limit to thirty-five for new recruits, forty-five for ex-soldiers and fifty for non-commissioned officers. The new appeal also pointed out that married men and widowers with children would also be accepted and would draw separation allowance at army rates. Kitchener was now contemplating raising four new armies consisting of thirty divisions, including those already in the field with the BEF. His appeal could not have been better timed if he had tried.

After the initial rush to the recruiting offices over the first three weeks of August, enlistments had fallen off mostly due to the mayhem at the recruiting offices and because of some confusion over how many men were actually required. Some of the public thought the hundred thousand was the full requirement. Just days before Kitchener's second appeal, reports of the severity of the fighting at Mons and Le Cateau began to appear in the British newspapers. The British national newspaper reports were about two or three days behind events on the battle front and ever mindful of censorship, they initially remained in keeping with the attitudes of the age where newspapers were expected to behave honourably and in the best interest of the country. Therefore, they highlighted the good and played down the bad news.

The Glasgow Herald reported: 'Fierce Attack on Our Troops in France' and 'Brilliant Response against Overwhelming Odds'. Among the column inches of the report, the only indication of the losses was at the end of a heroic retelling of the battle, where a sun-bronzed, wounded but stoic British soldier, still grasping his almost too hot to handle rifle, adds almost as an afterthought that he and his mate were among just thirty survivors from a force of 2000. At the same time as the battle reports arrived on the news-stands, the first batches of British casualties were arriving back in the south of England. As the retreat from Mons continued, each successive newspaper edition reported progressively grimmer news. The Times broke the full story of the retreat first. Published on 30 August, the famous Amiens Dispatch was a somewhat dramatic and inaccurate account of the military situation in France and the state of the British Army, then in full retreat and facing overwhelming odds. The headlines read: 'British Army in Critical Position' and 'Heroic Struggle British Outnumbered'. In later editions, it was 'Heavy British Losses' and 'Broken Battalions'. Then the long list of officer casualties were published and people quickly deduced that if a battalion had lost so many of its officers, then the casualties among the rank and file must also be very heavy.

The headlines were so alarming, questions were asked in the House of Commons regarding the newspaper's loyalty and code of conduct. Many MPs regarded the headlines as traitorous and demanded that action be taken against the newspaper. In fact, the dispatch had been passed to the government censors at the Press Bureau, but it had so alarmed the head of the Bureau that with a few through scores with a red pencil, he allowed it to be published almost intact. It cost him his job, but it served the purpose: the army needed men and within days of its publication recruitment figures soared. By the beginning of September, thanks mainly to the Amiens Dispatch, people in Britain were beginning to realise the extreme seriousness of the military situation in France. They also remembered the empty barracks and laughable reputation of the part-time soldiers of the TF guarding Britain's shores. In fact, the situation was far more serious than even they realised. There were no significant British forces whatsoever between the massive German armies and the Channel ports of Boulogne and Le Havre. Three days later British marines abandoned the Belgian Channel port of Ostend.

In response to the dire war news from France, fear of invasion and Kitchener's appeal for the second hundred thousand, the recruitment campaign was reignited with a bang. An unprecedented recruiting fever now took hold of the nation and raged throughout the last days of August and over the first fortnight or so of September. The outpouring of national fervour produced some extraordinary deeds of personal and collective patriotism. For a young single male of military age, there was simply no escaping the pressure to join the services. Newspapers were full of advertisements extolling the virtues of army or navy life or questioning their manhood or patriotism. Illuminated tramcars adorned with recruiting posters trundled through the Glasgow streets, while images of Kitchener and his challenging finger were plastered everywhere. Important local and national dignitaries made impassioned pleas, while the uncertain were cajoled and encouraged to enlist by their more adventurous mates or handed white feathers by stupid women and girls. Some men did not need much persuasion; three weeks without pay or on short time made army pay and allowances look very attractive. The effects can be seen over the weekend of 29 August, which was the Glasgow Trades' holiday. It was reported that the occasion was not observed to the same extent as usual. Too many people on short time meant they had neither the means nor the inclination to celebrate the event. The holiday traffic at the railway stations and at the Broomielaw was much lighter than normal. Glasgow Corporation Tramways also announced that the trams over the previous week carried a hundred thousand fewer passengers than the corresponding week last year.

At the end of August, the TF battalions were ordered to create a second line. This meant each battalion was to form a duplicate of itself, a new battalion that would accommodate those soldiers who had not volunteered for overseas service, those who were too young for active service (nineteen years) and those for whatever reason were unable to serve overseas immediately. Although initially the plan was for the second line to feed the first-line battalion with trained replacements, the second line would soon be required to take over the Home Defence duties when first-line battalions, now redesignated as Imperial Service battalions, were deployed overseas at short notice.

The national and local newspapers throughout Britain and Ireland began to encourage enlistment by introducing a competitive element into recruiting. They would publish weekly, sometimes daily, home nation recruiting figures, with headlines that appealed to national or civic pride. 'All honour to the lads who have put Scotland in the front. ... We must not let the sons of the Rose or Leek or Shamrock get in front of the proud Thistle.' Comparisons were made between nations and regions, and then cities and towns. 'Birmingham had already raised 8000 men, why can't Glasgow do the same? Is Glasgow to be shamed, are we still the second city of the Empire?' Soon this competitive recruiting ethos would spread to just about every social, major business and religious organisation. All would publish rolls of honour. The railways, the Paisley cotton mills, the Co-operative Society, Clydeside shipyards, even the Paisley Amateur Swimming Club got in on the action, proudly announcing that twenty-four of its members had gone to war, mostly with the Argylls and the HLI. The churches also got involved and in the case of the Roman Catholic Church individual parishes published rolls of honour as did Church-organised institutions like the Parkhead Reformatory for Catholic Boys, Tom Maley's old Slatefield Industrial School and St Aloysius' College. The industrial schools and reformatories were always fertile recruiting grounds for the military. Many of the boys were already institutionalised and found the home they never had within the regimental family. In the increasingly frenzied recruiting drive, everyone and every organisation had to be seen to be doing their bit.

The deteriorating military situation in France had a knock-on effect in Ireland, for the UVF in particular. With Carson holding back his UVF until his demand that Home Rule be shelved until after the war, many of the UVF were very uncomfortable about being prevented from enlisting by their leadership. The delay in discussing the adjournment of Home Rule back on 10 August put the pressure back on Carson. As early as mid-August, Carson was being warned that hundreds of UVF men were filtering away to join the 10th (Irish) Division or crossing to Scotland to join the military there. The news from France finally forced Carson's hand and on 28 August he offered Kitchener 36,000 men of UVF militia unconditionally.

SCOTTISH FOOTBALL

Almost inevitably, the recruitment spotlight shone on sport in general and on the game of professional football in particular. When those with an interest studied the recruitment statistics in comparison to middle-class sports, like rugby, cricket, amateur football and other amateur sports, the professional football players and their clubs appeared not to be doing 'their bit'. The professional game began to be regarded as a barrier to recruitment; it was seen as preventing thousands of fit young supporters from doing their patriotic duty and enlisting. Why were the professional players not following the examples set by the amateur players and enlisting? Were the football club directors preventing their players from enlisting? The accusations were being fired at all the professional clubs and their players throughout Britain, but in Scotland the two big Glasgow clubs attracted most of the heat. Celtic and Rangers both had massive support bases and it was felt that if some of the big name players at Parkhead or Ibrox were to enlist, many of their supporters would follow their heroes into the forces. One of the first letters to the editor referring to football supporters and enlistment appeared in the Glasgow Herald on 27 August. Under the headline 'Are We At War?', Query wrote:

> *I happened to be in Glasgow's Central Station on Saturday and couldn't help but notice the large crowd of young men waiting their turn at the booking office windows. The queue was for the Queen's Park Special and on enquiring I was informed that it was for a football match. I couldn't help but speculate what the young German and Austrian men were doing on a Saturday afternoon.*

On 31 August, under the banner headline 'Gather, Gather, Gather', the Glasgow Evening Times published a cartoon of St Mungo, patron saint of Glasgow. The figure was holding a fiery cross in one hand and a football in his other, while the background was a football stadium. The message to the SFA and Scottish League could not have been clearer. It was followed a couple of days later with another cartoon, this time of players, representing the major Glasgow football clubs. The headline was 'Footballers Fall-In'. The cartoon showed Celtic, Rangers, Queen's Park and Third Lanark players, followed by a crowd of supporters. The players were holding banners aloft; on the Celtic banner the slogan was 'J Quinn's Quick Firers', Rangers had 'J Smith's Sharpshooters' and Queen's Park 'Hampden Huzzars'. Jimmy Brownlie, the Third Lanark and Scotland goalkeeper, carried the 'Warriors' banner. The suggestion was obvious: the

Third Lanark, Queen's Park, Celtic and Rangers Banners.
(Glasgow Evening Times)

players should muster their supporters and lead them down to the recruiting offices to sign on.

At the same time, a number of letters appeared in the British and Scottish daily newspapers raging against the continuation of the game of association football itself during the current crisis. Written on 28 August, but printed in the Glasgow Herald three days later, a soldier's wife' wrote:

> *I have read an article in an English newspaper on Scotland and the War. 200,000 Scotch people attend football matches. There are 15,000 professional footballers in the United Kingdom. Such phrases ring in my Scotch ears and haunt me. Are 15,000 young, strong men to run about a field playing a game of ball while their brothers across the sea play a very different game – a game of life and death? Is that the way Scotland and England make war? Are you men, you Britons, who do this thing? I, a woman, challenge you to answer me. Are you men? Are we to wait for the five hundred thousand men who are needed? Is the Empire to wait for its sons? Happy and Proud I would be to be one of the five hundred thousand. As it is I am a soldier's daughter and a soldier's wife.*

Also on 31 August, the Glasgow Herald printed 'No Time To Play Games' and even the association football column was headlined with 'Apathetic and Unpatriotic'. The Herald reported increased gates at Scottish football games, which proved the football supporter had not yet awakened to the seriousness of the military situation. The paper highlighted the St Mirren versus Celtic game played at Paisley: 'At Paisley the crowd was a record one for a St Mirren-Celtic match.' In fact, according to the Herald's own report of the previous meeting of the teams at the end of January 1914 the gate was 16,000, while the number they reported attending this latest game was 15,000. At Ibrox Park in Glasgow, the same weekend, Rangers played Kilmarnock in front of a gate of 15,000, exactly the same gate as the corresponding game the previous season. In the Dundee Advertiser, Catholic Priest wrote under the headline 'Has The Nation Gone Mad?':

> Crowds of callous, thoughtless fools gather in their thousands to watch the awful farce of football. Has the country gone stark mad? Is the flag, under whose folds we enjoy glorious British freedom, of less importance now than a league flag or some other footballing trophy?

In England, the pressure on the FA was also increasing. The influential Lord Roberts VC and Earl Grey, the Foreign Secretary, addressed football crowds, condemning the game and calling for volunteers for the New Army. A statement issued from the Blackheath Rugby Club, a top English outfit of the period, announced that in view of the national emergency they had cancelled the remainder of their games for the season. They added that in the opinion of the club committee, all eligible able-bodied men should be offering their service to King and country and that all current rugby footballers fell into that category. Even the veritable WG Grace, the cricketing legend, added his penny's worth stating that: 'It was not a fitting time for able bodied men to play day after day with pleasure seekers looking on.' The cricketing season was by the end of August over for the year. Much of the opposition to the continuance of professional football stemmed from the snobbish middle classes, who regarded professional football as a spectacle suitable only for the proletariat and played by those who could not afford to play without being paid for their services. True blue sportsmen ignored games played for money and remained amateurs. Now the perception or concern of the middle classes was that many working-class men preferred to play and watch football rather than enlist.

Apathetic and Unpatriotic Football Supporters
(Glasgow Evening Times)

Chapter Four

SEPTEMBER

CELTIC FC

Having dropped more points at Paisley, a chastened Celtic squad boarded the train at Glasgow's Central railway station on Monday 31 August. The Bhoys were travelling to England for the replay of the Budapest Cup final or the 'World Championship' as some were unofficially calling the game, which was to be played the following night at Burnley. The bad-tempered match played back in May in the Hungarian capital had ended in a one-all draw after Burnley equalised with a sixty-fifth-minute penalty. At the final whistle, some players squared up to each other and had to be separated by officials. Normally the Parkhead faithful would have needed two or three trains to take them to Lancashire to support their idols but due to the war restrictions only the directors, Kelly, Shaughnessy, Dunbar and Colgan, travelled to Lancashire. Immediately prior to travelling to Burnley, sports reporters asked Willie Maley for his thoughts on the current pressure on football clubs and their players to contribute to the war effort:

> *I think it would be wise if this matter was taken up by all the football clubs of Scotland. Out of the six Glasgow clubs we could form a corps of 150 members who might on two or three days a week do two or three hours' drill under a competent instructor on some of the various playing pitches and so prepare themselves for any emergency which might arise. Such military training would in no way interfere with their football training, and would remove all fear of another 'Kipling' slight to our men, who I know from personal knowledge are keen to prove their desire to take their place, if needs demand it, beside their fellow-countrymen in defence of their country.*

The *Kipling*, Willie Maley was referring to, was none other than the JK Rowling of the day, Rudyard Kipling, author of *The Jungle Book, Soldiers Three* and *Kim*. He was known as the 'Poet of the Empire' and as an arch-imperialist he sympathised with the Ulster Unionists during the Home Rule debate. He was a close personal friend of Sir Edward Carson and of Cecil Rhodes, regularly spending the winter in South Africa. In February 1912, Winston Churchill and John Redmond spoke in support of Home Rule at the ground of the Belfast Celtic in Nationalist West Belfast. On the day, the politicians were cheered all the way up the Falls Road and into the stadium. In a letter to a friend, Kipling referred to the event and the stadium as 'that Kaffir reservation'. That same year he wrote the poem *Ulster 1912*, a celebration of the signing of the Ulster Covenant and a very public display of his anti-Catholicism. In the poem he describes Catholics and Catholicism as the 'evil powers of rebellion, rapine and hate'. For good measure he also threw in 'folly, sloth and spite'.

Burnley v Celtic at Turf Moor

A match between the Scottish and English cup holders would under normal circumstances have attracted a crowd in the region of 50,000, but the mill workers of Lancashire were on half-time working and some only on two days due to the loss of the German and Austro-Hungarian markets for cotton. As elsewhere in the country, thousands of local men had reported for duty with regular and Territorial Force units. The crowd of 10,000 that did turned up at Turf Moor was, under the circumstances, a respectable one. After the rough and tumble in Budapest, it was perhaps inevitable that the game would be a no quarter given or expected affair. Despite the physicality, Celtic so completely dominated a poor Burley team over the first half, the home crowd began to cheer on the Bhoys to show their appreciation. After the fracas in Budapest with Jimmy Lindsay, Peter Johnstone was targeted by the Burnley hard men for some special attention, which saw him forced to retire after taking a bad ankle knock. The injury would keep Peter out of the side for the next five league games, not returning to the side until 5 October against Raith Rovers. The second half saw Burnley redouble their effort, spurred on no doubt by the heckling of their support, but it was too little too late. The two goals, one from Patsy Gallacher and a particularly good effort by McColl in which he beat the two backs before getting off his shot, did not do the Celts justice, particularly when Burnley made the score 2–1 with a late and extremely dubious penalty. Joe Dodds played his best game yet in the hoops. A slightly subdued, but no doubt satisfied, Celtic returned to Glasgow as the Budapest Cup holders. However, the club had no trophy to show for their efforts, with the cup still resident in the city on the Danube. 'Celts Win the World Championship' was the headline but in a sign of the times *the Man in the Know* thought it more likely that the Russians or Serbians would get hold of the trophy before the Celtic would. He was not wrong!

SCOTTISH FOOTBALL

As the national recruiting frenzy grew, scores of letters were sent to newspapers. Numerous comments in the press and at public meetings by prominent national figures criticised the stance taken by professional football, and questioned its contribution to the war effort. The pressure on the Scottish football authorities to take some action had reached boiling point. The Scottish Football Association and Scottish League were seriously concerned about the matter, but were for a time uncertain how to react. Like just about everyone else, they expected a short war and initially they did nothing, awaiting the expected Government interference. The footballing authorities would have to be guided by the verdict of the civil and military authorities and whatever course was recommended, the clubs would have to follow. Independent action on the part of any one club was not felt desirable or necessary. While the Celtic were en route to Burnley, the Emergency and Finance Committee of the SFA met at Carlton Place in Glasgow. Celtic chairman, Tom White, as SFA vice-president was on the committee. They discussed the position of Scottish football in relation to the war and after some deliberation, it was decided to send a delegation to London. There they would consult with the relevant authorities to ascertain their exact position on the advisability of continuing or stopping the football season. The delegation would travel to London on 4 September and Celtic's Tom White would lead the party. A further SFA committee meeting was planned for the following Tuesday, 8 September, when the delegates' recommendations would be made to the full SFA council.

On 3 September, the Scottish League president, Thomas Hart of St Mirren, issued a statement in which he referred to the war cloud hanging over the nation at present and enjoined every club to do its utmost for recruiting members for the army currently being raised by Lord Kitchener. The League then subscribed £300 to the national relief fund inaugurated by the Prince of Wales. The Scottish League meanwhile would mark time, keeping its powder dry until it saw the outcome of the London consultations.

The same night Celtic were playing at Burnley, representatives of the six Glasgow first division clubs and the military recruitment officers for Glasgow, met at the home of Sir John Ure Primrose, former Lord Provost, staunch Unionist and chairman of Glasgow Rangers. Sir John had sat on the platform at Edward Carson's anti-Home Rule rally in Glasgow in 1913 and the policy of not playing a Catholic at Rangers is often dated from the beginning of his chairmanship in 1912.

The representatives discussed what steps could be taken under the auspices of the clubs to assist recruitment. The military authorities present wanted the clubs to back the formation of a Glasgow Footballers Battalion, manned by supporters and ideally led into the ranks by famous footballers. They stated that should enough recruits come forward they would guarantee that a battalion would be formed composed solely of footballers and supporters. The idea was for each of the six senior Glasgow teams to recruit and man a 160-strong infantry company. The Celtic company, for example, would be based around a number of the senior players, while the rest of the company would be made up of Celtic supporters. Rangers, Partick Thistle, Clyde and Third Lanark would do similarly. The amateurs of Queen's Park having already contributed very many players and members to the army were under less pressure, but agreed to fall in with the overall plan. The suggestion of a footballers' battalion was not well received by the clubs present. Instead they agreed to form a recruiting committee consisting of two representatives from each club chaired by Sir John Ure Primrose.

The committee later met in Celtic director John McKillop's Grosvenor restaurant, where they thrashed out their recruitment strategy. The clubs agreed to organise recruitment at their own grounds, the cost of which would be borne by the clubs. Every football ground would become a recruiting centre with facilities available for enrolling supporters on a match day. Recruiting leaflets would be given out, placards and posters would be put up and guest speakers would be allowed to address the crowd at half-time. A few days later, an appeal was published in the Glasgow newspapers:

> *Football's Bugle Call. Stirring Appeal By Glasgow Clubs. Glasgow's half dozen league clubs are making a whole-hearted effort to stimulate recruiting in the city. Patriotic handbills have been signed and issued by Queen's Park, Third Lanark, Rangers, Celtic, Clyde and Partick Thistle, intimating that eligible young men will be enlisted at the grounds of all six clubs. The stirring appeal should attract the youthful portion of the crowds who attend football matches to hurry to the assistance of their country in this hour of peril. MEMBERS AND FOLLOWERS OF THE FOOTBALL CLUBS OF GLASGOW, UP TILL NOW YOU HAVE LOOKED ON AT OUR GAME. WE NOW CALL ON YOU TO PLAY IT!*

One handout clearly and specifically encouraged supporters to enlist for the honour of the game:

> *We have shown you how, for the honour of our clubs and as clean sportsmen, we play to win. Obeying our Captain's orders; Fit in Body; Steady of Foot; Keeping our Heads when surrounded on all sides; Working in comradeship as one man, with a single, constant, determined, and sustained effort to overcome the resistance of our opponents and capture their goal with a clean, hard shot. We CONFIDENTLY call on you to bring into practice these lessons in the Great Contest of the Nations now raging, in which you are called to join in DEFENCE OF YOUR COUNTRY, YOUR MANHOOD AND YOUR FREEDOM. The Battle of Waterloo was said by the Duke of Wellington to have been won on the playing fields of Eton College. WHY SHOULD NOT HISTORY RELATE HOW THIS GREAT WAR WAS WON ON THE FOOTBALL FIELDS OF SCOTLAND?*

It would appear that few of the clubs were convinced that recruiting at football grounds was the answer, certainly the Celtic hierarchy were not convinced, but all the clubs recognised that the game had to be seen to be doing 'their bit' to encourage recruiting.

Under Britain's current system of voluntary recruitment, the decision whether or not to enlist was still a matter of principle, idealism and personal morale. The vast majority of the professional players, in both Scotland and England, were far from convinced about joining the army. Why risk their very lucrative but short careers in a war that may be over even before they could be fully trained as soldiers. In addition, all professional footballers were under legal contracts with their clubs, with everything that that entailed, until the end of the football season. As far as the Celtic players were concerned, Celtic Football Club was their employer and they, like most other professionals, were happy enough to follow the instructions and advice of their club and its solicitors. A few senior Scottish and English players did enlist early: Willie McAndrew, the captain of Clyde FC, enlisted in early September, as did John Fulton of Morton. Tom Maley's Bradford Park Avenue lost Donald Bell, one of the first top-class professional English footballers to answer the call. Several clubs lost players or staff who, having reserve commitments, were recalled to the colours. By the beginning of September, the Scottish football season was already well under way and with everyone expecting it to be a short war, few people within the game could see the point in senior professional players enlisting or the game being curtailed in any way. It was, after all, a business enterprise. There was no serious reason at this point why shareholders of clubs should be suddenly and needlessly deprived of their income any more than any other money-making concern in the country.

THE HOME FRONT

Elsewhere, recruiting efforts was going very well indeed. In the week since Lord Kitchener's second appeal on 28 August, over 174, 900 had enlisted nationwide, including 8500 young men in Glasgow. The highest single day's total over the week was recorded on 3 September when 33,200 men joined the army. On that day, 1014 enlisted in Glasgow, but only 114 in Dublin. In Paisley, Greenock, Coatbridge and Wishaw, long queues of men stood for hours on end outside recruiting offices. With the administration problems at the recruiting offices largely sorted, the increased numbers flowing through the enlistment process saw military resources again buckle. This time the various regimental depots were unable to keep up with the numbers arriving at the gates. The Glasgow recruiters, unable to pass the recruits onto the depots, had the enlisted men first accommodated in various public halls around the city including St Andrew's Halls at Charing Cross. When the halls filled up, the men were sent home having been told to report to their allocated regimental depot a few days later. At the bursting depots, no sooner had one batch of recruits been administered and dispatched, usually by train, to their training battalions, than the depot filled up again with more recruits. The chaotic scenes at recruiting offices and depots in Glasgow were repeated throughout the country.

The rush of recruits put military logistics and administration under enormous strain and what followed was absolute chaos, such as only politicians can create. In response to a very direct appeal within a mood of patriotic fervour and hysteria, scores of thousands of volunteers of all ages, including those underage and overage, from all occupations and all social classes, had answered Kitchener's second call and descended on the totally unprepared military. The entire recruiting system was a shambles. Once enlisted, hundreds of recruits were lined up at assembly points and allocated to battalions. If a recruit did not like the sound of the unit, he simply skipped into the next group of recruits and repeated the move until he was allocated to a battalion he did want to serve with. As the recruits were dispatched by the trainload to their training camps, mostly around Aldershot and Salisbury Plain, there was often no one in charge and no list of names. There were even cases of men just jumping on the trains without going through the enlistment process at all. The mayhem was such that an entire trainload of volunteers could arrive at a country railway station in the middle of nowhere and out would pour a thousand men of every class. They would be in every conceivable form of dress, including businessmen in city suits and bowler hats or trilbies, working men in dungarees and cloth caps, toffs in their straw hats, blazers and flannels, men in post office or railway uniforms, men in old army redcoats, and men without jackets wearing only shirts and braces. Some men obviously were far too old, others were obviously far too young, while others were unfit for active service. In very many cases, a blind eye was turned. So many underage boys did manage to enlist that questions on the matter were later asked in parliament. Hundreds of mothers up and down the country besieged their MPs constituency offices wanting their sons back. Some boys actually made it into action with the youngest recipient of the Victoria Cross a sixteen year old. Although there is now some dispute over his age, officially the youngest known British boy soldier to be killed in action was Private John Condon of Waterford. He was serving with the Royal Irish Regiment and was killed in May 1915, aged 14.

On arrival at their training camps, there were no uniforms, no weapons, no accommodation, insufficient training facilities and very few instructors. There were no commanders of any description and appeals were made for non-commissioned officers of any vintage to come forward immediately to help in the interim. There were cases of a thousand men being commanded by a lance corporal who was a veteran of the Zulu War. Men with any leadership experience, however spurious, were promoted on the spot. In some cases, the tall smart-looking chap in the blue suit and trilby would be made a sergeant and told to look after the remainder.

The rush to enlist was such that industries vital for the coming war effort were stripped of key workers. Mines, shipyards and engineering factories saw workers walk off the job with little or no notice to join in the great crusade. So many postmen had rejoined their units or reported to their TF drill halls that, the Post Office warned that postal services could be disrupted. The notion that it would be 'all over by Christmas' was prevalent and added to the urgency with which men, terrified to miss the great adventure, clambered to enlist. The bosses caught up in the patriotic maelstrom were forced to bite the bullet and support the enthusiastic volunteers. In the first heady six weeks of the war, it was regarded as unpatriotic to suggest anything that might dampen the martial ardour. Therefore, no one in authority was prepared to state that instead of volunteering for the services, some men would be contributing as much to the cause by staying at their jobs, producing the food, the guns, the shells and the ships. Coal was vital to the war effort and digging it out of the ground was just as important as firing a rifle, but thousands of miners like Celtic old Bhoy Tom McAteer, who hated being underground, took the opportunity to escape and simply walked out of the pits and into the military.

The inability of the War Office to cope with the flood of volunteers pouring into the military over the month of September saw civilians play an increasingly important role in raising and initially maintaining the locally raised units of the New Armies. A striking feature of their involvement was the formation of the pals battalions. City councils, local dignitaries, commercial organisations and civilian committees raised these units locally. The men who composed these battalions were all from the same district, shared an occupation or were from a common social background. Although largely an English phenomenon, the overall parochial nature of Scottish recruitment saw many locally raised units with the same parochial characteristics.

While the vast majority of men stepping forward to enlist were being earmarked for Kitchener's army, thousands of men were also joining the Regular Army and their local TF units. On 9 September, TF recruiters led by Sergeant Major George Cavan of the Highland Light Infantry arrived in the village of Carluke. Cavan was to die from wounds on 13 April 1918. After the recruiting rally, a number of local men stepped forward to enlist. Among them were William Angus and James Martin. The Martin family were well known in the town where Hugh Martin was an engineer employing a number of locals in his millwright workshop. James Martin was a thirty-three-year-old unmarried solicitor, who lived at home with his parents.

William Angus was born in February 1888 at Armadale, near Linlithgow, where his father George Angus was employed as a coal miner. A native of Carluke in Lanarkshire, George Angus moved his young family back to his home town soon after William's birth. The Angus family were Roman Catholics and William Angus was educated alongside his lifelong friend and Celtic legend, Joe Dodds, in the local Catholic school. In 1902 he left school and aged fourteen joined his father in the local pits. Like most boys of the period, Willie Angus was mad keen on football and was good enough to get a place in his local Carluke Rovers FC. In October 1910, Willie Angus got the chance of a lifetime when he was offered a trial for the Celtic. A lifelong supporter of the club, not only was it an opportunity to get out of the pits, but he would be living the dream, playing for the team he loved. Such was his pride in the Celtic, after he signed the forms he was photographed professionally while wearing the famous green and white hoops. His friend Joe Dodds had signed for the Glasgow giants in 1908, but had only cemented his place in the team in season 1910/11. Joe Dodds persuaded Willie to have a go at professional football, and while it is unknown how much influence Joe Dodds had in getting his mate a trial at the Celtic, an immensely proud Willie Angus would spend two seasons on the Celtic's books.

Willie Angus
(Courtesy of the Angus family)

In fact, Willie only played in a couple of trial or benefit games for the Celtic and failed to break into the first team. As a halfback, he was up against some stiff competition in 'Sunny' Jim Young and Peter Johnstone, both of whom were idolised at Parkhead and had the positions tied up. At this time, the Celtic had no reserve team as such, and players like Willie Angus were farmed out on loan to other clubs. In Willie's case, he, along with Willie McStay, went to the Vale of Leven in January 1912 in a vain attempt to save the Vale from demotion into a lower division. At the beginning of May 1912, Willie turned out for the Celts against a Dumbartonshire XI. The charity game was played for the benefit of St Stephen's RC school, Dalmuir. Willie was playing alongside Mulrooney, McGregor, McStay, Dodds, McMenemy and Nicol, Gallacher, Quinn, Gibson and Brown. The game ended in a 3–0 victory for the Celts and Father Brotherhood was delighted with the £100 raised. The game was also Willie's last chance to impress Willie Maley, unfortunately he failed to take it. At the end of season 1911/12, as was usual, Celtic FC conducted a cull of players it had decided would not make the grade. Among those released was Willie Angus, much to the disappointment of his pal Joe Dodds. Willie Maley thought young Angus was talented enough but perhaps just too quiet to make it in the rough and tumble of top-flight professional football. No other senior club came in to sign him and a bitterly disappointed Willie Angus returned to his old stamping ground, where he went back down the pits. He continued to play football as captain of junior side Wishaw Thistle. *The Man in the Know* was surer of Willie's abilities and at the time commented: 'No-one seems keen to pick up Angus the Carluke lad. He could give point to some already signed.'

Both Carluke men volunteered to join their local unit, the 8th (Lanark) Bn Highland Light Infantry TF, headquartered at Lanark. It was there that the latest batch of recruits were dispatched to begin the administrative process of enlisting. On arrival at the headquarters, Willie filled in the requisite forms and went through the medical examination. The doctor described him as twenty-five years of age, 5ft 6in tall with a 36in chest boasting an impressive 4in expansion. His physical development and vision were both described as *good* and he was regarded as being fit for military service. When at Celtic he was described as having an iron physique, and as a little swarthy determined man, all bone and muscle with a quiet manner. So quiet in fact while at Celtic, he had hardly a word to say. It was his quiet demeanour, rather than the lack of any skill, that failed to impress Willie Maley. After successfully navigating the enlistment process during which he took the oath and agreed to serve for four years, Willie Angus and his batch of new recruits were dispatched to the battalion then based at Dunoon on the Argyllshire coast to begin their basic training. Shortly after their arrival, middle-class James Martin applied for a commission and left to begin his officer training course.

While based at Dunoon, the 8th Bn HLI were engaged in coastal defence duties while at the same time training for war. However, the battalion was constantly plundered for trained men as other TF battalions that had been chosen for Imperial Service required additional men to make up their numbers prior to being posted overseas. One such battalion was the 8th Bn Royal Scots TF. The battalion recruited mainly in East Lothian and was headquartered at Haddington. After being reinforced by a company from the 6th Bn Royal Scots and another from 8th Bn HLI, including newly commissioned Second Lieutenant James Martin, they had the distinction of being the first Scottish Territorial Force battalion to be sent on active service, arriving in France on 5 November 1914. In early December 1914, two companies of 8th HLI comprising over 160 men were attached to the 7th Bn Royal Scots then training at Portobello near Edinburgh. Included among the HLI men was the brother of Celtic's Joe Dodds, Private Jimmy Dodds, a long-term member of the battalion.

On 5 September, newspaper headlines announced the loss of the cruiser HMS *Pathfinder* off the Firth of Forth with the loss of 259 lives; only eighteen of the crew survived. The Glasgow Catholic Observer noted that many of the men lost on the *Pathfinder* were Irish. Despite an Admiralty attempt at press censorship and the release of disinformation, eyewitness accounts undermined its efforts. The cruiser was attacked by a German submarine, U21, acting on information supplied by a German spy Karl Hans Lody. The agent, in the guise of an American citizen, was living and operating from Edinburgh's swanky North British Hotel and bicycling back and forth to the naval base at Rosyth. HMS *Pathfinder* has the dubious distinction of being the first ship sunk by a torpedo, the first combat victory of a modern submarine. The Glasgow Irish newspaper had begun to include a column dedicated to looking at the war from a specifically Irish or Glasgow Irish perspective. Initially titled 'War Notes for Catholics', the articles would continue throughout the war and highlighted the actions of brave Irish and Scottish regiments. A typical example was a story of the fighting Irish 'Killed to the Last Man':

> *I saw a handful of Irishmen throw themselves in front of a regiment of cavalry trying to cut off a battery of artillery. Not one of the poor lads got away alive, but they made the German devils pay in kind, and anyhow the Artillery got away. ... Every man of us made a vow to avenge the fallen Irishmen. Later, they were finely avenged by their own comrades, who lay in wait for the German cavalry. The Irish lads went at them with the*

bayonet when they least expected it. ... Some of them howled for mercy,
but I don't think they got it. ... In war mercy is only for the merciful.—

Private A M'Gillivray

As would be expected given the politics of their owner, Charles Diamond, the Glasgow Catholic Observer and the Glasgow Star both actively supported the British war effort throughout the conflict. The newspapers highlighted the Glasgow Irish community's contribution to the war effort, relief work and recruitment, Catholic heroics and medal awards, atrocities against Roman Catholics and the service of Roman Catholic chaplains attached to army or naval units, all stories designed to encourage continued Catholic participation. As the casualties mounted the newspapers printed photos, articles or short obituaries of the Glasgow Irish soldiers killed or wounded.

It was also reported that week in the Scottish Referee newspaper that the son of Celtic legend Tom Maley was with the colours. Joseph Maley, or Josie as he was known to his family and friends, was a useful centre half, who had played football for Mossend Hibs and Kirkintilloch Rob-Roy. His older brother, Tom Maley, had recently finished an engineering apprenticeship and was a reservist having joined the Royal Naval Reserve in 1913. He was expecting recall to the service as a naval artificer.

Meanwhile, the worthies of the Free Presbyterian Church wrote to the Glasgow Herald to raise their conscientious and decided protest against the practice of printing news and circulating newspapers on the Lord's Day. The newspapers were even sending newsboys to the doors of the churches at the end of divine services to advance sales. They felt any news, good or bad, would keep until Monday.

THE GLESGA PALS

In response to the Prime Minister's appeal made at the end of August, the Glasgow Corporation passed a resolution on 3 September that the city should raise two civic infantry battalions. At the same time, the Glasgow Chamber of Commerce also raised an infantry battalion alongside the 1st and 2nd City Bns. Although raised, equipped and maintained by the Chamber of Commerce, the battalion was initially known as the 3rd Glasgow Bn. The Glasgow Corporation would raise yet another battalion, the 4th Glasgow City Bn in March 1915. With the army training system at breaking point, completely overwhelmed by the sheer volume of new recruits, the cities and organisations throughout Great Britain raising the new battalions would be required to maintain their units from their own funds. That meant for the Glasgow city battalions, recruiting, feeding, clothing, equipping, accommodating and training each battalion of 1250 men until such time as the War Office was able to 'adopt' the battalion and bring it officially onto the war establishment. The cost of maintaining the three Glasgow civic battalions was met from the city's Common Good Fund. Although the first three city battalions were raised at the same time and under the same circumstances, each of the four battalions would reflect to some degree the social and religious differences present in Glaswegian society at the time.

It is difficult to determine with any certainty the exact numbers of Glasgow Irish volunteering for Kitchener's new service battalions in comparison to their Scottish fellows. In the servicemen's personal records that survived the London Blitz of 1940, the men's British nationalities are not recorded, neither in many cases are their religious affiliations. Indeed, the basic problem of defining a recruit's 'Irishness' is impossible to overcome: was he Irish by birth, by descent or was he a Glaswegian who simply decided to serve in an Irish regiment? However, the raising of the Glasgow civic battalions presents some interesting insights into the response of the Glasgow Irish to the developing emergency. The Glasgow Irish who volunteered to serve in the service battalions raised by the City Corporation answered the call to arms, not of the British or English, or Irish for that matter, but of their home city. Some reasonably accurate indication of their numbers can be gleaned from the recruitment records of the most socially representative battalion of the three raised and maintained by the city, the 1st Glasgow City Bn, later the 15th (Service) Bn Highland Light Infantry (1st Glasgow).

This battalion was raised exclusively, and in the space of twenty-four hours, from the employees of Glasgow Corporation Tramways. Prior to leaving the office at the end of the day, James Dalrymple, the general manager of the Tramways phoned around all the tramcar depots and asked if any of the men would be interested in joining a battalion made up entirely of men from the 'caurs'. On returning to his office the next morning, some sixteen hours later, there was a list on his desk with the names of 1100 volunteers, mainly from the motormen, conductors and permanent way men willing to enlist. Considering this figure amounted to 32 per cent of the traffic staff (3454) and just under 21 per cent of the Tramways entire staff (5331), it was a very significant contribution from the Tramways. In addition, some 500 Tramways staff had already been recalled as reservists a month earlier. The 1st Glasgow City Bn was probably the fastest recruited battalion in the history of the British Army. Indeed it was said at the time that the only reason it took as long as it did was because of the laborious military recruiting process as the men were sworn in at the Coplawhill tram depot.

Glasgow Corporation Tramways was staffed by a reasonable mix of skilled, semi-skilled and unskilled workers and offers a fair cross section of the 'working class' Glaswegians of the period. On average, a motorman-conductor with three years on the job could expect to be earning thirty shillings per week. It was a serious drop in wages to give up thirty bob for the seven shillings per week plus allowances of a private soldier. According to an original nominal roll of 15 September 1914, Roman Catholics made up 15.25 per cent of the original Tramways volunteers. Some eight months later, when the battalion had moved to England to complete the second phase of its training, a Roman Catholic soldier wrote to the Glasgow Observer complaining that the 200 Roman Catholics in the battalion could not get to divine service. Although 200 may be a rough estimate on his part, it still conservatively takes the percentage of Roman Catholics in the battalion to around 19 per cent. The increase in Roman Catholics over the intervening eight months from the original figure could be explained by the fallout rate of the original Tramways volunteers during their military training, which could be as high as 30 per cent. After the original 1100 volunteers, the battalion recruited outwith the Tramways, particularly for its 250-strong depot company of battle casualty reserves. As would be expected, there were initially no Roman Catholic officers commissioned into the battalion. It is interesting to note that a Glasgow Irish Tramways employee obviously took as little time, or gave as much consideration to, enlisting as his Protestant colleagues.

The other civic battalion, 2nd Glasgow, would later be designated the 16th (Service) Bn Highland Light Infantry. It attracted very many men who were either current or former members of the Protestant church led organisation, the Boy's Brigade. The Boy's Brigade was so closely associated with the 2nd Glasgow Bn it was later known by its subtitle the 'Boy's Brigade' battalion. Unsurprisingly, since it was so closely associated with the Boy's Brigade, it originally attracted only 8 per cent Roman Catholics recruits. The Chamber of Commerce battalion, 3rd Glasgow, which would soon be retitled as the 17th (Service) Bn Highland Light Infantry, drew a large percentage of its recruits from the business classes, students from the technical college and former pupils of the middle-class private schools of the city. Unfortunately, no detailed records of the Chamber of Commerce battalion's original muster rolls survive; however, given that the battalion attracted predominately the middle classes, it would be safe to assume that there were far fewer Glasgow Irish in the battalion than in the Tramways battalion. One middle-class Glasgow Irishman is known to have enlisted into the battalion; James Delargey Lavelle was the son of Baillie Lavelle of Coatbridge. Educated at the Jesuit-run Stonyhurst College, he was a civil engineer by profession. After three months serving in the ranks as No 16082 Private James Lavelle, he was granted a commission in the 12th (Service) Bn HLI, part of the 15th (Scottish) Division then training in the south of England. In April 1915, the Celtic starlet and future Scotland internationalist, Michael Gilhooly, also enlisted in the Chamber of Commerce battalion.

In March 1915, Glasgow Corporation would raise a third civic battalion, the 4th Glasgow, later the 18th (Service) Bn HLI. This would be a 'bantam' battalion manned by men of under normal regulation height for Regular Army service. Again, there are no relevant muster rolls available for the battalion, but in his annual club report of 1 June 1915, Willie Maley mentioned the battalion. He proudly stated that Celtic director John Shaughnessy had been appointed Colonel of the 18th (Service) Bn HLI and out of its full complement of 1600 men, fully 500 were Roman Catholics. Even allowing for some slight exaggeration on Maley's part, it suggests the percentage of Roman Catholics in the battalion at around 30 per cent was much higher than that serving with the other city battalions. Around the same time it was widely reported that over 300 Roman Catholics soldiers serving with the 18th HLI and training at Girvan, filled a local church while attending mass. There is some very credible evidence in the form of a personal letter written by the Lord Provost of Glasgow to suggest that Colonel John Shaughnessy used his personal influence to encourage the Glasgow Irish to join his battalion. This may be an example of a football personality using his position, in this case a director at Celtic FC, to influence club supporters to enlist.

The two civic battalions and the Chamber of Commerce battalion would later be designated the 15th Bn, 16th Bn and 17th Bn of the HLI. The city and its environs had already contributed thousands of volunteers to man three service battalions for Kitchener's Army. The 10th Bn and 11th (Service) Bn HLI were part of the K1 Army and were assigned to the 9th (Scottish) Division. The 12th (Service) Bn HLI was part of the K2 Army and was assigned to the 15th (Scottish) Division. The city would also raise the 13th Bn that was originally a part of the K4 Army, but was later transferred to a training reserve roll. The 14th (Service) Bn HLI was raised after the civic and Chamber of Commerce battalions, but was taken onto War Office strength before the civic battalions so was numbered before them.

In Edinburgh, after a confused start, the city council finally got its recruiting act together. Edinburgh had already provided enough recruits for three Kitchener battalions (11th, 12th and 13th Bns Royal Scots) when the Lord Provost announced that the city would raise its own City of Edinburgh battalion. As in most things, Edinburgh took a slightly different class-conscious approach to recruiting for the city battalion. The Provost issued an appeal for a thousand young men from the business and professional classes, naming solicitors, stockbrokers and advocates as his first choice, but university students and time-served superior craftsmen would also be considered. Labourers need not apply. Needless to say he had some difficulty recruiting sufficient numbers, but the battalion soon to be the 15th (Service) Bn Royal Scots (1st Edinburgh), was eventually brought up to strength when 450 men from a failed attempt to raise a Manchester Scottish battalion arrived en masse in Edinburgh to make up the numbers.

Catholic parishes were taking note of the Catholic men going off to war. Tiny Cardonald Parish recorded that seven members of its League of the Cross had immediately gone to serve. In Hamilton, it was noted that nearly every man in the district had joined the colours. Coatbridge stated that a large number of Catholic soldiers had left the town to join the colours of various regiments, notably the Dublin Fusiliers, the Royal Irish Fusiliers and the Inniskilling Fusiliers. From Govan, a large number of reservists for both the army and navy left St Anthony's for the scene of action. Cambuslang Parish stated, in addition to reservists and TF soldiers, three members of the Irish National Foresters were now serving with the colours, Brothers Millsop, Daniel Mitchell and Harry Dorman. In Glasgow, St Aloysius, Garnethill announced it had thirty-six men serving with the colours while St Joseph's, Woodside posted a long list of parishioners on active service at the church door. According to official, but unreliable, United Irish League of Great Britain figures, Irish Catholics made up 16.4 per cent of Scotland's recruiting total of 82,957 for the first three months of the war.

CELTIC FC

It was a weakened Celtic side that played Morton at Parkhead on 5 September. Peter Johnstone was unavailable and still trying to shake off the injury he picked up at Burnley. McMenemy dropped back to midfield as cover. Tom McGregor got his second League start for Alex McNair and Dublin-born 'Handsome' Billy Crone was brought into the forward line. Billy Crone was another example of a very powerful reserve player who could step into the breach at a moment's notice without causing a very marked drop in quality. Brought to Parkhead from Belfast Celtic in 1913, Billy was an Irish League internationalist and was the standby for McMenemy and Gallacher. On the day, Morton played with just two forwards and shocked the stadium when it went two goals up within half an hour. The first came after a high ball was flung into the box to be nodded on towards goal by Buchanan. McGregor on the post made a mess of the clearance and the ball went loose in the box. Shaw and Stanley Seymour both charged onto the ball, with Charlie Shaw managing to block Seymour's shot. The deflected ball fell to Stevenson, who, despite facing another diving attempt at a block by Shaw, slotted the ball home. The second was a goal scored from a header by Gourley guided in from a pinpoint cross, fired over by Englishman Seymour. The goal was scored while Celtic was down to ten men, McMaster off receiving treatment. Both goals came despite Morton seldom having the ball and after Celtic had a McColl goal disallowed for offside. A stunned Celtic resumed its attacks and Billy Crone had a golden opportunity to get one back but shot lamely past the post. However, a few minutes later he made up for the miss and got Celtic back into the game with a solo effort in which he created the chance and scored with a low shot. Just before half-time Billy Crone again stepped into the breach, latching onto a pass from McAtee to score his own and Celtic's second goal. The sides went in at half-time with two goals each and Celtic the more relieved of the two teams. Within seven minutes of the restart McAtee got his first and Celtic's third with one of his unstoppable shots. Celtic taking the lead seemed to take the heart out of Morton and the Bhoys were never thereafter in any danger of losing the game. Midway through the second half and shortly after McAtee scored his second goal, McMaster picked up an injury and was forced to go off permanently. Browning dropped back to replace him leaving Crone on his own. Andy McAtee produced another two of his thunderbolts in the closing stages of the game, taking his total to four. It was doubtful if Bradford in the Morton goal saw the ball on at least two of the occasions he was beaten by McAtee. However, the best goal of the game was quite correctly chalked off as being offside, the whistle having gone before McColl put the ball in the net in a manner not dissimilar to Henrik Larsson's sublime chip against Rangers almost ninety years later. With the game won, near the end McColl followed McMaster into the pavilion nursing an injury and the Celtic finished with nine men.

An appreciative but small crowd of 14,000 watched the impressive Celtic comeback. In a reflection of the ongoing national emergency, the corresponding game played on 14 February 1914 had attracted over 21,000 spectators. After producing four unstoppable shots each resulting in a goal, the following ditty about McAtee appeared in a Glasgow newspaper:

> *The Kaiser, they say, only once saw him play. And remarked, it is said,*
> *'Dearie me!' My German artillery's just fit for the pillory. They can't shoot*
> *like young McAtee.*

Elsewhere in the League, Hearts beat Kilmarnock 2–0, their fourth win in a row, which took the Edinburgh side to the top of the table. Rangers beat Falkirk 3–1 for their fourth win, and also on eight points, they were in second place to Hearts on goal difference. Clyde were third on six points, followed by Ayr United above Celtic, both on five points.

The night before the Morton game, Willie Maley had sat down at his desk in his home in Hyndland Avenue. He wrote a letter, under the heading 'Too Old at Forty', and addressed it to the editor of the Glasgow Herald. Willie had decided, as one completely familiar with the military, to enter into the recruiting debate. In his open letter he expressed his views on the treatment of Army veterans, married men enlisting and the upper age limit for recruits:

TOO OLD AT FORTY.

CELTIC MANAGER PROTESTS AGAINST AGE LIMIT.

The following letter appears in the "Glasgow Herald":—

MAINTENANCE AND THE AGE LIMIT

17 Hyndland Avenue, Glasgow,
September 4.

Celtic Manager's Age Bar Protest

Sir, – As the son of a soldier (who fought through the Crimean War), but who through the age limit is debarred from enlistment, I would like to offer my views on a point which has come specially to my notice. Much criticism is being levelled at married men, eligible by age, etc., for enlistment, who have not yet offered their services. Their diffidence in this respect deserved grave consideration.

A married man, earning a weekly wage only sufficient to keep the house from week to week, must ere he decide to let his patriotism carry him into the ranks, consider those he leaves behind him. Those of us whose memories are not so short as the average citizen carried away at present by the war fever, cannot forget the Crimean heroes who up to a few years ago were allowed to die in workhouses, and this in spite of the large sums still undisbursed lying at the credit of the Patriotic Fund raised at the time of that great war. If a married man goes out now it really is a paltry pittance his wife and family have to live on, and if he dies for his country or is permanently injured their position is very much worse. The Prince of Wales's Fund now being raised will not go very far to aid the cases I refer to, and after the war the married man's position will be doubly worse. Why does not this great government of ours, with the great wealth of the country at its back, boldly declare that all dependants of soldiers killed in the war will be properly and generously provided for? Surely when the country's very existence is at stake it would not be a big price to pay for the blood of thousands of men whose love for their families is keeping them back from what they feel is their duty? The War Fund will be administered as all other funds have been administered, and suffering will be rife. I hope my few words will lead to others venting what is a grievance with many good fellows anxious to show their love of country as honestly as their bachelor pals.

Another point, which personally affects myself, is this age limit. I, with many others I am certain feel that the proper test of a man's fitness for his country's call is his own individual fitness, and that the mere question of age should not debar him. How many of our leading officers are well over 60, and is a man of clean life not as fit as anyone between 40 and 50? Again, if he is not thought fit to go abroad and take his place in the fighting line, surely he is quite fit for home defence, where he could than release the younger men for the fighting and other arduous work abroad? I see mere boys being taken into the Territorials at present, and I cannot see how that class can be compared to say, the golfing men of 40 or 50 for fitness or handiness at a time like this.

W. Maley

It is obvious from the tone and content of the letter that Willie Maley fully recognised the extent of the emergency confronting the nation at the beginning of September 1914. As a patriotic British citizen he was himself prepared to enlist, but at forty-four years of age was too old for active service. It is obvious too that he fully understood the complexities of the military system and the financial and moral position of most married men regarding enlistment. His long and close association with the army ensured that he had a great deal of sympathy for veterans in general, but particularly for his father's old Crimean War comrades, who had been forgotten by an ungrateful nation and left to die in workhouses. Time and circumstances would prove Willie correct, and in time the government would address all the points he raised in his letter.

The Morton game was the first occasion on which the Celtic's military recruiting office, set up in the pavilion, was open for business. After recruiting leaflets were handed out before the game and at half-time, twenty-four young supporters came forward to volunteer for service after the game. At the other grounds, the military recruiters expressed themselves as equally well pleased with the numbers. The scheme apparently worked better at Parkhead than at the other grounds. Although they went along with the recruitment scheme, the Celtic directors appear to have been less than convinced. *The Man in the Know* also had an opinion:

> When a young fellow goes to a match on a Saturday afternoon he is at peace with the world, earning a decent wage and assured of fairly regular employment. Only in the event of him being turned away from his job or having his head turned by seeing some of his chums taking the shilling will he do likewise. Enlisting is contagious and infectious. Young fellows from offices and workshops are joining in batches. There is likely little will come of this football ground recruiting. The only fellows likely to fall in are those who are disgusted at their club's non-success. Instead of going home and beating their wives because their team lost, they will now set about beating the Germans for spite.

THE HOME FRONT

Saturday 5 September was Union Jack Day in Glasgow, organised in aid of the Soldiers and Sailor Families Association and the Territorial Force Association. Little paper flags fixed to a brass pin were sold around the streets and this was a popular method of raising funds for all manner of good causes. Begun by a woman, the flag days were tailor-made for women and children, allowing them to use their charms to coax money for the various causes. The first months of the war were characterised by the mobilisation of thousands of men who had volunteered for service in the armed forces. Often overlooked is the spontaneous and officially unsupported mobilisation of hundreds of thousands of woman all over the country. The suffragette leader Mrs Pankhurst immediately called off the woman's suffrage campaign when Britain declared war. Members of the women's suffrage societies, which included many Glasgow Irishwomen, would see voluntary war service as an opportunity to prove themselves to their menfolk. The women, members of thousands of diverse organisations, volunteered to support the servicemen and their families, both at home and abroad. The mobilisation of the women of Britain benefited from a pre-war membership boom in women's social, service and political organisations. The Glasgow Irish community with numerous well-established women's organisations, often Church-led, contributed in proportion. In Glasgow, thousands of young Catholic girls and young women belonged to numerous guilds and clubs, which imbued them with civic consciousness and a commitment to their community, albeit originally to their own Glasgow Irish community. The massively popular Ancient Order of Hibernians boasted its own very active and well-organised women's branch. For all these women, the step to war service was relatively easy. Women and their organisations took flag days to their heart.

As in most areas of social welfare, the Glasgow Irish had, of course, set up their own relief committees, shadowing the wider Glasgow committees. Throughout the war, all the various Glasgow Irish relief and social organisations would work very closely with both their Glasgow and national counterparts. This cooperation is a very good example of the war encouraging interaction between the Glasgow Irish and the wider Scottish community. In the event the Union Jack Flag Day raised an impressive £3800 for their cause.

Across the length and breadth of the country, over the first two weeks of September, recruiting continued apace. Posters pleading, challenging, threatening or shaming young single men into enlisting were everywhere. There was simply no escaping the war or the pressure to enlist. Everyone was talking about it and the newspapers were full of it, just page after page after page of war news. Special editions and magazines with coloured maps and portraits of the main personalities were published. Even in the cinemas and music halls everything took on a war flavour. The most popular song of the time was the marching hymn 'Tipperary'. In Glasgow, Coatbridge, Clydebank and elsewhere the trams were festooned with recruiting posters. Both local and national newspapers published recruiting figures daily, highlighting the scenes at recruiting offices in the major towns and parishes and reporting on how the various local communities and businesses were supporting the war effort. Civic pride and community spirit now had cities and towns competing with each other to see which could attract the greatest number of new recruits. Although most of the pressure to enlist was directed at young unmarried men, who it was felt should fill the ranks before married men with family commitments and responsibilities, married men were also coming under increasing pressure to enlist as the recruiting furore intensified.

On 3 September, the Glasgow Herald had announced that the Singer Manufacturing Company at Clydebank had found it necessary, on account of the European crisis, to dispense with the services of a large number of their employees, and also to further reduce the working week of others to just one day. It is understood that the dismissal of a large number of the young men had had a marked effect on recruiting in the burgh.

On 9 September, the Prime Minister received authority from parliament to increase the army by another five hundred thousand men. It was announced at the same time that all but 20,000 of the first half million recruits had been reached. Between 4 August and 12 September, 478,893 men had joined the Army, with an incredible 301,971 having enlisted in the two weeks after 30 August. The Glasgow Herald proudly announced that over 22,000 men from Glasgow had enlisted since the start of the war. On one single day, the Glasgow recruiting offices saw 1500 men pass through their doors. The newspapers also reported on how the local battalions and their training were progressing. On 10 September, the Glasgow Herald turned the spotlight on Paisley, Coatbridge, Clydebank and Dumbarton, all areas with large Glasgow Irish communities. In Paisley it was reported:

> *A further batch of fifty recruits left the town yesterday to join their various units. There is no falling off of enthusiasm in the men who are entering the ranks. From the works of Bow, McLachan and Co no fewer than 170 men have left to join the army or navy. Fifty-two men have left the service of the Paisley tramways company for service in the army. It is stated by the manager of the tramways company that nearly all the company's young men who are eligible for service with the colours have joined the army. About 1300 men altogether have been enrolled in Paisley.*

The surge in recruitment was not all down to patriotism. Since the start of the war, Scottish industry had contracted by a very significant 9 per cent, creating a ready pool of unemployed potential recruits.

That same night the Glasgow Stock Exchange Company of 'Lochiel's' 5th (Service) Bn Cameron Highlanders left Glasgow's Central Station for its training camp at Aldershot. The company was composed of 150 young men recruited from Glasgow's law apprentices and youths engaged in the city's accounting and architecture offices. Lochiel's service battalion had been assigned to the newly created 9th (Scottish) Division. Among the Cameron Highlanders leaving Glasgow that night was Edwin Garvie of Queen's Park FC. Amateur sportsmen, including football players, led by the middle-class gentlemen of Queen's Park FC were in the volunteering vanguard. Lance Corporal Edwin Garvie was among the first footballers to sign up for service; he was destined to die in a German POW camp from wounds received at the Battle of Loos in October 1915. Also en route to Aldershot with Lochiel's Highlanders was former Celt, John Young. The twenty-seven year old had gone back to labouring after football and now left his wife Maggie and five-year-old daughter May in their home in the Calton while he went off to war.

By the middle of September, so many men had enlisted, the difficulties of housing, feeding and clothing such numbers saw the military recruiting system reach breaking point. The military authorities were again forced to put the brake on recruiting and on 11 September upped the physique standards for recruits, including raising the minimum height for entry to 5ft 6in. The new physical requirements had the desired effect and immediately reduced the enlistment flow; however, a few recruiters worried about how they would reignite enthusiasm. On the British mainland, the month of September would prove to be the peak month for recruitment over the entire war, with a total of 462,900 men enlisting. All over the country, men had flocked to the recruiting offices, but the impressive figures were only possible thanks to the efforts of enthusiastic civilians. The locally raised battalions would come to form a very substantial part (38 per cent) of Kitchener's army. This amounted to 215 of the 557 service battalions raised prior to the introduction of national conscription in 1916, raised outwith the normal channels.

At the same time, the Royal Navy was also having some difficulty with excess numbers. So many men had come forward to serve with the various Naval Reserves that there were no places for 30,000 men on board ship. The Admiralty's solution was to form the Royal Naval Division.

The three brigades would be available initially for home defence and would fight as infantry, but the units would remain under the control of the Navy.

IRELAND

On the outbreak of war, John O'Brien MP, leader of the AFIL immediately recognised both the potential of the event itself and the upsurge of Nationalist Irish support for the British as a final opportunity to preserve at any price the unity of Ireland by uniting the Orange and the Green in a common cause. Towards the end of August, he followed John Redmond to the War Office, where he spoke to Lord Kitchener on the subject of raising an Irish Army Corps embracing all classes of Irish society, all creeds and all political opinions. The British warlord apparently gave O'Brien some tacit encouragement for his scheme, which was more than he did for Redmond. As a result of the meeting, on 2 September O'Brien spoke at an assembly of the AFIL at Cork Town Hall, when to an enthusiastic audience he suggested Ireland's cause was bound up in a British military victory and advocated Irish participation in not only the defence of Ireland, but in the fighting in France and Belgium:

> We are taking to-night – I don't conceal it from myself – one of the most momentous decisions in our history. If we make up our minds, for heaven's sake let there be no half-heartedness, let there be no qualifications or reservations. We have got to be honest friends or honest enemies of England. It won't do merely to say that we are willing to fight for Belgium, or to fight for Ireland, or to fight for France, much though we love those gallant nations (cheers). We have got to go further and to say, without putting a tooth in it, that we are ready to fight for England as well, in England's way (cheers). And in fighting England's battle in the particular circumstance of this war, I am convinced to the heart's core that we are fighting the most effective battle in all the ages for Ireland's liberty (cheers) as well as to save our towns and our homes and our women and children from the grip of the most appalling horde of brutes in human shape that ever cursed this earth since Attila met his doom at the hands of eternal justice.

In his speech, O'Brien had gone much further than John Redmond ever did in advising Irishmen to enlist voluntarily in the British Army. He considered that the future of an all-Ireland Home Rule settlement depended largely on the extent to which Irish Nationalist and Ulster Covenanters fought together on the battlefields of France. He would continue to advocate for voluntary enlistment until after the Easter Rebellion.

For the IRB element within the Irish Volunteers, the first six weeks of the war were difficult to say the least. Not only had they been sidelined by Redmond with regards to control of the Irish Volunteers, but Patrick Pearse, the senior IRB man within the Volunteers, believed the overall situation in Ireland was critical with Irish Volunteer bands playing British battalions off to war amid a never before witnessed public enthusiasm for the British and the army. Most of the weapons landed at Howth and Kilcoole were in the hands of Redmondites and the ammunition that remained in their hands turned out to be the dum-dum type, which could not be used. Irish cultural educationalist Patrick Pearse had been invited to the inaugural meeting of the Irish Volunteers in November 1913 and a month later he was sworn into the IRB by Bulmer Hobson. Over the course of the next nine months, he had become an influential figure and the most senior IRB man within the Volunteers' organisation. On 9 September, veteran IRB man Tom Clarke and the Supreme Council of the IRB called a meeting of separatists and select others. The meeting was held in the Gaelic League building at 25 Parnell Square in Dublin. Among those attending were IRB members Éamonn Ceannt, Thomas Clarke, Sean MacDermott and Patrick Pearse; Sinn Féiners Arthur Griffith and Sean T O'Kelly; James Connolly and Boer War veteran Major Sean McBride. At the meeting, it was resolved to expand the Irish Volunteers, James Connolly's citizen's army, Fianna and *Cumann na mBan*, to assist any German invasion of Ireland and to resist any attempt to disarm the Volunteers. It was also reportedly decided to stage a rebellion before the end of the war. The idea was to secure a place for Ireland among the nations attending any subsequent peace conference. Meanwhile the other leaders of the Irish Volunteers, including Eoin MacNeill and IRB men Bulmer Hobson and the O'Rahilly, had made their position abundantly clear, which was based largely on the IRB's own constitution that no insurrection should take place without the popular support of the Irish people. The widespread and obvious enthusiasm for the war shown by the Irish people highlighted and strengthened their case. From now on all three would be largely left out of the IRB loop. Despite operating from a much weakened position, it was felt by the physical force men that the war could still provide once in a lifetime opportunities to advance their cause. Little did they know that their circumstances were about to change dramatically!

KITCHENER'S ARMIES

When Lord Kitchener asked for his first hundred thousand volunteers from men between the ages of nineteen and thirty, those who stepped forward were assigned to newly created service battalions, which would make up six infantry divisions of the First New Army (K1). The new infantry divisions were designated the 9th (Scottish), 10th (Irish), 11th (Northern), 12th (Eastern), 13th (Western) and the 14th (Light) Division. The tiles bore no Nationalistic or politically motivated connotations, but were simply the British Army's Home Command areas and their main areas of recruitment. The 14th (Light) Division was designated as such simply because the division was composed of battalions from the Light Infantry and Rifle Regiments. It would be expected, therefore, that the 9th (Scottish) and the 10th (Irish) Divisions would be manned largely by Scots and Irish, respectively. For the most part the Glasgow Irish found it easier to enlist at a local recruiting office, but a number of men did travel to Ireland. The formation of a Third New Army (K3) would follow close on the heels of the Second. The Third New Army's six division would receive no titles being known simply by their numbers: 21st to 26th. A Fourth New Army (K4) would be created in November 1914, but later, April 1916, was broken up its battalions used as reinforcements for the first three New Armies. Fifth and Sixth New Armies would also be created. Due to the break up of the original Fourth New Army, the Fifth and Sixth were renumbered (New) Fourth and Fifth New Armies.

The 9th (Scottish) Division comprised new service battalions assigned to Scottish infantry line regiments, representing the whole of Scotland. At full strength of 18,000 men, the division was organised into three infantry brigades each comprising four infantry battalions. The 26th Brigade had the 8th Bn Black Watch, 7th Bn Seaforth Highlanders, 8th Bn Gordon Highlanders and 5th Bn Cameron Highlanders. The 27th Brigade had the 11th and 12th Bns Royal Scots, 6th Bn Royal Scots Fusiliers and 10th Bn Argyll and Sutherland Highlanders. The 28th Brigade comprised the 6th Bn King's Own Scottish Borderers, 9th Bn The Scottish Rifles (Cameronians) and the 10th and 11th Bns Highland Light Infantry. Attached to the division was the necessary complement of artillery, engineers, Royal Army Service Corps and Royal Army Medical Corps units.

Once the recruits had passed through the enlistment process (or otherwise) they were usually sent to the various regimental depots and from there were, in the case of the 9th (Scottish) Division's recruits, shipped by the trainload to the south of England and into training camps on and around Salisbury Plain. After going through the absolute chaos of arrival and reorganisation, the men were allocated to their various battalions and some form of military training began immediately. The training difficulties at this early stage were enormous. The men were accommodated in an assortment of barracks, tents and wooden huts, or, if they were lucky, were billeted on the local inhabitants. There were insufficient instructors and junior commanders, a total lack of stores of every description, but clothing and arms were absolutely lacking. The men trained for months in their own civilian clothing and carried wooden sticks and poles before anything that resembled uniforms or weapons arrived. At this stage, their appearance was certainly more comical than martial.

When the men of the K1 battalions started their intensive training, the age-old military training and indoctrination programme began to turn them from civilians into soldiers. Quite unawares, the men were also going through the bonding process that turned men into comrades. As the uniforms, kilts, glengarries and cap badges eventually began to be issued, the individuality of the infantry regiments and their battalions became more pronounced. It became obvious to bystanders that they were the Seaforth Highlanders, the Royal Scots, the HLI or the Argylls. On long route marches along the sunken lanes and through the sleepy villages of southern England, the newly formed pipe bands blasted out the ancient regimental marching and battle tunes and the men marched with a swagger in their steps.

As the British Army's totally unique regimental system instilled its *esprit de corps*, each man began to feel his place within the regimental family and recognised that he himself was now part the regiment's long history. He felt he was now a part of something that transcended the individual. From now until the end of their lives, be they long or short, these men were now more than individuals. No matter what or who they once were, now they were HLI, Leinsters, Seaforths or Dublins, and were connected through regimental tradition with the heroes of Waterloo, Talavera and Balaclava.

It would be another eight long months of incessant and rigorous training before the battalions of the 9th (Scottish) Division would be ready for war. It is worth noting at this point the potency of the British Army's regimental system, for it was a factor that many politicians from all political persuasions failed to consider. While the recruits of the Irish divisions remained committed to their political causes, if they indeed had any, the longer the men were exposed to regimental influences and traditions, so the influence of their political masters lessened. An example of this will be seen later when both Carson and Redmond attempted to subvert military tradition by creating their own forces within the British Army.

With the initial rush of volunteers, the new K1 service battalions quickly achieved their war strengths and more, except that is those of the 10th (Irish) and the 12th (Eastern) Divisions. The latter drew recruits from the agricultural districts of eastern England and it was felt only the harvest was keeping the numbers down. The 10th (Irish) Division on the other hand was in a very sorry state with insufficient volunteers stepping forward. By the end of August some battalions were barely into triple figures, while the best recruited, the 5th Bn Connaught Rangers, had attracted only 435 men, less than half a battalion's full war strength of just over a thousand all ranks. The Ulster-based battalions, the Royal Inniskilling Fusiliers and the Royal Irish Fusiliers, were both particularly weak. By the beginning of September, the second hundred thousand were about to be called forward to form the Second New Army (K2). These volunteers would man another six infantry divisions, the 15th to 20th. The Celtic divisions would be the 15th (Scottish) and 16th (Irish) Divisions. Like the 9th and 10th Divisions of K1, the two new Celtic divisions of K2 would be recruited from throughout Scotland and Ireland. However, it was obvious to the military planners that the new 16th (Irish) Division would not be feasible considering the woeful state of the 10th (Irish) Division. It was also clear to Lord Kitchener and the recruiters that the men currently serving with the two Irish militias had, except for the UVF until recently, been held back by their political leadership and without their active encouragement and support the new Irish battalions would never be filled. To complicate matters further, Carson and Craig would also be recruiting for their own Ulster division.

However, many men from both communities in Ireland were joining up. These were the men with little or no interest in politics and who just wanted to get into a fight or who needed a job. Some were going to the new 10th (Irish) Division's service battalions, but very many were also crossing to the mainland to join Scottish or English battalions and would be lost to the Irish divisions forever.

A few of the Glasgow Irish were going across the Irish Sea in the opposite direction. Bernard Gallacher and his nineteen-year-old son, also Bernard, both miners from Kirkintilloch, decided they would enlist together. On 11 September, they joined Kitchener's Army and asked to serve with the Royal Munster Fusiliers. After a tearful farewell to wife and mother, Mary Gallacher, the pair set off for the Curragh and the 10th (Irish) Division. On arrival in Kildare both were assigned to the Munster Fusilier's 6th (Service) Bn, then forming at Tralee, part of the 30th Brigade. Despite the arrival of the Kirkintilloch father and son team at Tralee, Lord Kitchener realised that he had to change his attitudes and tactics to recruiting and massaging Irish sensibilities. He decided to bend, but just a little. While Kitchener was wondering what he could offer the Irish, John Redmond was also thinking about concessions and about manning the newly announced 16th Division, which would be raised in Ireland.

THE WAR FRONT

While the Celtic were playing Morton at Parkhead and the women of Glasgow were selling their paper flags, the French Sixth Army stumbled into von Kluck's flank guard at the river Ourcq. Von Kluck, unaware of the French Sixth Army on his now exposed right flank, had executed a great wheeling movement, which had taken his army past Paris to the east of the city. This was contrary to the Schlieffen Plan, but apparently the German High Command had decided that it was unnecessary to bypass Paris to the west, and that the city could be dealt with later. After a stiff fight, the Germans retreated and the Battle, or the 'Miracle of the Marne' as it became known as, was over. During the next three days, the entire German invasion force retired onto a defensive line, which in the case of the German right wing, meant to positions behind the river Aisne. Despite its name, the battle was not won in the classic sense, but it was a strategic victory achieved through tactical manoeuvring. While the French were engaged in some ferocious fighting, the BEF, which had advanced onto von Kluck's other flank, saw little action, although it played the key role in the game of strategy. The very presence of the BEF north of the Marne made the German position untenable and ensured their withdrawal. The consequence was the failure of the German's strategic plan for a swift decisive victory in the west. It also signalled the end of the war of manoeuvre, from now on static defence would dominate the generals' thoughts. After six weeks of war, the cost in casualties had been enormous. The French had lost around a quarter of a million men. The BEF's losses were in the region of 14,000, with just 1700 lost during the advance to the Marne. The German losses are unknown, but there is no doubt that they were equally or even more horrific.

Among the British casualties was Private Thomas Highgate, a nineteen-year-old labourer from Shoreham, Kent. Thomas had joined the army eighteen months earlier and had opted to serve with the 1st Bn. Royal West Kent Regiment then based in Dublin. After crossing to France as part of the BEF, the battalion took part in the Battle and the retreat from Mons and on 5 September advanced into the gap between the German armies across the Marne. Thomas decided he'd seen enough slaughter and decided to desert. He was later found in civilian clothes hiding in a barn. After a hasty military trial, he was found guilty of desertion and on 8 September was executed by firing squad. He was the first of 346 men to suffer death by sentence of Courts Martial between August 1914 and March 1920.

SCOTTISH FOOTBALL

The four-man SFA delegation sent to London at the beginning of September had left Glasgow split 50/50 regarding whether to continue or to stop football for the duration of the war. Celtic's Tom White was publicly undecided, but the Celtic directors were in favour of continuing with the season. On their arrival in London, the delegation met the military authorities at the War Office and put the SFA unreservedly at the military's disposal. They were informed by the Under Secretary of State for War, who was also the Prime Minister's brother-in-law, Harold Tennant MP, that the War Office had no desire to see the game stopped. Indeed, they were eager to make use of football for recruiting purposes and for collecting money at matches to help alleviate distress among military families. Unsurprisingly, the committee arrived home unanimous in their opinion that football should continue. A few days later, the full SFA committee endorsed the report and recommended that recruiting measures similar to those already introduced at some grounds be extended to all Scottish football grounds. AG Adamson, director of Raith Rovers, resigned in protest, stating that he was ashamed of the decision to continue with the season.

However, the pressure on professional football was cranked up another notch when the newspapers published three broadsheet columns of rugby players who had enlisted. The two hundred players represented most of the famous Scottish clubs: Watsonians, Hawick, Glasgow High School, Glasgow University and others. In reaction to the pressure put on professional footballers to lead the way to the recruiting offices, the Celtic-minded *Man in the Know* vented his own opinion on professional footballers enlisting. His opinion almost certainly mirrored that of the Celtic boardroom:

> *There is a lot of nonsense written about our professional players just now. The patriots who write to the papers are most indignant because Celtic, Rangers, and other professionals are not joining the colours like their Queen's Park friends. These people cannot see that there is no comparison between the amateur and the professional player. Should the Queen's Park and Rugby players smell powder and return home safe and sound, as we all trust they will, they will find their situations awaiting them, and in many cases a better position found for them. But what is in front of the professional who happens to be ever so slightly lamed, or who may have lost his form to some extent. His club will be very sorry for him and all that sort of thing they will probably keep him on for the rest of the season, and after that, the deluge or rather the transfer list. Remember that most players are labourers or miners. They have no trade on their hands, and when their football days are over it is a case of working for a few shillings a week. So small blame to the lad who puts his three or four pounds a week before a wooden leg. We are still giving the last of our Crimean and Indian Mutiny veterans a swell funeral from the workhouse, and forty years hence we shall be doing the same for many who are risking life and limb in this Great War. We cheered our heroes on their way to South Africa, and then forgot all about them after filling up their places in workshops and offices. Let those who run down the footballer tell us what they are prepared to do for such as Joe Dodds, Andy McAtee, and others of their kind should they start shooting from the shoulder instead of from the instep, and come home with a ball in the knee or ankle joint.*

Obviously feeling the pressure on the professional game, he also thought that it would soon be an offence to play or even to write about football.

CELTIC FC

The weekend of 12 September saw the Celtic on a break from the League programme and 18,000 spectators at Shawfield watched in disbelief as Clyde knocked the Celtic out of the Glasgow Cup. Celtic knew they would be without Johnstone, but Alex McNair and Johnny McMaster had also dropped out through injury. For their replacements, Willie Maley brought in Billy Crone, and Alex Gray was hastily recalled from making grenades in a munitions factory. Tom McGregor kept his place at the back, McMenemy was dropped into centre half, while Smiler Browning joined him in midfield at left half. *The Man in the Know* was nervous and suggested that with a couple of Clyde stars also injured, a draw would be a good result for both teams. The 'Bully Wee' stunned the Celtic support by taking the lead in just three minutes. After the award of a free kick, Clyde forward Allan fired in what looked like a harmless hooked shot at goal. It was a strike that any other day Charlie Shaw would have stopped with one hand. Unfortunately for the Celtic goalie, this was not any other day and Charlie, much too everyone's surprise and dismay, and to his own embarrassment, fumbled the ball across the line. In response to the early setback, the Celts pressed hard to get an equaliser, but with the exception of Billy Crone hitting the post they never came close for the remainder of the first half.

Gallacher and McMenemy attack the Clyde goal

The visitors opened the second half as they finished the first with relentless pressure on the Clyde back line. However, without McMenemy and Browning in the front line, the Celtic attack lacked flair and penetration and was easily repelled by the Clyde defence. Half way through the second half Clyde got a second goal and Allan was again the scorer. Unbelievably, it came from another free kick and was due to another error from Charlie Shaw. On this occasion, he dropped the simple crossed ball at the feet of Allan who gleefully accepted the gift and slotted the ball home. Despite Celtic pressing hard for the remainder of the game, the Clyde defence stood their ground and time ran out for the Celts. Over the course of the ninety minutes during which the Bhoys had 75 per cent of the possession, the sum total of the Celtic attack was just two shots hitting the post, one each from Crone and McAtee, and a 'Sunny' Jim Young free kick that was diverted past the post by Gilligan when it was heading for the back of the net. In truth, the Clyde attack was not any better and if not for Charlie Shaw's two gifts, the match would probably have ended in a goalless draw.

The game was a disjointed stuttering affair for the Bhoys, where the men playing out of position disrupted the usual tight organisation at the back and interrupted the flow of play going forward. Patsy Gallacher was roughly handled at times, but more often than not got his own back. Charlie Shaw had a very rare poor game and the Celtic very unexpectedly went out of the Glasgow FA Cup. The Celtic fans left Shawfield scratching their heads; they had just witnessed the Bhoys sensationally knocked out of the Glasgow Cup for the second year in a row. The previous year, Third Lanark had taken the Celts to a replay at Cathkin Park after both teams failed to score at Parkhead. On that occasion, an amazingly freaky goal from McTavish delivered the mortal blow. This year the wounds were purely self-inflicted.

In the other Glasgow Cup first-round tie played that weekend, Partick Thistle beat Third Lanark 1–0 at Firhill in front of a crowd of 15,000. Clyde and Partick Thistle would meet in the cup final with Clyde, helped by old Celt Ebenezer Owers, the eventual winners.

In the League, Hearts had continued their impressive start to the season with their fifth straight win, beating St Mirren 5–0 and they were now in first place in the League table. Rangers in second placed, dropped their first point with a 1–1 draw with Dundee at Dens Park. Ayr United beat Aberdeen 1–0 at Somerset Park, maintaining their third spot in the league.

On Saturday 12 September, in response to either the dire news from the war front or the dire news of Celtic's defeat at Shawfield, old Celtic stalwart Willie McOustra joined the Scots Guards. Born in Stenhousemuir, the speedy winger was first tried out at Celtic Park versus the Kaffirs of the Orange Free State in September 1899. After turning out thirty times for the Celts and scoring nine goals, in February 1902 Tom Maley paid Celtic a sizeable fee to take Willie to Manchester City. However, a reoccurring knee problem saw his six seasons at Manchester blighted by injury and he turned out just sixty-seven times for the club. He played his last game for City in October 1907 before being offloaded to Blackpool FC. After two seasons with Blackpool, his professional career was over and Willie spent some time touring with the celebrity football team of the famous entertainment troupe Fred Karno's Army. After a year or so travelling around the country with Karno, Willie, like most working-class players of his day when their football career was over, was forced to return to his trade or lack of it. In Willie McOustra's case, he went back to working in the iron foundries. Towards the end of 1910, Willie was working as an iron moulder in Larbert and became involved in junior football at Stenhousemuir FC.

By the time the war broke out in August 1914, Willie was five years finished with top flight football and had moved into Glasgow where he was living with his wife, Elizabeth, and their three kids. Assigned to the 3rd (Reserve) Guards Bn based at Caterham, just outside the capital, Willie would spend the next six months there training for war.

Back on League business, Celtic paid their second visit of the season to the nation's capital when they meet Hibernian at Easter Road on 19 September. The Bhoys were forced to play with a make do and mend midfield and back line with McMaster and Johnstone both out injured. McGregor and Henry Jarvis were the replacements with Dodds moving up into the midfield to allow McGregor to slot in at the back. Shipyard electrician Henry Jarvis was brought in to the club to cover for the seldom injured Jim Young and subsequently spent most of his time on short-term loans to other clubs. It was his first appearance in the league for eighteen months. McNair was back in his usual position after missing the previous two games through injury.

Hibs were out of the blocks first and grabbed control of the midfield and held onto it for most of the game. They made several good goal-scoring opportunities but these were spurned by their forwards. Eventually and deservedly they took the lead through Wilson, who came in from the right to latch onto a cross from Smith and scored from close in. It would appear that the Hibs then took their foot off the gas or decided they would defend the one-goal lead, in either case Celtic eventually fought its way back into the game and with seventeen minutes to go scored the equaliser through Jimmy McColl, who burst through from the back. Most neutral observers thought the Hibernians deserved more than just a share of the points, but Celtic deserve some praise for their perseverance and refusal to quit. Overall it was a poor performance by the Bhoys. McMaster and Johnston were greatly missed and McNair looked as if he was back into the side too soon after injury. Henry Jarvis was a journeyman footballer and not quite up to the task at Celtic. Shortly after the game he was back on his travels, loaned out to Ayr United then Clyde. By mid-1916, Henry was in the army, but as an electrician he was soon returned to the shipyards to help build battleships. Gallacher and McAtee also failed to shine, while Celtic's saving goal came from the wing work of Browning and McMenemy and the strength of McColl. In the end Celtic were lucky to escape from Edinburgh with a point. Three points dropped in two visits was not good enough by any stretch of the imagination. With five games played, Celtic had slipped to eighth in the League.

THE WAR FRONT

After their retirement from the Marne, the Germans took up a strong defensive position along the Chemin des Dames ridge behind the river Aisne. With the realisation that the watered-down Schlieffen Plan had failed and that Germany now faced a prolonged war on two fronts, the Kaiser sacked von Moltke and replaced him with General Erich von Falkenhayn. On 12 September, the BEF was ordered to attack the Chemin des Dames ridge between Soissons and Craonne. The Battle of the Aisne began on 14 September when the British and French launched the first of a series of uphill frontal assaults on the heights. Among the battalions that attacked that day were the 1st Bn Queen's Own Cameron Highlanders, recently transferred into the 1st Division to replace the 2nd Bn Royal Munster Fusiliers. The Highlanders' objective was a sugar factory on the Troyon Ridge. As the Camerons advanced through the early morning mist, the German defenders opened up, pouring a colossal weight of artillery and small arms fire into the ranks of the closing British infantry. The attack withered and failed with the Camerons losing 147 men killed and over 400 wounded.

The result of the British Army's first large-scale assault of the war was over 1000 killed and 3000 wounded as they experienced for the first time the effect of modern military firepower. The Celtic regiments suffered alongside their English and Welsh comrades. In addition to the Cameron Highlanders, the Connaught Rangers suffered over 100 casualties, the Irish Guards 60, the Scots Guards 80 and the KOSB over 60. The Germans counter-attacked, but they failed to break through the hastily prepared defensive positions of the Allies.

Over the next fortnight the trenches became deeper and took on a more permanent look and in an effort to break the stalemate, each side attempted to turn the other's northern flank and what became known as the Race to the Sea began. A pattern of failed attacks, followed by equally disastrous counter-attacks resulting in catastrophic casualties was being formed. Cavalry units eager to exploit the anticipated breakthrough stood idle as the infantry were slaughtered. The battlefront was turning into one of stagnation and trench warfare. As summer turned to autumn, the weather worsened. The infantrymen suffered miserable conditions of constant heavy rain as their shell scrapes filled with water and the soaked men were subjected to constant shelling and small arms fire. Sir John French as a cavalry officer was determined to extract his force from the stalemate on the Aisne and get it onto the open plains of Flanders where there was still a chance of open warfare. Although there were still significant German forces in Belgium, particularly around Antwerp, the Allies assumed there was 150 miles of open country south from the Belgian coast and Sir John French decided that was just the place for the BEF. In addition, the British lines of communication would also be greatly shortened by being near the Belgian coast. The British were especially concerned at preventing the fall of Antwerp and were interested, above all, in barring the way to the Channel ports from which the Germans could threaten both the supply lines from England and the vital supply and communication hub that was London. With all that in mind, on 29 September Sir John French suggested to General Joffre the transfer of the British Army to its former place on the left of the line. Although it was never mentioned, both the British and the French recognised that it would be much easier for the British to get back to England should the worse happen. With the thought of the British bolting across the Channel, the French argued that although in broad agreement with the proposal the time was not right. Sir John French disagreed and curtly informed his French allies that the BEF would start to move north on 3 October.

The Germans meanwhile were thinking along the same lines and formulating their own plans for Belgium and the Channel ports. Having recognised the strategic mistake of not securing the ports when they had the opportunity, they set about correcting the error. A three-part plan was quickly formulated. First would be a major assault towards Arras, second a cavalry sweep across the Flanders plains to the coast and third the capture of the great port of Antwerp. By occupying the coastal corridor, the ports of Zeebrugge and Ostend would fall like plums. Next would be Ypres the most westerly town in Belgian Flanders and a major communications hub. Once Ypres had been captured, the route to the French coast lay open with Dunkirk, Boulogne and Calais ready for the taking. With the coast in German hands, the ports would provide havens for the German fleet and springboards for the invasion of England. The coast became the new glittering prize for the German strategists. Possession of Calais they reasoned, would win the war for them. On 29 September the German plan swung into operation with an assault on Antwerp.

RECRUITING SERGEANTS FOR THE BRITISH ARMY

On 18 September 1914, the Government of Ireland Act was finally passed. After thirty years of patient parliamentary work and peaceful agitation, John Redmond had achieved what the more illustrious Irish politicians O'Connell, Butt and Parnell had failed to do; he got a Home Rule bill on the statute book. Over the last six weeks of political wrangling, during which the Ulster Unionists had demanded that in view of the current crisis the bill be dropped, John Redmond had insisted that the Home Rule Bill progress to the statute book. Asquith agreed with Redmond, but after dropping the Amending Act, he introduced a new Suspensory Act. The new act would ensure that while the Home Rule legislation would be passed, the enactment of the *whole of Ireland* Home Rule Bill would be postponed until the end of what was still expected to be a short war. The Unionists were furious, however, with the enactment of the bill in limbo and with the question of partition still to be resolved, they decided to let the matter slide, but just for now.

Despite the delay in enacting the bill, it had received royal assent and was now officially on the statute book. The Irish both at home and across the diaspora were ecstatic. Bonfires were lit across the south of Ireland and John Redmond was widely acclaimed for what was a remarkable achievement. In Glasgow the Nationalists too were delighted. The Observer's headlines were 'Ireland's Triumph' and 'Congratulations From Irishmen Everywhere'. Among the hundreds of messages sent to John Redmond was one from the Glasgow Irishmen: 'Accept from Glasgow Irishmen warmest congratulations on enactment of Home Rule. Your splendid success consummates in triumph the longest, stiffest struggle ever waged by any race for nationhood and liberty', signed by Michael Quin (Home Government Branch).

The day previous there had been a meeting of the standing committee of the United Irish League in the House of Commons. President TP O'Connor MP was in the chair. The committee discussed Irish recruitment and a resolution was passed that it had been noted that thousands of Irishmen were enlisting into English, Scottish and Welsh regiments. There were figures for Irish recruitment from all over the country: from Lancashire not including Liverpool and Manchester, between 10,000 and 15,000 had been recruited, from Birmingham 3000, Newcastle upon Tyne 4000 and Glasgow between 5000 and 10,000. The standing committee was of the opinion that Ireland's cause would be better served if Irishmen joined Irish regiments, either in Ireland or where possible in newly formed Irish battalions in Britain. In time, the battalions would be brought together to form an Irish brigade, the formation of which had already been suggested by Redmond.

The figures may not have been far off the mark. In the early September editions of the Glasgow Observer a number of Glasgow parishes gave some indication of their Catholic parishioners now serving with the forces. St Roch's estimated 300 men at the front, St Joseph's Woodside 223, while St Patrick's claimed: 'A long list of men at the front is on the door of the church.' St Mungo's stated that: 'The billiard club may not open due to so many members being at the war.' The Cathedral parish of St Andrew also informed its parishioners that 'Another long list of servicemen is fixed to the door'. Two Catholic industrial schools, St Mary's and Slatefield, reported that hundreds of their former pupils were now on the front line and produced long lists.

With Kitchener still stonewalling over training and arming the Irish Volunteers en masse as an Irish defence force, John Redmond with Irish enlistment figures for the mainland in hand, and with the creation of an Irish army in mind, determined to have those Irishmen already recruited into English, Scottish and Welsh regiments transferred into Irish regiments. By the end of September some progress had been made in recruiting for the 10th (Irish) Division by drawing on the reserve battalions of the Irish regiments and by stripping their training depots of every available man. In response to John Redmond's request, recruits who were Irish born or the sons of Irishmen and who had enlisted on the mainland were, with their consent, transferred across to Ireland to top up the division. However, the 10th (Irish) Division was still the weakest of the K1 divisions, with a strength of 124 officers and 10,910 other ranks. Lord Kitchener himself had personally appointed Lieutenant General Sir Bryan Mahon as the divisional commander. Born in Co Galway, Mahon was the typical Ascendancy land-owning Irish Unionist. Although by reputation apolitical, he was a school friend of Carson and was Kitchener's spy in Ireland. He had been used by the Secretary of State as an intermediary between the Army and the Irish Nationalists. Mahon had a low opinion of the military usefulness of the Irish Volunteers. He recommended to Kitchener that they should be put under military discipline and control and used simply for home defence. He thought making them into Irish battalions might encourage recruitment and the battalions could then be tapped for drafts of battle casualty replacements.

Very many Irish Protestants and Catholics, fed up listening to politicians arguing, joined the 10th (Irish) Division. These men joined without any political encouragement or motive and were by definition therefore the least politically motivated of both traditions. Among them was a young man from Sligo, John Fallon. The seventeen-year-old father of the future Celtic stalwart Sean Fallon lied about his age and gave up a secure job as a baker to enlist on 5 September 1914. Assigned to the 5th Bn Connaught Rangers he was dispatched south to the regimental depot in Galway. On arrival, John was put through the usual administrative process before joining the battalion then based at Kilworth Camp, Fermoy, to begin his training. On arrival at Kilworth, he was assigned to A Company. Irish Nationalist gunrunner Hervey de Montmorency was another who'd decided he would do his own thing. The former Inspector or Commander of the Wicklow Brigade, Irish Volunteers wrote to Capt. George Berkeley (Irish Volunteers) in mid September stating that he is joining the Dublin Fusiliers as a Captain and hopes to be sent to the front. He is 'utterly sick' of the Volunteers, who have no officers and submit to a 'contemptible crew of leaders'. Money is spent paying the expenses of 'crazy creatures' who make 'bloodthirsty speeches'. He states that the Volunteers missed the 'greatest opportunity' when they failed to back up John Redmond's speech. He shudders to think what Home Rule means under the leadership of McNeill and O'Rahilly. Montmorency concludes that, 'it is better to be a captain in the British army than a Field Marshal in the Irish Volunteers'.

In the ongoing war of words between Unionists and Nationalists, some Unionists later highlighted that drafts of Englishmen were needed to fill up the division. The Nationalists gleefully pointed out that the drafts were of Irishmen or sons of Irishmen. There was one exception: the 10th (Service) Bn The Hampshire Regiment was drafted into the division as army troops and later drafted into the 29th Brigade to replace the 5th (Service) Bn Royal Irish Regiment that had been transferred out of the division having been rerolled as a pioneer battalion.

John Redmond liked to think of the 10th (Irish) Division as one in which Protestants and Catholics had combined in common purpose and the prime example of political barriers being swept away by a greater Irish patriotism. The 10th (Irish) Division was later described by him as 'the first definitely Irish Division that ever existed in the British Army', and when it deployed on active service in May 1915: 'For the first time in history the Irish people have put a national army in the field.' However, with the opportunity of making the 10th (Irish) Division into a distinctly Nationalist force gone, Redmond now pinned his hopes for a recognisably Irish Army on the new 16th (Irish) Division, part of Kitchener's Second New Army (K2).

Like K1, the K2 Army would consist of six divisions: 15th (Scottish), 16th (Irish), 17th (Northern), 18th (Eastern), 19th (Western) and the 20th (Light). The 15th (Scottish) Division began to assemble at Aldershot in mid-September and would remain there until the middle of November when it moved to Salisbury Plain. Like the 9th (Scottish) Division, the 15th (Scottish) Division would draw its men from the whole of Scotland.

The 16th (Irish) Division also began to form in September in Ireland with the divisional headquarters based first in Dublin and later at Mallow, Co Cork. The three infantry brigades were numbered 47th, 48th and 49th and were headquartered at, Fermoy, Buttevant and Tipperary, respectively. The 47th Brigade comprised the following service battalions: 6th Bn Royal Irish Regiment, 6th Bn Connaught Rangers, 7th Bn Leinster Regiment and the 8th Bn Royal Munster Fusiliers. The 48th Brigade comprised the 7th Bn Royal Irish Rifles, 9th Bn Royal Munster Fusiliers, 8th Bn Royal Dublin Fusiliers and the 9th Bn Royal Dublin Fusiliers. The 49th Brigade comprised the 7th Bn Royal Inniskilling Fusiliers, 8th Bn Royal Inniskilling Fusiliers, 7th Bn Royal Irish Fusiliers and the 8th Bn Royal Irish Fusiliers. The division would over the next nine months be allocated its artillery, engineers, medical and transport units.

In an attempt to encourage recruiting in Ireland and to placate the two Irish militia leaders, Lord Kitchener decided that he would make some concessions to both Unionists and Nationalists, but he remained determined that they would not be detrimental to military effectiveness. Kitchener again met with Carson who brought his lieutenant, Orangeman James Craig, along with him. After the pair reiterated their promise to the Secretary of State for War that they had 35,000 UVF men willing to enlist immediately and to serve abroad, Kitchener promised Carson that his UVF men would serve together, they would be commanded by their own officers and that the word 'Ulster' would accompany the number '36' in the divisional title. They could also have a divisional badge. However, that there were 35,000 UVF standing ready and willing to man the new Ulster division was something of an exaggeration on Carson's part. He was not prepared to send, nor indeed were the men themselves, willing to go to France leaving Ulster vulnerable to the Irish Volunteers, who were still only committed to providing a home guard.

Thousands of UVF men did answer Carson's call to man the Ulster division, but the Unionist militia also maintained a very powerful presence in the north of Ireland. By the end of September several thousand UVF men had indeed enlisted into the Ulster division. However, by the end of December, the division was still far from fully manned. The commanding officer of the 9th Royal Inniskilling Fusiliers was worried that as much as 30 per cent of his battalion would need to be brought in from outside Ireland. The newspapers also reported that some battalions had revived the old tradition of *beating up* fairs and markets by fife and drum looking for recruits. The whole of C Company of the 11th Bn Royal Inniskilling Fusiliers was raised on the British mainland by the British League for the Support of Ulster and the Union. It was also reported at the time that 120 men of the Glasgow Ulster Volunteers had left the city to serve with the Ulster division.

In the north of Ireland, the 36th (Ulster) Division was seen as more than a simple military formation. It was perceived as being primarily a political and overtly Unionist/Orange formation and an expression of Protestant Ulster's power, pride and if necessary its independence. Some also believed that the Ulster division was as committed to fighting for the continuation of Ulster in the Union as the survival of an independent Great Britain. In an attempt to emphasise the division's Ulster identity further, someone decided it would be a good idea to issue a unique divisional 'Red Hand' cap badge. The decision would cause some consternation in Dublin and in London and would prove to be a PR mistake. By the time the 18,000 strong Ulster division deployed on active service, 90 per cent of the men were Ulstermen. It also boasted one Catholic officer and thirteen Catholic other ranks.

After watching the formation of the Ulster division, John Redmond finally decided he had to make a leap of faith. It would be a much braver leap than Kitchener or Carson would ever have considered. Unfortunately, it was not recognised as such in London and would receive only paltry reward. On 20 September John Redmond made his celebrated speech at Woodenbridge, Co Wicklow, in which he said: 'The interests of Ireland, of the whole of Ireland, are at stake in this war.'

He drew out the high moral purpose of the struggle against the Germans and Prussian militarism:

> This war is undertaken in defence of the highest interests of religion and morality and right and it would be a disgrace for ever to our country, a reproach to her manhood, and a denial of the lessons of her history if young Ireland [note the allusion here to 1848 and the traditions of Irish nationalism] confined their efforts to remaining at home to defend the shores of Ireland from an unlikely invasion and shrinking from the duty of proving on the field of battle that gallantry and courage which have distinguished their race all through its history.

The crux of his message was reached when he said: 'Go on drilling and make yourselves efficient for the work and then account for yourselves as men, not only in Ireland itself, but wherever the fighting line extends in defence of right and freedom and religion in this war.'

Stirring words, which found a very positive response among very many young Irishmen, but for many others it was a very large leap from defending Ireland from invasion to fighting for the British overseas. Some went much further. Irish labour leader Jim Larkin described Redmond as an Irish Judas without the sense to collect his thirty pieces of silver' and asks 'is there no man available with a rope and a tree'.

When John Redmond made his Woodenbridge speech, he, like most other politicians, still believed that the war would be short. He certainly hoped that would be the case. It was in the Irish Parliamentary Party's interest that the war would be over as quickly as possible. It was politically very important for the leaders of constitutional Irish Nationalism to show their followers some physical results of their long-running Home Rule campaign. The Irish people needed to see their own parliament sitting in Dublin, dealing with Irish problems. The quicker the war was over the quicker that would happen. John Redmond assumed that within a few months, maybe a year, he would be back at the bargaining table facing hard-eyed Unionists determined to exclude Ulster from Home Rule. With that uppermost in mind, he had a number of additional motives for his dramatic move, both pragmatic and moral.

Firstly, he was painfully aware that the Irish Volunteers were desperately badly trained and equipped in comparison to the UVF. As he addressed the parade of Volunteers at Woodenbridge, he noted with concern that most of the men were armed with pikes and hurley sticks. The 36th (Ulster) Division would soon be issued with artillery guns. He still believed the British would train and arm the Nationalist Volunteers, who would then become the nucleus of an Irish army after the war and would be capable of confronting the UVF, should it come to shooting over the partition discussions. Once the British armed the volunteers, it would be very difficult for them to get the weapons back.

Secondly, he felt it was in the future interest of an *All Ireland* Home Rule settlement to support the Allied cause. By matching the gesture of the UVF, which had already pledged its unconditional support and whose members were now enlisting into the newly created 36th (Ulster) Division, he hoped to negate any moral advantage the Unionists may have gained in future discussions with the British government. He recognised the threat of Ireland being permanently partitioned and was vehemently opposed to it, fearing for the future of a Nationalist minority in what would be effectively an autonomous *Orange* state in the north of the island.

Thirdly, he hoped that Unionist and Nationalist soldiers fighting and perhaps dying together in what both sides saw as a noble cause would lead to Irish unity. He passionately wished for unity between the Irishmen of the north and the south.

Fourthly, Redmond was fearful of an anti-Nationalist backlash in England. The Unionists had a great deal of support in England and their cause had many powerful backers. Any sign of Redmond trying to take advantage of England's situation may have encouraged a Conservative/Liberal coalition aimed at defying the Nationalists. That in turn conjured up the spectacle of the UVF, at the behest of the British government, reinforcing the Irish Constabulary to maintain law and order. Where that particular scenario would have taken the Irish people is now pure speculation, but it is not too difficult to imagine a *Black and Tan* situation at the beginning rather than the end of the war. It is also no large leap of the imagination to consider that even the outcome of the war itself may have been very different.

Finally, he thought by defending the right of a small nation like Belgium to exist against the power of Prussian totalitarianism, Irish soldiers fighting in specifically Irish units alongside the military of other nations would vindicate the right of self-determination for their own country. In all, he felt justified to claim that 'Ireland's highest interests' lay 'in the speedy and overwhelming victory of England and the Allies'.

Leaving aside the purely Irish political dimension, John Redmond also felt that morally Irishmen should be involvement in what was being widely seen as a righteous war. For once,

Great Britain was not involved in a belligerent act of Imperial expansion, but was seen as fighting German despotism, military aggression and the possible domination of Europe. The Germans had launched unprovoked attacks on both France and neutral Belgium. The German invasion of Belgium in particular resonated among the Irish and Glasgow Irish as an assault on the rights and liberties of a small Catholic nation, very similar to Ireland. Like many middle-class Irish Nationalists, John Redmond was deeply upset at the atrocities perpetrated by Germany on the Catholic people of Belgium. His niece, who was a nun in the Irish Benedictine Convent in Ypres, Belgium, gave him a first-hand account of the suffering inflicted on the population and he was deeply moved. The Benedictine convent in Ypres was the home to British flags captured by the immortal Irish Brigade at the eighteen-century Battle of Ramillies. The convent was known as Les Dames Irlandaises and seems to have been established by James II. Although an allied victory, the Battle of Ramillies in 1706 saw the Irish Brigade attack and defeat two British regiments. Their captured colours were given to the Irish nuns in Ypres.

John Redmond was also briefed on what was being called the 'Rape of Belgium' by Tom Kettle. Professor Kettle was married to Mary Sheehy, an Irish suffragette, whose sister Hanna had married Francis Skeffington. The latter was murdered in Dublin by Captain Bowen-Colthurst in Easter 1916. A former IPP MP, Tom Kettle had been sent to Belgium by John Redmond to buy weapons for the Irish Volunteers and was still there when the war broke out. He was so horrified by German atrocities that he gave the arms to the Belgian Government and remained in Belgium for two months working as the war correspondent for the Daily News. In this role, he investigated numerous atrocity stories. Kettle's investigations and accounts were far from being sensationalist and were used by the Belgian Committee, which dealt with war crimes such as the German use of exploding bullets, murder and mutilation, dropping bombs and the destruction and confiscation of private property. Moved by the plight of Belgium, on his return to Ireland Thomas Kettle joined the British Army and advised other Irishmen to do likewise.

The British newspapers, of course, carried the harrowing stories, the details of which stirred an enormous feeling of hatred towards the Germans and sympathy for the Belgians. The German's allies, the Austro-Hungarians, were tarred with the same brutalities brush. They also were involved in an Imperial adventure in the Balkans in an attempt to dominate the small nations Serbia and Poland. The dreadful humanitarian record of the Ottoman Turks and their atrocities against ethnic minorities, particularly the Armenians, was appalling even by the standards of the times. These were all noble causes that John Redmond felt the Irish as a nation, distinct from the British, should be involved with and one that all Irishmen could unite around. Francis Ledwidge, a young Irish poet, echoed the thinking of very many Irish Nationalists who enlisted:

> I joined the British Army because she stood between Ireland and an enemy common to our civilization and I would not have her say that she defended us while we did nothing at home but pass resolutions.

Having crossed his Rubicon, John Redmond put much of his faith in Irish enlistment to give him the moral authority he needed to be able to outstare the Unionists and resist their aim for the permanent partition of Ireland. That said, he had no intention of simply filling the British Army with Irish recruits and wanted the Irish to enlist into battalions that would be overtly Irish, both in their manning and identity. Redmond's idea was that the newly authorised 16th

(Irish) Division would be manned entirely by the Irish Nationalists and would be a carbon copy of the 36th (Ulster) Division. Not only would the Nationalists be matching the Unionists in supporting the war effort in which he passionately believed, but also he thought that after the war an Irish Nationalist force that could militarily match the UVF would negate any advantage the militarily superior UVF gave Carson in negotiations. In the event that it came to shooting over Home Rule, the Nationalists, having been armed, trained and battle hardened with the 16th (Irish) Division, would be a match for the Ulster Unionist forces in the field.

John Redmond, who later confessed to having a 'lamentable ignorance of military matters', had already made several public references to the legendary *Irish Brigade*. This force of five Jacobite regiments of exiled Irishmen fought for the French over the

IRELAND'S NATIONAL ARMY

TO BECOME A PERMANENT FORCE IN THE COUNTRY.

MR REDMOND AND RECRUITING.

CARSON'S THREAT TO REVOKE HOME RULE ACT.

Ireland's National Army
(Courtesy Glasgow Observer)

course of the eighteenth century, mostly against the British. Unfortunately, when recruiting began for the 16th (Irish) Division, Redmond's insistence on calling the division the new 'Irish Brigade' caused utter confusion in the War Office and recruiting offices, both in Ireland and in centres of Irish populations in Britain like Glasgow. In addition, when Redmond requested that the 16th (Irish) Division be set aside for Nationalist volunteers as a specifically Irish brigade, Lord Kitchener ordered a single brigade (47th Brigade) to be set aside as Redmond wished. However, a British infantry division comprised three brigades, while an infantry brigade comprised four infantry battalions, 4000 men in total. The Ulster Unionists meanwhile, much more militarily aware, had insisted on the UVF serving together as an Ulster Division.

On 25 September, Prime Minister Asquith came to Dublin to help launch a recruiting appeal. In a Mansion House speech, which was addressed specifically to the Irish National Volunteers, he appeared to make a clear pledge on behalf of the government that there would soon be a southern Irish formation of the army along the same lines as the Ulster division, i.e. at least a full division of Irish Nationalists:

> *Don't let them [the Irish National Volunteers] be afraid that by joining the colours they will lose their identity and become absorbed in some invertebrate mass, or, what is equally repugnant, be artificially distributed into units which have no national cohesion or character. ... We shall, to the utmost limit that military expediency will allow, [a get out] see that men who have been already associated in this or that district in training and common exercises shall be kept together and continue to recognise the corporate bond which now unites them. Further, we are in urgent need of competent officers and when the officers now engaged in training these men prove equal to the test, there is no fear that their services will not be gladly and gratefully retained. But, I repeat, gentlemen, the Empire needs*

recruits and needs them at once. They may be trained and equipped in time to take their part in what may prove to be the decisive field in the greatest struggle in the history of the world. That is our immediate necessity and no Irishmen responding to it need be afraid he is jeopardising the future of the Volunteers.

Asquith also added to the confusion over brigades, divisions and corps by declaring, 'We all want to see an Irish Brigade, or, better still, an Irish Army Corps.' An army corps could be two or even three divisions and was a very sizeable formation indeed, comprising perhaps 55,000 men of all arms. Redmond, of course, heartily endorsed the idea of the two southern Irish 10th and 16th Divisions fighting alongside the 36th (Ulster) Division in such a formation. Finally, the Prime Minister added:

I have only one more word to say. Though our need is great, your opportunity is also great. The call I am making is backed by the sympathy of your fellow Irishmen in all parts of the Empire and of the world ... There is no question of compulsion or bribery. What we want, what we ask, what we believe you are ready and eager to give, is the freewill offering of a free people.

All this was effectively a double promise to deliver two of Redmond's objectives. First, that every inducement should be given to volunteers to join a corps that was distinctively Irish and have at least some degree of national cohesion and character. Second, Asquith pledged that the Volunteers would be given official recognition as part of an Irish defence force under the crown. Most importantly, the Prime Minister also pledged that there would be no question of compulsion. Nothing was asked or would be asked but the 'offering of a free people'. This last pledge in particular would not be forgotten. Later the Prime Minister twice assured Redmond privately that Lord Kitchener would announce the formation of the Irish army corps. However, promises to Redmond were one thing, when it came to facing down and commanding Kitchener that was another matter entirely. A letter preserved among Prime Minister Asquith's private papers dated 30th September 1914 reads:

Dear Mr Redmond,

I have spoken to Lord Kitchener on the subject of your letter, and he will have the announcement made that the War office has sanctioned the formation of an Irish Army Corps.'

Yours very truly,

H.H. Asquith.

In the event, despite the backing of Asquith and Lloyd George (who was himself at loggerheads with Kitchener over the creation of a Welsh corps), Kitchener's intransigence and Carson's disinterest in such a formation ensured the Irish army corps would never materialise. The Irish National Volunteers never enlisted en masse so never formed their own Irish National Volunteer division. However, it was vitally important politically to Redmond that the 16th (Irish) Division was seen to be distinctly Irish above all else. When it came to the nationality of the formation, Kitchener would not be Redmond's biggest problem. That arrived soon after the formation of the 16th (Irish) Division when it was announced that General Sir Lawrence Parsons had been appointed its commander.

Meanwhile, Sinn Féin and James Connolly and his Irish socialists, attempted to undermine the British recruiting efforts in Ireland with an anti-recruitment campaign. The split in the Nationalist ranks and the anti-recruitment campaign helped to further highlight and politicise Irish recruiting figures and enlistment patterns. For the next year, Nationalist politicians were required to justify perceived Irish recruiting shortfalls in comparison to other parts of Great Britain.

Although the vast majority of the Volunteers, both in Ireland and in Scotland, went with Redmond at the split, with the possible exception of the Belfast Volunteers, there would be no en masse enlistment from the Irish National Volunteers into the 16th (Irish) or any other division. In fact, many of the Volunteers left the organisation fearful of being coerced into enlisting, while others held off with the carrot of being armed and trained as an Irish Defence Force still a possibility. John Redmond's determined recruiting effort for his Irish brigade would be a constant uphill struggle to enthuse men for the British and Allied cause and would lead to accusations of him being nothing more than a recruiting sergeant for the British Army. It is probably fairer to say that he was recruiting for both the Irish and British causes, which meant that de facto he had to ask Nationalist Irishmen to serve in the British Army. It was not always the case. John Redmond, the IPP and the UIL vehemently opposed the British Imperial adventure in South Africa and Redmonites hooted Irish regiments as they left Dublin for the war against the Boers. It was the Glasgow Irish in the Home Government Branch, following Redmond's lead, that led to the then Celtic chairman, John H McLaughlin, being put under intense pressure to resign after he publicly supported the British war effort in South Africa.

GLASGOW'S IRISH VOLUNTEERS

John Redmond's call to fight wherever the firing line extended, split the Nationalist movement, including those based in Glasgow. In what was undoubtedly a reflection of Irish Nationalist opinion of the times, the vast majority of the Volunteers, both in Ireland and on the British mainland, would back Redmond and the IPP's move to support the British war effort. The size of the split is another indication of the popular mood, both in Ireland and among the Glasgow Irish. Although a highly motivated minority of around 12,000 remained with the old Irish Volunteers, the vast majority, 168,000 followed the lead given by John Redmond. Redmond's followers became known as the Irish National Volunteers. The same sentiment can be seen among the Glasgow Irish.

On Sunday 27 September, the winter session of the Home Government Branch of the UIL opened. The large meeting of the Glasgow Irish was held in the Watson Hall in Glasgow with the massively influential Arthur Murphy, brother of Celtic FC founding father Hugh and himself an early club committeeman, presiding. At the outset a motion was proposed and seconded to convey the thanks of the branch to the Irish leader and the Irish Party, to the Prime Minister and to the supporters of Home Rule in the House of Commons for the enactment of that measure.

The guest speaker to the meeting was David Mitchel Quin, editor of the Glasgow Observer. His subject was 'The attitude of Ireland Towards Great Britain after Home Rule'. The speaker said that Home Rule having now been placed on the statute book, it was a reasonable assumption that it would not be removed. On that assumption, what should be the attitude of Ireland towards the sister kingdoms and the Empire? He ventured to urge that Ireland ought to immediately assume and manifest an attitude of complete, sincere and unreserved loyalty to the United Kingdom and the Empire at large, which was applauded. All Home Rule leaders from Butt to Redmond had constantly argued that the concession of national autonomy to Ireland would evoke from Ireland a loyalty to the Empire, which had been previously withheld. Now that Ireland's demands had been conceded, the onus lay on the people of Ireland to be as good as their word. At every stage of the discussion on Home Rule the great majority of the people of Ireland had authorised Redmond and the Irish Party to conclude the satisfactory settlement that had been reached. They had approved of all that the Irish Party had done in the name of the Irish people. They had authorised Redmond to assure the Empire that Irish autonomy would lead to Irish loyalty and it was now up to the Irish people to deliver the goods. Questions were invited. The Sinn Féin delegates present, including IRB man Charles Carrigan, gave him a long interrogation. Although there was no record of the questions or answers, it was reported that the putting and answering of these questions infused considerable liveliness into the proceedings.

Reflecting the sentiment of the vast majority of the Glasgow Irish at the meeting, the following telegram was sent to John Redmond:

> *Cranks and extremists in Scotland are neither of account politically nor in the Volunteer movement here. Irish Volunteer companies in Scotland loyal to the Irish party have ever refused to be associated in any way with the Dublin Provisional Committee. We convey to you and the Irish party our heartiest congratulations on securing home rule. One hundred branches of the United Irish League in Scotland and their volunteer axillaries thoroughly approve of your policy regarding the war.*

The Glasgow Catholic Observer, of course, covered the meeting and the following Saturday the newspaper headline was 'Ireland and the Empire. Glasgow Irishmen Declare for Loyalty'.

That the Glasgow Observer should come out in support of the Redmonites is no surprise, since its proprietor, Charles Diamond, was a staunch supporter of the Irish Parliamentary Party, but the newspaper accurately reflected the majority opinion of its Glasgow Irish readers. The same edition of the Observer carried the story of the meeting of G (Bridgeton) Company, 1st Glasgow and West of Scotland Bn of the newly retitled Irish National Volunteers, which was of course organised by John Joseph Hinchey:

> *A meeting was called to discuss the actions of the breakaway section of the Dublin committee. The result of the meeting held in the Langholm Hall in Broad Street, Bridgeton was a strongly worded message sent to the Dublin Headquarters. That we the members of 'G' Company, Irish National Volunteers, condemn in the strongest terms the attitude adopted by a section of the governing body in Dublin and pledge our wholehearted support to Mr Redmond and the Irish Party and are in complete sympathy with their policies and we recognise no other leader or board not under the control of Mr John Redmond or his authorised representatives.*

All the office bearers of the Bridgeton Company, including the very active JJ Hinchey, signed the declaration.

At the end of September, the Glasgow County Volunteer Board instructed all Company Commanders of the 1st and 2nd Bns of the Glasgow and West of Scotland Irish Volunteers to determine the opinions of their companies regarding which committee they wished to recognise. Of the twenty-two volunteer companies based in Glasgow and district, eighteen voted to support John Redmond while four broke away. The editorial in the Glasgow Observer in mid-October commented on the split in the Irish Volunteers and the creation of the new Irish National Volunteers under John Redmond:

> The Irish Volunteer movement has now been place on a satisfactory footing and can proceed uninterruptedly with the work before it. Having rid itself of the small and insignificant discordant element, which all along has been seeking to create trouble and ferment strife, the organisation will find new life and vigour for carrying out its allotted task. Freed from this incubus, which had prevented the progress, it can proceed steadily in carrying out its aims and objectives. While graciously consenting publically to allow Mr Redmond's nominees to have a voice in the control of the Volunteers, this small minority of malcontents have all along in private sought to thwart and hinder the efforts made by the majority of the committee to place the movement on a proper working basis. The rupture such as it is, was bound to come and having now come, it is all for the good for the future of Ireland's military force.

The huge numbers who followed Redmond is testament to the influence that he and the Home Rule movement exerted over most Irish people, including the Glasgow Irish. However, for most of those who had joined the Irish Volunteer movement, their primary objective was not to achieve an Irish republic or indeed to fight for the British, but to defend the Home Rule Bill against Ulster Unionist opposition.

After the split in the Nationalist ranks, very many Catholic Irishmen from the whole of Britain did respond to Redmond's call. Persuaded by the arguments, particularly the cause of defending the rights and liberties of small nations, they joined Britain's new citizen armies. Reginald Dunne and Joseph O'Sullivan were two such Nationalist Irishmen, who became British soldiers specifically to help secure the freedom of small nations. In July 1922, the two men, now London-based IRA operatives, assassinated Sir Henry Wilson on his London doorstep. After shooting the man, who had been described after the Curragh Mutiny as an 'Anglo-Irish bigot', both were captured. They were caught because Joe O'Sullivan's wooden leg impeded his escape. Ironically, he had lost the limb fighting at Ypres in 1917 while serving with the London Regiment. Unable to escape his pursuers, Dunne came back for him and both were apprehended. At their trial, Reginald Dunne wrote a statement, but it was not allowed to be read to the court:

> We took our part in supporting the aspirations of our fellow-countrymen in the same way as we took our part in supporting the nations of the world who fought for the rights of small nationalities ... The same principles for

*which we shed our blood on the battlefield of Europe led us to commit the
act we are charged with.*

They were both hanged at London's Wandsworth Prison. The remains of Reginald Dunne
and Joseph O'Sullivan were repatriated to Ireland in 1976 when they were reburied in the
republican plot at Deansgrange Cemetery.

The Irish National Volunteers in the west of Scotland stagnated after the split. The
effectiveness of the Volunteer militias had been degraded by the recall of its ex-army instructors
and veterans. Over the next year or so, the Irish National Volunteers in the west of Scotland,
although still effectively up and running and conducting the odd route march, went into
hibernation as more and more members enlisted, were sucked into the expanding munitions
industries where they worked very long hours, or were later conscripted.

The split had left the Irish Volunteers in west central Scotland with only four companies,
all heavily infiltrated by the IRB. Like the National Volunteers, it too required reorganising.
The four companies comprising around 100 men formed themselves into a new A Company,
Glasgow Irish Volunteers. Shortly afterwards the IRB in Scotland was thrown into disarray when
its commander and Scottish representative on the Supreme Council, John Mulholland, resigned
over the suggestion that the IRB could stage an insurrection during the war. The rift was serious
enough to see lifelong advanced Nationalist Mulholland leave the organisation entirely before
the end of the year. It would be early 1915 before Glasgow's new IRB appointee to the Supreme
Council, Coatbridge-born Charles Carrigan, a socialist and Sinn Féin member, was in place.
Carrigan was at the same time a member of A Company, Glasgow Irish Volunteers. While the men
of the Irish Volunteers were in some disarray, it was the boys of the *Na Fianna Éireann* and later
the women of the Glasgow branch of *Cumann na mBan* who would largely take up the slack. A
slaugh of the Fianna was formed in Glasgow in 1910 and organised by Belfast-born IRB man Joe
Robinson, whose family lived in Glasgow. He would become a key figure in the Fenian movement
in the city and in addition to organising the Fianna, in 1914 he took an active part in the formation
of the Glasgow Irish Volunteers and was on the permanent committee of the Glasgow and West
of Scotland Regiment, where he represented the Clydebank Company. After the split in October
1914, he led the reorganisation of the Irish Volunteers in Glasgow.

In January 1915, Cathal O'Shannon, a member of the IRB Supreme Council, arrived in
Glasgow from Dublin. At a meeting in Joseph Robinson's house in Robson Street, Govanhill,
he warned that the ground was being prepared for an uprising against the British government
as soon as the time was opportune. Throughout 1915, a steady stream of weapons, explosives
and detonators were acquired by the IRB in Glasgow and its environs and transported across
the water. The materiel was gathered from assorted sources, including miners who had access to
explosives and detonators at the pits. Weapons and bullets were purchased from serving soldiers
and there were raids on ammunition and explosive stores. The most active Glasgow IRB men with
links to the Fianna included Barney Friel, Eamonn Mooney, Sean and Seumas McGallogly and
Seamus Reader.

CELTIC FC

Browning attacks the Dundee goal.
(Courtesy Dundee Courier)

On 26 September, the Celtic travelled to Dundee for the sixth game of the season. They were yet to win away from home and Dens Park was never a happy hunting ground for the Celts in the League. Indeed, the previous season, when they won 1–0 there, it was only the second time in some ten years that they had finished on the right side. The record for the last fifteen years made poor reading for any Celtic supporter: Dundee, nine wins; Celtic, three wins; and three draws. On the day, Celtic with a stiff breeze behind them started as if they wished to put the record right and only some stout defending by the home team kept the Celts at bay. Eventually the pressure was bound to tell and just before half-time McColl scored with a fine header. The Bhoys started the second half as they finished the first. Two minutes after the resumption and before the Dees had a chance to settle, Patsy Gallacher fired a powerful drive past Balfour to double the Celts lead. Three minutes later McColl added Celtic's third and his own second. The Bhoys took the opportunity to turn on the style with the wingers and midfield linking to produce some dazzling football. The Dundee defence was helpless and it was due to Celtic's showboating that the score was not increased. A surprising defensive lapse just before the end allowed Dundee to reduce the deficit. The 12,000 strong crowd were treated to the sight of Celtic in full flow and most enjoyed the experience.

On 28 September Celtic were due to play an away fixture against Clyde; however, the game was played at Parkhead due to a fire at Clyde's Shawfield Stadium. The fire destroyed much of the club's kit and equipment and the Clyde players turned out against Celtic in an odd assortment of footwear, having lost their boots in the fire. Celtic were in the mood for playing and put on a display of superb passing, attractive, entertaining football and were three goals up before half-time. The first from McMenemy coming after five minutes was a close range effort, which the Clyde goalie could not hold. The second from Browning came after a clever feint and a thunderbolt shot into the net after twenty minutes. The third and the last came from McColl just before half-time. After the restart the Bhoys played exhibition football but failed to add to their goal tally. Clyde were glad to hear the final whistle after ninety minutes of chasing shadows and the ball. The game was played in front of 15,000 spectators.

That week, after an approach by Ayr United, Celtic agreed the loan transfer of Alex Gray to the 'Honest Men' for the second time. The talented left-winger from Stenhousemuir simply could not break into the Celtic team. He rarely got the chance to shine since the position was occupied by the seldom-injured 'Smiler' Browning. At Ayr United he would join the other former or on loan Celts, Willie McStay, Bernie Connolly, Joe Cassidy and Archie McMillan.

THE HOME FRONT

While the BEF was fighting to the north-east of Paris, it had not gone unnoticed by the British citizenry that the roads to the Channel ports of Calais and Boulogne were wide open. On 30 September 1914, with the threat of a German invasion now a very real possibility, many towns and cities, including Glasgow, decided to form a Citizen's Training Force. The object of the force was to provide military training for men in the Glasgow district who were ineligible or for business or other valid reasons unable to enlist immediately in the armed forces. Similar home defence organisations were springing up all over the country. In London, the theatre and arts community decided to form themselves into a Corps of Artists and Painters. Its ongoing success was woefully undermined after a wag commented that they were 'longing for a brush with the enemy'. Around the same time, Willie Maley was in discussions with the Athletic Volunteer Force. As one of the largest and best organised, the Athletic Volunteers enlisted the services of the secretaries of the various cricket, cycling, golf, athletics and football clubs to form branches of the organisation. By the middle of October, Willie Maley was the honorary secretary of the Glasgow District of the Athletic Volunteer Force. Based at Celtic Park, he organised drill and shooting training for the volunteer athletes and the Beardmore rifle range.

On 30 September the first public indication that Glasgow was considering the formation of the Glasgow Citizen's Training Force was published in the Glasgow Herald. Those interested in joining the force were to make themselves known. It was quickly felt necessary to remind those wishing to apply for membership of the Citizen's Training Force that the force was intended for those men who were ineligible or unable to enlist in the active forces, but who wished to prepare themselves for any eventuality. It was vital that nothing should be done to prejudice recruiting for Kitchener's service battalions. The Citizen's Force was not to be regarded as a substitute for service in the armed forces.

With the newspapers full of stories of heroic last-ditch battles and invasion scares and the wonderful Home Rule news from Ireland, in the Garngad, William James Hilley decided to join the army. On 29 September, he walked into a recruiting office in Glasgow and followed his younger brother into the Royal Artillery. He was exactly the type of recruit the army was looking for: unmarried, twenty-five years old and an unskilled steelworks labourer. He tracked his brother to No 6 Royal Artillery's base depot at Glasgow, reporting there the following day.

By the end of September, Lody, the German spy, had achieved much of what he wanted to and feeling nervous decided to move on. He travelled from Edinburgh via Liverpool to Dublin, having decided to lie low in Ireland for a while but sent a final message back to his spymaster containing information on the busy ports. After landing in Dublin he made his way to Killarney in Co Kerry. Unknown to him he was being monitored by the British secret service and the Irish police arrested him at his hotel on 2 October.

During the last week in September, the Glasgow parishes sent representatives to the Belgian Catholic Relief Committee meeting in the Catholic Institute in Glasgow to discuss their contribution to the latest flag day. St Joseph's Parish sent a certain Miss Margaret Skinnider, local schoolteacher, active suffragette and future member of the Glasgow branch of *Cumann nam Ban*. This time it was Belgian Flag Day to be held on Saturday 3 October. The event would see the women and their collecting tins back on the streets in Glasgow and over thirty towns and villages throughout Scotland. On the day over 6000 women, including very many of the Glasgow Irish women and girls, were out in all districts of the city with their trays of Belgian flags and collecting boxes. In the event, good weather helped the Glasgow collectors raise over £5800. Later the contribution of Roman Catholic schoolteachers to the success of the Belgian Flag Day was widely acclaimed in the press.

WAR! AND FOOTBALL

There's gloom spread broadcast o'er the land.

And hearts are stirred today;

And every soldier, gun in hand,

Impatient waits the fray.

But still we will not be morose,

But, tighten up our belts,

We'll hope that Britain beats her foes

And go and see the Celts.

The German Emperor, they say,

Has sought this war for years;

And we must pay the price to-day

In men and women's tears.

But we must conquer Europe's dread, And his great ambitions smother;

We have one "Napoleon" at Parkhead,

And we do not need another.

James Conway

Chapter Five

OCTOBER

CELTIC FC

On Saturday 3 October the Celtic were at home to a Dundee team that they had outclassed only a fortnight previously. The Bhoys were again on top form playing one of their best games of the season. McMenemy was masterly and controlled the game from start to finish. The Celtic forward line played fast, skilful, attractive football, which at times completely mesmerised the Dundee backline. Dundee although well beaten, did contribute to the spectacle. It was one of those games were everything went right and while Charlie Shaw and his defence were never taxed, the Celtic forwards gave the Dundee backline a torrid time and the score could easily have been much higher. Smiler Browning got a hat-trick, while McMenemy got two and McColl one in a richly deserved 6–0 rout. It is not often the Celts pile on six goals. Prior to the Dundee game, they had not scored six goals in a League match since season 1909/10 when they defeated Queen's Park by 6–0. Unfortunately, just 10,000 spectators watched the superb game. Unsurprising, considering the recent dire news from France and growing casualty figures adding to the sombre mood. Elsewhere, Hearts dropped two points at Dumbarton, their first League loss after eight successive victories. A crowd of 16,000 watch Rangers beaten at home by Morton, while Ayr United continued to impress with a 4–0 drubbing of Hibernian.

On Monday 5 October, Celtic played their second game in two days when they travelled to Kirkcaldy to play Raith Rovers. Johnny McMaster was injured and Peter Johnstone finally fit again, covered his position. Joe Dodds, stepping up from the back, took Peter's place. The ever-reliable Tommy McGregor in for his fifth game in a row again filled Joe's place. In what became the closest of games the Bhoys attempted to play the Celtic way on a pitch that was not really suited to passing football. Celtic went into the lead after just five minutes through McMenemy but with more than a hint of an own goal. Raith Rovers was awarded a penalty for what looked to most observers an accidental handball against Tommy McGregor and the resulting spot kick was successfully put away. Jimmy McColl got Celtic's second while Walsh scored Raith's second equaliser within a few minutes of the restart. With all the goals scored in the first half, the second turned into a midfield battle with Raith Rovers playing a spoiling game where the ball spent a considerable amount of time in the crowd. Browning had a chance to win the game for the Celts in the final minutes of the match but missed when it looked easier to score. In a bizarre incident the referee RF Murray of Stenhousemuir took exception to the level of shouting from the crowd. After bringing the game to a halt, he addressed the crowd warning them if the barracking did not stop he would cancel the game. It is not clear what the barracking was about or why the referee had taken offence. The reaction of the crowd to the headmaster like telling off was also not recorded. The game however did continue and ended in a 2–2 draw. A very moderate crowd of 5000 turned out on a fine autumn day to watch the game.

Understandable when you consider the small Fife town had already seen thousands of her sons off to the war. With Celtic and Hearts having now both played nine games, the Tynecastle men sat on top of the league with sixteen points and Celtic three points behind on thirteen, followed by Rangers and Ayr United.

Saturday 10 October saw the Celtic on the Ayrshire coast where they took a full-strength side, less McMaster who was still out through injury. It was the same team and formation, which had drawn at Kirkcaldy. The record crowd of 10,000 spectators included a trainload of the Celtic faithful through from Glasgow. The 'Honest Men' had a good start to the season and before the game were only two points behind Celtic in the league table. The three Celts on loan at Ayr, McStay, Cassidy and Gray, were fired up and ready to show the Celtic directors what they were missing. In fine footballing weather and with a perfect pitch the crowd looked forward to seeing an exciting game. Unfortunately, it failed to happen. The first half turned into a slogging match and ended with both teams unable to get the upper hand. As opposed to fine passing and delicate footwork, hard charging and strong tackling were the features of the play. The second half began as the first half ended with both teams fighting hard for possession and manoeuvring for an advantage. McColl and Gallacher for Celtic and McStay, McLaughlin and Middleton for Ayr all took bad knocks through the rough play. With most of the play centring on the midfield Celtic's forwards contributed little to the game. Gallacher and McMenemy tried to get involved, while McColl was effectively marked out of the game. With twenty minutes to go Jimmy McMenemy burst through on the opponent's goal and looked set to score but Lyall in the Ayr goal threw himself onto the ball before the Celt could pull the trigger. The keeper sustained a bad cut to the head and bleeding profusely, had to go off for stitches. Richardson the Ayr striker took his place between the sticks. Even with Ayr down to ten men, Celtic could not take advantage as the home team refused to surrender possession of the midfield. Just as it looked as if the game would end in a scoreless draw, defeat for Celtic came at the hands of a future Parkhead favourite. Joe Cassidy picked up the ball on the right side of the field, cut inside and scored with a superbly struck shot. The goal came with only fifteen minutes to go and proved to be the only goal of a game. The game was for most of the ninety minutes a dour midfield contest with neither set of forwards in the match. Despite the fighting qualities of Ayr United, Celtic's class should have prevailed, unfortunately, too many Celts played below par and Ayr United deserved the victory. The travelling faithful dejectedly made their way back to Glasgow having watched the Celtic's third away defeat of the season.

The points dropped at Ayr left Celtic in third place in the table behind Heart of Midlothian still on top after a good home win against Motherwell. Rangers were second on the same points (thirteen) as the Bhoys but with a better goal difference. A delighted Ayr United was in fourth place through goal difference but on the same points total as Celtic and Rangers. That same Saturday the Celtic club went into mourning for the loss of one of its own. Director James Grant died at his home in Toome Bridge, Country Antrim. The genial Irishman who sported a magnificent beard was for the best part of twenty years one of the prime movers behind the scenes at Parkhead. Well aware of his limitations when it came to football, he was quite content to leave such matters to Willie Maley and James Kelly and never ventured an opinion as to team selection. In 1898 with permission from the board, he built a lavish private two-storey stand on the London Road side of the ground. The luxury edifice boasted padded seats and windows that could be shut if it rained. However, condensation meant the windows were useless and they were later removed. Ill for some years he underwent several operations. Ironically, he had been feeling better over the last few months than he had for a considerable time but a sudden relapse meant he was too weak to fight on.

THE WAR FRONT

Over the second week of October the BEF began withdrawing units from the Aisne and redeploying them north towards the Franco-Belgian border. The move would position the BEF between the extreme left of the French army and the remnants of the small Belgian army fighting desperately at Antwerp and hanging onto what little remained unoccupied of Belgium. On 9 October, in what was a stunning blow for the Allies, Antwerp fell to the Germans. However, despite taking the fortress, the Germans allowed the Belgian garrison of 50,000 men to escape, falling back first to Bruges, Ostend and finally to the line of the Yser, from Nieuwpoort to Diksmuide. Too late the Germans realised their blunder and rapidly advanced in an attempt to pin the Belgians, but they had missed their chance. In addition to the garrison abandoning Antwerp, tens of thousands of Belgian citizens who had already fled into the city to escape the Germans as they rampaged through the country were forced to flee again. The fall of Antwerp, occupation of Bruges and subsequent advance on Zeebrugge and Ostend had a chilling effect on England. It produced a reaction that far surpassed that of the apparent imminent fall of Paris at the end of August. Now it was London and not Paris that was threatened and the English felt menaced in their own homes. Never since the days of Napoleon Bonaparte had an enemy been so close to the English Channel. The arrival of the Germans on the Belgian coast heightened the likelihood of invasion and air raids on the south and east of England, while occupation of the channel ports presented the certainty of increased German submarine activity on Britain's supply routes.

By 10 October, the bulk of the BEF had been moved, largely by train, to concentration areas west of Lille with a view to advancing due east via Lille, turning the German flank or bursting through into the perceived gap. Just as the British were about to commence their advance, news arrived that Antwerp had fallen, more bad news was received on 11 October when it was learned that the Germans had taken Lille. All the bad news was offset by some good in that the Indian Corps had arrived in the south of France and was en route north. The 7th Infantry and 3rd Cavalry Division cobbled together in Britain had arrived in theatre on 6 October and would after the fall of Antwerp be attached to the BEF, forming IV Corps.

The fall of Lille meant the BEF's plans to advance due east were changed and the search for the gap saw their advance diverted to a north-easterly direction towards the Belgian medieval town of Ypres. The area of Ypres was once described as a shallow basin with the town in the middle. The hills forming the sides or rim of the basin are very low and partly wooded. The line of their crests runs approximately north to south, through the Houthulst Forest, Poelcappelle, Passchendaele, Broodseinde, Becelaere, Gheluvelt, and a nondescript rise that would become the strategic Hill 60 (south of Zillebeke) and St Eloi. The Messines Ridge begins around seven miles south of Ypres and is just 200 feet at its highest point. The feature would barely be considered much more than a slight rise in Scotland, but as the highest ground in the area it completely dominated the countryside for miles around and took on massive tactical importance. From Messines itself the ridge runs two miles north to Wytschaete before curving north-east. German advance parties had actually entered Ypres on 7 October, but

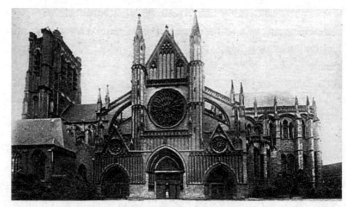

St Martin's Cathedral, Ypres

withdrew as the BEF began to arrive in the vicinity.

The British advance to contact began to 10 October with II Corps under the command of Horace Smith Dorian moving from the area around Bethune towards the Estairs and the La Bassee road. The following day the advance continued now in co-ordination with French forces. The III Corps under William Pulteney moved towards Bailleul and Armentières while the Cavalry Corps under General Edmund Allenby would secure the Messines and Wytschaete Ridges, south of Ypres. The newly arrived IV Corps under Rawlinson would secure Ypres itself. If successful, the manoeuvring would see the British forces in contact with Belgian forces on the Yser. The plan would be operational just in time, two German Armies had been ordered to descend on the channel ports and they too would be advancing via Flanders and Ypres. Over the next six weeks or so the British and Germans clashed in a series of vicious and costly fights around Ypres as both sides attempted to find a way past their opponents.

SCOTTISH FOOTBALL

Over the first two weeks of October, the fighting in France had quietened as the tactical situation took on a defensive posture. The British casualty rates lessened significantly as the BEF was moved out of the line on the Aisne and transferred north into Flanders. Over the same two- or three-week period the pressure on professional football also eased. The War Office's decision on continuance and the recruiting schemes put in place by the clubs had placated all but the most vociferous 'Stop Football' lobbyists. Remarkably, since the outbreak of war, ten weeks previously, the city of Glasgow alone had given over 30,000 of her sons to the military, this amounted to almost every available man between the ages of nineteen and twenty-four. A very large proportion of them were working-class football supporters.

In England, a certain Frederick Nicholas Charrington was far from content with the situation regarding professional football. The heir to a massive family fortune made from brewing, Charrington renounced his wealth and opened a charitable mission in London's east end. Even before the war he harboured a pathological hatred of football associating the professional game with a lack of morals and alcohol abuse. Later described as 'The Stop Football Fiend' Charrington launched a very public anti-football campaign and would almost single handily pressurise the War Office into a turnaround. He wrote to King George V suggesting he withdraw his patronage of the FA. He also wrote to the President of the FA Lord Kinnaird, urging him to resign. The highly regarded Arthur Kinnaird was himself a football legend. A Scotland internationalist he played in nine FA Cup Finals and was the proud possessor of five winners medals. When Lord Kinnaird wrote back explaining that the case for continuing football was too long and complex for a letter, Charrington turned up unannounced at Lord Kinnaird's home looking for his verbal explanation. Two of Lord Kinnaird's sons would later be killed in action. Undaunted, Charrington's vociferous campaign against professional football continued and he was later arrested at Fulham trying to stop the game and ended up in court the following Monday. However, all this adverse publicity had painted the professional game and its directors and players in a bad light and had begun to swing public opinion in favour of the stop football lobby. Although Charrington's verbal assault on the professional game was aimed at English football in the main, with the story being carried in the national newspapers, Scottish football too suffered from the fall out.

Frederick Nicholas Charrington

CELTIC FC

Perhaps in an attempt to silence or placate the stop football lobby, or more likely in support of the United Irish League (UIL) and Irish Parliamentary Party (IPP), the directors of Celtic Football Club got directly involved in the ongoing football continuance and Irish recruiting debate when they offered Celtic Park, free of charge to the UIL for what they described as a monster-recruiting meeting. On 12 October, the delegates of the Glasgow branches of the UIL met with Arthur Murphy in the chair. After sending a message of support to John Redmond, they issued an invitation to TP O'Connor MP to come to Glasgow. It was planned that he would address the meeting, organised for Celtic Park, in support of recruiting among the Glasgow and west of Scotland nationalists. However, TP O'Connor apparently disliked speaking outdoors and while he agreed to come to Glasgow, he rejected the idea of using Celtic Park stating that he wanted to address the meeting in a hall.

On Sunday 11 October Jimmy McMenemy, Johnny Browning and Joe Dodds were part of the Scottish League team that travelled to New Cross, London for a match against a Southern League side. Alex McNair, Johnny McMasters and Andy McAtee also travelled as reserves. The game played at the ground of Millwall FC on Monday afternoon ended in a 1–1 draw with both goals scored in the first ten minutes. The game went rapidly downhill afterwards with only one or two goalmouth incidents to excite the 5000 spectators. The Scottish team on the day was Brownlie (Third Lanark); Crossan (Hearts) and Dodds (Celtic); Gordon (Rangers), Wylie (Aberdeen), and Nellies (Hearts); Low (Hearts) and McMenemy (Celtic); Reid (Airdrieonians); Low (Hearts) and Browning (Celtic).

After the game the Celtic Bhoys travelled through to Aldershot where they visited friends and relations serving in the army. The Hampshire town was adjacent to the vast expanse of Salisbury Plain now a giant army tented encampment containing the best part of 200,000 men. Two of Joe Dodds brothers, William and Hugh, Garvie of Queen's Park and scores of Scottish amateur footballers were training with their battalions; part of Kitchener's Army and camped on the Plain. The Celtic supporters among the soldiers lionised the Celts and they turned out in their thousands to greet their football heroes. On his return to Glasgow, Jimmy McMenemy gave a quick interview to the Weekly Record. Jimmy spoke of his experiences in the London blackout, with the Londoners terrified of Zeppelin raids and of seeing loads of pitiful Belgian refugees. He'd seen old men; women and children all huddled together at the railway station and noted their haunted look that spoke of terrible experiences at the hands of the Germans. *"Vengeance is mine,"* said Jimmy, *"but I hope Kaiser Wilhelm gets his reward on this earth, and that when he does it is a good old British bayonet that gives it him."*

Saturday 17 October saw the Celtic play host to a young, tough to beat Falkirk team at Parkhead. The 20,000 strong crowd let out the biggest roar of the day at the unadvertised appearance of thirty-six-year-old Jimmy Quinn for the first time in the new season. The Celtic directors, Kelly, Dunbar, Colgan, Shaughnessy and White had been over the water at the funeral of fellow director James Grant and only announced the team late on Friday night. Jimmy was now semi-retired, but he had a gentleman's agreement with Willie Maley that he would train part time at Parkhead and be available to play if the Celtic were in dire need. Such an occasion arose with the loss of McColl through an accident earlier in the week. The Celtic favourite looked bulky, but fit, as he took to the field. In addition to it being his first game of the season, he only played two games throughout the previous season, so in modern terminology; he was less than match fit. That said he did play relatively well, spraying passes about and had two or three good attempts on goal. He even had a hand in the winning goal, but most fans could see he was not the rampaging Mighty Quinn of old. The game was described as colourless and fairly even, though most impartial observers agreed that Celtic just shaded it. They gained full points through a single goal scored by Patsy Gallacher, but the highlight of the day was most certainly the reappearance of the mighty Jimmy Quinn.

THE HOME FRONT

Since the invasion of Belgium, over 125,000 Belgians, almost all Roman Catholics, fled to Britain in fear of German atrocities. The Belgians, mostly peasants, had been driven from their farms with their only possessions what they could carry. On arrival in Britain many were totally bewildered by modern life and strange foreign customs after their own almost medieval lifestyles. The latest batches arrived in the south of England after the fall of Antwerp and these were the first to be dispersed to Scotland.

The day before the Celtic versus Falkirk game at Parkhead, over 1000 destitute Belgian refugees arrived in Glasgow's Queen Street Station. Although there were a number of Belgian Relief Fund organisations in the city, including the Catholic Relief Committee, they were set up to send aid to Belgium and not to deliver it to destitute people standing at their close mouths.

The Glasgow civic authorities had received very short notice from central government that the city was now the distribution centre for Belgian refugees sent to Scotland and as many as 3000 refugees were being sent to the city. Realising the scale of the problem, the Glasgow Corporation took on the responsibility of care for the refugees. Despite the short notice, the refugees were given a very warm welcome to the city and were met at the railway station by a number of the city magistrates, representatives of the city's Belgian Relief Committee and dozens of Roman Catholic priests and nuns. The refugees were showered with gifts of chocolate, cigarettes and money as they were transported in cars through the large crowds of well-wishers who had turned out to cheer them from the railway station. From Queen Street Station,

Belgian Refugees arrive in Glasgow
(Courtesy of Glasgow Evening Times)

they were taken to the City Halls in Candleriggs where they were given a meal and received gifts of fruit from the merchants at the adjacent fruit market. A further two trainloads comprising another 800 refugees were expected in the city later that day.

Most of the refugees arrived penniless and Glasgow's Roman Catholic community played a large part in the city's relief efforts. Prior to being distributed throughout Scotland where they would be supported by local communities and helped to find employment, the refugees were accommodated by the local charities like the Salvation Army and in Glasgow Corporation institutions. Many were also sent to city hotels like the Great Eastern Hotel in Duke Street. Over 200 Belgian families were placed with Glasgow Catholic households, while more were accommodated in the convent of the Little Sisters of the Poor on Garngad Hill, the convent of the Helpers of the Holy Souls in Langside, the Dalbeth convent on London road and in St Mary's Industrial School in the Calton. The refugees were eventually distributed throughout the whole of Scotland, but most went to the surrounding towns and villages like Hamilton, Coatbridge, Paisley and Kirkintilloch. Over 3000 refugees would arrive in Glasgow over that weekend. Despite the warm and genuine welcome they received, the British class system raised its ugly head when it was noted 'the last trainload to arrive in Glasgow contained Belgians of a better class than those that had already arrived.' The show of social unity and the financial generosity of the entire Glasgow community during the Belgian crisis was quite remarkable.

The Celtic football club would take a particular interest in the Belgian refugees and as soon as the emergency presented itself the Celtic directors donated £105 to the Belgian Relief Fund on behalf of the club. A devout Roman Catholic, Willie Maley was moved by the plight of the

Belgians and was among the Glasgow Roman Catholics who took refugees into their homes. On 20 October two young men Victor Colot and Francis Stolle arrived at the Maley home at Hyndland Avenue where Willie's mother Mary Ann looked after them. Francis Stolle was a seventeen-year-old student from Antwerp who only remained at the Maleys' for a few weeks before leaving for military service. Victor Colot was a twenty-year-old student from Monceau-sur-Sambre near Charleroi. He had fled from his home to Antwerp towards the end of August when two German regiments went on a drunken rampage through the town committing atrocities and burning down over 300 houses. Its unclear exactly how long he remained with the Maley family.

St Mungo—I'm nn muckle o' a haun' at foreign languages, but, thank guidness, I can aye manage the weans "Villy voo biv anither piece et jeely!"

St Mungo's Belgian Bairns.
(Glasgow Evening Times)

On 21 October the Celtic directors allowed three players to travel through to Hamilton to play in a benefit match for Belgian Refugees. Alex and Tom McGregor and Billy Crone made their way through to Hamilton at their own expense where they played in a league select against Hamilton Accies. The open, entertaining game was enjoyed by the Hamilton crowd in which were a number of refugees as guests of honour. Celtic legend Peter Somers, now a director at Hamilton Accies, had organised the benefit game and between £50 and £60 was made for Hamilton's Belgian Refugee Fund. The game ended in a 3–3 draw, which according to the 2000 crowd was about the right outcome. Billy Crone, Reid (Airdrie) and Graham (Hearts) scored for the league select. It was the first of many such gestures of support by the Celtic Club for the refugees. The entire country contributed to the relief effort for the Belgians, as scores of diverse organisations and associations swung into action organising their own fund raising events, even the military got involved. One such example was the 9th (Glasgow Highlanders) Bn HLI then training in Dunfermline. They organised a football match among themselves with Tom Maley's son Josie, described as being formerly of Queen's Park, pulling on a shirt.

That week's edition of the Glasgow Catholic Observer was unstinting in its praise for the city officials and the various Protestant churches and church-led organisations that were offering their assistance to the Catholic Belgians. It was noted that many ministers accommodated refugees in their church halls and manses. Over the course of the Belgian refugee emergency of 1914, in excess of 8000 destitute Belgian citizens would come to Glasgow. Although the Glasgow citizens who had dealt with the last influx of Catholic refugees into the city during the Irish Potato Famine were long dead, many of the current officials must have been able to draw a parallel. Although the welcome given to the Belgian Catholics was more wholehearted, generous and genuine than was ever given to the starving Irish masses who washed up on the Clyde sixty years before, the common humanity displayed by the average Glaswegian, who rose to both events, brought a great deal of honour to Glasgow's citizenry.

The same edition of the Glasgow Observer recorded that Councillor Patrick Dollan had addressed a meeting of the Home Government Branch of the UIL. His subject was 'Why Glasgow Irishmen should vote Labour'. His speech was marked by some quite heavy heckling, but overall it was a pleasant, lively meeting. Although they had already recorded the deaths of a number of soldiers in their death columns, that weekend's Glasgow Star and Glasgow Observer carried the first photographs of Glasgow Irish soldiers killed in action. Privates John Duffy and Malcolm Wilson were both twenty-five-year-old regular soldiers. Duffy was originally from Athlone, Co Meath, while Wilson was a native of Glasgow's Anderston district. Both were killed on 14 September as the 1st Bn Cameron Highlanders attacked a sugar factory on the Troyon Ridge above the Aisne. It was one of the first major British attacks of the war and the uphill assault resulted in the deaths of 147 men. John Duffy and Malcolm Wilson would be the first of very many men from the Glasgow Irish community to appear in the Star's and Observer's death columns. That same weekend the congregation of St Patrick's in Anderston were asked to pray for the 700 parishioners then serving with the army. In the Garngad, Fathers Crumley and Collins at St Roch's were praying for 400 of their parishioners in the services, now including two of the Hilley brothers.

The day the Belgian Relief game was being played at Hamilton, Tom Maguire, the old Celtic trainer, sat down and wrote open letters to the editors of the Glasgow Evening Times and the Glasgow Herald on the sensitive subject of recruiting. Tom was a former British soldier, who had served in India, Afghanistan and Egypt with the 72nd Highlanders, later the Seaforth Highlanders. During his service on the North West Frontier and during the Afghan campaign, Tom's regiment took part in some of the most famous exploits of the Empire's defenders. Many of the incidents were published in the popular Boy's Own comic books and were sung about in the music halls of the period. After seeing service in Egypt including the fight at Tel-el-Kebir, Tom retired from the army as a sergeant instructor, specialising in gymnastics and physical fitness, around 1884. At that time, the Army Gymnastic Staff were at the cutting edge of physical training techniques and on returning to Scotland, Tom was appointed Celtic's first full-time professional trainer.

Tom McGuire's letters to the newspapers on recruiting made the case for the Glasgow 'wee man', barred from enlisting into the army due to his lack of height. The regulation minimum for recruits at the time was 5ft 3in. The letters argued simply that the regulation height should be lowered to allow small men to enlist. Tom reasoned that there were thousands of jobs in the military that could be done by 'small men', which in turn would release men of full height for active service. Indeed very many of the small men were as hard as nails and perfectly fit and able to fight and were only rejected for the lack of an inch or two. At the time of writing, Tom had two sons training with Kitchener's battalions. Initially, there was no response to Tom's suggestion, but soon the nation would need all her men, even those regarded as being vertically challenged.

The Army recruiters were not the only people looking to attract the Glasgow Irish. In Glasgow that week, 50,000 Irish men and women were wanted but not for military service: 'Irish & Proud of it' had opened in the Coliseum theatre. Described as a 'gigantic production', the all-Irish show covered just about every aspect of Irishness with Irish songs, stories, wit, pathos, customs and dancing. Fifty Irish performers, plus a chorus of Irish boys and colleens, put on the show. There was even jaunting cars and a donkey, presumably an Irish one.

THE IRISH VOLUNTEERS

On 14 October, John Redmond presided over the first meeting of the National Committee of the new Irish National Volunteers in Dublin. The constitution of the new organisation was submitted. It stated that:

> The objectives of the Volunteers shall be to train, equip and arm a volunteer force for the defence of Ireland and the advancement and preservation of Irish rights and the maintenance of Irish national self-government.

The Provisional Committee of the Irish Volunteers had been divided into two unequal camps since Redmond's speech of 3 August and a week after the Woodenbridge speech, the minority broke away, seized the Volunteer's headquarters and issued its own manifesto declaring: 'Redmond, through his nominees, no longer is entitled to any place in the administration of the Irish Volunteers.'

The rump of the Irish Volunteers was now under the remit of the Dublin Provisional Committee led by Eoin MacNeill, but in the effective control of Padraig Pearse and the IRB.

John Redmond, like mainstream politicians of all hues, fatally underestimated the potential and commitment of his advanced Nationalist opponents, dismissing them as 'well known cranks and mischief-makers' or 'a handful of pro-German shirkers', and the IRB as a cabal of old diehards of a bygone era. In Dublin, the split had been much less clear cut than it was nationally; nearly 2000 out of 6700 volunteers broke away from Redmond. The breakaway group retaining the title of the Irish Volunteers were now under the complete control of Eoin MacNeill and Padraic Pearse, both of whom had their own plans for their Irish Volunteers, though not necessarily the same plans. Although overall the split on the ground was amicable enough, there were a number of flashpoints. On 1 October, the National Volunteers in Cork raided the armoury of the Irish Volunteers while the latter were drilling in the Cornmarket. The raid netted over 100 rifles that the Irish Volunteers could ill afford to lose.

The newly independent Irish Volunteers spent the month of October reorganising. Eoin MacNeill became chief of staff, Bulmer Hobson quartermaster and Michael Joseph O'Rahilly director of arms. Three key posts were in the hands of the IRB: Padraic Pearse was director of military operations, Joseph Mary Plunkett was director of military operations and Thomas MacDonagh was director of training. All three later became members of the secret IRB Military Council, which would organise, under the influence of Thomas J Clarke, the Easter Rising of 1916. In comparison to the UVF, the new Irish Volunteers were a massively inefficient military force, lacking finance, trained officers, weapons, equipment and now woefully short of manpower. In an attempt to rectify some of the shortcomings, the leadership would later become embroiled in a conspiracy with the Germans, led by none other than the very high profile Sir Roger Casement.

JOHN REDMOND'S IRISH BRIGADE

Once John Redmond had settled on the idea that the 16th (Irish) Division would be the new Irish Brigade and the nucleus of his Irish Army, he was determined that it would be 'nothing less than an identifiable Irish Brigade'. The man appointed to raise and train the new division was General Sir Lawrence Parsons, who was brought out of retirement, having seen distinguished service in India, Sudan and South Africa as an artillery officer. Parsons was, of course, an Anglo-Irish Ascendancy protestant, although untypically he liked to stress his Irishness. He described himself as being an Irishman from an ancient Irish family with deep roots in King's County and added that his ancestors had opposed the Union and supported limited Catholic emancipation. Indeed, Wolfe Tone described one of Parsons's ancestors as 'one of the few honest men in the Irish House of Commons'. In fact, the first of the Parsons settled in Ireland in 1590 when as commissioner of plantations he obtained considerable grants of land from the crown. General Sir Lawrence Parsons was typical of the Irish upper class, being the possessor of an outrageous sense of social superiority. He liked to describe recruits as 'Irish peasants' or if they came from the cities as 'disrespectable corner-boys or slum-birds'. General Parsons was above all an old soldier and as such was a member of an institution that held tradition at the very core of its being. On appointment, Parsons wrote to Redmond, telling him that he had been given the command because he was an Irishman and understood his countrymen and that 'we are both working in the same cause'. This was highly unlikely since he had signed the Ulster Covenant and privately regarded all Nationalist politicians as 'ex Fenians now MPs'. Belfast Nationalist Joe Devlin once described Parsons as 'a fool and an Orange fool at that'. However, a constraining factor was Parsons's wife, who exerted considerable influence over him and who was a dedicated supporter of Redmond and Home Rule. John Redmond and General Parsons would regularly clash over points when the general's view of military interests and Redmond's political interests collided. One of the most serious clashes was over colours and cap badges. Neither man could understand how important the symbols were to the other.

After Kitchener agreed that the 47th Brigade would be reserved specifically for Nationalists, Redmond's next request of the military authorities was that the entire 16th (Irish) Division and its composite battalions should have their own uniquely Irish badge and insignia. The division's traditionalist commander almost had a heart attack and of course objected vehemently. Regiments were the primary unit to which soldiers identified and, generally, loyalty to the regiment overrode all other loyalties. Regimental pride has its roots in tradition, with tales of the regiment's battle honours drummed into recruits at regular lectures. The bonding process was encouraged through regimental customs and regalia like their cap badges and gave the recruits a shared unique corporate image. Regiments were recognised by the general public mainly through their uniforms and badges. Many of the identifying badges and insignia held particular symbolism for that regiment. A tiger was superimposed on the cap badge of the Royal Munster Fusiliers to commemorate service and sacrifice in Bengal with the East India Company, while the Seaforth Highlanders stag's head badge and Gaelic motto *Cuidich 'n Righ* (Save the King) harks back to the regiment's clan origins. The readiness of men to die for their regiment was and is still a real facet of army life and regimental pride is the strongest force that keeps units going when their backs are to a wall. Regimental spirit is more powerful than religion and always more personal than mere politics. Although part of the regiment with its traditions and *esprit de corps*, an individual battalion within the regiment also had its own band, colours and customs, providing it with its own identity to which officers and men attached great loyalty. A man might be a loyal member of the Connaught Rangers or Scottish Rifles but within the regiment he would also be fiercely loyal to his own battalion. This would be particularly true for the new service battalions being raised for Kitchener's new armies. When the 1st Glasgow Bn heard it would be designated the 15th (Service) Bn Highland Light Infantry, it was immensely proud to be a part of the famous or some might say infamous HLI, but it was also proud to be known unofficially as the Glasgow Tramways battalion.

When Lord Kitchener decided to raise his service battalions, he deliberately chose not to raise new regiments, but grafted the new service battalions onto the existing regiments. This was done specifically to enable the new battalions to share the long traditions and *esprit de corps* of the old regiments. As far as General Parsons was concerned, John Redmond's plans for a new distinctly Irish national badge with no affiliation to any British regiment was politics interfering with military effectiveness. When it was pointed out to Parsons that the Ulster and Welsh Divisions had been given authority to issue their own badges, he stated that in his opinion the Ulster Division should never have been raised at all and that no unit should be getting these 'silly badges'. Eventually everyone that was anyone got involved in the row. Asquith, Lloyd George and Kitchener all voiced different opinions and the dispute simmered for months. Eventually, Kitchener overruled Parsons and told him to allow the badges. Various designs were then kicked around; Redmond wanted a simple Irish harp with Ireland scrolled beneath it. Parsons objected to the harp: with a crown it would cease to be specifically Irish, uncrowned it could appear disloyal. Still unconvinced about the whole idea, Parsons suggested a sprig of shamrock or a Celtic cross. By March 1915, Kitchener was sick of the entire badge saga; he overruled everyone involved and sanctioned a simple shamrock badge for the 16th (Irish) Division. Further arguments ensued between Redmond and Parsons with a major point of contention the appointment of regimental officers. Redmond wanted his Irish Brigade officered by Irish Catholic officers or at least officers with proven Irish Nationalist credentials. Parsons simply wanted potential officers, preferably with some previous military experience or training. Failing that, he wanted young men of the same class as himself. Unfortunately for John Redmond, very few of his nominees fitted the criteria set by Parsons either by class or military experience. For example, while private schools and universities in Britain had long established Officers' Training Corps (OTC) attached to them, most Irish Catholic private schools had no such organisations. Political expediency and military necessity clashed as General Parsons's stand on the young officers infuriated the Nationalists, as they watched young men of similar education and class and very little or no military experience given commissions in Britain.

The basic problem between Lord Kitchener, General Parsons and John Redmond was that they were working towards three completely different objectives. Kitchener and the War Office were trying to raise as many recruits as they could from an at best ambivalent Irish populous, while at the same time preventing John Redmond creating an Irish National Army. General Parsons, while no doubt leaning towards the Ulster Unionist cause, was in his own, blinkered and outrageously snobbish way, trying to raise and train an efficient British infantry division that would give a good account of itself in battle. Redmond, while hugely sympathetic to and determined to assist the British and Allied cause, was mainly concerned with rising and having trained and equipped an Irish National Army capable of facing down the military wing of Ulster Unionism after the war. He did not want Irish recruits to feel a part of British regiments; he wanted them to belong to Irish national regiments, commanded by Irish Nationalist officers. He wanted them to owe their ultimate allegiance to himself as Irish leader and to the new, as yet unimplemented, Home Rule constitution.

Irish Brigade Recruiting Poster

Meanwhile the battle for the Nationalists' hearts and minds continued unabated as John Redmond and the rest of the IPP leadership threw themselves into recruiting for the 16th (Irish) Division. It is important to note at this point that Redmond and the IPP leaders like Dillon and Devlin were recruiting for their Irish Brigade and not for the British Army generally. At no point did they encourage the National Volunteers or any other Irishman to enlist into non-Irish regiments. In addition, Redmond still wanted and needed a large Irish National Volunteer force to remain in Ireland under his command. At Wexford, Redmond laid stress on Asquith's pledge that the Volunteers would remain as a recognised permanent force for the defence of the country and who should have authority over Volunteers in a state? Surely, the elected and responsible government, but pending Home Rule, 'the policy and control of the Volunteers must rest with the elected representatives of the country.'

The Belfast Irish National Volunteers began recruiting in organised bodies after John Redmond visited the city. Nationalist west Belfast was bedecked with Union Jacks and other allied flags to greet him – testimony to the new complexion of relations between Irish Nationalists and Britain now that Home Rule was on the statute book, albeit suspended. At Clonard Picture House on the Falls Road, John Redmond addressed a rally of Belfast Irish National Volunteers and urged them to join the 16th (Irish) Division for service overseas – to 'strike a blow in defence of Ireland, where the real fighting is going on'. No one supported Redmond's recruiting policy more fervently than Joe Devlin, the popular and charismatic MP for West Belfast. Devlin assured his constituents that 'the war is Ireland's war quite as much as Great Britain's or any other part of the Empire's. However it may have been in the past, England today is fighting the battle of Ireland's liberty.'

Similarly, in the north, Edward Carson and the Ulster Unionists also maintained a large number of Ulster Volunteers. The 36th (Ulster) Division would eventually reach its full battle strength of 18,000, but there were still another 70,000 plus UVF that would remain in the north of Ireland. John Redmond and the Nationalist leaders initially at least managed to convince the majority of their followers that the war was just and that the covenant of Home Rule would be sealed through an Irish blood sacrifice. In response to their call, many thousands of Nationalists did, despite the administrative chaos, find their way into the army, but suspicious Irish Nationalists toiled with the nagging worry that the 'English were fooling us again'.

James Connolly and the Irish Labour Party added to Redmond's recruiting problems when it launched an 'Appeal to the Irish Working Class' asking them to remember that they and foreign workers belonged to the same class and had no cause to quarrel. It urged a revolutionary defeatist position, pointing out that the humiliation of Britain in the war could help open the way for 'an Ireland nationally free'. The Belfast division of the Irish Citizen Army declared: 'We have no foreign enemy except the treacherous government of England – a government that even whilst it is calling upon us to die for it, refuses to give a straight answer to our demands for Home Rule.' Big Jim Larkin left for America on 24 October and to mark the change of management, James Connolly had stretched across the front of Liberty Hall, Dublin a banner proclaiming: 'We serve neither King nor Kaiser but Ireland.' He then set about converting the citizens' army from a labour security force into a socialist-Marxist militia and began to train them for revolution.

THE HOME FRONT

By mid-October, recruiting for the Glasgow Citizen Training Force was well under way with negotiations over the use of TF facilities between the Glasgow Corporation and the TF Associations satisfactorily complete. On 22 October, it was publicly announced that Colonel John Shaughnessy, recently retired from command of the 7th Bn Scottish Rifles TF, had been offered and had accepted, command of the Glasgow Citizen Training Force. John Shaughnessy was, of course, the Glasgow Irish director of the Celtic Football Club. The choice was an inspired one since Colonel Shaughnessy was very well known in TF circles and no doubt his contacts and experience in the ways of the volunteer organisation, smoothed the way on many occasions.

The Celtic director, once appointed to command, took the leading role in the organisation and training of the Citizen Training Force. Since the formation of the Training Force, the city and its suburbs had been divided up into district companies and applicants to the central office were assigned to their nearest company. Training Force companies were established in Bridgeton, Burnside, Cathcart, Dennistoun, Hyndland, Langside, Kelvinside, Mount Florida, Parkhead, Partick, Pollokshaws, Pollokshields, Possilpark, Shawlands and the central district of the city. At the same time, attempts were being made to form companies at Ibrox, Carmyle, Broomhill, Stepps, Scotstoun, Springburn, St George's Cross, Crosshill and Maryhill. The Queen's Park Football Club attempted to form their own company from club members, their friends and staff, but the necessary numbers could not be raised. Those Queen's Park members who did agree to muster trained with the Mount Florida Company.

By the end of October over 1600 men had enrolled in the citizens' force. Training took place on two evenings during the week and every second Saturday. The evening training was company drills with route marches and there were field exercises on the weekends. Training consisted mainly of marching, rifle exercises and shooting practice. Drilling, which began after business hours, had commenced almost immediately in several of the districts. In the central district, the Business Company trained after office hours in Garnethill Public School in Renfrew Street. The St George's Cross Company, obviously concerned that their wives and daughters should be ready to protect themselves should the dastardly Hun come up the Clyde, placed an advertisement in the Glasgow Herald encouraging ladies to come along to shooting practice in their rifle range. Among the ladies who learned to shoot was Coatbridge's own Margaret Skinnider. She would later put her weapon training to use during the Easter Rising when she operated as a sniper and dispatch rider. On 14 November, at a parade of the Pollokshaws Company held in the drill hall of the 7th Bn Scottish Rifles in Copelaw Road, it was announced that the Glasgow Citizen Training Force could muster over 4000 members in over thirty districts in and around the city. The Pollokshaws Company was the strongest in the force, capable of mustering several hundred citizens.

In the autumn of 1914 Colonel John Shaughnessy was a very busy man. In addition to his commitments to his law firm, his place on school boards and now being the commanding officer of the Citizen Training Force, as a Celtic FC director, he was, alongside the other Celtic directors, deeply involved in the political debate surrounding professional football and the war. Colonel John was not the only Shaughnessy involved with the military. His younger brother Alexander was a member of the Legion of Frontiersmen. The Legion was a quasi-military organisation composed of adventurers, who saw themselves as the 'great white hunters', the Indiana Joneses of popular fiction. They were outdoorsmen or frontiersman, whose members were required to ride, shoot and survive in the roughest of terrains and direst of circumstances. Or as the recruiting poster went: 'Men who lived on or beyond the Frontiers of the Empire.' The Legion was yet another organisation trying to recruit enough men to muster its own battalion. Although recognised by the War Office, it received no official funding and members were expected the pay a 5/- entrance fee followed by an annual subscription of 2/5. Anyone who thought they might qualify for membership could contact trooper Alex Shaughnessy at his offices in Hope Street, Glasgow. The Legion was advertising for new members as early as 6 August 1914 and by the end of the month, Alex Shaughnessy and his Frontiersmen squadron had applied to Glasgow School Board for permission to drill twice a week in a local school hall.

The Frontiersmen would later raise the 25th (Frontiersmen) Bn Royal Fusiliers and would see active service in East Africa.

THE WAR FRONT

While the Celts were being seen off by the Honest Men of Ayr, in Flanders, Sir John French began his advance to contact. After the war, the official British military historians would designate the fighting around Ypres between 12 October and 22 November as the First Battle of Ypres. However, such was the intensity of the fighting all along the British line over the period, within the overall First Battle of Ypres it was decided to award a number of the savage encounters their own battle titles: La Bassée, Messines, Armentières and Ypres itself, which began on 19 October. The first three battles would last until the beginning of November, but the battle for the town of Ypres would stagger on until 22 November. Along the ridges, the names of the villages and hamlets, Hollebeke, Zillebeke, Gheluvelt, Hooge, Broodseinde, Messines and Passchendaele, would soon be engraved onto the British people's psyche.

The British Army, supported by the French on both flanks, began its eastward advance in Flanders on 12 October. The Allies made some progress; however, the Germans had expected it and remained largely on the defensive, building up their troop numbers. On Monday 19 October, I Corps under Douglas Haig arrived in theatre from the Aisne and concentrated around Hazebrouck, some fifteen miles south-west of Ypres. Sir John French was fairly satisfied with the progress of his plan thus far. The BEF had been fighting in Flanders for a week or so and had made some significant territorial gains, advancing the line eastward and at a relatively light cost of around 3000 casualties.

As far as the German High Command was concerned, its plans for Flanders were also ticking along quite nicely. Since the fall of Antwerp, new German units were arriving daily and already the Allied advance was being slowed and in some places completely halted. The last piece of the German battle plan fell into place with the arrival of the Fourth Army in theatre. The Fourth Army comprised mainly the young, barely trained, but hugely enthusiastic volunteers of early August, who had rushed to enlist in the same patriotic fervour that had gripped the British and French. The Germans were now ready to launch a massive all-out offensive stretching from Arras in the south to the Belgian coast at Nieuwpoort. The attack, if successful, would sweep westwards past the Allies and onto the French coast, capture Calais and the other coastal towns, knock Belgium completely out of the war and neutralise the BEF by cutting it off from Britain.

On the morning of 20 October, two German armies comprising five and a half army corps launched the attack along the entire Allied line from the Belgian coast to Arras. The pressure on the Allied line would be almost continuous for the next month. Utilising their vast superiority in artillery, the Germans kept up a continuous barrage, which both took its toll in casualties and deprived the men of rest. Over the course of the month, a number of concentrated attacks were launched at specific parts of the line in an attempt to bludgeon through the exhausted and shell-shocked defenders. On the coast, the Belgians were forced back and as a desperate last resort, they opened the lock gates on the River Yser, flooding the fenland at Nieuwpoort and drowning thousands of Germans.

Already weakened British battalions faced overwhelming odds as the German infantry attacked. The war diary of the 1st Bn Cameron Highlanders records that B Company faced three battalions of the enemy, who advanced with a band playing and the men singing. The Cameron men fired volley after volley at the advancing German ranks, but were completely overwhelmed by the sheer weight of numbers. All along the line, the story was the same: artillery barrages followed by mass infantry assaults. To the south of the line, the Royal Irish Regiment, out on a limb at Le Pilly, was completely surrounded. On 19 October, the strength of the battalion had been twenty officers and 884 other ranks. At roll call on 21 October there was one officer and 135 men. Information as to the fate of the battalion was later received from the Germans, when it was ascertained that 561 men had been captured, almost all had been wounded and barely 100 could walk. On 26 October, two companies of the 2nd Bn Royal Irish Rifles confronted three battalions of Westphalian infantry at the village of Neuve-Chapelle. Having suffered under an artillery barrage all morning, at midday with their ammunition expended the commanding officer ordered his men to fix bayonets and to attack. The battalion, accompanied by the walking wounded, charged into the Westphalians. In the ensuing hand-to-hand combat, which bore the hallmarks of a medieval battle, the Royal Irish lost seventeen officers and over 560 men, of whom 290 were taken prisoner, the vast majority suffering from wounds. Only thirty men managed to evade capture and make it back to British positions.

Between 20 and 29 October, the British line to the north and south of Ypres remained intact, but had been forced back almost parallel with the town. The centre of the line between Zillebeke in the south and Bixschoote in the north had held, and as a result of the redeployments to the north and south of Ypres, a pronounced bulge or salient in the line, which jutted eastward, had been created. The apex of the bulge, which would become the infamous Ypres Salient, was at the village of Gheluvelt, six miles east of Ypres.

Although the German attacks were being repulsed with heavy losses, the British were also sustaining severe casualties, particularly from the German artillery. From 29 October, the fighting in front of Ypres became almost continuous, both by night and day. The Germans launched yet another massive attack, having mustered sixteen German divisions for the assault. Battered and punch drunk British battalions, all desperately under strength, most with their walking wounded, cooks, grooms, officer's servants and storemen in the line, faced a withering weight of firepower. The thin khaki line bent and buckled and at Gheluvelt on 31 October it even broke for a time when the 1st Bn East Surrey Regiment was effectively wiped out (two officers and twelve soldiers were left out of over 1000 men). Before the Germans could exploit the breach, 364 men of the 2nd Bn Worcestershire Regiment retook the position at the point of a bayonet, losing over 100 men during the vicious fight.

Two miles to the south-east of Ypres, the Irish Guards were in the line near the village of Klein Zillebeke. The battalion moved into position late on 30 October and suffered almost continuous shellfire for the next sixteen hours as the men dug themselves in. Over the course of 31 October, the shellfire was so heavy, the Gordon Highlanders on the right of the Guards were shelled out of their positions and forced to retire along with the only two artillery guns available for support. At dawn on 1 November, the heavy shelling resumed, with entire lengths of trench line completely smothered in high explosive fire. Hundreds of men were blown to atoms and completely disappeared. It was noted at the time that the most depressing thing above all, was that there seemed to be no British guns available to reply. Between 31 October and 7 November, the Irish Guards lost sixteen officers and 597 other ranks killed, wounded or missing. The fighting raged up and down the line as the Germans pounded the British positions with their massively powerful artillery guns, but the wafer-thin line held. For ten days, the BEF outfought and outshot the Germans, but the small British force was suffering catastrophic casualties that it could not afford and could not readily replace.

Although British casualties in the weeks up to the end of October had been heavy, the wounded had been arriving home piecemeal; very many were also treated in French hospitals. Now the wounded were arriving home in a flood. The news of thousands of casualties arriving at railway stations spread like wildfire. People rushed to the railway stations and watched in horror and total disbelief as the wounded and dying arrived in trainloads. The scale of the casualties surpassed those previously seen and were such that existing military medical facilities were completely overwhelmed. Many public buildings were hastily requisitioned and turned into hospitals. In Glasgow, in addition to requisitioning Stobhill Hospital, the directors of the North British Locomotive Company based on Springburn Road placed the main portion of their administration building at the disposal of the Scottish branch of the British Red Cross Society. The additional facility added 400 available beds and would be needed until May 1918.

In the British newspapers, day after day, column after column of casualty figures filled page after page. The figures for officers were published first, but the public knew that if a battalion had lost over half its officers, the losses among the men would also be very heavy. As a very broad rule of thumb, for every soldier killed in action, two more will have been wounded. Over the period 10 to 31 October some of the casualty figures for the Celtic battalions were astonishing: the Gordon Highlanders 640, Royal Scots Fusiliers 670, Royal Irish Rifles 600, Royal Irish Regiment 550, Scots Guards 500, Black Watch 400 and Cameron Highlanders 400. These were losses from already weakened battalions. By the end of October, the regular British Army in Flanders was bleeding to death, several battalions had been effectively destroyed and most of those still in the line were so under strength under normal circumstances they would have been withdrawn. Sir John French was forced to request reinforcements from General Joffre, who sent French troops to take over the line north of Ypres. This allowed Sir John French to concentrate his massively overstretched forces into a much narrower frontage, but such was the scale of the losses, the British line was still precariously thin. With Regular Army reinforcements almost exhausted and Kitchener's new battalions far from combat ready, the British military authorities, in desperation, turned to the much derided and barely trained 'Saturday night sojers' of the Territorial Force to step into the breach.

One of the first TF unit ordered to France was the 14th (Country of London) Bn London Regiment TF, more commonly known as the London Scottish. The battalion was manned by middle-class, expatriate Scotsmen, who had paid a pound for the privilege of joining and an annual subscription to remain a member. The fees were designed to ensure only the right class of man joined the battalion, it really would not do to have any working-class east-enders in the ranks. Issued with new rifles immediately before embarkation, the battalion landed at Le Havre in France on 16 September soon after the British reoccupied the port. On their arrival, the London Jocks were split up into large work parties and placed on administrative duties. The next five weeks were spent labouring well behind the front line. On 30 October, the situation around Ypres was so desperate, the London Scottish were ordered forward, transported to Ypres in thirty-four London buses. They never even had the opportunity to zero or test fire their new rifles. After spending the day marching to Gheluvelt and back, they boarded more buses in front of the Cloth Hall and were transported a few miles south toward Armentières, debussing at the village St Eloi on the Messines-Wytschaete ridge. At 0800 hrs on Halloween, 31 October, they received orders to move onto Messines Ridge near the village of Wytschaete, where the Germans had forced a gap in the front line. The London Jocks were ordered to close the gap near Hun's Farm and Middle Farm.

In the light of a full moon, while Glasgow weans were knocking on neighbours' doors dressed as ghouls and goblins, the Germans launched their first attack to the accompaniment of their military bands. They advanced in closely packed ranks offering excellent targets in the half-light for the many fine marksmen of the London Scottish. Unfortunately, the new rifles, which had never before been fired, proved faulty. The magazines and ammunition were incompatible, causing constant jams or misfeeds. The magazines were quickly discarded and the Mark I rifles used as single loaders. Twice the London Jocks not only halted German attacks but forced the Germans back from the ridge, despite the fact that they themselves were in an open position, facing overwhelming odds in numbers and were armed with malfunctioning weapons and ammunition. Finally, the momentum and ferocity of a third German attack forced the London Scottish back off the ridge. The battalion had suffered very heavy casualties and the companies were cut off from headquarters. With both flanks about to give way, and to avoid the total destruction of the battalion, orders were given to withdraw towards Wulvergem. The companies withdrew independently, fighting for every inch and taking a heavy toll as they retired. The Germans had suffered such severe losses they were unable to hinder the retirement greatly or consolidate much of their gains. Exhausted, the Germans forces were forced to stop to draw breath. The actions of the London Scottish and others on the Messines Ridge had stopped the German breakthrough and given GHQ time to rush reinforcements into the area to secure the line. Later in the day, the battalion regrouped and the roll was called. Only 150 men were present but as stragglers rejoined, it was ascertained the battalion had lost almost 400 killed, wounded or missing. The performance of the London Jocks at Messines set the standard for TF units throughout the war. The Saturday night sojers had proved themselves worthy of their place alongside the regulars and the laughing and mockery stopped. By the end of the year, there would be twenty-three TF battalions on active service in France and Belgium, while more went to India and Egypt to replace regular garrisons, releasing them for active service.

CELTIC FC

On 24 October, the Celts faced a weakened Hamilton Academicals at Douglas Park for the twelfth game of the season. The Accies had two of their strikers calling off just hours before the game. Celtic fielded the same team as the week previous at Parkhead, which meant the second appearance of the season for the Mighty Quinn. Again he was greeted with a terrific roar from the crowd as he took the field. Two trainloads of the faithful had travelled through from Glasgow on specials, which took the crowd numbers to around 12,000. Hamilton set out their stall from the beginning, packing the midfield and defence and daring the Celtic forwards to break through, being happy to concede possession to the visitors. Celtic huffed and puffed but failed to make any great inroads through the packed midfield. Just a minute before half-time, Browning weaved his way into the box from the left wing only to be brought down. The referee awarded a penalty and Joe Dodds stepped up to take the kick. Dodds hit the ball well, firing in a low hard shot but Watson in the Accies goal saved both the shot and managed to knock the rebound out of play before Joe could follow up. The penalty was the last action of the half and the teams went into the pavilion level. The second half saw Hamilton continue with their spoiling tactics and Celtic struggle to master them. Browning and McAtee did their best and fired in a number of tempting crosses but were not supported in their efforts by their strikers. Although Hamilton saw little possession, they never gave the impression they were under any great pressure. With just ten minutes to go, Celtic stepped up a gear and in the space of five minutes, Gallacher hit the bar and a ferocious shot from Quinn knocked Watson off his feet. McMenemy latched onto the rebound but saw his shot go past the post. Just when it looked as if Hamilton had achieved their objective, Jimmy Quinn delivered the goods with just two or three minutes to go. Gallacher, having come to life in the last ten minutes, created a gap with a piece of wizardry. The mighty Quinn accepted the pass and fired a rising shot into the top corner, leaving Watson no chance. The roar from the travelling support could have been heard in Glasgow. Celtic came away with a 0–1 win and all the points having not played at all well, while most of the plaudits went to the Hamilton Academicals' defence.

Shaw, McNair and Dodds repel a Rangers attack.

The Celtic were the only team of the top six in the league to gain maximum points that weekend. Hearts drew 2–2 with the amateurs of Queen's Park. The Honest Men of Ayr were beaten 2–1 by Third Lanark, Greenock Morton drew 2–2 with Partick Thistle, Airdrieonians were beaten 4–3 by Dundee and the Rangers were beaten 2–1 by Raith Rovers. Hearts still led the league table with twenty-one points and Celtic were in second place on seventeen. Two points separated Ayr United, Morton, Third Lanark and Rangers in that order.

On Monday 26 October, Johnny McMaster and Peter Johnstone represented the Glasgow FA in an inter-city match against Sheffield. The Glasgow side was beaten 2–1 at the Hillsborough ground, but both Celts emerged from the game with their reputations intact. On 31 October, 30,000 spectators saw the Celtic take on their arch-rivals Rangers at Parkhead in the first Old Firm meeting of the season. Celtic had the measure of their opponents from start to finish, winning by 2–1. The Rangers were poor and never looked as if they believed any positive result was possible, coming into the game on the back of two consecutive defeats to Ayr United and Morton. Both of Celtic's goals came from free kicks, the first taken by 'Sunny' Jim Young from which Jimmy McMenemy prodded the ball past Lock in the Rangers goal. Patsy Gallacher scored the second, giving Celtic the victory. The Celts won without any great effort on their part and it was their fifth successive league win over the Rangers. That week, the Celtic directors arranged to have the Celtic's results wired to military base hospitals in France after they had received a request from wounded Celtic supporters.

THE HOME FRONT

In view of the scale of the casualties in Flanders and with the chaotic organisation of the new armies now largely in hand, the recruitment drive, deliberately choked off in mid-September, went back into top gear. The physical requirements including the regulation minimum height were reduced, but the flow of recruits had been interrupted and those men fired with patriotic zeal during August and early September had moved on. It would prove very difficult to kick-start the process.

With the BEF locked in a life and death struggle against the German hordes and the TF battalions en route to France and Belgium, football again came under severe moral pressure regarding recruiting. The gate of 30,000 at Parkhead for the Rangers game was enough to send the 'Stop Football' lobby into a frenzy of indignation. The thought of 30,000 fit young men watching football while the BEF was bleeding to death in France was to them a national disgrace. The national newspapers continued to print letters and editorials castigating professional football. The Glasgow Herald commented that the shame of football must be shared by all concerned – by shareholders who think more of their dividends, by the players themselves and by the youths who watched the games. Both the 'Stop Football' lobby and the newspapers ignored that fact that the 30,000 spectators who turned out to see the Old Firm encounter were less than half the number of those who had watched the corresponding game at Parkhead on 1 January 1914. Many of the missing supporters from both clubs had already enlisted and were in military training elsewhere. They also ignored the fact that many of the crowd were working in munitions or the shipbuilding industries. It was also noted at the time that a substantial number of the 30,000 spectators were already in uniform. However, the facts mattered little and professional football was now being regarded by the middle and upper classes as almost a disease, a dangerous obsession that encouraged a lust for pleasure and discouraged self-sacrifice. Even the cartoonists of the time got in on the act, Punch magazine taunting a footballer with the words: 'No doubt you can make money in this field, my friend, but there is only one field where you can get honour.' A Glasgow Evening Times cartoon showed a goalkeeper holding an artillery shell with the caption: 'Don't, wait until the goalposts are shattered.'

The Glasgow Catholic Observer of 31 October ignored the furore over footballers and recruiting. Instead it was the first edition to contain a half page of news in Flemish for its new Belgian Catholic readers. It also noted that, among others, John McKillop, Mick Dunbar and Tom Colgan of Celtic FC had all donated sizeable amounts to Glasgow's Irish Nationalist Volunteer Force Fund.

Just as the Celtic were kicking off against Rangers and the London Scottish were fighting to the death at Messines, the Glasgow Highlanders training at Dunfermline, quite out of the blue, received movement orders from HLI brigade headquarters. The battalion was to be held in immediate readiness to proceed on active service overseas. Taken completely by surprise, the next few days were chaos as preparations were made to move over a thousand men and their equipment to France or Belgium. On 2 November, the battalion received instructions to entrain that night by half battalion at 2000 hrs and 2130 hrs for Southampton. Telegram messages were sent to Glasgow ordering the second-line battalion at Greendyke Street to send 320 of the best-trained men to the first line battalion that evening. They would replace the same number of men who were either under nineteen years of age or for some other reason were unable to proceed on immediate overseas service. The Glasgow Highlanders entrained from Dunfermline as planned and recruits from Glasgow who had not yet joined the battalion were picked up at Edinburgh. They arrived at Southampton after an eleven-hour journey and went straight into a rest camp in the town. The rest camp was, in fact, some tents hastily thrown up in a city park that was now a sea of mud. New rifles were issued. The battalion had been training with the old, long Lee Enfield rifle. Now they were going into action they got the short Lee Enfield, which was one of the finest rifles ever manufactured. Josie Maley did not deploy with his battalion, but moved back to Glasgow having been seconded to the Glasgow Highlander's depot as an instructor. The battalion embarked on board the *SS Novia* on 4 November and sailed for Le Havre, arriving there the next day. The move from Dunfermline was so rushed few men got the opportunity to say goodbye to their family and friends. Private John Francis McKillop was among the Glasgow Highlanders who landed in France.

The recruiting effort, deliberately paused in mid-September to allow the administrators some respite, was now causing a great deal of concern. From a high of 462,900 for the month of September, the month of October showed a huge drop to just 136,800. The reasons for the drop were many and varied. The chaos at the recruiting offices and stories of overcrowding and discomfort at the depots and training camps had put many men off, while the deliberate raising of the physical standards had the desired effect. In mid-October, the height requirement was reduced back to the normal regulation standard of 5ft 4in and at the beginning of November would be reduced again to 5ft 3in. Another significant cause was the very real suffering caused to the wives and dependants of the volunteers when administrators, unable to keep up with demand, failed to get pay and allowances out on time. These were all factors that were within the control of the military authorities, but other factors they could not control. By mid-September, the immediate dampening effect of the war on trade was beginning to wear off and as the economy recovered so did the availability of work. Factories and mills on short time went back onto full time, and as war-related orders began to flow into commerce, employers began to take on more staff. Unemployment fell a full 2 per cent between the end of August and the end of September. In Glasgow on 28 August, there were just over 14,300 men idle. By the end of October, the number had fallen to 6800. Over the same period the number of young women who were unemployed rose. As a result of the increase in work available and with hundreds of thousands of male workers now in the army, wages began to increase. By the middle of October, recruiters were asking why a sturdy young men would enlist for 1/- a day, when there was now abundant work, sometimes paying over 6/- a day. The military authorities were now faced with the problem of how to reignite the enthusiasm for recruitment seen in August and September.

Just when the Allies thought it could not get any worse, the strategic and political situation regarding Turkey and the Dardanelles took a disastrous turn. After the outbreak of war in Europe, the crisis in Turkey went into limbo with no side attempting to force the issue. In fact, it was to no one's advantage at that time for the Turks to declare one way or the other. The Germans were perfectly happy with the current situation. Their armies were sweeping through Belgium and France and they expected a swift end to the war in the west. As long as that remained the case, Constantinople's importance and bargaining power would be greatly diminished. For Britain, her major concern was protecting the Suez Canal. With all available troops heading for France, it would be weeks before Indian troops could be got to Egypt. In the meantime, if nothing was done to antagonise Turkey further, she might even at this late stage still be persuaded to remain neutral. This delay allowed the Turks to mobilise, strengthen their defences, which included laying mines in the Dardanelles, and advance work already well underway to position the first sea mines in the narrows. It also allowed the Turks to see how the war in Europe was panning out before having to make the final leap. By the middle of August, the mining of the narrows was complete and the straits effectively closed. Despite the strategic hopes of the Allies, events in Europe were about to overtake them all.

By the beginning of October, the sweeping German advances across Belgium and France had been halted and then reversed at the Battle of the Marne, and the pattern of entrenched warfare that would soon stretch across Western Europe was beginning to develop. It was now to Germany's advantage that Turkey enter the war on her side, both to create a diversion for Russia and to help dissipate the Allied war effort building up against them in France. Instructions were sent from Berlin to their agents in Constantinople: the Turks must stop prevaricating and be driven into joining the war. The German Mission in Constantinople now turned its entire attention to compromising the Turkish position. As a first move, German agents staged some local raids against border posts in British-controlled Egypt, hoping that they would provoke a retaliatory attack. When this failed and in light of the Turkish government's continued indecision, the Germans tried another plan. On 27 October, three Turkish torpedo boats commanded by German officers entered the Black Sea, and just before dawn 29 October, bombarded the Russian town of Odessa. They sank the gunship *Donetz*, and damaged a number of steamships, among them the French ship *Portugal*. Simultaneously, an attack was launched on Sebastopol where the *Goeben* sank the Russian minelayer *Prut*. For the Turks the point of no return had finally been reached. The Russians withdrew their ambassador and embassy staff on 30 October. The British and French in a final attempt to avoid war, made an ineffective demand for Turkey to expel the German missions. This was of course impossible for the Turks, particularly with the *Goeben* and *Breslau* anchored in Constantinople harbour and capable of bombarding the city. The British and French embassies followed the Russians in asking for their passports. Hostilities would begin on 31 October and over the first week of November, Constantinople received declarations of war from Russia, Britain and France.

The die had been finally been cast and now was the time for decisive action and to launch a major attack that would reopen the straits. It was already infinitely more difficult than it would have been at the beginning of August, and it would only get more difficult as time went on. However, the allies were concentrating on events on the Western Front and the best opportunity for success was missed.

Chapter Six

NOVEMBER

THE HOME FRONT

The First Sea Lord, Winston Churchill, hammered the final nail into the coffin of British diplomacy with the Young Turks' government when on 3 November, against expert naval advice, he ordered the British naval squadron blockading the straits to bombard the entrance of the Dardanelles. The warships shelled the forts at Kum Kale on the Turkish mainland and at Sedd-el-Bahr on the Gallipoli peninsula. After a chance shot landed in an ammunition magazine setting off a massive explosion at Sedd-el-Bahr, the ships withdrew as ordered. Despite the fireworks, the show of force achieved very little and in fact not only did the Turks score a propaganda victory by claiming they had repulsed the mighty British Navy, the event seemed to concentrate the minds of both the Turks and their German advisers. Almost immediately action was taken to increase the Dardanelles defences significantly and from that point on the odds of any successful attack in the future decreased almost by the day. As far as the British were concerned, up to this point, the Dardanelles were largely a Russian problem. The main strategic concern for the British was the security of the Suez Canal. After what was a colossal and completely avoidable failure of diplomacy, on 5 November Britain and France officially declared war on Turkey.

The following day at dawn Karl Hans Lody was stood against a wall in the miniature rifle range at the Tower of London and shot. He had been captured three weeks earlier in Killarney, put on public trial on 2 November and three days later found guilty of espionage. Lieutenant Karl Lody insisted at his court martial that 'he would not cringe for mercy. He was not ashamed of anything that he had done; he was in honour bound not to give away the names of those who had employed him on this mission; he was not paid for it, he did it for his country's good, and he knew that he carried his life in his hands in doing so. Many a Briton was probably doing the same for Britain.'

The case was widely reported in the national press and Lieutenant Lody's stoic attitude and insistence that he was doing his duty impressed the British public. On the morning of his execution, he was reported to have said to the officer who escorted him from his cell to the execution ground: 'I suppose that you will not care to shake hands with a German spy'. 'No,' the officer replied, 'but I will shake hands with a brave man.' He even got a mention in the House of Commons as 'a patriot who had died for his country as much as any soldier who fell in the field.' Lieutenant Lody was the first person executed at the Tower of London since 1747, when the Catholic rebel, Lord Lovat, was beheaded there after the failed Jacobite rebellion of 1745–46. The Germans would later name a battleship after Karl Hans Lody.

In Glasgow, Saturday 7 November was Scottish Flag Day. Organised by the Scottish Patriotic Association, a sum of over £3000 was raised for Highland home industries to help the unemployed cottage industry workers, soldiers' and sailors' comforts and, of course, the Belgians.

CELTIC FC

On 7 November, the Celts took a short twenty-mile trip south-east to Kilmarnock, the home town of their captain 'Sunny' Jim Young. A crowd of around 6000, which included some hundred wounded soldiers, saw a highly competent Celtic defeat a lacklustre Kilmarnock at Rugby Park. The Bhoys were without Patsy Gallacher and Irishman Billy Crone got just his second league start of the season. Jimmy McColl was back in the side after being absent for the previous three games. The slippery park aided Celtic's slippery forwards and, even without Patsy Gallacher, they overran Killie. Celtic's first goal came from a dazzling McMenemy run and shot after twenty-five minutes. Jimmy McMenemy got a second when he headed home a pinpoint cross from McAtee. Celtic's third came after McAtee robbed Killie's Slimmon to slot a low shot past Miller in the Kilmarnock goal. At the other end, Charlie Shaw and the Celtic defence were well up to anything the Kilmarnock forwards could occasionally produce and Celtic cruised for most of the game. Kilmarnock got a consolation goal through a penalty when Peter Johnstone brought down Hamilton in the box with only ten minutes remaining. The Celts took maximum points at a canter.

Tuesday 10 November saw the Celts in the north of the city at Firhill. The Bhoys had been drawn against Partick Thistle in the first round of the Scottish League's War Relief Fund Shield competition. The Jags, probably in anticipation of a drubbing, rested some of their star players, while the Celts with so few reserves available were forced to field the same side that had beaten Kilmarnock. The sports writer of the Daily Record thought the Celts were in a 'Skilful Mood' and capable of taking liberties. For much of the first half the Bhoys put on a display of criss-cross passing that was a delight to watch but it lacked penetration and they seldom bothered the Thistle goal. *The Man in the Know* thought it was sod's law that a key man would be injured in the benefit game and sure as fate, Joe Dodds was carried off midway through the first half. The Celts were forced to play with ten men for the remainder of the game. Despite losing Joe, the Celts continued much as before and when the half-time whistle went the score, despite all of Celtic's possession, was still 0–0. Celtic kicked off the second half showing more determination to pressurise the Thistle goal and after ten minutes Andy McAtee scored for the Bhoys. The Thistle claimed offside but the goal stood. The Celtic fell back into their fancy game allowing the Jags to claw their way more into the game. The Celts got a couple of warnings before Partick Thistle equalised with a blistering shot after a dribbling run by Neil Harris. The last quarter of the game was all Celtic trying to make up for their squandered chances but it was not to be and Thistle held out for a draw. Despite the afternoon kick-off, a very reasonable crowd of 5000 spectators turned out to watch the benefit game and £120 was added to the relief fund. The draw meant the tie would have to be replayed.

IRISH RECRUITING

On Sunday 8 November, what was described at the time as a 'monstre meeting' of Glasgow Irish Nationalists was held in St Andrew's Halls. The meeting was organised by the Scottish branches of the United Irish League and the guest speaker was TP O'Connor MP, who was finally responding to Arthur Murphy's invitation to come to Glasgow. TP O'Connor was the Member of Parliament representing the Liverpool Irish constituency centred on the Irish enclave of Scotland Street. Liverpool Scotland was the only constituency outside Ireland to return an Irish Nationalist MP. The son of an Athlone shopkeeper and grandson of a non-commissioned officer of the Connaught Rangers, the former journalist and fervent Irish Nationalist represented the Liverpool Irish for over fifty years.

TP O'Connor was in Glasgow to explain the part played by the Irish Parliamentary Party in supporting the British war effort and why it was encouraging Irishmen to enlist. A number of Irish soldiers, including some wounded soldiers from Stobhill Hospital, joined the party on the platform and the audience of around 5000 was described as enthusiastic. After the singing of the national anthems of all the Allies, the meeting was opened by Scottish representatives proposing and seconding a resolution expressing adhesion to the policy of John Redmond in calling for the Irish people to support the aims of the Allies. TP O'Connor rose to support the resolution. He stated that he was first and foremost an Irish Nationalist and so he believed were they (drawing applause from the crowd). He considered from the Nationalist point of view the great struggle that every race and every nation had to gain respect for its religion and its language and the full development of its own national and racial qualities. He claimed that the Allies had done all they could to avoid war. In an attempt to demonstrate that religious differences could be set aside for the greater good, he next spoke of the internal religious divisions in France and highlighted the fact that the French had put their differences aside to unite in the national struggle for survival. He spoke of the German outrages in Belgium and dramatically introduced a young Belgian, whose family had suffered at the sacking of the Catholic town of Louvain. He asked the audience whether as Irish Nationalists they were hesitating as to which side they would take up in this war. He next addressed the claim that this was England's war and attempted to show that Nationalists enlisting for service in the British Army where not the imperial mercenaries of old. He said it was not only England's war; it was the war of Russia, France, Serbia and Belgium as well as England. Concerning Ireland and recruiting, there had been, he said, a subtle and steady but very dishonest campaign to underrate what had already been done, not only regarding Irishmen of Ireland but also of the Empire. To date, from the parishes of Glasgow a total of 7271 Irish recruits had been obtained and from Edinburgh 6383. When the other centres of population were added, the numbers would be no fewer than 30,000 Irishmen from Scotland. In the city of Liverpool and on Tyneside and elsewhere, thousands of Irishmen were joining English regiments. They were won to the Empire, but they were lost perhaps to Ireland, whom people were suggesting was not recruiting. Now, however, there was an Irish brigade in Ireland to which Irishmen could ask to be sent. It will become, he believed, one of the biggest and bravest in the British Army. He went on to say that when this great story would finally be told, it would be found that in this great crisis of the British Empire, as in so many others, the Empire had found her strongest defence in the arms of Irish soldiers and in the words of Irish statesmen.

TP O'Connor would justify the Irish Party's position on the war to Irish American dissenters by saying: 'The Irish Party, when they realised that on this occasion England was in the right, did not allow their historical wrongs to prejudice them.' Immediately after the meeting, the following telegram was sent to King George:

> *I have been requested by the largest and most enthusiastic meeting of Irishmen ever held in Glasgow today in the St Andrew's Halls to inform your majesty that a resolution was carried unanimously promising the fullest support both at home and in the field to the just cause of the allies and in token of national unity and loyalty to your own person.*

For the first time ever on a Nationalist platform in Glasgow, the audience sang 'God save the King'.

Telegrams expressing feelings of unity and loyalty were also sent to the King of the Belgians, the French President and Prime Minister Asquith.

Although there were undoubtedly other factors at work, including a special illuminated recruiting tram traversing the city, TP O'Connor's speech appears to have had an impact on the city's recruiting figures. On the six days prior to his appearance in the city, the daily recruitment figures were 111, 112, 131, 103, 101 and 70. On the four days after the meeting, the figures were 343, 273, 233 and 267. The highest figure over the ten-day period was the day after his speech. The day previous to TP's meeting in St Andrew's Halls, the Glasgow Observer published the first in a series of Catholic Rolls of Honour. It was a very long list of the names of 114 Roman Catholic men from St Alphonsus' Parish, Glasgow, who had enlisted up to that date.

Despite the fact that almost one million men had voluntarily enlisted since Kitchener made his first call in August, it still was not enough. On 16 November, the Prime Minister was back in the House of Commons. He asked for and received authority to raise another million men.

The horrendous casualty figures from Ypres and the disastrous recruiting figures for the month of October brought the subject of recruiting back into prominence with a vengeance. The political focus of the British government and of both protagonists in Ireland shifted back onto recruiting figures in general and on Irish figures in particular. They were not all necessarily focused on the figures for the same reason. The Unionists trumpeted the fact that the Ulster Division had reached 13,200 and pointed fingers at the 10th and 16th (Irish) Divisions. The UIL in Britain, fighting a rearguard action against Unionist propaganda on the reticence of the Irish to enlist, concerned itself with the number of Irishmen enlisting into British regiments as opposed to the Irish divisions.

In Glasgow, Scottish UIL delegates met in the Lesser City Halls on Saturday 21 November to discuss recruitment in Scotland. In particular, they were concerned at numerous reports of Irishmen attempting to enlist into Irish regiments but being sent instead to Scottish regiments. One report suggested that of 300 Irishmen in Stirling and district that desired to enlist into Irish regiments only forty were allowed to do so. Similar reports from other districts backed up the claim. The delegates agreed to communicate these facts to the Irish leaders. How much truth there was in the claims is impossible to ascertain; however, recruiting sergeants would undoubtedly push malleable or agreeable recruits towards their own regimental preferences.

Legendary Glasgow Irish socialist Harry McShane went through a similar experience when he enlisted in September 1914. On his arrival at Maryhill Barracks, Glasgow he volunteered for the Royal Engineers. Despite having engineering qualifications, and against his express wishes, he was assigned to the Highland Light Infantry and sent to Hamilton Barracks. Harry had not enlisted to fight the Germans, but to take the British Socialist Party's anti-war a message into the Army itself. After successfully arguing his point, he was eventually sent to the Royal Engineers depot at Chatham. After nine months military service he decided the anti-war message was lost on the eager recruits of the first hundred thousand and deserted while on a visit to Glasgow. His uniform was thrown into the Clyde. The confusion engendered by John Redmond's insistence on calling the 16th (Irish) Division the Irish Brigade most certainly did not help. At the same time, the headquarters of the 16th (Irish) Division was obliged to reply to

a letter from J Derrick, United Irish League organiser for Scotland, complaining of confusion by recruiting officers regarding the 16th (Irish) Division. The instruction that the 47th Brigade had been set aside specially for the National Volunteers led many recruitment offices in the UK and potential Irish recruits to believe only the 47th

Irish Nationalist Volunteers leave West Belfast for Fermoy

Brigade would be Irish and that only members of the National Volunteers could enlist into the brigade. The letter from divisional headquarters pointed out that the 47th Brigade was for National Volunteers but that the 47th, 48th and 49th Brigades were all purely Irish and open to all Irish recruits.

In West Belfast, Joe Devlin MP was also mustering support for the war among the Irish Nationalists. On 19 November, 600 Belfast Nationalist Volunteers, who had enlisted in John Redmond's Irish Brigade, left West Belfast for Fermoy, Co Cork. There they would undergo infantry training as members of the 6th (Service) Bn Connaught Rangers, part of the 47th Brigade. Hundreds of their friends and relations gathered to see them off and sang the 'Wearing O' the Green', 'A Nation Once Again' and 'Rule Britannia' accompanied by a number of Nationalist bands and pipers. The men were in great spirits and during a lull in the music chanted their favourite football anthem that 'the Belfast Celtic will be there.' Joe Devlin, other prominent Belfast Nationalists and several Roman Catholic clergymen were also at the railway station to see the men off. On 25 November, a second contingent of Belfast National Volunteers, 300 strong, would leave the city for Fermoy and the 6th Connaught Rangers.

In Dublin on the night of 20 November, the Irish National Volunteers were transporting around ninety rifles along the banks of the Grand Canal when the cart carrying the rifles was held up by a crowd of fifty men, some of them armed. Only two National Volunteers were escorting the weapons and they were unable to prevent the rifles being seized. The Irish Volunteers and the IRB were obviously collecting in some of their own.

THE WAR FRONT

On 11 November, twelve divisions of German infantry attacked the British line to the north and south of Ypres. The assault was launched after the most intense artillery barrage ever experienced by British troops. The German Army was the proud possessor of a magnificent artillery arm the quantity, quality and calibre of whose guns were far superior to anything the British could put in the field. When the German artillery bombarded the British positions, they blew entire platoons of men to atoms. Unable to reply in kind, the British soldiers could only suffer the punishment. In some places along the British line, a mile of front was held by the shattered remnants of a battalion (450 men). However, the Germans too were suffering and this would be their last throw of the dice. Advancing out of the early morning mist along the Menin Road marched the Prussian Guards Division, the same men who had so impressed the Celtic tourists as they goose-stepped along the Unter der Linden in Berlin. Unlike the British Guards, who were fighting soldiers who when on ceremonial duties dressed up in fancy red coats and bearskins, the Prussians were only parade-ground soldiers in magnificent uniforms and no match for the professionals of the British Army. That morning they advanced onto pulverised British positions largely held by punch drunk, woefully under-strength battalions, with their office clerks, drivers, cooks and grooms and walking wounded bolstering the line.

Immediately to the Prussian front were the battered remnants of the 1st Guards Brigade. It was a Guards Brigade in name only for its Guards battalions had been dispersed and their place taken by the battered remnants of the 1st Bn Cameron Highlanders and 1st Bn Black Watch. The brigade's fighting strength had been reduced from in excess of 4000 to around 800 bone-weary men. Through sheer weight of numbers, the 1st and 3rd Prussian Foot Guards broke through the 1st Guards Brigade, but having taken so many casualties their advance was spent and they moved into Nonne Bosschen (Nun's Wood) to take shelter from the British fire. Their breakthrough had created a thousand-yard gap and threatened to overwhelm the entire British line, since nothing stood between the Nun's Wood and the Channel ports. A hastily improvised defence followed by an accurate artillery bombardment pinned the Prussian Guards into the wood while a counter-attack was prepared. Led by the last of the reserves, comprising 300 men of the 2nd Oxford and Buckingham Light Infantry with a few odds and sods, the British light infantrymen swept into Nonne Bosschen. The 900 Prussian Guards, every man over 6ft tall and some over 7ft, fought hand to hand with the British infantry among the trees. The fight at Nonne Bosschen saved the desperate situation and a complete German breakthrough.

By 5 November, the depleted London Scottish, now rearmed with some replacement rifles picked up from the wounded, was pushed back into the line and had joined the badly mauled 4th Guards Brigade near Klein Zillebeke. On arrival, they were assigned to a stretch of the line known as 'Brown Road Wood,' south of the Menin Road. On 11 November, the Germans launched their main assault on the front line held by the London Jocks. As they poured across a clearing, the momentum of the assault saw them almost enveloped the right flank company. The German rush was only checked by a counter-attack led by the commanding officer and his headquarters staff. The battalion remained in the line until relieved on 15 November after nine days of almost constant shellfire. When the roll was called at Pradelles near Hazebrouck, less than 300 men answered their names. Among the London Scottish killed in action on 11 November was twenty-five-year-old Private Walter Crichton, the son of Walter Crichton, former secretary of Rangers FC. Walter Crichton is credited with moving the Rangers FC to Ibrox Park in 1887. His son has no known grave and is commemorated on the Ypres (Menin Gate) Memorial.

The same day that Walter Crichton was killed, Bridgeton boy Joe McAree, basic training now complete, boarded a cross-Channel ferry at Folkestone. He was part of a draft of 150 battle casualty replacements who had been assigned to the 2nd Bn Argyll and Sutherland Highlanders. It would take the draft ten days to get to the battalion then based at Armentières, but manning the front line at nearby Houplines. The 2nd Argylls had lost 170 men killed and over 300 wounded since the end of August and were now part of the 19th Brigade, attached to the 6th Division. After a couple of days of battalion admin, Joe and his draft, now assigned to their respective companies, went into the front line. The line was a single trench, knee deep in mud and slime. There was no fire step and the Germans were just 200 yards away. It was Joe's first tour in the front line, the first of many over what would be a long, cold, wet winter.

The Germans attacks in November had come within a whisker of achieving their aim. One more effort would have seen them through to Ypres and beyond, leading to the inevitable destruction of the British and French Armies and the war would have been won in the west. The fighting around Ypres stuttered on until the end of November, by which time the defences, bolstered by TF and French reinforcements, were beginning to solidify into the infamous Ypres Salient. The immediate crisis had passed; the Germans had exhausted themselves in their attempts to break the Allied line. The weather closed in and large-scale troop movements became impossible.

The BEF had held Ypres and halted the German thrust for the Channel ports, but at immense cost. The old regular Home Army and a number of Imperial service TF battalions that had made it to the front in time to get into the fight were completely destroyed. In six weeks of fighting around Ypres, the BEF had lost in excess of 58,000 men killed, wounded or missing.

The battle at Ypres was the last opportunity for open, mobile warfare and the classic image of stagnation and trench warfare began to appear. It was also the transition from the old chivalric ideas of warfare, of cavalry charges and military bands leading massed infantry into battle, to mechanised warfare and slaughter on an industrial scale. Even the Germans, who lost around 130,000 casualties, recognised that the battle was the end of innocence, calling the fight at Ypres the *Kindermort* (slaughter of the innocents). The original BEF had arrived in France in mid-August with around 90,000 men, now at the end of what would be known as the First Battle of Ypres, it had suffered over 86,000 casualties. Typical of the battalions, the 2nd Bn Highland Light Infantry had left Aldershot three months previously with a full strength of 1012 all ranks; now barely thirty fit men were left.

The medieval town of Ypres itself would become 'sacred ground', taking on almost a religious significance for the British Army. Even later in the war, when it made more strategic and tactical sense to give it up, the blood sacrifice of the colonial constabulary that was the Old Contemptibles had been such that it was emotionally impossible to do so. Once the situation at Ypres had stabilised, French battalions relieved the British units that had been holding the Ypres Salient. By the end of November, the BEF had redeployed a few miles south and was now holding a continuous twenty-mile sector of the front from a little south of St Eloi, past Armentières, Neuve-Chapelle and Festubert to the La Bassée Canal at Givenchy.

THE HOME FRONT

With the nation's focus firmly back on the recruiting effort, every avenue that might reignite the recruitment campaign was explored. The physical standards were dropped and the upper age limit increased to thirty-eight. The suggestion that small men well under the minimum regulation height might be accepted was first mooted. An appeal signed by the Prime Minister was distributed to all householders, who were asked to complete an attached form by giving the particulars of all men of military age who were living in the household and indicating whether or not they were willing to enlist. The great and the good, nationally and locally, held recruiting rallies and propaganda campaigns were stepped up. Recruitment posters changed from being an appeal to patriotism to emotional blackmail, such as 'What did you do in the war daddy?', or they appealed directly to women to encourage their husbands or sons to enlist. The distribution of white feathers increased significantly from the women of the Order of the White Feather. To the modern mind, it is difficult to understand the devastating effect on men that had been given a feather. The actions of the overzealous women would actually force the Admiralty and later the War Office to issue a badge to protect men engaged in vital war work.

With the panic over the loss of the BEF, calls for the introduction of universal national conscription grew. Muted at the start of the war, the concept now appeared firmly on the agenda. In response, in mid-November the anti-war socialists formed the No Conscription Fellowship. Fighting a rearguard action against what it saw as the militarism of civil and industrial society, when conscription was introduced in mid-1916, its members became conscientious objectors also known as conscies.

Garngad boy Patrick Hilley was one among many who responded to the critical situation at Ypres. In mid-November, he presented himself at a recruiting office and applied to join the Irish Guards. On his attestation form he was described as twenty-seven years of age, married with one child (Edward), a spirit salesman by profession and having no previous military experience. He nominated his wife, Mary, as his next of kin and gave his home address as 21 Wolseley Street in Oatlands. He sailed through the military medical examination, not that it was particularly difficult, and his overall physical development was described as fair. The only medical problem was the condition of his teeth, which were described as poor, but not sufficiently so to cause rejection. He had one distinguishing mark, a tattoo on his right forearm, the word 'Erin' within a shamrock. After taking the oath, he was accepted for service in the Irish Guards, given his shilling and a one-way ticket to London. He went back home to Oatlands, packed a bag, said goodbye to Mary and caught the midnight train to London. On 19 November, he reported to the depot of the Brigade of Guards at Caterham, near Croydon. There were now three Hilley brothers in the army. Back in the Garngad, another brother and future Celtic stalwart Hugh Hilley was incandescent as he watched yet another of his brothers enlist. Hugh was not only too young to enlist being not quite sixteen, but he was also too small. He knew of a number of boys who had managed to bluff their way into the army by lying about their age, but at a shade under 5ft 2in he knew he could not fool the military measuring stick.

SCOTTISH FOOTBALL

For professional football, the criticisms regarding its commitment and contribution to recruiting, despite the blessing of the War Office, had never entirely disappeared. Professional footballers and football supporters in general were still widely seen as failing in their patriotic duty. There had been a government-induced lull in recruiting over the second half of September and October as the military authorities, overwhelmed by the first half million volunteers, paused for breath. When they attempted to resume recruiting and on 5 November lowered the physical standards again back to 5ft 3in, they found the initial enthusiasm had passed. Those men who had stood for hours in lines outside recruitment offices but failed to get accepted in September had moved on with their lives.

The poor recruiting figures saw the armchair generals and patriotic do-gooders pick up their pens and notepaper again, and it was football and its supporters that were the main target. Some suggested football supporters should be charged double fare when travelling by public transport to games. Others that football supporters should simply be made to join the military and given no choice in the matter. On Friday 6 November, the working class leaning Glasgow Evening Times, in support of the footballers, published a long list of footballers stationed and training with Kitchener's Army at Aldershot. The columnist added that Aldershot was but one-seventh of the New Army and that if the whole list were published it would probably stagger those killjoys who, by libelling sportsmen in general and footballers in particular, fancy they have done their duty to their country and are now immune from military service.

On Friday 13 November, the very middle class Glasgow Herald published an article titled 'Patriotism First' castigating professional football as unpatriotic, in that it mitigated against recruiting. It argued that the clubs' selfish and greedy directors and players were more interested in profit and recompense than serving the nation. Compared to other sports, professional football was isolated in its contribution to the war effort, lacking national or patriotic spirit. The conduct of professional footballers was shameful, playing a game while brave men were dying on the battlefield.

In response to the article, that same day, Sir John Ure Primrose, president of Rangers, Tom White, chairman of Celtic, T Robertson, president of Queen's Park and Colonel JB Wilson, president of Third Lanark, gave an interview to the Herald on behalf of the SFA. The representatives set about explaining both the War Office's attitude and the SFA's position on the continuance of the professional game. The attitude of professional footballers to enlisting was

Young MEN of Great Britain. What Are YOU Doing?
(Courtesy of Jack Murray)

also highlighted and explained. In the article's introductory paragraph, the reporter put the Glasgow clubs and their supporters firmly at the centre of the controversy.

'Glasgow and the West of Scotland it was said was the cradle of Scottish football and in no other city in the United Kingdom was it possible for six first league clubs to thrive and prosper. If any shame were attached to the continuance of the sport, then the Glasgow public will also have to shoulder it in proportion to their interest in what has come to be regarded as a national pastime.'

The SFA's defence opened with the fact that they had sent a delegation to London to speak to the War Office and were willing to follow its guidance on the matter of continuing or stopping the season. The War Office had made it perfectly clear to the delegation that it was content to allow professional football to continue. They were informed in effect that 'if Lord Kitchener regarded the playing of football matches to be a mitigating factor against recruiting he would have said so and had he said so, the game would have been summarily stopped.'

As far as the SFA were concerned, that was the official position at that time. The SFA delegation had left London with a clear understanding of the War Office's attitude and should the War Office at a later stage consider the stoppage of the game expedient, they would advise the Association to that effect.

They further argued that the case against continuance of the game must be based on one or other of two grounds. Either the objection was emotional, or it could be contended that the game was militating against recruiting. To the emotional objection, the SFA argued that if it were said that it was incongruous to play football while soldiers were fighting and dying for their country, then it was equally incongruous that other sports or recreations or pastimes, such as horse racing, golf, music halls, picture houses and the like, should continue. Where would the final line be drawn? As to the objection that the sport was mitigating against recruiting, the SFA cited the Glasgow recruiting figures to prove the contrary. Glasgow had six first league clubs, more than any other city in the United Kingdom. The public interest in the game was proportionately high. Yet here, where football was so popular, the recruiting returns, instead of being poor, compared favourably with those of other British cities. In addition, at the insistence of the SFA, the various clubs had cooperated in several ways with the authorities in their recruiting efforts. The SFA issued a poster appealing to players and spectators who were physically fit and otherwise able to *join the army at once*. The clubs opened recruiting offices at their grounds with only mixed results. Furthermore, to assume that the 15,000 or 20,000 people who attended big matches had no interest in the nation's grave task was far from the case. Most of those present would have had a relative fighting at the front. The average size of matches was only around 4000; by the time one had deducted those who were under or over military age, and those who were unfit for service, there would be few eligible recruits left. The SFA further contended that a large proportion of recruits who had already enrolled in Glasgow were largely drawn from the ranks of the football supporters. The SFA and the clubs had also contributed handsomely to the relief funds.

The position of the professional football players was also explained and defended by the SFA. While it was admitted that had more professional players answered the call for men, much of the reproach of the game overall would not have been heard. The contribution of the amateur players, including those of Queen's Park of whom over fifty players associated with the premier Scottish amateur club had already enlisted, was acknowledged.

But what of the professional players who had shown a lack of anything like a general response? The first point made in the defence of the professional player was that contrary to popular belief, he was not a young and irresponsible individual who thought of nothing but sport. For most leading clubs, he was a fully grown man, alike in his physique and responsibilities. He was on average around thirty years of age and married with a family to support. Around one hundred footballers in Glasgow were receiving between £4 and £6 per week. This had allowed them to rise socially from their former positions as manual labourers or miners. To become proficient in their profession, the paid footballers had given up their former employment and became wholly dependent on football as their livelihood. Their professional life was short, between six and ten years at best. Thus, if they joined the army for three years, many would be too old to resume their profession when they returned. Should they be injured while on military service, they would most likely be unable to achieve the required fitness level for a return to top-flight football. Another man similarly injured in service, might still be able to resume his previous employment.

The SFA representatives also raised the question of player's contracts. Every schoolboy knows that a professional footballer is signed on for the season. The contract holds good under all circumstances and were the clubs voluntarily to close down, they would be faced with claims from the players for the continuance of their wages. The only way that the clubs could be relieved of the liability, would be if the clubs' directors stated the closures were by Government action.

On the subject of professional association footballers and the comparisons made with rugby players, the point was made that the rugby man was usually a middle-class 'high school' man while the association exponent was usually a working-class 'low school' man. The difference in economic status between them was wide and as a rule the rugby man had no dependants and was therefore a free agent. The association man was in most cases far from free. The actual circumstances of a typical Glasgow League club were cited. Of the twenty players on the club's books, thirteen were married men, three unmarried men had already enlisted and of the four remaining men, three had to support dependants, leaving only one free agent.

The SFA closed its defence of football continuance when Sir John Ure Primrose highlighted a fact that he personally felt may have influenced the War Office decision not to oppose continuance. Lord Kitchener had recently made it plain that he did not want the workers in armament factories and naval shipyards to join the Army. To those men his Lordship's own words were: 'You are doing your duty for your King and country equally with those who have joined the Army for service in the field.' It is a noteworthy fact that a large proportion of the supporters of our leading clubs were members of this class of workmen. The positions of the Celtic and Rangers clubs were stated. In Celtic's case, the ground was convenient for the homes of the workers at the giant Beardmore Forge engineering complex at Parkhead. The Rangers ground was adjacent to the Govan and Partick shipyards. It may be the case that the authorities had no desire to deprive these men of their customary Saturday afternoon recreation.

The interview ended when Sir John Ure Primrose suggested that if the Association felt any qualms on the subject, it would contact the War Office and request a definite pronouncement. On that final point the interview ended. The SFA felt its position had clearly been stated and hoped much of the heat would be taken out of the debate.

All of British football's governing bodies had rather lamely alluded to the sanctity of contracts and the legal difficulties of extracting both parties from player's agreements, of the footballers' personal circumstances, the benefit to morale, contributions to relief funds, etc. However, in reality professional football's only real defence was that it had the approval of Lord Kitchener and the War Office for the continuance of the game.

Back at the beginning of September, Tom Forsyth of Airdrieonians FC had not been satisfied when the SFA delegates returned from London with the War Office's decision that football should continue. He personally wrote to the Under Secretary of State for War asking for confirmation of the War Office's position. Tennant was undoubtedly a man under very severe pressure and as a politician well aware of the public mood regarding the continuance of football, he took his time to reply, but when he did respond the content of his correspondence was explosive:

> No objection is taken to occasional recreation, it is considered, however, that professional football does not come within that category, and it can only be admitted on grounds of contract or employment. It is much more desirable that professional footballers should find employment in his Majesty's forces than in their old occupation. With regard to the question of breach of contract, it is considered that this is a time when all should be prepared to make sacrifices.

Tom Forsyth immediately wrote an open letter to a number of newspapers including the Glasgow Herald, announcing Harold Tennant's pronouncement. On Saturday 14 November, Forsyth's bombshell letter was published in the column adjacent to the SFA's defence of professional football article. The members of the SFA committee must have choked on their breakfasts as they read their morning paper. The War Office had apparently changed its position on the matter, news of which had come completely out of the blue; there had certainly been no official announcement of any change. Had the newspapers not published Forsyth's letter, no one would have been aware of the change of position. The SFA called a meeting for 17 November to discuss the changed circumstances.

Elsewhere in the same edition of the newspaper, the latest recruitment figures for Glasgow were published. Since the outbreak of hostilities, the number of recruits to Kitchener's Army was 29,476, the City battalions 3300, the Territorials 5804 and the Naval Brigade 2000. It was a grand total of 40,580 and that did not include the thousands of Glaswegians who had joined the Highland regiments that had opened their own recruiting offices in the city. A very large majority of the 40,580 volunteers were working class and football followers.

CELTIC FC

The same day Forsyth's letter was published, Parkhead played host to Third Lanark. At that time, the Warriors were on good form and were regarded as a team who might stretch Celtic. After having being involved in the War Shield game at Firhill on the previous Tuesday, Celtic were without Joe Dodds, who was injured during the encounter. Tommy McGregor replaced him at fullback. Billy Crone got his third start of the season, as Patsy Gallacher remained unavailable. The game was apparently a bit of a bore with both sets of players content to 'kick the ball about'. Only Alec McNair received any praise from the sports commentators of the time. The 'Icicle' 'played a magnificent game in his own inimitable style' was one description. McMenemy and Browning were the only forwards on the park to show any signs of cooperation. A refereeing error disallowed a good Celtic goal after the Third Lanark and Scotland goalie Jimmy Brownlie dragged back a ball that had crossed the line. McColl made up for the error by scoring at the end of some slick passing and build-up play between Peter Johnstone and Browning. Midway through the second half, McAtee was brought down in the box and a penalty was awarded. With the opportunity to double Celtic's lead, Jim Young stepped up to shoot straight and not too hard straight into the arms of Brownlie. With only a few minutes left in the game, McAtee picked up a knock and was assisted to the pavilion. Despite being a man short, Celtic were never in any danger of losing their slender lead and the game finished with the Bhoys taking the two points. Only 7000 of the faithful watched what was a pretty mediocre game.

That weekend Heart of Midlothian was playing Falkirk at Tynecastle. At half-time the band of the Queen's Own Cameron Highlanders entertained the crowd while their recruiting team cajoled young men to enlist into the regiment. The game ended in a comfortable 2–0 win for Hearts. In their dressing room after the game, young Jimmy Speedie, a Boroughmuir graduate who was at the time was working as an insurance clerk, and who preferred to remain an amateur player, succumbed to the lure of the kilt. He announced that he would be enlisting immediately into the Cameron Highlanders. His surprise proclamation stunned both John McCartney and the Hearts board, but as an amateur there was really nothing they could do about it. Speedie's decision to serve with the 7th Bn. Cameron Highlanders meant that he would train with his battalion at Inverness and later Aldershot, and his services would be lost to the club. Elsewhere in the League, Rangers could only draw 1–1 at Dumbarton and in what was probably the game of the day, Morton dropped two points at Ayr. With fifteen games played, Hearts still occupied the top spot with twenty-seven points, Celtic were in second place, four points adrift. Morton and Ayr were in third and fourth on nineteen and eighteen points. Rangers were in fifth on sixteen points.

On 17 November, Willie Maley, wearing another of his many hats, this time that of a Scottish League selector, was part of the Scottish party that arrived in Belfast for the inter-league international between Scotland and Ireland. Celtic and Hearts between them provided seven of the starting eleven but due to a misunderstanding, the three Hearts players, Low, Gracie and Nellies, missed the ferry. Arriving in time for lunch, the Scots were feted by the Irish League and later taken on a guided tour of the paper mill at Ballyclare. Back in Belfast, the Scots party were just in time to catch the first house at the Hippodrome. The following day the missing players arrived off the ferry and the game kicked off as scheduled. The four Celtic players turning out for their country were: McNair, Peter Johnstone winning his first cap, McMenemy and Browning. The Scottish League

**Peter Johnstone and his
first Scottish League Cap**
(Courtesy of the Johnstone family)

won 2–1. Jimmy Gourley of Morton and Tom Gracie of Hearts, both winning their first caps, were the Scotland scorers. A crowd of just 7000 watched the game played at Distillery FC's Grosvenor Park, Belfast.

SCOTTISH FOOTBALL

In response to the War Office's surprise change of position, the 'Stop Football' lobbyists arranged a demonstration at Celtic Park during the Third Lanark game. At half-time a crowd of hecklers began shouting 'Stop football!', although they were largely ignored this reflected a very definite cranking up of pressure on the professional clubs. In the Glasgow Observer published the following Saturday *the Man in the Know* called them idiots, but he was obviously anxious, reflecting the very great concern in the Celtic boardroom. He wrote: 'If some people get their way there will be no play at Parkhead, Tynecastle, or anywhere else; football will die an unnatural death for the season one of these days.'

The War Office's revised position regarding football and yet more long casualty lists from Ypres led to yet another wave of letters to the newspapers with professional football again the main target. *The Man in the Know* called them the anonymous scribblers. He wrote that they were gentlemen who are:

> *convinced that football is the cause of a million or is ten million young men not joining Kitchener's Army. There are already thousands of young men already attested but unable to join their units because there was no room for them in an army training system full to overflowing. I know of a young friend who had joined a cavalry unit but had yet to see the tail of a horse or any vestige of a uniform. If the war goes bad for us then by all means stop football, but stop all racing, golfing, and motoring. Close down all the music halls, picture houses and tea rooms where so many of our unmarried young men spend most of their time.*

While Willie Maley and the League selectors were on their jolly to the Ballyclare paper mill, the SFA committee met in Glasgow to discuss Tom Forsyth's letter. The members of the SFA delegation who had gone to London and met Harold Tennant were outraged at the slur on their honour. The SFA later issued an indignant statement denying that they had not misunderstood or worse still had not misrepresented the War Office's position. They announced that circumstances had arisen that made it necessary to reconsider the future of the game. The SFA chairman called for an urgent meeting of the International Board of the English, Scottish, Irish and Welsh associations. The SFA's request was immediately agreed by the other associations and a date for the meeting was set for 3 December. The protestations of the SFA were not enough to placate the 'Stop Football' lobby and yet another wave of indignant letters arrived at the newspaper offices; some took on a very personal slant. One suggested that the Government arbitrarily send 'All Professional Footballers to the Front without the option of refusal.' In Edinburgh's Evening News, a letter was published from a 'Soldier's Daughter', suggesting that since Heart of Midlothian continued to play football while thousands of their countrymen were sacrificing their lives, they might like to adopt the temporary nom de plume 'The White Feathers of Midlothian.'

When Forsyth's letter was published, it also had an explosive effect in England. As in Scotland, the English game was also in financial trouble with attendances at games falling off a cliff. Some football clubs saw the problem coming. At the end of August, Celtic legend Tom Maley, then the manager at English first division side Bradford Park Avenue, watched the club's directors withhold the shareholders' dividend, fearing the war would drastically reduce gates. As early as mid-October the English players union was in talks regarding a cut in players' wages as part of a scheme to help clubs in financial difficulty. In defence of continuance, the FA produced a comparative table of match attendance figures showing the decline. It was an attempt to show that working-class football supporters were enlisting. On 17 November 1913, West Bromwich saw 35,000 come through the turnstiles. On 7 November 1914, the figure was 14,000 and on 21 November just 10,000. All the other clubs had seen similar falls. Taking attendance figures for just seven English clubs, the overall fall was from 126,000 in November 1913 to 55,000 in November 1914. Despite the attendance figures, the move to stop football only intensified and the last thing the FA needed was Forsyth's letter. The FA chairman, Charles Clegg, desperately announced that 'Special Recruiting Measures' would be introduced at all

English football matches to be played on 21 November. Although the results were mixed, overall they were bad and the special recruiting measures were deemed a disaster by the prejudiced press. 'Only ONE recruit from the special measures,' screamed the newspaper headlines. The poor figures gave yet another publicity coup to the 'Stop Football' lobby. The game did get some support from the Athletics News, who recognised the assault on the working class:

> *The whole agitation is nothing less than an attempt by the ruling classes to stop the recreation on one day in the week of the masses... What do they care for the poor man's sport? The poor are giving their lives for this country in thousands. In many cases they have nothing else... These should, according to a small clique of virulent snobs, be deprived of the one distraction that they have had for over thirty years.*

The beleaguered FA board was buckling under the pressure, but was looking forward to the international board meeting, where at least the four home football associations could present a united front.

Jumping onto the anti-professional football band wagon, Orangeman Sir John Lonsdale, Unionist MP for Mid Armagh and Charrington supporter, publicly announced that he would be asking the Prime Minister in Parliament: 'If in view of the failure of the special recruiting measures he would introduce legislation taking powers to suppress all professional football matches during the continuance of the war.' Professional football it seamed was on the edge of a precipice. At the same time the Prime Minister was announcing to the House of Commons: 'Since 10 August, over 700,000 men had joined the colours and the TF now stood at over 200,000, overall it was an encouraging recruiting condition.'

CELTIC FC

On 21 November, a second consecutive home game saw the visit of Ayr United to Parkhead. It was also the Celts second game against the Honest Men in six weeks, having lost to them on their previous encounter 0–1 at Ayr. After their

Jim Young and Patsy Gallacher in action versus Ayr United

victory at home, the Ayr men fancied their chances of repeating the feat. Patsy Gallacher made his welcome return to the team after being out for the previous two games. The teams ran out onto a chilly, misty Parkhead and Celtic managed to keep Ayr in the fog while they ran their visitors ragged. Ayr started bright enough and had one or two good shots on goal. One shot in particular fair warmed Shaw's fingers. In a classic sucker punch, Celtic's first goal came after an Ayr United attack broke down. Jim Young intercepted a pass, fired a long ball out to Browning, who went on to score Celtic's first after twenty minutes. This was followed five minutes later by Gallacher's first and Celtic's second. The Celts went in at the interval two goals to the good. In the second half the Celts scored twice, Patsy getting both, marking his return to the side by scoring a hat trick. Only Willie McStay, on loan from Celtic, Bell and Richardson played to form for the visitors. In addition to Patsy Gallacher both McAtee and Johnny Browning deserved praise for their performances. 'Sunny' Jim Young also put in a terrific performance, probably his best of the season so far. If the Bhoys had played badly at Ayr, they played very well at Parkhead and ran out easy winners by 4–0 against an Ayr United team that was totally outclassed in almost every department. The score margin did no justice to the performance; 10–0 would have been a more realistic indication of the gap in class. Only 4000 spectators watched the game, the closing stages of which was played in semi-darkness. The four goals scored took the Celts to the top of the goals scored list, but Heart of Midlothian still sat comfortably at the top of the football league.

The Hearts had also been in Glasgow that Saturday where 12,000 watched them beat Partick Thistle 0–2 at Firhill. The win kept the Tynecastle men four points clear of the Celts, with Morton nine points behind the leaders with a game in hand over both Hearts and Celtic. The Rangers were in fourth place a point behind Morton. With sixteen games played, Hearts were going very well indeed, having only dropped three points so far.

SOJERIN' WIE GEORDIE

In the newspapers, the debate over recruiting and who was or was not enlisting raged on. Recruiting figures throughout the United Kingdom showed a marked decrease and it was the Nationalist Irish and the professional footballer who were getting much of the blame. In London on 26 November, as promised, Sir John Lonsdale rose to his feet in Parliament and fired his question to the Prime Minister. Mr Asquith replied that he did not believe that there was any need for such legislation given the fact that the FA was currently liaising with the War Office on the issue of recruiting. Not satisfied, Lonsdale rose again to ask whether the Prime Minister was aware that only one recruit had been obtained at football grounds the previous Saturday, 'despite the most strenuous efforts'. The Prime Minister replied that he had indeed read the report in the newspapers, but was glad to say that in Scotland the response was very different. The difference that Asquith was referring to was Heart of Midlothian FC.

On Wednesday 25 November at Tynecastle football ground in Edinburgh, eleven Heart of Midlothian footballers felt compelled or were persuaded to enlist into the Army. The actions of the Hearts players, some of whom surrendered their £4 a week footballer's wages for the 1/- a day army pay, made newspaper headlines throughout the whole of the United Kingdom. The action which had the full support of the club directors, who agreed to set aside the players' contracts, stunned professional football, but delighted the public, the military and of course the politicians. The following day telegrams flooded into Tynecastle congratulating the club on its patriotic stance. The telegram boys were also frequent callers at the Edinburgh home of a certain Sir George McCrae. The telegram messages of congratulations and support included ones from (among others) Lord Kitchener, Winston Churchill, Arthur Balfour, Lloyd George, Bonar Law, Harold Tennant and last but by no means least the Prime Minister, who personally assured Sir George 'any help you need will be forthcoming'. In fact, the whole of Edinburgh and the east of Scotland were willing to help Geordie, even the Moderator of the Church of Scotland gave him an unheard of dispensation to recruit on the Sabbath.

The actions of the Hearts players and directors would lead directly to the spectacularly successful raising of the 16th (Service) Bn Royal Scots, also known and fondly remembered in Edinburgh as McCrae's battalion. The new service battalion was the personal project of Edinburgh worthy and former Liberal MP Sir George McCrae. The very epitome of the lad o' pairts, George McCrae had, through sheer hard work, business acumen and force of personality, climbed from the humblest levels of Victorian society through the stuffy deferential ranks of Edinburgh's notoriously class-conscious society until by 1914 he was one of the city's leading and most famous citizens.

Sir George McCrae had a long and affectionate association with the Heart of Midlothian football club. In recognition of the club winning the Scottish League Championship for the first time in 1895, the then Baillie George McCrae, serving as Treasurer of Edinburgh Corporation, presented the club with a handsome trophy; it was a personal gift from the treasurer, the Town Council gave them nothing. Sir George was also an original shareholder of the club and close associate of the chairman, Elias Furst, and club financial advisor Sir James Leishman.

After the plea by the Prime Minister for the leaders of civic society to get involved personally in the national recruiting drive, Sir George decided he would use his reputation and considerable influence to raise his own infantry battalion of 1000 men. McCrae had only recently resigned the command of the 6th Bn Royal Scots, an Edinburgh-based Territorial Force battalion. When he reapplied for a commission, he was appointed colonel and given permission by the War Office to raise, if he could, his infantry battalion. The news broke late on 19 November that Sir George had volunteered for active service, and the following day it was announced that he would be raising a battalion. Newspaper reporters besieged his Edinburgh home that afternoon for more information. After appearing at the door in uniform, he announced that he would indeed be raising a battalion and that recruiting for the second Edinburgh City battalion would begin on 27 November. He caused uproar when he said the recruiting campaign would be short, just seven days at most before the full complement would be reached. Seven days, how? The Lord Provost of Edinburgh had just taken almost seven weeks to raise his service battalion and had only done so with the absorption of hundreds of men from the Manchester Scottish. McCrae just smiled and winked at the reporters; he obviously knew something they did not.

As an astute businessman, Sir George McCrae, of course, recognised the powerful influence footballers had over their supporters. If some of the Heart of Midlothian players were to enlist into his battalion, hundreds of the club's supporters would follow them. It was not an original idea by any means and the secret to success would be to get the professional players actually to enlist. The question was how would it be done? Why would top-class professional footballers voluntarily surrender possibly years of their very short careers and £4 a week, for 1/- a day and risk a career-destroying injury or worse?

The story goes that the idea came to Sir George via his son Kenneth, who was a subaltern serving with the 7th (Service) Bn Queen's Own Cameron Highlanders. He had apparently spoken to former Hearts player Jimmy Speedie, who was serving with the same Cameron battalion. Jimmy informed young McCrae that several of the Hearts players had been discussing enlisting (just about every man of serviceable age was) prior to his own decision to enlist. The message was immediately conveyed to Sir George back in Edinburgh who thought, eh! That's handy!

George McCrae was staking his own personal reputation on raising the battalion, so it was very important that his project, carried out in the full glare of publicity, be successful. The day before Sir George's dramatic announcement of 20 November, the Hearts manager, John McCartney, had received a telephone call at his Tynecastle office from Sir James Leishman, asking him to meet him immediately at his shop in Edinburgh. James Leishman was another self-made Edinburgh worthy and like his great friend, Sir George McCrae, he too had a long and close association with Hearts FC. He too was a shareholder and although he declined an offer of a seat on the board, he accepted the position of financial advisor. In that massively deferential age, McCartney, of course, responded immediately to the summons by a knight of the realm, dropped what he was doing and went by taxi into the city. On arrival at the shop, he was ushered into Leishman's private office. Minutes later Sir George McCrae arrived unannounced and apparently unexpected. The two knights asked McCartney if he thought it was possible to get some of his players to join the battalion being raised by Sir George. A no doubt stunned and no doubt somewhat intimidated John McCartney said he would have to speak to the club directors. Unknown to the Hearts manager or the directors of the club, a number of the players had already been approached individually by Leishman and others. The clandestine meetings had been leaked to the press. The Edinburgh papers sensing that something was afoot reported on 21 November that 'thousands of men have a common bond of comradeship at Tynecastle, under the auspice of Heart of Midlothian half a battalion of excellent soldiers could be raised with ease.'

On 23 November, the Hearts chairman and John McCartney met Sir George McCrae and Sir James Leishman to discuss the Hearts players joining McCrae's battalion. The Hearts board of directors then met at Tynecastle when the chairman gave them an account of the meeting with McCrae and Leishman. After discussing the matter, the Hearts board agreed that no obstacle would be placed in the way of any players wishing to join the colours. In addition, should a player enlist, he would be paid half wages when unable to play and full wages if he played during the period of his current contract.

During their discussions with Sir George, it would no doubt have been pointed out to both the Hearts chairman and John McCartney that any player who enlisted into McCrae's battalion would be trained in and around Edinburgh for at least six months and, barring injury, would be made available to play for Hearts for the remainder of the football season. The point would not be lost on the Hearts directors, who had watched two first team regulars, amateur Jimmy Speedie and Geordie Sinclair, disappear off to their units, the services of both players being lost entirely to the club. The Hearts directors had done their bit. A message was sent to McCrae and

Leishman that they should come to Tynecastle to meet the assembled players. The decision of whether or not to enlist now shifted onto the players themselves.

The situation with the players at Tynecastle was an open secret and public expectation rose when the Glasgow Herald reported on 25 November that a 'strong effort is about to be made in Edinburgh today to enlist professional footballers'. The pressure on the players to enlist had been building for days and no doubt they were discussing it among themselves. The Heart of Midlothian footballers were like most professional players of their day, mostly working- or upper working-class lads, though some were better educated than the norm, who only wanted to play football. John McCartney later wrote that he addressed the assembled playing staff on the morning of 25 November and when the question of enlistment was put to them almost everyone stepped forward.

Sir George and Sir James arrived at Tynecastle that afternoon and brought with them a doctor. The playing staff was again assembled and after listening to a speech from Sir George, sixteen players stepped forward to volunteer. After a medical examination, six first team players and five reserves were enlisted and immediately sworn in by Sir James Leishman in his capacity as a Justice of the Peace. The remaining five players failed to make army medical standards.

In a massively deferential age, we will never know how much personal influence Sir George and or Sir James exerted, or how much coaxing or pressure was involved in the players' decision to enlist. It is difficult to believe that the Hearts lads were any more or less patriotic than their peers. The fact that they could enlist and still play out the season for Hearts would have been a very important factor. The pressure from two knights of the realm, newspaper reports and the expectation that something was about to happen at Tynecastle, or the example set by Jimmy Speedie, may also have played a part, as might the promise by Sir George McCrae

Welcome, my Heartie, I hope you have brought the rest with you!
(Courtesy of Glasgow Evening Times)

that they would all be allowed to serve together. Irrespective of their reasons or circumstances of their enlistment, nothing should ever diminish or tarnish their patriotic gesture.

The day following, a meeting was held at Tynecastle attended by the representatives of a number of east coast football and athletic clubs. The meeting was called to discuss McCrae's battalion and how the clubs could help to encourage recruiting. The Hearts chairman presided and opened the meeting by saying that the actions of the directors of Heart of Midlothian was nothing to be proud of, but was simply their duty. He hoped that others would follow their lead. Sir George McCrae and Sir James Leishman were also present at the meeting. Sir George spoke briefly saying that association football had stood on the brink of a precipice and that Hearts by their actions had saved the game. He trusted that the other clubs present would follow the lead so nobly given by Hearts. Sir James Leishman also threw in his tuppence worth saying:

I am not one of those who would damp down every form of recreation and I have no sympathy with the one sided and unjust criticism of football. There was possibly some little truth in the criticism, but so far as Edinburgh was concerned and he hoped the movement would not stop there, they had shown that the criticism was not just. To say the men were slackers or cowards was untrue. It was unjust to say so when the clubs were considering their position and asking for a lead from the government. He had never heard a more unfounded argument than that football prevented people form going to war.

Sir George also paid a personal visit to Easter Road in an attempt to recruit Hibernian players into his battalion. The Hibernian club operated with a very small squad of just fifteen signed players, most of them married, and his appeal was largely ignored. Only left back Sandy Grosert, who was already in the process of enlisting into the Royal Army Service Corps as a driver, stepped forward. Sandy would later transfer out of McCrae's battalion, preferring instead to soldier with the newly formed Machine Gun Corps. Later still he would be commissioned into the Gordon Highlanders, win a Military Cross and survive the war. The Edinburgh Evening News, disappointed with the response from Easter Road, commented: 'There must be something lacking at Easter Road.' They forgot to mention the size of the squad or that most of the players were married.

Sir George would get players from over seventy-five of the east coast clubs, including Hibernian, Falkirk, Raith Rovers, Dunfermline and the quaintly named Cow Punchers. The latter were officially Mossend Burnvale FC, but due to the state of their pitch they were landed with the agricultural nickname. Many young students from University of Edinburgh and its training colleges also decided to dance to Geordie's tune. Over 600 Hearts supporters followed their football heroes into the ranks of McCrae's battalion. Around 150 Hibernian supporters would join them. When the Hearts footballers agreed to enlist, the Tynecastle team was sitting very comfortably at the top of the League table; four points clear of Celtic and going very well indeed.

CELTIC FC

After the early and sudden death of big John Mulrooney back in August, on Friday 27 November, the Celtic family were again stunned to hear of the death of club legend Peter Somers, aged just thirty-six. The Celtic and Scotland internationalist died after an operation to remove his foot. Although the operation was successful, complications set in and Peter died in the early hours of the morning in a Glasgow nursing home. Motherwell born, Peter played for Cadzow Juniors before being brought to Parkhead in November 1897. Unable to displace Sandy McMahon, he turned out for Clyde before going to Blackburn Rovers in 1900. Despite being a regular in the Lancashire side's first eleven, Peter never settled south of the border and jumped at the chance to come back to Parkhead when Celtic called in August 1902. He came back into the first great Celtic side that would sweep aside all opposition for the next six years. Described as one of the most talented footballers in the history of the game, he was the brains of the six-in-a-row team and was titled Willie Maley's 'powder monkey', named after the men who served the guns on board battleships.

Maley credited Peter with bringing the 'forward' game to Parkhead. A combination of the English and Scottish styles, it did most to bring Celtic to the top of the game. Peter once taunted Jimmy Galt of Rangers, who was also a talented golfer: 'You teach me how to play golf and I'll teach you how to play fitba.' Peter played 219 times for the Celts and scored sixty-two goals. After leaving Parkhead in December 1909, he went to Hamilton Accies, where he later became a director of the club. At his funeral, in addition to James Kelly, Willie Maley, Mick Dunbar and Tom Colgan representing the club, Davie Adams, Willie Loney and Willie Orr represented his old team, while Jimmy McMenemy, James Young, Alec McNair and Joe Dodds represented the current Celtic squad. His old friend Jimmy Quinn was one of the pall-bearers.

The day after Peter Somers' death saw the Celtic away at Dumbarton. Despite wartime restrictions on travel and the government taking control of the railways, Celtic put on a special train for its travelling supporters. Calling at Rutherglen, Bridgeton, Central and Partick, the special would return from Dumbarton after the game. Both Hearts and Rangers had dropped points at Boghead recently. Rangers escaped with a very fortunate point, while Hearts suffered their first defeat of the season to the Sons of the Rock. Celtic took a full-strength team to Boghead and although Peter Johnstone was nursing a bad ankle knock, they proved too strong for the home team, outclassing them in every position. The Celtic started the game facing into the sun and playing against a stiff wind. With the exception of a few very brief spells in either half, Celtic controlled the match from start to finish. Playing a patient game, they held onto the ball, passing through the midfield, defence and back to Charlie Shaw in goal, play that greatly irritated the home section of the crowd. Andy McAtee and Jimmy McColl were the scorers in the first half with Brown pulling one back for Dumbarton right on the break. After the interval, the game went the same way with Celtic completely dominant. McColl grabbed his second, which made it three for the visitors and Celtic's fourth came through Jimmy McMenemy with twenty minutes to go. It could have been more, but the Celts were in a lenient mood and toyed with the opposition for the last part of the game. The game finished with a Celtic victory of 1–4. McAtee and Jim Young shared the man of the match plaudits. The 1000 supporters Celtic brought with them on their special train enjoyed their day out. A crowd of 7000 watched while the Bhoys sent a message to Tynecastle that the Celtic were back at their irresistible best.

The last Saturday of the month saw the League's leading clubs all win. Hearts beat Hamilton Accies 1–3 at Hamilton, Rangers won at Third Lanark, while Morton beat Airdrie 4–1. Hearts remained at the top of the League table, clear by four points from Celtic.

THE HOME FRONT

In that weekend's edition of the Glasgow Observer, *the Man in the Know* was worried. He felt the spectre of doom at his shoulder. Like in England, the recruiting drives at football matches had proved much less successful than the military authorities had hoped. Their failure showed the game in a bad light and gave ammunition to the 'Stop Football' lobby. Never convinced of their merit in the first place, *the Man in the Know* dubbed the football recruiting schemes fiascos. With the future of the game on the precipice, he blew off some steam with a rant and a dig at the middle-class letter scribblers:

*Our young men do not go to football matches with any idea of enlisting.
They have given the matter full consideration and many of them will enlist
later. Meanwhile they look on a football match as relaxation after a hard
week at the foundry or forge, and it is as reasonable to ask them to enlist
on a Saturday afternoon as it would be to expect their newspaper critics
to leave in the middle of a play or an opera, or mid way through a dinner
at their club and take the shilling. I do not say that that there are hundreds
of thousands who ought to be under canvas today. My point is that there is
a time and a place for everything, and those who go looking for recruits at
football matches ought to be under lock and key.*

The game, as had been suggested by Sir George McCrae, was still despite the enlistment of the Hearts lads, at the edge of a precipice. *The Man in the Know* wrote that there were very definite signs of a postponement. The English Association had cancelled the trial match fixed for Newcastle, which may have meant anything or nothing. Despite the 'Stop Football' cries reaching a crescendo, *the Man in the Know* tried to reassure himself that nothing definite had been announced from those who really mattered, the national associations. As an afterthought, he mentioned that Willie Donnelly, the old Celtic goalie, was presently in Dublin training with the Royal Dublin Fusiliers.

As the debate on recruiting figures raged, municipal efforts to encourage young men into the army continued unabated. Back in September, the old Celtic trainer Tom Maguire, himself a former Seaforth Highlander, wrote to the Glasgow Herald suggesting that a special battalion composed of small men should be formed. Nothing further was heard of his idea until November when Alfred Bigland, the Member of Parliament for Birkenhead, pressed the War Office for permission to form a battalion of men who were under regulation size but otherwise fit for service. A few days later, some 3000 men had volunteered, many of who had previously been rejected as being under regulation height. This type of unit became known as a bantam battalion and the event at Birkenhead did not go unnoticed in the Glasgow city chambers. In November 1914, Thomas Dunlop had succeeded Sir Daniel Stevenson as Lord Provost and by the beginning of December, Glasgow's new Unionist Lord Provost had contacted the War Office asking for permission to raise such a battalion. When news of the Provost's request was reported in the press, the Glasgow Rotary Club took up the idea of overseeing and organising the recruiting drive for the battalion. After tipping their hat to Glasgow's Lord Provost, who accepted their assistance, they formed a Rotary Club Recruiting Committee and led by its convenor JS Proctor, a Glasgow insurance company manager, arranged a number of recruiting meetings around the city.

At the end of November, the British press were printing heavily censored excerpts from Sir John French's despatch reporting the details of the fighting around Ypres in October and early November. The propaganda piece, of course, highlighted the positives and played down the negative. The headlines were: 'How the German Dash for Calais Was Frustrated', 'Desperate Days in Flanders' and 'Brilliant British Deeds'. The Glasgow Herald gave it a Scottish twist by highlighting the actions of Scottish regiments. At the same time, it was announced that with most of the original TF battalions either already on foreign serve or earmarked for foreign service, and their second-line battalions deploying to their war stations at home, recruiting would commence immediately for new third-line battalions. The new TF battalions were required to recruit and train replacements for their first- and second-line battalions. In response to the announcement of the third line, the County and City of Glasgow TF Association declared that an additional 4000 men would be required. All volunteers stepping forward for the third-line battalions were required to sign the Imperial service agreement agreeing to serve overseas.

On 30 November, it was reported that after a recruiting rally in Coatbridge, fifteen recruits signed on at the recruiting office, while eight signed on at the labour exchange. During the previous week, twenty-five men had signed on at the labour exchange. It was noted that Coatbridge had already provided over 2000 volunteers for Lord Kitchener's Army. Over the month of November, a total of 169,800 men enlisted nationwide, but of the now two million sanctioned, at the end of November the figure stood at just over one million. A remarkable figure no doubt, but well short of the target set by the government.

IRISH RECRUITING

The Man in the Know was not the only one feeling the hot breath of officialdom on his neck. Questions had already been asked in Parliament regarding the recruitment figures for Ireland and the government's official response to the Sinn Féin anti-recruitment campaign. In what was an ill-informed article, the Glasgow Herald of 25 November commented:

> *Liberally financed by Williamstrasse German agents have found willing instruments in those seditious Irish elements which at no period in our history have been absent and at every period of stress have been malevolently active. One would think at this juncture only a people cursed by blindness to its own interest and sunk fathoms deep in political incapacity would jeopardise its future by conniving treason. A majority of Irishmen may awaken before it is too late to the calamitous possibilities of the situation, which the extremists are engaged in creating, but they will need to bestir themselves. It is no doubt only a handful of misguided people who are promoting the anti-recruiting campaign, but they are doing so with tireless energy, scattering broadcast the most venomous attacks on Britain, the British forces and the cause to which Britain has committed all her resources. It is apparent that they have succeeded in checking recruiting in the South and West of Ireland. We do not blame Redmond or the accredited leaders of the Nationalists. We believe that they have sincerely tried to make Nationalist Ireland do as Unionist Ireland has done – its duty. The handicap on all intelligent effort in this direction is an ignorant peasantry, whose assiduously cultivated hate and prejudices are now being ploughed and sown by the agents of treason.*

The Herald article was all the more bizarre when you consider Scottish newspapers, including the Herald itself a few days earlier, were reporting that Glasgow's recruiting figures were disappointing, just 411 for the week, while at the same time reporting 'Dublin Doing Well' with 211 recruits this week and 247 the previous. In 1914, the population of Dublin was assessed at just over 300,000, less than a third that of Glasgow. In fact between 1914 and 1918, out of a population of 304,000, approximately 30,000 Dubliners joined the army. The Herald article finished by advocating the suppression of press freedom and censorship.

Ten days later a number of Irish printers contracted to print the anti-recruitment publications had their offices raided. The printers of Irish Freedom, Sinn Féin, Ireland, Irish Worker, Irish Volunteer and The Leader were warned that if they printed matter that the military authorities considered likely to cause disaffection or to interfere with recruiting, they would render themselves liable to trial under the provisions of Defence of the Realm Act (DORA). In December, Sinn Féin was banned, but was almost immediately replaced with Scissors and Paste and later with Nationality, both of which continued to espouse anti-recruitment articles.

The controversy over Irish recruitment figures had been rumbling on for months. The recruitment figures for the Unionist and Nationalist communities had been pawns in an Irish political game of chess right from the start, as both sides encouraged or held back volunteer recruits to suit their own political agenda. The Unionists, of course, took every opportunity to denigrate the Nationalist numbers and to talk up their own and inevitably a tit-for-tat war of words and gerrymandering of numbers ensued. At the end of November, the Nationalists launched an all-out media campaign in support of their own recruiting figures. With the Glasgow Irish enlisting fully in proportion to their fellow Glaswegians, the Glasgow Catholic Observer entered the debate on the furore over the recruiting figures with the article 'Has Ireland Done Her Bit' By WG Fallon, BA. It read;

> Before the war was declared there were in the three main branches of the Army about 47,000 Irishmen from Ireland and about 26,000 Catholics from Great Britain. I computed that the combined totals yield over 60,000 Catholic Nationalists from various parts of Britain and Ireland. Now let us learn what has been done since war was declared. But in the first place we must note the following. On August 1st the estimated population of Great Britain [i.e. England, Scotland and Wales] was 42,000,000 and the number of men between twenty and forty-five years of age was about 7,755,000. The corresponding figures for Ireland are:- Population 4,370,000; number of men between twenty and forty five years of age 772,000. But if the proportion for Ireland were measured by that of Great Britain, Ireland should have nearly 807,000 men between the ages stated. In other words, one of the fruits of enforced emigration during a period of seventy years is that Ireland today falls short of her due proportion of recruitable men by 35,000. Thus the call for Irish soldiers commenced under this disadvantage.
>
> In the second place, our British friends must get it into their heads that the economic conditions of Ireland are wholly different from those that prevail in Great Britain. Recent statistics show that large civic areas provide a disproportionately larger number of recruits than any other area with an equal population. In Ireland, Belfast, Dublin and Cork are the only large civic areas. And if we decide to make exceptions in the case of Derry City and Limerick the remainder of Ireland may be said to subsist on the agricultural industry. Now, as to this huge agricultural area, the Irish Department for Agriculture recently announced that their appeal to Irish farmers to put the land to the fullest use during the war period has received a gratifying

response. The result is that over large areas in Ireland agricultural labourers cannot be hired at any price. But when we remember that in normal times agricultural labourers provide twenty five per cent of Irish recruits we shall begin to understand that a contribution of recruits from Ireland proportionately equal to the number furnished by Great Britain is an economic impossibility. Even the anti-Irish 'Times' appreciates that handicap.

In the third place, Ireland requires careful handling. For over seven centuries she has been estranged, but with the passing of the Home Rule Bill to the statute book a wave of Imperial fervour swept over the island. Encouraged by every constitutional nationalist in Ireland, the War Office had an obvious opportunity. The War Office failed, lamentably failed in every respect to use the occasion. The 'Irish Brigade' could have been formed in August had the authorities so desired. Redmond did not request the formation of a Catholic Nationalist 'Brigade' merely an 'Irish Brigade.' The result now is that the Irish people have been allocated three months to grow suspicious. It took three months to promise to provide Catholic chaplains. Colours, a small request surely, has been refused again. But the reader will understand that the atmosphere of exulting joy is not as clear as it might have been. Therefore, when one valuates each unfavourable circumstance, it is satisfactory to be able to record that to the end of the first week of November some 36,000 men were recruited in Ireland and under the altered, though belated, conditions the weekly totals tend to increase. Admittedly, 36,000 falls short of Ireland's proportion. The 'Times' describes Redmond's campaign as 'a disappointment.' But is it? The Irish in Great Britain acknowledge Redmond's leadership, as do the Irish in Ireland. So if we care to deduct from Ireland's share the contribution from the Unionists of Ireland, and from Great Britain's share the contribution from the Nationalists of Great Britain, it will be found that the contribution of recruits from Nationalists – figuring at over 70,000 – falls short of the due proportion by only twelve or thirteen thousand recruits.

After very successfully adding to the confusion regarding overall recruiting figures, the writer signs off with a dig at the Ulster Unionists and their recruiting figure claims:

> *Hear the 'Morning Post of a few weeks ago and guess the game.' But surely, it wrote: 'The Ulster people may hope that this magnificent response [i.e., Orange recruits] to the call to arms ... will discourage any future attempt to separate this loyal Province from the rest of the United Kingdom.' Often we have read of the Ulster Volunteer – over one hundred thousand of them, I believe. Thirteen thousand have recruited – about one in eight.*

Meanwhile in Cork, Colonel Maurice Moore, accompanied by John Redmond's brother, Willie Redmond MP, who appeared in a Volunteer uniform, reviewed a parade of 3000 Irish National Volunteers. The Cork Volunteers were presented with colours and Willie Redmond in his address said:

> *The Volunteers appealed to all Irishmen to support the Volunteer movement. In this great European struggle Irishmen should be in the firing line, as many were already. In joining the Irish Volunteers it should be understood that no man would be compelled to serve outside Ireland, but if the occasion arose he was himself ready to take his place at the front and what he would say to the Volunteers was – 'Follow me.'*

The political situation in Ireland was also a great concern for the French government and while the British were trying to soothe French worries over the situation, it was reported in the world press that Sir Rodger Casement was in Berlin. Described as that notable Irishman, Sir Rodger had travelled to America to drum up support for the Irish Volunteers. While there, he met influential IRB leaders, who arranged for Casement to travel to Germany where he met the German Foreign Minister. He received assurances that in the event of a German invasion of Ireland they would come as the apostles of liberty. He also attempted to persuade the Germans that Ireland was on the cusp of revolution and that with German military assistance a full-scale armed rebellion against British rule could be brought about. Sir Roger had the Germans concentrate Irish POWs at Limburg Camp, where over the course of several months he attempted to recruit the Irishmen for yet another Irish Brigade, which would be armed, trained and transported to Ireland by the Germans. He had visions of a 3000-strong Nationalist Brigade landing in Ireland and leading the armed rebellion. Despite being offered preferential treatment by the Germans in an attempt to persuade them to join, only fifty-six of the 2000 Irish prisoners brought to Limburg took up the offer. The large majority of Irish POWs shouted Casement down and sent a delegation to the camp commandant stating they wanted no special treatment and that 'in addition to being Irish Catholics, we have the honour to be British soldiers'. The fifty-six went on to be trained by the Germans. Armed and dressed in Irish uniforms, they were later attached to a Brandenburg regiment. However, as the recruiting drive had transpired to be a disastrous failure, Casement and the Germans lost interest in the project. Most of the fifty-six who did enlist later reverted to normal POW status.

In Belfast, Wee Joe Devlin dispatched another contingent of Nationalist Volunteers to the Irish Brigade at Kildare.

THE WAR FRONT

After being rushed to France, the 9th (Glasgow Highlanders) Bn HLI, with Private John Francis McKillop in its ranks, arrived at Le Havre early on 5 November. By the time the Glasgow Highlanders arrived at St Omer a couple of days later, the situation at Ypres was still desperate. The battalion was ordered forward six miles south-east and into reserve positions at Wardrecques. There, alongside other newly arrived battalions, they were ordered to dig a new defensive line in case the line at Ypres failed to hold. For the next two weeks the men were billeted in a tile and paper factory at Wardrecques, while the line at Ypres held and the situation finally stabilised. Their time there was spent in training, which in reality meant route marches, usually in full pack and equipment and in some appalling weather. About that time, John Francis McKillop fired off a letter to his father, James McKillop, back in Glasgow:

> We are now within the sounds of the guns and have been marching a lot over the last few days. The weather has turned bitterly cold and wet and we can find little comfort, even after finishing a gruelling march and return, soaked to the skin, to a cold, draughty factory and guard duties of two hours on and two hours off. But it is astounding how a tot of army rum can bolster flagging spirits under such circumstances.

On 18 November, the battalion finally got a chance to test fire their new rifles, ten rounds at 300 yards, but there was no indication of whether they hit their targets or not. On Sunday 22 November, they were ordered to move and after fitting ice clogs to the shoes of their transport horses, the Glasgow Highlanders marched off along icy roads towards the sound of the guns. On 24 November, the battalion reached Bailleul and learned much to its delight that it was to be attached to the regulars, and alongside the 2nd Bn HLI to the 5th Brigade, 2nd Division. The next day as part of a divisional deployment into the front line, the battalion moved north to Mont Kemmel, one of the few features in the area south of Ypres that deserved the name of a hill. At dusk, two companies went into the front-line trenches, while the other two moved into reserve positions. For the first time, the battalion was on its own, and operating as an independent unit. The German trenches were on average 200 yards away, but in some places they were as close as just fifty yards. More of a concern was the fact that the Germans occupied the higher ground. The battalion war diary recorded the front-line trenches as being too shallow in places to adequately protect the strapping Highlanders. The war diary also noted that they did not attempt to deepen the trenches because the bottom was full of French dead, the bodies having been covered over with a few inches of earth. The Glasgow Highlanders spent two days and nights in the trenches enduring almost constant sniping and regular shellfire before being relieved by another TF battalion, the Liverpool Scottish. Miraculously the Glasgow Highlanders had suffered no casualties during their first tour of the front line.

As far as Sir John French and the BEF were concerned, the end of November saw the German firestorm weathered, and with the TF battalions moving into the line to reinforce what was left of the exhausted, regular battalions, the critical situation had stabilised. The remnants of the BEF were relieved by French forces that took over the Salient and the line to the north of Ypres, while the BEF moved to a shorter stretch of the front line between Messines and Cuinchy. The Germans too were exhausted and realising that no side was capable of mounting any large-scale attack, the High Command pulled several divisions out of the line, switching them to the Eastern Front to face the Russians, who were much more adept at winter warfare. The winter weather put a stop to large-scale military operations in France and Belgium and both sides switched their attentions to simply surviving the trench warfare.

Over the course of the Race to the Sea, the Germans had managed to secure and occupy most of the high ground, while the British and French forces found themselves occupying the lower ground. As the opposing forces began to dig in, the Allies found their positions were overlooked by the enemy. In addition to the obvious tactical disadvantage of the Germans being able to observe all movement, in northern France and Belgium the Allied positions suffered from high-water tables, making their trenches by necessity either very shallow or waterlogged, in some places both. In some areas, the water table was so high, it was impossible to dig any more than two feet before the shell scrapes became waterlogged and were impossible to occupy. The answer was breastworks, screens and earthworks that provided the British and French soldiers cover from view but not usually from heavy machine gun or artillery fire.

As the war on the Western Front, as it was now being called, stagnated, and the men on both sides settled into their waterlogged positions, the defence of the front lines became a matter of routine. The men manning the front-line positions did so on a rotation basis, usually four days in followed by four days in support positions then four days out, not necessarily in that order. With the onset of winter, the weather turned and the already bad conditions in the trenches became atrocious beyond the imaginings of sane people. The tactical situation along most of the line meant that the trenches filled with water and liquid mud simply had to be occupied. In places, some men took off their boots and trousers and stood for hours on guard, naked below the waist. The Highlanders took off their brogues and socks and slung their kilts over their shoulders so at least they would have something dry to wear when their shift was over. During their time in the line, the men were forced to dig constantly into the liquid mud that half-filled the trenches in an attempt to keep from freezing to death.

Their time in the line was absolutely exhausting with little opportunity for proper sleep. They were working in conditions previously considered to be unimaginable. If they were not shoring up the trenches, they were bailing water. If not bailing, they were erecting wire or they were on sentry duty or on stand-to or being fed. Because the German positions in many cases overlooked the Allied lines, movement over open ground in daylight was almost suicidal; therefore, communication trenches that connected the front-line trenches with the reserve and support trenches had to be dug. Specialist pioneer battalions had been hastily raised to help the infantry with the monumental scale of digging. Quickly, the front line actually became a system of trenches that took on the appearance of a spider's web. When the men did get the chance of some sleep, it was fitful at best, perched on a shelf dug into the side of a constantly collapsing trench wall. By the time the men were relieved, they were like zombies, soaked to the skin and completely covered in mud. As the soldiers stood for hours on end up to their knees in freezing mud and slime, thousands suffered from frostbite and trench foot. Only with a severe frost was there any relief from the energy and morale sapping mud.

The exhausting battles over the first three months of the war and the onset of winter conditions ensured there was no chance of any major breakthrough before the spring of 1915. However, the generals on both sides were concerned that the men might get soft without regular encounters with the enemy; therefore, almost daily, localised attacks across very narrow stretches of no man's land between the front lines were planned. This meant there was a permanent threat of attack and the need for constant vigilance.

The enforced lull in military operations meant that the part-time soldiers of the TF battalions, who had rushed to France at the height of the crisis in October and November, now had a chance to complete their training, though their experiences in the front line were often training enough. The much ridiculed Saturday night soldiers had and would again save the day for the British High Command as they manned the line, reinforcing what little was left of the Regular Army battalions.

The end of November saw the costly fighting around Ypres finally peter out. Although no one knew it at the time, it would not be the last or indeed the most costly fight in the area of the medieval Flanders town. Later the fighting around Ypres in the autumn of 1914 would be officially known as the First Battle of Ypres. The onset of winter also saw the annual winter storms in the English Channel and the threat of invasion subside, and with it the worst of the panic.

Chapter Seven

DECEMBER

CELTIC FC

The first day of December was a bleak wintry Tuesday, with cold drizzling rain and a bitter high swirling wind that seemed to blow in all directions at once. Celtic were playing Partick Thistle at Parkhead in the replay of the War Relief Fund Shield game that was drawn at Firhill. Only 3000 hardy souls braved the weather for the afternoon kick-off, while the Celtic directors had invited a number of wounded soldiers from Stobhill Hospital to join them in the director's room to watch the game. Shaw and McAtee carried slight knocks from the Dumbarton encounter but both felt they could last the pace. The game was pretty even for the first sixty minutes with Partick just leading by two corners to nil. Celtic then picked up the pace and as Thistle tired, the Bhoys quickly went ahead on corners. Once the Celts went into the lead on minor points, the heart seemed to go out of the visitors from Maryhill. Soon afterwards, McColl fired in Celtic's first goal. McMenemy then missed a good chance before McAtee got the second with a rocket shot into the roof of the net, which left Campbell in the Partick goal helpless. The Firhill men got a consolation goal with only two minutes to go through a powerful shot from Harris. Had Charlie Shaw not been carrying an injured wrist he would probably have held the shot. Celtic won the game by two goals plus three corners to Partick Thistle's single goal and two corners. The war fund was boosted by another £55. Over the two ties, the sum stood at almost £190, a very reasonable sum indeed.

The following day when Celtic and Rangers players arrived at Parkhead and Ibrox, they were greeted with notices posted on their pavilion wall. The proclamation was the Old Firm director's effort to encourage their players to enlist and it was unequivocal. 'Any player who joins the colours will be given full pay when they are available to take their place in the team, and half pay at other times—that is, when they are engaged in military service.' No Celtic or Rangers first team player took up the offer. There can be little doubt that the actions of the Heart of Midlothian players that enlisted was discussed in dressing-rooms the length and breadth of the country. The subject of following their lead and enlisting would also have been discussed in an informal way. The prevailing opinion appears to have been that circumstances for each player were different and therefore it was down to individuals to decide for themselves whether they should enlist. Jimmy Gordon of Rangers in an interview with the Weekly News warned that bullying football players and accusing them of being shirkers would not likely assist in recruiting. That week five more Raith Rovers players signed up with McCrae's battalion, James Logan, John Rattray, James Scott, William Wallace and William Lavery.

The first League game of the month was on 5 December and Celtic was required to make the long trek north to the Granite City to play Aberdeen. The Dons were struggling, sitting fourth from the bottom of the League and had failed to secure a victory at home since the middle of

September. An early kick-off compelled the Bhoys to travel up on Friday afternoon. With one exception, the Celtic side was unchanged from that which beat Dumbarton the week previous. Patsy Gallacher was out again, Tom McGregor was brought in and the team reshuffled. The game was played in atrocious conditions with a blizzard of snow and sleet making good football almost impossible but proved a great leveller between the teams. The conditions were with Aberdeen for the first half as the gale blew straight into the faces of the Celts but Aberdeen failed to take advantage. In the second half, Celtic began to take control of the game and with the blizzard behind them mastered the elements better than the Dons. 'Smiler' Browning scored the only goal of the game after sixty minutes. By the time the Celtic scored, the blizzard had worsened considerably and some of the players were close to collapse and just wanting the game to end. Despite the weather, a crowd of over 6000 hardy Aberdonians turned up for the game, a fitting tribute to the Scottish champions. However, only 1000 were left at the end to hear the final whistle. Willie Maley and the Celtic party returned home, with McMenemy hobbling having injured his ankle, to be greeted with the news that Clyde FC had been given permission by the Scottish League to play its remaining fixtures at Parkhead and that the Celtic director John McKillop had taken a turn for the worse and was very seriously ill.

That Saturday also saw the Hearts playing at home for the first time since the players enlisted. The visitors were the Hibernian in the first Edinburgh derby of the season. The directors announced that any man who had enrolled into McCrae's battalion would be granted free admission to the match. With typical business adroitness, Sir George turned it into a recruiting drive and organised his men accordingly. Prior to the kick-off, 800 men of McCrae's battalion preceded by the pipe band of the 9th Bn Royal Scots were wildly cheered as they marched around the stadium. At half-time they again mustered on the park while recruiters addressed the crowd. The game itself became almost incidental to the occasion, but over 12,000 spectators saw an entertaining game that ended with the Hearts taking full points, winning 3–1.

SCOTTISH FOOTBALL

As the four SFA delegates left Glasgow for the national association conference in London, *the Man in the Know* was confident that the associations would see sense. The League Championship would carry on as usual, with probably some reduction in the players' wages. The cup competitions would also be started and played to a finish, since so many clubs depended on the revenue brought in by a decent run in the cup. The howling of the 'Stop Football' fanatics would have no effect on curtailing the season, any more than the enlisting of the Hearts players. He thought it laughable that decent-living football players, married men many of them, were being coerced into joining the army, when the street lamps and corners were held up every day and hour by loafers with a soul above hard work and an eye for a watch, purse or bag. Perhaps the authorities were holding back these light-fingered gentry until our armies invaded Germany. He thought they could probably raise a corps from the Cowcaddens, Calton and Gorbals, enough to take a fair-sized German town.

On Thursday 3 December, the much anticipated meeting of the four international football associations took place in the offices of the FA in Russell Square, London. The English were in a fighting mood. Three days previously the major London clubs, including Chelsea, Tottenham, Arsenal, Fulham, Millwall and Crystal Palace, had met to discuss what they regarded as the unscrupulous, unwarranted and undignified attitude of a number of London newspapers to the continuance of football and the move by a number of London newspapers not to print match reports. After two and a half hours, the clubs decided that the sports reporters representing the newspapers would not be admitted into their grounds and passed a resolution expressing their willingness to discontinue the game simultaneously with the closure of all racecourses, cinemas, theatres, music halls and golf links.

The only subject on the international association's agenda was to consider the advisability or otherwise of continuing football during the war. Celtic's Tom White, as vice-chairman of the SFA, again led the three-man delegation down from Glasgow. The SFA's position was simple: it had already publicly given its word to cooperate fully with the War Office and the military authorities and to that end it would abide by its policy. The day previous, the War Office had already made it clear to Mr Clegg, the chairman of the FA, that as a conciliatory gesture to public opinion, the minimum required was that international games and cup competitions be cancelled. Clegg was a man under pressure, painfully aware of the importance, financially, of the FA Cup to football clubs. Most were already struggling to make ends meet having lost significant revenues through the reduction in their gate receipts.

The meeting was prolonged and at times heated. Eventually, after six and a half hours of debate, the FA in the same fighting mood as the London clubs wanted to concede nothing, while the SFA delegates wanted to give whatever the military authorities required of them. A compromise was eventually reached and a joint press statement was released. It declared:

> *It had been decided to recommend to each national association that the international matches for this season be abandoned. There is no evidence that the playing of football has hindered or is hindering recruiting. On the contrary, there is good reason to conclude that football has encouraged and assisted recruiting. In these circumstances this meeting recommends that; except as regards international matches, it is not right that football should be stopped or suspended. Further, the meeting is of the opinion that to deprive the working people of our country of their Saturday afternoon recreation would be unfair and very mischievous.*

Despite the prolonged debate and agreeing to issue the joint statement, the Scots delegation was far from happy at the apparent bartering between the FA and the War Office. Historically, in most matters the SFA tended to go where the FA led, this time, however, they decided that they would plough their own furrow. The day after the meeting at the FA offices, Tom White, Mr Steen and Mr Campbell went to Whitehall where they met with an old friend of the Celtic club, Irish Nationalist MP Thomas Scanlan. Tom was a former journalist with the Glasgow Catholic Observer, a solicitor and a close friend of TP O'Connor MP. In 1909, Tom won the old North Sligo seat of Celtic founding father, William McKillop, for the IPP, and in Westminster he took up the causes of Irish Land Reform and old age pensions. Tom escorted the Scottish football delegation to the War Office where he introduced them to the Under Secretary of State for War. The Scots delegates began by reiterating the wishes of the SFA to conform entirely to the policy of the War Office and asked Harold Tennant to state exactly what he required of Scottish football. Tennant's answer was the cancellation of both full international matches and the Scottish Cup competition. The delegation immediately acquiesced and told Tennant that they would recommend the cancellation of both to the full SFA council.

Harold Tennant MP

When the news broke, the FA was furious at the SFA delegates disassociating themselves from the conference vote. However, the die was cast and the damage to footballing solidarity already done. Even if Clegg wished to give up the FA Cup, further pressure had been applied to the FA when the English League authorities warned them that if they agreed to abandon the FA Cup, the League would buy their own cup and play for that. On 7 December, the full FA council voted to continue with football. They issued a bullish statement trumpeting their new motto 'business as usual', with the exception of the internationals. The FA really could not have chosen a worse or more insensitive war cry. For tens of thousands of upper- and middle-class families who had already lost sons or who had watched their sons and husbands enlist, it was far from business as usual. However, the FA immediately went on a PR offensive, organising a grand public meeting, which, launched amid great publicity, England's answer to the Heart of Midlothian recruiting campaign. The result was the 17th (Service) Bn Middlesex Regiment or the Football Legion, as it would be known. The FA felt the successful raising of the footballer's battalion and the sight of 1000 professional footballers and their friends marching off to war, would satisfy the 'Stop Football' cohorts.

When Tom White and the rest of the SFA delegates boarded the overnight train back to Glasgow, they must have wondered if they had overstepped their authority. They had left Glasgow with the remit simply to represent Scotland at the national association council meeting, nowhere was it agreed that they had been given any authority to represent or negotiate on behalf of the SFA with the War Office. Although Tom White and the delegates had promised Tennant both internationals and the Scottish Cup would be cancelled, the matter had still to be ratified by a vote of the full SFA council. The cancellation of the internationals would have little or no effect on most of the football clubs, particularly the smaller clubs, but the Scottish Cup was a very different matter altogether.

In addition to being the vice-chairman of the SFA and responsible for the interests of the whole of Scottish football, Tom White as chairman of Celtic would undoubtedly have consulted the rest of the Celtic board prior to travelling to London. They would have covered every possible permutation and outcome and how each would affect the Celtic club. No one would ever accuse the Celtic board of being less than business orientated, but with the entire game, at least according to Sir George McCrae, on a precipice, they obviously decided that if the Cup had to be sacrificed to save the League programme, half a pig was better than none. The board would have been perfectly well aware of how much the loss of the cup revenues would mean to Celtic. As Scottish Cup winners, the income from the previous season's cup run came to over £3300 or almost 25 per cent of the Celtic's revenue for the financial year. At a time when the game desperately needed finance, many would see the surrender of the cup as a major cash stream voluntarily being abandoned.

With the majority of Scotland's senior clubs being limited liability companies, money was, of course, a major factor in any decision regarding the abandonment of professional football. Many people had serious amounts of money tied up in the clubs. Although few directors made much money directly from their involvement with their club, indirectly, through the likes of catering or building contracts, there were business opportunities. In addition, many directors had entered contracts on behalf of their clubs giving personal guarantees to banks to cover liabilities.

By the beginning of December 1914 and just four months into the war, the professional game throughout Britain was hurting. Around 50 per cent of the male population that would normally have attended football matches and the revenue that they represented had been effectively sucked out of the game. Football clubs up and down the country were buckling under the financial strain of trying to manage their clubs normally, while operating with major financial reductions in revenue as a result of having fewer spectators. As early as the beginning of October, matches were being played at a loss. Some Scottish clubs even had difficulty finding the £50 guarantee that had to be paid to visiting teams. It was widely recognised that something had to done to help the needy clubs or they would not be able to complete their fixtures. By the beginning of December, the point of no return for the Scottish game had been reached.

The Man in the Know simply did not know what to make of the SFA delegates' offer to cancel the internationals and the Scottish Cup. He felt the internationals maybe, but even then the proceeds of those games could have been given to relief funds. But the decision to surrender the Scottish Cup left him completely perplexed. How could they differentiate between a League game and a Scottish Cup tie and why agree to the joint statement issued by the national associations, only to then independently renegotiate with the War Office? What was the national association council for, if not for the four home nations to act in harmony? He felt the SFA council should toe the national associations' line, face down the 'Stop Football' brigade and agree to carry on with the Cup as usual. It may be a personal rebuff for Celtic's Tom White, who had led the delegates, but to abolish the Scottish Cup competition would be a serious financial blow to the game at a time when every penny was desperately needed.

Although the interests and management of the Scottish game overall were the responsibility of the SFA, the day-to-day running and management of the Scottish football leagues was the responsibility of the Scottish Football League established in 1890. On 10 December, a special meeting of the first division committee was convened at the League offices in Glasgow. Among those committee members present was Celtic's man at the League, Willie Maley. The financial situation had reached critical mass and a decision had to be reached to help the failing clubs. After deliberations that lasted over three hours, it was announced that the committee was recommending a general all-round deduction of 25 per cent from players receiving 50/- per week and over, and 20 per cent from players receiving less than that sum, with a minimum of 30/- per week. Under normal circumstances, the players would have been up in arms at such a drastic reduction in their wages and indeed the Scottish Football Players' Union did discuss the matter the following week, but most professional footballers recognised the dire position their clubs were in. All agreed to the cut except the Ayr United players, who would only accept 12½ per cent. Players were also allowed to negotiate with their clubs how the deductions would be made, with the individual clubs retaining the deductions. Celtic, Dumbarton, Airdrieonians, Motherwell and Heart of Midlothian players took no part in the discussions, as they had already come to an agreement with their clubs.

At Parkhead, Willie Maley and the Celtic directors thought the scheme was badly thought out and would not address the problems of the poorer clubs. They also thought the cuts went too far and felt it was a serious mistake to allow each club to retain its own deductions instead of pooling the savings and then dividing them among those clubs in the deepest trouble. As it stood, it meant that the rich clubs, including Celtic, Rangers and one or two others, would still be drawing decent gates with a wage bill now lessened by 25 per cent. The poorer clubs, which may only have been drawing £40 at the gate but were still expected to pay out a £50 guarantee to a visiting club, were being asked to pay a few shillings less to each player out of nothing.

Celtic FC had already promised its players that any deductions that the League forced them to take from their pay packets would be made up to them at the end of the season in the form of a bonus. While the top paid footballers may have been more able to absorb such a reduction in their wages, the journeyman footballers on a very basic wage began to look closely at the pay, allowances and conditions being offered by the military and they began counting the pennies. It was effectively the beginning of economic conscription for the lowest paid professional footballers. Very many professionals also found themselves sucked back into industry, many into their old unskilled jobs.

The following day, the pressure on the players was cranked up another notch when 150 professional, west coast players and club officials, responded to an invitation from Ward, a former president of the Scottish Football League, to attend a meeting in the Bank restaurant in Glasgow. The topic? What else, football players and recruiting!

After the success of Sir George McCrae's recruiting drive in Edinburgh, where it was proven that football supporters would follow their heroes into the army, the west coast clubs and their professional players, particularly those of Celtic and Rangers, came under even more pressure to lead by example and enlist. The purpose of the meeting was to consider what steps could be taken to promote recruiting among professional players and the supporters of the west coast clubs. Directors and players from Celtic, Rangers, Partick Thistle, Clyde, Third Lanark, Ayr United, Hamilton Accies, St Mirren, Kilmarnock, Motherwell and Airdrieonians all attended. One helpful old footballer calling himself 'Forward' wrote to the Scotsman suggesting:

> *If the new football battalions were to be named after their football clubs, that might encourage players and supporters to join. The folk at home would enjoy hearing of the fighting exploits of the Celtic Irish Fusiliers or Rangers Highlanders on the field of battle.*

Also present at the meeting was Sir James Leishman, who travelled through from Edinburgh. Flushed with his recent success at Tynecastle, he thought he might be able to repeat the feat in Glasgow. He addressed the gathering, saying that he deprecated the personal attacks on players, but urged them to assist recruiting by enlisting and helping to raise their own 1000-strong battalion. He ended his speech by saying: 'For the love of heaven go on and let Glasgow flourish.'

Unfortunately for Sir James, the rough and ready west of Scotland was much less deferential than genteel Edinburgh and the Glasgow and Lanarkshire clubs refused to bow to upper-class pressure. The only outcome from the meeting was that the west coast clubs agreed to form yet another committee to oversee the project. The West of Scotland Football Recruiting Committee was set up under the chairmanship of William Wilton of Rangers and was based at Ibrox. In accepting the position Wilton stated: 'There has been a great deal of misunderstanding as to the number of men each club could give. At Ibrox for example we have only twenty professionals.'

At Parkhead, the Celtic had even fewer players and would play out the season with just nineteen, but field only sixteen players in the League. However, at the end of the meeting two senior professionals playing with Clyde FC, George McTurk and Celtic old bhoy Ebenezer (Ginger) Owers, stepped forward to say that they were willing to enlist, as did Alex Edward, the Scottish League referee, who also gave his name to Willie Wilton. In the event, no specific Glasgow or west coast footballers' battalion would ever be formed, and the West of Scotland Football Recruiting Committee withered on the vine at Ibrox. Ginger Owers and another Clyde teammate, Charlie Clunas, would soon join the 23rd (Sportsmen) Bn Royal Fusiliers. The recruiting team for the London-based battalion had opened an office at Glasgow's Central Station and had been recruiting for a fortnight. With the sportsmen's battalion training in the south of England, the services of both players would be entirely lost to Clyde. Lance Corporal Charlie Clunas was fated to die from wounds received in action in February 1916. Ginger Owers would be badly wounded on the Somme in 1916 and never played football again.

All the men who played football for one or other of the first division clubs were, in the eyes of the general public, lumped together as professional footballers and the general impression was that they lived pampered cosseted lives. They were thought to be young men who, with the exception of a few hours training during the week, spent their time on the golf course or in cinemas, killing time until Saturday afternoon when they would perform for ninety minutes. This was, of course, grossly unfair on the vast majority of the players. Even at the two wealthiest, best paying clubs in Scotland, Celtic and Rangers, only the first team squad, of perhaps sixteen or twenty players, were employed full time as professional footballers with their wages on a sliding scale. The remaining players on the clubs' books were part timers, reserves, brought in at very short notice to step into the breach when a first choice player was unavailable through injury. The second string players spent much of their time on short-term loans to other, sometimes amateur, clubs. These reserve players, alongside many of the players of the less wealthy clubs, like Kilmarnock, Dumbarton and Raith Rovers, would by necessity hold down ordinary jobs, with their football pay supplementing their occupational salaries. Even top players at the minor clubs, who were on full-time contracts, were paid very much less than the £5 or £6 paid to the top professionals per week by Celtic and Rangers, or even the £4 paid by Hearts.

In addition, with the exception of Celtic and Rangers, few of the Glasgow or western clubs were in the apparently happy financial position of Heart of Midlothian of being able to offer their players half wages if they enlisted and were posted away. In fact, Heart of Midlothian FC with one of the largest playing squads in the league (twenty-six) was also under some financial pressure. Its new stand had come in vastly over budget, and like other clubs it had, certainly over the first half of the season, seen its takings at the gate drop. The Hearts directors' offer of half pay was at the time largely an empty gesture since they already knew that their players had enlisted into a locally raised battalion that would be training in and around Edinburgh for months and would be available until at the very least the end of the season. At the end of every football season the professional players contracts ended and depending on their performances they were renewed or not with their pay and conditions renegotiated. At that point, the position regarding the Hearts players' pay could be re-examined. The way things were going there was very possibility that the season might yet be abandoned, or if it were allowed to play out, the current season 1914/15 would be the last until the end of the war. With the football season nearing the halfway point, very many of the journeyman players were simply playing out the season when they would reconsider their options, including after the reduction in wages, enlisting.

THE HOME FRONT

The month of December began with the worst storm seen in central Scotland for years. There were record rainfalls and one woman was killed in Glasgow when a wall was blown down on top of her. It was also announced to the British public that the war was costing a colossal £1 million a day. The effects of the war were making themselves felt on the British economy and people were beginning to feel the pinch of rising prices, particularly food and most worryingly in Glasgow, rents. Despite the assault on their living standards, the general public, already pressurised at every turn to help with the various relief funds, turned their minds and wallets in the run-up to Christmas to comforts for the troops at the front, prisoners of war and treats for the wounded in hospital. The pressure to give was immense; many large organisations had asked their staff to agree to deductions taken directly from their wages to go towards relief. The giant Beardmore's Foundry at Parkhead, for example, ran such a scheme. The hundreds of established church organisations looked for donations, as did Catholic churches, where the collection plate went around more than once. There were flag days just about every second weekend; between Union Jack Day on 5 September and Lord Robert's Day on 26 December there had been eight others. For the man in the street, there was simply no escaping the incessant demands for money.

From the start of the war, just about every British and Irish woman and girl had been knitting or sowing for the army and navy, socks of course, but with the onset of winter, mittens and balaclava helmets were also popular. Nationwide, tens of thousands of items of warm weather clothing were also handed in. The organisations running the various relief funds bought tons of tobacco, cigarettes, chocolate and Christmas puddings. Even the Royal family got involved with Princess Mary, the seventeen-year-old daughter of King George V and Queen Mary, setting up the Sailors and Soldiers Christmas Fund in November 1914. The aim was to give each person in uniform a Christmas gift from the nation. The response to her appeal was overwhelming and it was decided that the money would be spent on a brass box (very useful at the front) and although the contents varied most people got a combination of tobacco, cigarettes, a lighter, bullet pencil, sweets, chocolate and a Christmas card. Indian troops got spices and sweets. Amazingly, an estimated 335,000 boxes were delivered on time for Christmas 1914. When the fund closed in 1920, over 2.5 million boxes had been distributed.

Every district and social or charitable organisation was involved in relief and such was the scale of the effort it brought the postal service close to breakdown. The Glasgow Irish were, of course, deeply involved in the relief effort, with the Belgian refugees taking up most of their time and efforts. On the run-up to Christmas, the Glasgow Irish concentrated their efforts on Scottish and Irish regiments and the Glasgow Observer's Soldiers and Sailors Comforts Fund attracted sizeable donations. The Celtic directors donated £10 on behalf of the club to the Observer's comforts fund. The newspaper organised for foodstuffs like condensed milk, tea, sugar and biscuits and comforts like cigarettes and pipe tobacco to be sent both to soldiers on the front line and to prisoners of war in Germany. Very many people sent comfort parcels directly to their favoured regiments to be distributed among the soldiers. While the Glasgow Irish had been organising their own local parish-based relief events almost from the onset of the war, in mid-December they decided to stage an Irish Flag Day to be held at the beginning of February 1915 for the benefit of the Belgian refugees. The event was organised by the Glasgow branches of the Ancient Order of Hibernians, but it would be tens of thousands of women and children from across the whole of the Scots-Irish community that would be out rattling the tins.

On 16 December, a German cruiser squadron shelled the English coastal towns of Hartlepool, Scarborough and Whitby, killing 130 including a baby and wounding 300 more. The attack was largely a diversion while another German vessel laid over one hundred mines in British waters off Flamborough Head. On Christmas Eve, a lone German plane dropped a solitary bomb onto English soil near Dover. An attempt had been made three days previously, but the bombs dropped into the sea. The event concentrated the minds of the British people and the possibility of large-scale air raids by German Zeppelin airships became a nightmare scenario for people living along the east coast of Britain.

ROMAN CATHOLIC MILITARY CHAPLAINS

On 10 December, the Glasgow Daily Record reported that Father Stephen Thornton had been appointed chaplain to the battle squadrons of the North Sea Fleet. Stephen Thornton was born above the family pawnbroker shop at 49 Kent Street in the Calton district of Glasgow. His father was Matthew Thornton, a sixty-six-year-old widower, who had married Margaret Hughes, his twenty-six-year-old Irish servant, in December 1866. The Thornton family were among the oldest Glasgow families, Matthew Thornton himself being a portioner of the city. The couple would go on to have a family of six with Stephen being the third oldest, born on 20 January 1871. The Calton area was predominately, but not exclusively, an Irish Catholic slum. Very many Protestants also lived in the ghetto, which lay in the east of the city, along the northern bank of the river Clyde. The level of deprivation in the area at the time is now hard to imagine, with the child mortality rate one of the highest in the country. However, as pawnbrokers, the Thornton family were much more affluent than the vast majority of their neighbours.

Raised in the Calton, Stephen Thornton was educated by the Jesuit brothers at St Aloysius' College, before being admitted to Blairs College, Aberdeen, to study for the priesthood. From Blairs he went to France and afterwards to the Scots College in Rome, where he completed his studies and was ordained in December 1896. The following year he returned to Scotland to teach classics at St Peter's College, New Kirkpatrick, for a year. He then became a curate at Springburn, Glasgow, for a further year before ill health saw him retire on sick leave. His ailment was a chronic stomach complaint that would plague him throughout his life. In 1900, he returned to duty and was appointed assistant at St John's, Portugal Street, situated in the Gorbals Parish. His new parish lay south of the Clyde and just a mile or so from his home in the Calton. In the National Census of 1901, he is shown as living in the presbytery in Portugal Street, while his family were still in their home at Kent Street. With his father deceased, three of his brothers, John P, Thomas and Phillip, took over the family pawnbroker shop, while their Irish-born mother became head of the family. The Thornton boys were early members of the Celtic Club and John P Thornton's name appears on the attendance roll of the Celtic FC Ball held at the Windsor Hotel, Glasgow, in February 1894. The Thornton family was also related through marriage to Stephen J Henry, one of the early Celtic committeemen.

A son elevated to the priesthood is the apple of any Irish mother's eye, and Margaret Thornton would have been immensely proud of her son. Father Thornton remained at St John's for the next five years. There he found his vocation, administering to the poor and destitute, many of whom he would have known personally from his youth, having been raised in the area. In 1905, he got his first charge at the St Ninian's mission in Gourock. While there he developed a keen interest in sailing and became a member of the Royal West of Scotland Yacht Club. In 1908, he was transferred to Renton in the Vale of Leven. While serving on the parish school board, he worked closely with schoolteacher Mary Kelly, sister of James Kelly, the Celtic football legend and former club chairman. After six years, he was on the move again, this time to the new mission at Cadzow, a mining village on the outskirts of Hamilton. Stephen Thornton had only been at Cadzow a few months when war was declared and he watched as scores of his parishioners, former servicemen, were recalled to colours as reservists. On the outbreak of war he was appointed the military chaplain at No 3 Scottish General Hospital, Stobhill, Glasgow.

The unprecedented expansion of the British army meant the Army Chaplains Department was forced into a radical restructuring in order to meet the increased demand for chaplains. By November 1914, discussions with the War Office were under way regarding the number of chaplains required for performing adequately the necessary spiritual ministrations to the Catholic troops. As the negotiations dragged on, Catholic public opinion became enraged at the delay and the Irish bishops in particular clamoured for Irish chaplains for Irish regiments. The Irish bishops resolved that nothing should be allowed to stand in the way of 'a full and efficient number of Irish priests ministering to their wounded and dying countrymen on the field of battle. The stumbling block was Lord Kitchener who ignored the bishops and resisted attempts to enlist Irish support: *'They would only bring their priests with them and start wholesale proselytizing'*, he said. It took the personal intervention of Prime Minister Asquith's wife, Margot, aware of the consequences of ignoring Irish sympathy, who told Kitchener that he *'should give them their priests'*. After the discussions ended it was agreed that; four RC chaplains would be assigned to each division - one for each brigade and one for divisional troops. In addition, there was to be one chaplain for each Irish battalion and adequate provision for hospitals and base camps.

For Roman Catholic chaplains in the field, in addition to the usual priestly duties of conducting confessions and masses, a very large part of the job was tending to the wounded and dying and burying the dead, often in very dangerous situations and locations. How far any of the chaplains took the duty of tending to the spiritual needs of soldiers actually in battle was ultimately very much a personal decision. Anglican priests were officially not allowed to go into the front-line trenches; however, very many disobeyed. The question for Roman Catholic chaplains was more complex in that the sacrament of Extreme Unction meant the priest was required to be with the soldier almost at the moment of death. This, of course, meant that the priest himself needed to be in the thick of the fighting alongside the soldiers. In a letter to the senior Catholic chaplain at GHQ, Father T.A. Agius OSB, later wounded near Ypres in September 1917, described the battlefield application of the sacrament:

Roman Catholic Chaplain in the field

> *In the piteous work of clearing up the wreckage of battle the chaplains found to their hand a potent instrument in the Sacrament of Extreme Unction. Easy and quick to apply, this Sacrament could help men beyond the reach of human aid and put to precious use the last, often agonising moments of life. The physical alleviations, which other chaplains – in default of more practical opportunities – busied themselves in applying, were useless at that stage. But the Roman Catholic chaplains, not necessarily more patient, skilful, dedicated or courageous than their companions, could awake recognition in the last glimmer of consciousness and succour both soul and body in the extreme crisis. No wonder that, as they worked in aid posts and dressing stations, they caught the glances, curious yet longing, and heard whispered words which brought home to them a realisation of the immensity of their privilege.*

For Irish Roman Catholic soldiers, in particular, the mere appearance of a priest in their presence or the opportunity to attend a hastily set-up Mass, probably in a bombed-out shell of a house, was a great comfort in the final hours before a battle.

Meanwhile back in Cadzow, forty-four-year-old Father Thornton decided he would stage a recruiting event. He announced that on the day he was leaving to report for duty, he would march from Cadzow to Hamilton and invited the young men of the parish to join him. On the day, he marched with a dozen of his able bodied male parishioners to Hamilton dropping the recruits off at the barrack gates.

CELTIC FC

The rumour began midweek. The mighty Jimmy Quinn might make an appearance for the visit of the Queen's Park amateurs to Parkhead on 12 December. The faithful had feared that they had seen the last of the legend through his reoccurring knee injury. He had last played in October against Rangers but then he looked overweight and all of his thirty-six years. Now in semi-retirement, he promised Willie Maley he would continue to train and step in if needed. Gallacher and McMenemy were missing for the Celts and to the delight of the Celtic supporters, the mighty James did indeed step into the breach alongside Billy Crone. With so many of their regular players in the military, Queen's Park was forced to cobble together a team of youngsters. A crowd of around 7000 turned out in inclement weather to watch the game, a significant proportion to see the Celtic legend. Before the start of the game and again at half-time, the pipes and drums of the Cameron Highlanders entertained the crowd. A recruiting sergeant appealed to the crowd for volunteers but no one stepped forward. When the game kicked off, the Celtic took control of the match, dominating their amateur opponents for over an hour. Billy Crone scored a hat-trick before half-time, while Jimmy Quinn got two in the second half; had he been more agile he would have gotten more. With the points safe, the Celts took their foot off the gas. The Queen's Park youngsters managed a deserved consolation goal by Laidman. The game ended in a very comfortable 5–1 victory for the Bhoys. 'Handsome' Billy Crone had now scored five goals in just four League appearances. At half-time, accompanied by the music of the Cameron Highlanders, 130 ladies of the Ancient Order of the Hibernians took up a collection for the Glasgow Observer's Belgian Relief Fund and, despite the weather and smallish crowd, managed to collect £20. Willie Maley's brother Father Charles O'Malley was also in Glasgow during the week lecturing at the Deaf and Dumb Institute in West Campbell Street, under the auspices of the Caledonian Catholic Association. He delivered another £23 to the Belgian Relief Fund; the latest donation made it £117 in total from his St Margaret's Parish in Ayr.

Elsewhere in the League, Heart of Midlothian continued to chalk up the victories, the latest a 3–1 win over Airdrie at Tynecastle. Morton beat Clyde at home while Rangers won away at Kilmarnock. Hearts still topped the league followed by Celtic, Morton and Rangers.

On the afternoon of Tuesday 15 December, Celtic played Rangers in the semi-final of the War Fund Shield competition at Partick Thistle's Firhill ground. The full Celtic first team was on parade and the pulling power of the Old Firm was seen yet again, when despite the midweek afternoon kick-off a crowd of around 9000 turned up in Maryhill. The game was the usual dour hard-fought match between the two Glasgow giants both determined to win. Celtic dominated for much of the first half with McMenemy and Browning on the left wing raiding deep into the Rangers defence. After about twenty minutes, Browning was brought down in the Rangers box and a penalty was awarded. The Celts went into a deserved lead with the accurately struck penalty kick taken by Joe Dodds. Just before half-time Bowie scored a deserved equaliser after Shaw could only parry a long-range shot. The Bhoys launched a number of raids into the Rangers box and only keeper Lock's heroics kept the score even up to half-time. For much of the second half it was the same strenuous struggle. Then Rangers went into the lead after a powerful header by Reid beat Charlie Shaw. Try as they might, the Celtic just could not get back on terms and the Rangers ran out deserved winners by 2 goals to 1. The Ibrox men would meet Morton in the final. The real winner of course was the war fund, which was boosted by over £200 from the gate receipts.

An improving Airdrieonian side played host to Celtic at Broomfield Park, Airdrie, on 19 December. The home side set off at a cracking pace and for much of the first half Airdrie had the upper hand. Had they been able to press home their advantage, the end result would have been very different. Their forward play deserved more reward but in the Celtic defence Shaw or Dodds or McNair were consistently on hand to thwart their sustained attacks. Much against the run of play, Celtic managed to scrape a goal when McColl took advantage of a misunderstanding between the Airdrie goalie and one of his defenders just before half-time. The Celts went in at half-time somewhat shell-shocked but one goal up. The Airdrie front line had put in so much effort during the first half that after the restart they could hardly break into a run and as the Airdrie attack faltered, Celtic came more into the game. In what was the best move of the game, McAtee had a goal chalked off after the linesman saw an infringement by Browning prior to the goal being scored. It proved to be an excellent game of football and a day when the Celtic defenders were the heroes. There were no further scores and the game finished 0–1 to the Celts. The Bhoys left Airdrie somewhat relieved and feeling they had had a very close shave. The game was played in front of an estimated crowd of around 9000. The Celtic had put together an excellent run of wins that kept the pressure on the League leaders. The victory at Airdrie was their tenth successive win in the League. Elsewhere Hearts matched Celtic's win by beating bottom of the League Queen's Park at Hampden, while Hibs beat St Mirren at Easter Road.

A Christmas Day trip to Old Trafford was the next stop for a very busy Celtic squad. The Celtic board liked to keep the team playing and had long held the opinion that their performance dropped off when left idle for any amount of time. Despite the tight position at the top of the League with Hearts, and the fact that the team would be required to leave Manchester immediately after the game to get back to Glasgow in time to face Hamilton on Boxing Day, the opportunity of a friendly game with Manchester United with its additional revenue was too good to miss. Celtic was without Gallacher, McMenemy, Young and Dodds; the replacements were Joe O'Kane, Billy Crone, Tommy McGregor and Henry Jarvis. Henry slipped in at right half with McColl at inside left, while McAtee and Billy Crone occupied the right wing. The day was cold and crisp with the pitch soft under foot. New bhoy Joseph O'Kane led the forwards in his first senior start for the Celtic. In a dream debut, young O'Kane scored his first senior goal for the club after just five minutes and played well enough to convince Willie Maley he was Celtic material. The remainder of the first half was evenly balanced and the Bhoys went in at half-time a goal up. Celtic, playing with half the first team missing, continued to hold their own until midway through the second half when the home side equalised. Manchester won the game with a dubious goal, which saw Shaw impeded on his goal line while another Manchester forward scored. Offside was claimed, but the ref dismissed the Bhoys' pleas. The teams served up an exciting match and although it lacked the purpose of a League game, most spectators enjoyed the spectacle. The Manchester United officials were well pleased with the turnout of 15,000 for the game. The £300 taken at the gate proved Celtic was the most lucrative team to have guested at Old Trafford that season. The gate receipts were gratefully received at the Manchester club, which was suffering alongside most others from falling revenues. The Celtic party left Manchester as soon as was polite and travelled overnight back to Glasgow. They arrived back in the wee small hours and went into a city centre hotel for a few hours' sleep before travelling to Parkhead. That same day, Joe O'Kane was sent to Alex Maley's Clydebank on a long-term loan. Willie Maley's young brother had taken on the club at the start of the season and it was going well in the second division.

At Tynecastle on Christmas Day, Hearts played Leith in the semi-final of the East of Scotland Shield. Just 1500 watched the game, which ended in a 1–1 draw. The match would be replayed at the end of the season. That morning, McCrae's battalion had been issued with their new army boots and at noon, resplendent in their new uniforms and led by their own pipe band, marched around the city centre. That afternoon the battalion sat down to a full Christmas lunch. It is unknown if the Hearts players partook of the lunch and if they did, if it had any bearing on the Leith result.

SCOTTISH FOOTBALL

The day Rangers knocked the Celts out of the War Fund Shield, the full council of the SFA met at Carlton Place to hear the report from the delegates sent to the London conference. Prior to the discussion, a letter was read from the Scottish League's First Division Committee stating that to stop the Scottish Cup ties would not only be illogical, but financially disastrous to the clubs in the association.

Tom White laid the circumstances and facts of both the conference meeting and the delegates' visit to the War Office before the council. It simply boiled down to the fact that Tom White and the delegates believed that the SFA was honour-bound by the decision of 3 September to place themselves unreservedly in the hands of the War Office and to abide by its wishes. Now the War Office wanted the Scottish Cup and international games cancelled and it was their duty to accede to the request. Tom White finished by saying that the honour of the SFA was at stake and that he and the delegates believed that their recommendation to cancel the cup and the internationals would go far to mollify public opinion. There was no middle ground. It was feared that any contrary decision would imprint a stigma upon the greatest of all sports, from which it may never recover. Tom White then moved that the recommendations of the delegates be adopted, adding that their defence for playing football in Scotland during the war, and it was a good defence, had been that they were acting with the consent of Lord Kitchener and the War Office. The Kilmarnock and Motherwell members moved and seconded the motion that more time was needed to consider the matter. It was decided by seventeen votes to thirteen to defer the decision until Tuesday 22 December.

On Tuesday 22 December, the SFA Council reconvened and Tom White again moved the cancellation of full internationals and that season's Scottish Cup competition. Again, the logic of cancelling the cup was discussed, as was the SFA's word of honour given to the War Office. Eventually, the Scottish Football Association Council passed by just one vote, fourteen to thirteen, the London delegates' recommendations. The decision also meant that the Consolation Cup competition for clubs knocked out of the Scottish Cup in the early rounds was also cancelled, although the Qualifying Cup, which was already in its final stages, would be played to a finish. Their decision was not binding on the Junior Football Association, despite the fact that a junior representative seconded the motion to abandon the Scottish Cup. Three members abstained. Although the cancellation of the Scottish Cup hurt all the clubs, it was the big four, Celtic, Rangers, Hearts and Hibernian, which would suffer the largest losses, since they were the clubs most likely to have an extended run in the competition. It was later reported that both members of the Old Firm supported the cancellation. Heart of Midlothian had argued for the continuance of the Scottish Cup competition having already given their sacrifice to the War Office and to middle-class public opinion. The Tynecastle club's accountants were worried and had already informed the board that the cost of the impressive new 4000-seat stand, only completed in October, had come in at a cost of £12,780, twice the original estimate. They were also, to date, £400 down on gate receipts compared to last season, despite the team's excellent performances in the League. As for the ubiquitous *Man in the Know*, he was astounded by the decision and simply could not see the rationale.

THE WAR FRONT

On the Western Front, the men of both sides continued to suffer in appalling conditions and while those who manned the trenches would have been content to concentrate on surviving the conditions, the staff officers at GHQ had other ideas. Although it was recognised by both sides that no major breakthrough was possible, it was important both to dominate the land between the trench lines (no man's land) and to gain any advantage, however slight. It was also felt that the men would lose their fighting edge if left too long without fighting. All along the line, vicious localised attacks and counter-attacks took place almost daily as both sides sought an advantageous few yards of trench line or a mound a few feet higher than the surrounding area, with the same stretch of trench or mound taken only to be lost again. Even when there were no assaults, the British soldiers faced a sudden and violent death from German snipers, artillery or trench mortars. The Germans' advantage in artillery meant they could shell the British trenches with impunity and the daily bombardments brought abject horror with entire sections of trench obliterated, leaving nothing of their occupants to bury. Over the middle week in December 1914, on average the British were losing eighty-one men killed per day.

The 1st Bn HLI arrived in northern France from India on 7 December. There they were joined by a draft of reservists from Glasgow, including Patsy Gallacher's brother Willie. Just seven days later the 1st Bn HLI were manning the front line near Festubert. On 19 December, two companies of the battalion took part in an attack on a German trench line near Givenchy. After taking their objective at some cost, they were later forced to surrender their gains. At 0930 hrs the following day, the HLI trenches were subjected to a very heavy bombardment that saw most of the trenches blown in. The Germans followed up their bombardment with a bayonet charge overwhelming the defenders and isolating one of the HLI companies. After a successful counter-attack, the company was finally relieved after four days, two without food or water. When the battalion returned to Gorre and called the roll, two officers and fifty-four rank and file had been killed, sixty-three rank and file had been wounded and eight officers and 226 rank and file were missing. The final figure for rank and file killed over the four days was 164. Willie Gallacher was among those who survived the fight unscathed.

The TF had performed magnificently having stepped into the breach at the most critical moment in the war so far. By the end of 1914, there were eighteen TF battalions in France and Belgium, their volunteer soldiers having signed the Imperial force agreement. Their arrival in Belgium over the crucial weeks of November helped stabilise a critical military situation.

The arrival of the TF battalions had not come too soon. By the end of the heavy fighting in Ypres, the old regular British Army, which had gone off to war with a whistle and a spring in its step, had suffered 90 per cent casualties and had effectively ceased to exist. The men were not all dead; many had been wounded and many would return to fight again. Many had also been captured and were now doomed, if they survived, to spend four long hard years in captivity as POWs in Germany.

No section of British society escaped the shocking losses. Although the working classes suffered the most losses by numbers, the British and Irish aristocracy had suffered catastrophic losses within their own small tight-knit class. All the great landed families lost sons and heirs and would never be able to recover fully from the losses. However, with cavalry officers predominating at GHQ and in the War Office, the mood remained gung-ho, upbeat that come the spring, a breakthrough would be achieved somewhere along the line and the armies would resume the normal cut and thrust of mobile warfare. Artillery guns and their shells were proving to be something of an unexpected problem for the military planners. There did not appear to be enough of either and there were some reports reaching GHQ that the guns were restricted to firing just one shell a day. Throughout the winter and spring of 1914–15, the British were at a very serious disadvantage in artillery assets of both guns and shells. With the Germans being able to shell the British positions at will, the poor bloody infantry could only suffer in silence. Something needed to be done about the lack of artillery support, but for now it was down to surviving the atrocious winter conditions in the trenches and strengthening the defence line. In response to the artillery and the tactical situation on the front line, the battlefield area on both sides was becoming a maze of trenches. There were covered approaches to the front-line trenches. Reserve and support positions were linked together by communication trenches. As the year ended, it would be a long, very uncomfortable winter for all the soldiers on the front line; any thoughts of glory had given way to endurance and perseverance.

At just about the same time as the Celtic were taking the field in Manchester, at various points along the British-held sector of the front line, an astonishing event was taking place. The famous Christmas truce of 1914 is an example of common humanity overcoming the savage barbarity of warfare. It saw thousands of British and German soldiers climb out of their trenches to shake hands in the middle of no man's land. The truce was in fact a number of truces, but did not involve the whole of the front line; indeed forty-one British soldiers were killed in action on Christmas Day. The truces that did take place were in sectors of the line where the opposing forces were close enough to communicate and while most lasted a few hours, some went on for several days. The soldiers usually shouted obscenities across to each other, but on Christmas they were alternately singing Christmas carols and promising not to shoot. At Houplines, two miles east of Armentières, just 100 yards separated the opposing trench lines. The 2nd Bn Seaforth Highlanders and 2nd Bn Argyll and Sutherland Highlanders were manning that section of the line on Christmas Day. Late on Christmas morning, the Germans requested permission to gather in and bury their dead lying in no man's land. Local British commanders granted the request and just after lunch, the Germans climbed out of their trenches. Almost immediately British soldiers climbed out of their trenches and joined the Germans in no man's land. The soldiers met, shook hands and showed each other family photos. They swopped stories, fags, chocolate and cap badges. At some point, the subject of football and the Celtic's recent continental tour came up in the conversation. It was discovered that one of the Germans, a big sergeant, was a member of the Leipzig team that had toured Britain in 1913 and that had defeated the Celtic by 1–0 last summer. He expressed great regret that the war had spoiled his football career. In his autobiography, *Footslogger*, Lieutenant Colonel Graham Seton Hutchison, then a lowly lieutenant with the 2nd Argylls noted the incident: 'In the afternoon we advanced across our trenches to chat with the German. Most amusing, can this be war? Some played football against Glasgow Celtic.'

The incident was later reported in the Morning Post and in Glasgow, *the Man in the Know* picked up the story. Writing in the Catholic Observer, he commented that he thought he remembered the character. He was the big Leipzig fullback who had pulverised McMenemy and the other Celtic forwards as they attempted to push the ball through some very long grass. He recalled that the game in Leipzig was one that the Celtic players and officials unfortunate enough to have had a hand in it, would not soon forget. It was a joke that after having made the enthusiasts of Budapest, Berlin and Vienna crazy with their skill they would then go on to be beaten, literally beaten, at Leipzig. He thought the Celts had experienced German *Kultur* that day and no mistake. According to the German version of the Christmas football match at Houplines, the football game was between the German 133rd Royal Saxon Regiment and the Seaforth Highlanders. 'While swapping photos and fags, a Scottish soldier suddenly produced a football, teams were picked, caps were used as goalposts and a football game ensued.' Play was described as 'enthusiastic' but conditions were difficult in the hard frozen ground. At this stage in the war, the land between the trench lines was not the tortured, shell-scared wasteland it would later become. The game, which lasted about an hour, was played strictly by the rules despite there being no officials. The Germans roared with laughter when they spotted that the Jocks did not wear drawers under their kilts. According to their version, they won 3–2.

The Seaforths were not the only Highlanders playing football in that section of the line on Christmas Day. Although no football game was mentioned in *Footslogger*, according to a sergeant in young Joe McAree's 2nd Bn Argylls, the battalion was involved in a football match with the Germans. He wrote a letter home that was published in the Glasgow News in which he mentions the game. In his version, the Jocks won 4–1. Although both the 2nd Bn Seaforth Highlanders' and the 2nd Bn Argyll's war diaries record the truce and the Argyll's diary states that the opposing forces were the 133rd and 134th Saxon Regiments, neither record the playing of any game of football, nor do they mention the degree of fraternisation spoken of in *Footslogger*. The battalion adjutants, who were responsible for maintaining the war diaries, were perhaps nervous of the reaction of the general staff when they heard of the truce and simply downplayed the incident. When news of the unofficial truce got back to both the British and German High Commands, the generals were less than amused. Fraternisation was not to be tolerated under any circumstances and the men were ordered back into their trenches. According to the Argyll sergeant, a replay had been arranged for the following day, but the general staff would not allow it. After a few shots were fired into the air by both sides, common humanity was again forgotten and things went back to what at the time passed as normal. However, it was a reminder that despite the horrors and atrocities that opponents inflict upon each other, a man's a man fur aw that! At around 1100 hrs on Boxing Day, a German shell screamed through the house that the Argylls were using as an orderly room and the truce in the Houplines Sector was well and truly broken. The 2nd Bn Argylls were relieved late on Boxing Day by the Sherwood Foresters and moved back into billets at Armentières. The battalion remained out of the line for the next week and spent a peaceful New Year in Armentières. At some places along the line, the Christmas truce lasted well into the New Year.

CELTIC FC

On Boxing Day, the Celtic played host to Hamilton Academicals, taking to the pitch in the afternoon just twenty-four hours after running on at Manchester. The flags at Parkhead flew at half-mast to mark the passing of director John McKillop, who had finally succumbed to his long illness three days previously. The two McKillop brothers, John and William, were among the first to come on board the Celtic project back in 1887. William McKillop, a former honorary president of the club and IPP MP, had died suddenly back in 1909. John McKillop, who came onto the first Celtic board in 1897, had accompanied the Celtic tourists on their recent continental tour. Already unwell, he left the Celtic party at Dresden for the renowned German spa at Marienbad where it was hoped his condition could be improved but obviously to no avail. Like the rest of the non-player directors at Celtic, John McKillop left Maley, Kelly and Dunbar to look after the football. It was the passing of yet another of the originals at the Celtic club. His funeral at Dalbeth Cemetery in the east end of Glasgow was like a who's who of the Glasgow Irish and Irish Nationalists. John and Willie Redmond, Joe Devlin, TP O'Connor and Charles Diamond all sent wreaths.

Hamilton Accies were no pushovers and demanded every respect from the champions in what many regarded as a potential stumbling block for the Bhoys. The 6000 faithful who turned up for the game were greatly cheered to see the mighty Quinn return for his fifth start of the season; Jimmy was in again for 'Sniper' McColl. Right from the kick-off, the visitors failed to match Celtic in most departments. In the first half, two goals from Gallacher emphasised the Celts' superiority. The mighty Jimmy was on great form and reminded the faithful of what they were missing. The Accies came into the game a bit more in the second half and snatched a goal back, but Jimmy Quinn restored Celtic's two-goal lead soon after. The undoubted man of the match, Jimmy Quinn's contribution to the victory was a goal and a lay on for Patsy Gallacher. The 3–1 victory over Hamilton Academicals was the Celtic's eleventh successive league victory. On the day, the Celtic side was Shaw, McNair, Dodds, Young, Johnstone, McMaster, McAtee, Gallacher, Quinn, McMenemy and Browning.

Despite the Celts great winning run, the Bhoys went into the New Year in second place in the League table. Heart of Midlothian were still going strong and a 4–0 victory over Raith Rovers meant they led Celtic by four points, thirty-nine to thirty-five, with both teams having played the same number of games (twenty-one).

For the Bhoys and their legion of Glasgow Irish supporters, their next game was usually the highlight of the season, the Ne'erday clash with Rangers, this time away at Ibrox. The game would normally be one of the vital clashes of the season with the Old Firm usually fighting it out for the League title, but not so this time, since this was no ordinary season.

Scottish League First Division, 28 December 1914

Team	Played	Won	Lost	Drawn	For	Against	Points
Hearts	21	19	1	1	52	13	39
Celtic	21	16	2	1	51	17	35
Morton	20	11	3	6	44	28	28
Rangers	20	12	5	3	40	20	27
Ayr United	21	11	7	3	30	24	25
Partick Thistle	18	8	6	4	33	25	20
St Mirren	20	7	7	6	30	36	20
Third Lanark	20	6	6	8	32	24	20
Hibernian	22	7	9	6	33	41	20
Hamilton Accies	19	8	8	3	30	25	19
Falkirk	20	7	9	4	27	28	18
Dumbarton	21	6	9	6	32	42	18
Airdrieonians	20	7	10	3	27	33	17
Raith Rovers	21	5	10	6	27	35	16
Aberdeen	21	5	10	6	21	32	16
Kilmarnock	20	7	12	1	27	35	15
Dundee	22	5	12	5	19	45	15
Clyde	19	6	11	2	21	30	14
Motherwell	20	5	12	3	26	44	13
Queen's Park	20	3	12	5	20	43	11

Chapter Eight

JANUARY 1915

THE HOME FRONT

In Scotland, the New Year had been for centuries the major Scottish holiday of the year and celebrated much more so than Christmas. Although it was a seen as a time of renewal and of looking forward to the promise and possibilities of a new year, it was also for very many people a melancholy time, when people looked back at the highs and lows of the previous year. When at midnight the church bells rung out the old year, many a tear was shed as people remembered their auld acquaintances, very many of whom were, after five months of war, dead, wounded, missing or away from home serving in France or Belgium or in training camps around the country. The New Year celebrations of 1914–15 were unlike any others before experienced in Britain and Ireland. Many people felt a growing sense of foreboding, a concern that not only was the war not over, but there appeared to be no end in sight.

In addition, the Glasgow Irish reading their copy of the Christmas Eve edition of the Freeman's Journal probably agreed with the editorial that Ireland should have been celebrating a Christmas that restored the rights of the nation. However, this was not the case due to the awful effusion of blood, suffering and death that had visited many Irish homes that Christmas. Instead of Christmas prayers of goodwill among men, foremost in the prayers of many that Christmas was their loved ones fighting in the battlefields of Europe. Some soldiers managed to get a few days home leave over the holidays. It was noted in Cambuslang and Halfway that over the New Year the district had the look of an army camp, which was not surprising, since there were hundreds of local men, including 400 Glasgow Irish home from Kitchener's Army. Also home on leave for the New Year were 120 of Glasgow's Ulstermen who had volunteered for the 36th (Ulster) Division. They paraded alongside other members of the Orange Order at the new Orange Hall in Cathedral Street. Meanwhile, the Irish National Volunteers held a New Year's concert in the city.

The old custom of seeing in the New Year at Glasgow Cross was kept up in the traditional manner. A crowd, mostly youngsters, gathered around the Tolbooth steeple in the Trongate as the hour approached. At midnight the bells rung out 'A Guid New Year', which signalled much handshaking and exchanges of good wishes. Gradually the revellers dispersed on their first-footing expeditions. The working class of the city could normally expect a week off from their toil over the holiday, but pressure of work in the naval shipyards and large engineering concerns saw most back at work after just the weekend.

The Glasgow Herald editorial adopted a hopeful note for victory in 1915, but although it could not quite put its finger on it, it sensed that something had changed: 'We seem to be standing between two epochs, an old world receding with 1914 and a new earth emerging with its successor.' It went on: 'Whatever the future may bring, we may still affirm that 1914 was a cataclysmic year in relation to historical phenomena.' The Glasgow Herald published the year's final recruiting figures for the city on Friday 1 January 1915. In the five months since the appeal by Lord Kitchener, the city had contributed 32,900 to his new service battalions, 9000 to the Territorial Force battalions and 2500 to the Naval Brigade. The vast majority of volunteers had stepped forward in September with 14,500 passing through the recruiting offices. After raising the minimum height, the figures tailed off dramatically. In October 4,700 enlisted, November 3,800 and December, despite efforts to kick-start the recruiting drive, just 1,900. Recruiting in Glasgow for Kitchener's Army had, unsurprisingly, reached an all-time daily low on 31 December with just twenty-four men enlisting.

On the whole, however, the City Fathers felt a grand total of 44,400 for Glasgow compared favourably with any other city in the kingdom. Paisley too was doing its bit and the town's Roman Catholics were volunteering alongside their neighbours. At the end of January, the Paisley RC parishes announced that St Mirin's had contributed 467, St Mary's 153 and St Charles sixty-six, a total of 686 parishioners to the services.

For the volunteers of the service battalions, training progressed apace as the civilian volunteers were slowly but surely turned into soldiers. Uniforms, weapons and equipment were arriving in increasing volumes and battalions began to take on the look of proper military units. The holiday period saw most men get a few days furlough, or leave as it was more commonly termed. A battalion would normally be split into two halves, with the men in one half getting Christmas at home and the other getting the New Year. With the first volunteers of mid-August still only four months into their basic training, it would be months yet before they could be considered fit for active service.

It is a truism that an ill wind blows no one any good. The beginning of January 1915 saw the nation just five months into the war and already tens of thousands of men had been killed or wounded or were missing or prisoners of war, but the wind had blown some good into Glasgow and the industrial central belt of Scotland. All industries, particularly heavy engineering and the shipyards of the Clyde, received massive orders for ships, guns, munitions and their associated items. In 1914, it was estimated that 14 per cent of the Scottish workforce was employed in shipbuilding or closely related industries. Shortly after the outbreak of the war, three Clyde shipyards were designated as Royal Naval Dockyards and came under Admiralty control: William Beardmore at Dalmuir, John Brown at Clydebank and Fairfield's at Govan. All three yards were well experienced in constructing naval warships. As a result of the war, the three yards won contracts worth a colossal £16 million.

When Lord Kitchener made his first call for volunteers, thousands of skilled workers simply downed tools and enlisted. The Fairfield's shipyard alone lost over 1000 men to the New Army, mainly apprentices, platers, riveters and carpenters. It was a mistake the Admiralty did not repeat and later skilled shipyard workers were not allowed to volunteer for the armed forces. Indeed, the skill shortage would become so acute that many skilled men who had enlisted were sent back to their old jobs from France and Flanders. When conscription was introduced in mid-1916, skilled workers were exempted from the call-up.

In addition to the shipyard at Dalmuir, William Beardmore also operated a large engineering and armaments complex at Parkhead Forge, just a few hundred yards from Celtic Park. By 1900, the works covered an area of twenty-five acres and was the largest steelworks in Scotland, specialising in the manufacture of armaments and armour plate for warships. Situated in the east end of Glasgow, the Parkhead Forge was a major employer of the Glasgow Irish. A number of Celtic players were at different times employed at the Forge including Joe Dodds and Alex Gray. The expanded armaments facility at Parkhead Forge saw the number of Beardmore employees rise from around 3000 to over 20,000, while the expanding steel industry in the Clyde valley would employ another 24,000. The demand for war-related goods and services, known collectively as the munitions industry, saw steelworks, locomotive works and munitions factories all expand their operations or start from scratch. Munitions would eventually employ over 65,000, very many of them women.

The precision instrument maker Barr and Stroud, based at Anniesland in Glasgow's west end, also significantly expanded its 500-strong workforce to meet the sharp increase in demand for its rangefinders and binoculars. Celtic legend Willie Loney was employed at the Anniesland works. The manufacturing boom also reached down the supply chain to the thousands of small businesses supplying the war industries. Pay and conditions improved as various sectors were forced to compete with each other for scarce workers within a contracted local labour market. As a result of the boom, tens of thousands of new workers were sucked into Glasgow and its environs and into the expanding war industries.

By the beginning of 1915, the shortage and standard of affordable housing in Glasgow were becoming a national cause for concern. Even before the war began, Glasgow had a long-standing housing problem, one of the worst in Europe, with its population crammed mainly into privately owned one- and two-bedroom tenement flats. In Glasgow, there were over 44,300 one-roomed houses, of which 93 per cent shared a water closet, while in the city's 111,400 two-bedroom houses 62 per cent shared a water closet. There were thousands of good quality one and two room tenements throughout the city. However, with their china tiled entrances 'wally closes' and high rents, they were the preserve of the upper-working and lower middle classes and well beyond the means of the great majority of working-class families. There was therefore a desperate requirement for quality public sector housing with affordable rents, but the private property owners and vested interest parties, who dominated town councils, continuously blocked any move to improve the situation. In 1913, nearly a third of the town councillors had stakes in Glasgow's private housing, including its Liberal Lord Provost, Daniel McCauley Stevenson. With Glasgow's heavy engineering workshops and shipyards booming, thousands of workers from all over the country were being sucked into the city. Some skilled English workers were sent north by the government to help. On arrival in the city, they were appalled by the standard and cost of the available accommodation. The influx of war workers would quickly lead to a housing shortage and profiteering as private landlords hiked rents and evicted those tenants unable to pay, including the families of men fighting at the front.

Back at the beginning of November 1914, the Glasgow Women's Housing Association and the Housing Committee of the Glasgow Labour Party met to protest and discuss the problem of house factors raising rents. Agnes Dollan and John Wheatley spoke in support of the Labour Party's £8 housing scheme. The Wheatley Cottage scheme envisaged affordable publicly owned housing for workmen with a pilot scheme of 1000 cottages built at Riddrie in the north-east of Glasgow. By mid-January 1915, the Glasgow Eastern Argus was reporting that tenants in Shettleston were being warned that their rents would be being raised by a whopping £1 per week and in some cases £1 10/-. One factor reported that the scarcity of flats suitable for the working classes was such he had only one flat of the room and kitchen class on his books. In Govan, the women became organised into the Tenants Defence Association by engineer's wife Mary Barbour, a local Labour activist. The arrival in Glasgow over the previous few months of thousands of Belgian refugees also added to the problem. On 9 January it was reported that 250 'better class' Belgians had arrived in the city, who could afford a better standard of housing.

Rents were not the only cause for concern on the home front. The cost of basic foods had also risen considerably since the start of the war. Sugar, eggs and fish increased the most, while across the board the rise was an average increase of 19 per cent. The steep rise in the cost of living saw much of the benefit of the wage increase and overtime payments eaten up. In Dublin, the situation was even worse; there they saw even larger rises in the cost of living while attracting few of the increased trade benefits the war had brought to the industrialised cities of Scotland and England. The Board of Trade put most of the increase in costs down to transportation problems, a shortage of ships and increased transportation times. Amazingly, in 1914 the British mainland could only sustain itself using home-grown produce for a weekend, Friday evening to Monday morning. The Germans produced enough to sustain themselves for six or seven days. With such a large percentage of its food imported, around 60 per cent, it was absolutely essential for the British to maintain command of the seas, particularly the Atlantic supply routes to the Americas. Unsurprisingly, the Germans quickly began to plan a submarine campaign designed to cut off the supplies. The war at sea would become a very important element of Imperial Germany's military strategy.

Attitudes among the British labour force were hardening as the delusion that it would be a short war began to dissipate. The Labour leadership had gone along with the patriotic mood of the autumn of 1914, and declared an industrial truce but as it became increasingly apparent that industrial output would be as important as military strategy and as massively profitable government orders were placed with British businesses, the unions at grassroots level began to flex their muscles. With so many men sucked out of industry and into the military, a shortage of labour would add to the unions' arsenal as they confronted employers and the government. Railway workers and engineers would be the first to raise their heads above the parapet. On Clydeside, the Amalgamated Society of Engineers (ASE), concerned about an abrupt rise in food prices and the introduction of much better paid American engineers at Weir's of Cathcart, would fire the first shots. By the end of January, 10,000 men of the ASE were preparing to risk the wrath of public opinion by breaking the labour truce. They had already refused to work overtime and were prepared to strike for a 2d an hour pay rise. Shipyard workers, miners and dockers were all paying close attention.

Many industrial leaders, politicians and senior civil servants were also beginning to criticise the haphazard recruiting methods that had allowed so many workers in industries vital to the war effort to be sucked into the armed forces. Many felt that indiscriminate recruitment from industries such as mining, shipbuilding, engineering, railways and food production should cease, arguing that continuing to do so would injure the war effort. By the end of January 1915, over 15 per cent of agricultural workers were in the armed forces, while 115,000 coal miners had enlisted over the first few months of the war. Similarly, 17 per cent of railway workers had enlisted by the beginning of February and the totals would get worse as the year progressed. The general consensus was that some men would be of far more benefit to the nation digging coal or behind a plough than carrying a rifle. Some business leaders went so far as suggesting that only another one million men would be available for the army before further recruitment would cripple British industry. The points were put to Lord Kitchener at a Cabinet meeting towards the end of January, but as usual the Secretary of State for War refused to be swayed. He calculated that at least a further 1.5 million men would be needed by the end of 1915 and nothing should be allowed to interfere with recruiting. He won the argument on the day, but the problems would not go away. The Conservative Party was already becoming disenchanted with the conduct of the war and the political truce established in August 1914 was beginning to come under pressure. At the same time, the calls for the introduction of compulsory military service, conscription, began to gather pace.

On 19 January, the first Zeppelin raid over mainland Britain took place. Two people were killed at Yarmouth and another two killed in King's Lynn. At the time, the German Zeppelins were the ultimate terror weapon with British air defences initially unable to prevent attacks. The silent behemoths appeared in the night sky to drop bombs at will, indiscriminately killing and injuring women and children asleep in their beds. Although every loss is a tragedy, in fact, in the great scheme of things, the Zeppelins were as much about psychological warfare as physical destruction. It was a double-edged sword for the Germans for the raids proved to have massive propaganda and recruiting value to the British. The raids disgusted the British civilian population, who saw the tactic as one that epitomised German barbarity. This was exactly why the British were fighting the war.

In mid-January, St Patrick's announced in its parish notes that the congregation had lost twenty-three of its young Anderston men in battle.

By way of some light relief, the inhabitants of Shettleston and Tollcross had the opportunity to watch an unusual football match between Green's Carnival Celtic and a team of showmen from the north of England. The game was played at Germiston Park in Tollcross on Wednesday 20 January. The fun game attracted many locals and an element of farce was introduced when over the course of the game a number of hens from an adjacent yard invaded the park. On each occasion, cries of 'fowl' rang out around the spectators. That week also saw the opening of the Tollcross Cinema, which was designed to serve the Tollcross, Shettleston and Mount Vernon communities. The main feature was *The Million Dollar Mystery*, billed as the most expensive film ever made and serialised into twenty-one episodes. The cinema also staged live shows featuring assorted vaudeville acts. The first Saturday children's matinee attracted 800 east end weans

IRELAND

As the year turned, for John Redmond and Edward Carson it was still all about gaining and occupying the 'Loyal and Moral' high ground and that meant recruiting figures and public relations. For both parties it was a case of trying to prove who was contributing the most to the British war effort, while keeping the more extreme elements of both volunteer organisations under some control. John Redmond had the more difficult task, with the Irish Volunteer split at the end of September and the Irish Nationalists' natural aversion to anything British. John Redmond's fervent hopes of August and September that the two warring communities might be drawn together in a joint effort, so evidently possible, had now disappeared in an atmosphere of Orange mistrust. Although Redmond's gestures and overt support for the war effort had met with some success with the Unionists in the south, the Ulster Unionists had refused every Nationalist overture of cooperation and reconciliation and reverted to type, guarding their old walls. For the Irish Nationalists, the glittering prize of Home Rule had been achieved and the Bill was now on the statute book, but in suspension until the end of the war and with the Ulster question still to be resolved. This proved to be the worst possible scenario for Redmond as the initial euphoria of achieving Home Rule soon passed. As the war continued to drag on with no end in sight, the Irish people saw no physical evidence of the political freedom Home Rule had promised.

The war had also brought rocketing food prices to Ireland, even more so than on the British mainland, but with few of the additional jobs or increase in wages. In fact, outwith land reform and Home Rule, Redmond and the IPP had little to offer the vast majority of the Irish working class and that fact would become increasingly evident at the year wore on.

Irish Labour leader James Connolly was in Glasgow at the New Year where he met up with his old Marxist-socialist friend Arthur McManus. Arthur McManus was born in Belfast to Fenian parents who moved to Glasgow shortly after his birth. He became embroiled in class politics as a youth and was a member of the Socialist Labour Party. He was greatly influenced by James Connolly and being of Irish parentage, he was keenly interested in the Irish struggle for freedom. Connolly was in Glasgow to elicit help from his comrades in printing the recently proscribed Irish Worker newspaper. Arthur McManus agreed that the Irish Worker could be printed at the SLP's Renfrew Street printers. He personally worked hard at setting, composing and printing the newspaper. He even delivered the first copies to Dublin himself. The police quickly identified the source and the entire February edition was seized. McManus would later become the first chairman of the Communist Party of Great Britain.

On the Irish recruiting front, the insensitivities of Kitchener and the War Office did not make John Redmond's task any easier, but the 16th (Irish) Division was beginning to take shape. The major problem for Redmond and the IPP was the constant struggle against negative public relations. While Carson and the Ulster division were also having recruiting problems, the perception of unquestioned loyalty allowed their recruiting problems to remain largely out of the spotlight. With the connivance of the authorities, some of the Ulster Division's recruiting returns also showed evidence of creative accounting. With the weight of Irish history on their backs, John Redmond and the Nationalists on the other hand were under constant scrutiny. Another major recruiting problem for John Redmond was that with exception of the Tyneside Irish, the Irish in Britain were not rushing to join distinctly Irish battalions and, specifically, they were not rushing to join Redmond's Irish Brigade and that included the Glasgow Irish. Many did join and no doubt many more would have liked to do so, but it was just so much easier to join a Scottish battalion. The fact that the Glasgow Irish felt comfortable enough joining Scottish battalions also throws some light on how alienated and marginalised the Glasgow Irish of the pre-war period actually felt. The Glasgow Irish signing on with the Glasgow Tramways battalion within twelve hours is a case in point. Although the Glasgow Irish through the UILGB remained committed to Redmond and the IPP, they were increasingly refocusing their attention elsewhere, feeling their long-held ambitions on land reform and Irish Home Rule largely accomplished. From the onset of war, encouraged by their priests and political leaders, the Glasgow Irish threw themselves wholeheartedly behind the British war effort and as a result the community was more directly involved than ever before with the wider Scottish community. Redmond's problem with the Irish in Britain enlisting into Scottish or English regiments was that they largely disappeared into an anonymous mass of British men joining the army.

Much of Redmond's time and efforts now went into trying to gather in the evidence to prove that although the 10th and 16th (Irish) Divisions were still to be fully manned, that was because so many Irishmen had already enlisted and were serving elsewhere. In mid-January, an example presented itself when the Tyneside Irish won the three months' race with the Tyneside Scottish as to which would first complete a 500-strong infantry brigade.

On 16 January, Irish recruiting was the subject of an exchange in the House of Lords. The Sinn Féin anti-recruiting campaign and a perceived Irish recalcitrance to enlist led to questions being asked about what the government was doing about it. As usual the debate centred on recruit numbers, who contributed the most and who was failing to do their bit and why. Irish Catholic peer Lord MacDonnell said that if Home Rule had been place earlier on the Statute Book, there would have been no opportunity for that campaign to appeal to disloyalty. Viscount Midleton replied that recruitment from the whole of Ireland since the outbreak of the war was 54,000. According to Sir Edward Carson, Ulster had contributed between 16,000 and 17,000. If that were so, recruitment from the Nationalist part of Ireland was 38,000. From the whole of England, Scotland and Wales, 115,000 Irish Nationalists had enlisted since the passing of the Home Rule Bill. In total, 25,000 had enlisted from Scotland, 45,000 from Lancashire, Cheshire and North Wales, 20,000 from Yorkshire, 15,000 from the north of England, 5000 from South Wales and the Midlands and 5000 from London. With the figure of 38,000 from Nationalist Ireland and over 20,000 at the beginning of the war with the colours, beside the special reserves, over 200,000 Irishmen had enlisted. If, concluded Lord MacDonnell, an equal response had been made in other parts of the United Kingdom, we would have a force of over 2 million. The Marquis of Crewe said Lord MacDonnell's remarkable figures would stand close examination and added that every single Irish regiment was now at the front in Belgium.

By now the Irish recruitment figures had been so manipulated at all levels and by all parties with vested interests, they were almost meaningless. Only very broad conclusions could be reached using the statistics.

On the same day, the Glasgow Irish Nationalist's efforts on behalf of the Irish Brigade continued in Scotland with a recruitment rally held in the village of Newmains, Lanarkshire. Four men signed up, including P Gallacher, the president of the local UIL branch; J Conlon, secretary of the UIL and assistant secretary of the local Ancient Order of Hibernians (AOH); J Reilly, trustee of the AOH and J Brannon. Three of the men chose to serve with the Connaught Rangers and one the Royal Dublin Fusiliers. These latest recruits took the small parish's contribution of Catholic men serving with the army to fifty. A week earlier, it was reported that seven young men from the village of Balerno, John and Martin Wynne, Francis Byrne, Edward, Thomas and Francis McCue and John McGrory, had all enlisted into the Royal Dublin Fusiliers. On the other side of the coin the roll of honour posted on the door of St Patrick's, Coatbridge, showed that of the 375 parishioners already enlisted, only a fifth had enlisted into Irish regiments.

It was also reported that week that Willie Maley's brother Father O'Malley took part in a recruiting drive for the Ayr Citizen Defence Force. Alongside him on the platform was Sir John Ure Primrose.

On 23 January, the Glasgow Observer carried a report of a recruiting meeting at Drogheda during which Irish Nationalist scholar and former IPP MP Professor Thomas Kettle, now an officer serving with the Leinster Regiment, gave a recruiting speech. As a founding member of the Irish Volunteers, Kettle had given a rousing speech to the Glasgow Irish in Glasgow in April 1914, which helped to kick-start the expansion of Glasgow's Irish Volunteer battalion. He had been sent by John Redmond to Belgium on a Nationalist arms-buying mission, and was still there when the war broke out. He had seen at first hand the behaviour of the German Army during their rampage through the country. He was so appalled at what he had witnessed, that on his return to Ireland he promptly enlisted into the British Army. As a very high profile Irish Nationalist at the Drogheda meeting, Lieutenant Kettle explained his rational for enlisting:

> *Unless the sin committed against Belgium is punished, international law is an empty phrase. Having come to understand the martyrdom of Belgium, I made up my mind that I would rather see this war through as a sixth-rate soldier than as a first class man of letters. For my part I am fighting for Ireland. Break through the ring fence of the Navy and an attack on the East of England may very easily transform into an attack on the East of Ireland, with Drogheda becoming Scarborough. Some misguided people tell us, with the aid of maps, that as soon as Prussia has made England a protectorate she will present Ireland with a brand new independent republic, I will believe that upon one condition, namely that you find for me a vegetarian tiger. Prussianism is the end of all small nations, and Ireland has got to be defended on the Continent or not at all.*

In fact, John Redmond was not alone in having recruiting problems; Sir Edward Carson was also concerned about recruiting for his Ulster division. His promise of a division in waiting had simply failed to materialise and by the end of the year, there were still serious manpower shortfalls in some battalions. The progress of training was also falling short of expectations with the division beginning to fall behind others formed at the same time and operating under the same constraints of arms and equipment shortages. Given the UVF's much vaunted readiness for war, it should have been further ahead of the other divisions. Carson was also under some pressure from his Ulster Volunteers themselves. Although staunchly pro-British and fully supportive of the British war efforts and aims, the Ulster Volunteers had been formed specifically for the defence of Protestant rights in Ireland. Many of the volunteers were unhappy at the thought of being marched off to France, leaving the defence of Ulster immeasurably weakened while the rebellious Catholic Nationalists remained at home. Such a scenario they thought would see the

Nationalists both strengthen their political position and probably see them take over Protestant jobs to boot. The Unionists recognised that the Home Rule battle had been lost, but the question of Ulster remained to be answered and many of the volunteers thought their political position was weakened with their militia in France. In an atmosphere of diminishing enthusiasm for foreign service, the 36th (Ulster) Division was finding it increasingly difficult to recruit in Ulster, with many of the UVF refusing to leave old Derry's walls.

Meanwhile, like the majority of the new service divisions on the mainland, all three Irish divisions would continue to recruit and train, all with similar difficulties for the time being.

SCOTTISH FOOTBALL

The New Year found the management at the SFA effectively ostracised by the other British football associations after breaking ranks over the national cup competitions. The bickering, accusations and counter accusations would stagger on well into the New Year. Meanwhile Charrington and the others of the 'Stop Football' brigade kept up the pressure on football in general, but English football in particular, with their crusade. John McCartney, manager of Hearts, became involved in a war of words with the Bishop of Bristol over the matter. He pointed out to the bishop that there was a difference between amateur and professional sportsmen:

> *The lives of professional footballers were not of a lengthy nature and that being so they deserved and got good wages. It was their one chance to gain a competence. Working in a mine or factory, even till past the allocated span gave little opportunity to save. A wound or accident on the battlefield, perhaps very slight, might mean total incapacity for earning an income. If their ability as players gained them something tangible why should anyone object? The crusade against professional football was founded on imagination, propagated in ignorance.*

That the SFA acquiesced to the War Office request to surrender the Scottish Cup and full international games, plus the gesture of the Heart of Midlothian players appeared to placate all but the most vociferous of the 'Stop Football' lobbyists, certainly in Scotland. By mid-January, it was clear that the game in Scotland would continue until the end of the season, when the SFA stated that the situation would be looked at again.

The Scottish League accepted the SFA's decision to cancel the Scottish Cup competition and decided not set up a breakaway cup competition of its own. At the same time it also decided that League games would be brought forward a week from 13 February so as to fill up the dates left vacant by the cancellation of the Scottish Cup. However, the game itself continued to be in a precarious financial position with the Scottish League's cut in players' wages proving, as Willie Maley and the Celtic board had suggested at the time, of little help to the struggling clubs. Some indication of just how needy some clubs had become was the decision to stop employing neutral linesmen in League games. The move saved just a single guinea per week. It was also decided that the planned League international game between the Scottish and English Leagues would go ahead. The projected £1500 or £2000 that the game would pull in would give a welcome boost to some of the League clubs in dire financial need.

Although much of the pressure on the SFA to cease football for the duration of the war had largely dissipated, at least for the remainder of the current season, the moral and financial pressure on players to enlist remained. However, with the season halfway complete most senior professionals aimed to see out the remaining fixtures and reassess their position come April. As far as the League title race was concerned, most sports commentators were already seeing it as a two-horse race between the Celtic and Heart of Midlothian, and the clash between the two sides at Parkhead at the end of January as the title decider. They also felt that of the two teams, the Celtic had completed the more difficult part of their programme of fixtures while Hearts still had theirs to come.

The patriotic gesture of the Heart of Midlothian players in November had swung the support of the neutral observers behind the Edinburgh side, not that the Celtic ever commanded much support from the neutrals at any other time. Since its formation, the 16th Bn Royal Scots, as expected, remained based in Edinburgh while the battalion completed the first phase of military training. Therefore, although it was over a month since the Hearts footballers had enlisted, the players had been available for all the club fixtures. With twenty-one games played, Hearts still sat comfortably at the top of the League table on thirty-nine points, four points clear of Celtic on thirty-five. The leading two sides were followed by Morton and Rangers on twenty-eight and twenty-seven points respectively, but both had a game in hand over the top two. The New Year was a busy period for most of the major clubs. Three games would be played in just four days between 1 and 4 January, the results of which could have a major bearing on the title race.

On 1 January, soldiering was the last thing on the minds of the average working-class Glesga alpha male. There was an Old Firm game of fitba to be played and nothing would distract them from the fact. The Prussian Guards could be goose-stepping up Sauchiehall Street, but they would have to wait while the Celtic and Rangers fought out their own battle at Ibrox Park. The fitba-daft Glaswegians had the choice of three senior games in the city on New Year's Day, but for the vast majority there was no choice really. The Ne'erday Old Firm game saw 50,000 fans make the trip out to Govan and Ibrox Park. The Parkhead men and their followers were confident going to the home of their greatest rivals. Not only were they playing well themselves, but Rangers were regarded as being poor by their own standards. From twenty games played, the Ibrox side had won just twelve, lost five and drawn three. The Gers last game going into the Old Firm game had been a 1–1 draw away to Third Lanark. Despite the obvious disparity in League form, the Gers could take some heart from their victory over the Celtic in the War Shield game just a fortnight previous and both sides knew that Old Firm games were highly unpredictable. Both teams would field what was generally regarded as their strongest sides and despite their recent defeat to the Ibrox side, the Celts went into the game as firm favourites.

THE WAR FRONT

On the war front, after five months of fighting, the Allies were in a situation far removed from the one most of the commanders had expected or planned for back in the crazy days of August.

The first weeks of the war had been catastrophic for the French. A large slice of their country was occupied and they had suffered colossal casualties. The BEF, comprising much of the old regular British Army, was largely gone, killed, wounded, missing or captured, and the much maligned soldiers of the TF were helping to shore up the British military in France and Belgium.

The Germans too were not where they had imagined they would be at the start of 1915. The German battle plan of knocking France out of the war quickly and rushing victorious battalions eastwards to meet the Russian threat had failed miserably. The number of German dead was in the hundreds of thousands and the Germans were bogged down in France and Belgium. Mobile warfare had ceased and, completely deadlocked, they faced the possibility of prolonged siege warfare in the west, while the fighting on the Eastern Front sucked in more and more military assets.

The proven way to win battles was to outflank the enemy's positions, but with a line of continuous trenches stretching from Switzerland to the Belgian coast, this was impossible. The only alternative was to break through the opposing defences, but both sides confronted increasingly formidable defensive positions. It was now obvious to both the politicians and the British military planners that the war would not be over as quickly as they had so confidently expected back in August. Meanwhile, German, British, Belgian and French soldiers suffered horrendously as they manned their water- and mud-filled trenches during what was proving to be one of the coldest winters in years.

The war on the Eastern Front had also not gone the way of the German war planners. Russia, which the Germans thought would take six weeks to mobilise, stunned the Germans when it had four armies on the move within ten days and advanced into East Prussia. The Germans were relying on the Austro-Hungarians to occupy the Russians on the Eastern Front, but by the end of 1914, the Russians had driven the Austro-Hungarians back over 100 miles. In East Prussia, the German forces retreated ahead of a vast Russian army. In response to the threat in the east, the Germans rushed two divisions from the Western Front at the end of August. Two victories at Tannenberg and the Masurian Lakes stabilised the situation, but the Germans realised that the Austro-Hungarian military was weak and would need permanent support.

The war had also spread around the world. On 23 August 1914, Japan declared war on Germany in solidarity with Britain. One of the reasons for the action was Japan's intent to retake some islands in the Pacific Ocean that Germany had seized as colonies in recent decades. In South Africa, a minor Afrikaner rebellion had broken out at the start of the war against the British and was being put down by former Boer commanders. Action was also being planned against German colonies in East Africa.

At sea, the British were becoming increasingly concerned about the activities of German submarines. By the end of the old year, U-boats had sunk nine British warships while losing five of their own number. On 31 December, *HMS Formidable* was torpedoed and sunk in the English Channel with the loss of 537 officers and men. Although the first attacks on merchant ships had started in October 1914, the Germans had at that point no plans for a concerted U-boat offensive against Allied trade. They recognised the U-boat had several drawbacks as a commerce raider, and such a campaign risked alienating neutral opinion. That policy was by January 1915 under serious review.

In what had been a massive achievement of German diplomacy, Turkey, or the Ottoman Empire as it was then known, had entered the war at the end of October on the German side, and immediately blockaded the Dardanelles, effectively bottling up Russia and depriving her of year-round seaborne access to the west. In addition to cutting off a major source of imported wheat, in what was even more of a concern for the British, Turkey had become a threat to the Suez Canal and British interests in Egypt and Mesopotamia. The situation was an additional drain on resources, particularly manpower with the Australian and New Zealand Army Corps (ANZAC) having to be diverted to Egypt while en route to France. At the beginning of January 1915, the British government received a plea for help from the Russian Czar Nicholas. Under pressure from the Turks in the Caucuses and the Germans on the Eastern Front, the Russians wanted some kind of Allied demonstration against the Turks. Over the month of January, the British War Cabinet met several times to discuss military action in the eastern Aegean.

As the pros and cons of action against the Turkish mainland were kicked around the room, a number of scenarios began to emerge. The plan to force the Dardanelles, possibly followed by the threat and, if necessary, the bombardment of Constantinople by the Navy, could bring a number of advantages to the Allied cause. It could trigger a revolution in Turkey, which would see the downfall of the pro-German Young Turks. The only two Turkish ammunition factories, both in the neighbourhood of Constantinople and close to the coast, could be destroyed by a naval bombardment, which would make a continuation of the war impossible for Turkey. The pressure on the Suez Canal would immediately fall away. The German Berlin–Baghdad railway would be cut. A British invasion of Mesopotamia would not be a serious problem anymore and Germany would be cut off from the oilfields in the Middle East. Russia would be able to call back troops from the Caucasus, to use them on other fronts. German expansion towards the east would be stopped, which would end the threats to the English possessions in India. Hundreds of thousands of tonnes of Russian grain, which were blocked in the Black Sea, could be exported and become available for consumption in the west. Austria could be threatened by a combined operation of a Russian army over land and a move by British warships on the Danube, which would draw German troops away from the Western Front. Serbia would be saved. Greece, Romania and Italy, impressed by these successes, might well choose the Allied side. Bulgaria would then be reduced to a spectator and a united effort by the other Balkan countries could be planned against Austria.

It was indeed a considerable list of glittering prizes and they sparkled most in the mind of the First Sea Lord, Winston Churchill. However, there were also dissenting voices. Lord Fisher threatened to resign if the operation went ahead, while Kitchener blew hot and cold. The dissenters felt a Navy only plan would not work and that the operation would be a distraction, a drain on men and resources. The war needed to be won in France and Belgium and any sideshow would simply dissipate the efforts in the west. Churchill, through the sheer force of his personality, drove the plan through despite the detractors. On 13 January, the British War Council decided that the Admiralty should prepare for a naval expedition in February against the Dardanelles.

Apart from the naval considerations, the decision was taken that at least some boots on the ground, infantry, should be earmarked to occupy the Gallipoli peninsula. Churchill immediately offered his own Royal Marines Reserve battalions formed from excess naval reservists, and by March, these units would be reformed into the Royal Naval Division in the Aegean. By the end of January, the Dardanelles plan had taken shape. The forcing of the Dardanelles would be carried out in four phases: 1. Eliminate the forts at the entrance to the Dardanelles. 2. Sweep the minefields behind them. 3. Eliminate the forts in the Narrows. 4. Sweep the mines in the Narrows, to create a passage for the fleet. The Admiralty thought this operation would require eight ships, six of which might be lost. The two others might be damaged, but would succeed in forcing the Dardanelles. To defeat the two German battleships *Goeben* and *Breslau*, eight other ships would be needed. The potential losses were estimated as high as twelve ships. Messages were flashed to the fleet to prepare for action. Naval operations would begin on 18 February. No one thought to consult the history books: a similar operation had been tried in 1807 and had ended in abject failure.

CELTIC FC

On 1 January 1915, the Rangers ran onto Ibrox Park with the weight of history on their shoulders. Not for the past seven New Year's Days had they beaten the Celtic home or away. The Celts were at full strength for the crunch game. Rangers kicked off with a strong wind in their favour and after twenty minutes made it count when Bowie put the home side one up. After the restart, far from building on their success, the Rangers sat in, allowing Celtic to take the offensive. The Bhoys equalised fifteen minutes later through a fine shot by Johnny Browning. The Celtic continued to dominate the game for the remainder of the first half, but failed to add to their goal tally. The sides went in at half-time even, but it seemed to most observers that when the game restarted after the interval, Celtic with the wind at their backs would make short work of Rangers.

As expected, the Celtic started the second half as they finished the first. Time after time, the Celtic forwards raided deep into the Rangers box, but as often as they attacked, they were repulsed, forced back empty handed. Still, to the faithful it seemed only a matter of time before the Celts got their just rewards. As the minutes slipped by, the Bhoys began to get anxious and then overanxious as it began to appear that the Rangers just might hold on to salvage an undeserved point. With the game into its last fifteen minutes, yet another Celtic attack broke down in front of the Rangers goal. The Rangers defence punted a long ball deep into the Celtic half where Cairns of Rangers gathered it in. The Rangers man rushed into the Celtic box but had yet to pass Alex McNair. The two met in a crunching fifty-fifty tackle and it first appeared that Alex had won the ball, but Cairns refused to give up. He managed to retain the ball, at the same time forcing it into the path of the onrushing Reid, who, despite a desperate lunging tackle from Joe Dodds, rammed the ball across the Celtic goal line. It was then a matter of Rangers packing their defence and putting up the shutters. The Celts tried with increasing desperation to break the human wall. Numerous assaults were repulsed. When McColl missed a golden opportunity and Hempsey in the Rangers goal made two or three magnificent saves, it began to look like one of those days. The Celtic ran out of time and the referee blew the final whistle. Rangers had hung on to take the points and inflict serious damage to the Celtic's title challenge.

In a tactic all too familiar to the modern Celtic fans, Rangers had broken from a packed defence to score a breakaway goal then retreated back into their defensive wall, challenging the Celtic to break them down. Even when the Celtic forwards managed to get through, Hempsey, the Rangers goalkeeper produced some outstanding stops, saving the day for the Gers. The final result was a 2–1 dogged, but somewhat undeserved victory, for the Rangers. The Celtic side on the day was Shaw, McNair and Dodds; Young, Johnstone and McMaster; McAtee, Gallacher, McColl, McMenemy and Browning. The result was also a severe disappointment for James Hilley. Towards Christmas, he had been allowed a few days home leave, being due back at his Swanage base on 30 December. The Garngad's New Year celebrations plus an Old Firm clash were obviously too good to miss, so James lingered in Glasgow arriving back at his place of duty on 4 January 1915, four days late. It was his first offence and he was admonished, however he lost four days pay for the period he was absent.

After the game, the Celts had the dubious pleasure of a visit from Sir John Ure Primrose in their dressing room. The Rangers director and former Glasgow Lord Provost shook hands with all the players wishing them the compliments of the season and then spoke at length to Jimmy Quinn. Apparently, he had a great liking for the Celtic legend and in April 1914, on the occasion of Jimmy's semi-retirement, he had presented the mighty James with a case of pipes as a souvenir of his remarkable goal-scoring feats, particularly against Rangers. Jimmy was an inveterate smoker and would no doubt have been delighted with the gift. Big Peter Johnstone also wished a Rangers supporter the compliments of the season. The man challenged the 'Lanky One' en route to the dressing room at the end of the game. Instead of shaking him by the hand, big Peter had him by the throat. The defeat at Ibrox left Celtic four points behind Hearts. On New Year's Day, 6000 spectators watched the League leaders beat Hibernian 1–2 in the final of the Wilson Cup at Easter Road. The defeat left the Bhoys six points ahead of Rangers in third place, but both Hearts and Rangers had a game in hand over Celtic. The Bhoys would have little time to dwell on their Ibrox disappointment for just the next day, Saturday, they would be facing Clyde at Parkhead. Hearts, meanwhile, back on League business were playing away against a tough to beat Falkirk side at Brockville.

It was raining heavily in Glasgow when the Bhoys ran out at Celtic Park to face Clyde. A crowd of just 6000 braved the weather to cheer on the protagonists. Thanks to the fire at their stadium back in September, Clyde FC were still playing their home games at Parkhead and were now perfectly at ease playing at Celtic Park, this being their second game on the ground in two days. The Clyde team was somewhat depleted with three regulars, Ebb Owers, Charlie Clunas and Willie McAndrew, all now in uniform. Having joined the sportsmen's battalion of the Royal Fusiliers, Owers and Clunas had been posted to London to begin their military training; therefore, their services were entirely lost to the club. For Celtic, Johnny McMaster was out with a thigh injury and McGregor stepped into the breach, otherwise it was the same team that had lost to Rangers. The Celtic took a grip of the game from the kick-off and were superior to Clyde in all departments. There was never any threat to the Celtic goal, but as time went on the Celtic forwards were unable to get the goal required to settle the nerves. The Celts had a couple of goal-bound shots saved magnificently by McTurk in the Clyde goal, whose continued alertness kept the Celts at bay. Eventually the breakthrough came. Johnny Browning latched onto a perfect through ball from McAtee to beat McTurk and put the Bhoys into the lead just before half-time. The second half followed the same pattern of the first with Clyde dour in defence, while on their occasional forays into the Celtic half their forwards were forced to shoot from outside the box. Despite their superiority, the Celtic were still only leading by the single goal as the second half ticked away. The Celtic supporters' nerves were only settled when Browning got a second with just three minutes to go. Two goals from 'Smiler' Browning saw the Celtic comedian laugh all the way to the pavilion. It was workmanlike performance against a well-organised Clyde team, which saw the Celts run out winners by 2–0 and secure the points.

For the Celts, the dismal rainy afternoon in Glasgow brightened considerably when the news reached Parkhead that Hearts had drawn at Brockville. The Hearts game at Falkirk had been played on a pitch that was more like a half-flooded ploughed field. The Tynecastle men at first tried to play football, but after Falkirk took the lead, they wisely resorted to keeping the ball above the mud. Eventually relentless pressure from Hearts paid off and they got a deserved equaliser. As the game progressed and the condition of the pitch deteriorated further, it became something of a farce and neither side was sorry to hear the final whistle. The game ended with one goal apiece and the Hearts left a share of the points with Falkirk. Celtic's victory over Clyde, and with Hearts dropping a point, meant that the Tynecastle men's lead had been cut to three points, but still with a game in hand over Celtic.

On Monday 4 January, the footballers of the Scottish senior League played their third game in four days. The strain was beginning to tell with sports commentators seeing the tiredness in the players even before the start of the game. Considering Celtic had played on Christmas Day and Boxing Day, there were a few Bhoys with sore legs on display. For Celtic, thankfully, it was another home game, so at least there was no travelling involved. The Celts were without McMaster and Gallacher for the visit of Kilmarnock, with McGregor and Crone taking their places. The strain was also beginning to tell on the playing surface at Celtic Park, with it showing the effects of three games in four days. A younger and fresher Kilmarnock team held their own for most of the first half, but failed to threaten the Celtic goal. Celtic slowly but surely got on top of their opponents and the breakthrough came when Peter Johnstone sallied forward to score a rare goal for the lanky centre half. After the restart, Celtic continued to pile on the pressure and eventually it told when McColl got another goal for the Bhoys. The game ended in a 2–0 victory for the Celtic.

Meanwhile at Tynecastle, Heart of Midlothian notched up another good win by beating Hamilton Accies 3–0 in front of 7000 spectators. However, the result of the day was Airdrieonians 0–5 victory over Rangers at Ibrox.

On 9 January, Celtic were at Parkhead for the third home game in a row with their opponents Partick Thistle. The Jags had been on a good run of late, being unbeaten beaten since November. It was a cold windy day, but a sizeable crowd of 11,000 made the effort to turn out for the game. Among the spectators were two of Joe Dodds's brothers, Willie and Hugh, home on leave from Kitchener's Army. The Celtic faithful had barely time to snuggle down into their scarfs and bunnets when the visitors rattled one into the Celtic net. Unfortunately for them, Thistle failed to build on their confident start and retreated into their own half where they quickly found themselves under siege. Pinned back into their own half and subjected to a terrific bombardment of attacks, even when Partick Thistle did get hold of the ball, Patsy Gallacher chased and harried the Thistle backs to regain possession. One sports reporter described him as the nearest thing to perpetual motion he had ever seen. Despite all the possession in the first half, Celtic simply could not get the ball into the net, despite peppering the Thistle goal with shots from every angle. They hit the post twice and Campbell in the Thistle goal pulled off a number of excellent saves. Even Peter Johnstone attempted to get in on the act, encouraged by his goal against Kilmarnock five days previously. This time the halfback's four efforts on goal before half-time all went well over the bar. The Thistle defence was barely coping with the Celtic attacks and the Celtic faithful sensed a goal was coming. In the second half, the floodgates opened after the Bhoys made their first breakthrough. Patsy Gallacher eventually got a hat-trick, and McColl and Browning got one goal apiece. Joe Dodds was generally accepted as being the star man among the backs, simply for his tireless performance, which was rewarded by a goal from a penalty kick. The Celtic was vastly superior to Partick in every department with the Parkhead forwards slicing through the Maryhill defence almost at will. One commentator likened the Celtic forwards going through the Thistle defence as being better than the British cavalry going through the German infantry at Mons. It was a very bad example since it was completely untrue; however, in reality, the score could easily have reached double figures such was the gap in quality. The Celtic's 6-1 victory was an emphatic win for the Bhoys and one that helped exorcise some of the Ibrox demons. The Celtic side on the day was Shaw, McNair and Dodds; Young, Johnstone and McMaster; McAtee, Gallacher, McColl, McMenemy and Browning.

The joy of the win and satisfaction of another two points secured was dampened somewhat when news arrived at Parkhead that James Kelly's sister, Mary Kelly, had died. Mary was a popular schoolteacher in the Kelly's home village of Renton, where she had taught for most of her life. A keen and devoted Celtic supporter she was very often to be found at Parkhead during the football season. The funeral the following Wednesday in Alexandria was attended by the entire Celtic board. It had been an emotional couple of few months for the hierarchy at Celtic, first, big Mulrooney, next Peter Somers, then John McKillop and now Jimmy Kelly's sister.

While the Celts were putting Partick Thistle to the sword, Hearts were at Tynecastle where they faced third-placed Greenock Morton in what was being regarded as one of their toughest tests. The Hearts ran out winners by 1–0 with Tom Gracie scoring the only goal. The Scotsman thought Morton played as well as Hearts and deserved a share of the points, but the Edinburgh tabloids described the Hearts performance as 'sluggish' and after just a fortnight in khaki wondered if military training was agreeing with the Tynecastle men. Following a route march, some of the players had apparently suffered blisters from their new army boots and after having their feet bandaged were forced to play in football boots a size too big. The army boots had been issued to the men two weeks earlier on Christmas Day and it was an indication of the amateurism of the battalion that the boots should still be causing problems. The injuries induced by the players' military training so concerned the Hearts sixty-three-year-old trainer, Jimmy 'Duckie' Duckworth, that he announced that in future he would be accompanying his charges on their military training. The Tynecastle men's lead at the top of the League table was still three points with a game in hand over Celtic.

On 16 January, the Celts finally hit the road with a trip through to Falkirk. Over the last few years, Celtic's visit to Brockville had become one of the most physical encounters of the season as the Bairns countered Celtic's skill and finesse with a hard physical approach. The 10,000 spectators that turned up on the day, therefore, looked forward to a no-quarter given or asked for bruiser of a game. Celtic were without Alex McNair, who had an injured knee, but ever faithful Tom McGregor stepped into the breach. The Falkirk attack was pretty well subdued throughout; however, on a few occasions over the course of the game, they managed to create scoring opportunities. In fact, almost from the kick-off they came very close to opening their account when a well-struck shot came off the underside of the Celtic crossbar and bounced on the line before being cleared by Dodds. After that incident, the traffic was pretty much one way, with the Celts only being held by some pretty wild tackling. Again, despite having most of the possession, Celtic found it difficult to penetrate a stubborn defence. The closest the Celts came to a breakthrough over the first half was when Andy McAtee hit the Falkirk crossbar. The second half was more of the same until Andy McAtee fired in another of his trademark fierce shots. The ball was held by Stewart in the Falkirk goal, but Johnny Browning following in bundled goalie and ball over the line. The Bairns claimed the ball never crossed the line, but the referee awarded the goal. It would prove to be the only goal of the game and the Celts ran out winners but only just. As expected, it had been a dour hard-fought game of football on a heavy pitch where only Celtic's persistence and physical endurance saw them through. Unlike the Hearts, who could only manage a draw a fortnight earlier, the Bhoys escaped from Brockville with all the points. The Celtic side on the day was Shaw, McGregor and Dodds; Young, Johnstone and McMaster; McAtee and Gallacher; and McColl, McMenemy and Browning.

Meanwhile in Edinburgh, Hearts were rocking. They were two goals down at home to Dundee with only a half hour remaining. However, there was a late rally by the home side. Two goals from Tom Gracie and the winner right on the final whistle from Bryden snatched full points for the Tynecastle men. The Hearts poor performance was put down to a number of players with the flu.

The results of Saturday's games had left the League table unchanged at the top with Hearts now on forty-six points and still leading the Celts by three points. Greenock Morton was in third place on thirty-three points, but Ayr United had overtaken Rangers into fourth on goal difference. Celtic had played twenty-six games, and all four of their closest rivals had a game in hand. After a very tough three weeks, the Bhoys finally got some respite with a full week without a game. The next match would be a friendly against their Irish cousins, Belfast Celtic, on 23 January at Parkhead.

THE MALEY CLAN

Back in November when the 1st/9th (Glasgow Highlanders) Bn HLI received its deployment orders, the move overseas was so sudden no one got the opportunity to say their goodbyes. Now a large draft of Glasgow Highlanders, including Corporal Josie Maley, had been informed that they were about to be sent to join their battalion in the field. Determined to give them the send-off denied their battalion, on 13 January, the Glasgow Corporation threw a farewell dinner for the Glasgow men about to deploy on active service. At around 1215 hrs on a blustery wet afternoon, 157 Glasgow Highlanders, including Corporal Joseph Maley and ninety men of the 5th Bn Scottish Rifles TF paraded on Greendyke Street. Accompanied by the Glasgow Highlander's pipe band, they marched through streets lined with thousands of people the mile or so from Glasgow Green to St Andrew's Halls at Charing Cross. There they were treated to a slap-up meal, free cigarettes and cigars, a few beers and a variety show. Various music hall artists were engaged to entertain the men, the favourite being Miss Bessie Atwell, whose renditions of 'Where did you get that girl?' and the latest hit 'It's a long way to Tipperary' went down particularly well. The chorus of the latter could have been heard at Celtic Park. The Lord Provost appeared, made a stirring speech and wished them all good luck.

On Sunday 17 January, the extended Maley clan gathered in the home of Tom and Elizabeth Maley in Wilton Street. Having already seen Tom and Elizabeth's eldest son, Thomas, off to serve as an artificer with the Royal Navy at the end of October, the Maley family were now spending a few hours with Josie before he deployed on active service. Tom Maley was living at Bradford where he was managing English first division

Josie Maley, Glasgow Highlanders

Courtesy of the Maley Family

side Bradford Park Avenue. He had travelled home overnight to Glasgow after the Avenue's 3–1 win over Notts County. His eldest brother, Father Charles O'Malley, travelled up from his parish at Ayr. Willie Maley, his mother Mary Ann and his two boys Willie and Charlie had far less distance to travel from their home in Hyndland Avenue. The youngest of the Maley brothers, Alex, then manager of Scottish second division side Clydebank, would also not have far to travel. It had been a good weekend for the footballing Maley brothers with wins by Celtic and Bradford Park Avenue and a draw by Clydebank. As they say, two out of three ain't bad.

After a final few days' pre-embarkation leave, Josie bade a tearful farewell to his parents and siblings on 20 January at their home. A family legend tells of his young sister, Cissy, then aged twelve, tearfully running down Wilton Street after him. Josie picked her up and spun her around and around before continuing on his way back to battalion headquarters at Greendyke Street. At the Greendyke Street hall, it was a long day of kit checks and roll calls, followed by more checks and more roll calls. Final pieces of kit were issued and ill-fitting equipment exchanged. There was a constant procession of relatives and friends of Glasgow Highlanders already in France appearing at the hall door. They handed in letters and parcels to be delivered on their behalf and asked for messages of goodwill to be passed on: 'Tell so and so, that so and so was asking for them.' A long restless night was spent in bedrolls on the drill hall floor and the next morning the waiting continued. Corporals shepherded their men around the immediate vicinity of the hall in an attempt to keep bored soldiers out of trouble. Finally, at around 1900 hrs, as part of a replacement draft of two officers and 149 men, the Glasgow Highlanders, led by the pipe band, marched from Greendyke Street to Glasgow's Central railway station where they caught the overnight train to London. The legend of Cissy running after her brother in Wilton Street suggests all Josie's farewells were said in the privacy of his own home, so it is unlikely any of Josie's family was in the crowd at the station to see him off.

As always, the first few hours of the journey were spent singing songs, telling jokes and playing cards while the adrenaline of the departure still rushed. Soon tiredness took hold and the carriages quietened down as the men snatched a few hours of restless sleep. At London, the draft changed trains for Southampton and the south coast. By the time they arrived in the town it was well into the afternoon and they were crammed into the canteens set up by the Army, the Red Cross and some local church groups. By 1900 hrs, they had boarded the cross-Channel ferry for the overnight crossing. Just as dawn was breaking on the morning of 22 January, the Glasgow Highlander's draft landed at Le Havre.

**The Maley Girls. L to R
Peggy, Maurie and Cissy**
(Courtesy of the Maley family)

It took the new draft a full week to make its way from the base depot at Le Havre to the battalion's location at the front. They arrived at Bethune by train at lunchtime on 31 January, but the draft had not quite made it to the battalion just yet and had a sweaty five miles to march, carrying full kit before they reached the battalion's billets at the villages of Gore and Marais. The 1st/9th Bn Glasgow Highlanders had just returned to the villages from a tour of duty in the front lines in the waterlogged Le Plantin Sector, near Festubert. The battalion laid on a warm welcome for the new arrivals and as the draft approached Gorre they were meet by the regimental pipers and played into the village. The old sweats lined the road to cheer as the new boys approached. The sound of the pipes put a spring into their step even after five miles, and Corporal Josie Maley and his boys came swaggering into the village, kilts swinging and chests puffed out.

After settling into his billet at Gorre, Josie Maley would have been on the lookout for his old friend John Francis McKillop, but unfortunately he had missed him by about a fortnight. In mid-January, McKillop was among thousands of soldier incapacitated through trench foot and frostbite after standing for days on end in freezing cold, liquid mud. After passing through the regimental aid post and advanced dressing stations, he was admitted into a French military hospital. By the beginning of February, he was back in Glasgow recovering at home. Having had enough of roughing it with the troops, private school educated John Francis decided he would apply for a commission.

CELTIC FC

The date of the Celtic's friendly against Belfast Celtic had been freed up due to the abandonment of the Scottish Cup. After the Belfast Celtic game, it would be back to League business and Heart of Midlothian at Parkhead in what was being described by most sports commentators as a title decider. With the crunch game in mind, McGregor, Crone and Jimmy Quinn came into the side for Andy McNair, Jimmy McMenemy and Patsy Gallacher, all of whom were being rested. The Irish League champion's star man, Belfast bhoy Micky Hamill, was also out injured with a recurring knee problem. It was a cold misty unpleasant day for the estimated 5000 spectators who turned out to watch the friendly played on a treacherous Parkhead surface. The Irish League champions played open attractive football for the first half and might have scored, but they were never really in the game with Celtic playing at half pace. The mighty Quinn opened the scoring midway through the first half with a trademark twenty-yard screamer that had the faithful recalling Jimmy's halcyon days of yore. The pattern of the game in the second half was much the same as the first, with Jimmy getting two tap-ins to complete his hat-trick. Two minutes after he scored his third, Jimmy McColl got a fourth. The Belfast Celtic contributed to the spectacle, but their Scottish cousins took the honours without breaking sweat. In fact, the final result was of secondary importance to the Parkhead faithful compared to the gratification of seeing the Mighty Quinn show that there was still life in the old warhorse. After his scoring performance, few would have been surprised to see him back in the regular starting line-up. Despite their defeat, the Belfast Celts were delighted with the fixture and their share of the £108 taken at the gate. The Celtic side on the day was Shaw, McGregor and Dodds; Young, Johnstone and McMaster; McAtee and Crone; and Quinn, McColl and Browning. After the game, Willie Maley collected £6 from the Celtic players, which was donated to the Glasgow Observer's Belgian Relief Fund.

While the Bhoys were seeing off the Belfast Celtic at Parkhead, Hearts were also in Glasgow playing Third Lanark in the League. On the evening prior to the game, McCrae's battalion began a twenty-six-mile ten-hour route march that saw them get back to their Edinburgh billets at three in the morning. After a few hours' sleep, the Hearts players were on the train through to Glasgow. In the League, Third Lanark were lying in mid table, but only a couple of points separated them and fourth place. Over the season so far, they had proved a hard team to beat with ten draws and seven wins from their twenty-five games played and to date were undefeated at Cathkin Park. The best crowd of the day, 13,000, turned out to watch the League leaders go two up with goals scored either side of half-time. Third Lanark refused to concede defeat and as the Hearts took their foot off the pedal, the home side got one goal back. Third Lanark struck again well into the second half to grab a share of the points. Hearts had surrendered a two-goal lead and the sporting press attributed their loss of form to a reaction to inoculations and military training. The gap at the top of the League was now just four points with the same number of games played. Next up for Hearts would be the Celtic at Parkhead.

Just a couple of days before the Belfast Celtic game, death again came to call at Celtic Park when the news arrived that the seventeen-year-old son of Celtic old bhoy Hugh Goldie had died in service at Aldershot. Hugh Goldie was one of the 'Dons' brought into the Celtic at considerable expense soon after the club was converted into a limited company in 1897. He played twenty-seven senior games in the green and white stripes and even as a centre back had managed to score a single goal. On his arrival in Glasgow from Everton in May 1897, he brought with him his infant son Robert, born in Liverpool just weeks earlier. Seventeen years later Robert Goldie joined the 8th Bn Seaforth Highlanders at Kilmarnock and in September 1914 was posted to Aldershot with his battalion to begin military training. At the beginning of January 1915, Robert contracted pneumonia and was admitted to a military hospital in Aldershot seriously ill. After visiting their son in hospital, Hugh and Grace Goldie retuned home, thinking all was well. Just a few days after receiving a letter from Robert stating that he was recovering, a telegram arrived stating that their son had died suddenly on 19 January. Robert's remains were brought home to Crookedholm and he was laid to rest with full military honours at Kilmarnock Cemetery.

The very day Hugh Goldie's son died, Celtic old boy Pat Slavin enlisted at Fauldhouse, West Lothian. Pat had arrived at Celtic Park from Fauldhouse Hibs in the desperate days immediately after the Arthurlie debacle of January 1897. Celtic stalwart Davy Russell, who also lived in Fauldhouse, probably cleared nineteen-year-old Pat's path to Paradise. Young Slavin performed well at outside right for the reserves in the Combination League and was promoted into the first team for a Glasgow League game against Third Lanark. Playing alongside his hero Davy Russell, Pat scored his first senior goal in the Celts 3–1 victory. Impressed with his performance, the directors put Pat into the side again for the last league game of the season against St Mirren at Love Street. The game was meaningless, but Pat failed to shine in the 2–0 defeat by the Buddies. The loss saw the Celts relegated to fourth position in the league behind winners Heart of Midlothian, Hibernian and Rangers. It was the lowest league position Celtic had ever occupied at the end of a season. It also turned out to be player legend James Kelly's last Scottish league game for the Celts. Exactly a month later he would become a director of the newly formed Celtic Football and Athletic Company.

Pat Slavin was undoubtedly a very talented outside right, but unluckily he arrived at Celtic at a monumental time in the history of the football club. The directors of the new company were ruthless in their determination to achieve instant success. They invested big money to bring into the team the best players from around the country and had them in place for the start of the new 1897–98 season. The star players were known collectively as the 'English Dons'. In order to help pay for the new men, the reserve team was disbanded and Pat Slavin was among the journeymen players cleared out to make way for the 'Dons' including ironically Hugh Goldie. Pat was picked up by Motherwell and in a season plagued by injuries, went on to play nine times for the 'Steelmen' over 1897–98. Back in Fauldhouse, he returned to working as a quarry labourer. By way of hobbies, he joined both the St John's Dramatic Society as a stage manager, and the 10th Bn Royal Scots TF as a part-time soldier. By 1914, Pat had married, moved to nearby East Benhar and attained the position of foreman at the local Bellbrae quarry.After signing on with the Royal Scots, thirty-seven year old Pat Slavin was dispatched to Glencorse Barracks near Penicuik to begin his military training. Having man management experience and having previously soldiered with the TF, Pat was quickly promoted to Corporal and posted to the 3rd (Reserve) battalion Royal Scots then based at Weymouth.

In January 1915, Mr Charles McCallum of Furnace Row, Bo-Ness watched as another two of his sons went off to war. Charles McCallum was first generation Glasgow Irish, his parents arrived in Glasgow from Ireland during the Great Famine and then moved east to Bo'Ness where his father found work as a miner. Charles McCallum's sons Charlie and John joined three McCallum brothers already serving. On the outbreak of war, Alexander and Archibald McCallum, were already members of the 10th Bn Royal Scots TF based at Linlithgow and were embodied with their battalion. The youngest son Owen McCallum, joined the Royal Engineers. Now Charles McCallum's two eldest sons had also enlisted. Charlie who joined the Royal Army Medical Corps (RAMC) was a married man with six children. He had recently moved his young family from Bo'Ness to Lochore, Fife, where he was employed as a miner. Charlie was trained in First Aid and was a member of the mine rescue team. On enlisting, he was dispatched to Aldershot where he was posted into the 44th Field Ambulance, 43rd Brigade part of the 14th (Light) Division. In this case, a Field Ambulance was a medical unit and not a vehicle used for transporting the wounded. Each division had three Field Ambulances attached, one for each infantry brigade. The Field Ambulance was responsible for the first links in the medical evacuation chain that stretched from the Regimental Aid Post on the front line, through the Advanced Aid Posts and Field Dressing Stations to the Main Dressing Station stationed some few miles back from the front line. Finally, the Field Ambulances would transport the wounded several miles back to the Casualty Clearing Stations. John McCallum was the eldest of the McCallum brothers. He was married with four children and lived at Carriden, near Bo-Ness where worked for the Colt-ness Coal Company as a miner. On enlistment he decided to join the Royal Scots and was ordered to reported to Glencorse Barrack. Three days later he was posted to the 3rd (Reserve) Bn Royal Scots at Weymouth.

The eagerly awaited day of the Celtic versus Hearts game finally dawned. By lunchtime on 30 January, the centre of Glasgow was awash in maroon and khaki as the Hearts brought trainloads of supporters through from the capital. Thousands of soldiers from local camps and military hospitals also flooded into the city. It was reckoned that every wounded soldier from Stobhill Hospital capable of walking had made his way to Parkhead where he was allowed in free. The Celtic pavilion was packed and was like a who's who of Scottish football. Among the old Bhoys present were Hugh Clifford and Davie Russell. The Tynecastle team, led by Tom Gracie, who had recently recovered from a bout of the flu, came to Glasgow's east end at full strength. Celtic fielded a full-strength team less Jimmy Quinn in for McColl in what proved to be the mighty Quinn's last major competitive game for Celtic. It had been frosty in Glasgow over the previous week, but a thaw on Saturday morning saw the playing surface at Parkhead soft and treacherous underfoot.

As the players took to the field, the Tynecastle men were given a very warm ovation from the Celtic support, in recognition of their patriotic gesture of enlisting into the Army. Hearts set their stall out from the start, defending stubbornly, obviously content to soak up the pressure and hoping for a goal on a counter-attack. Celtic, of course, immediately went onto the attack, forcing two corners within the first two minutes. After just five minutes, Nellies punted a ball out from the Hearts box, which fell to inside left Graham. The Hearts forward raced upfield, dribbled the ball past Jim Young and played a one-two with Willie Wilson, who had managed to catch up. On getting the ball back, he found himself with a clear sight of goal but still a good twenty-five yards out. As the Celtic defenders closed in he let fly. The ball screamed into the top right corner of the Celtic net out of the reach of Charlie Shaw's left hand. The large Hearts contingent roared as their favourites now had two points to defend.

There followed prolonged periods of Celtic aggression with the Hearts defending as if their lives depended on it. Despite all the possession, Celtic failed to penetrate the defence and resorted to long-range shots that were either wide of the mark or dealt with comfortably by Boyd in the Hearts goal. Patsy Gallacher had a couple of good runs, beating defender after defender, but the final pass or shot went awry. The Hearts managed one or two attacks and on one occasion caused some panic in the Celtic defence that was eventually sorted out by Jimmy Dodds. Half-time came and went and the pattern of play of the first half began to repeat itself. The Hearts defenders, Crossan and Currie, were indomitable in defence, but were frequently overrun only for the Celtic forwards to squander the chances they had created. As the game wore on and play opened up, the Celtic created many more scoring opportunities, but each was squandered in turn. The old warhorse Jimmy Quinn faded towards the end and Jimmy McMenemy found the heavy-going tiring. Gallacher and Browning were the most effective for Celtic.

Currie, the Hearts left back, heads away from Gallagher, the Celtic forward, in the great match at Parkhead.

Mr. A. Edward, the referee in the match between Hearts and Celtic.

Boyd, the Hearts goalkeeper, kicks clear, with M'Menemy close in, after Gallagher had centred.

Celtic v Hearts 30 January 1915

Ten minutes after the restart, Celtic finally got the breakthrough. The Celts had already had a number of ineffectual shots on target when Jimmy McMenemy fired in a low hard shot that Boyd was forced to divert round the post for a corner. McMenemy took the corner kick, placing the ball towards the back post where Andy McAtee met it with his chest and diverted the ball into the net. The Hearts players screamed for handball, but the referee, who was well placed to see the incident, allowed the goal to stand. Celtic controlled the remainder of the game, but again failed to turn the sustained pressure into a winning goal, despite a number of clear-cut chances. It was the old story yet again. Celtic had most of the ball, clever midfield and wing play but few goals to show for the effort and skill. There were a number of controversial incidents, one when Patsy Gallacher was bundled off the ball by Boyd having beaten four of the defenders and looked almost certain to score, but no penalty was awarded by the referee.

The game ended in a draw with the visitors relieved to leave Parkhead with a share of the points. It would be difficult to determine whether the final score was the result of dogged, skilful defending or inept chance-taking by wasteful attackers. It was probably as much of one as the other. Despite the fact that Celtic should have won the game, a draw was probably a fair result. A crowd of around 55,000 with at least 10,000 in uniform watched an excellent, fast-flowing game of football. The Celtic team on the day was Shaw, McNair and Dodds; Young, Johnstone and McMaster; McAtee, Gallacher, Quinn, McMenemy and Browning. The Heart of Midlothian team was Boyd, Crossan and Currie; Briggs, Scott and Nellies; Low and Wattie; and Gracie; Graham and Wilson.

Politically, it was probably a good result for the Celtic, since a convincing victory would have left them open to the charge that the Hearts players were drained after their military training during the week. The crowd was by far the biggest of the season with the soldiers being admitted free. The last time there were so many soldiers at Celtic Park was during the victory parade and military display of the Indian and Colonial troop in August 1902 at the end of the Boer War.

The draw meant Hearts remained at the top of the league by four points; both clubs had played twenty-seven games. With only eleven more games to go, the task of overhauling Hearts was still a formidable one.

Chapter Nine

FEBRUARY

THE HOME FRONT

In yet another step towards total war, on 4 February the German government announced an escalation of submarine warfare in an attempt to blockade Britain. From 18 February, this would include unrestricted attacks on all ships heading into British waters. When the war began, President Woodrow Wilson pledged neutrality by the United States, a position most Americans favoured. Britain, however, was one of America's closest trading partners and when the Germans announced unrestricted naval warfare against all ships, neutral or otherwise, the Americans protested. The move would interfere with American trade and led to tension with America.

Great Britain imported vast amounts of foodstuffs and raw materials that were needed for the war industries. The German move to blockade British imports threatened the very existence of the nation. Great Britain was much more dependent on imported food supplies than Germany: pre-war free-trade policies had allowed a 'grain invasion' from America and Canada to shrink the domestic agricultural sector, after which British farmers largely concentrated on dairy and meat production. By 1914, Britain was importing 78 per cent of its wheat and flour and 52 per cent of its cereals and pulses. Despite British farmers specialising in meat and dairy produce, even these were imported in large quantities: 35 per cent of the meat, 43 per cent of butter and 74 per cent of cheese were imported. British trade was protected by the Royal Navy, which was the largest and most powerful navy in the world and the British were immensely proud of it. Since the days of Nelson, it had dominated and controlled the oceans of the world.

In addition to surface ships, by 1914 most major navies of the world possessed a number of new-fangled submarines in their fleets. By the outbreak of the Great War, the French possessed the most submarines (123), followed by the British (fifty-seven), with the Germans (thirty-eight) in third place. Despite some advances in design, including diesel engines, most were still highly unreliable and dangerous to operate and were largely restricted to coastal operations. All that would quickly change as the Germans grasped the value of the *Unterseeboot*, from which the famous 'U-boat' derived its ominous title. Although up to this point there was no deliberate German plan to attack merchant shipping, in the six months prior to the opening of the commerce war in February 1915, U-boats had sunk nineteen ships, totalling 43,000 gross registered tonnage. On 1 February, in response to German submarine attacks on British ships, the government issued instructions to all British ships to fly neutral flags.

With the British enforcing a distant blockade of Germany and its surface fleet confined to port under the direct order of the Kaiser, the key to the German blockade strategy would be its fleet of submarines. The Germans were the first nation to employ U-boats as a substitute for surface raiders, attacking Allied merchant shipping and warships and they would come to dominate undersea warfare during the Great War.

The threat to the British food supply added to the escalating cost of food. The trade unions calculated that from the start of the war the price of basic foodstuffs had risen by over 20 per cent. When war broke out, the trade unions had called an industrial truce. The estimated 72,000 workers on strike in July 1914 fell to nil at the start of February 1915. The official *History of the Ministry of Munitions* would later comment: 'The first six months were a time of peace in the labour world, such as had never existed before and has not existed since.' That peace was rudely shattered in mid-February when Clydeside engineers came out in what became known as the 2d an hour strike. It was an unofficial strike, against the advice and wishes of the union. In addition, the newspapers of the time were reporting on industrial unrest across the whole of Scotland with Glasgow engineers, carters and dock labourers, Kilmarnock engineers, Dundee jute workers, Edinburgh saddlers and leather workers, Scottish railwaymen, and farm labourers all demanding higher wages to counter the steep rise in the prices of what they termed the necessities of life.

In another assault on the pleasures of the people, the effects of alcohol on war workers' output appeared on the addenda. The question of how much, how often and at what strength alcohol should be consumed became a matter for public debate. On a lighter note, the famous Scottish comedian Harry Lauder appeared at the Pavilion Theatre. The Harry Lauder Pipe Band toured the country with him playing at venues in the same town. The band was used to drum up recruits, very often at football games.

On 14 February, reacting to the air raids on the English coastal towns, Archbishop McGuire of Glasgow instructed that a pastoral letter be read out in all the Catholic churches throughout the Archdiocese of Glasgow. The letter was effectively a recruiting call for Roman Catholic men to enlist. It contained the following references to the war:

> *It is paganism we have to fight, with its characteristic disregard for human life and property of law and justice, of honesty and truth childhood and womanhood, of art and learning; with its resolve to trample on the rights of all opposed to its tyranny: with its cynical maxim that the end justifies the means; and such an end to do for Europe what has been done in Germany. ... It is Christianity against paganism, the cross and its civilisation against the crescent and its barbarism – against the even worse, because deliberate and calculated, barbarism of the [German] War Lord.*

> *We must not shrink from the task or from the sacrifice, which it will bring with it. Young men who are free cannot content themselves with applause for others who go to the front; they should go to the front themselves. Families ought not to content themselves with sympathy for others whose dearest are in the fighting line; they should encourage their own dearest to go there. Thank God reasonable provision is to be made for the women and children left behind, and for men who return disabled.*

The letter concluded with:

> *Let us remember that we are not fighting for military glory, nor do we seek revenge even for the murdered women and children of Belgium, and our*

*own East Coast, keeping in mind the warning of St Paul – 'Not avenging
yourselves, dearly beloved: Revenge to Me, I will repay, saith the Lord.'
Glory is not a word for Christian lips, but duty is – the duty of defending
ones' country, his liberty, his altar, and his home.*

Extracts of the archbishop's letter were also published in the Glasgow News on 15 February.
In the same edition under the banner headline 'Irishmen and the War', the newspaper published
the recruiting figures collated by the UILGB at the behest of John Redmond from the various
Scottish Catholic parishes. A detailed breakdown by parish for Glasgow and Coatbridge districts
was published in the Glasgow News on the same day. (See Annex A.)

The Glasgow Herald of 15 February also ran a version of the story under the banner 'Irishmen
in the Army':

*According to statistics prepared by the United Irish League authorities the
numbers of Nationalists from Roman Catholic congregations in Glasgow
and district who have joined the Navy, Army and Territorial Force since
the beginning of the war are as follows:*

Glasgow and District	*8470*
Coatbridge and District	*1825*
Dalry and Kilwinning	*56*
Dumbarton	*252*
Duntocher and Old Kilpatrick	*125*
Dalmuir	*130*

On Saturday 20 February, the Glasgow and Country Board of the Irish National Volunteers
meet to discuss various matters relating to the governance of the organisation. Back in October,
after Redmond's Woodenbridge speech, a meeting of delegates representing twenty-two
companies of the Irish National Volunteers determined to ascertain the views on the Volunteer
movement. The decisive question was put: 'Which committee does your company desire to
recognise?' Eighteen voted for John Redmond's committee and four for the Provisional
Committee led by Eoin MacNeill. After the split, and as a consequence of most former regular
army instructors being recalled to the colours, it was reported that the dearth of military
instructors had caused some companies to become disorganised. On 6 February the Glasgow
Observer carried a special report entitled 'The United Irish League of Great Britain'. Should
the Irish League in Great Britain continue in existence? The question was being asked in the
light of the passage into law of the Home Rule Bill. The point was made that the United Irish
League GB was very different from its Irish counterpart, and that the purpose for which it had
been established, the passage of the Home Rule Bill, had been achieved. To retain it threatened
to isolate and segregate the Irish in Great Britain.

At the beginning of February, Willie Angus's number came up on the latest 8th Bn HLI
draft list. Having completed his basic training, Willie had come to the attention of his superiors
and was appointed lance corporal. The Lanark battalion was plundered of men yet again with
this latest draft earmarked as reinforcements for the 8th HLI Company attached to the 8th Bn
Royal Scots then fighting in France. After a one-week furlough back home in Carluke where

he said goodbye to family and friends, Lance Corporal Angus and his draft of battle casualty replacements left for France. On 16 February, they embarked at Southampton and landed at Le Havre the following day. As instructed, the draft made its way to No 1 Infantry Base Depot at Rouen. The HLI men remained at Rouen where they completed an additional phase of training before being dispatched to join their new battalion, arriving around 24 February. Willie Angus, however, was among thirty men who had been exposed to spotted fever and would be kept quarantined until 12 March.

IRISH FLAG DAY

Irish Flag Day Poster

The Glasgow Irish community and indeed the Catholic community all over Britain and Ireland felt a great empathy for the Belgians, both the refugees in their midst and the Belgians suffering under the heel of the Germans. Much of the relief efforts conducted by the Glasgow Irish over late 1914 and 1915 were directed towards their cause. In mid-November 1914, a committee of ladies belonging to the Ancient Order of Hibernians (AOH) had decided that they would conduct an Irish Flag Day with the monies raised going to the relief of the Belgians. Although the original idea and most of the heavy lifting for the Irish Flag Day would come from the women of the AOH, the men took the lead in organising the event and handling the funds and collections. The driving force behind the Irish Flag Day was James McGhee, Provisional Secretary for Scotland of the AOH and secretary of the Irish Flag Day.

On the run-up to the day on 6 February, there was the inevitable intervention of Nationalist and Unionist politics with a heated debate over the design of the Irish Flag. The Unionists thought it should be green, superimposed with an Irish harp with a crown; the Irish Nationalists favoured the harp but with no crown. The final design was a gold harp without a crown on a ground of dark green. The collectors comprised 8000 women and girls from all over Scotland, 4000 in Glasgow alone. In addition to the women associated with the AOH, Catholic schoolteachers played a large part in the running of the day, but the event drew together all classes and creeds in aid of the Belgians. There was some trepidation regarding the wisdom of organising yet another flag day, the eleventh such event since the first back in September. Many felt the format was played out and that something different should be attempted.

In the event, the decision to go ahead with the flag day was taken and in preparation for the event over 13,000 collection boxes were issued with 2,750,000 paper flags. Dozens of Roman Catholic schools, their teachers and pupils were all involved on the day. In Glasgow, the following were all involved: St Roch's, St Francis', St Luke's, Our Lady and St Francis', Charlotte Street; St Conval's, Pollokshaws; St Saviour's, Govan; St Joseph's, Tollcross; St Columba's; St Mungo's and St Mungo's Academy; St Bride's, Cambuslang and St Bridget's, Baillieston.

The morning of 6 February was cold, dull and drizzly but the weather improved somewhat as the day progressed. Most of the female collectors dressed up for the event with thousands of girls in traditional Irish costume. Their numbers were increased by a great number of young boys and girls who contributed to the success of the day. In Glasgow, the planned parade set off at 1500 hrs from the offices of the AOH on North Frederick Street. Led by two members on horses and the Rory Oge O'More War Pipe Band, the procession included a number of charabancs and coaches containing dignitaries, some dressed in character, with a couple of Irish jaunting cars. The Kenmure Industrial School Brass Band, the Springburn group of little Irish colleens, St Mungo's district brake and the Parkhead Minstrels followed, bringing up the rear. The parade route was from North Frederick Street, George Street, Duke Street, Parkhead Cross, Great Eastern Road, London Road, Bridgeton Cross, Govan Street, Nelson Street, King Street, Jamaica Street, Union Street, Bothwell Street, Sauchiehall Street, Renfield Street, St Vincent Street, George Square and back to North Frederick Street.

Irish Flag Day Colleen
(Courtesy of Glasgow Evening Times)

In Ayr, Father O'Malley as the local flag day convenor was deeply involved in the success of the event, while in Greenock the success of the day was greatly enhanced by the visit of Celtic to play a League match against Morton with thousands of their Glasgow Irish supporters in the town.

Despite the unfavourable weather, the Irish Flag Day was an unprecedented success, collecting over £5500 and the organisers went to some pains to stress that the success was in no small part due to the help they received from very many Protestant ladies, who had been involved in organising similar events. The convener, David Mitchel Quin of the Glasgow Observer, was also moved to comment:

> On all hands this Irish enterprise on behalf of suffering Belgium elicited from the Scottish public not merely the financial response but also a neighbourly sympathy and friendliness very striking, very gratifying, and calculated, we hope to produce enduring result in the maintenance and extension of reciprocal good feelings.

CELTIC FC

On 6 February an estimated crowd of 10,000 watched the Celtic take on St Mirren at Parkhead. In the previous season's corresponding fixture, the Buddies had run out winners by 2–0. Arriving at Parkhead in good form, the visitors had high hopes of at least securing a point. In the first half the Celts played into a stiff breeze, but despite having the elements against them, Jimmy 'Sniper' McColl scored twice. After the break, the Celts, with the wind in their favour, again dominated the game, but stout defending by the St Mirren backline kept the Bhoys at bay. With just three minutes to go, the St Mirren forwards broke away to score a late goal when a short-range shot from Brannick beat Charlie Shaw. The goal ensured a nervous few minutes until the finish for the Celtic faithful. McMaster at wing half received the plaudits and was the man of the match. *The Man in the Know* thought he was the best left half at Parkhead since the great Willie Orr. However, Johnny had picked up a knock after colliding with Joe Dodds, which would keep him out for the next game against Morton. The Celtic side on the day was: Shaw, McNair and Dodds; Young, Johnstone and McMaster; McAtee, Gallacher, McColl, McMenemy and Browning.

At Tynecastle, 8000 spectators watched Hearts beat Kilmarnock 3–1, with, according to John McCartney, most of the first team players ill with assorted ailments. However, Tom Gracie, who scored Hearts' second goal, was, according to the Scotsman, more like his old self. Rangers saw off Falkirk 3–0 at Ibrox Park. No change, therefore, at the top of the League table.

On 13 February, the Celts travelled to Greenock minus Johnny McMaster, but with two special trainloads of supporters for the second League game in February. Morton were having a good season, currently occupying fourth place in the League. Although they never saw themselves as outright League winners, they did see themselves among the placed horses at the finishing post. A victory over Celtic on the day would put them well in the running. It was a wild day at Cappielow with a strong wind blowing in from the Firth of Clyde. From the start, Morton pressed hard, fast, and close, giving the Celtic players little time to settle on the ball. Despite the close attention, a goal from Patsy Gallacher midway through the first half, which had more than just a hint of offside about it, opened the scoring for the Celts. The Morton players protested vehemently, but the referee, Humphrey, dismissed their pleas. After the restart, Morton opened strongest and driven forward by their midfield, their forwards created a few longer-range shooting opportunities and the wingers sent over some tempting crosses, but generally the Celtic defence was never under any great pressure. Midway through the second half, a fine solo effort by 'Sniper' McColl ended Morton's hopes when he fired in Celtic's second goal. Near the close, Seymour managed to pierce the Celtic defence and had only Shaw to beat, but Charlie charged him down, forcing the little Englishmen to chip over the bar. It was a hard-fought contest, but the better team undoubtedly won. Gallacher and McColl were the stars on the day, both showing a hunger and desire for the ball. Both their goals were the result of their determination and drive. Alex 'Icicle' McNair and Tom McGregor were steadfast in defence and made a major contribution to the victory. The Morton management found consolation in the best gate receipts of the season, thanks to the Celtic's travelling support boosting the crowd to over 10,000. The Celtic side was Shaw, McNair, McGregor, Young, Johnstone, Dodds, McAtee, Gallacher, McColl, McMenemy and Browning.

That same Saturday, League leaders Heart of Midlothian was playing away to the Steelmen at Fir Park. McCrae's battalion had spent the Thursday night before the game wandering around the Pentland Hills lost in a blizzard. The battalion was in a very serious predicament and was only rescued when two former gamekeepers with local knowledge stepped out of the ranks to lead the battalion off the hills, thereby saving many lives. The entire battalion got the Friday off to recover from the ordeal. The crowd of 9000 that turned out at Fir Park saw an entertaining game between Hearts and Motherwell. The home side was the more aggressive over the first twenty minutes without greatly threatening the Hearts goal. Hearts then came more into the game and, notwithstanding Motherwell going down to ten men midway through the first half, failed to capitalise on the advantage despite having Pat Crossan back in the side after injury and playing his best game of the season. Over much of the second half, Motherwell continued to hold its own defensively until the closing stages, when the relentless Hearts pressure finally told and Harry Wattie scored to secure for Hearts a narrow and somewhat undeserved 0–1 victory.

Earlier that week, yet another Celtic old bhoy Thomas Clifford took the plunge and enlisted into the Royal Scots Fusiliers. On his attestation form, he lied about his age, claiming to be thirty-four when he was in fact forty. Kilbirnie born, Tom had had a season at Luton Town when he signed for the Bhoys in August 1901. He remained on the Celtic books for three seasons but failed, like so many others, to make the breakthrough into the first team and was offloaded to Motherwell in 1904. That week, Celtic goalie Charlie Shaw also took the plunge, this time into the world of business when he opened a newsagents and tobacconist shop at Bridgeton Cross. Patsy Gallacher was another Celtic player forced to confront the changing circumstances brought on by the war. In mid-February, he went back to work as a ship's carpenter, building dreadnoughts at Clydebank. At the same time 'Smiler' Browning found himself employed Monday to Friday in an engineering shop, while Jimmy McCall returned to his old trade of riveting. In fact, by this time most of the Celtic players were gainfully engaged over the working week in occupations other than football.

On 13 February, it was reported in the press that Rangers FC had to date sent sixty-nine footballs to military units. That same Saturday, *the Man in the Know* commented on the footballs that Celtic had sent to the front-line units:

> *Celts' Gifts to Soldiers.*
>
> *No club has done more than Celtic to make our soldiers happy at the front by sending out footballs and none has received less credit. That is because they do not advertise at Parkhead. Their charitable and sportsmanlike actions are done by stealth and we would hear nothing of them but for an occasional acknowledgement such as appeared this week from the 7th Cavalry Brigade. A football from Maley reached them a few hours before they were due in the trenches, and they made the most of their time, to the astonishment of a number of cows and the detriment of the farmyard. It is pathetic to read that when their ten day spell in the trenches was over the soldier writer hoped that: the survivors' would enjoy many a good game with the ball provided by the Celtic club.*

Saturday 20 February saw the Celtic take on Dumbarton at Parkhead while Hearts faced Rangers at Tynecastle. The gap between Hearts and Celtic at the top of the League was still four points, but Rangers were considered a major obstacle for Hearts in the dash for the title. The Sons of the Rock were sitting in the middle of the League table when they arrived at Parkhead to face the champions. Johnny McMaster was back after missing the Morton game, but was not up to scratch, obviously still suffering from the injury picked up against St Mirren. Otherwise, a full-strength Celtic side took to the field. From start to finish, it was a case of backs to the wall for Dumbarton. On twelve minutes after some clever wing play, Browning squared the ball to McColl, who smashed his shot past the Dumbarton keeper. McColl had scored his twenty-first goal for the season and the only goal of the game. It was a workmanlike performance from the Bhoys as they attempted to break down a stubborn Dumbarton defence. On the odd occasion that Dumbarton ventured forward, McNair and his backs ensured one goal would be enough for Celtic. A crowd of around 5,000 watched the game and the loudest cheer of the day was not when McColl scored, but when the half-time score at Tynecastle was raised on the board. In Edinburgh, the Rangers led Hearts by 0–2.

In the capital, Hearts went on to suffer only their second defeat of the season and the first at Tynecastle when they went down 3–4 to Rangers. The visitors from Glasgow were four up with only ten minutes to go, when Hearts, in an amazing rally that belied their supposed military fatigue, scored three goals in eight minutes, hit the post and even missed a penalty, but it was too late to grab the equaliser. The crowd of 16,000, which included 1000 travelling Rangers fans, witnessed a truly astounding match and one that most neutrals agreed Hearts deserved something from. The Hearts lead at the top of the table was cut to two points. It is not often the Rangers are cheered by the Parkhead faithful, but this was certainly one of those rare occurrences.

McCrae's Royal Scots were now well into the first phase of their military training with long route marches and tramps over the Pentlands or Braid Hills the order of the day. The battalion had also received a painful course of inoculations a couple of days prior to the Rangers game. After the defeat, John McCartney announced that Crossan, Wattie, Currie and Briggs had all been sick at half-time and had only played on because there was no one else available. The typhoid jabs were notorious in military circles and very often men reacted badly, suffering for days with nausea and sickness. When it was suggested that the Hearts slip was due to military training, *the Man in the Know* was having none of it:

> *Heroes or Martyrs?*
>
> *Of course over training is put down as the cause of the leader's defeat and we are told that ninety minutes of Swedish drill on Saturday morning finished the soldier lads for the rest of the day. If Hearts win the league they will be heroes, but if they lose the race for the championship, it will have been down to their military training and they will be seen as martyrs.*

He thought, therefore, that should Celtic take the League flag yet again, they would get no credit for the achievement. The Glasgow Observer also reported that Private John Francis McKillop, nephew of the recently deceased Celtic director John McKillop, had arrived back in Glasgow. He had been repatriated home from a French military hospital to recover from severe frostbite and trench foot.

A try by Gallagher. the Celtic forward, in the match with Partick Thistle at Firhill. From left to right the players are: Bulloch Gallagher, Hamilton, and Morrison. All of them played a conspicuous part in a strenuous match.

A Patsy Gallacher raid into the Thistle defence

The Celtic's last game in the month was an away tie at Firhill on 27 February. It was a tricky game for the Celtic and one that took careful planning. Partick Thistle were going well in the League, sitting in sixth place, three points behind Morton, but with two games in hand. A sizeable crowd of 30,000 hardy annuals, including around 4000 soldiers, braved wintry weather to watch the game and to listen to the Harry Lauder Pipe Band, which put in an appearance as a part of a recruitment drive. From the kick-off, the Jags were the more aggressive and pressed the Celts back into their own half. Several chances presented themselves, but wild shooting saw the opportunities squandered. After weathering the Thistle's early storming play, the Celtic came more into the match and soon settled into their usual attacking game. McColl opened the scoring for the Bhoys after latching onto a precisely judged through ball from McMenemy. A second goal for Celtic came after Patsy Gallacher was brought down in the box and Joe Dodds stepped up to score from the penalty kick. Throughout the game, Partick Thistle had plenty of the ball, but never threatened to breach a solid Celtic defence. The Celtic side on the day were Shaw, McNair and Dodds; Young, Johnstone and McMaster; McAtee and Gallacher; and McColl, McMenemy and Browning. Apparently, not a single recruit was enlisted at Firhill.

Hearts, meanwhile, were playing away to city rivals Hibernian. The Edinburgh derby at Easter Road was watched by 15,000 spectators. According to the Glasgow Herald's sports commentator, Hearts had by far the best of the exchanges and, but, for a marked weakness in front of the goal, might have won with ease. The game ended in a 2–2 draw, all the more disappointing for Hearts since they completely dominated from start to finish and really should have won convincingly.

THE WAR FRONT

Over the winter of 1914/15, Germany was forced to bolster Austria-Hungary's forces fighting the Russians on the Eastern Front. Russia's rapid mobilisation and initial successes on the battlefield caused the German war planners great concern. Also of concern was the poor performance of the Austro-Hungarian Army. The German Supreme Command was obliged to move significant forces from the west to the east to reinforce its allies. German leaders would later describe their alliance with Austria–Hungary as 'like being shackled to a corpse'. The situation on the Eastern Front and the transfer of troops there would force the Germans to remain on the defensive in the west in 1915, while pressing forward in the east. Although they would achieve no major or strategic breakthrough there, once Russia had been defeated, the full weight of their forces could be redeployed against the British and French in the west. The Germans had been victorious at Tannenberg and the Masurian Lakes and the Russians were now under pressure from German and Austro-Hungarian forces in Poland. After Turkey's entry into the war, the Russians faced yet another enemy on its border. The Russians looked to their allies to help alleviate some of the pressure by engaging with the Ottoman Turks.

Officially a part of the Ottoman Empire, on the outbreak of the war, Egypt was in a curious position. It had been under the governance of the British since the early 1880s when they took control of Egypt to protect the strategically important Suez Canal. The canal is 101 miles long and connects the Red Sea and the Mediterranean. It was a vital supply route for British trade, allowing shipping to use the shorter route from India and other Asian and African parts of the Empire rather than go around the Cape of Good Hope.

When Turkey entered the war, the security of the Suez Canal became a major concern for the British. In mid-December 1914, Egypt was declared a British protectorate and was consequently at war with the enemies of Britain. By January 1915, there were over 70,000 British and Empire troops in Egypt with over 30,000 specifically assigned to protect the Suez Canal zone. At the beginning of December 1914, the 1st Australian and New Zealand Army Corps (ANZAC) arrived in Egypt en route to France. It was decided that the ANZACs would remain in Egypt both to train for war and to help bolster its defences. On 9 February, the British War Council decided as a precaution, to send troops to support the Allied naval operation in the Dardanelles where the Greek island of Lemnos had been occupied as a base for the Allied fleet. On 19 February, the Allied fleet began the bombardment of the outer forts at the mouth of the Dardanelles.

On the Western Front, the horrors of winter warfare in the trenches continued as incessant rain fell over northern France and Belgium adding to the torment of the soldiers. On 1 February, at Cuinchy, near La Bassee, Catholic Irishmen Lance-Corporal Michael O'Leary won one of the most celebrated Victoria Crosses of the entire war. Born at Macroom, Co. Cork, O'Leary was an excellent example of the adventurous Irishman. He first served in the Royal Navy, and then moved to Canada where he joined the North West Mounted Police before retuning to Britain to serve with the Irish Guards. Recalled as a reservist at the start of the war, he arrived in France on 23 November 1914 when he was assigned to No1 Company. Alongside his comrades, O'Leary suffered the atrocious winter conditions in the trenches and managed to get himself awarded a Mentioned in Dispatches. On 1 February, the Irish Guards in the line at Cuinchy, took part in a localised engagement when they assaulted German positions about 200 yards to their front. After an artillery barrage, O'Leary's company went over the top. Outstripping his comrades O'Leary was first on the enemy line and proceeded to clear two German machine gun positions. His Victoria Cross citation read 'For conspicuous bravery at Cuinchy on the 1st February, 1915. When forming one of the storming party which advanced against the enemy's barricades he rushed to the front and himself killed five Germans who were holding the first barricade, after which he attacked a second barricade, about 60 yards further on, which he captured, after killing three of the enemy and making prisoners of two more. Lance-Corporal O'Leary thus practically captured the enemy's position by himself and prevented the attacking party from being fired upon.'

O'Leary was later reported as saying that he attacked the second barricade because "he was intent on killing a German to whom he had taken a dislike" and was described as returning with his prisoners "as cool as if he had been for a walk in the park". Back in Inchigeela, near Macroom, his father apparently wasn't impressed; he told the local newspaper that he was surprised he only got eight.

Michael O'Leary was promoted sergeant in the field and shortly afterwards sent home. When on furlough O'Leary was feted and cheered as no VC hero had ever been. He received a tumultuous welcome in Cork, where the Mayor and the entire town turned out. John Redmond and the IPP then trooped Michael around Ireland where

Sergeant O'Leary VC at Hyde Park, London
(The Illustrated War News)

he spoke at numerous nationalist recruiting meetings. At some of the meetings he received a less than warm welcome from Irish Volunteers and Sinn Fein hecklers in the crowd. He received the award from the King at Buckingham Palace on 23 June. The greatest day in his life, however, would come on June 26, when Londoners turned out in tens of thousands to acclaim him in the streets. To honour him the London Irish organized a demonstration in Hyde Park, at which over 60,000 people were present. O'Leary drove from the Strand to the Park in an open carriage, cheered all along the route by thousands of admirers. Michael O'Leary was commissioned in October 1915 into the Connaught Rangers.

IRELAND

In Ireland, recruiting for the three Irish divisions went on apace, as did the propaganda battle between Nationalists and Unionists. The perceived shortfalls in Irish recruiting led several political commentators on the mainland to question the Irish recruiting system itself and why nothing was being done to create more enthusiasm. Suggestions were made to John Redmond, including one from the Permanent Under Secretary at the War Office, that perhaps a joint appeal by himself and Sir Edward Carson might be effective. That John Redmond had made such an appeal at the beginning of the war and had been ignored by Carson and the Unionists seemed to have been forgotten.

For several weeks, John Redmond had again been exerting pressure at Westminster for recognition and equipment for his National Volunteers. By now the Volunteers were disgusted and demoralised by the way they had been treated and as a direct result their attendance at drills and parades had fallen off. By mid-February, those Volunteers who had been enthused by the various appeals had already enlisted, while those disillusioned and disaffected had begun to drift away from the Volunteer movement. Eoin MacNeill's Irish Volunteers saw a steady increase in enlistment. They had never ceased to drill regularly and were gaining new followers as Nationalist discontent spread through the country. Over the whole of 1915, the Irish Volunteers were actively sowing sedition throughout Ireland by publishing anti-British recruiting posters and anti-war leaflets, and sending organisers abroad to enrol and train Volunteer recruits, while the leadership was active in organising and attending anti-recruitment meetings. James Connolly, while fighting the good fight for his Irish General Workers Union members and achieving some significant pay increases, was at the same time already planning his own socialist revolution in Ireland.

In addition to Redmond pleading for official recognition for his Volunteers, Major General Sir Lovick Friend, then Commander-in-Chief of Ireland, also threw his weight behind the scheme. In addition to soldiering, General Friend was a typical Victorian gentleman sportsman playing cricket and, unusually for his class, football. He played in goal for the army engineers team that was beaten 3–1 in the final of the 1878 FA Cup by the Wanderers. Lord Arthur Kinnaird, who in 1914 was the president of the FA, played in the winning Wanderers side.

General Friend wrote to the War Office suggesting that the Volunteers be recognised as an auxiliary force with special duties. He estimated the adoption of his plan would release 20,000 troops from Ireland. He privately showed John Redmond his message to the War Office and urged Redmond to lobby the Prime Minister. Redmond wrote personally to Asquith and, always impressed by Redmond's arguments, Asquith instructed Tennant to speak again to Kitchener on the matter. No sooner had the instructions been given, than Redmond received a letter from TP O'Connor on the same subject. He had spoken to Tennant, who had informed him that Kitchener would not consent to the proposals regarding the Volunteers and the reasons he had given were even more disturbing than the decision itself. Tennant had stated that Kitchener's view was that the creation of such a force would lead directly to civil war and perhaps to revolution. Kitchener pointed to the existence of another armed force in the north of Ireland, and that the creation of a second armed force must mean civil war. TP O'Connor pointed out to Tennant that this might be an excellent argument for disarming both forces, but it was not an argument for leaving one armed and the other unarmed. Tennant then said that Kitchener's strong opinion was that there were revolutionary forces in Ireland that the constitutional Nationalists could not control and of whose existence perhaps they were not even aware. After speaking to Tennant, O'Connor told Redmond: 'We are dealing with an Irish Orangeman [Kitchener] who takes the Irish Orange view, and who is determined in every way to strengthen the forces against us and weaken the forces for us.'

The letter from TP O'Connor had exposed a much more alarming aspect to Kitchener's attitude, and revealed the extremely serious apprehensions that had arisen among Redmond's colleagues as to the future of their party. As the combined effects of smears and insults to Irish Nationalist sensitivities mounted, recruiting as a popular movement in Ireland was slowly but effectively strangled. As the months passed, Redmond's gamble with Nationalist support, based on the assurances given by Asquith and his government, looked to be in trouble as no worthwhile results were forthcoming. As the war dragged on and it became increasingly obvious that Redmond's gamble had failed, his support for the British war effort began to bring irrevocable discredit upon both himself and the Irish Parliamentary Party.

The 36th (Ulster) Division also continued to have recruiting problems with the division being accused of recruiting without permission in Liverpool during February. By March, the situation was so serious the divisional commander wrote to Edward Carson and his Unionist MPs, pleading for help in recruiting. Meanwhile, in the north of Ireland, Joe Devlin was still doing his bit to raise Redmond's Irish Army. On 12 February, he was reported in the Irish News as saying: 'By taking part in this war effort, his supporters intended to claim a full and an increasing part share in the work and glory of the Empire, which the blood and brains of Irishmen have done so much to create.' A few days earlier, 100 Derry Nationalist recruits en route from Derry to the Irish Brigade at Fermoy had received gifts of pipes, tobacco and cigarettes and a 'Good Luck' message from wee Joe.

Chapter Ten

MARCH

CELTIC FC

At the beginning of March, Heart of Midlothian's lead at the top of the League table was down to just one point. Both Celtic and Hearts had seven games left to play. With four games at Parkhead, it was considered by the football pundits that the Celts had the easiest run-in. Hearts had three games at Tynecastle.

The remaining fixtures for both clubs looked like this:

HEARTS		CELTIC	
Dumbarton	Home	Hibernian	Home
Partick Thistle	Home	Raith Rovers	Home
Clyde	Home	Airdrieonians	Home
Airdrieonians	Away	Queen's Park	Away
Aberdeen	Away	Aberdeen	Home
Morton	Away	Third Lanark	Away
St Mirren	Away	Motherwell	Away

After allowing their five-point lead at the top of the table to slip to just one, a number of sports commentators had been writing about the Hearts losing their edge and blaming too much military training as opposed to football training. If indeed any of the power brokers at Tynecastle felt that was the case, it is inconceivable that the board, with its close business and personal ties to Sir George McCrae, would not have aired its concerns and discussed the effects military training was having on the performance of the football team. The Heart of Midlothian directors having acquiesced to Sir George McCrae's plea for support in raising his battalion, would have demanded his support in return to ensure the team be given the best possible chance to bring the League Championship flag back to Tynecastle for the first time since the 1896/97 season. As a Heart of Midlothian supporter himself, Sir George would have picked up any disquiet among the 600 Hearts supporters who had followed their heroes into his battalion. As they watched Hearts lead at the top of the League fall away, their supporters, both in and out of McCrae's battalion, were no doubt asking, with the League flag almost in their grasp, what the hell were the Hearts footballers doing wandering around the Braid Hills just hours before vital football games?

In early March something was done. It had already been reported in mid-February by the press that arrangements were being put in place for the Hearts players to be allowed to train under the club trainer at least twice a week over what was left of the season. Now it was announced that all heavy marching for the soldier-players would be curtailed.

As usual, *the Man in the Know*, never a man to mince his words, had his own opinions on what he subtitled 'Hearts playing Sodjers':

> *Every week Tynecastle enthusiasts are told to prepare for defeat because the 'we are seven' section have been route marching and all that sort of thing during the week, though you only have to speak to a Kitchener's man to learn that military training has made a man of him, that he feels like digesting horse nails and doing ten miles before breakfast. No, we are sportsmen and patriotic enough to wish the Hearts success in their fight for the flag, but this twaddle of aches and pains make us sick.*

On 6 March, the Celts faced Hibernian at Parkhead and 13,000 spectators made their way to the east end of Glasgow to watch the game. After their draw with Hearts the previous week, many pundits expected the Hibs to stretch the champions and for about twenty minutes they were indeed a match for their hosts with both sides threatening the other's goal. The Bhoys opened the scoring after Patsy Gallacher was brought down in the box and Dodds converted the penalty kick. Almost immediately after the restart, Hibernian struck back to level the score at 1–1. The Celtic then stepped up a gear to a level the Hibs simply could not match. Browning and McAtee added a goal each to take the Celtic in to the pavilion at the interval leading 3–1. After the restart, Celtic continued as they left off and two goals from Jimmy McMenemy sealed the Hibernian's fate. The Celtic then took their foot off the pedal and gave the spectators a demonstration of football wizardry, entertaining to watch, but producing no more goals. The resulting 5–1 victory sent a powerful message to the capital. The Celtic team on the day was Shaw, McNair and Dodds; Young, Johnstone and McMaster; McAtee, and Gallacher; and McColl, McMenemy and Browning.

At Tynecastle, a very impressive crowd of 15,000 watched Heart of Midlothian send out their own message as they put Dumbarton to the sword. The Daily Record sports reporter 'Donovan' thought the victory was the first fruits of the concession made by the military authorities in allowing the soldier-players to trip along to Tynecastle to practise two nights a week. He thought it wonderful how much tuning up could be done in an hour or two by the trainer, Jimmy Duckworth. Two goals by Tom Gracie and one from Graham saw the Hearts three goals to one up by half-time. Gracie got his hat-trick when he added another goal in the second half, which saw the Hearts running out easy winners by 4–1. After the game the Heart of Midlothian directors declared themselves well satisfied with the performance of the team. With Celtic and Hearts both winning, the gap at the top of the League remained one point in Hearts' favour. One of the by-products of the Hearts directors' decision to allow their players to enlist was an upsurge in support for the team. As a consequence, their home gates improved drawing in many previously uncommitted supporters.

On 9 March, yet another sudden death shocked the Celtic family. Wine and spirit merchant Patrick Colgan, brother of Celtic director Thomas Colgan, was found dead at his place of work in John Knox Street, Dennistoun having suffered a brain haemorrhage. Belfast-born Pat was an ardent politician and gave many years of valuable service to the cause of Irish Nationalism.

At one time, he was the secretary of the Archbishop Walsh branch of the National League in Parkhead. He was also for a time the secretary of the Home Government Branch. His funeral cortege to Dalbeth was like a who's who of Celtic FC and Glasgow Irish Nationalists and included in addition to the Colgan family, Willie Maley, James Kelly, Thomas White, John Shaughnessy, Michael Dunbar, Arthur Murphy and James McKillop.

On Saturday 13 March, Celtic played Irish League side Glentoran FC at Parkhead. The friendly game was arranged at short notice to fill a vacant date in the fixture list caused by the cancellation of the Scottish Cup. Thanks to the enterprise of the Celtic management, the Glasgow footballing public got a chance to see another Irish League team at Parkhead. A crowd of 6000 watched the game, which saw the appearance of veteran Jimmy Quinn and the first appearance in green and white hoops of Patrick McCabe. A mad Celtic fan, it was a dream come true for Pat when he signed for the team he loved on 9 March from East Stirlingshire. The young left-winger, described as 'cleverly', was also wanted by Liverpool and Clyde. At Parkhead, Willie Maley saw the youngster as a potential standby for the ever reliable Johnny Browning. On the day, Glentoran made an early show, but Celtic's class soon told and two goals from the Mighty Quinn and one from Pat McCabe saw off the visitors. Towards the end of the game, Charlie Shaw received an injury and went off to be replaced in goal by Joe Dodds. The Celtic side on the day was Shaw, McNair and Dodds; Young, Johnstone and McMaster; and McAtee, Gallacher, Quinn, McMenemy and McCabe. The Glentoran side was Murphy; McCann and Granger; Ferrett, Scraggs, and Emerson; and Lynar, Moore, Boyd, Duff and Lindsay. Young McCabe impressed Willie Maley, but would have to wait until October 1916 before he would get a chance to shine in the first team. It would be his only other appearance in the hoops and by December 1916 he was serving with the Scots Guards. Meanwhile he was sent back on loan to East Stirling.

That same weekend, at Broomfield Park, Airdrie, a crowd of 10,000 watched an in-form Airdrieonians hold Hearts to a 2–2 draw. Hearts had led by two goals after just nine minutes, but Airdrie got one back just before half-time. The second half was a fast-flowing end-to-end encounter with either side just as likely to score. Halfway through the half, a bad mistake by Hearts goalkeeper Jimmy Boyd allowed Airdrie a soft equalising goal. Airdrie then went down to ten men, and Hearts launched a series of increasingly desperate attacks, but try as they might they could not get back their lead and the game finished in a draw. The result saw Hearts increase their lead over Celtic to two points, fifty-six to fifty-four, but Celtic now had a game in hand, Hearts having played thirty-three games to Celtic's thirty-two.

FOOTBALL AS USUAL?

Saturday 20 March saw the worthies of the four national football leagues meet in Glasgow. The Royal Hotel on George Square was the venue and J McKenna of Liverpool FC presided. The meeting was called to discuss the ongoing financial crisis facing the professional game and the enlistment of professional footballers into the military. Top of the agenda were, of course, recruiting and how the clubs might be able to save money. The introduction of special war agreements with the professional players, including the abolition of close season wages and a new maximum wage, were discussed.

As far as recruiting was concerned, the surrender of full international matches and the Scottish Cup, had largely taken the sting out of the 'Stop Football' cohorts in Scotland; however, English football was still in deep trouble. The raising of the Footballer's Legion (17th Bn Middlesex Regiment) formed back in November in a blaze of publicity had been a disaster. The recruiting drive had begun well enough and around thirty-five professional footballers enlisted on the first day, but the recruiting campaign faltered and by the middle of March 1915, only a hundred or so professional footballers had enrolled into the battalion. The figures were so bad, the battalion's commanding officer wrote to the English League warning that he would go public with the facts and figures. A week later he did exactly that. The newspaper headlines screamed: 'Are Players Without Patriotism?' and 'A Serious Indictment'. Not only did Lieutenant Colonel Grantham highlight the fact that despite there being 1800 professional footballers in the English leagues, only 122 had enlisted. He alluded to the fact that some clubs and their directors had actively prevented their players from enlisting. He also stated that with the formation of the Footballer's Battalion public opinion had calmed down regarding the patriotism of professional footballers under the belief that professionals were enlisting into the battalion. The revelations in Lieutenant Colonel Grantham's letter, whose son had been killed in action a fortnight earlier, reignited the debate with a bang. It was effectively the straw that broke the camel's back of English football. The English public's perception was that the Footballer's Battalion was manned entirely by professional footballers, but that never was the case. In fact, at the time of the colonel's letter, the battalion was fairly well recruited with almost 900 men in the ranks. With its perceived failure went the FA's hopes of carrying on anything like 'business as usual'. The FA finally recognised the writing on the wall and capitulated to Charrington and his cohorts. The 1915 FA Cup final was held at Manchester well away from it historic home at the Crystal Palace in London. The Admiralty had already commandeered the famous old stadium for training the Naval Brigade. Arrangements were put in place to reorganise professional English football onto a regional basis with players only paid travelling expenses. The 'Stop Football' fanatics had won their war in England and at the end of the 1914/15 season, professional football was effectively suspended.

The Glasgow meeting ended with nothing definite decided but it was agreed that the leagues would meet again at Blackpool after the season had finished and a date at the beginning of July was pencilled in.

THE WAR FRONT

On the Western Front, as winter slowly released its grip on the land, the generals' minds began to turn to offensive action. Over the winter months, more British divisions had arrived in France and the BEF was split into two armies. Following months of suffering in the miserable conditions of the trenches, most of the ordinary soldiers were eager to see the situation moved forward. The Battle of Neuve-Chapelle would be fought over 10 to 13 March and was launched with the aim of capturing the Aubers Ridge. The feature lay a mile or so ahead of the British, and despite being barely twenty feet higher than the surrounding area, it gave an observation advantage to its occupiers. Capturing the ridge would threaten the German Army occupying the strategically important city of Lille.

The village of Neuve-Chapelle lies on the road between Bethune, Fleurbaix and Armentières and the front lines ran parallel to the Bethune–Armentières road. It was the first large-scale organised attack conducted by the British during the Great War and was undertaken by Sir Douglas Haig's First Army. The plan was to attack using three infantry brigades, two British (23rd and 25th) from the 8th Division and the Garhwal Brigade of the Meerut Indian Division. They would assault along a very narrow frontage of just 4000 yards, break through the German lines and advance as far eastward as possible towards the Aubers Ridge. Reinforcements would then take over the assault, and capture and occupy the ridge.

On the morning of Wednesday 10 March at 0730 hrs with a roar that shook the earth, the most destructive and withering artillery action of the war up to that time began. More shells, mostly shrapnel, were fired by the 342 guns assigned to the operation during the thirty-five-minute barrage than were fired over the course of the entire Boer War.

At 0805 hrs, the first wave of assaulting British and Indian infantry went over the top. In the centre and on the right of the assault the artillery had done its job, cutting the barbed wire defences and pulverising both the German trenches and the village itself. The assaulting troops from the 25th Brigade and the Garhwal Brigade were soon through the German lines and fighting around the village itself. However, on the left (north) of the village, the wire and German trenches had survived the bombardment intact. The 23rd Brigade had been assigned to this sector of the assault and leading the attack was the 2nd Bn Scottish Rifles. The battalion recruited mainly from Glasgow and Lanarkshire and had attracted very many of the Glasgow Irish into its ranks. As the Scottish Rifles closed with the German trenches, they ran into the uncut wire and were scythed down in swathes by machine gunfire to their front and flank. The men tore at the wire with their bare hands in an attempt to fight their way through, but over the course of an hour the battalion lost most of its officers and hundreds of men killed or wounded. Eventually, a new artillery fire plan was launched onto the uncut wire and trenches and a single company of the battalion got through the gap and overran the German positions.

In the second wave of the 25th Brigade, the 2nd Bn Rifle Brigade and the 1st Bn Royal Irish Rifles swept through the captured German lines and into the village, clearing the enemy before them. The village had been pulverised by the artillery, even the village churchyard was devastated, the very dead blown from their graves. Broken coffins and ancient bones lay scattered about amid the fresher dead, the slain of that morning in grey-green forms sprawled among the tombs. All that was left intact in that once fair village were two great crucifixes reared aloft, one in the churchyard, the other over against the château. From the cross, the figure of Christ, intact though all pitted with bullet marks, looked down in mute agony on the slain in the village.

After fighting their way through to the edge of the village, both battalions halted, dug in and awaited reinforcements. Both battalions had taken casualties during the assault, the Rifle Brigade having lost thirteen men killed and sixty wounded. The Irish Rifles had lost fifty men killed and 100 wounded. In the afternoon, after some delay due to a breakdown in communications, the advance was continued by fresh troops with the British line pushed forward a mile almost to the Aubers Ridge itself. As darkness fell, the advance was halted having reached the limit of effective artillery support.

On 11 March, having fully recovered from their surprise, the Germans made a number of counter-attacks that were beaten off and over the course of the day little progress was made by either side. That night significant German forces arrived in the area to reinforce their defences. On 12 March, the British launched another assault. The Rifle Brigade and the Irish Rifles were again ordered to attack. Their first assault failed, being immediately met by savage crossfire; the second went later in the afternoon and once more failed, this time with even more casualties. Between 10 and 12 March, the Royal Irish Rifles lost 409 men killed, wounded or missing. Among the 377 casualties suffered by the Rifle Brigade was Irish Republican Maud Gonne's nephew, twenty-one-year-old Lieutenant Thomas Percy Pilcher, killed on 12 March while leading one of the Rifle Brigade's platoons.

Maud Gonne was the daughter of a wealthy British Army officer. After her widowed father died in 1886, she and her sister spent some time in London before moving to France. There she met and had an affair with Lucien Millevoye, a journalist and politician whose marriage had broken down. The affair with Millevoye ended in 1898, but not before she bore him two children and joined the Irish Republican Brotherhood. In 1900, she returned to Ireland where she founded *Inghinidhe na hÉireann* (Daughters of Ireland), a women's Republican movement, and opposed Boer War recruitment for Irish regiments. Together with William Butler Yates, she founded the Abbey Theatre in Dublin. In 1902, she played Yeats' Cathleen ni Houlihan, symbolising Ireland's struggle when she shed the appearance of an old crone to become 'a young girl with the walk of a queen'. In 1903, she married Major John MacBride, who had formed an Irish brigade to fight the British during the Boer War; after the birth of their son Sean, their marriage failed. Major John McBride would be executed after the 1916 rising. In 1918, Maud was interned and she spent some months in Holloway Prison in London. On her release, she organised relief during the War of Independence, and alongside the sister of Sir John French, Charlotte Despard, assisted Republican prisoners and their dependents during the Irish Civil War. Imprisoned without charge by the Free State government in 1923, she was released after going on hunger strike. Maud's son Sean McBride became Chief of Staff of the IRA in 1936. Maud Gonne died on 27 April 1953 and is buried in the Republican plot at Glasnevin Cemetery.

By the end of 12 March, it was clear that the British could not gain control of the Aubers Ridge, while the Germans could not recapture Neuve-Chapelle. Sir John French ordered that the ground won be held and consolidated. The result of the fight was that the British line had been advanced about a mile along a narrow frontage. Although the main advance had been halted, sporadic fighting continued on and off for the next five days or so. The 1st Bn HLI took part in the assault on 11 March and remained in the line until relieved on 18 March. The battalion suffered over seventy men killed that last day, and 104 during their time in the line. The gains had come at a considerable cost, with the Celtic regiments suffering serious casualties in men killed, wounded or missing. The 2nd Royal Scots Fusiliers had lost 307, the 2nd Bn Scot Rifles 469, the 1st Bn HLI 300 and the 1st Bn Royal Irish Regiment 409. With the Royal Scots Fusiliers, Scot Rifles and the HLI all recruiting from Glasgow and Lanarkshire, the casualties hit the city and its environs hard. By 19 March, the wounded from the fight at Neuve-Chapelle were arriving in Glasgow and long casualty lists began to appear in the Glasgow newspapers. Among the 170 men killed from the Scottish Rifles, ten were native Irishmen, thirty-six were born in Glasgow's Barony Parish, nine were born in Govan and another dozen were listed as being born in Glasgow district. Of the 104 killed with the 1st Bn HLI, thirty-seven were listed as Glaswegians, six men were from Coatbridge and five were native Irishmen.

L/Corporal Willie Angus 8th HLI
(Courtesy of the Angus Family)

In his report to Lord Kitchener, Sir John French estimated British casualties over the three days of the battle, 10th to 13th, to have been over 12,600 all ranks killed, wounded or missing. Although the British broke through the German front line and captured the village of Neuve-Chapelle, they failed to capture the vital Aubers Ridge. Neuve-Chapelle demonstrated that it was quite possible to break into the enemy positions, but also showed that it was not easy then to exploit the hard-won gains by breaking through and beyond them. The main lessons of Neuve-Chapelle were that despite some successes the artillery bombardment was too light, with too few high explosive shells available to suppress the enemy defences and cut the barbed wire. There were too few good artillery pieces. The reserves were too few to follow up success quickly. Command communications took too long and the means of communicating (wire) was too vulnerable.

On 1 March, the 8th Bn Royal Scots as part of 22nd Brigade, 7th Infantry Division, had taken over the Pincantin Sector of the front line and on 10 March the battalion had played a minor role in the Battle of Neuve-Chapelle where it manned forward trenches, but was not required to take part in the advance. Having spent three weeks in quarantine, Willie Angus and the remainder of the draft arrived at the battalion on 12 March while it was still in the area around Neuve-Chapelle. On arrival, the HLI men were posted into D Company, which was the HLI Company. Lance Corporal Willie Angus and the men of the new draft would have had their first taste of trench life a couple of days later when the battalion went back into the front line. Over the course of the next four days, three men were killed and another half dozen wounded. Among those who died from his wounds received during that tour in the line was Lance Corporal William Brooks from Carluke. Willie had arrived in France along with Willie Angus and the new HLI draft.

In London, another old Celt was about to receive his marching orders. On 24 March 1915, at Caterham Barracks, Willie McOustra's name appeared on the draft list. He was one of a 100-strong draft posted to the 2nd Bn Scots Guards. The battalion was in France with the BEF, part of the 20th Brigade, 7th Infantry Division. The 2nd Bn Scots Guards had been involved in the Battle of Neuve-Chapelle and on 12 March they had suffered over 200 casualties during an attack. After being withdrawn from the line, the battalion went into rest billets in the village of Laventie where it had a chance to reorganise and lick its wounds.

At Caterham, Willie's draft left the depot on 25 March for Southampton, sailed overnight and the following morning landed in France at Le Havre. After a long train journey and a final approach march, Willie McOustra and his draft caught up with the battalion on 27 March when they marched into Laventie. The weather was cold and frosty, but the long march up to the village worked up a sweat. After a few hours being messed about by the battalion clerks and quartermaster staff, the men were allocated to companies and went off to find their company headquarters.

TURKEY and the DARDANELLES

At the Dardanelles, the Anglo-French naval operations that had begun in mid-February were not going according to plan. The Turkish mobile artillery pieces proved to be impossible to destroy from the sea and the numerous trawlers whose task was to sweep the waters clear of sea mines were badly damaged by the mobile artillery units operating on both the Gallipoli and Asiatic sides of the Dardanelles. It was becoming increasingly apparent that the Royal Navy would need Army support, boots on the ground, specifically to capture the Gallipoli peninsula, the heights of which commanded the Dardanelles Straits. On 4 March, the ANZACs arrived on Lemnos, having been transferred from Egypt. Six days later the British War Council decided to assign the 29th Division to the operation.

On 12 March, General Sir Ian Hamilton waited nervously outside Lord Kitchener's office. He had received a summons, quite out of the blue, to the War Lord's office and he was very uneasy. The last time he had felt this nervous was when his headmaster had summoned him unexpectedly and now, like then, he could not help but wonder what he had done wrong. Corfu born, Scotsman Ian Hamilton had worked closely with Kitchener during the South African War. He later described the meeting in his diary:

> After standing for a few moments in front of Kitchener's desk, K looked up and said in a matter-of-fact voice, 'We are sending a military force to support the fleet now at the Dardanelles and you are to have Command.' At that moment K wished me to bow, leave the room and make a start ... but my knowledge of the Dardanelles was nil; of the Turk nil; of the strength of our own forces nil ... Although I had met K almost every day over the last six months and although he twice hinted that I might be sent to Salonika; never once to my recollection did he ever mention the Dardanelles.

Ian Hamilton managed to summon up enough courage to ask Kitchener a few pertinent questions to which he got short, sharp answers. Within forty-eight hours, he was on board a British warship en route to the Dardanelles having managed to acquire a single map of the area. It was a portent of things to come and set the stage for what was already doomed to become a completely inadequate military operation.

By 17 March, Ian Hamilton was in theatre and in time to watch the latest Anglo-French naval attempt to force the Dardanelles. About fourteen miles from the mouth of the straits, the channel narrows to just one mile across. The bottleneck had been sown with an extensive minefield and was covered by Turkish artillery. The attack was another disaster with three battleships sunk and two other ships badly damaged. General Hamilton, while on board ship, took the opportunity to check out possible invasion beaches on the Gallipoli peninsula. After the latest naval failure, Hamilton sent a telegram to Kitchener stating that only a combined naval and army operation could hope to succeed. On 22 March, the decision to mount a combined operation was taken; unfortunately, it would take a month for Ian Hamilton to organise his army and that could only be done in Egypt. Ian Hamilton departed for Alexandria, telling the Navy he would be back in a month with the army. The Turkish defenders on Gallipoli, under German military expertise, would put that month to very good use.

CELTIC FC

On 20 March, Celtic Park was the venue for the twenty-fourth League international between Scotland and England. The gates were opened at 1.30 pm and soldiers were admitted at half price (3d) at two special gates, one in Janefield Street and one on the London Road side of the ground. The band of the Westthorn Reformatory provided entertainment before the game and at half-time. Seats in the Grant Stand were sold out days before the game. The Celtic contributed four players, McNair, Dodds, McAtee and McMenemy. Heart of Midlothian contributed two, Nellies and Wilson. Charlie Shaw and Johnny McMaster were unused reserves. On the day, the Scotland side was completely outplayed by its opponents and went down to a surprising 1–4 defeat. Scotland captain Joe Dodds scored the Scots' only goal from a penalty kick.

While the Scots were being completely outclassed at Parkhead, Willie Maley took the remnants of the Celtic team down to Clydebank to play his wee brother Alex's side. This latest incarnation of Clydebank FC had only been formed in May 1914 and had been due to join the Scottish Third Division at the start of the new 1914/15 season. However, for the start of the new season the Second Division had been expanded from twelve to fourteen clubs and with the local shipyards booming, Clydebank was promoted up a division without having to kick a ball. Under the youngest of the four Maley brothers, the Bankies had done well in their first season and now sat in fourth place in the League, seven points behind the leaders, but with a game in hand. The Celtic were turning out on the Bankies' new Clydeholm Park, the first senior club to do so. With four of the Celts stars on international duty and Patsy Gallacher injured, the Parkhead side was always going to be something of a scratch team. Willie Maley therefore took the opportunity to try out two new lads, Higgins and Glachan. The Celtic team on the day was Shaw, McGregor, Higgins, Glachan, Johnstone, McMaster, Crone, McColl, Quinn, Browning and Wilson. The 3000-strong crowd that turned up on the day were disappointed to learn that their local hero, Patsy Gallacher, was injured, and would only run the line for the Celts. However, the appearance of the famous Jimmy Quinn went some way to make up for their disappointment. When local reporters pointed out that Jimmy had only played a half dozen times this season, Willie Maley assured them that the mighty one had been training at Parkhead and was as fit as a fiddle.

From the kick-off, the Celtic, with a stiff breeze at their back, went immediately into the attack, but after about ten minutes, Clydebank broke out from defence. A long ball landed at the feet of on-loan Celt Joe O'Kane, who cleverly trapped it and shot past a helpless Charlie Shaw to put the Bankies one up. Both sides then attacked alternately and both went close to scoring with good efforts. During one Celtic attack, Jimmy Quinn fired a hard shot towards the Clydebank goal. The goalie seemed to have the shot covered before a wicked deflection diverted the ball into the net. Five minutes later, after Clydebank had again been pressing, 'Handsome' Billy Crone broke up field to score the Celtic's second goal. Just minutes later the Mighty Quinn went on one of his rampaging runs of old, swerved past three players to fire in an unstoppable shot. The goal took the Celts into the interval somewhat undeservedly two goals to the good.

At the restart, the Celts resumed where they had left off, but despite having most of the possession for the first twenty minutes failed to break through. The Celts then got a warning shot fired in by Joe O'Kane, which Charlie Shaw just managed to hold. As the Celtic attack faltered, Clydebank took control of the mid-field and began to dominate the game. The last twenty minutes saw the Celts completely torn to ribbons as the Bankies ran riot. A goal from Wilson and an eighteen-yard screamer from Thompson brought the sides level. Worse was to come, this time at the hands of Joe O'Kane when the Maryhill lad scored twice in quick succession to get his hat-trick. The game ended in an embarrassing 3–5 defeat for the Celtic. Just to rub salt into the wounds, Billy Crone picked up an injury. *The Man in the Know* was impressed with young O'Kane, and thought he would be called into the first team squad come August. The Clydebank game was the last time the Mighty Jimmy Quinn turned out in a competitive match for the Celtic. Despite the defeat, some solace was to be had in the nature and quality of Jimmy Quinn's last competitive goal.

In the League that weekend Hearts beat Partick Thistle 3–1 at Tynecastle. The visitors started off strongest and went into the lead midway through the first half, before Hearts came back just before half time to level the score. In the second half Hearts produced a brilliant display and scored twice to gain a well deserved victory. Elsewhere, Morton beat Motherwell 2–0. Clyde achieved a surprise 3–1 victory over Ayr United at Firhill and Aberdeen beat Airdrie 3–0 at Pittodrie. With three players on international duty at Parkhead, Rangers had the weekend off.

That week also saw Willie Maley attending the AGM of St Peter's Amateur Athletic Club, Partick, of which he was an honorary member. He was given a vote of thanks for his support for the club and in his acceptance speech noted that eight members of the club had enlisted into the military.

The Celtic's last game in the month was played at Parkhead on 27 March. With Gallacher and Crone both out injured, Peter Johnstone was catapulted into the forward line, at his old position of inside left, Joe Dodds taking Johnstone's place in midfield alongside McMaster, while Tom McGregor filled in at the back. The visitors, Raith Rovers sitting third bottom in the League, came to Glasgow with a full-strength side. The Fifers kicked off with the wind at their backs, but were soon pinned into their own half by a series of concerted Celtic attacks. After ten minutes, McColl scored from short range after a ferocious shot from McAtee could only be palmed away by the Rover's goalie. Fifteen minutes later, the Bhoys got a second goal when a long ball fired forward by Tom McGregor was latched onto by McColl who raced through to score. Jimmy McMenemy picked up a knee injury and was forced to retire for the remainder of the half. McMenemy reappeared for the second half, but was a passenger for the rest of the game. A blizzard sprung up during the later part of the game, which made conditions difficult for all the players. Celtic continued to pressurise the Raith defence and only good goalkeeping kept the Celts from scoring on several occasions. Raith Rovers then broke away to threaten Charlie

Shaw's goal, but an excellent chance was squandered. Five minutes later with Celtic ignoring the warning, Raith again broke. This time the chance was taken and Celtic's lead was reduced to the minimum. With only fifteen minutes to go, the roles were suddenly reversed; Raith Rovers were doing all the attacking and on two occasions Shaw's goal was severely threatened. Finally, the Parkhead faithfuls' nerves were settled when Celtic broke upfield and McAtee whipped in a cross, which McColl met with his head to bullet the ball past the helpless Raith keeper.

The highly entertaining game ended with a somewhat flattering 3–1 victory for the Bhoys and a hat-trick for Sniper McColl. Peter Johnstone, showing his versatility back in the forward line, looked uncomfortable at times, while the attack was fettered throughout the second half by McMenemy's injury. As for Raith Rovers, many teams have played a lot worse at Parkhead and left with a share of the points. The Celtic team on the day was Shaw, McNair and McGregor; Young, Dodds and McMaster; and McAtee, McMenemy, McColl, Johnstone and Browning.

With the Celtic not playing League football over two weekends in mid-March, the League table at the end of the month showed the Bhoys still in second place on fifty-six points, but now had two games in hand, with five games left to play. Heart of Midlothian on sixty points headed the table by four points and had just three games left.

THE HOME FRONT

Shells! The announcement by Lord Kitchener that the failures of the army at Neuve-Chapelle were in part down to a lack of shells sparked a furious debate both in Parliament and in the country at large. On St Patrick's Day in Liverpool, IPP MP TP O'Connor entered both the shells and labour dispute debates proclaiming 'Give Kitchener Shells'. He stated that for the first time in forty years their St Patrick's Day gathering was strictly non-political:

> *On Monday the whole world heard the frank language in which Lord Kitchener described the great need for shells. Every factory in the country should be working full time. Every employer should be allowing fair participation in his enhanced profits, encourage his workers to put into their work their best labour and best will. What would be the conscience of the man who, if an employer, through greed, and if a workman, through temper, imperilled thousands of lives and added millions to the burden of the nation?*

From the start of the Great War, the BEF had suffered from a general lack of artillery ordnance, both guns and ammunition. The problem was that in 1914 there was very little stock of high explosive shells (HE) in the British arsenals. Experience from the Boer War was that shrapnel shells (holding 375 balls per 18-pounder shell) predominated and it was assumed that they would be the ordnance of choice for future wars.

To add to the government's concerns over the manufacture and supply of shells, the Glasgow engineers, many of whom were engaged in munitions work, had, by the beginning of March, been on strike for a fortnight for their 2d an hour. At Parkhead Forge, 900 steelworks labourers had managed through negotiations to secure an increase of 2/- per week, with double time for

Sunday and time and a half for overtime. At the Acme Steel Foundry in Shettleston, cranemen, hammermen and labourers were given an advance of a halfpenny per hour, and steels smelters 5/- per week, with time and a half for overtime instead of time and a quarter. In all about, 1700 men were affected by the increases.

In response to the increasing militancy of the workers, many of whom were disobeying their union leaders' calls for negotiations, the government set up arbitration courts. The Glasgow engineers having refused an employer's offer of a halfpenny an hour increase, agreed to abide by the ruling of the arbitration court and accepted an award of 1d an hour and 10 per cent on piece rates. Industrial unrest on the Clyde would not cease with the engineers or steelworkers and over the next twelve months, the discontent would escalate over wages, work practices and dilution of skills. DORA already gave the government considerable powers, but over the first six months of the war, voluntary agreements were preferred with the unions. The need for munitions and the lack of the unions' control over their members would see the government increasingly take control of industrial manpower and move inexorably towards compulsion.

Chief among the grievances of the Glasgow working class were the scale and frequency of rent increases. At the beginning of March, a Glasgow Corporation resolution was sent to the Secretary of State for Scotland asking the government to inquire into the causes for the massive increase in rents in the city. With the overall cost of living spiralling, the number of complaints from Glasgow tenants threatened with eviction for non-payment of rent by their private landlords had soared. Labour councillors, John Wheatley and Pat Dollan, among others on the Corporation, publicised the situation by highlighting the cases of wives and dependants of soldiers evicted from their homes while their husbands and fathers were fighting at the front. Such cases provided an additional source of moral outrage, especially when the rhetoric from the government of the day was that everyone had to make sacrifices. With little progress appearing to have been made by their political leaders, across the city the women themselves were becoming organised to confront the landlords.

The St Patrick's Day celebrations in Glasgow were described as modified. Formerly it was the custom to hold Irish Nationalist demonstrations, but due to the political truce, no party meetings were arranged. Many people displayed sprigs of shamrocks in the streets, while in the Catholic churches throughout the city, morning services were attended by large congregations. In Paisley, the members of St Mirin's held a patriotic revue and Irish concert in the Clark Town Hall. The revue was presented by Catholic school children dressed in character costumes.

In Bridgeton, the Glasgow National Volunteers were still drilling and conducting shooting practice at their Broad Street hall, but with so many men now with the army, the main focus of the Corps had switched to the expansion of the Boy Scouts attached to the Corps. Honorary Secretary JJ Hinchley commented: 'It is most encouraging to note the wholehearted manner in which the Irish people of Bridgeton have responded to the request to send their boys, and it shows the patriotic spirit in its true colours.' The Bridgeton Corps suffered another body blow at the beginning of March when it lost two of its military training instructors. Glasgow's Irish Volunteers too were encouraging the participation of boys, but heavily influenced by the IRB the Fianna were not learning to tie knots and light fires. They were learning to shoot, raid explosives dumps and smuggle arms and explosives past customs officials at ports like Ardrossan and Stranraer.

In Glasgow City Chambers, the councillors were discussing among other things reducing the maximum speed of motorcars. That week the City Tramways Committee was petitioned by a deputation from the Women's Suffrage National Aid Corps in support of the proposal that during the war, owing to the scarcity of men to act as conductors, women should be employed in that capacity at the same wages and on the same conditions as the men. The matter was later remitted to the tramways manager, Dalrymple, who stated that he was still 300 men short of his full staff, and that the conductors and motormen were practically working seven days a week. He promised that he would give serious consideration to the matter.

COLONEL SHAUGHNESSY and the WEE MEN

At the start of December 1914, Glasgow's newly elected Unionist Lord Provost, Thomas Dunlop, had sought permission from the War Office to raise a bantam battalion. The Glasgow Rotary Club took up the idea of overseeing and organising the recruiting drive for the battalion and formed a Rotary Club Recruiting Committee. A number of recruiting meetings were arranged around the city over January and February 1915. The meetings were held to ascertain how many men were interested in joining a Glasgow bantam battalion. The idea was to enrol 2000 names before approaching the War Office for official permission to form the battalion. The potential recruits were required to be between the ages of nineteen and thirty-eight, of sound health and physique, between 5ft and 5ft 3in in height and boast a chest measurement of 35in when fully expanded. Within a few weeks, the Rotary Club had 1700 names on its list and when presented with the figures, the War Office gave Glasgow permission to raise its own bantam battalion. The full Corporation met on 11 March and agreed to raise and equip the battalion. A special subcommittee was formed, headed by Provost Dunlop, to oversee the project. The new battalion, 4th City of Glasgow, was to be known as the 18th (Service) Bn Highland Light Infantry. In a rare show of political correctness for the period, it was also agreed that the term 'bantam' would be dropped, as it may prove offensive to the vertically challenged potential recruits. The following day, Thomas Dunlop wrote to the General Officer Commanding in Chief Scottish Command recommending Colonel John Shaughnessy as the new battalion's commanding officer.

On 15 March, the Celtic director, John Shaughnessy, with sixteen years' service in the Volunteer and Territorial Forces, was offered and accepted the command of Glasgow's new battalion. As one of the leading Roman Catholics in the city and a director of Celtic FC, Colonel Shaughnessy's appointment was as much a political decision as a military one, driven by Lord Provost Thomas Dunlop's wish to recognise, acknowledge and encourage the support of the Glasgow Irish community. The newspapers, of course, splashed the news that the wee men of Glasgow were to get the chance of getting into the fight. Since the outbreak of the war, Colonel Shaughnessy had been busy overseeing the setting up and training of the Glasgow Citizen Training Force. John Shaughnessy's appointment was not without some controversy and at least one letter was sent to the War Office suggesting Shaughnessy's private life and those of his two brothers were not without scandal and as such he was unfit to command the battalion. The

Lord Provost immediately came to Colonel Shaughnessy's support and while he agreed that the private lives of the brothers may leave something to be desired, their conduct did not affect John Shaughnessy, in whom he and the recruiting committee had complete confidence.

On 17 March, the special subcommittee, with John Shaughnessy and Proctor from the Rotary Club in tow, motored down to Girvan on the Ayrshire coast to meet the town council. The sleepy seaside town had been chosen to billet 1400 recruits while the battalion carried out the first phase of its training. Billeting was the term used when accommodating soldiers outwith barracks. Usually public buildings, like schools or halls were used, but very often individuals were required to accommodate soldiers in their homes. That same night the deputation was back in Glasgow in time for John Shaughnessy to join in the somewhat subdued St Patrick's Day celebrations among the Glasgow Irish. A couple of days later, the Corporation lobbied the War Office for permission to put the bantams into the kilt. The Lord Provost thought the kilt made a wee man look broader. Glasgow Irish councillor Patrick Dollan moved that there were more important social matter matters, housing for example, needing their attention. With all arrangements in place, it was time to start enrolling the volunteers and the Rotary Club handed over their list of 2000 names to the Corporation's special subcommittee. To gain recognition from the War Office, the new battalion would need to enrol 1350 men into its ranks, a figure that included a first-line reserve of 200 men.

In the Garngad, on 19 March 1915, Hugh Hilley celebrated his sixteenth birthday and after watching three of his elder brothers join up, he was desperate to get into the army. Even his neighbour, Hughie McGrory, future Celtic great Jimmy's older brother, was talking about joining. Some of Hugh's mates had already managed to get into the army while still underage. Jimmy McAteer from Villiers Street in the Garngad was just a year older than Hugh, but was already a month with the 12th Bn Royal Scots and was training with them in Aldershot. Hugh's main problem was his height; at a shade under 5ft 2in, he was too small to pass the minimum height requirements for military service. At his home in Millburn Street, young Hilley was taking a keen interest in the bantam story in the newspapers, particularly in the enlistment conditions, and particularly in the minimum height requirements. He wondered to himself when they would begin recruiting.

As soon as the Rotary Club list was scrutinised by the Corporation subcommittee there were problems. The Corporation recruiters removed around 800 names from the list for various reasons, mostly because the individuals were ineligible because of their youth. Notices were then sent to the 1200 remaining volunteers, warning them that they would soon be asked to report to the Army Recruiting Office in the Tramways building in Bath Street. The list was arranged in alphabetical order and the notice to report was sent out in rotation. The first 200 were asked to attend on 24 March for a medical examination and then 200 each day until the list was exhausted. It was planned to send those who passed the medical to Girvan in daily batches, where on arrival they would be billeted in private houses. In the event, only around half the number asked to attend on the first day turned up and only thirty-three men passed the medical. The result was enormously discouraging and warning bells began to ring. Although the expected failure rate for the army medical was around 40 per cent, a 33 per cent pass rate was appalling. The following day was a bit better, but only sixty-one men were added to the battalion roll and questions were being asked of the Rotary Club Recruiting Committee. Proctor could only suggest that perhaps it had been a bad idea to drop 'bantam' from the title. On 25 March, the first batch of just twenty bantams were dispatched down to Girvan. By the end of the third day of recruiting and 600 names into the Rotary Club list, the number successfully passed into the ranks had risen to just 134. It was decided to abandon all hope that the Rotary Club list might provide sufficient recruits. Recognising the potential for a disastrously embarrassing episode for the city, at the end of March recruiting for the battalion was thrown open to the whole of west central Scotland.

After opening up recruiting for the bantam battalion, recruiting figures improved dramatically. The wee men came in from just about every parish, but particularly from the districts where the mining industry was a significant employer. The ideal miner was a small, stocky, immensely strong individual, well suited to working in the cramped conditions found underground. A glance through the enlistment rolls of the battalion shows the names of the Lanarkshire mining villages regularly appearing. A number of wee men from Celtic legend Jimmy Quinn's mining village of Smithston, near Croy, joined the battalion and were cheered off on the train to Glasgow by most of the village. On Friday 26 March, Colonel Shaughnessy inspected fifty-six men who had successfully enlisted prior to them moving to Girvan. A crowd of friends, relations and interested spectators gathered in front of the Tramways Offices to watch the inspection before the men set off for St Enoch's station where they entrained for the Ayrshire coast.

GIT AFF THE BEVVY

Prior to the outbreak of the Great War, one of the main political and social issues in Britain was the level of consumption of alcoholic drinks. Convictions for drunkenness regularly exceeded 200,000 each year and local newspapers were full of reports of the misadventures of those who had enjoyed more than a drop or two. In response, anti-drink groups, temperance societies such as the Catholic League of the Cross, had been campaigning against the demon drink for decades and with some limited success such as the Temperance (Scotland) Act of 1913. Before its introduction, it was not uncommon for pubs to open their doors at 5.00 am and to keep them open until midnight. The new Act had delayed the opening until 10 am and brought forward the closing time to 10 pm.

In Glasgow in 1914 over 1700 premises held liquor licences and the city fully deserved its hard-drinking reputation. Concerned at the effect drinking was having on industrial output, at the end of August 1914, the Government had introduced the Intoxicating Liquor (Temporary Restriction) Act. This gave any licensing authority that chose to apply for it, the power to curtail drinking hours drastically. In Dublin, so concerned at the increase of drunkenness since the outbreak of the war, the licensing authorities were considering closing public houses at 8 pm. At the end of October 1914, Lord Kitchener, alarmed at the amount of alcohol soldiers were drinking when off duty, appealed to the public not to treat soldiers to drink. Despite widespread support for restrictions of some description, especially among women, and an ongoing debate on the subject, over the first months of the war the restriction powers were never applied universally.

By March 1915, the Government was so concerned about excessive drinking among shipyard and munitions workers that the then Chancellor of the Exchequer, David Lloyd George, a long-time temperance supporter, was moved to say, 'We are fighting Germany, Austria and drink; and as far as I can see, the greatest of these deadly foes is drink.' Lloyd George started a campaign to persuade national figures to make a pledge that they would not drink alcohol during the war. In mid-April, Councillor John Wheatley suggested that the figures for the number of people arrested for drunkenness for Glasgow, down by over 1400 since the start of the war, be sent to Lloyd George. Under pressure from Lloyd George, the King, to set an example to his people, took the pledge for the duration of the war. In April, under the direction of the Scottish Temperance League, 3200 canvassers visited almost every home in Glasgow with a view to signing everyone over the age of fourteen to the pledge. The same message was issued from every church pulpit. By July, the Central Control Board (Liquor Traffic) had been established under DORA and it made Orders that covered most industrial areas including Clydeside. Public houses could only open for five hours per day, over lunchtime and between 6 pm and 9 pm, although a reasonable amount of time after 9 pm was allowed to consume any drinks already bought. The air in the boardroom at Parkhead must have been for once 'blue' as the Celtic directors; almost to a man involved in the liquor trade, discussed the assault on their businesses and incomes.

IRELAND

On 8 March, the Belfast Regiment of the National Volunteers paraded at Celtic Park, Belfast. The Volunteers were attired in uniform, and were equipped with rifles and bayonets. Also on parade was a nursing contingent numbering around eighty. The parade was inspected by John Dillon MP, Colonel Moore and Joe Devlin MP. At the end of the parade, Joe Devlin commented that 1500 Nationalist Belfast men had returned to the army as reservists, while another 1500 had joined up as recruits. Several thousand spectators watched the parade at Celtic Park. That same day the Irish Times announced that Irish Parliamentary Party MP Dr John Esmonde and two of his sons, John and Geoffrey, had joined the Irish Brigade. In all, five Nationalist MPs or in Tom Kettles case a former MP would join the Army.

On 14 March, John Redmond spoke at a mass meeting of 5000 Irish Nationalists in Manchester. The leader of the IPP spoke of a new political world that parties would come back to after the war and as usual, he spoke of Irish recruiting figures:

> With Home Rule an established fact, this year's St Patrick's Day should have been one of triumph, congratulation and jubilation, but alas for Ireland, they met at a time of suffering and deep tragedy. The shadow of war and death were hanging over their people, and Ireland was shouldering her right and honourable part. The official recruiting figures to 15 February showed that there were 99,704 Irishmen from Ireland with the colours. The Irish in Great Britain had added 115,000 to the colours, and the proportion of Irishmen who had come from the Dominions was

surprisingly large, making a grand total of at least a quarter of a million. He was sorry Irish recruits had not all joined Irish regiments and Brigades.

Every Irish soldier who gave his life on the battlefield died for Ireland as truly as any of Ireland's martyrs in the past. (Cheers) Ten years ago the Kaiser might have been right in counting on a divided nation. Dissatisfaction in South Africa, Ireland, Egypt and India, but he had forgotten the march of events and ideas, and had not realised that the rule of the people had been substituted for the rule of an ascendancy class. (Cheers)

In Ireland, a large St Patrick's Day Nationalist demonstration was held at Strabane. The speakers stressed that with Home Rule now an established fact, all Irishmen should stand by the noble cause of the Allies. The statement was greeted with loud cheers and great enthusiasm. Later in the parade, Union Jacks were carried, a thing never before seen during a St Patrick's Day parade.

In camps across the island, the three Irish divisions continued to recruit and train for war. Although the first two came into being in August 1914, the battalions had gone through a prolonged recruiting drive, which saw the men at differing stages of training. In addition, as stores and equipment increasingly arrived at the battalions, trained men were often seconded to other specialist tasks, for example, as machine gunners, signallers, transport, etc. Discipline could also prove problematical. Many men who only months earlier were civilians with no thought of joining the army, had some difficulty in understanding the constraints of military discipline and were unable to cut themselves off from their former lives. From time to time, they felt obliged to return home. If they had no leave they took it and if they had leave, they often overstayed it, often with what appeared to them to be a perfectly reasonable excuse. By March, having completed the individual and battalions training phases, the 10th and 36th Divisions were progressing to their brigade training. The 10th Division was concentrated around Newbridge, Kildare and the Curragh, where field training progressed throughout March and on into April. The 16th (Irish) Division was also slowly, but surely, beginning to fill.

Around this time it was noted that yet another barrier to recruiting throughout the whole of the UK and Ireland was the increasingly lucrative wages to be had working in the rapidly expanding munitions industries. Recruiters were reporting that men were asking why they should enlist for 1/- a day when they were being offered £2 10/- a week for working in a factory or forge. Plus, they were being promised that they would not be asked to serve in the army. Indeed, around this time, the shortage of skilled men for the expanding munitions industry saw the army forced to return skilled, enlisted men, now at the front, back to their civilian employment.

Chapter Eleven

APRIL

THE HOME FRONT

At the beginning of April, Celtic chairman, Tom White, in his guise of vice-president of the Home Government Branch of the United Irish League, gave a lecture at the Tinplate Workers Hall in Watson Street, Glasgow. Arthur Murphy was in the chair and the subject of Tom's lecture was 'Is the Labour Party Justified in Preaching a Peace Policy at the Present Juncture?' Tom White was referring to a recent Labour Party Conference at Norwich at which peace proposals were formulated and discussed. Tom's lecture sought to show that the Labour Party was not competent to give its views on the matter. At the same time, he was working with Arthur Murphy in organising a visit to Glasgow of veteran Irish Nationalist John Dillon MP. On 10 April, posters and newspaper adverts publicising the event announced that 4000 seats would be available for Dillon's lecture at St Andrew's Halls on Sunday 18 April.

Back in the Garngad, Hugh Hilley had spent a couple of days hovering around the army recruiting office in Monkland Street in Townhead. The office was just a stone's throw from the foot of the Garngad Hill, and a ten-minute walk from Hugh's home in Millburn Street. It took him a few days to muster the courage, but when he presented himself at the recruiting office on 9 April, he managed to convince the recruiters (not that they took a lot of convincing) that he was a month older than the nineteen years that was required to be eligible for active service. In fact, Hugh had only three weeks earlier celebrated his sixteenth birthday, but at just a shade under 5ft 2in, he was exactly the right height for a bantam and managed to bluff his way through the application process. After passing the army medical, which involved a doctor checking his eyesight and teeth for any obvious defects and his chest for TB, the final step was to take the oath. At last, Hugh Hilley was in the army. He was given his shilling, issued with joining instructions and the next day found himself parading outside the Tramway Offices in Bath Street. When everyone had been checked in, the new recruits were marched off to St Enoch's railway station where they caught the train for Girvan and the Ayrshire coast. On the day Hugh joined the bantams, another eight men from the Garngad did likewise.

At the end of April, the bantam battalion was fully up to strength and shortly afterward there were enough recruits to form two reserve or depot companies 400 strong. The recovery from the disastrous start was quite remarkable.

The Glasgow Corporation had issued the bantams with uniforms and equipment, though weapons and ammunition were still in short supply. Route marches played a big part in the early stages of training. The battalion commanders organised for the Glasgow Police Pipe Band to come down for a few days to accompany the battalion on their marches, hopefully drum up some recruits and provide some entertainment at night. The news that the Glasgow police were coming to visit the battalion would have had a good few bantams sweating at the thought of being recognised.

By April, the various TF divisions embodied back in August 1914 were coming to the end of their training period. Many of the divisions had been pillaged for battle-ready battalions during the crisis of October and November, but with new battalions drafted in as replacements, they were now ready for active service. On 13 April, the telephone rang in the headquarters of the 51st (Highland) Division TF in Bedford. The Highlanders had been based in and around the town for the last eight months, training for war. The telephone call was from the War Office, warning that they should prepare for active service overseas. On 29 April, movement orders were received and over the next few days the division embarked from Southampton and Folkestone for Le Havre and Boulogne and by 5 May the Highland Division was concentrated in billets in and around Lillers. On arrival in theatre, the division was attached to the Indian Corps.

The month of April saw the highly visible arrival of women in the mainstream British workforce. After considering the suffragette petition to allow female tram conductresses, James Dalrymple authorised a controversial experiment that saw two female clerical workers become the first Glasgow Tramways conductresses. Resplendent in their green straw hats, military-style tunics and ankle-length Black Watch tartan skirts, the two were the first of generations of the fearsome Glesga clippies. The women were immortalised in Glasgow folklore thanks to their sharp, biting wit and war cry of 'cumoangitaff'. By June, 250 women were employed on the trams or in training with 1400 applicants waiting in the wings. By the end of the year, the experiment was declared a success and soon over 700 women would be employed, not only as conductresses, but also as motormen, driving the trams. The clippies worked eight hours a day, six days a week and soon they would be fighting, supported by John Wheatley, for equal pay for doing exactly the same job as the men they had replaced.

IRELAND

On Sunday 4 April, John Redmond took the review of some 25,000 Irish National Volunteers at Phoenix Park, Dublin. The contingents had travelled to Dublin from every part of Ireland and, led by their bands, proceeded directly from the railway station to the park where they were formed up in military formation on the famous fifteen acres. The mobilisation of the Volunteers stirred memories of another parade from over a hundred years previously, when on the same spot Grattan's Volunteers mustered. The Volunteers consisted of four divisions, each representing an Irish Province. John Redmond, Joe Devlin and Colonel Moore mounted the saluting base while the Volunteers marched past en route to another muster at the head of O'Connell Street. A crowd of well over 100,000 spectators lined the park and route to O'Connell Street. There another saluting base was set up within a stone's throw of the Parnell Memorial. Another immense crowd, including a number of dignitaries, awaited the arrival of the Volunteers. There were no speeches during the parade; however, John Redmond later gave an interview to the press. The main thrust of the interview was again the training and arming of the Irish Volunteers and the contribution of the Irish to the recruiting effort. He highlighted the fact that the latest government figures, including those of the Ulster Volunteers, showed that 50,000 Irish Volunteers were serving with the colours. It was a very honourable record for Ireland. He also rubbished the suggestion that all enrolled members of the Volunteers should go to the front. Only a certain number of Ulster Volunteers went or could go to the front and the same was true of the Irish Volunteers. He reminded the press that at the start of the war he had offered the Irish Volunteers as a home defence force. Despite the apparent acceptance by the government and by all parties in the House of Commons, to date the offer had not been utilised, despite the fact that it would release 20,000 regular troops then stationed in Ireland for active service. He failed to recognise that Kitchener had no intention of redeploying the 20,000 regulars out of Ireland, not with 25,000 Irish Nationalists parading about in uniform and an increasingly vociferous anti-British campaign being conducted by the IRB-controlled Irish Volunteers. The Weekly Irish Times correspondent noted that only the Belfast divisions were fully armed, equipped and well drilled. It thought the fine fellows who made up the Volunteers had the makings of at least ten battalions for Kitchener's Army.

In addition to the IPP leadership conducting recruiting drives for the two southern Irish divisions, a number of current and former Nationalist MPs and their families led by example and enlisted. William Redmond MP, younger brother of the IPP leader, enlisted at the age of fifty-one, one of the first Irish Volunteers to do so. In November 1914, he gave his famous 'Follow Me' speech to the Cork Volunteers. He was commissioned into the Royal Irish Rifles in February 1915. William Archer Redmond, the MP for East Tyrone, was the son of John Redmond. He joined the 7th Bn Leinsters in mid-February 1915. After his enlistment in January 1915, fifty-year-old Stephen Gwynn, poet, Protestant and Irish Parliamentary Party MP for Galway Borough, author and journalist, joined General Parson's Officer Cadet Company as a private solder. He was commissioned in mid-April and was shortly afterward transferred to the 6th (Service) Bn Connaught Rangers. As a medical man, Dr John Joseph Esmonde MP for North Tipperary, joined the RAMC at the beginning of March 1915 and was awarded a captaincy. At the same time, two of his sons joined him in the army. Dr John Esmonde would die shortly afterwards and his Parliamentary seat would be won by his son John Lymbrick Esmonde, then serving with the Leinster Regiment. Geoffrey Esmonde would be killed in action serving with the Tyneside Irish in October 1916. Professor Thomas Kettle, a former IPP MP for East Tyrone and Irish Volunteer gunrunner, joined the Army in November 1914 and by January 1915 was an officer serving with the Leinster Regiment. Daniel Desmond Sheehan, All-For-Ireland League MP for Mid Cork, followed William O'Brien's advice to enlist. In mid-November 1914, Sheehan joined Redmond's Irish Brigade. The former Glasgow Catholic Observer chief reporter was gazetted lieutenant into, and practically raised, the 9th (Service) Bn Royal Munster Fusiliers. Three sons followed him into the military; one aged only sixteen at the time. Two of his sons, Daniel Joseph and Martin Joseph, were killed serving with the Royal Flying Corps. His brother-in-law, Sergeant Robert O'Connor, would be killed serving with the 2nd Bn Leinster Regiment in July 1917. His brother would be very badly wounded serving with the Irish Guards. After the war, Sheehan wrote:

> I served and I suffered and I sacrificed, and if the results were not all that we intended … we enlisted for worthy and honourable motives and we sought … the ultimate good of Ireland in doing so.

The end of April, found John Redmond still writing letters to the press still trying to get across the message that the Irish Brigade was really three brigades. He announced that the brigades at Fermoy and Buttevant were full, but the brigade at Tipperary was still in need of recruits. For the four weeks ending 16 April, about 6000 recruits had enlisted in the whole of Ireland. Later John Redmond presented Irish wolfhound mascots to each of the 'three' Irish Brigades.

In Ireland itself, like on mainland Britain, the people were suffering from rising prices. The war had initially impacted negatively on the Irish economy. The normal markets for linen were closed, supplies of steel and other materials needed for shipbuilding were diverted to military projects, agriculture was disrupted and prices fluctuated. However, the slump was to prove short-lived. As a factory inspector in Belfast reported at the end of 1914, the demand for fine linen was soon replaced by orders for bandages, army bedding, shirts and tents. Belfast had never been a major centre for naval construction and, according to the records, comparatively few vessels were built in the city in the war years. However, this hides a major shift in activity and the city became a major repair centre. In the south, agriculture boomed, as it had during the great wars against Revolutionary and Napoleonic France, and for the same reasons. Since other supplies were cut off, Ireland became Britain's larder. The importance of Irish agricultural exports would increase significantly as the war progressed, notably after the adoption of U-boat warfare by the Germans. In general, as with the rest of Britain, this was a period of high demand and high profits for Irish farmers and industrialists. Even the urban poor benefited to some degree. With so many Irishmen serving with the colours, their wives were enjoying significantly increased incomes due to the army pay and separation allowances.

Politically, however, as the war dragged on with no end in sight, Redmond, the IPP and the Home Rule movement were slowly losing the battle for Irish hearts and minds. John Redmond's carefully thought-out plan based on a short war was slowly, but surely unravelling.

SCOTTISH FOOTBALL

While the furore over footballers and recruiting was going on, William MacAndrew, secretary of the Scottish Football League, had been collecting data from the First and Second Division Clubs. His idea was to compile a list of football players who were then serving with the colours or were engaged in what was termed at the time government work at home. The footballers listed on the return were players held on the club's books and not necessarily regular first team players. The number of players in service assigned to Heart of Midlothian, for example, was sixteen; however, only six then seven were regular first team players. Government work was considered to be any occupation that contributed directly to the war effort, such as mines, shipyards, steelworks, foundries, munitions factories, etc. It was obviously an attempt by the Scottish League to show the general public that professional football was contributing to the war effort.

The League secretary's list was published in Scottish newspapers on 9 April and showed that, to date, from the First and Second Divisions, 202 players had enlisted and 111 were employed on government work. The figures did not include those from Celtic FC, which refused to participate in what the club saw as pandering to the media and an obvious public relations exercise. The figures for the First Division were that 128 had enlisted and sixty-five were on government work. The Celtic weren't the only people unimpressed with the League's public relations exercise. Writing to the editor of Dundee's Evening Telegraph and Post on 12 April, *Hamish* disputed the figures presented by the Scottish Football League. As an example he highlighted the figures assigned to Dundee FC. Of the eight players recorded as having enlisted, he claimed two were recalled reservists and four no longer actually played for Dundee FC. According to *Hamish* to date only one Dundee FC player had actually enlisted.

First Division

Club	Service	Government work
Aberdeen	14	1
Airdrieonians	1	0
Ayr United	5	8
Clyde	8	5
Dumbarton	5	0
Dundee	8	0
Falkirk	10	3
Hamilton Accies	0	4
Heart of Midlothian	16	0
Hibernian	2	1
Kilmarnock	5	6
Morton	5	3
Motherwell	0	5
Partick Thistle	1	8
Queen's Park	26	6
Raith Rovers	7	2
Rangers	2	6
St Mirren	9	5
Third Lanark	4	2

While Celtic refused to submit data for the club, the club's figures were in fact, two enlisted (Gilhooley and O'Kane) and nine in government work.

CELTIC FC

On 3 April, the Celtic took on Airdrie at Parkhead and 10,000 of the faithful watched the Bhoys move to within three points of Hearts with a comfortable 3–0 win over the visitors. In what was described in the press as an excellent display, McColl and Browning scored during the first half, while McMenemy got Celtic's third after the restart. The Airdrie side repeatedly threatened, but could not break through the Celtic's sturdy defence. In the end, the Celts prevailed somewhat easily. Heart of Midlothian meanwhile, made the journey north to the Granite City to face Aberdeen. Tom Gracie was ill and missing from the side for the first time that season, Wilson was also out. On the day, the Aberdeen Evening Express correspondent thought Hearts played fine football throughout, but despite chances being created by both sides, neither team could score and Hearts left a vital point behind in Aberdeen. The illness that kept Tom Gracie out of the side at Aberdeen was much more serious than anyone realised. In March, Tom had been diagnosed with leukaemia. Tom only informed John McCartney and insisted that he continue to both play football, and to train with McCrae's battalion. In the race for the title, the Celts were now just three points behind Hearts, on fifty-eight and sixty-one respectively, but the Bhoys still had two vital games in hand.

The first of Celtic's outstanding fixtures was on Tuesday 6 April against the amateurs of Queen's Park, in a keenly contested match at Hampden. Over the course of the first half, the amateurs gave as good as they got and deserved to go in at half-time all square at 0–0. In the second half, the Celts stepped up a gear and went into the lead from a fine headed goal by Jimmy McMenemy. It was to be followed shortly after by another, this time a powerful shot from Jimmy McColl. Queen's Park again came more into the game and on several occasions threatened the Celtic goal. Towards full time, in what was the best move of the game, Patsy Gallacher scored Celtic's third. The 0–3 victory took the Celtic to within one point of Hearts with one game still in hand.

On 10 April, the 'soldier footballers' of Hearts, as the Scottish press were now calling them, just managed to catch the train through to Greenock from Edinburgh in time. McCrae's battalion had been on night manoeuvres and had spent most of the night on the Braid Hills. No nominal roll exists listing those men involved on the exercise so it is not known for certain that the players were on the hills. If they were, then the order to curtail military training for the Hearts lads during the League run-in had been wilfully disobeyed. What John McCartney, the Hearts board or indeed the Hearts supporters both within McCrae's battalion and back in Gorgie, thought of Sir George McCrae and his promises are unrecorded. If asked, there would be little doubt that the supporters who followed the players into the battalion would have preferred to see their heroes abed the night before the vital game as opposed to tramping around the hills with them. Their opponents, Greenock Morton, were having one of their best ever seasons and sat comfortably in fourth place in the league, just one point behind Rangers in third. A good crowd of 10,000 turned out at Cappielow to watch the clash. Morton dominated the play from the kick-off and went into the lead after twenty minutes from a free kick. Just before half-time, Nellies missed a penalty, shooting past the post and squandering the chance to go into the pavilion at half-time all-square. The second half developed along the same lines as the first, but Hearts were awarded another penalty twenty minutes after the restart. This time Tom Gracie drove the ball straight at the keeper, squandering yet another opportunity to equalise. With just minutes to go, Morton scored again, putting the game beyond Hearts and inflicting massive damage to their chances of winning the League.

Meanwhile at Parkhead, a full-strength Celtic were facing an Aberdeen side who were in seventh place in the League, but only four points separated them and the bottom side. The week previously, in what was one of their best performances of the season, they had held Hearts to a score-less draw at Pittodrie. At Parkhead a crowd of 15,000 turned out to watch the third last game of the 1914/15 campaign and a game that the Celtic really needed to win. Straight from the kick-off, the Celtic went into the attack, determined to stamp their authority on the game and to take both points. After just ten minutes, Jimmy McMenemy got the breakthrough with a fine goal. The Celtic continued to dominate the game, but failed to add to the score despite their dominance. Numerous corners were won and Andy McAtee hit the post with a fierce shot, while Jimmy McColl struck the goalkeeper square in the chest with a shot just as powerful. Despite the chances and the dominance, Aberdeen managed to fight off the Celtic forwards making it a nail-biting finish for the Celtic supporters. The game ended with a low score, but it was a convincing 1–0 victory, which took the Bhoys to the top of the League for the first time that season. With thirty-six games played, Celtic led the pack with sixty-two points, one ahead of Hearts, but still with their game in hand to play. Rangers were in third spot, having played thirty-seven games for forty-eight points. Greenock Morton sat just one point behind Rangers, having also played thirty-seven games.

THE BELGIAN RELIEF FOOTBALL MATCH.

From left to right the members of the group are: Back row: Graham, Hendren, Ross, Smith, Nellies, Brownlie, Reid, and Dodds. Centre row: Meaney, Allan, Briggs, Thomson, Gordon, and M'Nair. Front row: Lady Dunedin, Low, Crossan, Currie, Paterson, Walker, Meredith, Hodkinson, Crone, Duckworth, and Miss Violet Vanbrugh. (From photo by J. R. Coltart, 8 Dalmeny Street, Leith.)

Belgian Relief Match Teams
(Courtesy of Jack Alexander)

On the evening of 14 April, both the Celtic and Heart of Midlothian were called upon to provide players for a charity match. Celtic sent three internationalists, McNair, Dodds and Billy Crone, through to Edinburgh to play in an International XI side versus an Edinburgh XI. Hearts contributed seven players, two for the internationalists and five for the Edinburgh select. Also included in the internationalists side was forty-year-old Billy Meredith of Manchester United. The legendary Welsh internationalist had a long and controversial connection with Celtic's Tom Maley from their days at Manchester City and the payments scandal of 1905. The Edinburgh XI was made up mainly of Hearts and Hibernian players.

Over 22,000 spectators turned out at Tynecastle to watch the match played in aid of the Belgian Refugee Funds. The game turned out to be a cracker with the reporters commenting that it was worth travelling half the length of the country to watch. The Edinburgh forwards took much of the credit for their dash and endeavour, while the internationalists' backline of Brownlie, McNair and Dodds took the credit for nullifying their efforts. Meredith, with his trademark toothpick *in situ*, produced some clever play. At half-time the sides went into the pavilion with honours even. The second half followed the same pattern of exciting end-to-end play and after thirty minutes a twenty-five-yard shot from Sunderland's Thomson beat Willie Allan in the Edinburgh goal. The internationalists scored a second after some clever wing play involving the veteran Meredith, who sent Gordon of Rangers through to score. The final score was 2–0 to the internationalists, but for sixty minutes it was anybody's game; however, on balance it was a fair and popular result. The match ball was later auctioned, pulling in another £7 15/- for the fund. The internationalist team was Brownlie (Third Lanark), McNair (Celtic), Dodds (Celtic), Gordon (Rangers), Thomson (Sunderland), Nellies (Hearts), Meredith (Manchester United), Walker (Hearts), Reid (Rangers), Crone (Celtic) and Hodkinson (Blackburn Rovers). The Edinburgh team was Allan (Hibernian), Crossan (Hearts), Currie (Hearts), Briggs (Hearts), Paterson (Hibernian), Ross (St Bernards), Low (Hearts), Meaney (Leith), Hendren (Hibernian), Graham (Hearts) and Smith (Hibernian).

The following Saturday, 17 April, Hearts travelled through to Paisley for their final game of the season, while Celtic went to Third Lanark for their second last game. It was a must-win match for the Tynecastle men. The advantage was with Celtic, but mathematically, Hearts could still win the League, but they simply had to beat St Mirren and hope the Celtic tripped up at Cathkin Park. Historically, the odds were against them; Hearts had not taken even a point at Love Street for a decade. On the day, 9000 spectators watched Hearts launch attack after attack over the course of the first half with Graham, Briggs, Brydon and Wattie all having good tries at goal. The efforts of the Hearts forwards were thwarted by an outstanding display of goalkeeping by Irishman O'Hagan in the Buddies' goal. The second half was more even with both goals threatened in turn. Twenty minutes after the restart, the Buddies scored through Clark. The Hearts again rallied and despite relentless pressure on the St Mirren goal, failed to make the breakthrough. The game ended with the final score 1–0 to St Mirren. Garngad man and fervent Celtic supporter Hughie McGrory (no relation to Jimmy of immortal memory), played in the game. He had come to St Mirren as a halfback at the start of the season from Blackburn Rovers and was delighted to have a say in the defeat of Hearts.

The Celtic, meanwhile, travelled across the city to Cathkin Park, knowing exactly what was required of them. Going into the game, the Bhoys knew a win would secure the League Championship. Right from the kick-off and against the wind the Celts fell into their stride, and after eleven minutes 'Sniper' McColl opened the scoring. Ten minutes later 'Smiler' Browning added a second. In the second half, Third Lanark came more into the game and tested Charlie Shaw on a number of occasions, but further strikes by Browning and McMenemy saw the Bhoys extend their lead to four. A crowd of 20,000 spectators saw the Celts retain their League Championship flag and secure their twelfth League Championship title in what was the strangest of football seasons.

A week later, the Celtic took a full-strength team to play their last match of the 1914/15 League season against the Steelmen of Motherwell. Although the League Championship was already assured, a win would add yet another record in the competition to the Celtic's collection – sixty-six points for thirty-eight matches.

The game at Fir Park was played out in front of 12,000 spectators. Motherwell snatched a goal after just two minutes play and then defended their lead as if their lives depended on it. Eventually, relentless Celtic pressure told when Johnny Browning equalised just before half-time. The second half was a repeat of the first with Celtic constantly on the attack, but Motherwell was resolute in defence with Allan, Penman and Kelly outstanding. The Motherwell defence held out to the end and deserved most of the plaudits for their fighting performance. For the Celtic, despite all the dominance and pressure, the game ended in a disappointing 1–1 draw. However, with the League Championship won, the result was a disappointment only in that the club missed out on a new record for points won. The Celtic side on the day was Shaw, McNair and Dodds; Young, Johnstone and McMaster; McAtee, and Gallacher; and McColl, McMenemy and Browning.

Scottish League, First Division Season 1914/15

Team	Played	Won	Lost	Drawn	For	Against	Points
Celtic	38	30	3	5	91	25	65
Hearts	38	27	4	7	83	32	61
Rangers	38	23	11	4	74	47	50
Morton	38	18	8	12	74	48	48
Ayr United	38	20	10	8	55	40	48
Falkirk	38	16	15	7	48	48	39
Partick Th	38	15	15	8	56	58	38
Hamilton Acc	38	16	16	6	60	55	38
St Mirren	38	14	16	8	56	65	36
Hibernian	38	12	15	11	59	66	35
Airdrieonians	38	14	17	7	54	60	35
Dumbarton	38	13	17	8	51	66	34
Kilmarnock	38	15	19	4	55	59	34
Dundee	38	12	17	9	43	61	33
Aberdeen	38	11	16	11	39	52	33
Third Lanark	38	10	16	12	51	57	32
Clyde	38	12	20	6	44	59	30
Motherwell	38	10	18	10	49	66	30
Raith Rovers	38	9	19	10	53	68	28
Queen's Park	38	4	29	5	27	90	13

That same weekend, Sheffield United met Chelsea in the forty-fourth final of the English FA Cup. The game was played at Old Trafford, Manchester, since its usual venue at Crystal Palace had been requisitioned by the Admiralty for training the Royal Naval Division. It was the first time Chelsea had made the final, while Sheffield had already carried off the trophy in 1899 and 1902. Over 50,000 spectators watched the game, many travelling up from London. The game ended with Sheffield picking up the FA Cup for the third time after a 3–0 victory over Chelsea. With so many spectators in uniform, the game would later become known as the Khaki Cup Final.

HEROES or VILLAINS

With the Scottish League Championship won and lost, the commiserations, celebrations and accusations began. On the day, the Heart of Midlothian people, of course, made no direct comment about their failure to win the League despite their obvious disappointment after leading the race for so long. On 20 April, manager John McCartney spoke to Edinburgh's Evening News:

> They played at times so tired and sore that they could hardly stand; yet they took Celtic to the last day of the season and left Rangers floundering eleven points behind. They gave their best throughout and that is all that anyone could ask.

Although John McCartney never directly attributed the team's failure to the military training affecting the players' performances, the suggestion was there. The Edinburgh press was more forthright in its opinions. Military training with trench digging, route marches and the likes, was blamed for the failure and for what was in its opinion a grave injustice.

According to the Edinburgh Evening Standard: 'Hearts, have laboured these past weeks under a dreadful handicap, the likes of which our friends in the west cannot imagine. Between them the two leading clubs [Celtic and Rangers] have not sent a single prominent player to the Army. There is only one football champion in Scotland, and its colours are maroon and khaki.'

The Scotsman on 28 June 1915 argued: 'It is practically safe to assume that but for the war, the club would have finished in the position it held at the top of the League table for thirty-five weeks out of the thirty-seven constituting the season.'

At the club AGM at the beginning of July, chairman Elias Furst, stated in his report: 'That so many of our players joined the Army was, I am convinced directly the means of the club losing the League Championship. I think everyone would admit that.'

In fact, not everyone did admit that. With two league games left to be played, neutral football commentator *John O'Groat* writing in the Weekly Record on 17 April, thought there were two major factors that contributed to the Hearts failure to maintain their excellent early season form. The first and most serious was the loss of team captain Bob Mercer; the other a badly arranged programme of matches that left Hearts a run of four away games at the close of the campaign. He thought the loss of Bob Mercer's presence and steadying influence, particularly towards the end of the season was critical in the failure. While, the final four difficult away games came at a time when the energy and vitality of any team was naturally beginning to ebb. He made no mention of the effect of route marches, trench digging or Swedish drills.

The positive or negative effect of infantry training on professional athletes is debatable. Some commentators suggested while stamina might be gained, some speed or sharpness was lost. Certainly, the effect on ordinary working-class recruits was nothing other than remarkably positive. Few had ever eaten or lived as well and with the physical exercise and fresh air, the vast majority of working-class men blossomed, putting on inches in height and pounds of hard muscle. Infantry training at that time concentrated on stamina and lower body strength with the favoured exercises Swedish drills and the ubiquitous route march. The marches started off short and light, and the distance and weight carried in packs was gradually increased. Eventually the men would be expected to march at speed twelve miles carrying full kit weighing around 40lb and be capable of going immediately into battle. There were, however, a couple of danger times for recruits' health and well-being. The first was the issue of new boots and the second their inoculations. Inoculations very often left men feeling extremely unwell. Many were so badly affected they were bedridden for days. The army's hard leather boots, if not properly fitted, could literally cut a man's feet to ribbons, but old sweats usually looked after recruits and soon properly broken-in boots became like slippers.

The suggestion was that the Hearts players were often worn out or suffered from lack of energy going into games and their performances suffered accordingly. Yet the battalion, while based in Edinburgh, had disciplinary problems. Some of the men were going over the wall of their billet after lights out when they were supposed to be in bed. Jack Alexander in his excellent book on McCrae's battalion reported: 'There was no guard on the stone wall that divided the school from Greyfriars Churchyard.' That wall could be crossed, and the cemetery gates were (in the words of Cpl Veitch) 'eminently scalable'. For the married, the thirsty, the lonely and the brave, this was their way out and, inevitably, their way back in. Boer War veteran Archie Ewing, a former Argyll and Sutherland Highlander, re-enlisted in August 1914 and by February 1915 had been appointed a company sergeant major with McCrae's battalion. Archie spent long nights in a local hostelry preventing as he put it, his charges being 'treated' by the public with free drinks. His onerous duty often lasted long past closing time and resulted in him returning to his billet singing his head off and arguing with the sentries.

The statistics show that over the second half of the season the performance of Hearts did indeed tail off. Between 15 August and 26 December when the battalion was mobilised the team's record was: played twenty-one, won nineteen, lost one and drawn one. Goals for fifty-two, against thirteen. Points gained thirty-nine. After mobilisation between 2 January and 17 April: played seventeen, won eight, lost three and drawn six. Goals for thirty-one, against twenty. Points gained twenty-two.

Heart of Midlothian dropped only its fourth league point on 2 January 1915, when it drew 1–1 at Falkirk. McCrae's battalion had actually only fully mobilised a week earlier and at this time was still largely in an administrative phase. Therefore, Hearts had lost a point before serious military training had even started.

Further analysis of the Hearts performance in games after they had been mobilised, and that they narrowly won or lost, shows that the team actually performed well during the second half of games. For example, in mid-January, a late second half rally saw Hearts come back from being 2–0 down to win 3–2 against Dundee. In mid-February, Hearts won 1–0 at Motherwell, the winning goal coming late in the second half after prolonged periods of sustained Hearts pressure. There was the narrow defeat by Rangers also in mid-February when Hearts came back from being 4–0 down at half-time to lose 4–3. In fact, they would have won that amazing game had they neither missed a late penalty nor hit the post. The 2–2 draw at Airdrie in mid-March was an occasion when Hearts completely dominated the entire game and should have won. The point was not lost through any tiredness or lack of sharpness on the part of Hearts, but through a goalkeeping error. Goalkeeper Boyd wasn't a member of McCrae's or any other battalion. Similarly, over Hearts last three League games, the Tynecastle men dropped five points out of a possible six at a time when, according to newspaper reports, heavy marching and training had already been curtailed for the best part of a month. On 10 April at Greenock Morton, Hearts missed two penalties; Nellies missed the first and was not involved in any military training, while a desperately unwell Tom Gracie missed the second. The game and points were lost in the final minutes when Morton scored a second goal while Hearts desperately sought an equaliser. In should be noted that most of the teams the Hearts were playing had also given players over to military service. According to the unreliable Scottish League list, of the last three teams Hearts played, Aberdeen had 14 men in service, Morton 5 and St Mirren 9. The Hearts management was also willing to provide seven senior players for the latest Belgian relief match. The game was played in Edinburgh, just two days before their vital last game of the season against St Mirren in Paisley.

While the Hearts lads were engaged in serious military training from around the middle of January, at the same time, if not before, the cut in footballers' wages saw most of the Celtic players back in normal full-time work; Patsy Gallacher went back into the shipyards at Clydebank, while Tom McGregor and Jim Young were employed full time in iron foundries. Peter Johnstone initially went to work in his tobacconist's shop before being kicked out by his wife Isa. He decided it was probably safer to go back down the pit. Jimmy McColl worked as a riveter and Johnny Browning was employed first in an engineering shop, then in Denny's Shipyard at Dumbarton. A ten or twelve hour shift of hard physical graft in an Edwardian shipyard or iron foundry would be regarded by most commentators as every bit as strenuous, tiring or dangerous even as most forms of military training.

It should also be noted that over the course of the entire 1914/15 football season, the Celtic played a total of fifty-four games, Hearts played forty-six. Over the period of the League campaign, Celtic played fifty games, including friendlies and used all nineteen players from a squad of nineteen. Two young players also got a trial versus Clydebank FC. Over the same period, Hearts played forty-three games and used nineteen players from a squad of twenty-six. In addition, both teams contributed individual players to a number of relief and League international squads.

In reality, Heart of Midlothian never lost the League; they were simply beaten to the finish line by the sheer consistency of Celtic. The Hearts' misfortune was not the effect of military training on their form, but facing a team that refused to admit defeat. After losing to Rangers at the New Year, Celtic dropped only one point until after the League race was won. That point was lost in the 1–1 draw with Hearts at Parkhead, and most neutral sports correspondents agreed that Celtic was the better team and really should have won. Echoing the opinion of *John O'Groat* of the Weekly Record, *the Man in the Know* pointed out that football teams often taper off towards the end of the season. As an example, he cited Manchester City and Oldham Athletic, which promised to fight out that season's English League Championship between them. Both had faltered through no fault of military training, to be overtaken and beaten in the race for the title by Everton FC.

The Heart of Midlothian team was exceptionally talented and did well to hold the lead at the top of the table for so long. Unfortunately for the Tynecastle men, the Celts did better in reducing that lead and getting to the top of the table with two games in hand. In an ordinary year and against an ordinary team, Hearts would have gained the honour they deserved, but this was not an ordinary year and this Celtic side was no ordinary team.

As the Celtic slowly but surely closed the points gap at the top of the table, a bias in favour of Hearts, was clearly manifest. The supposedly neutral Scottish football supporter–if such exist where the Celtic were concerned, would, given the action of the players in joining McCrae's battalion, much have preferred to see Hearts win the race for the title. While this may be understandable, a much more sinister bias was also evident within the game itself, with a director of Third Lanark FC asking the sports correspondent of the Weekly Record to write an anti-Celtic article appealing to the patriotism of both his own side and Motherwell FC to defeat the Celtic over the last two games of the season. Still regularly referred to as The Irishmen, the appeal to the patriotism of the Third Lanark and Motherwell players can only suggest that the Celtic were seen by the director in question as being somehow un-British or un-Scottish. John O'Groat refused the request and in his column asked why there should be such anxiety to see the Celts lose the race for the championship? He surmised it was not all about Hearts and not all about patriotism and more about simply wishing to see the Celtic beaten.

The Celtic victory was much better received among the tens of thousands of Celtic supporters in the trenches. Private Kelly of the 2nd Bn Scottish Rifles, manning the line near Bois Grenier, wrote home to friends in Castle Douglas telling of how he and his mates celebrated the news that the Celts had captured the League Flag again. They decided to stage an impromptu concert in their dugout, with biscuit boxes and mouth organs for the musical accompaniments. Hearing the Celtic supporters singing, the Germans deduced that the Celtic had won the League and joined in the celebrations. Kelly wrote:

> We were only ninety yards from the German trenches, they shouted over to
> us in good English – 'Good old Jimmy Quinn! Roll on, Cowcaddens! When
> are you going back to Glasgow, Jock?'

Corporal Josie Maley also got the good news. The 9th Bn Glasgow Highlanders were in the line near Festubert when he penned a letter to *the Man in the Know* in which he commented on the Celtic's successes: 'So the good old Celtic got hold of the League championship and the Charity Cup once more. Well done, Celtic!'

The Man in the Know also picked up a number of reports of where, on recognising the Glasgow accents in the trenches opposite, the Germans had shouted across no man's land the news that Celtic had won the League. He wrote:

> One has to take a great deal of what passes as war news with a pinch of
> salt, but the story of the Germans and the Celts is probably one of the few
> truthful yarns spun for our edification. I can well believe the story knowing
> that English and Scottish football results are carried in German sporting

papers, and that all over the continent – at Copenhagen, Berlin, Budapest and Vienna the football enthusiast can go over the Celtic's season's record and tell every match won and lost.

THE HOME FRONT

On 17 April, the very same day the Celtic won the Scottish League Championship, the inspirational founding father of Celtic FC, Brother Walfrid, passed away. Glasgow Catholics, particularly those in the Calton and Bridgeton, heard the news with profound regret. His was already a legendary name in the east end where for many years he had laboured as a Marist teacher among the poorest of the district. Born Andrew Kerins at Ballymote, Co Sligo, his drive and personality had led in November 1887 to the foundation of the Celtic Football Club. Transferred by his order to a new position at St Anne's Spitalfields, London, in August 1892, he only returned to Glasgow on a couple of occasions. On one such visit in August 1897, just a few months after the club was converted into a limited liability company, he attended the Celtic Sports Meeting at Parkhead. The visit to Parkhead, perhaps, provides some insight into his thoughts and opinions regarding the conversion of his charitable idea into a privately owned business venture. After retiring from teaching, he moved to the Brother's College at Grove Ferry, Sussex, where in 1913 he suffered a stroke. He then was moved to the Marist Brothers Provincial House at Dumfries, where after a prolonged illness he passed away in his 76th year. It was said of him that until the end of his days he never lost interest in the goings on at the Celtic Club.

Sunday 18 April saw veteran Irish Nationalist John Dillon in Glasgow at the invitation of the Glasgow and district branches of the United Irish League. He was the principal speaker at a large demonstration of Glasgow Irish Nationalists held at St Andrew's Halls. Around 5000 Glasgow Irish packed into the hall to hear Dillon speak on the subject of Ireland's attitude to the war. He began by highlighting the contribution of the Glasgow Irish, stating that no class of the community had contributed so many recruits in proportion as the Irish of Great Britain. In Scotland, 27,511 Irishmen or sons of Irishmen had joined the Colours in addition to the 10,000 already serving. From Glasgow alone, 9000 men had enlisted, which raised a cheer from the audience. However, he had come to Glasgow for another purpose, he announced. Firstly, to thank them on behalf of the responsible leadership of the Irish cause in Ireland for their support and for setting an example of the highest patriotism to the people at home, not only for their cheerful readiness to face sacrifice for the cause, but for their keen political instinct, which was so characteristic of them. It took a keen political instinct to realise what their duty was at this time. More cheers from the audience. The Irish had a long and bitter memory, but there was the call of duty. And what were the reasons why Ireland was bound to take its full share of the sacrifices and sufferings of this terrific struggle? The first was that she was honour bound. (Cheers) Ireland had long pledged her honour that when her demands were granted, England would find in Ireland a loyal and faithful friend in the hour of danger. (Cheers) The British Government, relying on their honour, and in spite of threats and enormous pressure, passed the Home Rule bill. Was it to be said that they had broken a troth and were now to set an example of perjury and broken faith? Ireland had kept her word. (Cheers)

He then went on to describe as a small, but noisy faction, those who opposed this policy and had declared that it was time to strike. These young men were never numerous and were now a dwindling number. Many of them preached neutrality, but how could anyone remain neutral in a struggle like the present. Others still, whose numbers were very minute, had sent a message to the Kaiser of Germany, stating that if the Germans landed in Ireland there would be a rising in their favour. (Laughter)

Dillon then went on to talk about the recruiting response in the south of Ireland. He highlighted the fact that there were two main reasons why recruiting in the south had not been as great as in Scotland and Britain. Firstly, the south of Ireland did not have even half the number of men of military age as England and Scotland. That was due to the enormous drain of emigration, leaving only the old and children. Secondly, it had taken some time to impress upon the people in Ireland their true situation, particularly those who had seen the blight of English rule there. Today, however, with only a small exception, Ireland was substantially heart and soul with the Allies in the present struggle. But for the evictions and the clearances, Ireland would have raised 400,000 men. John Dillon then alluded to the conviction, now held by most of the Irish leadership, that there had been a determined effort by those at the War Office who were responsible for recruiting in Ireland, to stop Nationalist Irishmen from enlisting. This would enable the enemies of Home Rule to claim that the Irish were no help at all to the British war effort. Within recent weeks, recruiting had been placed in the hands of civilians, men of capacity and business, and it was now going like a house on fire.

Dillon also mentioned the incident at Birdcage Walk, London, in July 1914 when John Redmond and he were walking back from the King's conference at Buckingham Palace. As they were passing Wellington Barracks, hundreds of men from the 1st Bn Irish Guards rushed to the gates of the barracks to cheer both men rousingly. Hundreds more appeared at the windows of the barrack blocks waving bed sheets. The battalion was 90 per cent Roman Catholic and was overtly Irish Nationalist in its political sympathies. John Redmond acknowledged the Irish guardsmen's rousing rendition of 'A Nation Once Again' with a smile and a wave. John Dillon stated that the incident had brought home to him and to many doubting Nationalists that the King's uniform might cover a true Irish heart. (Cheers) As a final point, Dillon advised those interested to scan the casualty lists, where they would find the names of those fighting. There they would find Irishmen fighting with the Black Watch and other Scottish regiments. His main reason for coming to Glasgow was to ask them to join the Irish Brigade. Irishmen ought to stick together, for he felt sore to see other regiments get the honour and glory of Irishmen. The meeting end with the singing of the British national anthem and, of course, 'A Nation Once Again'.

On the industrial front, the concerns over the lack of munitions and workers' militancy saw the introduction of Munitions of War Committees, which, with the agreement of the trade unions, would see workers asked to surrender many of their hard-won employment rights to help secure the supply of munitions. In mid-April, after considering the details and ramifications, the trade unionists on the Clyde led by the engineers agreed to support the formation of the Glasgow and West of Scotland Munitions of War Committee. The Glasgow Herald of 19 April announced that the government had commandeered 300 to 400 tramway workers in Newcastle to manufacture munitions.

Also on 19 April, the Lord Provost chaired a meeting of the senior Glasgow clubs at the city chambers. They met to discuss a football match between the League Champions and a Rest of the League select. The aim of the match was to raise funds for the Belgian refugees. It was a cause that the Celtic were happy to be associated with and a date was set for the game to be played at Hampden Park on 15 May. After the lack of goodwill and good sportsmanship displayed when Celtic won the League, *the Man in the Know* thought it would be an opportunity to note and appreciate the sporting spirit, if such a thing existed of a Glasgow crowd where the Celtic were concerned. A suggestion had been mooted that week that the champions might go to Belfast at the end of April to play a game, but with German submarines lurking in home waters, no one was too keen at the thought of sighting a periscope in mid-channel.

THE WAR FRONTS

The Gallipoli Landings

After the failed naval assault on the Dardanelles of 18 March, General Ian Hamilton had spent a month at Alexandria reorganising and gathering in the men and materiel required to mount a seaborne invasion of the Gallipoli peninsula. As the British scoured the Med for supplies and equipment, German and Turkish spies sent fulsome reports back to their spymasters. With the element of surprise completely lost for the invaders, the defenders on Gallipoli put their intelligence warnings to good use.

The Mediterranean Expeditionary Force (MEF) comprised British, Australian, New Zealand, Indian and French troops. The ANZAC contingent numbered around 30,000 men, including an Indian Brigade, while the French contributed 16,500. The British element comprised the 29th Division, the last of the Regular Army divisions, and the Royal Naval Division. The Royal Naval Division comprised 10,000 naval reservists, while the 29th Division comprised 17,500 regular soldiers, eleven of whose twelve battalions had been on garrison duties across the Empire when war broke out. Among the regular Celtic battalions of the 29th Division were the 1st Bn Royal Munster Fusiliers, 1st Bn Royal Dublin Fusiliers, 1st Bn Royal Inniskilling Fusiliers and the 1st Bn King's Own Scottish Borderers. Also attached to the division were the 5th Bn Royal Scots, a Territorial Force battalion based in Edinburgh. The 29th Division had left the UK in mid-March and arrived in Alexandria over the first week of April.

Ian Hamilton's plan for the seaborne invasion involved the French division landing on the Asiatic shore at Kum Kale as a diversion, while the remaining Empire forces would simultaneously assault a series of landing beaches designated S, V, W, X, Y and Z at the south of the Gallipoli peninsula. The ANZAC forces were assigned to Z Beach about fourteen miles from the tip of the peninsula. On the day they were mistakenly landed a mile further north at Ari Burnu. The next beach to the south, Y Beach, was assigned to the 1st Bn King's Own Scottish Borderers (KOSB) and a battalion from the Royal Marines. The landing beach was not actually a beach at all, but a narrow strip of shingle below a 200-foot cliff. The initial landings on V, W and X Beaches were assigned to the 29th Division's 86th Brigade of four fusilier battalions. The 2nd Bn Royal Fusiliers were assigned to X Beach, where they would be followed in by the 1st Bn Border Regiment. The 1st Bn Lancashire Fusiliers would land on W Beach.

Gallipoli Landings Map

The 1st Bn Royal Munster Fusiliers and 1st Bn Royal Dublin Fusiliers would land on V Beach at Cape Helles, situated at the southernmost tip of the peninsula. Inspired by the fact that the Gallipoli beaches lay within sight of the ancient ruins of Troy, an old collier, *SS River Clyde*, was transformed into an assault ship to be used as a Trojan horse. The idea being to run her aground on V Beach when the soldiers of the Royal Munster Fusiliers, a company of Royal Dublin Fusiliers and the Hampshire Regiment hidden inside would burst from the ship's hold straight onto the beach. At least that was the plan. The 2nd Bn South Wales Borderers plus attachments were assigned to S Beach. All units were tasked on landing to drive inland, thereby creating a wide bridgehead or toehold on the southern tip of the peninsula.

On Sunday 25 April, the Allied invasion fleet appeared off the Gallipoli shore and while the French troops landed on the Asiatic coast, 55,000 British and ANZAC troops set out on rowing boats for the landing beaches on the Gallipoli peninsula. With the exception of the landing on S Beach, the operation was a disaster. On landing, the ANZACs were tasked with driving inland and taking the heights that dominated the narrow neck of the peninsula. However, they found themselves in the most inhospitable terrain imaginable with steep cliffs and deep gullies, which made progress slow and torturous. Their slow progress allowed Turkish reinforcements to be rushed into the area and after some fierce fighting, they prevented the ANZACs from capturing the strategically vital Sari Bair heights.

At Y Beach, the KOSB and the Royal Marines eventually scaled the cliff without interference. Ian Hamilton's idea was that the KOSB and Marines would then drive south four miles to take the Turkish forces from the rear and link up with the southernmost beaches. Unfortunately, the idea was not delivered with enough clarity to the two commanding officers at Y Beach, who on arrival at the top of the cliff sat on their hands for the rest of the day and did nothing.

The 2nd Bn Royal Fusiliers were the first battalion ashore on X Beach, where their landing was opposed by just twelve Turkish soldiers, who promptly got off their mark. Following them in were the 1st Bn Royal Inniskilling Fusiliers and the 1st Bn Border Regiment. After reorganising, the battalions moved south with a view to joining up with the landings at V and W Beaches just a mile away.

At W Beach, the Lancashire Fusiliers waded ashore from their boats and into hell. Caught up in wire entanglements positioned under the waterline they were scythed down in droves by well-positioned Turkish machine guns. The subsequent fight for W Beach passed into military folklore as the action in which six Victoria Crosses were won before breakfast. Despite the carnage on the shoreline, the Lancashire lads, with the help of the 4th Bn Worcester Regiment, created and held a narrow beachhead. A quarter of the battalion were killed on the Gallipoli shoreline, while hundreds more were wounded. In recognition of their gallant deeds, Ian Hamilton directed that the beach was to be known as 'Lancashire Landing'.

At first light, the battleships *HMS Queen Elizabeth* and *HMS Albion* bombarded the Turkish positions around V Beach for an hour. Towards the end of the bombardment, the *River Clyde* (with sally-port exit doors cut in its bow sides for the 2,000 men of the 1st Bn Royal Munster Fusiliers, 1st/ 2nd Bn Hants, 2nd Bn Royal Fusiliers and W Company 1st Bn Royal Dublin Fusiliers) was run aground. Unfortunately, the *Clyde* beached about twenty yards from shore and the ensuing delay while a pontoon of boats was created, allowed the Turkish defenders to reoccupy their trenches. Three companies of the 1st Bn Royal Dublin Fusiliers in six boat tows also arrived on the beach at the same time as the *River Clyde*. The boats were rowed in for the last few hundred yards after being set adrift by steam pinnaces. The Turks opened up a murderous weight of fire on the Dublin Fusiliers rowing ashore. In a scene that predated the carnage on Omaha Beach by thirty years, Turkish machine gunfire cut men to pieces while still in the boats, some of which simply drifted away with their cargoes of dead and wounded Irishmen. Some men jumped over the side and struggled ashore, only to be cut down as they reached the beach. Many of the wounded fell face down into the shallow water and, weighed down by their packs, they were unable to rise. Their comrades who had made it to the safety of a low bank some fifteen yards up the beach came back to help them, but were themselves shot down. The commanding officer of the Dublin and Munster Fusiliers on the bridge of the Clyde watched in horror as his men were cut to pieces on the shoreline. He later estimated that of the 240 men who had rowed ashore, barely forty made it without being wounded. The sea for a distance of fifty yards was red with blood. Later figures showed fifty-three men had been killed and over 150 had been wounded, some of whom would later die from wounds.

Inside the *River Clyde*, the men could hear the bullets ricochet off the hull of the ship. It took just five minutes to create a pontoon bridge between the *Clyde* and the shore. The sally-port doors were opened and the men of the Munster Fusiliers poured out. Like the Dublin Fusiliers, the Munsters charged into a wall of machine gun and mortar fire. The carnage was such the dead and wounded soon blocked the gangways and had to be cleared away over the side before those still inside could follow. The weight of fire onto the gangways and pontoons was such that several of the pontoons were displaced and as a second wave of Munsters attempted to get ashore, they too were cut down, many of the wounded falling into the sea where they drowned. The Munsters lost fifty-five men killed and another 100 wounded.

Also on board the River Clyde that morning was Tipperary-born, Father Willie Finn, RC chaplain to the Dublin Fusiliers and the 86th Brigade. As Father Finn was about to follow the men out of the ship, he was advised not to go. He replied, 'A priest's place is beside the dying soldier.' He stepped onto the gangway and immediately received a bullet through the chest. Undeterred, he made his way across the pontoon, receiving another bullet in the thigh and still another in the leg. By the time he reached the beach he was riddled with bullets, but in spite of the great pain he must have been suffering, he heroically went about his duties, giving consolation to the dying troops. It was while he was in the act of attending to the spiritual requirements of one of his men that shrapnel shattered the priest's head, killing him instantly.

From the Kilkenny Journal 2 October 1915:

> Pte. P. Delaney, in a letter to his father.... Sent a photo of heroic Father
> Finn and the place were he is buried with six hundred of the Dublins.
> 'Father Finn was a father to the lot of us. We had many a chat with him
> about old Ireland and Home Rule. He was the bravest of the brave and
> died looking after the dying and wounded. He was a great man and worthy
> son of gallant Tipperary.'

After the debacle of the daylight landings, hundreds of men were put ashore from the *River Clyde* at night with barely a casualty. Over the next three days, the beachheads were merged and expanded through a series of engagements, including a vicious fight involving the Munsters on 26 April during which they cleared the village of Sedd-el-Bahr and Hill 141. On being relieved the following day, the remnants of the battalion returned to V Beach. The roll was called. Of the officers, five had been killed and twelve had been wounded, and of the other ranks, 600 had been killed or wounded. The Dublin Fusiliers were also involved in the fighting and like the Munsters suffered more casualties.

The First Battle of Krithia was fought over 28 to 30 April. Again, the regular soldiers of the 29th Division took the lead, alongside the French division. Their objective was to capture the village of Krithia and the vital heights of Achi Baba. The dark brooding ridge, 720 feet high, towered over the southern portion of the peninsula and from its slopes every inch of ground back to the beaches could be seen. The capture and control of Achi Baba was vital for the MEF's continued advance and would allow the Allied artillery to range across the entire peninsula. On 28 April, in what was another inept badly coordinated operation, the 29th Division actually advanced onto the slopes of Achi Baba, but was so weakened both during the assault and by the casualties sustained during the landings, that it was unable to repulse a determined Turkish counter-attack, which forced the men off the slopes.

The Allies retreated to their start positions, where ominously they began to dig trenches. The allies had sustained 3000 casualties from an attacking force of 14,000. Again, the Dublin and Munster Fusiliers were badly mauled. This time the two battalions had to be temporarily amalgamated. The Royal Dublin Fusiliers were down to just one officer and 374 other ranks. The amalgamated battalion was known as the 'Dubsters'.

Further to the north, the ANZACs were fighting their own desperate battle, clinging to rocky outcrops and the sides of ravines on a beachhead just 3500 yard long and 1200 yards deep. Desperately in need of water and food, the officer commanding, General Birdwood, considered the situation untenable and advised Ian Hamilton to evacuate the position. Hamilton replied that an attack at Krithia, commanded by General Hunter Weston, was imminent and would relieve the pressure. He advised the ANZACs to dig, dig, dig and stick it out. Hunter Weston would never get to the ANZACs, but they did hold on, suffering over 4500 casualties over 26 and 27 April. From then on, the ANZACs were known as *'Diggers'*.

Overall, the Gallipoli landings were a disaster. The only positive was that the Allies were ashore and they did have a toehold on the peninsula, but the casualties had been catastrophic. Adding to Ian Hamilton's worries was the logistics of keeping the Expeditionary Force sustained in the field, now that the operation looked like it would take longer than expected. Chief among his concerns was the resupply of water. There were very few natural sources of water available on the ground won by the allies, and water had to be shipped in from as far away as Egypt. Hamilton was already aware that half his force was employed resupplying the other half, which was digging in and defending the beachhead. Meanwhile the men went thirsty in temperatures that were already climbing towards summer highs of ninety degrees. Hamilton also needed reinforcements to replace the men lost and ammunition, particularly high explosive shells. Things were not going according to plan on Gallipoli, not that there was any great plan in the first place.

The Western Front

On the Western Front, the stalemate and sporadic local fighting continued, but at Ypres the fighting had taken an ominous turn. The Second Battle of Ypres began on 22 April, and a new terrifying weapon was introduced to the battlefield, poison gas! That morning as a prelude to their attack, the Germans first released a major discharge of gas against four miles of Allied positions defending the Ypres Salient. French Colonial troops bore the brunt of the first gas attack and the sight of the mysterious choking yellowish-green gas cloud rolling across the front lines terrified the troops, who broke and fled from their positions. Canadian troops rushed into the area and stabilised the situation, but lost 2000 men gassed. A second gas attack was launched on 24 April against the Canadians. The men attempted to improvise gas masks from wads of cotton, handkerchiefs or field dressings soaked in urine. Sustained German pressure over the next week all along the salient saw the Allies being forced to retreat towards Ypres and they surrendered the vital high ground to the east of the city. The fighting along the Ypres Salient would continue on and off for the next three weeks. The use of poison gas had come as a tactical surprise to the Allies, who condemned its use as barbaric and reprehensible. Having gotten that off their chests, they immediately began the development of their own chemical weapons. The introduction of poison gas to the battlefield was, as far as the British and Irish public were concerned, yet another example of the barbarity of the Germans and of German *Kultur*.

The war had also moved into another dimension, underground. In an attempt to break the stalemate, both sides reverted to the medieval siege warfare strategy of mining under the enemy lines, placing explosives and blowing them up. The British first formed a tunnelling company in February 1915 under the command of the Royal Engineers to counter German mining operations. Civilian sewer workers from Manchester formed the nucleus of the first company. The call then went out to infantry battalions for soldiers with mining experience to be seconded to the new mining units. With extra pay on offer, there were no shortage of volunteers. By April, additional mining companies had been formed and tunnelling operations were well under way.

In some areas, both sides mined and countermined intensively. For the infantry above ground, the wait for underground explosions was nerve-racking indeed; for the men underground, hard physical graft often came accompanied by sudden death with cave-ins a constant hazard. There were also many underground encounters, as miners, breaking into an enemy tunnel, met the Germans underground. Very often these encounters included vicious hand-to-hand fighting with bayonets, knives and sharpened shovels in the cramped tunnels and chambers. The blowing of mines below enemy front-line positions became a regular feature of local actions. Infantry tactics developed to involve the rushing and capturing of the crater formed by an explosion. The craters were often a dominant ground feature, as the lip of earth thrown up was usually higher than the ground in the area, giving possible observation over the enemy positions. Crater fighting would become a highly dangerous and unpleasant feature of many local actions in 1915. Tunnelling would, for the remainder of the war, form an integral part of British tactical planning. Canadian and Australian units would also form their own tunnelling companies.

For the soldiers on the ground, April saw a change in the weather as spring finally sprung. Conditions improved to the point where the Glaswegians, always critical of the weather, were complaining about the heat, having forgotten the horrendous winter they had just spent freezing in liquid mud-filled trenches.

Chapter Twelve

MAY

SCOTTISH FOOTBALL

After what had been the strangest football season ever, on the evening of 4 May 1915, the SFA held its annual general meeting at Carlton Place, Glasgow. Duncan Campbell (Morton FC) presided. After adopting the minutes of the last annual general meeting and amending a number of rules relating to the Scottish Cup, the secretary and treasurer submitted their reports. Among the items in the secretary's report were the facts that there were 114 clubs and fourteen associations on the SFA roll. Eighty-four clubs registered 1598 professional players, a decrease over the previous season of six clubs and 156 players. The report showed that football had not shirked its duty under the abnormal conditions of the season just finished. Approximately 1500 Scottish players had enlisted, while 2000 non-playing staff had also joined the colours. Clubs and associations had contributed over £5000 to various relief funds, while collections at matches were estimated to be around £1000.

According to the treasurer's report, the SFA's income over the year was £3155 and its expenditure £5625, therefore a loss of £2470 was incurred. In addition, £1000 had been contributed to the Prince of Wales's War Relief Fund and £250 donated to the Belgian Relief Fund. Another £1000 was allocated to a SFA Benevolent Fund, taking the loss for the year to well over £4000. With cash held standing at £7000, the total assets of the SFA stood at £12,400. The office bearers were voted in. The Earl of Rosebery was re-elected patron and Sir John Ure Primrose, Bart, as honorary president. The retiring officials – D Campbell (Morton), president; Thomas White (Celtic), vice-president; and T Steen (Ayr United), treasurer – were all unanimously re-elected.

Immediately after the AGM, an extraordinary meeting was held to discuss altering a number of association articles that required to be changed due to the wartime conditions. It was subsequently agreed that the SFA Council, at their absolute discretion, be empowered to suspend the game entirely or in any district or districts. Correspondingly, agreements between players and clubs would be suspended during any such suspension period. The council were also given the power to suspend or abandon any or all of its competitions. The players' agreements with their clubs were also amended and adapted to reflect the changing conditions. Players signed by the clubs were to be engaged for a period of not less than four weeks. The engagements could be terminated by the club on any reasonable ground, on four weeks' notice in writing to the player, stating the ground upon which the agreement was terminated. The clubs' ability to engage players was also curtailed. A soldier serving with the colours or a sailor serving in the Royal Navy could not be approached at any time without at least fourteen days' notice being given, in the case of the army, to his commanding officer, and in the case of the navy, to his port or fleet management committee.

CELTIC FC

Over the first eight days in May, the six senior Glasgow clubs played out the Glasgow Merchants Charity Cup competition. In a throwback to the origins of the competition, corner kicks were a part of the scoring system. On May Day, the Celtic met Queen's Park at Hampden Park in the first round and 8000 spectators watched two Patsy Gallacher goals. Celtic beat the amateurs by two goals and four corners to one goal and four corners. At Parkhead, Third Lanark beat Clyde 1–0 in the other first round game. Rangers and Partick Thistle each had byes into the semi-finals. On 4 May, Third Lanark lost 3–0 to Rangers and the following day 10,000 watched Celtic and Partick Thistle play out a 1–1 draw at Firhill; however, Celtic went through by the narrowest of margins, 4–3 on corners. The winning corner was gained with just two minutes left on the clock.

On 8 May, Celtic and Rangers met in the Glasgow Merchants Charity Cup final at a blustery Ibrox Park. Over 30,000 turned up to watch the latest Old Firm encounter and £864 was added to the Charity Cup kitty. The Celtic was without Johnny McMaster, who had been injured during the Patrick Thistle game, and as usual the ever reliable Tom McGregor stepped into the breach. Before the start of the game, Major RM Christie, ex-president of the SFA, made a recruiting speech to the crowd. He was keen on getting some football supporters into the 13th (Service) Bn HLI then stationed at Gosport. The game was described as an exhibition of prolonged bad temper, with at least two players in danger of being sent off. *The Man in the Know* called it 'peppery' and noted that for a charity game there were many uncharitable things done. After about twelve minutes, Joe Dodds, somewhat against the run of play, fired the Celts into the lead with a twenty-yard belter. Patsy Gallacher was clogged midway through the first half and was forced to retire for medical treatment. While the wee man was off receiving attention, Rangers pressed their advantage and scored two goals through Cairns and Cunningham. The interval came and the Celts went into the pavilion with Rangers leading by 2–1. Patsy Gallacher reappeared after the restart and the Celtic, now with the wind at their backs, took control of the game. Despite Celtic having most of the ball, Rangers managed to go further ahead when they broke upfield to force a valuable corner point. With ten minutes to go, the Ibrox men were still leading by two goals and one corner to one goal. Just five minutes from time, a fine shot from Johnny Browning put the Celts level on goals, but as the few remaining minutes ticked away it looked as if Rangers would hold on to win by a corner kick. With less than two minutes left on the clock and all seemingly lost, Andy McAtee gathered in the ball and raced up the wing. Jimmy McMenemy kept pace with him through the centre, to head in Celtic's winning third goal from Andy McAtee's inch-perfect cross. The Charity Cup was remaining at Parkhead for a fourth consecutive year and the season ended on another high note for the Celtic.

The Man in the Know commented that the Rangers found the manner of their defeat a 'trifle galling' as they watched their last chance of a trophy disappear into the Celtic's silver cabinet. The last gasp goal reminded him of a previous occasion the Celtic had deprived Rangers of a cup in the dying seconds. The location was old Cathkin Park and the occasion was the final of the British League Cup. The trophy was the Glasgow International Exhibition Cup, which Rangers had won the year previous. The trophy had been put up by Rangers to raise funds for the Ibrox disaster of 1902. The final had gone into extra time with the sides level at 2–2. With seconds left on the clock, Willie Loney forced a corner that was whipped over by Davie Crawford. The ball was meet by the Mighty Quinn, who planted it into the Rangers net. The winning goal was so last gasp there was not even time to kick off. The Rangers directors had asked repeatedly for the cup to be put up for competition and it was generally felt that they would rather win this cup than the Scottish Cup. *The Man in the Know* thought that perhaps some day the Celtic would put it up for a worthy cause. How wrong he was: the trophy still sits in the silver cabinet at Parkhead over 110 years later.

IRELAND

The morning of the Charity Cup final, the newspapers broke the news of the sinking of the cruise liner *Lusitania* off the coast of Kinsale. The ship was the largest passenger vessel on the transatlantic service and had left New York for Liverpool on 1 May. Having already announced unrestricted submarine warfare and the possibility of attacks on neutral shipping, the Germans had published in American newspapers a warning to passengers crossing the Atlantic on British ships that they did so at considerable risk of being sunk. On 7 May, German submarine U-20 fired one torpedo at the liner; the torpedo struck and appeared to cause a second explosion, which many believed was the detonation of contraband munitions destined for the British Army that were stored in the hold. The damage caused to the ship was so severe it rolled over and sank in just eighteen minutes. Of the 1959 people on board, 785 passengers and 413 crew died, including 128 American citizens. In 2008, divers exploring the wreck discovered millions of rounds of US-made ammunition and thousands of shrapnel shells in the hold.

Back in February 1915, the IRB members of the Irish Volunteers had formed a Military Council comprising seven members: Thomas Clarke, Sean MacDermott, Padraic Pearse, Éamonn Ceannt, Joseph Plunkett, James Connolly and Thomas MacDonagh. Plans were drawn up to stage a rebellion, perhaps as early as September 1915. The plans were kept secret from other advanced Nationalists and Irish Volunteers leaders. The advanced Nationalists had also stepped up their anti-recruitment campaign, but it was not without its risks and consequences. On Sunday 16 May, Sean MacDermott was arrested under the Defence of the Realm Act regulations after delivering what was regarded as a seditious speech in the Square at Tuam. Although only thirty-one years of age, he had already demonstrated considerable talents as a political organiser, having run an election campaign for the Sinn Féin candidates in his native Leitrim in 1908 and had been an organiser for the IRB since at least 1908. At the time of his arrest, he was the commercial manager for the suppressed newspaper Irish Freedom. Copies of the newspaper, banned since December 1914, were found on the brake that he was using as a platform and were confiscated. His arrest caused quite a stir in the town and he was taken under escort to the local police barracks. He was later sentenced to four months' hard labour in Mountjoy Gaol. McDermott's arrest may have been a factor in the postponement of the September uprising. The same day that Sean McDermott was arrested in Tuam, Sinn Féiner John Milroy was arrested after giving an anti-recruitment speech in Custom House Square, Dublin. He was found guilty and sentenced to three months' imprisonment in Mountjoy. The influence of the anti-recruitment campaign in Ireland should not be overestimated. Although only 23,015 men enlisted there between mid-December 1914 and mid-May 1915, compared to almost 45,500 between August and mid-December 1914, recruitment figures for the British mainland also reflected a similar fall.

In mid-May, John Redmond was still writing letters to the press with regard to the Irish Brigade. In his latest, he emphasised once again that the Irish Brigade was in fact three brigades, composing the 16th (Irish) Division. In a piece of gross exaggeration, he stated, 'They are entirely composed of Irishmen and are largely officered by Irishmen.' The brigades at Fermoy and Buttevant were recruited up to strength, but the 48th brigade at Tipperary was still in need of recruits.

Corporal John Fallon and sister
(Courtesy of the Fallon family)

Based at the Curragh, Newbridge and Kildare, the 10th (Irish) Division was coming to the end of the brigade training phase and daily expected a warning order to move to England to start divisional training. When the order did arrive, the division was instructed to concentrate at Basingstoke, Hampshire. At the Curragh, the 5th Bn Connaught Rangers, part of the 29th Brigade, moved out at 1500 hrs on 4 May. By 1700 hrs, the battalion was boarding a ferry at the North Wall, Dublin. As usual a farewell delegation of dignitaries was at the docks to see the battalion off and an Irish ladies' committee gave out presents of pipes, cigarettes and chocolates to the men. The crossing from Dublin to Holyhead was without incident, although a German submarine had been sighted off Holyhead that same afternoon. After some delay at Holyhead, it was 1130 hrs the following day before the 5th Bn Connaught Rangers reached Basingstoke and marched into New Park Camp, Hackwood. Soon after their arrival, Private John Fallon received the good news that he had been promoted and was appointed 'Paid' Lance Corporal. No doubt, the extra tuppence a day would come in handy. The month of May was spent training in and around Hampshire and included brigade marches, night operations, shooting practice at Ash Ranges and field exercises. The Irish battalions spent the whole of 27 May practicing drill and polishing their personal kit. The following day, the 10th (Irish) Division was inspected by the King at Hackwood Park.

THE WAR FRONT

Gallipoli

On 1 and 3 May, the Allies repelled two major Turkish attacks, but despite inflicting horrendous casualties on the attackers, the Allies also suffered heavy losses that they could ill afford.

Irrespective of the fact, Ian Hamilton ordered Lieutenant-General Sir Alymer Hunter-Weston, commander of 29th Division to launch a quick counter-attack. Reinforced by two ANZAC brigades, the frontal attack went in on 6 May, but little progress was made, mainly due to a lack of command and control. The following day Hunter-Weston tried again, another frontal assault in broad daylight, with the same results. A third and final assault was to be launched on 8 May. Ian Hamilton suggested that a night attack should be tried, but Hunter-Weston disagreed. This time a little progress was made, between 200 and 300 yards, but at the cost of all available artillery munitions and more heavy casualties. In fact, none of the assaults actually reached the Turkish trenches, being broken up by outposts manned by machine gun teams, snipers and shellfire. When the offensive was called off after three days of fighting, Krithia and Achi Baba were not much closer, while Hunter-Weston's unimaginative frontal assaults cost 6,500 casualties, about 30 per cent of the troops engaged. With the serious losses, the situation back to stalemate and with stocks of artillery munitions almost depleted, Ian Hamilton, like Oliver Twist, asked for more, four more divisions and 25,000 shells, particularly high explosive. While they awaited Kitchener's reply, the tactics were changed to one of bite-and-hold, small-scale stealth assaults, which proved much more successful in gaining ground and infinitely less costly in lives than large-scale frontal assaults. However, even a blind man could see that the campaign at both ANZAC and Cape Helles was stagnating. Ian Hamilton's request for more shells arrived on Kitchener's desk at about the same time as the 'Shells Scandal' broke in the British newspapers. His initial reply to Ian Hamilton's requests was not encouraging.

The Battle of Festubert

The British Generals on the Western Front had a couple of months to get over the disappointment of Neuve-Chapelle and now decided they would have another go at breaking through the German line along the Aubers Ridge. The British attack was in support of a simultaneous French assault on Vimy Ridge further to the south.

Willie Angus and the 8th Bn Royal Scots as part of the 7th Division were in a support role for the assault. On the night of 8/9 May, the battalion marched into assembly positions in reserve trenches behind Rue Petillon. The attack was an unmitigated disaster. A shortage of shells led to an ineffective artillery barrage prior to the assaults going in, and in most places the attacking infantry had barely left their trenches before being cut down. The Meerut Division, and the 1st and 8th Divisions were all very badly cut up. After the attack, the Royal Scots moved back, first to Rouge-de-Boat and then on 10 May they marched to Essars. Two days later, they moved into billets at Les Choquaux. Despite the disaster at Aubers, the general decided they would have another go just a week later and a couple of miles to the south at Festubert. The next week was spent preparing for the attack that would be launched from the area between Givenchy and Richebourg.

Corporal Josie Maley and his draft had joined the Glasgow Highlanders at Gorre at the end of January and the battalion as part of 5th Brigade, 2nd Division, spent the next three months being shuttled around the area taking their turn in the front line and being used for myriad administrative tasks around the rear areas. By the beginning of May, the battalion was based at Annequin and taking its turn manning the front line in the Cuinchy Sector. On 6 May,

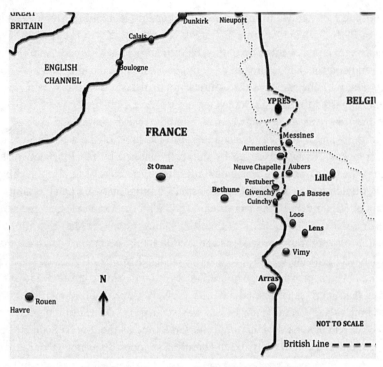

British Section of the Front Line May 1915

the Glasgow Highlanders moved into billets in the Collège Des Jeunes Filles in Bethune, but unfortunately for the boys all the girls were gone. The town was a major administrative hub for the British and was buzzing with activity and rumours of another big push.

The Big Push as far as the 2nd Division and the Glasgow Highlanders were concerned would be known to posterity as the Battle of Festubert. The battle was in fact, phase two of the earlier failed assault on the Aubers Ridge. The Highlanders had been stood by in support positions during that assault, ready to exploit the breakthrough that never came. They then marched to Richebourg on 11 May and spent the next few days at hard labour, digging trenches behind the front line.

On 13 May, it poured with rain and the British artillery opened their fire plan with a total of 433 guns and howitzers firing along a narrow 5000-yard frontage. The guns had three objectives: howitzers would attempt to blow gaps in the enemy breastworks and destroy trenches, the 4.5in guns would target the enemy support lines, while the majority of the eighteen pounder field guns would attempt to destroy the enemy wire, firing shrapnel which was worse than useless. Firing day and night for the next two days, over 101,000 shells were fired, a high proportion of which were duds and failed to explode. On 14 May, the commanding officer of the 2nd Scots Guards went forward to look at the ground his battalion would assault and cross. When he came back, he was less than happy. At least six rows of barbed wire still remained in place, strung across the battalion frontage and largely untouched by the shelling.

The battle plan involved the breaching of the German line in two places by prolonged bombardments followed by infantry assaults from the Rue du Bois and north of Festubert. That from the Rue du Bois was to be carried out by the 2nd Division, which would attack with the 6th Infantry Brigade on the right and the 5th on the left. The 7th Division was on the right of the 2nd, and the Garhwal Brigade of the Indian Corps, with the Sirhind Brigade in support, on the left. The 5th Infantry Brigade now consisted of five battalions, although they were not up to full strength: the 2nd Ox and Bucks, 2nd Worcesters, 2nd Royal Inniskilling Fusiliers, 2nd HLI and the Glasgow Highlanders. The 5th Brigade would attack on a frontage of two battalions. The 2nd Inniskilling Fusiliers (right assault) and 2nd Bn Worcestershire Regiment (left assault) would lead the attack with the Glasgow Highlanders behind the latter and the Ox and Bucks behind the former. The 2nd Bn HLI was in immediate reserve until the enemy's line was captured, when they would dig communicating trenches to it.

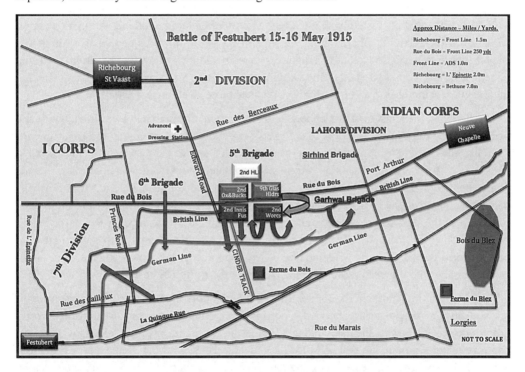

Battle of Festubert 15 – 16 May 1915 Map

The Glasgow Highlanders were ordered to send three working parties of fifty men each to act with the Worcesters. These parties were handed over to that battalion at 1730 hrs; therefore the whole of No 4 Company was detached from the Glasgow Highlanders for the opening phase of the attack. The 2nd Division's assault area was split by a cinder track, which ran between the Rue du Bois and the German positions at the Ferme du Bois. The 5th Brigade would assault on the left or east of the track as far as Port Arthur and the 6th Brigade on the right or west. Prior to zero hour, the Worcesters were to move out of the front trenches and crawl as far forward as they could without being detected. The 150 Glasgow Highlanders from No 4 Company were to follow them out and remain there to secure the ground gained. The remaining Glasgow Highlanders companies would then move forward to occupy the vacated front-line trenches and breastworks.

On 15 May, after the necessary administration had been completed, the men got a few hours to themselves. Army chaplains, including a number of Catholic priests serving as chaplains, moved among the men. Joe Maley took the opportunity to attend a trench-head Mass, where he took Holy Communion. He then managed to get off a couple of quick letters. In one to his family, he told them he was just getting ready for a couple of days fighting, but he was in the pink of condition, well and happy, and concluded: 'I hope all are as happy and well as I am. I expect,' he added, 'that in a week or so I'll be getting a spell of leave, and then I will see you all and have a day or two at Millport.'

The reference to his imminent leave was probably due the fact that his company commander had just informed him that he had been accepted for a commission with John Shaughnessy's 18th HLI and would be posted back to Officer Training School in Scotland within a few days. Josie also wrote a letter to Charlie Quin, *the Man in the Know*, in which he said everything was in place for his transfer to Colonel Shaughnessy's team and it was now just a matter of waiting patiently. He also commented on Celtic winning the League: 'So the good old Celtic got hold of the League Championship and the Charity Cup once more. Well done, Celtic!'

At 2000 hrs, the Glasgow Highlanders, less No 4 Company, marched from Richebourg and occupied three lines of breastworks to the rear of the Worcesters occupying the front line. By 2230 hrs, the entire 5th Infantry Brigade was in position and in the darkness the men awaited zero hour. After a prolonged, but as it transpired completely ineffectual artillery barrage, the attack went in at 2330 hrs. As the first wave of infantry rose into the assault, the Germans occupying the positions in front of the Worcesters, fully alert and awaiting the attack, opened fire. Most of the Worcesters were caught in the open and barely advanced a few yards before being cut down in droves by German machine gun fire. Some attempted to go on and were accompanied by the Glasgow Highlanders of No 4 Company, but it was suicide, and within twenty minutes the Worcesters were falling back into their original positions.

On the right of the attack, the Inniskillings did have some limited success and managed to take and hold, at some considerable cost, a portion of a German trench line. Meanwhile, shortly after midnight 15/16 May, the badly mauled Worcesters were ordered to attack again. This was contrary to the original plan that had the Glasgow Highlanders taking up the attack if the first assault failed, but the Worcester's commanding officer informed brigade headquarters that he would not be able to reorganise his shattered battalion quickly enough to keep to the new zero hour of 0200 hrs.

The Glasgow Highlanders were then ordered to put in the assault at 0315 hrs, but the survivors of the Worcesters were now back in the front line and the narrow communication trenches were choked with their dead, dying and wounded men. The Glasgow Highlanders were, therefore, unable to move forward and unable to make the deadline. Eventually, at around 0300 hrs, in an attempt to get forward, the leading Glasgow Highlander companies climbed out of the trenches and crossed open country under heavy small arms fire to reach the front line. On arrival, they had great difficulty getting into cover with so many of the Worcesters in the line of breastworks. Confusion reigned for the next few hours as what was left of the Worcester

Regiment were eventually withdrawn and the Glasgow Highlanders fully occupied the front-line breastworks. Throughout 16 May, a number of localised attacks and counter-attacks took place along the entire battle area. Plans for a renewed general attack were issued and then cancelled, and reissued only to be cancelled again.

For the Glasgow Highlanders, the day was spent in the front-line breastworks under almost continuous shellfire. Most of it was ineffectual, but one or two did strike home and cause considerable casualties. One large-calibre shell found its mark when it detonated inside a dugout in which a section of Glasgow Highlanders was sheltering. Of the ten men in the dugout, a half dozen were blown to pieces with the remainder very badly wounded, some dying later. The sight was such that when two men went to help the wounded, they could not bear to do more than glance inside at what was left of the bunker.

Corporal Joseph S. Maley
(Courtesy of the Maley Family)

At some point early on the morning of 16 May, Corporal Josie Maley was wounded on the top of his head by shrapnel. Later, a Glasgow newspaper story reported that he was seen hit and fall by friends who carried him unconscious, but alive, back to the regimental aid post (RAP) positioned in the shelter of a ruined house to the rear of the battalion's positions. The medical officer patched him up, but only very rudimentary first aid could be carried out this close to the front lines. Josie was then stretchered to the main dressing station (MDS) a mile or so to the rear. There, more elaborate medical treatment was available and the doctors took some time to stabilise the wound before Josie was transported by field ambulance back along the medical evacuation chain to No 33 Casualty Clearing Station (CCS) based at Bethune. A CCS was a major medical facility with the means to conduct major surgical operations. Josie apparently never recovered consciousness; he lingered on into 17 May before succumbing to his head wounds. Corporal Joseph Stanislaus Maley, aged twenty-two, was buried in Bethune Town Cemetery.

The day after Josie Maley was fatally wounded, Alex Dickson, also 9th HLI, who had been on the books of Rangers FC, was killed by shellfire. His parents lived in Linthouse, Govan. Despite never actually taking part in any attack, the Glasgow Highlanders suffered five officers and 207 other ranks killed, wounded or missing over the three days of 15–18 May, mostly as a result of shellfire.

Also involved in the fight at Festubert was Willie Angus and the 8th Bn Royal Scots. The 7th Division would take part in the first assault, but the Royal Scots would again be spared the worst of the fighting when they began the attack in reserve positions near the Rue Cailloux, north of Festubert. When the attack went in, the leading battalions captured the first line of German trenches, but suffered heavy losses. In mid-afternoon, the 8th Royal Scots were ordered up into the captured trenches with instructions to hold onto the gains. Just hours earlier and just 2,000 yards away, Josie Maley had been fatally wounded.

For the next thirty-six hours the shellfire was incessant and the losses were very severe. At some point during 18 May, Willie Angus was caught up in a blast, which saw him take a shell splinter in his right leg near his knee. The medics of 23 Field Ambulance patched him up and passed him onto No 7 Casualty Clearing Station based at Morville. The following day he was passed further down the medical chain to No 1 Canadian Stationary Hospital at Wimereux and the day after that to No 10 General Hospital based at Rouen. Although serious enough to see him passed all the way down the medical chain to the large stationary hospitals well back from the front line, Willie's wound kept him in hospital for just one week before he was transferred on 29 May to a convalescing facility nearby.

Meanwhile back at Festubert, the Royal Scots had continued to suffer under the intensive artillery shelling. Finally, after dark on 18 May they were relieved and moved back to Bethune. The thirty-six hours spent holding the captured German trench line had cost the 8th Royal Scots thirty-six men killed and over 140 wounded. Among the dead were eight men of the 8th Bn HLI Company, three of whom were from Carluke. After its experiences at Festubert, the battalion managed a few weeks out of the line moving from Bethune to Lillers on 19 May and to Essars on 2 June.

Also on 18 May, the 1st Bn Irish Guards took part in an attack near Le Touret, where the battalion lost over 400 men, killed, wounded or missing. The disastrous assault on the Vour L'Avoine Farm cost the Irish Guards over half their effective strength. The battalion was withdrawn from the front line and sent to the rear to lick its wounds and to reform. A few days later, word of the losses arrived at the Guards depot at Warley. Immediately drafts of replacements were mustered and sent to the 1st Irish Guards to make up the losses. Among those warned about a posting to the 1st Battalion was now fully trained Patrick Hilley. A few days' home leave was awarded to men on draft, but not before they signed the Active Service notification form. This meant failing to return on time from their pre-embarkation leave meant they would be charged, not with absence, but with desertion, a much more serious crime. Pat got back to Warley on time and with a draft of fifty battle casualty replacements, they made their way to France embarking at Southampton on 31 May and landed at Le Havre on 1 June 1915. There were now two of the Garngad's Hilley brothers in France. Pat was just three weeks behind his brother Edward. Meanwhile, Gunner James Hilley, probably acting under John Redmond's directive that Irishmen should if possible enlist or transfer into Irish regiments, was attempting to work his transfer from the 17th Division to the 10th (Irish) Division.

Celtic old Bhoy, Willie McOustra with the 2nd Scots Guards, was also involved in the fighting at Festubert. In the first wave of the 7th Division's assault, the Scots Guards went over the top at 0312 hrs on 15 May and by 0530 hrs their assault had taken them through the German front line and on into their support trenches. Shortly afterwards, the Germans launched a counter-attack. F Company, Scots Guards, advancing ahead of the line was attacked, surrounded and effectively destroyed. Thirty odd men managed to fight their way out and join a unit on their right. Their last stand would later be described in detail in the British press. The German counter-attack swept on and around 0800 hrs came up against Willie McOustra's G Company, then in the area of the third German support line. The fighting was at very close range and at times became almost medieval in its ferocity. Individual hand-to-hand fights using bayonets, picks and shovels made the fighting intensely personal. At around 0900 hrs, the

Grenadier Guards came up in support just as the Scots had beaten off the Germans. Support units were fed into the battle over the course of the day and at 2030 hrs, the Scots Guards were relieved and moved back to occupy an orchard near the old German front line that had been taken in the first rush. When the men were mustered, only 300, including Willie McOustra answered their names.

The fighting at Festubert stuttered on until the 25 May, when Sir John French ordered Sir Douglas Haig to pull the plug. Festubert could only be regarded as any kind of a success when compared to the abject failure of the attack at Aubers a week or so earlier. The ground captured was insignificant, about a mile in depth and 3000 yards long, while the loss of men (16,000 casualties) and the ammunition expended was vastly out of proportion to the advantage gained. The problems already identified months earlier at Neuve-Chapelle were again apparent, particularly the supply, quality and type of artillery ammunition, which was woefully inadequate.

CELTIC FC

Monday, 10 May, saw Willie Maley travel south to Liverpool. He was representing the club at yet another funeral; this time it was that of an old footballing friend, Newcastle-born Tom Watson, the architect of Sunderland and Liverpool football clubs. On Saturday 15 May, the newly crowned League Champions took on a Scottish League XI at Hampden Park. The charity game was organised by the Lord Provost of Glasgow, who was present, and the proceeds of the gate

Jim Young in action v Rest of the League

would benefit Belgian refugees in the care of the Glasgow Corporation. The day broke sunny but windy and the Celtic started the game playing into both. The Bhoys were under the cosh for the first fifteen minutes or so. Gourley of Morton went close and then Charlie Shaw was forced to save from Cunningham of Rangers. Once the Celts weathered the storm, they began to exert their own pressure. After twenty minutes or so, Andy McAtee broke down the right wing and fired over a cross into the penalty box. The wind caught the ball, whipping it high into the air, giving Kerr in goal a difficult catch. The Queen's Park man jumped and caught the ball cleanly, but before he could steady himself he was shoulder charged (perfectly legally) still holding the ball, into the net by Jimmy McColl. The select went back onto the attack and again Shaw was forced into a save from Gourley. At the half-time whistle the Celts were leading by a single goal. At the interval the Lord Provost addressed the crowd, pleading for recruits for the city's

TF battalions, while at the same time, the crowd was entertained by the pipes and drums of the 7th Bn Scottish Rifles. When the second half got under way, the select had most of the play, but were unable to break through a stubborn Celtic defence. When they did manage to do so, they found Charlie Shaw on the top of his game and an insurmountable barrier against all efforts. Browning and McAtee fired in a couple of efforts at Kerr but the select goalie was not greatly tested. The final whistle went with the Celts winning by the single goal.

Charlie Shaw was the undoubted man of the match, after one of his best ever performances in the Celtic goal. Overall the game was described as a dull, rather insipid affair. Still, the Lord Provost and the managers of the Belgian Refugees Fund were not complaining, over £1500 had been added to their coffers. The Celtic team on the day was: Shaw; McNair and Dodds; Young, Johnstone and McMaster; McAtee and Gallacher; McColl; and McMenemy and Browning. The Scottish League XI team was: Kerr (Queen's Park); Crossan (Heart of Midlothian) and Craig (Rangers); Gordon (Rangers), Reilly (Falkirk) and Nellies (Heart of Midlothian); Low (Heart of Midlothian) and Gourley (Morton); Reid (Airdrieonians); and Cunningham (Rangers) and Morton (Queen's Park).

While the Celts were turning out in the Belgian Refugee Fund game, the stadium at Parkhead was staging the sixteenth annual inter-scholastic sports meeting under the management of the Scottish Amateur Athletics Association. Willie Maley, of course, had a long connection with the athletic association. A few days after the Belgian relief game, Patsy Gallacher, now working in the shipyards as a carpenter, refereed the game between St Mirin's League of the Cross and St Mirin's Young Men's Club. The game was played at Ralston Park, Paisley the ground of Abercorn FC. The Young Men's Club won 4–0 and everyone was well pleased with the Celtic wizard's performance as a ref.

The final whistle at Hampden Park on 15 May also brought the 1914/15 football season to a close. In what must be regarded as the most remarkable season in the history of the game in Scotland, the Celtic emerged as League Champions, having taken the flag in the face of unexampled public bias in favour of the Heart of Midlothian. They won the Glasgow Charity Cup, beating the Rangers at their own ground and as holders of the Scottish Cup retained the trophy. In a fitting showpiece finale, the Celts beat the Scottish League select. The only footballing shadow on a magnificent season was the fact that the Glasgow FA Cup had eluded them once more.

THE HOME FRONT

The annual May Day demonstration in Glasgow was held on Sunday 2 May. It was organised on a larger scale than previous occasions, with over 160 Labour and Socialist organisations taking part. The day transpired to be a beautifully, bright Sunday and tens of thousands of spectators crowded into the rallying point at Glasgow Green. The procession, led by the bands and banners of the various bodies taking part, assembled in George Square before marching through the city to the Green. There were twelve platforms and at each speakers delivered addresses on the various aspects of Labour and Socialist doctrine. Among the speakers on the Glasgow Housing

Committee platform were Councillors Kerr, Izatt and John Wheatley, who spoke about the fair rents problem. Councillor John Stewart spoke at the Trades Council platform on the subjectof the workers' opinions and the decision to go to war. Councillor Alex Turner addressed the efforts to obtain better wages, hours and conditions of labour. He noted that those urging the workers to make sacrifices were not themselves making sacrifices in the same proportion. On 17 May, the Glasgow Herald announced that the Glasgow and West of Scotland Armaments Committee had introduced a scheme under DORA to deal with bad timekeeping by workmen employed in shipyards and engineering shops. The scheme provided for the imposition of fines by trade unions on any of their members whose timekeeping was

Forward, May Day 1915

poor and did not have an adequate excuse. Employers were authorised to deduct the fines from the wages of the penalised. The fines ranged from £1 for the first offence, £2 for a second and £3 and dismissal for a third offence. Non-union workers were subjected to the same penalties.

On 22 May, the King paid a surprise visit to Glasgow. Arriving largely unannounced, he toured the great Clydeside industrial complexes including the shipyards at Clydebank, Port Glasgow, Govan, Dalmuir and Greenock. The following day it was the turn of Dumbarton and Denny's shipyard where he was introduced to the foremen of the yard, but apparently Celtic's Jimmy Browning now employed at the yard as a riveter, was not included among those worthies presented. From Denny's yard the King travelled to Scotstoun and Yarrow's shipyards. The afternoon was spent on Glasgow Green where the King reviewed the troops and presented medals. Among the medal presentations were two Victoria Crosses. The first was awarded to Ayrshireman Private Ross Tollerton of the Queen's Own Cameron Highlanders and the second was presented to Drummer William Kenny of the 2 Bn Gordon Highlanders. Willie Kenny was an Irish Catholic born in Drogheda, Co. Louth. A professional soldier, he had seen service in South Africa and India. His Victoria Cross was won in the desperate days of October 1914. His citation reads 'For Conspicuous bravery on October 23rd, near Ypres, in rescuing wounded men on five occasions under very heavy fire, in the most fearless manner and for twice previously saving machine guns by carrying them out of action. On numerous occasions he conveyed urgent messages under very dangerous circumstances over fire swept ground.'

As usual, rumours of a soldier's wounding or death reached home before any official notification reached the family. One of the first things men did when they had the opportunity, particularly after a bad time on the front line, was to write letters home to their loved ones and friends. As the son of the famous Tom Maley, Josie would have been well known throughout the battalion and the news of his wounding would undoubtedly have been mentioned in letters. As a result, the rumours of Josie Maley's wounding were even mentioned by *the Man in the Know* writing in the Glasgow Observer, who was desperately hoping that the rumours were false. Too soon, of course, the notification of Josie's death, in the form of an official War Office brown envelope, arrived at his parent's home.

The report of Josie Maley's death was published first in the Glasgow Herald on 26 May and on 29 May in the Glasgow Observer. The announcement in the Observer was accompanied by a short poem written by the staff poet John Conway. His verse, under the nom de plume JC, was usually dedicated to the Celtic or its star players. Sadly, not this time:

> *Hearts thrill with pride, and yet are sad;*
> *We mourn war's grim mischance.*
> *There's a hero sleeping tartan clad,*
> *in a quiet grave in France.*
> *God speed you, tall young Highlander*
> *Though the brave are falling daily.*
> *No manlier heart in the trenches there,*
> *Than Corporal Joseph Maley*

> *John Conway, Bridgeton*

Once the news of Josie's death arrived back at his battalion, his friends and company commander took the time to write to Tom and Elizabeth Maley to offer their condolences. Lance Corporal JJ O'Halloran and Private Peter Dougherty, both Glasgow Highlanders, and described by the Glasgow Observer as scions of well-known Glasgow Catholic families, wrote expressing their sorrow at Josie's death, adding that he died nobly in the cause of freedom and honour. As the son of Celtic legend Thomas Maley and nephew of Willie Maley, Josie's death was felt deeply at Parkhead, especially among the older members of the playing squad, like Jimmy Quinn, Jim Young and Jimmy McMenemy, who had been at the club for ten years or so and remembered Josie playing about the place as a boy. A fulsome tribute was paid to Josie at the Celtic club's AGM at the beginning of June 1915.

Thomas and Elizabeth Maley.
Bradford circa 1912
(Courtesy of the Maley Family)

Later, in Josie's parish church of St Charles, a Requiem Mass was celebrated. In addition to the Maley family, friends, representatives of the Celtic team and two comrades from the Glasgow Highlanders attended. John Francis McKillop and John Lee were both home recovering from injuries received in France. Like Josie Maley, John Francis too was in the process of applying for a commission. He would be commissioned into the Queen's Royal West Surrey Regiment in 1916. He saw further war service in Salonika, Egypt and Palestine before returning with his battalion to France. Lieutenant John Francis McKillop was badly wounded in October 1918 and was awarded a Military Cross. John F McKillop MC would later become a director of Celtic FC.

For a number of years after Josie's death, an entry appeared in a couple of the Scottish newspapers' memorial columns. They were inserted by his family, commemorating their Highland Laddie on the anniversary of his death. Tom and Elizabeth Maley never got over the loss of their son. Ten years later, Tom was still searching out Glasgow Highlanders who had been at Festubert with Josie at the time of his death, desperately trying to piece together his son's last hours.

By May 1915, most of Kitchener's K1 and K2 service battalions were coming to the end of their military training. After the best part of eight months' army and regimental indoctrination, the civilian volunteers of August and September 1914 had been transformed into soldiers and were battle ready. As befitted its position as the senior new army division, the 9th (Scottish) Division was the first new army division to be deployed on active service. The vast majority of the soldiers would have got a few days' home leave before deploying to France. Very many of the footballers who answered Kitchener's first call would be deploying. Included in the roll call were Garvie of Queen's Park, Speedie of Hearts and former Celt, John Young. Also deploying on active service was Gunner James Hilley and Joe Dodds brother Lance Corporal Willie Dodds. The infantry battalions embarked from Folkestone and landed at Boulogne, while the artillery left from Southampton landing at Le Havre. On 8 May, Edward Hilley moved from Borden to France with his artillery guns, landing at Le Havre on 10 May 1915, the first of the Garngad brothers to get into the fray. By 15 May, the entire division was concentrated around St Omer and two days later marched to Bailleul. On arrival, the infantry went into the front line where they learned the do's and don'ts of trench warfare from experienced troops, while the artillery brigades were attached to the battle-hardened regulars of the 6th Division artillery for instruction on their gun lines near Armentières. At the beginning of July, the division took over a section of the line around Festubert for the first time. Edward Hilley remained with the 50th Brigade RFA throughout the war and the brigade remained attached to the 9th (Scottish) Division until the Armistice of November 1918.

Also en route to France in mid May was the 14th (Light) Division. Charlie McCallum, now employed as a stretcher-bearer, and his Field Ambulance embarked from Southampton and landed at Le Havre. While the infantry of the division were gaining experience in the trenches, the Field Ambulances practiced their medical evacuation procedures. By mid June, the Field Ambulance was operational having set up their medical facility to the west of Ypres.

A CRASH OF OVERWHELMING MAGNITUDE

Early on Saturday 22 May, the Leith men of the 7th Bn Royal Scots TF with a company of the 8th Bn HLI attached, paraded at Larbert Railway Station. The 7th Bn Royal Scots were part of the 52nd (Lowland) Division TF. Training complete, the division had been ordered to join the MEF fighting on Gallipoli. The division was to be transported by rail south to Liverpool docks from where it would embark for Gallipoli. At Larbert Railway Station, the Royal Scots battalion of just over 1000 men were split into two half-battalions and allocated to two trains for the journey to Liverpool. When the troop trains arrived at the station, they reflected the social norm, with first, second and third class carriages. When the soldiers boarded, it was officers into the first-class carriages, sergeant majors into second class and soldiers crammed into third class. The wooden-framed decrepit third-class carriages were lit with high-pressure gas cylinders, which were stored under the carriage. They had been pressed into service though wartime necessity. Conditions in the third-class carriages were awful and made worse by having eight or nine soldiers with full kit crammed in. Among the soldiers of B Company, 8th Bn HLI, squeezed into the train was twenty-nine-year-old Private James Dodds, the eldest brother of Celtic's Joe Dodds. All four of the Dodds brothers had been long-term members of the 8th Bn HLI's Carluke company. Indeed at the beginning of the war there was some concern at Parkhead that Joe Dodds might be required to report for military service. With three of his brothers serving in the military, Joe was the only son left at home to care for aging parents.

At 0342 hrs, the train carrying Jimmy Dodds and his half-battalion pulled out of Larbert Station. By 0517 hrs, the troop train was at Carstairs where the steam locomotive took on water. It took another sixty-five minutes to cover the forty-eight miles to Lockerbie, much quicker than the first leg of the journey and it was now within striking distance of the Scottish border.

At around the same time as the troop train was approaching Lockerbie, signalman James Tinsley hopped on board a local train that would be stopping at his place of employment, the signal box at Quintinshill near Gretna Green. The thirty-two-year-old Yorkshireman was already officially late for work, for he was due to start his shift at 0600 hrs. However, he was not greatly concerned since he had a private arrangement with the colleague he was about to relieve, George Meakin, that allowed each an extra half hour in bed before the start of an early shift. The signal box at Quintinshill controlled a section of the main west coast line between Scotland and England. In addition to the two main north–south lines, there were two sidings or loops, one each side of the two main lines and adjacent to the box. The loops were designed to allow slow moving trains to be pulled off the main lines to allow faster moving trains to pass.

When James Tinsley arrived at the signal box on the northbound local train there was much going on. In addition to the local train, a locomotive pulling empty coal wagons occupied one of the sidings and a freight train occupied the other. Signalman Meakin had put both trains into the loops to allow two northbound expresses and the southbound Royal Scots troop train free passage. With the two loops occupied, Meakin used a crossover track to switch the slow local train from the northbound line to the southbound line to allow the free passage of the first northbound express through Quintinshill. Once the first northbound express had passed through, the local train would need to be moved back onto the northbound line to continue its journey, before it would again be sidelined further north to allow the second northbound express free passage. This was the position of the trains at Quintinshill when James Tinsley hopped off the local train just as it was crossing over onto the southbound line and climbed the steps of the signal box, ready to take over from George Meakin.

The handover between two experienced signalmen went smoothly enough and by 0636 hrs the signal box had been officially handed over to Tinsley. George Meakin, with his ten-hour shift finished, took a seat in the corner of the box where he began to read the morning paper delivered to him by Tinsley. At 0638 hrs, the first express hurtled through on its way north and

Tinsley then spent the next few minutes signing on duty and updating the signal box register. Both took some thought, as his falsified signing on time of 0600 hrs had to be in sequence with the train movements prior to him actually coming on duty at 0630 hrs. It has been suggested that Tinsley was not functioning normally that morning. He apparently had a history of suffering from fits and the entries in the book were never correctly completed. At 0646 hrs, Tinsley was offered and accepted the second northbound express train into his section of the line. He then offered it to the next section to the north and, returning to his register, he recorded the details of the northbound express.

At 0649 hrs, the time inside the signal box stood still as amid a cacophony of shrieking whistles and screaming brakes the Royal Scots troop train ran headlong into the stationary local train. The local train had been forgotten about by Tinsley and left on the southbound line. The result of the heavily laden troop train hitting the 120-ton locomotive at around forty miles per hour was complete carnage. The wooden carriages were smashed to matchwood and on impact the pressurised gas cylinders exploded, causing a fire to spread throughout the wreckage. Such was the force of the impact, many of the smashed carriages were derailed and thrown onto the northbound line. Scores of Royal Scots were killed instantly, while scores more were seriously injured and trapped alongside the uninjured inside the wreckage. Those trapped and conscious faced a slow, agonising death as the fire spread rapidly towards them. Among those hopelessly trapped and conscious was Jimmy Dodds. He would later recount how, with his hair, face and chest on fire, he only escaped death when a second violent crash freed him. The second crash was the second northbound express train. There had been no time to switch the signals to stop or even slow the express, which careered through the wreckage of the troop train that had fallen onto the northbound line. Jimmy Dodds was saved from the wreckage and taken to Carlisle, where the town's hospitals were overwhelmed by the number of casualties. Doctors were called in from the surrounding areas and a number of institutions were requisitioned as makeshift hospitals. Jimmy Dodds would spend many months recovering from his injuries. He was eventually discharged from the military in mid-1916.

The final number of fatalities was 230, including 212 Royal Scots, two 8th HLI, five other military personnel, three railwaymen and six civilians on the express, and two civilians from the local train. When questioned as to how such a crash could happen, James Tinsley's only answer was that he had simply forgotten that the local train was on the southbound line. Subsequent investigations found that both Tinsley and Meakin had failed to follow set procedures and both were charged with culpable homicide. On 15 September 1915, both James Tinsley and George Meakin were sent to trial at the High Court of Justiciary in Edinburgh. After hearing two days' worth of evidence, the jury was out for just eight minutes before returning a unanimous guilty verdict. They were both awarded prison sentences. Meakin received eighteen months while Tinsley received three years. The train smash at Quintinshill was and still is to date Britain's worst railway disaster.

Meanwhile, the other half-battalion of Royal Scots arrived at Liverpool, where they joined the 52nd (Lowland) Division. Only twenty officers and 477 other ranks of the 7th Bn Royal Scots boarded the Empress of Britain, which sailed for Gallipoli on the evening of 23 May. Over the next week, the remainder of the division followed them east.

COLONEL SHAUGHNESSY and the WEE MEN

COLONEL AND HIS RIGHT-HAND MEN.

Leaders of the command are depicted in this interesting snapshot. Reading from left to right the names are:—(1) Captain A. C. Macgowan, adjutant; (2) Colonel J. Shaughnessy; and (3) Major W. Gillespie.

Colonel Shaughnessy 18th Bn HLI

Colonel Shaughnessy's bantams were also on the move in mid-May. The battalion, now well over 1000 men strong plus two reserve companies, fully equipped and resplendent in their new uniforms, relocated a few miles along the coast to Gailes, near Irvine, where the men occupied a newly constructed hutted camp built on the local links golf course. The site was open to the bracing southwesters blowing off the Firth of Clyde, but it fair cleared lungs more used to the poisonous fumes of the Scottish industrial heartlands. The battalion's training would began in earnest when the wee men would be taken step by step from individual skills, to section, platoon, and company level training.

The recovery in the battalion's recruiting figures after the disastrous start had been remarkable. Unfortunately, there are no surviving muster rolls or records for the bantam battalion, but Willie Maley would mention the wee men during the Celtic club's AGM in May 1915, commenting that fully 500 of the 1600 recruits who had volunteered were Glasgow Irish. With no surviving muster rolls available, his figures should be taken with some caution, but if he was exaggerating, it would only have been slightly. Some indication of the large number of Roman Catholics who had volunteered to serve with Colonel Shaughnessy can be gleaned from a report in the Glasgow Observer at the beginning of May that over 300 Roman Catholics of the 18th HLI, led by Colonel Shaughnessy, had packed into a special service held in the Church of the Sacred Heart, Girvan. Reportedly, the singing of 'Faith of Our Fathers' and 'Star of the Sea' was inspirational, while a Miss Shaughnessy presided at the organ.

Taking Willie Maley's figures with a pinch of salt, but allowing a very conservative 25 per cent, there was still a far larger proportion of Glasgow Irish enlisted into the 18th Bn HLI than in any of the other service battalions raised by the Glasgow Corporation or the Glasgow Chamber of Commerce. There is some compelling evidence to suggest that Colonel Shaughnessy used his prominent position within the Glasgow Irish community and at the Celtic club to encourage Roman Catholics, very many by definition Celtic supporters, to enlist into his battalion. The Lord Provost of Glasgow in communication with military authorities on 22 July 1915 stated that: 'Colonel Shaughnessy is a Roman Catholic and has brought a large number of his co-religionists into the regiment with him.'

In comparison, the 15th Bn HLI, originally the most socially representative battalion, was initially comprised of 15 per cent Roman Catholics. In mid-August 1915, a letter was sent to the Glasgow Observer from some disgruntled Roman Catholics serving with the battalion. They had recently arrived at Salisbury Plain and were complaining that the battalion's 200 Roman Catholics had no access to Roman Catholic services. That figure would suggest a percentage of 20 per cent.

Entrenched firmly at the very bottom of the social scale, the Glasgow Irish suffered more than most from the effects of deprivation and malnutrition. One of the most obvious effects of both being stunted growth. Of course, the majority of the bantams were not Glasgow Irish and stunted growth was also a characteristic of the working class generally. British officers were astonished when they first saw the size and physique of the Australian and New Zealand soldiers. When Hugh Hilley enlisted, he was described as being just less than 5ft 2in in height with a 31in chest. His underdevelopment is hardly surprising when you consider his home in Millburn Street was sandwiched between the Millburn Steelworks, the Tharsis Sulphur and Copper Works and the giant St Rollox Chemical Works.

By the middle of June, the bantams were ready to progress onto the next training phase. Battalion and brigade level training was conducted largely in the field and much more space was required than was available on the golf links at Gailes. The battalion's next stop would be at Masham in north Yorkshire.

A NEW NATIONAL GOVERNMENT

Sir John French's report after the Battle of Neuve-Chapelle expressed the view that the attack had been hampered by a lack of shells. He also expressed his views to a Times newspaper correspondent. While there was some truth in the fact, the lack of shells was really more about Sir John French shifting the blame away from his own tactical mistakes. The supply of munitions was the responsibility of the War Office and ultimately of Lord Kitchener. Lloyd George, the Liberal Chancellor, had been fighting with Kitchener for control of the supply of munitions since the beginning of March, believing that the War Office was not up to the task. He saw the latest information as an opportunity to wrest control of the supply of munitions from Kitchener. Lloyd George spoke to Lord Northcliffe, the powerful newspaper baron, and encouraged him to publish the details of the report in his newspapers. On 15 May, an article appeared in the Times, written by the Times official military correspondent and based on information given to him by the BEF Commander-in-Chief. The article placed the blame for the shortage of shells fairly and squarely on the shoulders of Kitchener and the War Office. The resulting furore became known as the 'Shells Scandal'. The British public read in their newspapers that their soldier sons were losing their lives unnecessarily as a result of a shortage of shells. Adding to the government's woes was the resignation of the First Sea Lord. Lord Fisher gave up his position at the Admiralty after a serious disagreement with Winston Churchill over the conduct of the campaign in the Dardanelles. Furthermore, the increasingly heated debate between those advocating volunteerism and compulsion highlighted a profound division within the government. Under pressure, Herbert Asquith decided that a coalition government with himself at its head should be formed. One of the first casualties was Winston Churchill, who was dismissed after the failure of the naval attacks on the Dardanelles.

Chancellor Lloyd George would be given the responsibility for a new Ministry for Munitions, while Lord Kitchener would remain Minister for War. But with a view to forming as broad a coalition as possible, Asquith asked certain Opposition and Labour leaders to join. During the night of 18 May, while at home, John Redmond received a message from the Prime Minister. The message informed Redmond that the coalition was to be formed and that the Prime Minister was anxious that he should join. In itself it was a very remarkable offer and highlighted the improvement in Anglo-Irish relations that an Irish Nationalist should be offered a position in the British Cabinet. However, the message also contained the information that Sir Edward Carson was being put forward by the Conservative and Unionists.

The choices put before him involved enormous consequences, whichever way he jumped. But, John Redmond quickly decided that the principles and history of the Irish Parliamentary Party prevented him from taking office in an English government, which meant that he could not accept a place in the Coalition. The next morning (19 May) he sent his reply to the Prime Minister. He went on to assure the Prime Minister of the continued support of the IPP in the prosecution of the war. Later that same day he sent a second message to Asquith recommending that, in view of his own refusal to serve in the coalition, Edward Carson should not be given a place. He explained that from an Irish point of view his inclusion would do infinite harm to the Allied cause in Ireland. Asquith tried twice more to persuade John Redmond to join the new National Government, but to no avail. Redmond called a meeting of the IPP in Dublin on 25 May where his decision not to join the Coalition was fully endorsed. After the meeting, he again contacted Asquith stressing his serious objection to the inclusion of Edward Carson. He explained that: 'For the Irish people, it will mean to install in power the leader of the Ulster revolters, who just the other day, was threatening hostilities to the forces of the Crown and the decisions of Parliament.'

The reorganisation of the government meant that there would be a degree of negotiations between interested parties for key posts. As Asquith tried to balance his new government, Redmond warned him that the current arrangements for the governance of Ireland must be left unchanged. Ireland would react very badly to the existing office bearers being replaced by Unionists. In the event the new coalition contained Nationalist Ireland's most passionate enemies: Andrew Bonar Law, Arthur Balfour, Austin Chamberlain, Walter Long and Lords Landsdown and Curzon. Despite Redmond's warning, Sir Edward Carson was given the position of attorney general. The Freeman's Journal could barely contain its fury at 'the scandal of Sir Edward Carson's selection as the guardian and director of criminal law in England.'

When John Redmond was offered a place in the Coalition government, like his decision to support the British war effort with the Irish Volunteers, his decision not to accept a place split the Irish Nationalists. The Glasgow Irish leadership for the most part would have been happy for Redmond to join the government. The Home Government branch president Arthur Murphy and other leading Glasgow Irishmen's thoughts on the matter were printed in the Glasgow Observer and Glasgow Star. Arthur Murphy argued that:

> *Quite evidently there is a feeling in the country in favour of a Coalition Government. It is in the best interest of the country that the best brains of all parties should be brought to the solution of the war problem. So far as Ireland is concerned, I would support Mr Redmond's acceptance of Cabinet office. It cannot possibly prejudice Home Rule, since the Coalition Cabinet must leave office before Home Rule is further dealt with. Meanwhile Irish interests in the Army and elsewhere will suffer unless the Cabinet should possess some spokesman who will speak for such Irish interests. Everything considered I would support Mr Redmond's acceptance of office.*

Arthur Murphy
(Courtesy of Glasgow Observer)

James McGhee, Provincial Secretary of the AOH, Glasgow, stated: 'Much as I would be against the Irish Leader taking office in the Cabinet, I see no other course open under the circumstances but to accept to safeguard the Home Rule Bill.'

James Stafford, National Vice-President, AOH said: 'Should a Coalition ministry be formed I would welcome the inclusion of Mr Redmond as representing Ireland, but before accepting office the new Government should be fully pledged to carry Home Rule for Ireland.'

Thomas O'Hare, BL, Glasgow said: 'I think Mr Redmond's acceptance of office would place the Irish Party in a difficult position. While the Irish people, in common with others, have done and are doing, all in their power for the success of our arms, there still remains unsettled those vital questions which in the past have prevented members of the Irish party taking office.'

Stephen Power, Grand High Chief Ranger, Irish National Foresters, and Secretary in Scotland of the INF stated: 'I think it is rather early for any Irish member to take office in the British Government. I should like to see the Irish Parliament open first.'

On 27 May at a meeting of the North Dublin Executive of the UIL, a resolution was adopted approving John Redmond's action in not accepting a seat in the Coalition Cabinet and that the national organisation should be resuscitated in its full vigour until an Irish Parliament was sitting in College Green.

At Westminster, the Parliamentary Labour Party's decision to accept a place in the coalition government with the support of the TUC, also created a split in the socialist movement, with the ILP opposing the move. Many of the rank and file members were also unhappy at the decision. On 29 May, Forward put the case under the heading 'The Beginning or the End of the Labour Party'. When the dust finally settled and the new Coalition Cabinet finally met, it contained twelve Liberals, eight Conservatives and the Labour leader, Arthur Henderson. Lord Kitchener also had a seat. Although the Liberals held most of the key posts, the presence of so many

Conservatives and Unionists in the Cabinet was seen by the Irish Nationalists as a very definite threat to Home Rule.

Aside from the purely Irish Nationalist aims and ambitions, John Redmond and the IPP also recognised the formation of the coalition as a threat to their liberal tendencies. Redmond opposed the idea of coalition government, believing that a homogeneous government and a responsible opposition able to criticise the government were essential. The formation of any coalition inevitably means some degree of compromise by all parties. Almost from the outbreak of the war, the Conservatives and their Unionist allies had been agitating for mandatory military service and the introduction of national conscription. John Redmond and the IPP worried that in a mood of compromise, national conscription would be introduced. The Nationalists opposed conscription because they saw it as inherently undemocratic. They regarded universal military service as the imposition of state power over an individual's free decision to enlist voluntarily and a Unionist political measure to undermine Liberal reforms. They also worried that it represented a slide towards British militarism and the threat of military dictatorship. Redmond later warned Asquith that the imposition of conscription on Ireland would be an impossibility. Just to crank up the pressure, on 18 May Kitchener was back again: he wanted another 300,000 men.

After a pretty traumatic month for Prime Minister Asquith, finally, the government received some good news. As a result of prolonged negotiations, Italy entered the war on the side of the Allies on 25 May with a declaration of war against Austro-Hungary. Despite being a reluctant member of the so-called Triple Alliance since 1882, Italy had declared for neutrality at the outbreak of the war. Over the months that followed, both sides wooed the Italian government to come over to their side. The Italian decision to enter the war on the side of the Allies was based on promises and assurances, which included that after the war, it would be given control of the territories bordering Austria–Hungary, Dalmatia and numerous islands along the Adriatic coast. Italy's entry into the war opened up a new 400-mile front, stretching along the mountainous Austro-Italian border including the high Alps, and it drew Austro-Hungarian troops away from the Eastern Front.

CELTIC FC

On Wednesday 26 May, a Celtic party comprising James Kelly, Tom Colgan and Willie Maley attended a reception at the city chambers in George Square for the official presentation of the Glasgow Merchants Charity Cup. Sir John Ure Primrose invited Lord Provost to present the trophy, Thomas Dunlop made a speech saying that they had been through a year of war and stress and that the future of football was uncertain. He went on to say that probably unless the war terminated shortly, the game would be more or less abandoned. He hoped, however, that that would not prevent them from making some effort to retain at least the group of charity matches, from which Glasgow institutions had benefited to the tune of £37,000. The sum to be allocated that year, despite the untoward circumstances under which the competition was played, amounted to £1450, which was the same as last year. This splendid total was secured by all the players cooperating heartily and giving their services absolutely free. In addition, the recent charity match on behalf of the Belgian refugees in the care of Glasgow Corporation had brought in something in the region of £1000. He congratulated the Celtic on their success. Willie Maley accepted the Charity Cup on behalf of the club, remarking that 'this, the thirteenth win was as sweet as the first.'

In allocating the funds the following grants were made to Catholic charities: £70 to St Mary's hospital, Lanark; £20 to the Little Sisters of the Poor, Garngad; £15 to the St Vincent de Paul Society; £10 to Dalbeth House; £10 to the Children's Refuge, Bellevue, Rutherglen; £10 to Nazareth House; £5 to the Prisoner's Aid Society: £5 to St Elizabeth's Home; £5 to St Mary of Egypt's Home and £5 to the Sisters of Mercy, Garnethill. The Glasgow Herald of 27 May carried the story of the presentation of the Charity Cup to Celtic on page 11, on page 13 it carried the story of Josie Maley's death at Festubert.

The same day that Willie Maley accepted the Charity Cup, Celtic starlet Joe O'Kane attested at an army recruiting office in the Glasgow Tramways offices in Bath Street. As a carpenter to trade, the nineteen year old decided he would serve with the Royal Engineers. After successfully passing the army medical, he was assigned to No 219 Field Company. Joe had been on the Celtic's books since June 1914, but it was only after the school benefit game at Maryhill in August that Willie Maley finally made up his mind about the boy. He was sent down to spend the season at second division Clydebank FC, then being managed by Willie Maley's younger brother Alex. The Maryhill youngster did well at Clydebank, firing three goals past Charlie Shaw when Celtic went down to play a friendly and got stuffed 5–3. The intention had been to bring young O'Kane into the full Celtic squad for season 1915/16. So much for that idea! Within a few days of attesting, No 93470 Sapper Joe O'Kane was en route south to the Royal Engineer's training centre at Deganwy in North Wales.

Around the same time, young Michael Gilhooley also enlisted. On the Celtic's books since 1912, the Edinburgh-born lad signed on with the 17th (Chamber of Commerce) Bn HLI then training at Prees Heath, Shropshire. Within days of arriving, No 2800 Private Michael Gilhooley had been assigned to C Company and secured a place in the battalion's football team.

Yet another young Celt young was at the time considering his military options. Govan born, John Joseph Cassidy had spent the season impressing at Ayr United. Now, with the season over, twenty-one-year-old Joe pondered a monumental decision. Should he put his blossoming football career on hold while he enlisted, or hold off to see what the close season would bring? While he was thinking, he volunteered for the workers army and became employed in the shipyards as a riveter. At the end of May, he joined Charlie Shaw, Jimmy Wilson, Henry Jarvis and Tom McGregor in a Celtic five-a-side that represented the club at Greenock Morton Sports. The Celts were beaten 1–0 by Rangers, who then lost in the final to the home side.

Chapter Thirteen

JUNE

CELTIC FC

The annual general meeting of Celtic FC was held in the pavilion at Celtic Park on the evening of 1 June. There had never been a season like it and there was plenty to report for the officers of the club. Unfortunately, much of the report was not to do with profit or loss, or the quality or quantity of success of the football team. Colonel Shaughnessy travelled back to Glasgow from the bantams' camp at Gailes to chair the meeting. In the week before, Celtic's chairman Tom White had been very seriously ill with pneumonia and prayers had been said for his recovery at his own St Mary's chapel in Pollokshaws. By the time of the AGM, Tom White was out of the danger, but still recovering from his brush with death, was unable to attend. The previous nine months had been a tragic period for the Celtic family. The deaths of John Mulrooney, James Grant, Peter Somers, John McKillop, Mary Kelly and Patrick Colgan all came over a five-month period, while Josie Maley's death had been announced in the press just a few days previously. At the start of the meeting, the deceased were mentioned by both Colonel Shaughnessy and by Willie Maley. Among the great and the good of the Celtic family, Maley also remembered one of the Celtic club's original supporters, Barney Dempsey. The sixty-seven-year-old Irish-born wine and spirit merchant passed away on 26 May. Willie Maley noted: 'A Celtic general meeting without our grey-haired old friend, proposing or seconding some motion will be strange to us who have met him all these years.' All the tragedies saw the Celtic manager and directors regularly in black ties and the championship flag at half-mast.

After the opening formalities, Willie Maley made his report, giving full justice to the players for their effort over the course of a difficult, but ultimately successful season. It was announced with a great deal of pride that over 300 footballs had been sent to soldiers at the front. He asked the club members to note: 'All the balls were paid for from club funds and not from collections from supporters,' whom the club felt were harassed, both privately and publicly, for subscriptions for all sorts of war funds and had enough to do at present. Maley added, 'We could all be generous with other people's money, but that was not the Celtic way.' This was an oblique reference to a statement made during the Rangers AGM that the club had sent 168 footballs to the military, failing to mention that the money to pay for the footballs had come largely from collections from the spectators. In addition to the considerable cost of so many footballs, the Celtic over and above donated £380 to charities, including the various war funds. Like the footballs, the money came from Club funds and 'not a penny from the track'. This was a reference to the custom of supporters throwing coins onto the track or into sheets carried around the track in response to an appeal. While on the theme of charity, Maley mentioned that he had looked at the club's financial records and discovered that over twenty-five years the Celtic had given to various good causes over £7000 and had in addition played around 150 games for charity.

Having refused to participate in the flawed Scottish League's roll call of players in service or in government work back in April, Willie Maley and the directors felt it necessary to clarify the position of the Celtic first team players concerning their personal circumstances. He stated: 'It will please the many friends of the club and confound our enemies to learn that every one of the Celtic players are doing their share towards the defence of the country at this present time.' Of the players currently on the club's books, two youngsters had already enlisted, Joe O'Kane and Michael Gilhooly. Three married men, McMenemy, Shaw and Johnstone, were in sole charge of a business, which prevented them from enlisting. One player, Joe Dodds, had three brothers at the front and was the sole support of aging parents at home. The rest of the team was engaged in government work: Gallacher, Browning, McColl and McMaster were in the shipyards; Young, McNair, McGregor and Crone were employed in engineering works or iron foundries and Gray was in Beardmore's making grenades. Andy McAtee was back to the pits. The Mighty James Quinn, still on the peripheries of the club, was also back in the pits. Willie Maley also took great delight and pride in announcing that Colonel Shaughnessy had been honoured by the city of Glasgow with the command of the 18th Bn Highland Light Infantry and of the 1600 men on the battalion roll, fully 500 were of the faith.

The Celtic had managed to win the League using just sixteen players over the course of the season and even then, Crone, Gray and Jarvis had between them only appeared seven times in total. The Mighty Quinn himself had appeared just six times. The total number of appearances over the season for each player is as follows: Browning, thirty-eight; Crone, five; Dodds, thirty-six; Gallacher, thirty-three; Gray, one; Jarvis, one; Johnstone, thirty-two; McAtee, thirty-eight; McColl, thirty-three; McGregor, fifteen; McMaster, thirty-three; McMenemy, thirty-six; McNair, thirty-five; Quinn, six; Shaw, thirty-eight and Young, thirty-eight. The goalscorers were McColl, twenty-five; Gallacher and Browning, fifteen; McMenemy, thirteen; McAtee, nine; Quinn, six; Crone, five; Dodds, three and Peter Johnstone and Morrison (Raith Rovers), one each for a total of ninety-one.

The war was now ten months old and it had impacted on just about every facet of people's lives. This included the game of football and of course Celtic FC. The major football clubs were first and foremost businesses, and their life's blood was the supporters, the spectators coming through the turnstiles. Few industries could have been so directly impacted by the war and the expansion of Britain's armed forces as professional football. Over the 1913/14 season, Celtic's nineteen home league games saw approximately 343,000 spectators come through the turnstiles at Parkhead. That is an average of 18,052 per game. Over the 1914/15 season, Celtic's nineteen home league games saw the numbers drop to approximately 245,000. That was a massive 98,000 down on the previous season. The average gate per home game dropped to 12,894, down 5158 spectators. (See Annex B) for detailed figures. Rangers FC suffered a larger fall at 120,000, but the difference between the two Glasgow clubs was the unprecedented number attending what was seen as a title decider with Heart of Midlothian. The game played at the end of January 1915 saw 45,000 come through the turnstiles at Parkhead, 35,000 up on the corresponding game played on Tuesday 24 March 1914.

Despite all the difficulties of the season, the club still managed a profit of £362. The revenue for the season was significantly down by £6000 at £8230, with expenditure also down at £7867. From the bank balance of £4078, it was decided to pay a 5 per cent divided and to place £2000 into a contingency fund. The board voted themselves £350 in directors' fees and the players were given back the 25 per cent reduction in their wages ordered by the Scottish League. They were also given a £20 bonus for winning the League Flag.

The £6000 drop in revenues can be put down to four main factors: the drop in home gates (98,000), the early exit from the Glasgow Cup, no Scottish Cup and a poor return from the annual Celtic sports meeting back in August 1914. During the season, the team played in total fifty-four games; thirty-nine were won, eight drawn and just seven lost. The team was accorded a vote of thanks for winning the Budapest Cup, the League Flag and the Glasgow Charity Cup and for their victory against the Rest of Scotland team. Only the Glasgow Cup was a cause for some regret, the Glasgow Football Association trophy had eluded the Celts since 1911. The total for trophies won since the inception of the club twenty-seven years previous now stood at:

Scottish FA Cup	nine wins
Glasgow FA Cup	nine wins
Glasgow Charity Cup	thirteen wins
Scottish League Championships	twelve wins

The retiring directors, Colonel John Shaughnessy and James Kelly JP, were both unanimously re-elected. Also officially retiring but unable to be re-elected to the team was the Mighty James Quinn. The rampaging centre forward was the spearhead of Willie Maley's great six-in-a-row side and the darling of the Celtic support. Even towards the end of his career, his appearance in the side could pull in extra thousands at the gate. On retiring, the Mighty James had been at Celtic Park for over fourteen years. He had made 273 first class appearances and scored 216 goals. In what was his last season, he managed, despite being a shadow of his former self, to score four times and make a significant contribution to the success of the season. Typically, his last goal in the hoops was scored in his old rampaging fashion in the friendly game at Clydebank back in March. The generation of the Celtic faithful who saw the Mighty James at his peak doubted if they would ever see his likes again. The Glasgow Observer's house poet

The Mighty James Quinn

James Conway felt compelled, in this year of strife and sorrow, to mark the occasion in verse. His reference to Celtic supporters in France and the Dardanelles is interesting.

Bid you goodbye? The heart rebels!
Of all our idols, thou wert king;
From France and the far off Dardanelles
The fond farewells come echoing.

And we at home will miss you too,
The many brilliant games you played;
The modest, daring lad we knew,
Who led the Green and White Brigade.

Our greatest centre had you been
In peaceful days before the war;
Yet must I grieve that I have seen
The passing of an Emperor.

Your well won fame will never die,
We harbour kindly thoughts of thee
Our idol in the days gone by,
Our toast through all the years to be.

James Conway

It is interesting to note how some of the other senior clubs performed financially over what was the strangest of seasons. The Celtic's greatest and closest rivals were, of course, Rangers FC. On 24 May at the Trades Hall in Glassford Street, Rangers had held their AGM. The directors announced that the income for the year was £9271, which included £326 carried over from the previous financial year. This was a drop of over £4000 on the income for the previous season. Total expenditure for the season was £9137, leaving the club just £134 in credit. The club had donated £182 to the War Relief Fund and sent 164 footballs to the military. The directors also announced that the proposed building of a new stand was postponed, and that no dividend would be paid to shareholders. In view of the uncertainty over the continuation of football next season, none of the twenty first-team players had to date been re-engaged.

In Edinburgh, the Heart of Midlothian had, under the circumstances, managed a very impressive profit of £724. The club suffered a relatively small fall in its home league gates, due mainly to the popularity of the team, particularly after the players enlisted, with a total of £5829 being taken at the turnstiles. The gate was also helped by the fact that Edinburgh was a major garrison town and a concentration area for many thousands of soldiers. In the previous season, £6101 was taken at the gates during home league matches. The wages of the twenty-six players on their books cost the club £4303, an increase of almost £300 on the previous season. The club raised £187 for the various war funds and sent seventy-eight footballs to the front in answer to appeals from soldiers. For the start of the 1915–1916 season the playing staff would be cut to seventeen. Of the previous season's first team players, Boyd, Nellies, H. Graham, W. Wilson and Bob Mercer were re-engaged.

Third Lanark announced a decrease in income of over £1200, but still managed to record the small sum of £73 in credit at the end of the season. They made a point of thanking the players for their understanding and the 7th Bn Scottish Rifles for helping them out by providing stewards, saving the club having to pay for police. At Firhill, Partick Thistle also posted a very small profit from a much-reduced annual income. Clyde, Motherwell and St Mirren were all just in the red, while some clubs were not weathering the storm at all well, Raith Rovers posted an operating loss of £1130, while at Dundee FC the loss for the year was just over £1100.

The Celtic fans had a final cause for celebration that season when their adopted Parkhead junior team won the Scottish Junior Cup. The Celtic took a great interest in the local side, allowing them to train at Celtic Park under the guidance of Willie Quinn the Celtic trainer. A crowd of 35,000 crammed into Firhill on Saturday 22 May to watch the Parkhead beat Port Glasgow Juniors 2–0 to take yet another trophy back to the east end.

After the Celtic's impressive financial performance over a very difficult season, at the end of June, Willie Maley was voted onto the Scottish League's business committee. Although he had been the Celtic's representative at the League for some time, the business committee comprised the real powerbrokers at the League. The move was well timed, for the Scottish League was due to meet the other British football leagues at Blackpool to discuss whether football in any form should be played over the next season.

On 28 June, Celtic Park was taken over by the Scottish Amateur Athletic Association, an organisation with which Willie Maley had a long-term connection. The athletic meeting was held in aid of the Belgian Refugee Fund and was conducted under bad weather, with incessant rain spoiling much of the programme. As a consequence, the crowd was nothing like what the meeting would have attracted with better conditions. Celtic beat Rangers 2–1 in the five-a-side football competition. The 1/4th Bn Scottish Rifles won the Military Marathon. The Celtic directors, in typically generous fashion, donated £25 to the Belgian Fund. That same afternoon Celtic's twenty-four-year-old wing wizard, Patsy Gallacher, married his sweetheart Mary Josephine Donegan at St James' Church in Renfrew. Reflecting the wartime circumstances and the state of the Scottish game, Patsy annotated his marriage certificate by writing 'carpenter' under the occupation heading, and not 'professional footballer'. Jimmy McColl would follow him up the aisle just a few days later when he married the girl-next-door at St Saviours Church, Govan. He too annotated his certificate with his civilian employment as a riveter.

THE HOME FRONT

The cost of living had continued to rise over the spring of 1915. On 3 June it was announced that the price of electricity would go up by 10 per cent due to the increased cost of coal, while the cost of wholesale meat at Perth reached record highs. On Saturday 5 June, the stokers in Coatbridge Corporation Gas Works went on strike, claiming an extra 9d per shift. The town was plunged into darkness while homes and businesses resorted to candles for light. The dispute was settled when the men accepted 6d immediately with the other 3d going to arbitration. In addition to the cost of food and utilities, the pressure on the Glasgow housing stock also continued to rise. House owners and their factors saw property as a commodity and took advantage of the current market conditions of high demand and shortages.

The east end of Glasgow became the centre of attention nationwide over the month of June. The pressure on Glasgow's private housing stock had begun to blow, with the rate of evictions soaring. The Glasgow Irish town councillor John Wheatley took up the case of the McHugh family living at William Street, Shettleston. The wife and five children of a serving Irish

The Shettleston Eviction Case.

Wild Scenes—Factor's House Stoned—Women Pickets—Eviction not yet attempted—But Kitchener refuses assistance.

The Shettleston Eviction Case

guardsman were being threatened with eviction from their home for non-payment of rent. The eviction was ordered despite the fact that the Miner's Union had offered to pay the rent. On the evening of 16 June, a huge crowd of between 3000 and 4000 mainly women and weans, gathered outside the McHugh's house where they were addressed by Councillor Wheatley. He said that this was a fight for a poor woman and poor women should undertake it. At the end of the meeting, 500 women made their way to the ILP rooms where they volunteered for picket duty. The following day crowds gathered outside the factor's office, which was guarded by the police, and an effigy of the factor was burned. The police advised the factor not to execute the warrant. A day or so later, Wheatley again addressed the crowd, stating that the sole object of the agitation was to make it illegal for any soldier's dependants to be ejected from their home during the war. Wheatley then sent a telegram to Lord Kitchener: 'Numerous cases of absent soldiers' dependants here threatened with eviction for non-payment of rent; appeal for and await your suggestion of protective measures. – (signed) Councillor Wheatley. City Chambers, Glasgow.' If Wheatley thought he would get any support from the British War Lord, he was soon to be disappointed. The following day he got his reply from the War Office:

Yours yesterday.

Separation allowance cannot be increased to assist in payment of rent, and no action feasible by War Office. – Secretary of State.

Wheatley had not asked for an increase in the separation allowance; he had asked for the non-eviction of soldiers' wives and children, while the breadwinners were at the front risking their lives. The case received widespread publicity, even in the English press. Under pressure from Wheatley, Glasgow City Council began an investigation into the case. The McHugh case in the end came to nothing after the woman chose to move out of her house. It was, however, one of the first salvos fired in what would become a battle between rapacious Glasgow landlords and their tenants, rallied and advised mainly by Glasgow's socialists.

Within weeks of the McHugh case, Mary Barbour and the Tenants Defence Association were organising the first of the rent strikes in Govan, which was to become the bastion of the housewives' struggle. In every window of every house there were notices that read: 'We are not removing.' Within weeks, thousands of the notices were being displayed in street after street. Soon all of Glasgow was involved, from Parkhead to Govan, from Pollokshaws to Calton. Even more affluent areas, such as Cathcart, became embroiled in the action.

The threat of eviction through the sudden arrival of a factor with an eviction notice accompanied by police was a constant concern and strategies to prevent this were put into place. In each close, a single woman who lived there was posted as sentry, allowing everyone else to go about their normal daily business. When a factor was spotted, the sentry would give warning by ringing a bell. Immediately everyone within the building would run to defend their neighbour against the factor, carrying their weapons of choice: flour, peasemeal, wet clothes, rotting food or whatever they had to hand. Mary Barbour and her comrades organised the women so effectively that Willie Gallacher named the protesters 'Mrs Barbour's Army'. John McLean was active in many districts but mainly in Ibrox where he was supported by Pat Dollan and Harry Hopkins of the Amalgamated Society of Engineers. The trade unions also became officially involved at this point. William Reid, shop steward and tenants' leader, stated that: 'The temper of the men was such that, in the event of wholesale evictions taking place … they would not hesitate not only to prevent evictions, but to influence Parliament by every other means in their power.' By this, they meant strike action. This coordinated community action between industry and the home was the real strength of the rent strikes' success.

Demonstrations were organised. Mrs Barbour understood the importance of respectability and decorum during these marches. Demonstrators – men, women and children – all presented themselves in good order, wearing their best 'Sunday' clothes. A nationalistic flavour was introduced when Union Jacks appeared in strikers' windows and on marches there were homespun placards declaring, for example: 'Our Husbands, Sons and Brothers are fighting the Prussians of Germany. We are fighting the Prussians of Partick'.

The action continued throughout the summer and into autumn and by October it was estimated that there were 20,000 households on rent strike. The screw was tightened further when, encouraged by John Wheatley, Harry Kirkwood, convenor of shop stewards at the giant Beardmore complex at Parkhead, warned Glasgow City Council that any future evictions would be seen as an attack on the working class resulting in industrial action. Scottish MPs were lobbied to ask questions in Parliament, where the strikers received the support of Lloyd George concerned at the potential disruption to the munitions industries. The government took notice and ordered an official inquiry into the whole question of house rents in Glasgow.

Before the inquiry could begin, eighteen Partick tenants were issued with summonses to appear in court on 17 November. They had refused to pay an increase of 2/- a month on their rents of £2 per month. The Woman's Housing Association organised a protest march to the court and the workers from five Glasgow shipyards and one large engineering factory joined them. On the day, Glasgow was shrouded in its infamous smog. The sight of thousands of men and woman marching through the gloom en route to the court provided an eerie spectacle. John McLean and Willie Gallacher had platforms erected outside the court where their oratory raised the temperature still further. By the end of the demonstration that day, the landlords' court actions lay in tatters and all legal action against the striking tenants had collapsed. The sheriff hearing the cases, realising that some kind of legislation on rents was about to be introduced, decided not to proceed with the actions.

Eight days later the government rushed through parliament a Rent Act, which restricted rents to pre-war levels. Mrs Barbour's Army had won. Mary Barbour was the public face of the rent strike and is rightly regarded as the leader of the housewives who fought the battle on the streets, but she was supported and advised by many others including John Wheatley,

Pat and Agnes Dollan, John McLean, Willie Gallacher, Helen Crawford, Mary Laird, Jessie Stephens and Mary Ferguson. Although somewhat in the background after the McHugh case, John Wheatley was regarded by the likes of Pat Dollan as the brains behind the campaign. The success of the rent strikes had far-reaching effects lasting well beyond the end of the Great War. The 1919 Housing and Town Planning Act, commonly called the Addison Act, codified for the first time a programme of council housing for the shelter and well-being of manual workers throughout the UK. This act was to become both the beginning and the peak of council housing reform in Britain. The Glasgow rent strikes, now largely forgotten, were one of the most important social protest movements in the history of Britain.

The Glasgow Observer over the month of June under its Parish Notes printed details of the latest losses suffered by a number of Catholic parishes. St Joseph's, Woodside noted that three young men had fallen, John Byrne, Jas Boland and Patrick Costello. The addition of these names brought the total number of fatalities for St Joseph's up to forty. Thirteen men had enlisted the previous week. The latest casualty list contained the names of five St Aloysius, Springburn parishioners. James Boland, John Madden, James Love, James Brennan, and John Dougan all wounded. The parish now had 400 men serving with the colours. Father McHugh, attached to the 6th (Renfrewshire) Bn Argyll and Sutherland Highlanders TF, spent much of his time writing to the relatives of the killed and wounded of Johnstone, Neilston, Barrhead and Paisley. Christy O'Reilly and Daniel O'Connor were just two of twenty-two Argylls killed between 15 and 20 June. That month a new military detention wing opened in Barlinnie Prison. Father Malloy from St Joseph's Home on the Garngad Hill was appointed the officiating clergyman for the Catholic soldiers spending some time in what was known locally as the 'Big Hoose'.

On 1 June, Glasgow's Italian community was also dragged into the war. The Italian Consulate in Bothwell Street issued a mobilisation order for Italian men between the ages of twenty and thirty-nine. The men were to report themselves to the Consulate where they would be medically examined. Those found to be fit for service were sent to Italy. It was estimated that there were at the time in Glasgow around 500 Italians eligible for military service.

THAT IT HAD COME TO THIS!

On the morning of 18 June, which happened also to be the 100th anniversary of the Battle of Waterloo, Lieutenant Colonel George McCrae rode at the head of his 1000-strong battalion down the Mound, Market Street and into Edinburgh's Waverley railway station. After seven months' military training in and around the city, it was time for the battalion to move onto the next phase, brigade training at Ripon. The 'Hearts' battalion, led by the battalion's pipes and drums, was taking its leave of Auld Reekie. The railway station itself was thronged with family, friends and well-wishers there to say their goodbyes. Sir James Leishman and the Heart of Midlothian directors were there, as were John McCartney and Jimmy Duckworth. Even team captain Bob Mercer, injured since the start of the season, managed to hobble along to see the boys off. There were the usual handshakes and backslapping, tears and long desperate hugs from mothers, wives and sweethearts. Then carriage doors slammed shut and the train's whistle blew a long warning; after a hiss of steam and a first clanging jolt, the train began to pull slowly away from the platform.

Some insight into the private thoughts or perhaps the conscience of John McCartney and the Heart of Midlothian board, regarding their involvement in the enlistment of their young footballers, might be glimpsed when John McCartney later recalled that for him, when the troop train was pulling away from the platform: 'There was a moment, a long moment, of unexpected silence, disbelief, I think... That it had come to this. I could not move. I stood quite still. I heard the cheering start again. The finest men I ever knew had gone.'

It must have been incredibly difficult for a footballing man like John McCartney to watch his team disappear off to war. Like Willie Maley, McCartney believed in building a team and that was not done overnight, the right blend took years to achieve. By the start of the 1914/15 season, he had undoubtedly built a very fine team at Tynecastle and one that, had it been given the chance, would have matured into a side that could have, over a number of years, challenged the Old Firm for the dominance of Scottish football. McCartney, like Maley at Parkhead was completely dedicated to and absorbed in what he regarded as a life mission at Tynecastle. He must surely have been somewhat disturbed at the hijacking of his very capable team, just when it was on the brink of success. The prevailing circumstances in mid-1915 and later the ultimate sacrifices of the Hearts lads, meant that even after the war, John McCartney's innermost feelings regarding the circumstances around which the Hearts players enlisted will never be known. But, his comment 'that it had come to this' is in itself perhaps enough.

THE WAR FRONT

The Western Front

After the fight at Festubert, the 8th Bn Royal Scots had a fortnight or so out of the line. It was, of course, too good to last and on 6 June the battalion took over a stretch of the line behind Le Plantin near Givenchy. Lance Corporal Willie Angus had just twelve days respite at the convalescing base before being declared fit enough to return to active service, and on 9 June he returned to his battalion via the No 1 Infantry Base depot. On arrival, Willie reported to his company headquarters and received the good news that he had been promoted to full corporal. The next day the battalion moved into the front line at Windy Corner near Givenchy. This proved to be a difficult section of the line to hold and was subject to constant mining, sniping and mortar fire. In the Royal Scots section of the front, the opposing trenches were only about sixty or seventy yards apart. That night a trench raid was planned for a party of twenty men from A Company and a party of fifteen 'bombers' (grenade men) under the command of Lieutenant James Martin to attack a large shell crater a few yards short of the German front line. The crater had been manned and fortified by the Germans in an attempt to get forward a few yards and to deny it to the British. The German line immediately behind the crater was on a raised banking that overlooked the open area of no man's land between the front lines.

The raid went in over the night of 10/11 June, but it failed. There were no casualties so it was decided to try again the following night. This time while the raid was going in, the Germans exploded a mine, after which the raiders rushed back into their own trenches. When a head count was conducted, it was discovered that James Martin was missing. A number of men crawled back into no man's land to find him but to no avail.

During the stand-to on the morning of 12 June, James Martin's body was spotted lying beneath the German parapet and within a few yards of the German trenches where it had been blown by the blast of the mine explosion. At first, it appeared that the Carluke officer had been killed, but after a few minutes he was seen to move. As the day wore on, Martin recovered some of his senses and lying exposed in the June sun was heard to plead for water from the Germans. James Martin was lying so close under the German parapet they could not actually see him without exposing themselves to British fire; however, after hearing him they raised a number of trench periscopes through which they spotted the wounded officer. Their response was to lob a bomb over the parapet. The section of the British line immediately opposite the wounded officer was buzzing at the development. Because he was a popular officer among the men and because of the outrage at the Germans throwing a bomb at a wounded man, various plans for a rescue were kicked around, but all agreed that it would be suicide to attempt anything until nightfall, though few thought he would last that long.

Willie Angus and D Company were positioned further along the trench when they heard what had happened to James Martin. Willie went up to the section of line opposite where James Martin lay and after having a look at the situation volunteered to go get him. At first permission was refused, since anyone attempting to cross the fifty yards of open ground would be shot down, but Willie was insistent and eventually his commanding officer sought permission from his superiors to risk the life of a soldier in what appeared a forlorn hope. Permission was received just after lunchtime, brought to the line by the brigadier general himself. A fire plan using all available rifles and machine guns was ordered to cover the German trench line. It was around 1400 hrs before everything was in place and Willie was ready to go. A fifty-yard length of rope had been tied around his waist to pull him back into the trenches should he be shot.

It is difficult to understand what was in Willie Angus's mind when he volunteered for what was so obviously a likely suicide mission. Numerous people, including a number of senior officers, tried to dissuade him. Even his commanding officer felt it necessary to get permission from higher authority to allow a soldier to volunteer for almost certain death. Just before Willie went over the top, a senior Canadian officer, who had heard of the rescue attempt, also arrived at the trench. The officer was concerned that an enlisted man was going to what appeared his death in an attempt to save an officer. He took Willie to one side for a final word. The Canadian wanted to reassure himself that Willie was not being coerced or browbeaten into the action and he wanted to give Willie a final chance to pull out. Willie was warned that he was going to his death. Willie's reply is, perhaps, an insight into his mindset: 'It doesn't matter much sir, it's as well now as later.' Many men had adopted the same fatalistic attitude to life in the front line. After watching their mates killed at random by artillery or trench mortar fire, there seemed little anyone could do to prevent their own death. To very many men it appeared inevitable and only a matter of time.

What follows is an account of Willie's heroic rescue for which he was awarded the Victoria Cross, not only Britain's highest award for bravery, but widely acknowledged throughout the armed forces of the world as the most difficult to win and the most prestigious. The account is by the Commanding Officer of the 8th Bn Royal Scots, Lieutenant Colonel Gemmell, who witnessed the incident and wrote to Willie's father in Carluke.

Dear Mr Angus,

A most heroic action was performed by your son Lance Corporal William Angus. On a certain night I had to send a small party out to attack a German barricade. The Germans exploded a mine, and when the party got back Lieutenant Martin (whom I expect you will know as he comes from Carluke) was missing. In the morning, Mr Martin was seen lying on the parapet of the German trench, and shortly afterwards he was seen to move his arms. Your boy at once volunteered to go out and bring him in. It seemed so hopeless that I could hardly bring myself to consent, thinking it would be better to wait until dark and then try and rush the trench. However, we made arrangements for covering fire with rifles and machine guns and, with a rope fifty yards long, which was the distance Mr Martin was away, your son crept out. Owing to the clever way he crept and the height of the parapet, he got to where Mr Martin was lying without being seen. He took Mr Martin by the shoulders and raised him up a bit. The Germans must have seen or heard him – they weren't six feet from him – but luckily the parapet was high and our fire made them keep down their heads. They then threw bombs and hand grenades, which burst all around your son and Mr Martin. Mr Martin was seen to stagger to his feet, and assisted by your son, made a dash for our line. He got about thirty feet and fell, but managed to crawl in. Your son took a slightly different road and had at least a dozen bombs thrown at him. We saw he was wounded and he fell, but thank God he managed to get back to our line also. No words can describe one's feelings over a deed like this. Your boy went gladly to what was almost certain death, determined to try and rescue his officer. That he ever returned was a miracle. The General has sent forward his name for the Victoria Cross, and that he will get it there is little doubt, as no braver deed has ever been done in all the history of the British Army. Your son has no fewer than forty wounds, many of them serious, some very slight, but I am glad to say that the doctors say there is no fear of him, and he will recover from them all. Mr Martin, you will be glad to hear, will also recover. Just in closing may I say how proud we all are to have such a man as your son in our battalion, and to have seen such a deed as this has been the privilege of few.

Lieutenant Colonel Gemmill.

When Willie Angus staggered back into his own trenches, he was immediately attended to by the battalion medics, who rushed him to the regimental aid post. After receiving first aid from the regimental medical officer, he was taken to No 23 Field Ambulance based at Hinges. Willie's forty wounds were spread across his head, face, shoulders, left arm, the left side of his body, right foot and thigh. Three wounds were particularly serious, his left eye, his right foot, leg and thigh. He would later tell Willie Maley that after the first bomb blew off part of his foot, he did not really feel any more of the wounds. By 14 June, he had been admitted into No 13 Stationary Hospital at Boulogne. The large stationary or general hospitals located mainly on the French and Belgian coasts were state of the art for the times. Some had over 1,000 beds and were staffed by doctors and specialists covering all medical disciplines.

The Glasgow Catholic Observer newspaper carried the story on 26 June. The Victoria Cross was not yet official, but there was no doubt that he would get it. As a Glasgow Irish Roman Catholic, the newspaper took a particular delight in the award and would follow the subsequent recovery of Willie Angus closely. The Celtic Club too were delighted with the award to its former player and *the Man in the Know* was fulsome in his praise for Willie Angus. Willie Maley, writing on behalf of the Celtic, addressed a letter of congratulation to Willie's father George Angus. He says:

> I beg to offer you, on behalf of my club, and personally, our sincerest congratulations on the brilliant achievement of your son, Willie. That he may come back to you all safe and sound is now our most earnest prayer, and we trust that you may all be long spared to each other to happy and prosperous days. I can safely say that no club ever had a more willing or conscientious player, and one who always showed by his cleanness that fine spirit which has in his army life enabled him to do the deed which has earned him a world's acclamation, and, I am sure brought great pride to the folks at home who have followed his career anxiously.

The same edition of the newspaper also carried the sad news that Celtic's old trainer and former Seaforth Highlander Tom Maguire had died suddenly. *The Man in the Know* recounted Tom's tenure as trainer at Parkhead in the days of Doyle and Madden and noted that Irishmen had long been doing their bit, in Tom's case in Afghanistan. He also mentioned that the Celtic directors had behaved in their usual generous fashion by making sure that the widow and family of the club's old servant were well looked after. He noted also that Joe Dodds' brother had been badly burned in the Gretna train smash a month earlier, and had all but lost his arm.

On 29 June the official notification of the award of the Victoria Cross was published in the London Gazette. The citation was typically understated:

> No 7709 Lance-Corporal William Angus, 8th (Lanark) Battalion, The Highland Light Infantry (Territorial Force) – For most conspicuous bravery and devotion to duty at Givenchy on 12 June 1915, in voluntarily leaving his trench under very heavy bomb and rifle fire and rescuing a wounded officer who was lying within a few yards of the enemy's position. Lance-Corporal Angus had no chance whatsoever in escaping the enemy's fire when undertaking this very gallant action, and in effecting the rescue he sustained about 40 wounds from bombs, some of them being very serious.

It is difficult today to describe the prestige of the award and the esteem the recipient of a Victoria Cross was held in by the nation. This was a time when the term hero was only very rarely applied and seldom outwith an act of physical bravery in which the hero would have actually risked his life. A man from the lower classes who won a Victoria Cross became a working-class hero at a time when there were very few. For the winner of a Victoria Cross to come from a small community like Carluke was undoubtedly the biggest thing that had ever happened in the community and put the town firmly on the map. When it was clear that Willie would survive his wounds, Carluke began planning a civic reception for their hero son. Willie's heroics had made him a national personality and the national newspapers covered his story. People would write and publish poems about him and his actions and his portrait and citation appeared on a range of cigarette cards and on the cover of magazines and boy's comics.

Cpl Willie Angus in hospital

While still in hospital at Boulogne Willie wrote to his sister:

> I am still in France and they might keep me here for some time yet. They are doing their best to save the sight of my left eye. The best of eye specialists in the world are in this hospital. They have given me great hopes of getting my sight all right, so I will just have to hope for the best. My other wounds are getting on all right, but it will be a long time before I am able to get up and walk about. However, I will get on all right, never fear, and some day your battered old brother will come back to Carluke as cheery as ever.

Unfortunately for Willie, on 6 July the doctors gave up the fight for his eye and it was removed. As Willie stated in his letter, the remainder of his wounds were progressing satisfactorily, so five days after the removal of his eye he was transferred by the hospital ship, St David, back to England where he was admitted into the military hospital at Chatham.

While Willie Angus was performing his heroics at Givenchy, a few miles to the north, a fervent Celtic supporter was not as lucky. Company Sergeant Major Tommy Burns was an old Slatefield schoolboy, who had been advised to join the army by Tom Maley when the Celtic legend was superintendent of the school. Tommy took to the life with the Gordon Highlanders and by August 1914 was the regular army recruiting sergeant based in the office at Glasgow Cross. When war broke out, he was posted back to his battalion. As a platoon sergeant, he had been awarded the Distinguished Conduct Medal for 'Conspicuous gallantry on 14 December 1914 in an attack on the German trenches near Kemmel, when he conducted the advance of his platoon with great coolness and ability under heavy fire after his officer had been wounded.' While Tommy was winning his Distinguished Conduct Medal at Ypres, a medal very often awarded in place of a Victoria Cross simply to preserve the exclusivity of the Victoria Cross, the Slatefield Industrial School published in the Glasgow Observer a roll of honour listing the names of over 150 former schoolboys who were on active service with their regiments. On 17 June 1915, the Gordon Highlanders were being relieved from their front-line positions near Hooge, and as they moved out of their positions, the Germans launched a gas shell barrage. Company Sergeant Major Tommy Burns and twenty of his men were killed or later died from the effects of gas or wounds. Tommy's body was never recovered and he is commemorated on the Menin Gate memorial to the missing of Belgian Flanders.

The Gallipoli Front

After stopping off at Alexandria, the bulk of the 52nd (Lowland) Division arrived at Mudros over the fortnight 29 May to 11 June. They likewise landed piecemeal on Gallipoli, but by 14 June, two complete infantry brigades (155th and 156th) were ashore and the 157th Brigade would land on 3 July.

Since the landings at the end of April and the First Battle of Krithia, little tactical progress had been made; however, Ian Hamilton had received some fresh supplies of artillery ammunition, and additional infantry in the shape of a French division and the British 42nd Division TF. Reinforced, the Second and Third Battles of Krithia were fought over the month of May and into early June, but still no breakthrough onto the heights of Achi Baba was achieved. General Hunter-Weston had persisted in his suicidal daylight, frontal assaults with predictable results and correspondingly high casualties.

With June came the scorching temperatures of a Turkish summer. Much of the fighting had been conducted over the plain or lower slopes of Achi Baba with the result that the no man's land between the trench lines was dominated by the Turks, who held the higher ground. With the forces unable to clear the area of fallen soldiers, the bodies of men from both sides lay where they fell, decomposing in the heat. The conditions encouraged swarms of bloated flies, which fed on the putrefying flesh; they spread disease and made life for the living almost intolerable.

Having arrived on the peninsula at the end of April with a medical unit, Welsh international goalkeeper Leigh Roose experienced the full horrors of Gallipoli. An eccentric gentleman footballer, Roose turned out on one occasion for Celtic when he stood in for Davy Adams in a Scottish Cup semi-final against Clyde in March 1910. Managed at the time by Willie Maley's wee brother Alex, Clyde won 3–1 and two of their goals were down to the Welshman's goalkeeping errors. Leigh exchanged insults with a number of Celtic supporters after the game and later slipped out of Glasgow on the midnight train to London. Now serving with the Royal Army Medical Corps (RAMC) on Gallipoli, Leigh was at the sharp end, working in appalling conditions which he described in a letter to an old footballing friend:

If ever there was a hell on this occasionally volatile planet then this oppressively hot, dusty, diseased place has to be it. If I have seen the fragments of one plucky youth whose body... or what there remains of it... has been swollen out of all proportion by the sun, I have seen several hundred. The bombardment is relentless to the extent that you become accustomed to its tune, a permanent rata-tat-tat complemented by bursting shells... and yet at night the stars are so bright in this largest of skies that one cannot help but be pervaded with a feeling of serenity, peculiar as that appears.

True to form, the eccentric Welshman would later completely vanish from his medical unit. The RAMC had no idea where or even exactly when he had gone missing. It was assumed that he had either deserted, been killed or been taken prisoner. Having received no communication, his family feared the worse, that Leigh was yet another casualty of Gallipoli. Years later they bumped into someone who had played cricket with him in Egypt in early 1916. In fact, in the spring of 1916, Leigh had made his way from Egypt back to England where he joined the 9th Bn Royal Fusilier as an infantry soldier under the surname of Rouse. In August 1916, he was serving as a Lance–Corporal with his battalion on the Somme.

By the time the 52nd (Lowland) Division was landing on Gallipoli, many of the earlier reinforcements had already been lost, so the arrival of the Lowland Scots did not greatly increase the size of the force Ian Hamilton had at his disposal. Just a week after the division arrived, another attempt was made on the Turkish front line. This time the French troops on the right of the line managed to push the Turks back a few hundred yards. Ian Hamilton was under immense pressure from Kitchener and Churchill to drive the campaign forward. No one at the War Office or Admiralty expected the Gallipoli operations to be prolonged. Neither had they planned for it to require substantial, additional manpower and materiel, especially not artillery shells. Ian Hamilton ordered Hunter-Weston now appointed commander of VIII Corps to plan another assault for 28 June. By the end of June, the Gallipoli campaign had cost some forty-two thousand casualties, killed, wounded and sick.

Gehenna

The attack of 28 June was given primarily to the badly weakened infantry battalions of the 29th Division and to supplement its numbers the 156th Brigade was attached for the assault. The brigade included the 4th Royal Scots, 7th Royal Scots (after Quintinshill, there were only two companies) and the 7th and 8th Bns Cameronians (Scottish Rifles). The assault would be known as the Battle of Gully Ravine; however, the Turkish trenches to be attacked by the Scottish infantry were on an adjacent feature known as Fir Tree Spur, while the 29th Division assaulted Gully Spur and Gully Ravine.

During the night of 27 June, the 156th Brigade, which had not been in action yet, moved up into the front line. As 28 June broke, it became another blazingly hot windless day. It was an inauspicious day for a battle: exactly one year earlier Gavrilo Princip had stepped off a pavement in Sarajevo and shot dead Archduke Ferdinand and his wife. Due to the lack of artillery shells, the General Staff decided to concentrate the greatest weight of the artillery barrage on the objectives of the 29th Division. After a completely ineffectual artillery barrage against the Turkish trenches on Fir Tree Spur, the Royal Scots and 8th Cameronians (Scottish Rifles) went over the top. The 4th and 7th Royal Scots reached their objectives, but to their right, the 8th Bn Scottish Rifles' uphill assault on the Turkish trenches resulted in carnage. Of the 900 men who went into the assault, 307 were killed and 160 wounded within a few minutes. Some men actually fell wounded or dead back into their own trenches. The 7th Bn Cameronians (Scottish Rifles) were the immediate reserve for the assault and they too were drawn into the carnage. With only two companies involved in the attack their casualties were fourteen officers and 258 men, with more than 150 killed. The inability of the Scottish Rifles to take their objective resulted in the Royal Scots being subjected to enfilading fire from their right flank and they too were badly cut up and forced to retire back to their own line.

Despite the losses, the brigade commander, W Scott Moncrieff, was ordered to attack again later in the day. After failing to convince his superiors of the futility of the assault, the brigadier went up to the front line to lead the remnants of his brigade himself and was killed. Many thought Scott Moncrieff committed suicide being unable to live with the loss of so many of his men. The losses to both the Royal Scots and the Scottish Rifle battalions were so severe they were amalgamated to form two composite battalions. The 156th Brigade lost nearly half of its total strength and was effectively destroyed. The loss of this brigade caused the commander of the 52nd Division, Major General Egerton, to question the competence of his commanding officer, Lieutenant General Hunter-Weston. Major General Egerton was particularly incensed at a comment attributed to Hunter-Weston when he reportedly said of the casualties suffered by the 156th Brigade at Gully Ravine: 'He was delighted to hear that the pups had been well blooded.' Hunter-Weston was a master of a foxhounds and blooding pups is a fox hunting metaphor relating to inexperienced hounds. A few days after the battle, General Sir Ian Hamilton visited the 52nd (Lowland) Division. As he was led around the battalions, Major General Egerton would introduce each by saying: 'These are the remnants of the.......' After the fourth such introduction he was rebuked by Ian Hamilton.

With two Glasgow battalions of Cameronians involved, the Glasgow Irish community suffered its full share of the losses. When the casualty lists from Gallipoli were published, the city was plunged into mourning. Almost every district had lost men. Although the city had already suffered very many casualties up to this point in the war, they had largely been from the professional soldiers of the Regular Army and the losses had been geographically spread out. This time it was the Saturday night soldiers of the TF, most of whom had joined their local battalions, and the casualties came in clusters. The Garngad lost fifteen men killed on 28 June with more dying from their wounds over the next few weeks. Everyone in the Garngad was related to someone or knew someone who had been lost or wounded at Gully Ravine. The McMath family lived directly across from the Hilleys in Millburn Street; they lost their son Dan. The Heath family from 85 Garngad Hill lost two sons serving with the 8th Scottish Rifles. Two men from the same close in Turner Street were lost, while dozens more part-timers from the district were wounded. Special prayers were said in St Roch's for the dead, wounded and missing.

IRELAND

On 1 June, the 10th (Irish) Division was back on ceremonial duties at Hackwood Park when Lord Kitchener inspected the division. The divisional commander received complimentary telegrams both from the Palace and from Lord Kitchener, expressing their pleasure at the standard of the troops. Training continued throughout the month, but it became increasingly obvious that the men had reached their peak and were battle ready. In mid-June, 1200 men from the 16th (Irish) Division, then at Mallow, were transferred into the 10th (Irish) Division.

John Redmond was furious when he heard of the transfer of men between Irish Divisions. The men had been taken from the uncompleted 49th Brigade and when Redmond protested, he got a frosty reply from the War Office. In fact, Redmond jumped the gun, since every man transferred was a volunteer who had stepped forward when it was announced that the 10th (Irish) Division was about to be deployed overseas. Their move followed a general impression among the men of the 16th (Irish) Division that they were being kept permanently in Ireland to be used to fill up the depot companies of the Irish battalions of the Regular Army. On 25 June, a sign that something was in the air was seen when the Irish division was issued with up-to-date 1914 pattern equipment. Sure enough, two days later the division was warned to hold itself in readiness for active service in the Dardanelles.

For John Redmond, his major concerns over the composition of the new British Cabinet and Coalition government continued. Sir Edward Carson was now a Cabinet minister. Almost half of the members of the reconstituted Cabinet were Unionist politicians. Even since the war, the Unionist leaders in Ulster had renewed their unconditional pledges to stand by Carson's threat of repealing the Home Rule Act. Irish resentment and distrust would inevitably be felt most keenly in the Nationalist counties of Ulster. They were now apparently threatened by the advent of a Government pledged to concede all that Carson and the Conservatives and Unionists demanded, including national conscription.

Chapter Fourteen

JULY

SCOTTISH FOOTBALL

On 3 July, the representatives of the English, Scottish, Irish and Southern Leagues met in the Winter Gardens, Blackpool, to discuss the continuation of professional football. Among the Scottish delegates to the conference were Elias Furst of Heart of Midlothian and Celtic's Willie Maley, now a member of the all-powerful business committee. After some debate, which included a motion by Willie Maley that each country be allowed to select its own brand of football and set up any competition it chose, a resolution was passed in favour of continuation of football on lines to be recommended to the governing bodies in the three countries. Resolutions, which were unanimously adopted at the conference, were as follows:

> *This conference, having carefully considered all the arguments in favour of and against the continuation of the game, are satisfied that the best interest of the nation, those engaged in the war, and preparing munitions of war, as well as a considerable number of people who are, by various reasons, unavailable for the purposes of the war, will be served by the continuance of the game.*

> *Having regard to the varying conditions experienced by the League here represented, the conference is of opinion that each League should be left to carry out such programme as may be thought most advisable in such way as should best recommend itself to the League concerned.*

> *That each League consider the desirability of approaching its national governing association to discontinue registration of professional players, during the ensuing season, and that for such period all professionals be made amateur players as in the case of professionals who have joined the Army and Navy, and who thereby automatically become amateurs.*

A special meeting of the Scottish Football League was held in Glasgow on Thursday 8 July, at which the delegates to the recent conference of the four national leagues at Blackpool submitted their report. After a lengthy discussion and consideration, the committee adopted the following resolution:

> *That in any football which the League may carry on during 1915–1916 no player shall be engaged unless such players are regularly employed throughout the week during the term of his engagement in work other than football, or in any connection with football, and no club shall allow its interests to interfere with the work of players engaged in Government work.*

A committee was appointed to see that the foregoing resolution was properly carried into effect. The committee also decided that the competition be carried through as in former years, with the same number of clubs, and to reduce the guarantee to £30. The maximum wage to be paid to all players was fixed at £1 per match played by the club. Football was to be played only on Saturdays or holidays, and kick-offs were to be at 4 pm instead of 3.30, as formerly.

The Celtic was not convinced about a number of the proposals, particularly the £1 wage for the players. The club felt £2 would have been more appropriate, since they saw the measure as one designed to benefit the country clubs. While many clubs were suffering from a severe fall in gates, others were not and Celtic felt the £1 wage took advantage of the players. The League had made it impossible for players to earn a living solely by playing football, but many of the footballers were unskilled workers who might only earn £1 10/- per week at civilian employment. Even with the £1 from playing football, they were still left well short of their previous earnings and well short of those of skilled artisans. The players were being penalised simply for being professional footballers. The Celtic would continue to fight the players' case and eventually the SFA and Scottish League agreed that if the clubs could afford it, players could be paid a maximum of £2 per week.

The Man in the Know was, of course, delighted that the game would continue, but he was also concerned about the quality of football the new conditions would produce. He feared that players reduced almost to amateur status would not treat the games with as much seriousness or importance or that they might simply fail to appear on a Saturday, especially if overtime pay was available at their place of work. He had visions of Willie Maley running around Glasgow trying to gather in a team while the faithful waited at Celtic Park for a game that may or may not take place. He also noted that the League had allowed Aberdeen and Dundee to participate in the competition, but decreed that no player could be taken off government work, even an hour early, to travel north. He thought the Celtic faithful would resign themselves to the fact and would not be too upset at Celtic taking on the northerners without the likes of Gallacher, Browning and McColl, all three of whom were helping to build ships. The Glasgow FA Cup competition and the Glasgow Merchants Charity Cup competitions would carry on as normal, with the same restrictions applied.

The same could not be said of the Scottish Second Division. The minor clubs had been losing money hand over fist and could not contemplate another such season. The lower division clubs suggested the creation of two sectional leagues, East and West, but the first division clubs refused to accede to the suggestion. That was the end of the Scottish Second Division; it ceased to exist for the duration of the war. Alex Maley at Clydebank called a meeting of the western clubs to discuss setting up a competition. To save money and travel, only local clubs would participate. With the likes of Albion Rovers, Wishaw Thistle, Vale of Leven, Renton, Clydebank and Dumbarton Harps taking part, a cheaply conducted competition might stimulate local interest and generate some cash.

Maley's suggestion was taken up and the SFA allowed its members to form two regional competitions, the Western League and the Eastern League. The West of Scotland League was formed on 28 July 1915 and consisted of six ex-Second Division clubs (Abercorn, Albion Rovers, Arthurlie, Clydebank, Johnstone and Vale of Leven) and six non-League clubs (Dykehead,

Renton, Royal Albert, Wishaw Thistle - all ex Scottish Football Union - Stevenston United from the Scottish Reserve League and Dumbarton Harp).

In mid-July the English FA finally caved into the 'Stop Football' brigade, went the whole hog and announced the abandonment of professional football. The English League had just minutes earlier by the most slender of majorities voted for paid wages, but the FA overruled the League. No player would be paid for the pleasure of chasing a football in England. Only expenses could be paid to players and the game in England went back to the good old, bad old days of the paid amateur. The English League itself would be divided into regions, which would carry on their own competitions.

COLONEL SHAUGHNESSY and the WEE MEN

On 29 June, Colonel Shaughnessy, Private Hugh Hilley and the bantams moved by train from Gailes to Masham in north Yorkshire to begin the next phase of their training. Other towns and cities around the country had also raised bantam battalions and now they were being brought together, formed into brigades and allocated to the newly created 35th (Bantam) Division. On arrival at South Camp, Masham, the 18th HLI was assigned to the 106th Brigade alongside the 17th Bn Royal Scots, 17th Bn West Yorkshire Regiment and the 19th Bn Durham Light Infantry. The 104th and 105th Brigades made up the division.

For the first time, all the bantam battalions came under the eye of professional soldiers, many of whom were returning to duty after being wounded during the first nine months of the war. It was something of a culture shock, particularly for the officers who up to that point had been cocooned in the parochial atmosphere of their own mess and under the benign supervision of well-wishers and friends. For the 18th Bn HLI attached to the 106th Brigade, this meant the battalion came under the command of their new commander Brigadier General H O'Donnell.

It is unclear exactly what happened, but within four or five days of their arrival, Colonel Shaughnessy had managed to fall foul of his brigade commander. Brigadier General O'Donnell spoke privately to him and suggested that for the good of the battalion he might relinquish command in favour of a Regular Army officer. He could if he wished take over as second in command. Colonel Shaughnessy rejected the idea, stating that in his opinion he had a good relationship with his men and that replacing him with a new unknown commanding officer would not benefit the battalion. Thinking the matter finished, John Shaughnessy got on with his job. On 12 July, he was sent for by the general officer commanding of the 35th Division, Major General Pinney, who informed him that Brigadier General O'Donnell, had with his approval, decided that he would be superseded and the position of second in command was still open to him.

Brigadier General O'Donnell had apparently decided that John Shaughnessy was more of an administrator and organiser, and much too close to his men. He felt that while Shaughnessy was energetic and keen, he had brought the social club mentality of the old Rifle Volunteers into the new service battalion and he was not considered to be the correct man to lead the battalion on active service.

John Shaughnessy fired off a letter to the Lord Provost of Glasgow relating what was happening. Thomas Dunlop was furious and there followed a flurry of letters and telegrams back and forth between the military and Glasgow's Lord Provost.

To Sir Bruce Hamilton, commander of the Fourth Army:

> *Surprised to learn that Brigadier 106 Infantry Bde. proposes to sack Colonel Shaughnessy. His influence had a great deal to do with the raising of the battalion. His appointment was after a recent inspection by Sir Spencer Ewart. In my opinion he is a very efficient officer. Would urge you to reconsider.*

And later: 'I am in receipt of your telegram the contents of which has greatly perturbed myself and the committee who raised the 18th Bn HLI.'

From Sir Bruce Hamilton, 22 July: 'Greatly regret that while recognising the good work done by Colonel Shaughnessy, it has been necessary purely on military grounds and in the interests of the efficiency of the battalion to recommend the appointment of another officer.'

To Sir Bruce Hamilton, 22 July:

> *Dear General,*
>
> *I can hardly find words to tell you how upset I have been since receiving your telegram today indicating that you have arranged to supersede Colonel Shaughnessy. In view of all that Glasgow has done at this present time in the way of recruiting, I and the recruiting committee feel hurt that it should have been done so hurriedly and without consultation or letting us know of the proposed change. Colonel Shaughnessy is an officer in whom both myself and the committee have the utmost confidence. Colonel Shaughnessy sacrificed himself and his business for duty to his King and country and to be turned down in this way seems to us to be a most extraordinary procedure.*
>
> *If not already too late I would respectfully urge upon you to reconsider the proposal. I might point out that Colonel Shaughnessy is a Roman Catholic and brought a large number of men of his own persuasion to join the regiment and to separate them from him seems to us to be the greatest injustice. I would also point out that a change of this kind might operate very strongly against recruiting in the city.*

Despite the Lord Provost's pleadings, the decision had been made and in the event, Colonel Shaughnessy did, of course, do the honourable thing. He pointed out that the battalion already had a very efficient second in command, and surrendered his own command. Subsequent offers of appointments saw him find his niche in the army recruiting organisation and John Shaughnessy would be appointed Recruiting Officer for Glasgow. Colonel Shaughnessy was not the only commanding officer to lose his battalion. In the autumn of 1915, there were wholesale removals of commanding officers of locally raised battalions and brigades in the 38th (Welsh) Division 'in the interests of efficiency' as the formation prepared to go overseas.

For the Glesga wee men, the next six weeks were spent on the Yorkshire Moors where, overseen by professional military instructors, their training intensified. The syllabus included trench-digging, artillery cooperation, musketry, bombing (grenades), close-quarter fighting and route marches, of course. The regular army instructors introduced some realism by liberally pouring warm bullock's blood over everything including the troops themselves. In late August, the entire division moved south to Salisbury Plain and they moved onto the final phase of their training. Hugh Hilley meanwhile had managed to keep a low profile and was doing well enough in training to avoid being conspicuous. By the time the battalion moved to Salisbury Plain, he had had the best part of five months' training under his belt and was thriving in the healthy outdoor lifestyle, vigorous exercise and regular wholesome food.

On arrival at Salisbury Plain, the battalion began a training circuit that involved rotating through various training activities and necessitated regular moves around the area and into different accommodation. The quality of the accommodation ranged from mouldy bell tents, leaking wooden huts to their own bivouacs under the stars. Pleasant enough in the last days of summer and a south of England autumn, but by late October it was becoming unpleasant. Life was also about to take an unpleasant turn for Hugh Hilley.

Over the course of the first mad patriotic rush of recruits, thousands of underage boys managed, with or without the knowledge of their parents and a nod and wink from the recruiters, to join the army. At first, it seemed like an adventure, a lark for spirited patriotic young men whose only fault was their eagerness to serve their country. The civil and military authorities knew it was happening and even the press colluded by printing tongue in cheek cartoons of boys duping the recruiters and carrying stories of spirited boys eager to fight the Hun. However, the numbers of boys involved and the realities of the war were daily being forcefully driven home by ever lengthening casualty lists. The realisation that it would not be a short war also took something of the shine off the adventure. Now the mothers wanted their boys back and questions would be asked in the House of Commons regarding the matter. All battalions were obliged to scour their units for the boys and if found, return them to their homes.

Around the end of October, Hugh Hilley was called into the battalion orderly room and was asked to produce his birth certificate. A few days later the certificate arrived from Glasgow and Hugh's fate was sealed. After no doubt a tearful interview with his new commanding officer, Hugh was discharged from the army under King's Regulations Paragraph 292: 'Having made a mis-statement as to his age on enlistment.' The regulation applied only to a soldier serving in the United Kingdom who, on enlistment, had stated his age as eighteen years or upwards. The free discharge application was made by the boy's parents, on the ground that he was less than eighteen years of age. On 19 November, his discharge was completed and he was given a travel warrant to get him home to Glasgow. After he was discharged from the bantam battalion, Hugh Hilley's soldiering days were over. By the time he was officially old enough for active service, the war itself was about over.

Once settled back home in the Garngad, Hugh would take up football again, expending his considerable energies on the field as opposed to the battlefield or the trenches. He would play football for St Roch's Guild team and later star for junior club St Anthony's, with whom he won the Glasgow Junior Charity Cup in June 1921. His performance in the cup final earned him banner headlines in the Glasgow newspapers. Just a few days' earlier, Hugh Hilley's boyhood dreams had come true when he signed professional forms for Celtic FC. Just a month later, Hugh's joy was complete when he was joined at Parkhead by another Garngad boy. His lifelong friend and neighbour Jimmy McGrory had also caught the eye of the Celtic manager. Hugh Hilley would play on and off with the Celtic for the next nine years. Over his time at Parkhead, he made a total of 195 appearances for the club. Hugh's younger brother Cornelius would also go on to play professional football. It is interesting to note that when Hugh signed for the Celtic in May 1921, during his medical examination he was measured at 5ft 8in and that was tall enough for the Scots or Irish Guards. His time in the army, with all the exercise and regular food, may not have been wasted after all.

Hugh Hilley of Celtic c1921

WAR FRONT

Gallipoli Front

After the Battle of Gully Ravine, Hunter-Weston, buoyed by the very limited success of his latest frontal assault and despite the horrific casualties, decided to continue with his unimaginative battle plan. Before his next assault could be launched, the Turks launched their own attack over 1–5 July. Like the Allies, the Turks failed to break through the front line and they fell back to their own trenches leaving thousands of dead and dying. Over 28 June to 5 July, Turkish losses were estimated to be 16,000, with 10,000 killed. After the latest series of assaults, no man's land was littered with thousands of unburied bodies of British, French and Turkish soldiers decomposing in the scorching heat. Since June, a plague of flies had bloated themselves on the putrefying corpses and by July virtually every soldier on the peninsula suffered from varying degrees of dysentery, some fatal. Such was the scale of illness, the already inadequate medical facilities almost collapsed. The situation had become so bad a truce was agreed in order to bury and burn the dead.

On 12 July, Hunter-Weston finally got the chance to launch his own attack. The 52nd (Lowland) Division's 155th and 157th Brigades would lead the assault with the already badly mauled 156th Brigade in immediate reserve. The Glasgow Territorials of the HLI were to the forefront. The attack would be the usual full frontal trench-to-trench assault going over in broad daylight after an artillery barrage. Like the result on the 28 June, some small gains were made, but at far too high a cost. Despite the limited success of 12 July, reinforced by units of the Royal Naval Division, the 52nd (Lowland) Division was ordered to renew its attack on 13 July. The result was depressingly similar to the day previous. The 52nd (Lowland) Division had concentrated on Gallipoli on 3 July 10,900 strong, by 13 July the division had lost 4,800 killed men and wounded. Major General Egerton described the operation of 12 to 13 July as 'a wicked and useless slaughter of his men'. The comment led to his dismissal. The 52nd (Lowland) Division, months in the training, had been destroyed in just ten days, with battalions reduced to companies and companies to platoons. Despite the sacrifice and slaughter, the few yards won saw the Allies no closer to taking the vital heights of Achi Baba. On 20 July, Hunter-Weston claimed illness and invalided himself home, probably much to the relief of the men on the ground. Most of his contemporaries thought he jumped before he was pushed. He would return to active service in time for the start of the Somme battles of 1916 when he commanded VIII Corps. His divisions suffered some of the highest casualty rates of all those involved in the battles. In October 1916, he was elected the Unionist MP for North Ayrshire.

Meanwhile, Sir Ian Hamilton asked for and received yet more reinforcements. It had been decided that with Helles and Anzac stalemated, a new front, further up the peninsula was the answer. Five fresh divisions (90,000 men) were allocated to the MEF. Three, the 10th (Irish), 11th and 13th, were New Army and two, the 53rd and 54th, were TF. The place chosen for the new front was at Suvla Bay about five miles north of Anzac Cove, with the landings scheduled for 6 August.

The Western Front

On the Western Front, the months of June and July were strategically quiet with the Allies recovering from the battles of Ypres, Aubers Ridge, Festubert and the French Second Battle of Artois. The local, almost daily fights over a few yards of no-man's-land continued of course. After almost a year of conflict, the armies on the Western Front were slowly and painfully learning how to adapt to the new tactical realities of entrenched warfare. The German generals' policy since the collapse of the Schlieffen Plan was to hold their hard-won gains in the rich industrial and mining sector of north-eastern France and Belgium while they and the Austro-Hungarians launched a series of major offensives on the Eastern Front. This meant the consolidation of the German front lines in the west, consisting of well-constructed trenches with deep bunkers, barbed wire defences, reinforced concrete gun emplacements and selected strongpoints. This defensive policy forced the British and French onto the offensive. The Allied generals were faced with the problem of how to overcome deep fields of barbed wire, reinforced strongpoints, machine-gun beaten zones and support trench networks from which fresh reinforcements could be rushed into an area under pressure. Military tactics had failed to keep pace with advances in technology and out-of-date military tactics had failed so far to break through the German's in-depth defensive positions, resulting in failed assaults and massive casualties. Recognising the problem, the Allied generals turned to new technology to help break the deadlock and the land-ship, later titled the 'tank', was already on the drawing board. On 24 June, Sir John French and the French commander-in-chief, General Joffre, met at Chantilly to discuss a major offensive to be launched in the late summer. This attempt to eject the Germans from French and Belgian soil would use some of the new technology; the assaults would be preceded by poison gas!

Tactically, for the men in the trenches, the stalemate meant falling into a routine of rotations through front, support and or reserve line duties then a similar period out of the immediate danger area where they could get a chance of some rest, if they were lucky a shower and maybe, depending in what sector of the line, even some recreation. However, even when out of the line and at rest, sudden violent death could visit. At the beginning of July, the 2nd Bn Argylls with Joe McAree in tow took over trenches at Burnt Farm, near Rue-du-Bois. The location was just a mile or so from the place where Josie Maley had been mortally wounded. Over the period of the duty, the battalion lost six men killed and another dozen wounded. The battalion was relieved in the front-line trenches on 8 July and moved back into billets at Gris Pots. Soon after arriving at their billets the cry went up for a game of football and Joe McAree with several of his mates grabbed a ball. No sooner had the game kicked off than a German long-range shell screamed onto the pitch. One officer spectating and five footballers were killed and a half dozen other footballers were wounded by the same shell. Joe took shrapnel to his stomach and died from the wound. He left a young wife, Catherine, and one child at 124 Greenhead Court, off Green Street, Calton. He was a member of the

Joe McAree, a rare footballer
(Courtesy of Glasgow Observer)

St Alphonsus congregation and had four brothers serving with the colours. The week after Joe McAree's photo and obituary appeared in the Glasgow Observer, *the Man in the Know* commented on his death in his sports column when he described Joe as an old Slatefield boy, a protégée of Tom Maley and a rare footballer.

IRELAND

For John Redmond and the IPP, the first year of the war had been a mixture of triumph and disaster. Having achieved Home Rule for Ireland, the war and the Ulster Unionists' intransigence had seen the creation of an Irish parliament sitting in College Green postponed until the end of the conflict when Carson's Amending Bill would be addressed. He recommended patience; much had been achieved and not through armed force, but through the democratic will not just of Irishmen, but of the whole of the United Kingdom.

It had been a whole year since Redmond staked his political leadership and the future of his party on his belief that Irishmen should take a full part in the conflict. His loyalty to British democracy and what he regarded as a righteous cause had brought scant reward for his own cause. Tens of thousands of Irish Nationalists had, at his call, joined the British Army and were even then preparing to go into action overseas. As the war dragged on, the outlook for Nationalist Ireland had undeniably become politically less favourable. With the collapse of the Liberal government and the elevation of its Unionist enemies into the Coalition, even Home Rule itself seemed less secure. In an atmosphere of increasing mistrust, the Lord Mayor of Dublin, in response to a requisition signed by thirty members of the corporation, summoned a special meeting of the municipal council to consider a resolution demanding that the Home Rule Act be put into operation for all Ireland on 17 September as a right of the Irish nation.

The Irish Volunteers over the summer months continued with the anti-recruitment campaign while encouraging recruits into their own ranks. At the insistence of John Redmond and John Dillon, the British authorities ignored Unionist demands that the Irish Volunteers be suppressed. Redmond advised that making martyrs of what was a tiny proportion of Irish public opinion could tip very sensitive Irish sensibilities into something more extreme. The Irish Volunteers were, therefore, allowed to continue and it was a common sight to see both the Irish Volunteers and Connolly's Citizen's Army marching through Dublin in uniform and with weapons on their shoulders. The Volunteers' director of organisation, Padraic Pearse, while publicly appealing for recruits, wrote that the Volunteers envisaged no military action in the near future. 'But,' he warned, 'what if a future Unionist or Coalition British Government repudiated the Home Rule Act, or Conscription was forced on Ireland, or an attempt made to disarm the Volunteers.' Most Dubliners ignored them. If they thought the reasons for their parades and training were important that was their business. Unknown to the Dublin populous, the vast majority of the Irish Volunteers and indeed Eoin MacNeill, the parading and training had a much more serious purpose known only to an inner conclave of the IRB. At the end of July, news reached Ireland of the death of the old Fenian Jeremiah O'Donovan Rossa in America. The IRB decided it was just the occasion for a large public demonstration of Irish Nationalism. Thomas MacDonagh, now commandant-general of the Volunteers, took charge of the arrangements while American mathematics teacher, Éamon de Valera, recently promoted from captain to commandant, would supervise transport arrangements for 1 August, the day of the demonstration.

If Irish politics was entering a somewhat uncertain and confused period for the leadership, the rank and file were similarly somewhat perplexed. On 2 July, a man named Francis Ryan, who was in prison at the time, had his Dublin house broken into. Two women were caught with Ryan's property in their possession. Among the items were nineteen rounds of rifle ammunition, which Ryan, a member of the Citizen's Army, promptly identified as his property. The police later searched his house and found a Mauser rifle. He was then charged under DORA of having, without the permission of the military or naval authorities, the rifle and ammunition. His defence was simply that he had acquired the rifle before the ban on importing arms had come into force and that, as everyone knew, there were thousands of rifles in Dublin. If the police wanted to charge anyone, they should start with the political leaders and not the rank and file. The Crown decided not to press for a heavy penalty and the court bound Ryan over to keep the peace. The court also confiscated the rifle and the ammunition.

At the beginning of July in Basingstoke, the 10th (Irish) Division was a hive of activity. It had just received movement orders and sun helmets and khaki drill clothing were issued to the men. On 6 July, embarkation orders were received and two days later the bulk of the division entrained for Devonport where they embarked for Gallipoli. In the case of the 5th Bn The Connaught Rangers with the exception of an advance party, the battalion embarked on the *Bornu*, total strength seventeen officers and 786 other ranks. The advance party of twelve officers, and 159 non-commissioned officers and men, mostly A Company including Corporal John Fallon, entrained for Liverpool on 8 July and embarked on the *Mauretania*, sailing the following day. Alongside John Fallon looking over the ship's rails as it made its way down the Mersey, were the fighting father and son duo from Kirkintilloch, Bernie and Bernard Gallacher with the 6th Bn Royal Munster Fusiliers. The bulk of the 5th Connaught Rangers on board the *Bornu* also sailed on 9 July. As the vessel moved down the harbour, the juvenile delinquents on board the training ships gave the Connaughts a rousing cheer. In response, the drums of the battalion played 'Brian Boru' and other Irish tunes. The *Mauretania* arrived in theatre on 16 July and landed the troops on Lemnos four days later. From the pier, they marched about a mile to bivouacs. After a three-day stopover in Alexandria, the *Bornu* arrived at Lemnos on 28 July and the following day disembarked its passengers, the 5th Bn Connaught Rangers joined A Company in bivouacs. Training for the division began on 30 July with drills and route marches. After three weeks on board ship, the men found the training difficult, made worse by the intense heat and lack of drinking water. Even when in bivouacs there was no rest for the men. Flies were a constant torment. They swarmed over food making it almost impossible to eat or indeed sleep. Already, just two days after its arrival, the battalion had 10 per cent of its strength reporting to the sickbay suffering from severe dysentery. Very many more, less seriously affected with enteritis, suffered in silence. If the men thought it was bad on Lemnos, worse conditions awaited them on Gallipoli. After the furore over badges and flags, the battalions of the 10th (Irish) Division were ordered to sow badges of their own design onto their sun helmets or shoulders. The Royal Irish Rifles improvised a green and black patch; the Leinsters stencilled a large black 'L' onto the side of their helmets. The 5th Connaughts decided they wanted an elaborate cloth shamrock with a '5 CR' device; this would take too long to produce and they would go into battle without them. The 7 Bn Munster Fusiliers made do with a green shamrock shoulder patch.

Meanwhile, Ian Hamilton's plans to open up a new front at Suvla Bay to break the stalemate at Helles were well advanced. The officer given command of the operation was the somewhat elderly Sir William Stopford. At the start of the war, he had been Lieutenant of the Tower of London, dozing through the ceremonial duties and looking forward to a leisurely retirement. In what must be regarded as one of Lord Kitchener's most bizarre decisions, sixty-one-year-old Stopford was unceremoniously summoned from the Tower and given command of one of the most critical operations of the entire war. Within days, he had been dispatched to the Dardanelles, given command of IX Corps and instructed to break the deadlock at Gallipoli. To be fair to Kitchener, he had first offered to Hamilton, Lieutenant General Sir Brian Mahon, then commanding the 10th (Irish) Division and already en route to theatre, but Ian Hamilton felt Mahon had reached his ceiling and asked for either of two experienced senior officers from the Western Front, but Kitchener refused the request. The next senior officer on the list just happened to be Sir William Stopford. The new commander of IX Corps had been a staff officer throughout his career and had no experience of commanding troops in action. For an operation that would require drive and a high degree of man management and leadership qualities, the choice, based entirely on military protocol, really could not possibly have been any worse.

The month of July saw the 16th (Irish) Division and the 36th (Ulster) Division a similar position. Both formations were now largely recruited up to strength, but their progress was being hampered by a lack of equipment and materiel. Both formations suffered being pillaged for their attached units particularly artillery, engineering and signals units. The 36th (Ulster) Division would move to England later in July to begin field training, but the 16th (Irish) Division would needs wait until September before following them over the Irish Sea.

CELTIC FC

In the light of the introduction of the National Registration Act, it is worth looking at the charges levelled at the Celtic club regarding placing their players in 'starred occupations' to prevent them from enlisting or later from being conscripted into the military. Back in December 1914, most professional football players had responded to the cut in their wages by returning to their old employment. By mid-January 1915, Gallacher, Browning, McColl, Jarvis and McMaster were back in the shipyards. 'Sunny' Jim Young, as a time-served iron turner, was working in a Kilmarnock engineering shop, while McGregor and Crone were employed as iron moulders. McNair and Dodds were also employed in iron foundries, while Andy McAtee was back in the pits. All were, therefore, doing what was regarded as government work. Three married men, Jimmy McMenemy, Peter Johnstone and Charlie Shaw, were in sole charge of their own businesses. Peter Johnstone would soon go back to the pits. Alex Gray was working for Beardmore's at Parkhead Forge making grenades as early as September 1914. The vast majority of the Celtic first team squad were therefore engaged in government work, purely as a result of the financial and political pressure applied by the SFA, Scottish League and the War Office. As early as January 1915, the civil and military authorities accepted that government work was an honourable and increasingly vital alternative to enlisting. The players were, therefore, already employed in what would later be regarded as starred occupations well before the enactment of the National Registration Act, which first introduced the starred system of exempted skills and jobs.

The Ministry of Munitions would soon launch a nationwide recruiting campaign for an army of war workers, men and women, whom it wished would leave their non-vital current jobs to take up employment in vital industries such as shipbuilding, mines, transport, engineering shops, iron foundries and the soon to be created government munitions factories. It would, therefore, have taken very little effort for a ship's carpenter like Patsy Gallacher to get a job in the shipyards, or Jim Young to get a job in an engineering shop and it certainly would not have needed any pulling of strings, inside connections or calling in of favours. The suggestion that Willie Maley or any of the Celtic directors used their influence to have players placed into starred occupations is clearly unfounded.

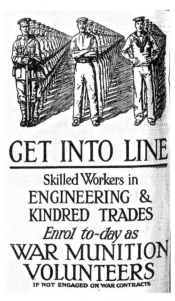

GET INTO LINE

Skilled Workers in
**ENGINEERING &
KINDRED TRADES**
Enrol to-day as
**WAR MUNITION
VOLUNTEERS**
IF NOT ENGAGED ON WAR CONTRACTS

War Workers Fall In!

Over the first months of the war, professional clubs throughout the whole of Great Britain were thinking along the same lines as Celtic when it came to their players voluntarily joining the armed forces. As businessmen, the Celtic board of directors and manager Willie Maley obviously did not want to see the club's best assets, the players, sucked into the recruiting maelstrom. Over the course of the war, the Celtic club would at different times, have its commitment and contribution to the war effort questioned in the Glasgow press. The allegations were clearly absurd since, in addition to Colonel John Shaughnessy actually serving as an army officer, most Celtic board members had close family and friends in the armed forces almost from the first shot. While it is probably fair to say that Willie Maley was first and foremost the manager of Celtic, he was from a military family himself and as a typical Edwardian middle-class male, every inch a British imperialist and intensely patriotic. He would personally ensure that the Celtic club did its bit for the war effort, but he did not feel the need to trumpet the club's or indeed his own efforts. It would also be fair to say that Maley and the Celtic board had a strained relationship with the Glasgow press almost since the creation of the club. It was long felt at Parkhead that the Celtic never quite received the praise the club deserved and it was too often quickly and unfairly criticised. The modern phenomenon, commonly known as the Celtic paranoia, is almost as old as the club itself. As a result of this strained relationship, Willie Maley and Celtic used *the Man in the Know* column in the Glasgow Observer and Glasgow Star to put their points across to their public. Unfortunately, for the most part the only people who read the Glasgow Star or Observer were Roman Catholics, mostly from the Glasgow Irish community. The Celtic board and Willie Maley refused to justify the club's position or policies to the mainstream Glasgow media. As a result, much of what Celtic as a club contributed during the war was lost to the general public.

With most professional players now engaged in work other than football during the week, and with no close season wages available, Saturday afternoons over the summer of 1915 saw the various sports days take on increased significance for footballers, both as a potential income from the five-a-side prizes and as a way of keeping relatively fit. Only from July were the Scottish football clubs allowed to sign players for the 1915/16 season, when it was more certain that football would be allowed to continue. The Celts would start the new season with a squad of sixteen players: Shaw, T McGregor, McNair, Dodds, Young, McMaster, Johnstone, Wilson, McAtee, Gallacher, McColl, McMenemy, Browning, Pat McCabe, Joe Cassidy and Barney Connelly.

For the Celtic, the first year of the war ended as it begun with a death. In mid-July, word reached Glasgow that old Bhoy Peter Meehan had died in Nova Scotia, Canada. The Broxburn miner had arrived at Parkhead in May 1895 from Sunderland FC and helped the club to League and Charity Cup success. On 28 November 1896, he alongside Barney Battles and Johnny Divers refused to strip for Celtic trainer JJ Mullen versus Hibernian unless the press box was cleared of reporters from the Scottish Referee sports paper. The infamous three-player revolt saw Peter transferred to Everton FC having turned out twenty-five times in Celtic colours. After his British football career ended, he emigrated to Canada where he hoped to reignite his footballing career. A reoccurring old injury saw him forced back to the pits. *The Man in the Know* recalled Peter's contribution to the Celtic cause and noted the last time he saw Peter was in February 1905, the day they buried Barney Battles and 40,000 Celtic faithful had lined the route from the Sacred Heart, Bridgeton to Dalbeth Cemetery.

By the beginning of August, the Celtic management were already focusing on the new football season. Traditionally, the start of the season was signalled with the staging of the annual Celtic Sports meeting. This year however, Willie Maley planned something much more than the usual athletics events. Utilising his long-standing personal contacts with the military, Maley was planning for the Celtic Sports to be as much about patriotism and recruiting as athletics and five-a-side football. Military bands were booked to provide the entertainment; Army display teams would give demonstrations of infantry assaults and grenade throwing and Glasgow's first Victoria Cross winner, Henry May of the 1 Bn. Cameronians (Scottish Rifles) would put in an appearance. Hundreds of wounded soldiers from Stobhill hospital, British and Belgian received invitations to come to Celtic Park as guests of honour. Arrangements were made for Bantam battalion recruits still training at Gailes to come to up to Parkhead and the running track was adapted to allow a mobile recruiting platform to traverse the track throughout the event. The army also provided scores of military athletes to take part in the athletic meeting. Willie Maley was determined that the 1915 Celtic Sports would provide an occasion for a great military event and recruiting rally. He was determined that the general public would be left in no doubt of the Celtic club's commitment to the British war effort. Over the course of the 1915–1916 football season, the commitment of both the Celtic club and its Glasgow Irish supporters would be sorely tested.

KING FOOTBALL

There is no game like football, no matter what they say.
And many a sacrifice I've made to watch the Celtic play.
There's no game with half the charm, tho' scribblers may malign.
Why, all out Tommies play it when behind the firing line.

There is no game like football, as brave young Angus knows.
His football training helped him when he faced his German foes.
He played the game with gallant heart, and everyone applauds.
But none could be more proud of him than comrade Joseph Dodds.

There is no game like football, when the Allies reach Berlin.
When Kaiserdom is crushed at last, and peace is ushered in.
We will welcome back our gallant lads, each to his native shore.
And football will be football still when this dreadful war is o'er.

James Conway

THE HOME FRONT

At this point of the war, the most crucial industrial sector was munitions. Although the 'Shells Scandal' had effectively brought down the Liberal government, in fact the armaments industry had been among the more innovative sectors of industry. The shortfalls in output and resulting shortages experienced on the front line were the result of the unprecedented rate of usage and additional high orders placed by the government with private firms that simply never had the capacity to fulfil the orders. The shortfalls in weapon production were indeed very serious ranging from 12 per cent for rifles to 55 per cent for machine guns and 92 per cent for high explosive shells.

On 2 July, the Munitions of War Act became law. Like DORA, the Munitions of War Act was a piece of emergency legislation designed to increase government control over the workforce and the direction of the British war effort. Its main feature was to suspend trade union rights in war-related industries for the duration of the conflict. Strikes in factories engaged on war work were made illegal and all labour disputes were to be submitted to compulsory arbitration. Most contentious was section seven of the Munitions of War Act under which it became a penal offence for workers in controlled establishments to withdraw their labour or to leave their current job to work at another without the consent of their current employer. Employers were given the power to issue or refuse the certificates of discharge, thus making it impossible to gain work elsewhere without the permission of the previous employer. Other clauses of the Act made it an offence for a worker to refuse to undertake a new job regardless of the rates of pay on offer and the Act also made it an offence for a worker to refuse to work overtime, whether overtime was to be paid or not. The Act allowed for munitions tribunals to be set up to deal with transgressors against the Act. On the Clyde, the workers took to calling it the 'Slavery Act'. From a Clyde engineers strike emerged the Clyde Workers' Committee and the beginning of the legend of Red Clydeside.

The informal industrial truce of the start of the war, which had become a formal agreement between the TUC and the government in March, was now embodied in statute. It became a statutory requirement to accept arbitration of disputes and dilution of the workforce when the government and employers saw fit to introduce unskilled labour rapidly into essential industries. The Ministry of Munitions under the direction of Lloyd George would eventually manage over 250 government factories and supervise another 20,000 controlled establishments. From a situation where 500,000 shells were produced in the whole of 1914, the British armaments industry became capable of producing 76.2 million shells per year in 1917. However, the impact of the Act on labour relations was questionable: apart from Russia, no other Great Power suffered as many wartime strikes as Britain.

As a result of the drive to expand the war industries and particularly the munitions sector, it was quickly realised that there was a shortage of workers in the industrial centres where war and munitions production were concentrated. The Glasgow conurbation stretching along the length of the Clyde valley was one such. In some areas, the loss of labour was critical. By mid-1915, 23.8 per cent of the male employees in the chemicals and explosives industry had enlisted, 23.7 per cent from electrical engineering, 21.8 per cent from the mines, 19.5 per cent from engineering trades, 18.8 per cent from the iron and steel industry and 16.8 per cent from small arms manufacturing. The government, therefore, moved to reinforce the industrial labour supply, even at the expense of the army's manpower requirements. Indeed the army found itself having to return to civilian life many of the skilled workers who had been allowed to enlist at the start of the war. In mid-1915, when the subject of acute labour shortages came fully into the public consciousness, enlistment was still entirely voluntary. The War Office and the government finally realised that some men were more valuable at home producing the weapons, munitions and the materials of war as opposed to standing in a trench with a rifle. The new Ministry of Munitions began a major recruitment drive of its own to attract an army of workers into the war industries.

On 3 July, the offices of the Glasgow and West of Scotland Armaments Committee opened at 45 Renfield Street to enrol men then engaged in merchant work and who were qualified to undertake war work. The response to the committee's campaign after a week or so was poor in comparison to other places outwith west central Scotland, since nationally 46,000 had volunteered for war work. The explanation was simply that most men in the Clyde area were already engaged in some form of war work. However, it was noted that over 6000 Scottish schoolteachers volunteered to work in a war-related industry during their summer holidays. Suitable employment included munitions, agricultural work, manual labour, Red Cross work, nursing, laundry work, and sowing and mending soldiers' garments.

In the spring of 1915, enlistment had averaged 100,000 men per month, but this could not be sustained. The upper age limit had been raised from thirty-eight to forty in May 1915 in an effort to keep the numbers up, but it became clear that voluntary recruitment was not going to provide the number of men required. The June enlistment of 114,000 slipped to 95,000 in July. So began a prolonged argument between the military and industry over the nation's pool of available manpower. It became increasingly apparent that only compulsory military service and the mobilisation of the nation's womenfolk could satisfy both demands; however, the Liberals were not going to surrender their principles just yet and a half-way house known as the Derby Scheme would be tried first.

The Munitions Act was a major step forward in Lloyd George's philosophy of total war, as both the wider population and British industry were sucked into the war effort. In mid-1915, there was no formal or official list or category of occupations that would or could legally exempt a worker from enlisting or prevent him if he wished to do so. On the other hand, neither could a worker be protected from public pressure to enlist. Some industries, vital to the war effort, did attempt to regulate the flow of their workers into the army. The railways, for example, stipulated that any railway employee who wished to enlist had first to obtain the written consent of the company employing them. However, this did not prevent 17 per cent of railway workers enlisting. As early as December 1914, the Admiralty had adopted an idea proposed by the Vickers armaments company to issue badges to its Royal Dockyards workers to protect them from overzealous recruiters, but the badges did not prevent men from enlisting.

From the Factory to the Field
(Glasgow Evening Times)

In July 1915, the government introduced the National Registration Act. This Act created a register of every adult in the country between the ages of fifteen and sixty-five. Registration Day would be 15 August 1915. Everyone within the specified age group was to complete a form giving their name, age, nationality, marital status and employment details. From the information contained in these returns, the government formulated its division of labour policy based on a starred system in which specific trades or skills were exempted from military service and non-starred men identified as available for military service. The system would be controlled by local tribunals to whom an individual or employer could apply or appeal. The system was pretty flexible and if a good enough case could be made, just about anyone could be considered essential to his particular occupation or employer. Over the course of the war, the need for specific trades or skills changed and men considered essential one month might find themselves liable for military service the next. The National Registration Act, which introduced the register, was seen by many, including the Irish Nationalists, as a prelude to national conscription and was therefore politically contentious. As a result, neither the Act, nor later National Conscription, would ever be introduced into Ireland.

The trade unions were also active in Glasgow at the beginning of July. The Scottish Trade Union Congress held a conference in the Christian Institute to debate three main topics: the cost of living, war relief and after war problems. Over 200 delegates attended, including the former Labour leader, now Sergeant J O'Connor Kessack. Wages for skilled artisans in particular had risen considerably with £10 not unheard of, but for women and the unskilled, wages had not risen as high or as fast. It was noted that the Co-operative Society had estimated that since the start of the war the cost of living had risen by at least 35 per cent.

In response to Kitchener's appeal for another 300,000 men in mid-May, on Sunday, 11 July, Archbishop Maguire of Glasgow made another appeal for Catholic recruits. What was described as a 'stirring letter' was read out at Masses throughout the Archdiocese of Glasgow. The letter urged young Catholic men to enlist and exhorted their parents to facilitate such enlistment:

> Our cause is a noble one; we are not fighting to gain money or land; we are not fighting for glory or revenge. We are fighting for peace. Will not you, young men of the diocese, help to hasten this peace, which can only be gained by the sword? Will not you, fathers and mothers, let the young men go? You will, and God will bless you. You will answer the call of our King – a George who by his devotion to duty has ennobled a name to which some of our Kings brought little credit – it is in his name that Lord Kitchener speaks. You will answer him not by any poetry of words but by the rhythm of marching feet. 'We are coming, three hundred thousand more.'

The success or otherwise of the Archbishop's appeal to Glasgow's Roman Catholics is impossible to ascertain.

That same weekend, the men of the 15th (Scottish) Division, training finished, moved to France. Just six weeks or so after the men of K1 deployed on active service, the units of the second hundred thousand men in K2 followed in their footsteps. Among the units of the 15th (Scottish) Division that deployed was the 12th Bn HLI with Lieutenant James Delarge Lavelle, the eldest son of Glasgow Irishman John Lavelle, Baillie and the first Roman Catholic Provost of Coatbridge. As a Stonyhurst-educated civil and mining engineer, James enlisted first into the 17th (Chamber of Commerce) Bn as a private soldier, but in September 1914 applied for and was granted a commission in the 12th Bn HLI. His younger brother Patrick Joseph Lavelle was a medical student at Glasgow University when war was declared. He applied for a commission and was gazetted 2nd Lieutenant in the 5th Bn Royal Scots Fusiliers. The TF battalion formed a part of the 155th Brigade, 52nd (Lowland) Division. The 12th Bn HLI landed at Boulogne on 10 July and by 16 July was with the 46th Brigade billeted in the area of Lozinghem. The remainder of the month would be spent in and around the front line learning the ropes under the supervision of experienced troops. Just as James Lavelle was en route for Lozinghem, Pat Lavelle and the 5th RSF were in action on Fir Tree Spur on Gallipoli when over 11-13 July the battalion lost seven officers, and 61 other ranks killed; one officer and 139 other ranks wounded. Lieutenant Pat Lavelle escaped the engagement unscathed.

A YEAR OF STRIFE AND PAIN

As the first anniversary of the war drew close, the original perceptions that it would be a short war had been dispelled. However, that fantasy had been replaced by another equally as illusory, with people now believing that the war could not last another year, but when asked no one could say how or why it would end within the year. By August 1915, 2 million men had voluntarily enlisted and the war was now costing the British taxpayer a colossal £3 million per day.

The first year of war saw civilian life in Great Britain and Ireland transformed. Events and circumstances on the War Front forced increasing demands on all sections of the British community. The Defence of the Realm Act of 1914 and its amendments heralded unprecedented and unimaginable change as the government attempted to control and manipulate people's lives. The energies and skills of schoolchildren to the elderly, middle class ladies to Glasgow shop girls were increasingly mobilised. Every sector of British industry increasingly turned their manufacturing capacity to the production and supply of war materiel and in the quest to maximize output, workers saw many of their hard-won rights and conditions eroded, while owners and shareholder accepted a cap on their profits. The war had brought the nation together in a national crusade to beat the Hun in what was still being seen as righteous and necessary war. The commitment of the Roman Catholic Church in Scotland to British war aims guaranteed the support of the Glasgow Irish. However, the Glasgow Irish needed little encouragement from their priests and political leaders to get involved in the fight. Founded on a well-established tradition of military service, and based on an ethos of duty and honour, the Glasgow Irish male had from the outset of the war been drawn into the conflict. Their voluntary recruitment figures fully matched or indeed surpassed that of their Protestant contemporaries. The community's patriotic and loyal reaction to the crisis and their immediate wholehearted contribution to wider community's relief efforts brought them increased respect and acceptance from Scottish society.

In Ireland, the old divisions remained with the political truce called at the start of the war, holding, just. Irish Home Rule was an established fact, but its suspension until the end of the war left the IPP with nothing to show for its efforts. The formation of the Coalition government left the Irish Nationalists significantly weaker with John Redmond, politically, unable to accept a seat in the new Cabinet. Sir Edward Carson and his Conservative-Unionist allies had joined the Coalition and now working from inside the government, were significantly stronger. Already, their calls for universal conscription were becoming both incessant and in view of falling recruiting numbers, increasingly difficult to resist. John Redmond was already warning that conscription should not be introduced in Ireland. Very significant numbers from both side's Militia forces were serving with the British Army, the 10th (Irish) Division was already in the field and the 16th (Irish) and 36th (Ulster) Division were both about to take the field. Sinn Fein continued with their anti-recruitment campaign with only limited success, while the IRB within the Irish Volunteers continued to plan rebellion behind the scenes.

Over the course of the year, the conflict had spread worldwide with the main belligerent nations fighting in Africa, the Middle East and Asia. Germany had lost most of her colonies, while British and French colonial troops poured into Europe to assist their colonial masters. Italy had joined the Allies in May, and by the end of the month, Italian troops were fighting the Austrians on their shared border. The British and French had opened up another front at Gallipoli, but it, like the Western Front, it was already stagnating and was only serving to dissipate the military effort and spread scarce resources even thinner. The British Navy still ruled the waves and had created a very effective blockade of the German ports but the Germans retaliated with a submarine campaign against merchant fleets plying the trade routes of Britain and France. The sinking of the Lusitania had proved to be a public relations disaster for the Germans. To placate the Americans, the U-Boat campaign was suspended, but just for now.

The problem of maintaining vast numbers of men and animals in the field, including the incessant need for battle casualty replacements, served to turn the war into a vast logistics exercise for both the generals and their respective governments. The first of the New Armies formed under the old voluntary methods were now in the field. They were completely unique, a product of a set of political, social, economic and military circumstances and conditions that only existed over the first year or so of the war. The New Armies could not have been conceived or raised at any other time. They would be the last major manifestation of Edwardian Liberalism as Britain adjusted to the demands of twentieth century warfare. It was now clear to the British political and military leadership that military factors alone would not win the war. The decisive factor would be the nation's ability to marshal all its economic, social and political capacities to enable it to endure longer than its opponent. The age of Total War had arrived.

The Celtic,

Glasgow Irish

and the

Great War

The End of Innocence

Season 1915– 1916

Planned publication August 2016

Annex A

Roman Catholic Enlistments by Parish.

Extracted from returns submitted by one hundred branches of the United Irish League or in the absence of a branch, the Roman Catholic parish priest, of Irishmen who have gone from the country into the Navy, Army or Territorial Force since the start of the war. The return showed 25, 747, and this is apart from 10,000 Irishmen from Scotland who were in the services prior to the war, and the thousands of Scottish Catholics, notably from Highland districts. The return showed a grand total of 50,000 Irish and Scottish Gaels in the fighting ranks.

Listed below are the Roman Catholic Parish statistics for Glasgow and Coatbridge.

Glasgow and District:

St. Andrew's Congregation, 200; St. Alphonsus', 89; St. Anne's 270; St. Charles, 120; St. Columba, 115; St. Francis, 550; St. John's 365; St. Joseph's 510; St. Aloysius', 340; St. Mary's, 356; St. Luke's 370; Sacred Heart, 600; St. Mungo's 314; St. Margaret's, 428; St. Michael's, 200; St. Patrick's 320; St. Paul's, 84; St. Roch's, 520; St. Saviour's, 350; St. Peter's 380; St. Anthony's, 270; St. Agnes', 125; Holy Cross, 26; Maryhill, 150: St. Aloysius, Springburn, 237; Pollockshaws, 152; St. Bride's, Cambuslang, 245; St. Columkille, Rutherglen, 235; Shettleston and Carntyne, 150; St. Joseph's, Tollcross, 85; St. Charles', Newton, 60; St. Joseph's, Milngavie, 22; Cardowan and Stepps, 32.

Coatbridge and District:

St. Patrick's, 300; St. Mary's, 200: St. Augustine's, 498: All Saints', 130; Airdrie, 245; Chapelhall, 46; Whiterigg and Darngavil, 24; Longriggend, 30, Bellshill and Mossend, 250; Baillieston, 100; Glenboig, 73.

Source: Glasgow News 15 February 1915.

Annex B

Comparison Celtic FC League gate figures seasons 1913–14 and 1914–15.

Date	Team	Gate	Date	Gate
16 Aug 13	Ayr Utd	20,000	21 Nov 14	4,000
30 Aug 13	Falkirk	30,000	17 Oct 14	20,000
13 Sept 13	St Mirren	6,000	6 Feb 15	10,000
29 Sept 13	Clyde	20,000	2 Jan 15	6,000
4 Oct 13	Aberdeen	15,000	10 Apr 15	15,000
18 Oct 13	Dundee	25,000	3 Oct 14	10,000
1 Nov 13	Kilmarnock	13,000	4 Jan 15	8,000
22 Nov 13	Hamilton Accies	15,000	26 Dec 14	6,000
6 Dec 13	Third Lanark	10,000	14 Nov 14	7,000
20 Dec 13	Motherwell	16,000	22 Aug 14	18,000
1 Jan 14	Rangers	75,000	31 Oct 14	30,000
10 Jan 14	Dumbarton	11,000	20 Feb 15	5,000
24 Jan 14	Airdrie	16,000	3 Apr 15	10,000
14 Feb 14	Morton	21,000	5 Sept 14	14,000
24 Mar 14	Hearts	10,000	30 Jan 15	45,000
13 Apr 14	Queens Park	14,000	12 Dec 14	7,000
18 Apr 14	Hibernian	12,000	6 Mar 15	13,000
25 Apr 14	Partick Thistle	8,000	9 Jan 15	11,000
28 Apr 14	Raith Rovers	6000	27 Mar 15	6,000
Totals		**343,000**		**245,000**

Differential between seasons 1913-14 and 1914-15 equalled 98,000 missing spectators.

Note: The home game versus Rangers in season 1913–14 was on New Year's Day. The home game versus Rangers in season 1914–15 was on 31 October.

Source: Glasgow Herald.

Annex C

Battalion types, Scottish and Irish infantry regiments, recruiting areas and depot locations

Regular Bns.

1st and 2nd   Initially full-time, professional soldiers

Reserve

3rd Reserve	Regular soldiers on administrative attachments, Recruits.
3rd (Extra Reserve)	Ex soldiers and special reservists liable to be called
4th (Extra Reserve)	up in an emergency

Territorial Bns.

5th, 6th, 7th, 8th, etc.   Initially part-time soldiers.

Service Bns.

5th–17th (or higher)   Initially, civilians volunteering for the duration of the war. After the introduction of National Conscription in 1916, conscript soldiers would serve with all types of battalions.

The Scottish and Irish Infantry Regiments of 1914, their county affiliations and depot locations were as follows.

Scottish Infantry Regiments

The Royal Scots	Edinburgh and East and West Lothian. Depot at Glencorse, Midlothian.
Royal Scots Fusiliers	Glasgow and Ayrshire. Depot at Ayr.
King's Own Scottish Borderers	Galloway, Dumfries-shire, Selkirkshire, Roxburghshire. Depot at Berwick.
Cameronians (Scottish Rifles)	Glasgow and Lanarkshire. Depot at Hamilton.
Black Watch	Perthshire, Dundee, Angus and Fife. Depot at Perth.
Highland Light Infantry	Glasgow and Lanarkshire. Depot at Hamilton.
Seaforth Highlanders	Ross-shire, Sutherland, Caithness, Western Isles.

Depot at Fort George, Ardersier, Inverness.

Queen's Own Cameron Highlanders   Inverness-shire and Morayshire.

Depot at Inverness.

Gordon Highlanders   Aberdeen, Banffshire, Deeside.

Depot at Aberdeen.

Argyll and Sutherland Highlanders   Argyllshire, Stirlingshire, Dunbartonshire, Renfrewshire.

Depot at Stirling

Irish Infantry Regiments

Royal Irish Regiment   Tipperary, Wexford, Waterford, Kilkenny.

Depot at Clonmel.

Royal Munster Fusiliers   Cork, Kerry, Limerick and Clare.

Depot at Tralee

The Connaught Rangers   Galway, Sligo, Roscommon and Leitrim.

Depot at Renmore.

Inniskilling Fusiliers   Omagh, Fermanagh, Donegal and Derry.

Depot at Omagh.

Royal Irish Rifles   Belfast, Down, Antrim and Tyrone.

Depot at Belfast.

Royal Irish Fusiliers   Monaghan, Armagh and Cavan.

Depot at Armagh.

Leinster Regiment.   Offaly, Meath, Louth and Laois.

Depot at Birr.

Royal Dublin Fusiliers   Dublin, Kildare, Wicklow and Carlow.

Depot at Naas.

Battalions of the Argyll and Sutherland Highlanders and the Royal Munster Fusiliers

The battalions raised by the Argyll and Sutherland Highlanders and the Royal Munster Fusiliers showing the designations of their regular, reserve, extra reserve, Territorial Force, first, second and third line and service battalions.

Argyll and Sutherland Highlanders

Regular   1st Battalion Argyll & Sutherland Highlanders

2nd Battalion Argyll & Sutherland Highlanders

Reserve   3rd (Reserve) Battalion Argyll & Sutherland Highlanders

4th (Extra Reserve) Battalion Argyll & Sutherland Highlanders

Territorial Force   1/5th (Renfrewshire) Battalion Argyll & Sutherland Highlanders

1/6th (Renfrewshire) Battalion Argyll & Sutherland Highlanders

1st/7th (Stirlingshire) Battalion Argyll & Sutherland Highlanders

1st/8th (Argyllshire) Battalion Argyll & Sutherland Highlanders

1st/9th (Dunbartonshire) Battalion Argyll & Sutherland Highlanders

2nd Line Unit	2/5th (Renfrewshire) Battalion Argyll & Sutherland Highlanders
	2/6th (Renfrewshire) Battalion Argyll & Sutherland Highlanders
	2nd/7th (Stirlingshire) Battalion Argyll & Sutherland Highlanders
	2nd/8th (Argyllshire) Battalion Argyll & Sutherland Highlanders
	2nd/9th (Dunbartonshire) Battalion Argyll & Sutherland Highlanders
3rd Line	3/5th (Renfrewshire) Battalion Argyll & Sutherland Highlanders
	3/6th (Renfrewshire) Battalion Argyll & Sutherland Highlanders
	3/7th (Stirlingshire) Battalion Argyll & Sutherland Highlanders
	3rd/8th (Argyllshire) Battalion Argyll & Sutherland Highlanders
	3rd/9th (Dunbartonshire) Battalion Argyll & Sutherland Highlanders
New Army	10th (Service) Battalion Argyll & Sutherland Highlander
	11th (Service) Battalion Argyll & Sutherland Highlanders
	12th (Service) Battalion Argyll & Sutherland Highlanders
	13th (Service) Battalion Argyll & Sutherland Highlanders
	14th (Service) Battalion Argyll & Sutherland Highlanders
	15th (Reserve Service) Battalion Argyll & Sutherland Highlanders

The Royal Munster Fusiliers raised the following battalions over the course of the Great War. Note the additional extra reserve battalions to offset the absence of the Territorial Force organisation in Ireland.

Royal Munster Fusiliers

Regular	1st Battalion Royal Munster Fusiliers
	2nd Battalion Royal Munster Fusiliers
Reserve	3rd (Reserve) Battalion Royal Munster Fusiliers
	4th (Extra Reserve) Battalion Royal Munster Fusiliers
	5th (Extra Reserve) Battalion Royal Munster Fusiliers
Service	6th (Service) Battalion Royal Munster Fusiliers
	7th (Service) Battalion Royal Munster Fusiliers
	8th (Service) Battalion Royal Munster Fusiliers
	9th (Service) Battalion Royal Munster Fusiliers
	1st (Service) Garrison Battalion Royal Munster Fusiliers
	2nd (Home Service) Garrison Battalion Royal Munster Fusiliers

Abbreviations

General

AGM	Annual General Meeting
AFIL	All For Ireland League
AIF	Australian Imperial Force
ANZAC	Australian and New Zealand Army Corps
AOH	Ancient Order of Hibernians
ASC	Army Service Corps
BEF	British Expeditionary Force
BDE	Brigade
BN	Battalion
CAV	Cavalry
CEF	Canadian Expeditionary Force
CO	Commanding Officer
C of E	Church of England
C of I	Church of Ireland
COL	Colonel
C of S	Church of Scotland
COY	Company
CPL	Corporal
CSGT	Colour Sergeant
CSM	Company Sergeant Major
CSS	Catholic Socialist Society
CYS	Catholic Young Men's Society
DIV	Division
DMP	Dublin Metropolitan Police
DORA	Defence of the Realm Act
FA	Football Association
FC	Football club
FP	Field punishment
GHQ	General Headquarters
GNR	Gunner
GOC	General Officer Commanding
GSO	General staff officer
HLDRS	Highlanders
HQ	Headquarters
ILP	Independent Labour Party
INF	Irish National Foresters
INL	Irish National League
INV	Irish National Volunteers

IPP	Irish Parliamentary Party
IRA	Irish Republican Army
IRB	Irish Republican Brotherhood
ITGWU	Irish Transport General Workers' Union
LCPL	Lance Corporal
LOL	Loyal Orange Lodge
LT	Lieutenant
LT. COL.	Lieutenant Colonel
NCO	Non Commissioned Officer
NUDL	National Union of Dock Labourers
NUWSS	National Union of Women's Suffrage Societies
OC	Officer Commanding
ORs	Other Ranks
OTC	Officer Training Corps
POW	Prisoner of War
PTE	Private
QM	Quartermaster
QMS	Quartermaster Sergeant
RC	Roman Catholic
REG	Regiment
RIC	Royal Irish Constabulary
RSM	Regimental Sergeant Major
SF	Sinn Fein
SFA	Scottish Football Association
SGT	Sergeant
SL	Scottish League
SPR	Sapper
SR	Special Reserve
TF	Territorial Force
TPR	Trooper
UIL	United Irish League
UILGB	United Irish League of Great Britain
UVF	Ulster Volunteer Force
WO	Warrant Officer
YMCA	Young Men's Christian Association

Index

Bibliography and Sources

Primary Sources

Cork City and Country Archives PR12 (44A) Capt. George Berkeley Papers (Irish Volunteers)
Glasgow City Council Papers Vol. 3. E–H. 1915.
Glasgow City Council D-TC 19 (Raising City Regiments) 1914 Glasgow City Archives, Mitchell Library, Glasgow.
Glasgow City Council D-TC 19.2.26 (Col. John Shaughnessy) 1915 Glasgow City Archives, Mitchell Library, Glasgow.
Glasgow Corporation Minutes (Magistrates) CI. 3.51. 1914 (Raising 1st and 2nd Glasgow Bns.) Glasgow City Archives, Mitchell Library. Glasgow.
Glasgow Corporation Minutes (Magistrates) CI. 3.51. 1915 (Raising 18th Bn. HLI) Glasgow City Archives, Mitchell Library. Glasgow.
Glasgow Corporation Minutes (Magistrates) CI. 3.51. 1915 Glasgow City Archives, Mitchell Library. Glasgow.
Glasgow Corporation Office for Belgian Refugees 1914–1919 D-CA12/2-4 and D-CA12/1 Burials of Belgian Refugees who died in Scotland, 1914–1919. Glasgow City Archives, Mitchell Library, Glasgow
Glasgow Valuation Rolls 1914 (Mitchell Library, Glasgow)
Lord Provost Letter Books 1915 GI/1/28 Glasgow City Archives, Mitchell Library, Glasgow
Lord Provost Letter Books 1915 GI/1/28 Glasgow City Archives, Mitchell Library, Glasgow
Monthly Recruiting Figures, Sept 14–Feb 1915, Statistics of the Military Effort of the British Empire (His Majesty's Stationary Office, London 1922)
Military Service Pensions Collection MA/MSPC/RO/603 Scottish Brigade (Military Archives, Dublin, Ireland)
National Census: 1841, 1851, 1861, 1871, 1881, 1891, 1901 and 1911 (General Register Office, Edinburgh)
National Census of Ireland 1901 and 1911 (National Archives of Ireland, Dublin)
Personal Maley Family Papers May 1915 and April 1922
Redmond Papers Ms.15258. (National Library of Ireland, Dublin, Ireland)
Register of Births, Deaths and Marriages (Registration House, Edinburgh)
WO 95. Various War Diaries 1914-1915. (National Archives, Kew, London)
Kew, London).
WO 98. Victoria Cross Registers (National Archives, Kew, London)
WO 363 and 364. Soldiers Attestation, Discharge and Pension documents 1913–1920 (National Archives, Kew, London)
WO 372. Service Medal and Awards Rolls Index, First World War (National Archives, Kew, London)
WO 339/25901. C493352. Commissioned Officer's Records (Col. John Shaughnessy) (National Archives, Kew, London)

Newspapers/Periodicals

Belfast Evening Telegraph, Belfast News Letter, Burnley Express and Advertiser, Clydebank and District Leader, Clydebank Press, Coatbridge Express, Coatbridge Leader, Daily Mail, Dundee Courier, Edinburgh Evening News, Evening Telegraph and Post, Freeman's Journal, Forward, Galway Express, Glasgow Catholic Observer, Glasgow Daily Record, Glasgow Eastern Argus, Glasgow Evening Times, Glasgow Examiner, Glasgow Herald, Glasgow News, Glasgow Star and Examiner, Golden Penny, Greenock Telegraph, Hamilton Advertiser, Hansard, HLI Chronicle, Illustrated War News, Irish Independent, Irish News, Irish Times, Irish Worker, Kildare Observer, Kilsyth Chronicle, Labour Leader, London Gazette, Motherwell Times, Paisley Gazette, Poblacht Na-h Eireann (Scottish Ed), Scotsman, Scottish Referee, Scottish Sport, Sunday Post, The Outpost (17th (S) Bn. HLI Vols. 2 and 3, The Times, Weekly News, Weekly Record, West Lothian Courier.

Books, Articles, Reports and Other Sources

Alexander, Jack. McCrea's Battalion (Mainstream Publishing. Edinburgh, 2003)

Allison, Sidney. The Bantams (Howard Baker. London, 1891)

Arthur, John W and Munro, Ion S. The Seventeenth Highland Light Infantry (Chamber of Commerce Battalion) 1914–1918 (David Clarke, Glasgow, 1920)

Balantine, Ishbel. The Singer Strike, Clydebank, 1911 (Glasgow Labour History Workshop, Clydebank District Library, 1989)

Banks, A., A Military Atlas of the First World War (Leo Cooper, Barnsley, 1997)

Barnes, Money R. The British Army of 1914 (Seeley Service & Co. Ltd. London, 1968)

Beckett, Ian. Home Front 1914–1918 (The National Archives, Kew, London, 2006)

Bowen, Desmond and Jean. Heroic Option (The Irish in the British Army) (Pen and Sword. Barnsley, England, 2005)

Bewsher, Major F.W., History of the 51st (Highland) Division, 1914–1918 (Edinburgh, 1921)

Campbell, T and Woods, P. The Glory and the Dream (Mainstream Publishing, Edinburgh, 1986)

Chalmers, T., History of the Fifteenth HLI (John McCallum, Glasgow, 1934)

Chalmers, T., History of the Sixteenth HLI (John McCallum, Glasgow, 1930)

Cooper, Bryan. The 10th (Irish) Division in Gallipoli (Naval and Military Press, Uckfield, East Sussex, 2009)

Cousins, Geoffrey. The Defenders A History of the British Volunteer (Fredrick Muller, London, 1968)

Coyle, Stephen. Na Fianna Eireann in Scotland (SRSM article)

Craig, Jim. A Lion Look Back (John Donald Publishing Ltd, Edinburgh, 1998)

Crampsey, Robert. The Scottish Football League First 100 Years (Glasgow, 1990)

Dangerfield, George. The Damnable Question (Constable & Co. London, 1977)

Darragh, James. The Catholic Hierarchy of Scotland (John Burns & Sons, Glasgow)

Devine, TM. Clanship to Crofters' War (Manchester University Press, 1993).

Edmonds, Sir James E., Military Operations in France and Belgium, 1914, vol. I (London, 1933)

Edmonds, Sir James E., Military Operations in France and Belgium, 1914, vol. II (London, 1933)

Edmonds, Sir James E., Military Operations in France and Belgium, 1914, vol. I (London, 1933)

Edmonds, Sir James E., Military Operations in France and Belgium, 1915, vol. I (London, 1927)

Edmonds, Sir James E., Military Operations in France and Belgium, 1915, vol. II (London, 1928)

Emden, van Richard. Boy Soldiers of the Great War. (Headline Book Publishing. London. 2005)

Ewing, Major John, History of the 9th (Scottish)Division (Edinburgh, 1919)

Finnan, Joseph P. John Redmond and Irish Unity, 1912–1918. (Syracuse University Press (Sd) 2004)

Fisher, John. Gentleman Spies (Sutton Publishing, Stroud, Gloucestershire, 2002)

Fitzpatrick, David Ed. Ireland and the First World War (The Lilliput Press, 1988)

Fraser, Hamish. Scottish Popular Politics: From Radicalism to Labour (Edinburgh University Press, 2000)

Fraser, Hamish and Maver, Irene, Eds. Glasgow 1830–1912 (Manchester University Press, 1996)

Fraser, Hamish and Morris, RJ. People and Society in Scotland Vol. II, 1830-1914 (John Donald Publishers Ltd, Edinburgh, 1995)

Gallagher, Tom. The Uneasy Peace: Religious Tension in Modern Scotland 1819–1914 (Manchester University Press, 1987).

Gillion, Captain Stair. The K.O.S.B. in the Great War (Thomas Nelson & Sons, Ltd, Great Britain, 1930)

Greaves, Desmond C. The Life and Times of James Connolly (Lawrence & Wishart Ltd, London, 1986)

Grayson, Richard S. The Belfast Boys (Continuum UK, London, 2009)

Grayson, Richard Edit. (Staniforth J. H. M. Letters) At War with the 16th Irish Division (Pen and Sword. Ltd, Barnsley, 2012)

Grieves, Keith. War, Armed Forces and Society, The politics of manpower, 1914–18 (Manchester University Press. 1988)

Gwynn, Stephen. John Redmond's Last Years (Edward Arnold, London, 1919)

Gwynn, Denis R. The Life of John Redmond (London, 1931)

Handley, James Edmund. The Irish in Scotland (Cork University Press, 1945)

Handley, JE. The Celtic Story (Stanley Paul, London, 1960)

Hannan, John. The Life of John Wheatley (Spokesman, Nottingham, 1988)

Harris, RG. The Irish Regiments A Pictorial History 1683–1987 (Nutshell Publishing Co, Tunbridge Wells, 1989)

Haythornthwaite, Philip J. The World War One Source Book (BAC, London, 1992)

Historical Section of the Committee of Imperial Defence. Principal Events 1914¬–1918 (His Majesty's Stationary Office, London)

Horne, John and Kramer Alan. A History of Denial (Yale University Press, London, 2001)

James, Brigadier EA. British Regiments 1914–1918 (Naval & Military Press, Heathfield, East Sussex, 1998)

Jarvie, Grant. Sport in the Making of Celtic Culture (Leicester University Press, London, 1999)

Jeffery, Keith. Ireland and the Great War (Cambridge University Press, 2000)

Johnson, Christina. Developments in the Roman Catholic Church in Scotland 1789–1829 (John Donald Publishers, Edinburgh, 1985)

Johnstone, Tom and Hagerty, James. The Cross on the Sword, Catholic Chaplains in the Forces (Geoffrey Chapman, London, 1996)

Karsten, Peter. Irish Soldiers in the British Army, 1792¬–1922: Suborned or Subordinate? Journal of Social History, Vol. 17, No.1 (Autumn, 1983) (Pub. Peter N. Sterns)

Kee, Robert. The Green Flag (New York: 1972).

Kiberd, Declan. 1916 Rebellion Handbook (The Mourne River Press, 1989)

Knox, William. An Industrial Nation: Work, Culture and Society in Scotland 1800–present (Edinburgh University Press, 1999)

Laffan, Michael. The Partition of Ireland 1911–1925 (Dundalgan Press, 1983)

Lenman, Bruce P. Integration and Enlightenment. Scotland 1746–1832 (Edinburgh University Press, 1992)

Levenson, Leah and Natterstad, Jerry H. Hanna Sheehy-Skeffington: Irish Feminist (Syracuse University Press, 1989)

Levenson, Samuel. James Connolly - A biography. (Quartet Books, 1977)

Livingstone, Thomas. Tommy's War (The Diaries of a Wartime Nobody) (Harper Press, 2008)

Lucy, John F. There's a Devil in the Drum (Naval & Military Press Ltd, 1998)

Luney, Derek. Men That God Make Mad (Vintage Books, London, 2007)

McConnel, James. Recruiting Sergeants for John Bull? Irish Nationalist MPs and Enlistment during the Early Months of the Great War (SAGE Publications, 2007)

McCorry, Helen. The Thistle at War (National Museums of Scotland Publishing, Edinburgh, 1997)

McCartney, John. The 'Hearts' and the Great War (Bishop and Sons Ltd., Edinburgh, 1918)

McCracken, Gordon A. Bygone Days of Yore: The Story of Orangeism in Glasgow (County Grand Orange Lodge of Glasgow, Glasgow, 1990)

McCance, Capt. S. Royal Munster Fusiliers 1861 to 1922 (Naval and Military Press, Uckfield, East Sussex)

MacDonald, Catriona MM and McFarlane, EW. Scotland and the Great War (Tuckwell Press, 1999)

McFarland, 1990; Bradley 1995; 1881 Census of Scotland.

McFarland, Elaine. 'How the Irish Paid Their Debt' The Scottish Historical Review, Vol. LXXXII. 2. No 214. October 2003

McLean, Iain. The Legend of Red Clydeside (John Donald Publishers Ltd. Edinburgh 1983)

McShane, H and Smith, J. No Mean Fighter (Pluto Press Ltd., London, 1978)

Moloney, Alison and Jim. Life After Victoria 1900–1909 (Pen and Sword Books Ltd, Barnsley, 2008)

Moncrieff, George Scott. The Mirror and the Cross (Catholic Book Club, London, 1960)

Mooney, Major Barnes. The British Army of 1914 (Seeley, Service & Co, Ltd, London, 1968)

Novik, Ben. Conceiving Revolution (Irish Nationalist Propaganda during the First World War) (Four Courts Press 2001)

Oats, Lt. Col. L.B., Proud Heritage, The Story of the Highland Light Infantry 1777–1918, Vol. 2–3 (Thomas Nelson, Edinburgh 1951 and House of Grant, Glasgow, 1961)

O'Cathain, Mairtin. Irish Republicanism in Scotland 1858–1916 (Irish Academic Press Ltd, 2007)

O'Drisceoil, Donal. Peadar O'Donnell (Radical Irish Lives) (Cork University Press, 2001)

Philips, W.A. The Revolution in Ireland (Longmuir and Green Co., London, 1923)

Pinney, Thomas, Ed. The Letters of Rudyard Kipling 1911–19, Vol. 4 (University of Iowa Press, 1999)

Piper, Leonard. Dangerous Waters. The Life and Death of Erskine Childers (Hambledon and London, London and New York, 2003)

Poblacht Na-h Eireann (Scottish Edition), November 18,1922 (National Library of Ireland)

Reid, Col. A.K., Shoulder to Shoulder, ed. Alex Aitken, 1988, unpublished history of the Glasgow Highlanders in the First World War.

Reader, Seamus. Irishmen in Scotland (An Toglac, St Patrick's Day Issue, 1962)

Reader, Seamus. Irishmen in Scotland (An Toglac, Summer, 1964)

Record of the 5th (Service) Bn. The Connaught Rangers 19 August, 1914 – 17 January 1916 (Naval and Military Press, Uckfield, East Sussex)

Richardson, Neil. A Coward if I Return, A Hero if I Fall (O'Brien Press. Dublin, 2010)

Riddoch, Andrew and Kemp John. When the Whistle Blows (Haynes Publishing. Yeovil, Somerset, England, 2008)

Royle, Trevor. The Flowers of the Forest (Birlinn Limited, Edinburgh, 2006)

Ryan, AP. Mutiny at the Curragh (MacMillan & Co Ltd, London, 1956)

Ryan, Meda. Tom Barry: IRA Freedom Fighter (Mercier Press, Cork, 2005)

Sellwod, AV. The Saturday Night Soldiers (White Lion Publishers, London, 1966)

Simkins, Peter. Kitchener's Army (Pen and Sword, Barnsley, England, 2007)

Smout, TC. A Century of the Scottish People 1893–1950 (Fontana Press, Glasgow)

Smyth, JJ. Labour in Glasgow 1896–1936 (Tuckwell Press, 2000)

Stewart, Lt. Col. J and Buchanan, J., The Fifteenth (Scottish) Division, 1914–1919 (Edinburgh, 1926)

Swift, Roger. Irish Migrants in Britain: 1815-1914: A Documentary History (Cork University Press, 2002)

Swift, Roger and Gilley, Sheridan, Eds. The Irish in Britain 1815–1939. (Rowman and Littlefield, 1989)

Thomson, Lt. Col. R., History of the 52nd (Lowland) Division (Glasgow, 1923)

Victor, Rickard, Mrs. The Story of the Munsters (Hodder and Stoughton, 1918)

Vignes, Spenser. Lost in France. Tempus Publishing, Stroud, England 2007)

Various. The Highland Light Infantry Chronicle, Vol. X, No. 2 (John Horn Ltd, Glasgow, April 1910)

War Office – Weekly Casualty Lists (Various dates August 1914- July 1915)

Weir, Alec. Come On Highlanders! (Sutton Publishing, Stroud, Gloucestershire, 2005)

Westlake, Ray. Kitchener's Army (Spellmount Ltd, Staplehurst, Kent, 1998)

Westlake, Ray. British Regiments at Gallipoli. (Leo Cooper, London, 1996)

Westlake, Ray. British Regiments in France and Belgium 1914. (Leo Cooper, London, 1997)

Westlake, Ray. British Regiments in France and Belgium Jan–June 1915. (Leo Cooper, London, 1997)

Wilson, Brian. Celtic A Century with Honour (Collins and Sons, Glasgow, 1988)

Yeats, Padraig. A City in War Time. Dublin 1914–18 (Gill & MacMillan, 2011)

Young, Derek. Scottish Voices from the Great War (Tempus Publishing Stroud, England, 2006)

Young, James D. Socialism Since 1889: A Biographical History (Pinter Publishers, London, 1988)